Women and Faith

Women and Faith

Catholic Religious Life in Italy
from Late Antiquity to the Present

Edited by
Lucetta Scaraffia
and
Gabriella Zarri

HARVARD UNIVERSITY PRESS
Cambridge, Massachusetts, and London, England 1999

Copyright © 1999 by the President and Fellows of Harvard College
All rights reserved
Printed in the United States of America

Originally published as *Donne e Fede: Santità e Vita Religiosa in Italia,*
© 1994 Gius. Laterza & Figli Spa, Roma-Bari. English-language edition
arranged through the Eulama Literary Agency.

Library of Congress Cataloging-in-Publication Data

Donne e fede. English.
    Women and faith: Catholic religious life in Italy from late antiquity to the
present / edited by Lucetta Scaraffia and Gabriella Zarri.
      p. cm.
    Includes bibliographical references (p.   ) and index.
    ISBN 0-674-95478-5 (alk. paper)
    1. Monastic and religious orders for women—Italy—History.
2. Women in Christianity—Italy—History. 3. Women—Italy—Religious life.
I. Scaraffia, Lucetta, 1948–   . II. Zarri, Gabriella, 1942–   .   III. Title.
BX4220.I8D6613 1999
282'.45'082—dc21   99-19455

Contents

Introduction   *1*
Lucetta Scaraffia and Gabriella Zarri
Translated by Keith Botsford

1   Female Asceticism and Monasticism in Italy
    from the Fourth to the Eighth Centuries   *8*
    Franca Ela Consolino
    Translated by Keith Botsford

2   Mystical Marriage   *31*
    E. Ann Matter
    Translated by Keith Botsford

3   Society and Women's Religiosity, 750–1450   *42*
    Giulia Barone
    Translated by Keith Botsford

4   Women, Faith, and Image in the Late Middle Ages   *72*
    Dominique Rigaux
    Translated by Keith Botsford

5   From Prophecy to Discipline, 1450–1650   *83*
    Gabriella Zarri
    Translated by Keith Botsford

6   Spiritual Letters   *113*
    Adriano Prosperi
    Translated by Keith Botsford

7   The Convent Muses: The Secular Writing
    of Italian Nuns, 1450–1650   *129*
    Elissa B. Weaver

8   Little Women, Great Heroines: Simulated and
    Genuine Female Holiness in Early Modern Italy   *144*
    Anne Jacobson Schutte

9   Models of Female Sanctity in Renaissance and
    Counter-Reformation Italy   *159*
    Sara F. Matthews Grieco

10 From the Late Baroque Mystical Explosion to the
    Social Apostolate, 1650–1850   *176*
    Marina Caffiero
    Translated by Keith Botsford

11 Mystical Writing   *205*
    Marilena Modica Vasta
    Translated by Keith Botsford

12 Female Dynastic Sanctity, 1650–1850   *219*
    Sara Cabibbo
    Translated by Keith Botsford

13 Sacred Imagery and the Religious Lives
    of Women, 1650–1850   *231*
    Karen-edis Barzman

14 "Christianity Has Liberated Her and Placed Her
    alongside Man in the Family": From 1850 to 1988
    (*Mulieris Dignitatem*)   *249*
    Lucetta Scaraffia
    Translated by Keith Botsford

15 A Voyage to the Madonna   *281*
    Emma Fattorini
    Translated by Keith Botsford

16 Sisters and Saints on the Screen   *294*
    Giovanna Grignaffini
    Translated by Keith Botsford

    Notes   *303*

    Index   *367*

Introduction

LUCETTA SCARAFFIA and GABRIELLA ZARRI

"I believe in God, the Father Almighty . . . ": as is well known, so begins the Apostles' Creed, the Catholic, Christian profession of faith, thus immediately underlining the masculine nature of the divinity within a religion that had from its earliest days been characterized by its openness to the presence of women. Indeed, with conversion Christians became "neither male nor female; for ye are all one in Christ Jesus."[1] Here is a hypothesis of spiritual equivalence, but one lodged within a monotheistic religion that gave the symbols of female devotion scant space, and in a social context in which, at least until the nineteenth century, women occupied a segregated place in public life, one subordinated to male authority.

From this contradiction derives the importance and ambiguity of the relationship between women and Christian religion: the contradiction explains the extraordinary attention this theme has drawn from both feminist theorists and female scholars, especially historians, studying the past of women.[2] The abundance of research one might call "scientific" on this theme can also be explained by the exceptionally rich and well-preserved documentation on women's religious orders, which is rare for a field in which it is generally difficult to find sources by or about women. Alternatively, the wealth of research in this field may be motivated by the same premise on which the reflections of feminist theoreticians are based: the intuition that it is precisely in the field of religion, the highest and most complex symbolic representation of a society, that one must seek out the causes of women's role in the Western world.

Indeed, we should not forget that feminism came into being only in the Western world, and as an effect of the expansion of democratic rights to all citizens. For all its secularization, the society that saw the rise of feminism is

1

recognizably heir to the Christian religion. It was Christianity that first assured equal spiritual dignity to women and men, through the repeated recognition of female figures whether in the Gospels—one need only think of Mary Magdalene—or in the Pauline and patristic commentaries. Christianity did lay down a theoretical base, though one often misunderstood and contested, for the equality of the sexes. It is not by chance that it is in the Christian religion, through the demand to be admitted to the priesthood, that the final battle for women's equality with men has been fought in Western society.

To understand the deeply innovative potential of this demand, we must remember that our culture is based on the exclusion of women from the priesthood and war: that is, from two of the three functions—priesthood, war, and reproduction—which Georges Dumezil identified as fundamental to Indo-European civilization. Now that women have taken an active part in war, the male priesthood is the last vestige of an old order in which women's social role in society is exclusively defined by the third function, the reproductive. That complex construction of female devotional symbols which over the centuries found a home within the Christian tradition only emphasized this dichotomy. The Virgin and woman saints were above all represented as images of maternity, and hence of fertility and protection against illness—"Women can recognize themselves in the first function only through a divinity which is both purely feminine and authorized by the established system"[3]—and were excluded from the more important cults and rituals. Socially and symbolically, women's access to religion was confined to a strictly delimited area.

In historiographical terms, even before the growth of the feminist movement, women scholars from many countries had brought out the specificity of female religiosity within their more general studies. One cannot overlook the fundamental research of Eyleen Power and Régine Pernoud on medieval women,[4] of Romana Guarnieri on the heresy of the Free Spirit, and of Natalie Zemon Davis on women and the Reformation in France.[5] In recent decades, however, the subject of the relationship between women and religiosity has, because it is now linked to more polemical, theoretical problems, received more intensive attention.

From its original research into traces of female presence and intervention in the religious domain, mostly in the context of experiences that were both heterodox and considered by their contemporaries to be heretical or due to witchcraft,[6] feminist scholarship on this theme has gone on to make an explicit request for a revision of the fundamental point, the very image of a single God of the male gender. Luce Irigaray in fact argues that just as man needed an image of God to define his own gender, so the true liberation of women can only come about through constructing a symbol of feminine divinity, symbolically the most powerful possible point of reference.[7] "Women," she says, "lack a mirror to become women. To have a God and establish one's own gender go together. God is that Other we absolutely need to become ourselves."[8]

This proposal for a radical rethinking of religion is significant in that it is the logical conclusion of decades of reflection on a tormenting problem in feminist thought: is the Christian religion principally responsible for the oppression of women or it has been, though ambiguously, one of the few outlets for some women to accede to culture, to public life, and—sometimes—to power? The answers so far given to this question fall into three main groups.

First there are Christian feminists, who reread the Gospels and the patristic literature—including that, almost always hardly known, written by women— and trace there a feminine presence and theological openings for women that have been forgotten or suffocated by the Church's misogyny.[9] These Christian feminists propose a "return to origins."

A second group is polemical and accusatory. Its rigidly dogmatic outlook condemns the entire normative and theoretical ecclesiastical patrimony, not to speak of clerical practice, as antifeminist. Its attention is focused on the repression of women, whether practical—in the decisions of the inquisitorial tribunals, for example—or ideological, via the hierarchy's knowing complicity in overlooking the works and writings of women, such as Catherine of Siena or Teresa of Avila, who had imposed themselves by their exceptional lives and talents.[10]

Alongside these two contrasting positions, the last few decades have seen the publication of a series of interesting studies using documentation from the relatively abundant sources regarding nuns and especially women distinguished by their saintliness—often the authors of mystical texts and letters of great historical, theological, and literary interest. These studies allow us to draw up a preliminary, though of necessity provisional, set of conclusions about the relationship between women and the Christian religion, one that takes into account its contradictory aspects. What this research shows above all is early Christianity's emancipatory potential for women.

The Christian revolution in the perception of the body, which through chastity could "free itself from the clutches of the animal world"[11] and thereby become an instrument of redemption and spiritual evolution, made it possible for women to find, by choosing virginity, a way out of the subjected state to which the role of wife and mother condemned them. Indeed, virgins avoided the burdens and physical sufferings that weighed on fertile women in an underdeveloped society; they had time and energy to devote to study and the spiritual life. Their engagement in the life of the spirit was favored by the fact that continence "had the advantage of being compatible with extreme simplicity"; by choosing this path, "women and uneducated Christians could acquire the same reputation as more learned men."[12]

Many women, virgins and widows, welcomed the possibility of an active social role, so much so that by the second century one could already speak of women as having a real importance within Christian society. They were bene-factors and often functioned as a sort of "intermediary" or "guide" to the pagan families converted through their patient teaching. Although, as the era of persecutions came to an end and the Church was fully established, the misogyny of the Christian hierarchy often prevailed, women who chose vir-ginity did thereby retain a way of affirming their own identity, which other-wise would have been totally absorbed in the burden and requirements of their biological role. We should also remember that discrimination against women was compensated for by their symbolic glorification. At about this same time the cult of the Virgin, which had little basis in the gospel tradition, began to make itself evident.

The essays in this collection consider the history of the institutions within which these women lived, many of which they themselves founded or reor-ganized. This area of research, thanks to abundant documentation, has now been thoroughly studied and therefore allows us to suggest a periodization of religious phenomena that we consider to be particularly significant for the history of women.

The theoretical problem of a periodization in women's history that is inde-pendent of and different from periodization in history as a whole has been set out by Joan Kelly in regard to the Renaissance.[13] The question of whether there was a Renaissance for women, and when and in what areas women participated, has drawn the attention of a number of scholars, both men and women: they have asked whether the history of women can be characterized as having its own development and rhythm. Does female protagonism and action emerge with particular vigor in periods of religious and social divisive-ness? Do "revolutionary" moments bring about decisive changes in the social and cultural life of women? So far, research on religious movements and on successive models of sanctity in which it is easy to find analogous charac-teristics has enabled us to prove that indeed institutions and models chal-lenged in times of fresh openings and social crises do, once the revolutionary crisis and subsequent reaction are over, reconstitute and impose themselves as elements of a new order, a fact identified by Reinhart Koselleck as charac-teristic of the broader phenomenon of bourgeois revolutions.[14]

The periodization we propose as a chronological scansion of the religious processes that have been studied takes into account this finding in general historiography. It seems to us particularly significant in showing women's participation—though more as mediators than revolutionary protagonists—

in movements that tear apart the fabric of society and culture. In religious movements, in fact, it was mostly women who offered the principal discourse on reform: whether in an operative sense—as with Catherine of Siena or Teresa of Avila, to mention two of the most noted examples—or in a mystical or prophetic form, as with Bridget of Sweden. In periods in which the ecclesiastical and hierarchical fabric is being put together again, such women develop models of role reversal and opposition, like the mystical prophets and "false" saints of the modern age. Thus, while in the first case women exert themselves in the same direction as history in general—indeed often accelerating it and giving it direction—and are thus accepted and glorified by the ecclesiastical hierarchy, in the second they are swimming against the current and are thus marginalized and repressed.

The religious and cultural literature by or especially about women is an immense theme. Here it has been studied in hagiographic writings, rules and instruction manuals, the literature produced by the religious women themselves in the form of texts and letters, trial records, and the iconographical representation of models of sainthood. As a result, with the significant exceptions of the mystical marriage and the Marian cult, the broad theme of symbolic culture and the vital contribution to the construction of a Christian culture made nearly always indirectly by women through symbolic culture has been left somewhat in the background.

But that symbolic culture reveals a profound participation by women in the religious movements that at different times, starting in the eleventh century, scholars have identified with the "feminization" of religious life. This term obviously expresses many different themes. Feminization—in the sense of promoting new congregations and massive religious observance in a period of secularization, a period in which one sees the withdrawal of men and their ideological opposition to religious society—can legitimately be discussed only in terms of the nineteenth century. Nonetheless, in the thirteenth and fourteenth centuries the femininization of religious life shows how intensely women participated in the devout practices promoted by the mendicant orders and how much more aware society and Church were of the mystical and prophetic phenomena in which women were prominent protagonists.

As important, too, was the role played by the Church: not only at its origins but also at different periods of its history. It consented to the expression of a cultural and public role played by women, and this—as in the case of virgins who, though refusing to enter convents, chose not to marry—in turn advanced their social status.

The Church's repeated confirmation of the concrete reality of divine incarnation—at the Council of Ephesus in 431 the completeness of Christ's human nature was affirmed, and at the same time Mary's title of "Theotokos" was authorized—reinforced not only the role of the mother of God, but also its concrete character, the material representation of the divine through image and relic, of the physicality of the suffering Christ. This shift particularly appealed to women, excluded as they were from written culture, and also created a culture with strong "feminine" characteristics.[15]

We find traces of this feminine culture, concrete and full of emotional meanings, throughout Christian history: from Saint Bridget, whose realistic visions of the birth of Jesus contributed to the conception of the Nativity scene, one of the most significant icons in the Christian imagination, to Margaret-Mary Alacoque, who in her mystical ecstasies invented a devotional symbol of exceptional good fortune, the Sacred Heart. This feminine symbolism, closely tied to the body and daily life, and thus accessible to all, enjoyed great success. Few texts can offer a more realistic image of the incarnation than Saint Bridget's meticulous description of Mary as she wraps her newborn child in his swaddling clothes:

> Then the Child crying and, as it were, shivering with cold from the hard floor on which He lay turned a little and stretched out His limbs, seeking to find His mother's warmth and love. The mother then took Him in her arms . . . She then sat down on the floor and laid the Child on her lap and at once she began to bestow on him much care, tying up His small body, His legs and His arms with long cloths, first the linen garments and then the woolen ones. Then she enveloped the head of the Child, tying it up with two linen garments.[16]

Beginning in that period in the Reformation when almost all Protestant churches returned to an iconoclasm of Hebrew origin, thus putting down a further plank within their antifeminine culture, our principal emphasis on the femininity of Catholic Christian culture arises explicitly from our choice of Italy as central to the essays in this volume. Given the presence of the Church and the papacy, Italy may be considered to exemplify the whole of Catholic society.

As far as the female protagonists of Christian religious life are concerned, their direct relations with men were almost always in the form of relations as a couple. As has already been observed, the couples formed by Mary and her Son, or a female saint and Jesus, were asexual.[17] Christ was mainly represented as a child or in his death-agony; the woman fulfilled a maternal or succoring function. Any possibility of a sexual involvement was put aside. Equally sexless were the other couples displayed in the Christian tradition, those in which God did not intervene: the mother who converted her saintly son, like Helen and Constantine or Monica and Augustine; the brother and sister who entered religious life, like Ambrose and Marcellina or Benedict and Scholastica;

the husband and wife who chose chastity, like Cecilia and Valerian. The couple can be constituted by the founders of a religious institution, like Clare and Francis, Francis of Sales and Jeanne de Chantal, or more recently Father Gemelli and Armida Barelli. These were couples marked by a distinctive, spiritual sort of fecundity reached through intense collaboration: never entirely equal, they were always anchored by a hierarchical link that explicitly acknowledged male superiority.

Equally asexual, but more disquieting because less decisively built around male superiority, were the mystic-confessor couples, which might also sometimes be configured as spiritual mother–disciple relationships. In these instances direct communication with God allowed the woman to accede to an understanding superior to that of the ecclesiastic. It was not by accident, therefore, that in the thirteenth and fourteenth centuries the ecclesiastical establishment dedicated itself with much effort to defining the dependent relation between a nun and her confessor; in fact, the latter's role increasingly became that of a spiritual director who exercised total control over the woman's life.

The Christian religion was therefore configured as a male religion—one male God and a celibate hierarchy from which any feminine presence was excluded. But at the same time, especially in Catholicism, it offered women a certain visibility and social presence through the choice of a virginal religious life; it paid special attention to the material and imaginary aspects of culture considered traditionally feminine. It remains a religion simultaneously masculine and feminine, contradictory in its attitude toward women. If it has, until now, managed to control that ambiguity by here opening and there closing access, it must now face the final reckoning, one already implicit in the earliest formulation of the equality of the sexes: women's access to the priesthood.

Translated from the Italian by Keith Botsford

Female Asceticism and Monasticism in Italy from the Fourth to the Eighth Centuries

FRANCA ELA CONSOLINO

From the age of Constantine onward, martyrdom being by then impracticable, adhering to an ascetic ideal that might, as martyrdom had, guarantee salvation took a number of forms. But as far as women were concerned (women's role among the desert anchorites turns out not to have been significant) there were no substantial differences throughout the empire. Furthermore, while the practice of ascesis for men—involving a drastic distancing from their home environment and organized in various forms of cenobitic life—fairly soon led to the elaboration of rules setting down the principles of monastic cohabitation, many women dedicated to God remained in their native towns, if not in their own homes.

The delay with which female asceticism regimented itself into various forms of monastic life under the discipline of a rule (the first written evidence of such a rule for a community of women religious goes back to that of Caesarius of Arles, completed in 534), is noteworthy; a cenobitic model never entirely replaced relatively free forms of domestic ascesis. The very fluidity of the situation made it possible for the ecclesiastical hierarchy to maintain greater control over women than they did over men, or to be justified in their intervention by the known weakness of the female sex.[1]

The greatest and often insuperable difficulty in reconstructing the initial stages of female monasticism lies in the partial or total silence of our sources. The many texts that, between the end of the fourth and the beginning of the fifth centuries, exhorted women to remain virgins and widows to remain chaste, do make a few passing references to this nascent institution. But rather than dwelling on the concrete facts of daily life, they instead insisted on the earthly and supernatural virtues of consecrated chastity. For posterity's sake, they set out the various arguments that motivated such a choice, without specifying the way of life in which it could be worked out. Even in the following period it is barely possible to reconstitute monastic forms and norms in their integrity. If and when, in the period we are examining, a rule was adopted, it was never rigidly prescriptive. While there was no continuity of development on the institutional level, on the theoretical plane—where the thinking of the Church fathers was simultaneously a presupposition and a key to interpretation for women's monastic experience from late antiquity onward—there was one. For this reason, we must start with an analysis of patristic thought, with particular attention to the Latin fathers whose influence prevailed uninterruptedly throughout the Middle Ages and beyond.

Why Chastity?

The point of departure for any argument exalting chastity and recommending its practice lies in the words of Paul of Tarsus, who saw in the renunciation of sex a necessary condition for putting a true distance between the Christian and things of this world:

> But I say to the unmarried and to widows, It is good if they abide, even as I.
> But if they have not continency, let them marry: for it is better to marry than to burn . . .
> And there is a difference also between the wife and the virgin. She that is unmarried is careful for the things of the Lord, that she may be holy both in body and in spirit: but she who is married is careful for the things of this world, how she may please her husband.[2]

Virgins and widows were the two basic constituent parts of female monasticism, and the Church fathers turned to Paul to discourage marriage for both groups.

Fairly early on, we find women taking vows of chastity in the first Christian communities. The Acts of the Apostles make reference to the four virgin daughters of the deacon, Philip of Caesarea, who all possessed the gift of prophecy;[3] an epistle from Ignatius of Antioch to the church in Smyrna during the Trajan period mentions, though not very clearly, a relationship between virgins and widows, speaking of "virgins called widows."[4] Some fifty years later, Policarp of Smyrna, writing to the Philippians, defines widows as "the altar of God."[5]

The text that perhaps best testifies to the importance assumed by virginity during the second century and its relationship to the preaching of the apostle is a part of the apocryphal Acts of Paul, known as the Acts of Paul and Thecla, whose earliest version must go back to the last decade of the second century.

The protagonist is the virgin Thecla of Iconium.[6] After hearing from her own house Paul preach, she left her betrothed to follow the apostle. Condemned to burning, she survived thanks to a providential thunderstorm that extinguished the flames, and was thus able to rejoin Paul and follow him to Antioch, where she refused the hand of the young and powerful Alexander. He took his revenge by throwing her to the wild beasts who, however, spared her. Fearing retaliation, Alexander freed her, and Thecla was able to rejoin Paul in Myra and obtained his permission to return to Iconium to teach the word of God; thence she moved to Seleucia, where she made many converts.

Although Tertullian denied the authenticity of these Acts,[7] Thecla was much revered, especially in the Greek East.[8] In the *Symposium* of Methodius of Olympus (ca. 311 C.E.), she leads the choir of virgins, and Gregory of Nyssa named his sister, Macrina, a consecrated virgin who had made her own house into a monastery, after her.[9] The successive developments of the Thecla legend are interesting examples of a changing historical context. After having preached in Seleucia, Thecla, followed by a few noble ladies, supposedly withdrew to a mountaintop to devote herself to the ascetic life. At the age of ninety she was attacked by a band of mercenary thugs who dragged her down from the mountain, which in turn opened up to receive her. The evolution of the legend is in perfect accord with the affirmation of new forms of behavior: her refusal to marry in that part of the legend which goes back to the end of the second century responds to the need to spread the Christian message with greater zeal; the later Thecla offers a model of ascetic behavior that belongs to at least a century later.

Though the importance accorded continence and chastity during the second century should have been a distinguishing social trait among Christian groups, it was not until the middle of the third century that the Church paid specific attention to consecrated chastity and how best to lead such a life. In Carthage, where the gift of visions was granted to a lay, married woman, the martyr Perpetua (d. 203), not even Tertullian—despite his eventual, somewhat confused conclusion on the total prescription of chastity—had treated virgins as a category apart. A text such as *De virginibus velandis* did no more than extend the same precepts of modest comportment and discreet clothing usually applied to widows and married women.

The first writer to consider virgins as a specific group within the ecclesiastical community—still in Carthage, but fifty years later—was Bishop Cyprian (d. 258), who composed for them *De habito virginum*, a brief and eminently practical treatise, in which he affirmed the superiority of the virgin status and laid down minute details for their lives. Considerably later, and in a Greek context, came the first theoretical work centered on the exaltation of virginity, the *Symposium* or *On Virginity* of Bishop Methodius of Olympus (d. 311?), a treatise inspired by the homonymous Platonic dialogue, in which ten virgins take turns praising virginity.

Methodius was writing at the end of the third century, when martyrdom was still the preferred path to sanctity. When the persecutions ended in Constantine's reign, renouncing the world came to be configured as a sort of bloodless martyrdom *(sine cruore martyrium),* and in the newly established order of merit the palm was awarded first to virginity, followed by continence in widows, and marriage. By the latter half of the fourth century, a proliferation of writings, in both East and West, exhorted virgins and widows to take vows of chastity.[10] Though these works coincided chronologically with the first instances of female monasticism and tended to encourage it, they showed little interest in its organization and were primarily concerned with the heightened dignity of those who repudiated the world and consecrated themselves to God.

In promoting the ideal of consecrated chastity, the Church fathers—sometimes using arguments advanced in earlier diatribes—made great play of its absolute value, and of the advantages chastity offered and the ills it avoided. Because sexual attraction was a consequence of the Fall, a virginal life, which imitated that of the angels, offered those who practiced it a privileged position, an earthly anticipation of the joys of paradise. The woman who chose to dedicate herself to God overcame the weakness of her own sex and became a *mulier virilis,*[11] capable of competing in virtue with men. Marriage, by contrast, established to populate the world, was no longer necessary now that the goal had been achieved. Refusing a physical maternity, therefore, not only freed virgins from the risks of pregnancy but also offered them a rich spiritual maternity with a view to the afterlife.

Besides these general considerations, the Fathers offered a few practical recommendations, suggestions not so much as to how they should conduct their daily lives, but rather as to how they should use their detachment from the world and safeguard their chastity: by staying at home, by not ever going out alone, by fasting, by confining themselves mainly to their rooms *(in cubiculo),* there to await their heavenly Bridegroom while reading Holy Scripture day and night. The consecrated virgin must be aware of her womanly attraction to men and must therefore behave in such a way as not to attract their attention. Her only relationship with the external world should be limited to acts of charity.

The Church fathers advocated a middle way: one that would avoid a condemnation of marriage itself, as proposed by the Encratites,[12] and yet not put chastity and the married life on the same plane, as had the monk Juvinian at the end of the fourth century, drawing on himself the wrath of Jerome and provoking worried responses from other Eastern fathers. The Church hierarchy was of one mind in its belief that though chastity was a greater good, marriage was still desirable. But in the heat of argument it remained true that marriage was disprized. In the West the extreme point of this downgrading of marriage was in Jerome; at the opposite extreme was Augustine, the only Western father who also wrote on matrimony. Augustine differed from the others in not centering his discourse on chastity, but rather by accompanying chastity with humility, for, in his words, "It is easier for the humble married . . . to follow the Lamb, than proud virgins."[13]

The instructions given virgins largely agreed with those given that other category of women vowed to God, the widows, whose existence had already been a part of the Jewish tradition. There were only a few treatises devoted specifically to Christian widowhood, whereas there were many parenetic, or hortatory, texts (preferably in epistolary form) addressed to widows. These praised the *univira,* the woman who knew but one man, while at the same time placing a high value on an arduous choice that implied a renunciation of well-known pleasures. The Fathers tended to give a restrictive interpretation to the Pauline precepts that widows should remarry,[14] arguing that the apostle was referring only to the weakest, for fear of the scandal that might affect the Church through their eventual yielding.

Proselytization and the Elitist Mentality in the Propaganda of Ambrose and the Latin Fathers

Because exhortations to chastity were based on a large fund of commonplaces, if we want to understand the particular value of an individual contribution, we have to keep in mind to whom they were specifically addressed, and for certain works, we know this. At the same time we have to consider their ideal audience, who may not always be the same as the first. One distinction of paramount importance is the hierarchical position of the various authors within the Church. In the Latin West, for instance, two monks, Jerome and Pelagius, both of them unconstrained by pastoral obligations and linked to the senatorial aristocracy of Rome, were far freer in choosing their female interlocutors than those who found themselves locked into more demanding positions, whose more rigorist positions were no accident. Far more delicate was the position of a bishop like Ambrose, who, alongside Jerome, is the one among the Latin fathers who paid the most attention to female chastity. His position of prestige and influence among his colleagues, both near and far, proved determining in the success of this campaign, which bore fruit not only in his diocese of Milan but also in other cities, such as Vercelli, Trent, and Florence.

From Ambrose one cannot expect clear and explicit statements. When he seeks to spread an ideal that he proclaims accessible to all, he neither makes nor could make any distinctions among the undifferentiated female population he is addressing. In the absence of direct indications, there are still a few hints in some of his writings that can help us distinguish, within that vast audience, a more limited circle of women by whom his message might be understood in its entirety. Ambrose was not the first Italian bishop to concern himself with virgins and widows. Zeno, bishop of Verona from 360 to 370, had already referred to them in his *Tractatus de pudicitia* and *Tractatus de continentia,* but the originality of Ambrose consists in dealing with virgins and widows as classes of their own, clearly distinguished from married women, and in allotting them a specific role in the ecclesial community.

Less than three years after his election as bishop, the former governor of Liguria Emilia wrote his first text exhorting chastity, the *De virginibus,* a treatise in three books commissioned by his sister Marcellina, a consecrated virgin who headed a community of women dedicated to God in Milan. The work was closely linked to Ambrose's pastoral activity and derived from a fusion of several homilies delivered during Epiphany and connected to the ceremony of *velatio* and the feast in honor of the virgin and martyr Agnes. The public to whom the homilies were originally addressed was likely to have been the community of the faithful come to church for the liturgical celebrations. But the text, in the form in which we read it, was the final stage of the work and was destined to be read by, and circulated among, the Western Catholic Church.

During his peroration, the bishop of Milan referred to a few exemplary cases and did not gloss over contemporary reality. Lamenting that his urging of virginity had not had the hoped-for success in Milan, he observed that adepts came to him from other places to take the veil at his hands: virgins wishing to take their vows came from the regions of Piacenza and Bologna, but there were also some "virgins brought as slaves from the furthest reaches of southern Mauritania."[15] This reference to Moorish slaves formed a sort of pendant to the mention of the virgins of Piacenza and Bologna and showed, on the one hand, that virginity knew no geographical limitations and, on the other, that a central role was played by the bishopric of Milan, to which virgins from all over flocked to take their vows.[16] Unfortunately, we know nothing about these slaves, not even how they came to be in Milan. But we do know that the rules applying to men denied access to the monastic life to those in servitude, and it is probable that when the Moorish maidens took the veil, they too were enfranchised. If this was the case, Ambrose's recruiting would have found fertile ground among women of unfree status, for whom monastic life offered emancipation.

In the exhortations he delivered, Ambrose managed to find the right example to reach even members of the upper classes. He spoke of a rich and noble virgin who refused the earthly bridegroom proposed by her family, arguing that no ordinary man could compete in prestige, wealth, and dignity with the King of Heaven. In defending her freedom of choice, the maiden appealed to her legal rights, which allowed her to refuse a husband who did not please her. To those who objected that had her father still been alive she could not have gotten out of the wedding, she said that that may well have been the reason for his premature death.[17] The example served two purposes for Ambrose: girls whose fathers had died were informed of their legal rights, and reluctant parents were warned of the risks involved in setting obstacles to vocations. Given that in his *De virginitate,* written slightly later, Ambrose defended himself against the charge of preventing young women from marrying, one must suspect that Milanese families—especially the richer ones, those interested in the transmission of their property—did not look with favor on their daughters' consecration.[18]

In *De virginibus* the bishop of Milan touched on Scripture and on the history of recent persecutions to offer examples for his thesis, but he also supported his argument by citing an exemplary consecrated virgin in his own family, his sister Marcellina, whose praises he sang because her virtue was equal, indeed superior to, that of his other examples.[19] With a play on the words *parens* and *auctor,*[20] which refer also to physical begetting, Ambrose suggested that Marcellina, granddaughter of the virgin and martyr Soteris, inherited the virtues of her female line.[21] He used the glory of his family to increase his own prestige as bishop and give greater emphasis to his advocacy of asceticism, which was an area of great significance in his pastoral action. But his recall of Soteris had an added significance: as the cult of martyrs gained in strength (and Ambrose, along with Damasus, was one of its most ardent promoters), Ambrose sought to supply a martyr in his own family; invoking Soteris' passion, he could point to her natural successor in his own sister.[22]

De viduis, which he wrote shortly after *De virginibus,* performed the same parenetic function for widows as the other had for virgins. The work bore no dedication, argued in generalities, and sought its models in Scripture; but in a few places it is possible to find clues to the kind of public Ambrose sought to address. One aspect on which Ambrose dwelt was that of a widow's financial means, on which her eventual largesse depended. He stated that it is not what she possessed that counts but the spirit in which the gift was made. The widow in the Gospels who offered the only two coins she possessed was of greater worth than a rich woman who could give far more, *quia liberalitas non cumulo patrimonii, sed largitatis definitur affectu.*[23] Ideally, a widow's behavior should combine the old Roman value of fidelity to the departed spouse, the care of her domestic attachments, and a reasonable practice of charity. There remained the daily difficulties to which a woman alone is exposed, and Ambrose, with the help of Scripture, minimized them:

> When Simon's mother-in-law fell ill of a great fever, Peter and Andrew prayed to God for her . . . You too have relatives who can pray for you. The apostles are your family, the martyrs are your family . . . Be you likewise ready with compassion, and you shall be as family to Peter. It is not blood that ties one of us to another but virtue which makes us a family, for we walk not in the flesh, but in the spirit. Therefore love you being in the same family as Peter, being related to Andrew, so that they may pray for you, and your desires be lessened.[24]

If the bishop of Milan found nothing better than Peter's family and being related to Andrew to invoke against the obstacles of daily life, this must mean that in terms of organization there were no ecclesiastical structures within which (perhaps by giving them economic support) those women, so forcefully dissuaded from undertaking a second marriage, could be accommodated. Ambrose's arguments were offered as valid for all widows, but in fact they would be convincing only to women of sufficient means who could sustain themselves independently after the deaths of their husbands.

Toward the end of his life Ambrose found, in Florence, one ideal woman he could address. This was the widow of a religious (in all probability, a former member of the papal court, a curial, who had been elevated to a bishopric) called Giuliana. She had convinced her son to become a priest and her daughters to be virgins. She had invited Ambrose to inaugurate a basilica, which she had dedicated to Lawrence the Martyr. This was a wonderful opportunity and Ambrose took the best possible advantage of it by offering the basilica a few relics of the martyr Agricola and using the occasion to deliver a homily, the *De exhortatione virginitatis,* which was to be the last (in the year 393) of his parenetic texts and a *summa* of his teachings.[25] Rather than cite the heroines of the Old Testament, Ambrose this time built his whole text around the figure of Giuliana, offering her to the faithful as a living and concrete example of widowhood and using her to weave a eulogy of virginity.

Moving on from generic, distant examples to one close to home, Ambrose therefore sought out a well-known (if only because she was a bishop's ex-wife) and wealthy (she could afford to restore a church) woman. His final image of her—that her entire family was dedicated to the service of God and thus brought prestige to the community of believers—was significant.[26] He described a Christian triumph, which was fairly rare for Ambrose, and this triumph showed the advantage consecration could bring in the eyes of the world as well. This reproduction on earth of a heavenly vocation became an insistent theme in writers such as Jerome and Paulinus of Nola, both of whom wrote portraits of women who got the best of both worlds, fame on earth and glory in heaven.

That personalization of his message which took place in Ambrose only with Marcellina and Giuliana, Jerome practiced at all levels: when he exhorted women to take vows of virginity and widows to remain chaste, his letters were addressed to aristocratic ladies, already showing the elitist nature of such writings. Besides the usual commonplaces about the importunities of marriage, Jerome reminded his ladies of the value system of the *nobilitas.* Thus Julia Eustochium, bride of the King of Heaven, must *discere sanctam superbiam* when faced with the wives of notables on earth;[27] whereas Demetriades, heiress to that very powerful *gens,* the Anicius family, showed herself equal to her family's tradition, giving luster to their house—to the titles of her consul ancestors she added the only missing title, that of having a virgin in the family. Pelagius made the same observation.[28] The appeal to widows was of the same order: they should not neglect their hereditary traditions, from which a daughter seeking to remarry would be deviating.

Jerome's teaching, especially given his notoriety and the huge circulation of his writings, was probably most effective in his portraits of female saints. The protagonists of these stories were women who belonged to the same high, aristocratic circles as his audience, making for a perfect correspondence between his subjects and his exhortees. His examples were immoderate; indeed, at times, they tended to strike his readers with their *outrance.* Take the case of the widow Lea, whose death coincided with that of the great Praetextatus,[29] the pagan *consul designatus,* who in Jerome's eyes was guilty of scant affection for Pope Damasus.[30] Seeing a precious opportunity for a good argument, the aggressive monk opposed—and it was a winning contrast—the illustrious dead man to this woman who had spent much of her life within the four walls of her own bedchamber.[31] Even more incisive was the way in which he exhorted Paula to accept the premature death of her young daughter Blaesilla, who, a widow within a few months of her marriage, had vowed herself to the strictest asceticism and died weakened by vigils and fasts. To Paula, overcome with grief, Jerome proposed as a model her relative Melania the Elder, who, having buried her husband, suffered the loss of her two young sons without tears, thanking God because, relieved of that terrible burden, there were no longer any obstacles to following Him.[32]

These exemplary portraits had in common their protagonists' disdain for the world. Epistle 108, which is a biography of Paula, who claimed descent from Agamemnon and the Gracchi and who abandoned Rome and her young children to follow Jerome to the Holy Land, was a good example.[33] The narrator accented the bitter humiliations to which Paula subjected herself; he showed how the radical nature of some of her decisions (most prominently, her quitting Rome) gained no favor with her highly placed relatives. But among the twists and turns of his arguments, it is possible to discern an appreciation of that aristocratic world to which Jerome, in theory at least, was utterly indifferent. He pointed out, in fact, the distinction Paula enjoyed even as a nun and was insistent on the subject of the honors granted his subject, both in her lifetime and after, when she was privileged with a burial place along the path that led to the grotto of the Nativity, in full sight of the pilgrims come to pay homage to the Savior's crib.[34]

A like ambivalence can be seen in the portrait Paulinus of Nola painted of his relation Melania the Elder[35]—she whom, before Jerome's break with Rufinus, he had pointed to as a worthy model for Paula.[36] Leaving her son (who was probably still a minor) in Rome, Melania had moved to the Holy Land, from which she returned twenty-eight years later to encourage the monastic vocation of her granddaughter, Melania the Younger. Paulinus's portrait referred to her return to Italy: the noble lady was praised because she was equal in virtue to Martin of Tours and because she disdained worldly nobility. But Paulinus also lingered with satisfaction on the deference—more consonant with her rank than with her humble appearance—paid her by the rich and noble relations who came to render her homage.

Cases like those of Lea, Paula, Macrina, and the two Melanias show us an inherent contradiction in the attitude of the Church fathers. Their preachings insisted on the seclusion in which a woman consecrated to God should live; nonetheless, they did not want the didactic impact of these examples drawn from among illustrious ladies to be lost. The success of their propaganda on behalf of asceticism required them to spread the word, to make sure that these women's exemplary sacrifices should not remain ignored by the world. Jerome's attitude demonstrates this. During his stay in Rome (when he might have contented himself with the spoken word), he preferred to put down in writing his "unveiling" of these holy lives, which otherwise might have re-mained hidden to outside eyes. Fasting and vigils were edifying only when some well-known personage made them known, or when an already famous woman renounced the world. Even greater was the impact of charitable ac-tions, which affected the social fabric.

The only category of women who could command attention for this sort of activity was the aristocracy, which explains why sources on the early stages of female monasticism and on ascetic communities in which women of high birth did not play a leading role are so scarce.[37] Furthermore, offering aristo-cratic examples to aristocratic women could, by producing vocations and gifts, help reinforce the Church, its image, and its finances—the more so because their exclusion from the priesthood kept at bay the risk that these *clarissimae feminae,* or noteworthy women, would manage their capital of prestige and property in their own names. Perhaps, as the Fathers argued, to refuse marriage was a privilege given to few women.

Even in those treatises dedicated to aristocrats, Augustine distinguished himself from the world of the senatorial nobility (which was, at least by proclivity, Ambrose's world too) and from the general tenor of elitist proselytization that characterized the writings addressed to this milieu, such as *De bono viduitatis,* commissioned from the bishop of Hippo by Juliana Anicia, daughter-in-law of Sextus Petronius Probus and mother of Demetriades, the young Roman aristocrat whose taking the veil had so shocked the senatorial aristocracy of Rome.

Nevertheless, one thing that did link Augustine with the other Latin fathers was his anti-Pelagianism. Pelagius, whose epistle *De castitate* was not addressed exclusively to a female audience, had also composed, a few months before Ambrose,[38] another epistle to Demetriades, at the request of her family.[39] In this epistle Pelagius eulogized the Anicius family and put the exemplary value of her vocation in its proper light. But Pelagius was also making a pressing appeal to Demetriades' sense of responsibility, reminding her that she should seek her betterment only from herself. In a worried letter also signed by his friend and colleague Alipius, Augustine differed from Pelagius and warned her mother, Juliana, against the risk that Demetriades might attribute to her own merits that which was in fact God's grace.[40] Years later, Demetriades would again be warned against pride in the brief *De vera humilitate,* which has come down to us anonymously and may be the work of Prosper of Aquitaine.[41]

Not ever mentioned, but no less real for that, was the subtle danger Peter Brown has observed: that the reference to individual responsibility might make the laity less easily regimented by ecclesiastical institutions.[42]

The Search for Models: From the Old Testament to the Martyrs

The Bible not only possessed the necessary authority to justify theological and disciplinary positions, it served the Fathers as a rich repertory of exemplary figures. The area of sexual behavior was no exception. Alongside instances of conjugal virtue (Sarah, Susanna, Queen Esther), the Bible offered perfect examples of widows: the prophetess Ann; the widow of Sarepta; the saviors of their people, Deborah and Judith. The Old Testament lacked figures of women who had chosen to remain virgins, but Miriam, Aaron's sister, the maiden whose timbrel had guided her people in the crossing of the Red Sea,[43] was, because unmarried, such a virgin and from Athanasius[44] onward the Fathers accentuated her virginity, pushing their interpretations so far as to see in her, as she bore the same name (in Hebrew), a precursor of the Mother of Christ.[45]

For all that, the Old Testament would not have been of much use in giving a value to virginity had it not been for the fact that, at the very end of the fourth century—thanks to a decisive contribution from Ambrose, often in combination with an exegesis of the Forty-fourth Psalm—a new, allegorical reading of the Song of Songs had been made, in which the female protagonist is a figure of the virgin and Christ is the spouse. It was still Ambrose, though his interpretation was somewhat forced, who proposed that the Sulamite woman be the concrete model for women consecrated to God.[46] Identifying the consecrated woman with the heroine of the Song of Songs, enriched by Origen's interpretations of the beloved wife as a figure for the soul enamored of Christ, was an essential aspect of the spirituality of female monasticism.

Martyrs who added virginity to the merit of the bloody sacrifice of their lives were also useful in the argument for chastity. Particularly apt was the case of a confirmed saint like Agnes,[47] with whose name, on the occasion of her feast,[48] Ambrose opened his *De virginibus,* offering her as a double example of virginity and martyrdom.[49] This double investiture was probably the reason Agnes enjoyed such great literary success. She was also celebrated by Damasus, another exalter of virginity, and was likewise the subject of a Prudentian song, a pseudo-Ambrosian hymn, and a *passio,* whose authorship is, not just accidentally, attributed to Ambrose.[50]

To take his defense of chastity to its extreme, in *De virginibus* Ambrose recalled two cases in Antioch in which virgins committed suicide to avoid rape: the sisters Bernice and Prosdoce, who drowned, together with their mother, Domnina, to avoid their persecutors; and their sister, Pelagia, who jumped from the roof of her own house.[51] Ambrose was not alone in singing their praises, but he was recounting persecutions that had come to an end;[52] for consecrated virgins, the risk of being raped hardly existed at all, and such cases as were recorded no longer served to instruct virgins as to how they should behave but rather illustrated their total dedication to chastity. The situation in Augustine's Africa was vastly different. There, the Donatists held that martyrdom for the faith offered immediate entry to paradise, and the menace of Barbarian incursions made the rape of consecrated virgins quite possible. In *The City of God,* having suspended judgment on Bernice and Prosdoce, martyrs venerated by the Church, and perhaps suicides by divine inspiration, the bishop of Hippo wanted to make sure that the example of the virgins of Antioch was not followed by contemporary women.[53] He pointed to the case of Lucretia, that outstanding example of matronly chastity, to show that Christian women living in the sight of God did not—even if they suffered rape—have to kill themselves to prove their innocence.[54]

If, at the end of the fourth century, it was churchmen who sought a sanction for the choice of chastity in the acts of the martyrs, the tables would shortly be turned, for the kind of "novel" that is the hagiographic legend offered readers examples of women who, whether virgins or married, accompanied their profession of faith with an extreme defense of their chastity, and by so doing recalled the behavior of the aristocratic heroines of late antiquity praised by such authoritative writers as Paulinus of Nola and Jerome.[55]

The principal model, who could be imitated in different ways by all women, remained the Virgin Mother, Mary. Her perpetual virginity was increasingly accentuated until—thanks to the ascetic propaganda of the fourth century—it became an incontestable fact.[56] Although many apocrypha give us information about the Madonna unavailable in the canonical texts (especially important in this context is the proto-gospel of James, written ca. 200, which demonstrated her virginity *post partum*), the Marian model was rounded out by the exegeses of Origen. Origen picked up the Eve-Mary parallel made earlier by Irenaeus of Lyons and noted how the angel's blessing of Mary annulled the curse placed on Eve, so that every virgin soul was blessed in Mary.[57]

While not pronouncing himself directly on her virginity after giving birth, Origen tended toward a positive answer, finding it logical that for women Mary should have the primacy in chastity, as Christ had for men.[58] Origen also attributed to Mary a self-awareness gained from reading the Law and the prophets meditating on Scripture.[59] This was another aspect of Origen's portrayal taken up later, when, with the affirmation of female asceticism, the Virgin became the principal model to which all should conform (a model whose formation begins with the figure of Mary sketched by Athanasius in his epistle to the virgins).[60]

In the Latin West Ambrose was equally important. With Athanasius as his guide to Mary's life, he not only proposed her as a model in *De virginibus*,[61] but in his commentary on Luke, referring to the trembling with which the Virgin greeted Gabriel's visitation, he observed: "Learn to recognize a virgin by her comportment . . . May women learn to imitate her modest way of life: alone within her house, so that no man could see her, or seek her out, save the angel . . . Learn, O virgin, to avoid lascivious speech; Mary feared even the angel's greeting."[62]

If imitating Mary made all virgins into mothers of Christ, Mary is said to have made her vow of chastity before her betrothal to Joseph.[63] Apart from a Nativity homily of doubtful authenticity attributed to Gregory of Nyssa,[64] the first to speak of such a vow was Augustine, who concluded in *De sancta virginitate:* "Christ, born of a virgin who had decided on that state before knowing who was to be the fruit of her loins, preferred to approve her holy virginity rather than impose it. He wanted virginity to be a free choice even in the very woman in whose womb he took on the form of a servant."[65]

Mary, identified with the Church, was both physical mother to and spiritual daughter of Christ: we find this formulation ("Virgin Mother, daughter of your Son") again in Dante, in Saint Bernard's Prayer to the Virgin.[66]

Female Monasticism in Italy

With one important exception—that of the aristocratic ladies of Rome between the fourth and fifth centuries, prominent partly in the city and partly in the Holy Land—our information on female monasticism in Italy, both at its origins and in the period which concerns us here, is discontinuous and partial, making a full reconstruction of its evolution difficult. Nevertheless, because there seem to be few marked differences between monasticism in Italy and elsewhere, what we know about the latter throws some light on points that remain obscure.

Although by the fourth century consecration to God was already sanctioned by the ceremonial *velatio,* we have no testimony in regard to older rituals, and the prescribed age at which vows were taken probably varied from one place to another.[67] Furthermore, consecrations to God did not necessarily imply that virgins left their own homes; domestic monasticism seems to have long coexisted with the cenobitic form. From Jerome's letters we learn that his sister lived at home in Stridone,[68] as did Cromazio's sisters in Aquilea.[69] We also know of a community of virgins at Emona, in Pannonia.[70]

Italy was no exception. To win over the resistance of parents, Ambrose reminded them that a virgin daughter, unlike one who is married, does not abandon them,[71] but he himself mentioned the twenty virgins of Bologna who left their homes and lived in community.[72] It is hard to imagine that other Milanese virgin, he maintains, "of illustrious family, powerful by virtue of her wealth, and mother to the needy," living in a convent. Mallia Dedalia was the sister of the Christian Neoplatonist Mallio Theodoro and the recipient of a Claudian panegyric and of Augustine's *De vita beata;* she was given the honor of burial in the sacellum, or chapel, of Saint Satirus next to the martyr Victor.[73] By 414 Ambrose's Epistle 130 offered a clear option between the solitary and the communal life—with a preference for the latter—that left little room for presumption or pride.[74]

Alongside these two approved forms of female ascetic monasticism, a third grew up that caused the Church fathers some embarrassment. These were the *virgines subintroductae,* or secret virgins, who had entrusted the governance of their own chastity to cohabiting with ascetics. There is evidence of such cohabitations already in the third century. Two letters "Ad virgines" attributed to Clement of Rome (d. ca. 101), but whose composition should probably be assigned to the first half of the third century, warned against the inherent risk of *nimia familiaritas,* or excessive familiarity, between persons of the opposite sex. During his episcopate (249–258),[75] Cyprian of Carthage—called upon to pass judgment on the scandalous conduct of certain virgins who, while continuing to call themselves virgins, had been found in bed with men, one of them a deacon—condemned every kind of promiscuity.[76]

But that disciplinary problems persisted even after that time is attested to by Canon 13 of the Council of Elvira (300–303), which took up the question of penance for fallen virgins. Condemned by the Council of Neo-Cesaream (held between 314 and 325), cohabitation between virgins and male ascetics was nonetheless still practiced in the early stages of monasticism. The evidence lies in interventions by Jerome,[77] in two minor works by John Chrysostom,[78] and, still in the course of the fifth century, in a brief work from the pen of the otherwise unknown Asterius, bishop of Ansedonia.[79]

Augustine gives us eyewitness accounts of a few female monastic communities in Italy at the end of the fourth century. He also mentions that in Egypt there are communities of "women who serve God with love and chastity. Segregated in their habitations, and as far away from men as possible, they are united to them only by pious charity and the pursuit of virtue . . . They exercise and maintain their bodies by working wool, and the clothing they make they consign to their brothers, in turn receiving from them the means necessary to their survival."[80]

These communities are not limited to the desert, for Augustine has seen them in both Milan and Rome, where many widows and virgins living together and earning their living through wool and linen, are directed by serious and experienced women, capable not only of putting order into and regulating the habits of daily life, but also of educating souls.

Regarding female monastic communities in Rome, we also have the testimony of Jerome, who mentions *crebra virginum monasteria,* or monasteries thick with virgins, in the Holy City.[81] But we do not know to which monasteries he refers, nor where they were, for he only mentions a few members of the Roman senatorial aristocracy who practiced a quite particular sort of monasticism, functioning partly in Rome and partly in the Holy Land. A small number of texts tell us about these holy ladies; they are of varying length, and by far the most important of them are Jerome's letters.

Jerome attributed the honor of introducing monasticism to Rome to the noble Marcella, who—widowed after seven months of marriage—transformed her own house on the Aventine into a monastery following the example, preached about at length by the exiled Athanasius while in Rome, of Anthony and Pachomius.[82] There gathered about her other women who had turned their backs on a worldly life to live in poverty and chastity. The virgin Asella, already fifty years old when Jerome wrote her eulogy in 384,[83] actually shared Marcella's house, and Lea, the widow Jerome had contrasted to Vettius Praetextatus, was also part of her circle.[84] Asella's example likewise influenced another member of her family, Paula, who (once widowed) dedicated herself to an ascetic life and took with her her daughter Julia Eustochium to whom Jerome's first letter on chastity was addressed.[85]

While Marcella, her ward Principia, and Asella remained in the city, Paula and her daughter followed Jerome to Bethlehem, where she founded both a male and a female monastery near the grotto of the Nativity, as well as a *diversorium,* or hostel, along the road for pilgrims. Marcella died, loaded with debt, in 404, leaving her daughter Julia Eustochium in charge of the monastery.

A similar case, though involving a much stronger personality, is that of Melania the Elder, the noblewoman related to Paulinus of Nola, who actually resided in Jerusalem. Both women were imitated by their granddaughters: Paula the Younger—consecrated a virgin by her mother (the principles of her education had been laid down by Jerome)—won over her father and joined her aunt in the monastery founded by her grandmother. Melania the Younger convinced her husband Pinianus to live in chastity and—encouraged by her grandmother, and having liquidated what little was left of her fortune—moved to the Holy Land.[86] Aristocratic converts to asceticism also included at least one penitent sinner, Fabiola,[87] a supposed descendant of Fabius Maximus. After one divorce and the death of her lover, she made public penitence and, together with Paula's son-in-law, the senator-monk Pammachius, founded a *xenodochium,* or hospital, in Ostia.[88]

At all events, while on Eastern monasticism we have that hugely rich dossier, Palladius's *Historia Lausiaca,* there is nothing in the West remotely similar, either as to variety or wealth of information. In fact, the only testimony we have is that of women belonging to the Roman *nobilitas* who embraced the ascetic life. A partial explanation is that Western sources all derive from figures deeply linked to the aristocratic world, whose values, if not indeed extraction (as was the case with Paulinus of Nola), they shared. But the very fact that these female aristocratic saints were able to monopolize the attention of ecclesiastical writers, rendering them blind and deaf to any other manifestation of feminine sanctity, also demonstrates—in a politically precarious period, which makes the authority of the Church, by contrast, even more solid—the considerable prominence these converted senatorial wives, with whom the outstanding ecclesiastical writers came into contact, had in the religious life of the West. Naturally, the economic power of these noble ladies did not come amiss: their rich patrimony represented a not negligible source of support for the charitable and propagandistic activities of the Church. It remains, however, that the only female examples of the ascetic life in the Latin world during the fourth and fifth centuries were aristocratic: a sign that the phenomenon was of such importance, at least for those who wrote about female asceticism, as to be all-embracing.

If we know just about everything about these Roman noblewomen, we know next to nothing about the convents of Rome itself. The most consistent information comes from the *Liber pontificalis,* whose chapter on Leo III (795–816) passes in review all the religious foundations in his care. For the preceding period, we have to rely on sparse literary or epigraphic evidence, with the additional inconvenience that we cannot even locate certain monasteries, and that the presence of a tombstone belonging to a nun is not sufficient proof of the existence of a convent at the place where the stone was found.[89]

The only source on female monasticism in Italy between late antiquity and the Middle Ages that is not completely fragmentary is the correspondence of Gregory the Great. Though the letters regarding nuns and monasteries are not numerous, the concrete problems they address give us some idea of the situation at the end of the sixth century.[90] We discover, for instance, that the pope intervened in the most varied kinds of administrative affairs, both in Rome and elsewhere; that some abbesses address him directly; and that the bishops concerned often receive his instructions as to how to proceed. It was Gregory who appointed the abbess to rule over the monastery of Luni;[91] it is he whom that *gloriosa femina,* Adeodata, petitioned directly for the consecration of a community of virgins in Lilibaea in Sicily.[92] He intervened in a disciplinary matter in a Palermo convent. There he brought the nun Marcia, unjustly transferred elsewhere, back into the community and compelled the nun Victoria to submit to an examination by the *defensor* Fantinus (after Victoria had supplanted the abbess and given away convent property to obtain the priorship, and thus to succeed her).[93] These records all show that certain monasteries, rather than appeal to their local bishops, appealed, or preferred to appeal, directly to the pope.

Concerned to avoid situations that could cause material discomfort and thus threaten a proper monastic life, Gregory moved three Roman congregations from their crumbling buildings to more suitable lodgings;[94] gave part of a donation to enable the nuns of Rome to buy winter clothing;[95] and sent to Abbess Adeodata in Africa a ship with supplies and charged the *notarius,* Hilarius, *rector patrimonii Africani,* with its supervision.[96] On occasion, Rome also offered legal assistance: the *rector* of the Syracusan patrimony, Romanus, was asked to support Abbess Thecla in her suit against the *vir magnificus* Alexander.[97]

There are also instances in the *Registrum epistolarum* that deal with practices not yet or not fully established. The epistle to Bishop Maximinian of

Syracuse, which prohibits the election of abbesses under the age of sixty,[98] reveals the absence of any specific rule fixing the age at which nuns could be elected. Gregory's intervention in sending as soon as possible a man above suspicion to Sardinia to look after the fiscal and money affairs of a monastery, so that nuns should not incompetently meddle in male affairs, indicates that such affairs were usually handled by people outside the convent, in keeping with the growing tendency toward enclosure in the first rules for female congregations.[99]

This enclosure must not always have been rigid or sufficiently protected. There was clearly a problem with nuns being abducted or voluntarily leaving their convents, sometimes taking with them the dowry that belonged to the community. The pope demanded that both nuns and goods be returned to their original communities, and that their partners, if laity, be excommunicated and, if religious, be confined to a monastery to repent.[100] Other decisions of the pope likewise aimed to make the protection of nuns stricter and more secure against all possible risks, such as his denying access to any convent by the physician Anastasius, whose presence caused *multa mala;*[101] or his epistle to the bishop of Naples asking that soldiers not be quartered in Abbess Agnella's convent;[102] or his approval of Bishop Januarius of Cagliari when the latter refused to allow a men's monastery to be placed alongside a women's;[103] or, further, when he invited the Neapolitan *dux,* Guduin, to mete out exemplary punishment to a soldier who had raped a nun.[104]

As far as the economic resources of the convents are concerned, Gregory's letters show that a number of monasteries (obviously not all female) came into being as the result of testamentary dispositions and on the basis of the patrimony of the departed.[105] Although in two cases in the letters the private property of the nuns became the property of the community,[106] there were exceptions: the pope's three aunts, all nuns, lived in their own house and kept their own patrimony.[107]

A trace of continuity with late-antique Rome is maintained in the social impact that an aristocrat's taking the veil could still have at the end of the sixth century. Commenting with satisfaction on the decision of the patrician Maria to become a nun, the pope foresaw that through her others would be won to the Church: *multos per illam venire ad ecclesiam.*[108]

Of the convents in Lombard Italy we know about through Paul the Deacon, from epigraphs or from imperial acts (not all of the latter of proven authenticity), all but two are royal foundations.[109] The phenomenon is not limited to the valley of the Po, for in Benevento, Theodorada, the wife of Duke Romuald, caused a church to be built beyond the walls in honor of the apostle Peter, and also founded a cenobium with many servants of God.[110] But it was at the court in Pavia that this practice was particularly successful. By the middle of the seventh century we can already discern a clear link between the dynasty and the construction of sacred edifices. The Catholic Aribertus (653–662), the grandson of Theodelinda and heir to Rodoaldus, commissioned an *oraculum Domini Salvatoris* beyond the western Marenca gate of Pavia, which he caused to be decorated and ornamented, and to which he made a sufficient donation.[111] Here were buried Kings Pertaritus, Cunipertus,[112] and Aribertus II.[113]

Turning to feminine monastic foundations, the "Carmen de synodo Ticenensi," at verses 11–15, recalls among the achievements of Pertaritus (d. 688) the construction of a convent whose first abbess was his sister: "He built a cenobium to which he assigned servants of Christ, and placed at their head his famous sister, that she should rule over them with maternal love."[114] We can identify this monastery, which is also recalled by Paul the Deacon,[115] as that of Saint Agatha on the Mountain (S. Agata al Monte);[116] King Cunipertus's daughter, Cuniperga, whose funeral epigram, mutilated at its conclusion, has survived,[117] later became its abbess. That powerful link with the crown, attested to by the fact that the Lombard princess was the abbess of the same convent which had been the charge of her paternal aunt, was further emphasized in the epigram by an allusion to the physical resemblance between Cuniperga and her father.

King Cunipertus, whose wife, Rodelinda, had built at Alle Pertiche, outside Pavia, a basilica in honor of the Holy Mother of God, did not put only his daughter in a monastery.[118] Paul the Deacon notes that, having heard his wife praise the beauty of Theodote, "a maiden of the most noble Roman extraction, elegant in body and with long blond hair reaching almost to her feet," the king feigned indifference before his queen, but on the first possible occasion, "bidding the maiden Theodote to appear before him, he lay with her, and then immediately sent her to the monastery within the walls of Pavia which bears her name *(quod de illius nomine appellatum est)*."[119] The monastery of Santa Maria della Pusterla, which later took the name of Theodote, existed thanks to an otherwise unknown layman called Gregory, as is evidenced by a later Act.[120] Cunipertus's donation to the monastery of Santa Maria, attested to by an Act of 891, could have been the "dowry" offered by the king to the convent to which he consigned Theodote.[121]

Among the epigraphs of Pavia is the fairly ample funeral epigraph devoted to a Theodote, abbess of Santa Maria della Pusterla, who was *mater virginum* and looked after her flock, making sure they were protected from the snares of the enemy.[122] Besides caring for the spiritual welfare of her nuns, this Theodote devoted herself to intensive building, renewing the old, crumbling buildings and putting up new ones.[123] Dedicating the epigraph was the new abbess, also called Theodote, and from the tenor of her dedication it seems likely that the older Theodote in some way arranged her succession. Since Paul the Deacon says that the monastery took on the name of Cunipertus's daughter, it would be reasonable to suppose that she is the Theodote who ruled long and well, embellishing and enlarging the monastery; but it remains difficult to be certain, and against the identification of the abbess with Theodote, the most noble, Roman, hence "Byzantine" maiden, there is a telling fragment at the beginning of the inscription, which reads "regali linea splendet."[124] Whatever the case, the notable enlargement of the convent during the abbess's reign is the most significant precedent to the work undertaken at the San Salvatore monastery in Brescia, some fifty years later, by the abbess Ansperga, daughter of the last Lombard king, Desiderius, and sister of Adelchis.

The other lay foundation, the monastery of Santa Maria, went back to the beginning of the eighth century. It was built by a senator in 714, or shortly thereafter, in his own house at the western edge of the city.[125] Another royal foundation is that of Santa Maria fuori Porta, sometimes known as Santa Maria delle Cacce, which also allegedly went back to the beginning of the eighth century,[126] because its foundation is linked to Epifania, the daughter of King Ragimbertus, who reigned for only a few months in 700.[127]

The best-chronicled case we have is that of Desiderius and Ansa, who founded San Salvatore in Pavia, a convent that, together with other churches, was placed under the jurisdiction of the eponymous monastery in Brescia, where Ansperga was abbess.[128] The founding document of the Brescian monastery, in the names of Desiderius, Ansa, and the coregent Adelchis, specifies that monastic property be inalienable; that not more than forty religious celebrate the divine offices; and that the abbess be chosen from within the congregation. The sovereigns took care to remove the convent from the jurisdiction of the bishop of Brescia, giving the abbess the right to choose the bishop who would ordain priests for the celebration of mass.[129] Besides the donations of Desiderius, of Queen Ansa, and of Adelchis, the abbess dealt with acquired[130] and bartered goods for her convent, whose power grew to cover neighboring institutions.[131] It is as though the dynasty had made San Salvatore a place of safety for all those goods it wished to preserve from the vicissitudes of politics.

The Rules

We know very little about the early rules that governed female monasticism in the West, and the little we do know refers mainly to communities founded by leading figures of the Roman senatorial aristocracy. Although these founders were not always abbesses (for instance, Melania the Younger was not), the management of a new community generally fell on the prestige and resources of the founders, and her authority, as Elizabeth Ann Clark has demonstrated, rested on her social and economic prominence.[132] Her preeminence was underlined in the way functions within the convent were meted out. In Paula's convent, for instance, the nuns were divided into three different sections according to their social rank, though the aristocratic group had been forced to give up their servants—these at one time having been forced to choose a monastic life alongside their mistresses.[133] The willingness of Paula and Julia Eustochium to undertake the most menial tasks derived not from specified norms but from the desire to be first even in self-humiliation.[134] Melania the Younger's biographer does not seek to conceal the fact that in her convent on the Mount of Olives she was served by a virgin.[135]

Contrary to what happened in the convents known to Augustine, one must conclude that for this category of high-born ascetic ladies, work was performed not so much for practical ends and maintenance but because it served to keep idle thoughts at bay. To this end, both prayer and the *lanificium* were recommended to Demetriades by Jerome; he invited her to make wool for her own use or as an example to other virgins, or to make gifts to her mother and grandmother that they could exchange for more valuable gifts destined to support the poor.[136]

Even reading the rules gives us little by which to reconstruct life in a "normal" convent, especially since for a considerable period rules written specifically for women's communities did not exist at all. The first rules of which we have any knowledge in the Latin West are those of Pachomius, translated by Jerome in 404, and the brief version of the Basilian rule, accessible through Rufinus's Latin translation.[137]

Another text of considerable influence in the West, if not in Italy, is the Augustinian rule. We have two versions: one for women, added to Epistle 211, which is a severe reprimand *(obiurgatio)* written by Augustine between 420 and 425 on the occasion of a revolt against an abbess who had succeeded her sister as the superior of the convent at Hippo. This rule, which is known as the *Regularis informatio* and which in part of the manuscript tradition is graphically separated from the letter itself, is the feminine version of his *Praeceptum ad servos dei,* which Augustine had written in 397. This second version has only minute differences from the other, primarily changes of gender. One version was obviously adapted from the other, and today, after much critical work on the question, we can conclude that the male version came first.[138] Even if this is a text originally written for men, the fact that it was adapted for women is an important indication of the criteria by which the lives of religious were expected to be inspired.

The *Regularis informatio* provides for all goods to be held in common;

they are available to whoever needs them. Rich nuns are exhorted not to complain or otherwise boast of their wealth, while the poor are urged not to glory in their improved station in life. They must listen to God's word being read during meals. The treatment of the nuns should be adapted to their previous habits so that each may offer what she can give. Nuns should keep their hair covered and dress modestly, but the text prescribes nothing like enclosure: at most nuns are told not to go out alone and not to exchange looks with men they might meet or provoke them; if a nun proves petulant or arrogant on this score, her sisters are to reprove her, and then, if there is further testimony, to bring her before the superior, or a priest, or the bishop. Clothing is to be kept in a single wardrobe and made available as needed. Provision is made for one bath a month, but the nuns are to go to the baths at least in threes; and these groups of three are to be picked by the superior—a matter requiring a series of specific recommendations.

The male version of the Augustinian rule is the basis for the first female rule, composed by Caesarius of Arles for the convent of which his sister, Caesaria, was abbess. She and a companion had previously been sent to Marseilles to be trained in the religious life according to Cassian.[139] The explicit purpose of the rule, which is stated at the very beginning, is to transmit the teachings of the Fathers and adapt them to the female sex. Caesarius blends Augustine's *Regula ad servos dei* with another work of uncertain authorship that he considers Augustinian, the *De ordine monasterii*.[140] The second part of Caesarius's rule follows Augustine step-by-step, adding, however, a prescriptive section of his own that clearly provides for enclosure and is the most original part of the work. It is the first text in which enclosure is explicitly considered and this aspect was accentuated by his successor, Aurelianus of Arles (547–551). Having made a number of modifications over the years, Caesarius thought it opportune to issue a *recapitulatio*, which he placed at the end of the rule; to this were later added a few measures concerning the divine office, and the whole was solemnly promulgated on June 22, 534.

The rule of Caesarius, which removed monasteries from the jurisdiction of the local bishop, had considerable success in Merovingian France. We do not know how it fared in Italy, where, within twenty years, there had appeared two works devoted to male monasticism, the *Regula magistri* and the rule of Saint Benedict. We now know that the latter did not take immediate root and, more important, that it did not exclude the reading of other texts for the edification of monastic communities. Throughout the period that concerns us here, male monasteries were based on a mixed system, a custom that prevailed at least until Benedict of Aniane, to whom we owe the most ancient and complete collection of monastic rules.[141] *A fortiori*, the same must have happened for women's congregations, as can be proven by what occurred in Gaul.

In the second half of the sixth century we have the *Regula tarnantensis,*[142] and, half way through the next century a rule for women attributed to Columbanus.[143] In this same period, Bishop Donatus of Besançon drew up a rule for the nuns of Jussa-Moutier, a convent in his episcopal city, and their abbess Gauthsrude, half of which is made up of borrowings from the rule of Saint Benedict, one-quarter from fragments of Caesarius (particularly the scrupulous observance of enclosure), and the final quarter from either the rule of Columbanus or original material.[144] The same happened at the monastery of Charmalières in the Auvergne, whose nuns lived under a combination of the rules of Caesarius, Columbanus, and Benedict.[145] Between the end of the seventh and the beginning of the eighth centuries, and still in Gaul, we have the text of another rule for nuns, to which is added a fragment mixing passages from Jerome, Caesarius, and Benedict.[146] Before 629, and of mixed character, is yet another rule composed by Waldebert of Luxeuil in the first part of the seventh century, transmitted to us in Benedict of Aniane's collection under the title *Regula cuiusdam ad virgines;* he considers Benedict and Columbanus to be equally authoritative.[147]

In the absence of local documentation, it is reasonable to extend what can be observed in France to the Italian situation. Despite the more frequent use of Benedict, the real authority to rely on for practical matters is Caesarius, the only one to write explicitly for female communities. It is no accident that from Caesarius onward enclosure becomes increasingly rigorous; this is in perfect agreement with the preoccupation with preserving chastity that emerges in the letters of Gregory the Great.

Translated from the Italian by Keith Botsford

CHAPTER 2

Mystical Marriage

E. ANN MATTER

Like so many traditional spiritual nuclei, the concept of mystical marriage derives from Judaism. As early as the formative period of the Talmud (fifth and sixth centuries C.E.) the relations between God and Israel were conceptualized as a spiritual marriage. The idea is especially prominent in interpretations of the Song of Songs, which is seen as a song of spiritual love directed either to the love between God and Israel (celebrating Moses' revelation of the Torah on Mount Sinai) or to the love revealed when the Ark of the Covenant was placed in the temple in Jerusalem.[1]

The celebrated first-century rabbi Akiba was referring to this already ancient tradition when, developing his argument for the inclusion of the Song of Songs in Holy Scripture, he said that "the whole world is not as valuable as the day on which Israel was given the Song of Songs; all scripture is a holy text, but the Song of Songs is the holiest of the holy."[2] With these words Akiba sought to justify the inclusion of such an unequivocally secular book in the Bible. Incorporating the Song of Songs in Scripture gives both Christianity and Judaism expressive legitimation for the use of a sexual and matrimonial language to describe the relationship between God and his people.

The idea of a marriage between God and the Church (defined as the incarnation of God's people) occurs very early in the Christian tradition, for instance in Ephesians 5:25–32:

Husbands, love your wives, even as Christ also loved the church, and gave himself up for it; That he might sanctify it, having cleansed it, by the washing of water with the word, That he might present the church to himself a glorious church, not having spot or wrinkle or any such thing; but that it should be holy and without blemish. Even so ought husbands

31

also to love their own wives as their own bodies. He that loveth his own wife loveth himself: For no man ever hated his own flesh; but nourisheth and cherisheth it, even as Christ also the church; Because we are members of his body. For this cause shall a man leave his father and mother, and shall cleave to his wife; and the twain shall become one flesh. This mystery is great: but I speak in regard of Christ and of the church.

This letter, probably written by a disciple of Saint Paul, and beyond doubt in the first century, sets up a clear parallel between human marriage and the mystical marriage of Christ and the Church. Indeed, according to this text, human marriage—which is here alluded to by a reference to Eve as Adam's wife in Genesis—derives its sacramental power from the relationship between Christ and the Church. The idea that spiritual love confers a special importance to human love is a major part of the Christian tradition of mystical marriage.

The Christian writer with the greatest influence on the development of the concept of mystical marriage was Origen of Alexandria, a third-century theologian best known in the Latin Middle Ages for his exegesis of the Song of Songs in both a series of homilies and a commentary. Only parts of these texts have survived, in Latin translations by Jerome and Rufinus of Aquila.[3] Origen, a pupil of the Platonist philosopher Ammonius Saccus, spent a large part of his life in Palestine, where he had regular contact with the Jewish scholarly community.[4] His exegesis of the Song of Songs, which shows the clear influence of the Hebrew tradition, at the same time develops a fresh reading of the text, one which privileges the role of the believer's soul:

This little book is an epithalamion: that is, a wedding song. I believe Solomon wrote it in dramatic form, as a bride speaking to her husband, which is the word of God, fiery with divine love. In truth, he loves her greatly: whether as a soul made in his own image, or the church.[5]

Origen hastens to underline the spiritual nature of the text: the husband is understood to be God, the Beloved is the Church or the soul. The real story of mystical marriage in the Christian tradition begins with this interpretation of nuptial love in the Song of Songs as a paradigm of the love between God and the soul of the Christian believer. This reading likewise legitimizes the idea of a devout life as a marriage with God.

Medieval exegesis is greatly indebted to Origen, for his reading of the Song of Songs builds an exegetical and conceptual bridge between the tradition of biblical commentary and the tradition of mystical marriage. Though most of the medieval commentaries on the Song of Songs follow the definitive "allegorical" interpretation of Cassian—that is, the ecclesiological interpretation—another, "tropological" or moral reading, favoring the soul as the Beloved, flowered especially in the twelfth century.[6]

The remarkable homilies that Bernard of Clairvaux wrote about the Song of Songs are texts of an extraordinary significance for the concept of mystical marriage. Bernard wrote his eighty-six homilies between 1135 and his death in 1153. At the time, he was both abbot of Clairvaux and one of the most important theologians of the day. He was particularly involved in the campaign against the Cathars and in condemning the trinitarian theology of Gilbert of Poitiers.[7] Despite this litigious and worldly life, Bernard set down a spiritual interpretation of the Song of Songs; his homilies were preserved, much read, and appreciated for his knowledge of the life of the soul, which reaches toward spiritual union with God.

For Bernard, this search is a special prerogative of monastic life. Indeed, his first homily begins with a distinction between the "spiritual food" offered to the cloistered and the food offered to all:

> To you, brethren, I say things that differ from those who live in the world. The latter are offered milk, not food, in conformity with the teachings of the apostles. To those who live the life of the spirit, solid food is offered, as the Apostle Paul teaches us . . . "Howbeit we speak wisdom among the perfect" [1 Cor. 2:6], and I am sure you are to be found amongst these.[8]

Bernard's first homily contains a reading of the Song of Songs that is also a guide to the spiritual discipline of the Cistercians. The third homily, especially, offers a complex interpretation of the opening words of the Song of Songs ("Let him kiss me with the kisses of his mouth"), which Bernard sees as a description of mystical union. The homily begins with an image of Experience, perceived metaphorically as a book:

> Today, we read in the book of experience. Direct your attention inwards; each must take conscious account of that whereof we speak. I want to know if to any of you it has been given to say, in his own words [*ex sententia*] "Kiss me with the kisses of your mouth." It is not given to just anyone to say this with real ardor, but if anyone has, even once, received this spiritual kiss from Christ's mouth, he will again seek out this intimate experience, and willingly repeat it."[9]

This kiss of divine intimacy, this kiss from the mouth of Jesus, is not one to be savored right away; it must rather be the culmination of the three kisses that constitute mystical ascesis—the kiss of the feet, of the hand, and finally of the mouth. Bernard derives the representation of these three kisses in the first words of the Canticle, in which the Latin repeats three times variations on the lexeme *os, oris.* "*Osculetur me osculo oris* sui." The kiss of the feet is identified as the beginning of penitential devotion, as an expiation of sin. The kiss of the hand helps the poor sinner in his spiritual ascent; it is Jesus who here reveals himself as a friend and guide to the penitent soul. These two preliminary kisses prepare the soul for the ultimate spiritual gift, the kiss of the mouth, which can only be attained after the purification of the first kiss and the help of the second. This final kiss, the result of tears and prayer, brings out Bernard's poetic style at its most passionately rhetorical:

> tunc demum
> audemus forsitan
> ad ipsum os gloriae
> caput attollere,
> pavens at tremens dico,
> non solum speculandum,
> sed etiam osculandum.[10]

> Then, at last,
> let us (perhaps) dare
> raise up the head
> to that mouth of glory
> (I speak fearfully and trembling)
> not only to catch sight of it,
> but even to be kissed.[11]

Though reading the Song of Songs as a celebration of marriage between the soul and God flourished particularly within monasticism, the idea of the mystical marriage was widespread in medieval society. We know this from the many public ceremonies that made reference to the idea, for instance, the annual celebration in Venice of the "marriage" between the doge and the sea; the "marriage" between the new doge and the abbess of one of the most prominent Venetian convents; and the "marriage" between the new bishop of Florence and the abbess of an important convent.[12]

Francis of Assisi used the concept of marriage to express his devotion to poverty, and the documents of the first Franciscans attest to his marriage with "Lady Poverty." In Thomas of Celano's second *vita*, Francis is described as the groom in the mystical marriage with Lady Poverty with specific references to Scripture, to Ephesians and Genesis:

> Considering poverty and the disdain of the entire world as particularly dear to the Son of God, [Francis] sought to wed poverty in perpetual charity. He became the lover of her beauty; not only did he leave father and mother, but he put aside everything else to devote himself to poverty as to a spouse, for thus the two could become one in spirit. He therefore

drew her to himself with chaste embraces, and not for a single hour did he forget that he was wedded to poverty.[13]

Another early Franciscan text, the *Sacrum Commercium Sancti Francisci cum Domina Paupertate,* contains a collection of stories specifically based on mystical marriage.[14]

Generally speaking, however, the idea of a mystical marriage between God and the soul of the believer was most commonly found in medieval women's religious communities. The monk, the friar, the bishop, and the doge of the Middle Ages might conceive of themselves as participants (sometimes even as the bride) in a mystical marriage, but this way of understanding the spiritual life was far more common in women's communities. Not only could medieval nuns more readily (that is, without a change of gender) envision themselves as the spouse of Christ; by such mystical marriages they also acquired prestige, a status superior to that of ordinary women.

As early as the fourth century, Christian theologians urged nuns to consider their lives as a marriage to Christ. Jerome, for instance, insistently pursued this line in his Epistle 22 to Eustochium, in which he cited the Song of Songs no fewer than twenty-five times to illustrate the spiritual marriage of a virgin consecrated to Christ.[15] With the development of cloistered life in the Middle Ages, mystical marriage became an integral part of women's monastic life. To understand the classic version of this idea, we have only to focus our attention on nuns' lives between the twelfth century and the early modern period.

The Virgin Mary, the spouse of God in a mystical marriage celebrated in the liturgy and in some twelfth-century commentaries on the Song of Songs was an ever-present model for nuns.[16] An anonymous German text from that century, the "St. Trudperter Höhe Lied," offers a Mariological interpretation of the Canticles, proposing a consistent parallel between the Virgin Mary and nuns as brides of Christ. Most probably written by a confessor of a community of cloistered nuns, the "St. Trudperter Höhe Lied" uses the *topos* of the mystical marriage to urge the nuns to desire the *minnichlichen götes erken-nusse* (the loving wisdom of God). The text gives us a Virgin Mary who functions as a model for the pious soul; nuns are exhorted to seek to become, like her, daughters of God, mothers of Christ, and brides of the Holy Spirit.[17]

Another anonymous German text from the twelfth century, the *Speculum virginum,* is structured as a dialogue between the priest Peregrinus ("Pilgrim") and a "virgo Christi," Theodora. Its main thesis considers the form of monastic life and especially how nuns can become worthy of their role as brides of Christ. The *Speculum virginum* concludes with an antiphonal poem with the title "Epithalamium Christi virginum, Alternatim," in which Christ and the nun exchange praise and words of love.[18]

Though one might think that the idea of mystical marriage in the twelfth century was merely the result of male and clerical preaching to nuns, the next century makes it clear that nuns made this tradition their own, a fundamental part of their own self-knowledge. One need only note that two thirteenth-century saints, Clare of Assisi and Gertrude of Helfta, thought of their monastic lives as marriages to Jesus. Clare, one of Francis of Assisi's first disciples, condemned by her sex to the life of the cloister, urged Agnes of Prague to think of herself as a bride, a mother, and a sister of Jesus Christ.[19]

Gertrude, writing in a Cistercian convent at the end of the century, organized convent life in seven steps, seven "Exercitia spiritualia," the last three of which were so formulated as to coincide with the monastic hours. The fifth, which is the first of the last three, the "Exercitum divini amoris," seeks to introduce the desire for an *unio mistica* as part of the daily devotions of the nun. The "Exercitum divini amoris" begins with an invitation to contemplate the celestial Bridegroom:

> When you want to ready yourself for love, remove from your heart all disorderly affection, every obstacle and phantasm, and choose your day and the opportune hour for your design—at least three times daily, morning, noon and night—, making amends for not having loved the Lord God with all your heart, your soul and all your strength. Then, with all your affection, your devotion and your intent, conjoin yourself with God in prayer, as though you saw your bridegroom, Jesus, present; for without a doubt he will be present in your soul.[20]

Gertrude follows up this invitation to spiritual discipline with repeated invocations to God in which the word *amor* is frequently present: "O amor Deus, o amor." This use of an explicitly erotic term—*amor* (love) rather than other words for love such as *dilectio* or *caritas*,—indicates the consummation of this mystical marriage between the nun practicing this discipline and God. It is evident that mystical marriage was a concept fully integrated into the spiritual life of Gertrude.

In effect, self-representation as the bride of Christ became a near-essential component of female spirituality in the late Middle Ages. Rudolph M. Bell has examined the lives of nearly two hundred nuns, canonized or beatified, who lived between the thirteenth and sixteenth centuries.[21] All the nuns included were famous for their spiritual powers *in imitatione Christi*. Their complex spirituality sought to assure union with the divine Bridegroom and required that they have the capacity to endure long periods without food. Bell defines this as "holy anorexia" and finds its origin in the childhoods of these saints, especially in their relationships to their mothers.

Another American scholar, Caroline Walker Bynum, offers an explanation of this phenomenon based on medieval spirituality rather than on modern psychology.[22] She sees the prolonged fasting of the saints of the late Middle Ages and the early modern period as the result of the nuns' extreme identification with Christ. This identification was made possible because of the symbolic affinity between a woman's body and Christ's: women's bodies, like Christ's, could suffer for others (as Jesus suffered), and women could nurse their children, as Christ feeds the faithful with his body in the Eucharist. The point of contact between mystical marriage and the refusal to eat lies in the intense identification of the nun with Jesus. Bynum offers many instances of the connection between spiritual marriage and food, or between spiritual marriage and the body, pointing out, for instance, that Angela of Foligno, Adelheid Langmann, and Catherine of Siena all married Christ in visions of the Eucharist, and that Alice of Schaerbeek claimed to have been infected with leprosy by God, thus making her mind a marriage bed suitable to receive her divine husband.[23]

I find Bynum's explanation more convincing than Bell's because it pays greater attention to the complex symbolism of medieval religious culture. Nonetheless, I would like to consider the phenomenon of mystical marriage in the late Middle Ages from another perspective. To the extent in which they were part of a veritable explosion of female sanctity, one determined by the needs of the time, mystical marriages were largely governed by the relationship between nuns and their confessors and spiritual directors. As John Coakley has shown, spiritual directors exercised powerful control over women mystics, and simultaneously exploited them in order to gain reputations as churchmen.[24] In speaking of medieval feminine mysticism, we cannot overlook the fact that women's words were often preserved and interpreted by men, and for that reason we cannot exclude the possibility that mystical marriage was a male construct.

As we have already seen, the idea of mystical marriage originated as an allegory of the religious community (Judaic or Christian) as the bride of God and only gradually transformed itself into a form of personal mysticism. It is evident that spiritual directors played a major role in the tradition: from Jerome to the anonymous authors of "St. Trudperter Höhe Lied" and the *Speculum virginum,* and before the English "Haili Meidhad,"[25] it was the teachers and confessors who encouraged nuns to think of their lives in religion as a marriage to Christ. It remains for us to verify what happened when women appropriated this tradition for their own uses. This would require that we search out the many specific references to the innumerable mystics who refer to this spiritual convention, but Caterina Benincasa, known as Catherine of Siena, remains an outstanding example in this regard.

The difference between the way in which Catherine of Siena spoke of her mystical marriage to Jesus and the way in which her confidant, Raymond of

Capua, wrote about it in his *vita* of Catherine is of particular interest. As Karen Scott noted, Raymond made many changes in the story, transforming Catherine from a rustic, independent, and autonomous woman into a "little saint" in the traditional mold.[26] Concerning Catherine's mystical marriage, Raymond speaks of a vision in which Jesus approached her dressed as a bridegroom, a pope, or a bishop. After the marriage, Raymond asserts, Catherine continued to see the ring given her by Jesus, a ring that no one else could see.[27] In his legend and his insistence on the sanctity of Caterina Benincasa, Raymond follows and imitates the hagiography surrounding another Catherine, Catherine of Alexandria, the legendary virgin and martyr of the early Church.[28] The moral of Raymond's fable is the recognition of the sanctity of his Catherine.

In her letters, however, Caterina Benincasa spoke of her mystical marriage to Jesus in a very different way, dwelling constantly on the humanity and Passion of Christ. She did not get married with a silver ring, she says, "but with the ring of his flesh."[29] In other letters, Catherine speaks in concrete detail of that flesh:

Note well that the Son of God married us in the circumcision, cutting off the tip of his own flesh in the form of a ring and giving it to us as a sign that he wished to marry the whole human generation.[30]

Gentle Jesus wed [the soul] with his flesh, for when he was circumcised, so much skin was taken from the circumcision that a ring was made from the extremity as a sign that he wished to marry the whole human generation.[31]

In developing her thesis of the corporeality of feminine mysticism in the late Middle Ages, Bynum bases herself on these texts.[32] What most interests me, however, is the way in which Raymond transformed Catherine's theologically complex, indeed severe, model of mystical marriage into a fantasy of a virginal female. Raymond's model, in fact, is the one that prevailed in the women's monastic tradition. The kind of mystical marriage that flourished in convents after Catherine—that is, in the early modern period—conforms strictly to the exemplum offered by Catherine of Siena, the Raymondian Catherine.

The triumph of this new model brings about a new phenomenon: the use of mystical marriage as a form of resistance against the intellectual and spiritual restrictions attendant on the strictly cloistered life, a subversion of the limitations on freedom imposed on religious women.

The limitations imposed in the early modern period brought about a huge change in the possibilities available to a woman who devoted herself to the religious life. As Katherine Gill has noted, a traveler to any part of Italy in the closing years of the fifteenth century would have observed a great number of "open" monasteries from which daily emerged—for works of charity and welfare—women who were known as *pinzochiere, mantellate,* tertiaries, or simply *mulieres religiosae.* A century later, our hypothetical traveler would have observed hardly a single woman walking alone through the streets of the same city, and certainly no nun or woman in religion. This great change was brought about by the imposition of a strict, cloistered life for women religious. The change was gradual but found its culminating statement during the last session of the Council of Trent.[33] In fact, this constriction on the liberty of women religious is clearly manifest in the repression of Lucia Brocadelli of Narni after the death of her patron, Ercole d'Este. When Ercole's son, Alfonso, became duke of Ferrara, Lucia Brocadelli, the court prophet protected by his predecessor, was forbidden to leave her convent. All at once, at the age of twenty-nine, Lucia saw her whole notable political and spiritual influence vanish.[34]

The power that Lucia Brocadelli lost—that is, her spiritual reputation and her public voice—would have been inconceivable for a woman in the seventeenth century. The conventual restrictions imposed by the Council of Trent turned all nuns into cloistered nuns. No diminution in the production of spiritual texts written by women occurred, however, as a result of this change. On the contrary, and perhaps ironically, the imposition of strict enclosure in the early modern period brought about an explosion of creativity. From the late sixteenth through the eighteenth centuries, theater, music, and literature flourished in women's convents in a manner never before seen in that context.[35]

The nuns of those centuries wrote religious literature of all kinds: treatises on spirituality, accounts of visions, prayers, and autobiographies. Why such an artistic flowering came about is still partly unexplored and subject to investigation. I would like to advance the hypothesis that in this repressive atmosphere mystical marriage offered nuns a chance to express an artistic and spiritual autonomy otherwise denied them.

Teresa of Avila shows us how a mystical marriage offered a defense of her intellectual freedom. All of her works were written under the supervision of the Inquisition and at least once she was forced to break off her autobiography. *Libro de la vida,* a text that took final form in 1565 after ten years' work, begins with the notation that it was written under the orders of her confessor.[36] In the middle of this constant scrutiny Teresa nonetheless found a way to express her most intimate experiences: for instance, her famous vision of the angel with his dart, the tale of a mystical union and the model for the Bernini statue in Santa Maria delle Vittorie in Rome:

I saw that in his hands he had a golden dart, and on its metal tip, it seemed, a small flame. It seemed that he several times thrust his dart into my heart and that it penetrated to my entrails. When he took it out, I thought he had cut [my entrails] with it, leaving me burning with a great love of God. The pain was so great that I let out some sobs; and the sweetness this pain gave me was so excessive that I didn't want him to stop, nor would my soul have been contented with anything less than God. Even if my body allowed itself to partake of it, even greatly, it was not a physical pain. It was so sweet a coupling of the soul and God that I pray Him, in his bounty, to give a taste of it to whomever thinks I lie.[37]

In her *Testimonies,* or *Relations,* autobiographical fragments mainly written after the publication of her *Vida* in 1565, Teresa speaks explicitly of the spiritual power connected to such visions. In a "testimony" from 1572, she tells how Jesus appeared to her in a vision when John of the Cross gave her, for mortification, a tiny fragment of the Eucharist:

His Majesty said to me, "Fear not, my daughter. No one will be able to separate you from me," and made me understand that what had happened was of no importance. Then he appeared to me in an imagined vision, as on other occasions, very interiorly, gave me his right hand and said, "Behold this nail as a sign that from this day henceforth you are my wife. Until today you have not merited this, but from this moment on not only shall you protect my honor as the honor of your Creator, your King, your God, but you will protect it too as my true wife. My honor is yours, yours mine." This grace had such an unconfined effect on me that I couldn't contain myself and remained as in ecstasy.[38]

Visions such as this one, in which Jesus reassures the nun of his presence, became an important theme in female monastic literature of the early modern period. Here, Teresa follows in the footsteps of Catherine of Siena, imagining her marriage to Jesus in terms closely linked to his Passion. In the century following, nuns were to use Teresa as a kind of model of the spiritual life, often without taking into account the severe asceticism that had been a part of her visionary experiences. As in the case of Catherine of Siena, for whom, thanks to Raymond of Capua, a ring of flesh had become a silver ring, the figure of Teresa, read symbolically, became an authoritative legitimation of the visionary life.

The Italian Capuchin Maria Domitilla Galluzzi, for example, wrote her confessor in 1626 about a vision of Christ clearly inspired by Teresa of Avila's words:

And because I had so many doubts, the permission Your Reverence gave me, many months after I had fathomed it [the Passion], was of great comfort to me: that is, to read a few things by Saint Teresa, wherein it suddenly happened to me, without effort on my part, as the supreme good. And I thought it expedient to lift up these raptures publicly to the said saint, since he [God] spoke to her almost the same words, that is, saying to her: "you have enough credit, my daughter, let us now close the door on the malicious." And this too was of great comfort to me, to know that such words can come from God.[39]

In another letter, written in 1634, Maria Domitilla speaks of a vision of Saint Teresa that comforted her and gave her permission to undertake extraordinary prayers and penances. In this vision Teresa told her, "Daughter, charity and humility made me much beloved of God."[40] Here we have two examples of the importance of Teresa's mystical marriage to Maria Domitilla Galluzzi. In the first case, Teresa inspired in Domitilla a vision of Christ; in the second, the Spanish saint appeared in person to the Italian nun. On both occasions a mystical marriage legitimated the expression of a strong and creative personality living a life that in other regards was highly constrained. Maria Domitilla Galluzzi was only one of the many nuns for whom the possibility of a mystical marriage enriched and made possible an inner space.[41]

Mystical marriage, then, is a *topos* within medieval Christianity drawn from a long and complex history including biblical exegesis, liturgy, public ceremonies, mysticism, and monastic life. In all the changes we have seen, however, it always retained a liberating potential—for in both its communal and its intimate and personal forms it always implied a link with God, indeed the mystical union, which medieval Christianity interpreted as the ultimate power.

Translated from the Italian by Keith Botsford

CHAPTER 3

Society and Women's Religiosity, 750–1450

GIULIA BARONE

From the Lombards to the Franks

For most Italians, the Lombard presence in Italy can be summed up in a few works of art: Alessandro Manzoni's *Adelchi;* a few magnificent jewels whose craftsmanship is now barbarian, now Byzantine; and two splendid but enigmatic monuments, the so-called little temple of Cividale and the frescoes of Santa Maria *foris portas* of Castelseprio. These works are few, far too few. But even the specialist does not have many other sources at hand: a collection of laws, the most interesting and rich of which came from the Germanic sovereigns who settled on the territory of the former Roman empire; a work of history by Paul the Deacon, which was composed, however, when the Franks had already conquered the kingdom; and a few documentary archives, essentially concentrated in the eighth century.

It is from this extremely limited number of sources that scholars have sought to sketch a schematic view of what the female religious experience was in the Lombard period.

Chapter 1 noted the phenomenon of the great royal foundations, but the picture would be incomplete if one did not take into account those forms of female monasticism that, barely institutionalized, seemed to prevail in the kingdom during the eighth century.

The Lombards' long period of drawing progressively closer to Christianity and the Latin Catholic rite in particular came to an end during the reign of King Cunipertus, around 680. But the profound transformation this worked in society becomes perceptible only at the beginning of the next century, thanks to the abundant legislation that marks the long reign of Liutprand— and, to a lesser degree, the reigns of his successors, Ratchis and Astolfus—and the simultaneous increase in documentation that has been preserved.

Thus in Pavia, alongside the convent of Santa Maria Theodote, celebrated because of its rich royal endowment, we also have the foundation of Saint Agatha and, later still, in the eighth century, the senator's convent, so called after its founder, who turned his own house into a monastery, naming as first abbess his daughter.[1] As is always the case in the peak years of Lombard rule, names are not of much help in assigning individuals to one ethnic group or another; indeed, in this particular wealthy family the father bears a Roman name (Senator filius Albani), while the mother is called Theodolinda, and her daughter, the future abbess, Sinelinda. The one sure thing is that the family belonged to the ruling milieu, to which by this time the descendants of the vanquished Romans probably belonged, and was profoundly imbued with Christian values.[2] The founding document in fact begins with a long introduction in which the apostle Paul is invoked as *auctoritas* to explain the parents' decision to devote their own daughter to divine service rather than matrimony: in spiritual terms, chastity will be far more fruitful for her than marriage, and her prayers will help the souls of her parents.

We know of other convents: in the eighth century in Lucca (Santa Maria); near Florence (San Bartolomeo), in the duchy of Spoleto—at the instigation of Duke Gisulph II; in Verona, where we know that in 745 two women founded a small convent whose traces were then lost; and in Lodi (San Giovanni). Of particular interest are also the foundations of Salto, near Cividale, and the Versilia monastery, the work of the nobleman Valafredus, who, together with his children and other relatives became a monk of Monteverdi, which he founded and endowed richly.[3]

Our meager knowledge of female monasticism and the paucity of documentation (often, we only know of these institutions through their founding charters) is common to all Europe in the early Middle Ages and until the early centuries of the High Middle Ages (tenth to thirteenth centuries). Many, indeed nearly the quasi-totality, of female foundations are "private" in the same sense as the senatorial monastery mentioned above. An aristocratic family would offer part of its fortune for the creation of a monastic community. Generally, its dimensions were small and the office of abbess would go to a woman of the founder's family. The daughters and sisters who either did not wish to marry or did not find appropriate marriages lived out their lives in the monastery.

The family's extinction or its impoverishment, or the lack of suitable candidates to head the convent, would lead to the rapid and definitive disappearance of the convent. These very characteristics tended to render the foundations almost "invisible" in the documentary sense. The religious within the community were often not highly educated; the archives of the nobility suffered many vicissitudes, and most of them were lost; there were few links with "major institutions" (the papacy, the empire, the royal dynasties) that could have enhanced the monasteries, making their existence more secure and lasting. For all these reasons it is easier to postulate the existence of female communities than to document it. Even if one can assume that certain nuns and abbesses enjoyed *fama sanctitatis* within their communities, history has left no trace of them.

Fortunately, the Lombard eighth century, with its private and public documents, was rich in legislative activity, which is, far more than foundation documents, our principal source for determining the involvement of women in religious life. Indeed, as the century progressed, laws regarding women who intended to take the veil or had already done so (even if not consecrated to God by a priest) became ever more numerous. The Lombard sovereigns took the veil to be a definitive decision from which there was no turning back. A subsequent marriage was, therefore, severely condemned as were any relations with men. However, given the extreme dependency, juridical and economic, of the Lombard woman on her *mundoaldo*[4]—the legal representative and administrator of her property—Liutprand sought to avoid forced vows or confinement to convents; his intent was to prevent the *mundoaldo* from taking advantage of the psychological prostration of recent widowhood to induce women to take the veil. The term of a year (of Roman origin) in which no decision in this regard was allowed was supposed to allow a woman to choose her destiny freely. In reality the *mundoaldo* had an interest in coercing the woman. Given the absence of an adequate law on this matter, a good part of the property of a "handmaiden of the Lord" could finish irrevocably in his hands. Later, the Lombard kings were to put precise limits on the quantity of goods that a woman could dispose of if she took the veil, protecting her family, especially the children, if any.[5]

This whole complex of laws, which we cannot analyze here, shows how widespread the phenomenon was. If the number of women intending to consecrate themselves to the religious life had not been constantly increasing, the monarchs would not have felt so frequent a need to intervene. At this point, however, the phenomenon was still largely parainstitutional. Had there been many convents in the Lombard kingdom, as there were among the Franks, or if the bishops had been able to exercise direct control over the religious, there would have been no need for the sovereign to intervene and sanction the definitive value of such a choice or to repress the abduction of, and violence against, women consecrated to God. The laws all suggest an increasing number of "house nuns," that is, women who took the veil while continuing to live at home—a phenomenon already widely present in late antiquity—who therefore continued to be exposed to "worldly temptations."

The case of the major royal foundations, and especially that of the monastery of San Salvatore (later Santa Giulia) in Brescia, is obviously different. A few years ago, Stefano Gasparri put forward the hypothesis—perfectly credible in a number of respects—that King Desiderius and his wife, Ansa, had used what was originally a foundation like many others, and whose abbess (once again) was their daughter, to construct a solid basis of power for the ex-duke, now king of the Lombards.[6] Voluntary donations by relatives and clients, confiscated goods, lands that through one means or another ended in royal hands: this huge property-complex flowed into the abbey's patrimony and was thus indirectly controlled by the sovereign.

Nor did matters change greatly with the advent of the Franks. The "great" monasteries of the Lombard kingdom continued to enjoy the favor and protection of the new rulers, while continuing to be strictly controlled by them. San Salvatore was given in appanage first to the mother of Emperor Ludovic (Louis) II, then to his daughter, and finally, in 868, to Empress Angilberga.

The "strategic" character of these monasteries was reinforced by the Frankish kings. So that the tolls they collected should provide for their clothing, Lothar I gave the nuns of the Brescia convent the ferries across the Po at Piacenza, thus allowing the monastery to control the most vital north-south passage of the time. Santa Maria Theodote in Pavia also received rich privileges from the same king, in the form of fishing rights in the Po and Ticino, together with other concessions. This policy has been interpreted as proof of the perfect dovetailing of these rich female foundations with the administration of the Frankish empire; the privileges were granted to compensate the monasteries for Lothar's lengthy stays in Pavia, for housing and maintaining the king and his numerous following was a considerable financial burden.

Ludovic II pursued an identical policy toward the Pavian and Brescian monasteries: to the latter he granted a privilege of free trade throughout Italy and exemption from duties for all merchants operating in its name, while the former received the proceeds from a ford across the Po. In this manner, through their wives and daughters, the Carolingian emperors wound up controlling not only monastic institutions of great prestige, but also vast properties and highly strategic traffic routes.[7]

The Post-Carolingian Era

During the ninth century the great wave of monastic foundations, principally for men but also for women, that characterized the end of the Lombard era and the early years of Frankish domination seemed to have run its course. The aristocracy of that phase of the Middle Ages had a wide variety of reasons to enter the monastic life. There was a spontaneous search for individual salvation, but as often the decision was influenced by external factors: there was, for instance, no easier way in which to rid oneself of a political adversary than to confine him to a monastery. But other motivations came into play: the uncertainty of the times; the loss of political prestige; or even—in the interpretation Victor Fumagalli gives of the extinction of certain great noble families in the ninth century—an existential crisis resulting from the waning of a great political project.[8]

When male members of a family chose the cloister, the monastery became the only possible solution for their wives and nubile daughters; the monastery preserved a dignified standard of living and guaranteed a degree of safety their man (or men) were no longer in a position to provide. This was certainly the case with the wife and daughters of the former Lombard king Ratchis and with the family of Valafredus, the founder of Monteverdi.[9]

Even during the great flowering of monasticism, a convent remained immeasurably smaller than a male foundation. Wilhelm Kurze has noted that where between the eighth and ninth centuries the number of monks at Nomantola would have added up to some twelve hundred (a figure borne out in other areas of Europe), the female abbey founded by Count Winigis in 867 had room for no more than twenty;[10] and when fourteen years later the convent was further endowed, the number of handmaids of the Lord still rose to only thirty.

This disproportion between male and female communities characterized the entire Middle Ages, and has not yet yielded a satisfactory explanation, especially considering the almost exclusively aristocratic interest in monasticism in this period. Certainly one of the elements that worked against female communities was their inability to offer liturgical memorials on the same scale as their male counterparts. During the ninth century, and even more in the tenth, monks tended ever more frequently to take major orders and, having done so, as priests they were able to say masses in memory of the founder or benefactor of the community and were not limited to mere prayers.[11] This sort of "memorial specialization," like that of Cluny, where masses were uninterruptedly offered for the "friends" of the abbey, was impossible for female communities. In this sense, the social role of women was limited and consequently the initial endowment of the convent and the dowries brought by individual nuns were always essential to the very survival of the community.

This does not alter the fact that in some cases female communities were apparently entrusted with guaranteeing the "memory" of the aristocratic family that founded them. Such seems to have been the role of Gandersheim, Quedlinburg, and Gernrode in tenth-century Saxony. There are, however, no significant parallels at the same time in Italy or Burgundy, apart from the minor exception provided by Santa Giulia in Brescia, whose famous necrology has survived.[12]

There is another element which probably played an essential role in keeping the flow of female monastic vocations at a reduced level. It has been said, perhaps with some exaggeration, that the choice of entering into religion was—given that society almost automatically destined her for marriage—just about the only real choice a woman could make herself. In fact, many ecclesiastics lamented the way in which parents offered to God girls whom, through poverty, illness, or deformity, men did not want. Put that way, the argument is too radical. Men, too, were "automatically" directed toward marriage—if, that is, an impairment made them unable to bear arms. But certainly the value of a woman, in a society in crisis or in a state of demographic stagnation, was powerfully linked to her reproductive capacity: in general, freedom of choice for women was proportional to levels of population growth.

But, to return to monastic foundations, in the Tuscany that Kurze studied there were sixteen in the eighth century, three in the ninth, and not a single one in the tenth until 978.[13] In such a situation—when many ancient foundations (Montecassino, Farfa, and others) were vanishing, destroyed by Saracens or done in by troubled politicosocial conditions—female monasticism was obviously even further downgraded. Even the brief flowering of Greek monasticism in Rome only further masculinized the monastic picture, for in Greece women's communities were in number and size even less important than in the West.

It should not be forgotten, however, the history of sanctity in Italy being our subject, that in this stage of history a woman became a saint only if she was a nun or, if a lay person, because she was very powerful. To this one must add that in Italy the Lombard monarchy, in constant struggle with the Church, had in practice put a stop to the flourishing cult of queen nuns such as Radegunda, Batilde, and Clotilde, so characteristic of the Franks or, in another form, of Ottonian Germany.[14]

One would have thought that the pious Theodelinda, as described in the *Historia Langobardorum* by Paul the Deacon, or in the letters addressed to her by Pope Gregory I, would have had all the attributes necessary for a sovereign to become the object of a cult: she was a Catholic in what was largely an Arian court; she founded churches (including the Church of Saint John the Baptist in Monza, to which Paul the Deacon linked the fortunes of the kingdom); she was educated and generous. Nonetheless, two elements were probably missing from her canonization: she did not, at the end of her life, become a nun, so that she could not be seen as a saint; and neither of her kingly husbands, Authari and Agilulf, was converted from what seems to have been a tenacious Arianism. In the Carolingian period, in contrast, the odor of sanctity that clung to Clotilde had much to do with the baptism of her husband, Clovis.

There was no great change in the Carolingian period, which is marked by a drastic diminishment, if not the total disappearance, in the model of the holy queen. In the Carolingian ninth century, the admired figure was the queen who was *consors regni,* the consort, the queen who shared the power of the emperor to whom she was bound. The most famous example in Italy was that of Angilberga, the wife of Ludwig II, a woman whom all the sources describe as highly capable and influential, and whose rise was well recorded in the archives.[15]

The notable great ladies of the tenth century—a period, we should not forget, for which narrative sources are fewer than for the Carolingian period—were almost all at some remove from any idea of sanctity. As is true of all the areas under permanent Byzantine influence, Rome in the tenth century was a city in which women handled property with notable autonomy and sometimes had a decisive influence on politics. Rome was painted in somewhat gloomy colors by the historian Liutprand of Cremona, and his reconstruction of the history of Rome was influential in making the tenth century known as the Iron Century.[16] Modern historians often cite it as the "Age of Pornocracy."

Liutprand's great ladies—women like Stephania, Theodora, and even more prominently Marozia—liked to flaunt the ancient and aulic title "senatress"; they were all purportedly women without modesty, more than capable of unscrupulously using their own wiles and charms to seize power for themselves, their husbands, or their children.

By contrast, the second half of the tenth century offers us a princess, Adelaide, a queen of the *Regnum Italiae,* whose saintly reputation was to be ratified in the next century by a papal canonization. Queen and empress, her links to Italy were only political, for she was born in Burgundy and it was to Burgundy that she retired after an eventful life.[17] Within the tradition of chronicle and hagiography, the life of Adelaide presents some aspects of a novel and some elements of the life of a saint.[18] Married when very young to Lothar, king of Italy, she was still very young when she was left a widow with an infant daughter. Because her marriage had conferred on her a certain legitimacy, she fell prey to the persecutions of Berengarius (Berengar II of Ivrea), who himself sought the Italian crown. Confined to a fortress and subjected to all sorts of vexations, the young widow kept up her spirits and decided to escape. Pursued, she hid in the marshes of the Po, was concealed by a fisherman, and was then taken under the personal protection of Adalbert of Canossa, an act by which he later gained the favor of the Ottonian court.[19] There followed, at the age of nineteen, her marriage to Otto of Saxony, formerly king of the Germans, to whom (at least in some versions) she "transferred" the royal crown of Italy.

The marriage was certainly politically significant, and a few years later, in 962, alongside her second husband, she was crowned empress of the Holy Roman Empire. Her husband, considerably older than herself and a widower, already had two sons to whom this marriage seemed a threat to their own positions. A series of rebellions ensued that embittered Otto and damaged his kingdom. Adelaide was widowed a second time in 973, but this did not put an end to her political role. Although her relations with Otto's young son, Otto II, and his Greek, Byzantine wife, Theophanu, were at first poor—which contributed (in the eyes of hagiographers) to her status as a "martyr" to motherly love and patience—in the last years of Otto II's reign she returned to prominence. When Otto II died in 983, Adelaide and Theophanu, her stepdaughter-in-law, made common cause to protect their grandson and son, the three-year-old Otto III, whose crown was finally recognized by all the rival princes of Germany. For a few years, the two women shared the burden of conducting the empire's affairs until, feeling herself close to death, the Burgundian princess withdrew to the Abbey of Selz on the Rhine, which she had founded and staffed with Cluniac monks, and selected as her last place of residence.

It is thanks to Cluniac hagiographers that Adelaide's sanctity was recognized by the Church. The queen had already received a highly favorable report in the Life written by Abbot Maïeul, but her real fame rests on her Life as written by Odilo of Cluny, with whom she had been in close contact.[20] In the Cluniac abbot's *Epitaphium,* Adelaide is seen as a model sovereign: she was both just and merciful; she loved peace but also knew how to defend order in a human society that God intended to be ruled by someone whose power was ordained by Himself; she bore every adversity with patience, protected the Church, founded monasteries (her assistance in founding Cluniac monasteries in the Po Valley is proven); and at the end of her life she prepared herself serenely for a Christian death.[21] Such is the idealized portrait that Odilo drew of the Holy Roman empress Adelaide, yet her cult remained almost exclusively restricted to the Abbey of Selz and in limited fashion to the Cluniac order. In the current state of research there would be no basis for the hypothesis that her model of sanctity had an influence on Italian society at the time.

Religious Italy has little to rival this obviously preeminent woman who goes well beyond any purely feminine notion of sanctity. Take, for instance, one of the few women in tenth-century Italy who did enjoy a certain reputation of sanctity, Abbondanza of Spoleto. At best, her story is not particularly trustworthy and tells us little about her. We know that her pilgrimage to the Holy Land, undertaken to accompany her father, was fundamental to her religious experience, and that after his death she led a chaste life, used her property for the service of the poor, and, most important, founded the Church of Saint Gregory of Spoleto. In effect, her hagiographic survival rests on the frescoes in that church, which relate a few episodes of her life.[22]

The Triumph of Monasticism and Signs of the Gregorian Reform

The great monastic and canonical reform pushed through by the Carolingian monarchy—which modern historians, somewhat simplifying the issue, connect with Benedict of Aniane and his works—was almost completely ignored in Italy. The tradition connected to a few early medieval great abbeys, such as Montecassino and Subiaco (which could boast of having been founded by the father of Western monasticism, Benedict of Nursia), but also Bobbio, Nonantola, and Saint Paul Without-the-Walls in Rome, was simply too powerful, and the central power, which should have helped to impose uniformity on the various monastic observances, was too weak. Nevertheless, Italy was richer than other parts of Europe in lively cathedral churches. In the tenth and eleventh centuries, their libraries contained treasures unknown elsewhere, and their schools, with instruction in grammar and rhetoric for the benefit of the local clergy, were both better distributed and more lively.

The Cluniac movement, based on the monastery founded in Burgundy in 910 by William the Pious, was also slow to impose itself on Italy, even though it enjoyed the support of such patrons as Otto I and Adelaide, or the *princeps Romanorum*, Alberic. Its influence, in fact, was probably less great than history long claimed.[23]

What was lively and precocious in Italy was the rediscovery of the ascetic model associated with the Desert Fathers, that early monasticism with strong eremitic connotations characterized by manual labor and an unusually stringent asceticism, which had reached the West through the writings of Jerome and Cassian of Marseilles in the closing stages of antiquity. In the last years of the tenth century, at the court of Otto III, a few of the great "hermits" of the day met. Among them were Nilus of Rossano, a celebrated Italo-Greek monk, and Romuald of Ravenna, called on against his will to found a reformed Benedictine congregation later known as the Camaldolese.[24]

But this new phase in the history of monasticism had no major effects on the world of women. From its earliest days, the eremitic life had been a strictly masculine endeavor. It was thought too dangerous for women (and also for the men with whom they might have come into contact), who were seen as lacking the physical energy necessary to support so austere a life.

As we move through the eleventh century, however, women's foundations become more and more numerous in the available documentation. This is due to the spread of private churches and monasteries (*Eigenkirche* and

Eigenklöster) and the contemporaneous settlement of great aristocratic families in Italy. The relationship between aristocracy and monasticism in this period has been well analyzed by Cinzio Violante and Guiseppe Sergi, and with some simplification it can be broken down into several essential characteristics.[25]

An aristocratic family founds a religious establishment on its own property and retains the right to name its superior, who is nearly always chosen from within the family. In return, the charitable foundation engages itself, as explained earlier, to pray for its founders and benefactors, living and dead. At the same time it plays a role as a form of "cement" for family identity, which is particularly important when large families tend to divide themselves into various branches, with only scant relations among them. The church or monastery, founded by common ancestors and generally chosen as a place for burial, becomes—as the family castle is for other reasons—the ideal center of the world of that family. Furthermore, the property that constituted its original donation often winds up being the only part of the family property that long remains common property. In this respect, and within the limits just stated, even female monasticism had its raison d'être. This explains the number of such foundations in the pre-Gregorian age that Paolo Golinelli lists in Emilia.[26]

But the first half of the eleventh century is important for other reasons, too. It is precisely during this period that the underlying premises for essential changes in ecclesiastical structures were being set out. These were to have a profound effect on religious ideals in the period that followed.

Halfway through the eleventh century accusations against the clergy of the time, regarding simony and concubinage, became ever more strident. This is not the place to detail the reasons for or the results of the struggle for reform, but a few points have to be made to make it possible to understand the next stage. The struggle against married clergymen, the ever more explicit demand that the celebrant consecrate the host *con mani pure* (that is, without having had relations with women), and the final triumph of the principle of ecclesiastical celibacy had a decisive impact on models of sanctity and spiritual ideals. What had been themes dear to monastic morality in the patristic era now became weapons against a corrupt clergy. This battle was fought in Italy jointly by a part of the Church hierarchy and by a lay elite that was especially strong in cities like Florence and Milan.[27] Reading in the sources, one comes to see that women participated as much as men in this passive resistance against an unworthy clergy; they too were involved in what was called at the time a liturgical strike, refusing to accept the sacraments from impure priests.

The eventual victory of reform along these main lines (henceforward the clergy must be celibate, if not virgin, and without an economic relationship of any sort with the secular power) nonetheless marked a decisive defeat for the laity. By its acceptance of the earthly dimension, the laity was condemned to a fundamental inferiority. It is true that at the same time the Church declared the substantial equality of all states before God. Thus married lay people were not denied the possibility of pursuing perfection, but in the eyes of the faithful sexuality had acquired a connotation of "impurity," which had been fundamentally extraneous in previous ages. In my opinion, this is the source of that deep misogyny which Georges Duby found in so many texts of the feudal era;[28] and it is certainly the most convincing reason for the "overvaluation" of virginity for which women were often responsible.

The Gregorian and post-Gregorian eras, like all periods in which ecclesiastical structures are subject to a powerful "hierarchization," were, as J. Tibbets Schulenberg pointed out many years ago, sparing in figures of holy women.[29] Another model of sanctity, that of the bishop-saint, was spreading through Europe and was destined for great and lasting success; and, naturally, it had no female pendant.[30] The New Monasticism triumphed during the twelfth century; the Camaldolese and the Vallombrosans continued to flourish and to them were now added the Carthusians and Cistercians, whose diffusion in the next century reached parts of Europe never touched by the old monasticism, such as east-central Europe, or regions it had barely affected, such as southern Italy. But few women enjoyed the successes visited on their male counterparts among the religious orders. Even in this period, all we find in Italy are a few pale figures of exemplary nuns such as Agnes and Giovanna da Bagno of Romagna, for whom the male Camaldolese (on whom they depended) assured a minimum of saintly reputation.[31]

The exemplary woman in Italy, the one long remembered after her death, exalted but also maligned in her lifetime, was neither a saint nor a nun, but the "Great Countess," Matilda of Canossa, marchioness of Tuscany. This noblewoman, descended from two great aristocratic families and related to the imperial family through her mother, a great landowner on both sides of the Appennines, which provided her with the key to Italian politics, was, while she remained for a long time the imperial vicar in Italy, the genuine and vital ally of Gregory VII and his successors in the struggle for ecclesiastical reform. Twice married, apparently against her will, to men who made her the object of morbid and gossipy curiosity on the part of contemporary chroniclers, childless and abandoned, in the encomiastic literature written about her she is described as a true *miles Christi* in the Gregorian sense, one who applied all her energy and political capacity to serving the Roman Church, which she made the universal legatee of all her domains. Matilda was the heroine of *De principibus canusinis,* which Donizone of Canossa dedicated to the lords of his town; she was also the figure exalted in Rangerio of Lucca's

Vita Sancti Anselmi, as one of the "great" personages of the Gregorian period; to Matilda was likewise dedicated the commentary on the Song of Songs
in which Giovanni of Mantua compared her to the example of female spiritual
perfection, the bride of the Song.[32]

This want of female saints reflects the "marginality" of women in the
religious domain. But in a new period, new ideals of sanctity would no longer
exclude women.

Women in Heretical Movements

The part played by women in the heretical movements between the eleventh
and twelfth centuries has long been the object of study and debate, though
in Italy, from some points of view, it was—compared to the better-known
Cathar movement in Provence—fairly marginal. However sparse and not
always verifiable the testimony we have about Italian heretics (the Monteforte
group, the Waldensians, the Cathars, and the Free Spirit movement), one
thing is certain: they all contained a substantial feminine element. In at least
one case, that of Monteforte, a woman, the chatelaine, seems to have played a
fundamental role in guaranteeing the development of the sect.[33]

Apart from among the Cathars, however, active participation by women,
with parapriestly functions, was prohibited. Among the Waldensians the
preachers were all men; and even among the Cathars the task of linking the
different groups was left to the *perfecti,* not the *perfectae.* The women, as one
might expect, given the social structure of the period, were relegated to an
almost purely domestic and sedentary life. Unfortunately, although what we
know about Peter Waldo derives from somewhat late sources, one need only
refer to the religious choices he made to understand the limited role of
women among the Waldensians. When he decided to give up all his worldly
goods and preach the word of God *against the heretics,* his daughters were
steered toward monastic vocations—an affectionate father was bound to consider this the only "safe" choice.

Among the Cathars the situation of women was in some ways different:
once she had received the *consolamentum,* a woman was as much a *perfecta* as
a man; and it is not by mere chance that historians have noted a number of
Provençal noblewomen who were remarkably influential in their family circle and contributed decisively to the success of the movement in southern
France.[34] One proof of the importance of this phenomenon is the zeal with
which Dominic of Guzmán applied himself to bringing these noblewomen
back to orthodoxy. It should be remembered that the first Dominican foundation, at Notre Dame de Prouille, was created for the benefit of these new
converts. Women's disaffection and their progressive movement into the Sec-

ond and Third Orders created for them by the Mendicant friars was a real contribution to reabsorption of the Cathar phenomenon into the faith.[35]

What were the reasons for this strong feminine presence in both orthodox and heretical movements in this phase of the Middle Ages? Some thirty years ago, Gottfried Koch offered a possible explanation: that the female population outweighed the male; that young women who could not find husbands, and instead married older men, became widows at an earlier age; that mortality among men was high owing to war or to warlike games such as jousts; and that all these reasons compelled women to make their own way in a society in which marriage was no longer a sure thing.[36] Koch's thesis, which attracted many, has generally been rejected as too "materialistic."

Nonetheless, as already noted, women's vocations and especially those of young women not yet married seem especially widespread in those periods of historical development in which the biological role of women seems less important: that is, in periods of demographic growth. This observation, however, would only explain a greater social openness toward autonomous choices for women; the world of heterodox movements, less structured and hierarchical than the traditional ecclesiastical model, certainly seems to have offered women at least a minimum participation, a possibility of speech and action that the orthodox tradition, ever faithful to Pauline teaching, had always denied them.

In one aspect, heretics and Gregorian reformers were in agreement: in their search for a more perfect ascesis. Both condemned the materiality of the body and, along with that, love, marriage, and procreation, all of which were seen as concessions to the weakest, basest forms of human nature. One could say that while the traditional, Catholic condemnation of the body devalued woman, seeing her with a misogynist eye as Eve the temptress, the heretical world and particularly the Cathars assigned no such negative primacy to women: for them, any form of physical relationship that brought about the creation of other human and therefore carnal beings was a sign of imperfection. A legitimate marriage was no better than a free or an adulterous union; in fact, it could even be seen as worse, in that marriage was traditionally associated with procreation and the rearing of the young.

Mary and the Positive Feminine

Despite its prominent role in recent studies, the history of the relationship between women and religion in the twelfth century was not marked solely by misogyny. It cannot be denied that in many ways, in Italy, this was a more negative than positive period for women. As regards property, the revival of trade and the readoption of Roman law governing it both marked a clear worsening of the situation for women. Ever more decisively excluded from inheriting property, forced to content themselves with a dowry, even within marriage women were theoretically denied any capacity to manage or control family property.[37] In a more strictly religious or spiritual sense, however, there was an evident positive reevaluation of the feminine element. There emerged, with ever greater authoritativeness, the figure of Mary: as the necessary vehicle of salvation for humanity, the beloved of the Divine Son, and, unique among all creatures, the one assumed into heaven.

This does not mean, of course, that until then Mary had been a marginal figure: one has only to note that there is practically not a single early medieval or Byzantine crucifixion scene without her presence, alongside John, at the foot of the cross, and no one can deny that tradition gave her a role as the "privileged intercessor" to her divine Son. It remains true, nonetheless, that early medieval religiosity, strongly impregnated with Old Testament elements, emphasized the role of God the creator and judge: in the representations of the Last Judgment or the Apocalypse, Mary hardly appears.

But, bit by bit, a religious attitude came into being based on reading the Gospels; the humanity of Christ, from his birth in poverty to his death on the cross, became a subject of daily meditation. In this new spiritual climate, which probably reaches its apogee in Bernardine mysticism, in which the soul seeks union with its divine Spouse and takes root in the ever more common *sequela* or *imitatio Christi*, the figure of the Mother of God assumes ever greater importance: a theological importance, but also an affective and emotional one. Evidence of this new attitude comes from the numerous foundations dedicated to the Virgin. It is not easy to date this tendency—in the empire there were already Marian cathedrals in the eleventh century—but between the twelfth and thirteenth centuries the Île-de-France was covered in white Notre Dames built in the new Gothic style, and in Italy from 1200 onward a great many cathedrals were dedicated to Mary, often superseding older devotions.[38]

Another image was soon added to that of the Virgin mother: Mary as Queen of Heaven, crowned in person by her divine Son. The motif of the coronation of the Virgin spread first in France and reached Italy in the thirteenth century, finding its grandest statements in the great churches in Rome dedicated since late antiquity to Mary: Santa Maria Maggiore and Santa Maria in Trastevere. There one can still see today, in the cool shadows of their naves, the story of Mary and her coronation in the splendid mosaics created by the greatest artists of late-thirteenth-century Rome, Pietro Cavallini and Jacopo Torriti.

The spread of Catharism in some ways favored Marian devotion: in denying the Incarnation and condemning any positive vision of its material nature, the Cathars naturally attached no importance to the Virgin. As a result, her role became ever more central to the teaching of the Church. When, in the thirteenth century, the Church tried to "reconquer" for the faith the many who had strayed, the Marian confraternities, actively promoted by the preaching of the Mendicant friars, had a major role in gathering back the faithful.[39]

A form of religiosity in which the affective and emotional elements became predominant; and the spread of mysticism, in which the feminine element is built in—in seeking union with God, men and woman alike think of themselves as brides;[40] both these played a role in giving the Marian cult a new dimension. The more favorable demographic conditions of the thirteenth century also helped give female religiosity a much broader role than in the past.

In recent years, there has been much debate over the part played by the development of poems about courtly love toward the end of the eleventh century. Some interpretations of this poetry, traditional in its general lines, have been optimistic; others have followed Robert Fossier in offering a more pessimistic, misogynistic view.[41] In the French historian's view, Occitan love poetry sees women more as objects than subjects: objects, moreover, of a love that is anything but ennobling. My own view is that, despite its limitations, the Italian version of Provençal courtly poetry—whether that which arose at the court of Sicily's Frederick II and his sons, or that emerging in the new urban culture, such as the Florentine *Stil nuovo*—shows an objective, positive reevaluation of what it is to be a woman. It would seem unimportant here to analyze, much less resolve, the vexed question of whether Dante's Beatrice or Petrarch's Laura were in fact real women. They exist within the poetry, and the contemporary reader of the *Vita nova* or the *Canzoniere* could not help getting a richer and more multifaceted view of women than had prevailed in the preceding centuries. That courtly poetry should be, as Georges Duby sustains, no more than a masculine game through which men sought, in women, a way to become more civilized and refined, is, as Duby admits, only one aspect of the problem.[42] What is certain is that in thirteenth-century society women had begun to *exist*.

The Mendicant Orders

The creation of the Mendicant orders without any doubt represents a decisive turn in the history of Italian and European religiosity. The two major orders—the Franciscan and the Dominican—were founded at about the same time and were officially recognized by the Church during the reign of Honorius III (1216–1223), though in fact they corresponded perfectly with the desires expressed by the Fourth Lateran Council (1215) animated by the great reformer pope Innocent III. Though founded with different characteristics and aims (the Dominicans were clerics dedicated to antiheretical preaching, while the Franciscans were a lay and clerical fraternity whose principal activity was the itinerant preaching of moral values), they soon became the buttresses of the Church in the thirteenth century.

Both were highly centralized; both—as opposed to earlier monastic orders, which had excluded only personal property but had managed extensive landholdings possessed in common by the monks—renounced all property or fixed income; and both were active in preaching. The direct intervention of the Holy See, which overwhelmed the two orders with privileges, soon gave them further tasks: as spiritual directors of conscience, through confession, and, when the Mendicants were given the ungrateful role of inquisitors *heretice pravitatis,* as repressors of heresy.[43]

As already pointed out, the Dominicans immediately founded women's communities of their own. In Rome, for instance, the first of these was that of the nuns of San Sisto, destined to become one of the richest and best administered of all urban convents. For that matter, the story of Saint Francis of Assisi is inseparable from that of Clare, his aristocratic fellow townswoman who, touched by his words, left family and home to follow his example of *sequela Christi*.[44]

As far as the women's branches of the Mendicant orders are concerned, two problems were soon evident. First, Franciscan and Dominican nuns could only partially develop the evangelical message of their founders. As women, and thereby excluded from sacramental functions, they had to content themselves with a style of life that differed only in its greater austerity from that of more traditional nuns. The Mendicant women's communities had to accept dowries; normally, to enter a convent, nuns had to demonstrate that they entered with a dowry and would not become an intolerable charge on their monasteries. Clare's fierce resistance to the official hierarchy and indeed the papacy is well known through her insistence on remaining faithful to the absolute poverty demanded by Francis. But the *privilegium paupertatis* granted to San Damiano and a small number of other communities does not affect the overall picture.[45]

Indeed, the growing success of the Mendicants made their women's communities centers for aristocratic recruitment: two of the three Poor Clare foundations in Rome (San Silvestro in Capite and San Lorenzo in Panisperna) were created by one of the most powerful baronial families of Rome, the Colonna; in Naples, Santa Chiara—especially in the days of Robert and Sancia (early fourteenth century)—was closely linked to the court; in the 1220s in Bologna, Diana degli Andalò headed the Dominican convent, thus establishing a link between the new order and one of the most illustrious families of the city; and later, at the end of the fourteenth century, Corpus Christi, founded in Venice by the Dominican Giovanni Dominici, contained the fine flower of that city's nobility.

There is another element, however, that we should not underestimate. For all these good signs, the truth is that early on the Mendicants, too, had to face the same problems with which the Cistercians had been faced earlier: it was nearly impossible to keep relations between women's communities and those of the male branch, entrusted with the spiritual care of such communities, harmonious. As their brothers had already found out, both Dominican and Franciscan men felt the weight of spiritual counseling that many thought perilous to their souls. Too frequent contacts with nuns who, being cloistered, ended up totally dependent on whoever kept them in touch with the outside world; administrative problems; misunderstandings arising from a very different kind of religious sensibility: all these led those in charge of these orders, by the middle of the thirteenth century, to seek to disburden themselves of this weighty responsibility.[46] The Holy See was compelled to intervene to retain the link between the men and the women, but it is clear that many convent chaplains envied their brothers who were able to exercise their apostolate anywhere in the world.

Italy seems to have been a particularly difficult country for relations between monks and nuns. There were no double monasteries or exceedingly few during the early Middle Ages, not a single foundation comparable to Robert d'Arbrissel's at Fontevraud, or Gilbert of Sempringham's in England, during the twelfth century;[47] a similar attempt to create double communities, in the context of the Benedictine reform of Forzaté, had but a brief existence—the women's communities flourished, while the men's became extinct within a few decades.[48]

For all their limitations, the Mendicant communities, to be joined at the end of the thirteenth century by the Carmelites and the Augustinians, gave a tremendous impetus to feminine religiosity in Italy. However, women's most innovative and original experiences were to come not in the cloister but in the lay world, especially in the towns.

The New Forms of Lay Religiosity

Women's growing need to express the evangelical message in a concrete, realistic fashion was certainly the determining factor in the success of penitential societies, confraternities, and, above all, the Third Orders. These last were Mendicant tertiaries, groups inspired by the religious message of the Franciscans and Dominicans but living in the secular world. All these ways of life reveal the same need: to translate into action the love of their neighbors so insistently promoted by preachers, for this love, for a layman or a laywoman, could only take the form of active charity.

Penitents and tertiaries took up a way of life marked by moderate asceticism (refusing all finery, games, and excessive enjoyments of the table, while adhering completely to the precepts of the Church concerning sexual morality, and thus engaging in long periods of abstinence) and participated more intensely in religious life (which now involved an obligation to pray several times daily, attendance at mass not just on Sundays and feast days but at meetings whose fundamental purpose was to listen to homilies prepared for such pious associations, and more frequent recourse to the sacraments). Their practices in fact reflected a way of life akin to that of the religious, which continued to be the one model of Christian perfection. How did this active charity by the laity manifest itself? And what part did women play in it?

From the twelfth century onward and in nearly all parts of Italy there was a burgeoning of hospital foundations.[49] At this stage in the Middle Ages, of course, the terms *hospitale* and *hospitium* were largely generic and concealed many different realities. Such institutions might be no more than simple shelters in which gathered and found a welcome all those who found themselves, whether temporarily or permanently, homeless. Among the former might be foreigners, most particularly those traveling for a religious purpose, such as pilgrims, whose number rose steeply from the end of the eleventh century.[50] The second group consisted of the poor in both their traditional guises (orphans, widows, the occupationally disabled) and the new ones typical of Italian cities in the late Middle Ages (the socially marginal, peasants freshly arrived from the country, unemployed artisans or wage earners, the once-rich, fallen on hard times in ever more frequent economic crises).[51] Besides offering hospitality and support, the *hospitalia* began to perform tasks more similar to those of a hospital in the modern sense: care of the sick, the wounded, and sometimes the incurable, as was done at the leprosaria, which become ever more common starting in the twelfth and thirteenth centuries.

The increased number of these *hospitalia* is probably due more to the new lay spirituality and its need for action than to religious institutions. True, one should not think of these institutions as having modern dimensions. The archives reveal the existence of scores of such hospitals in every urban center, but these were often tiny institutions, with something like a dozen beds and without regular medical personnel. There are, of course, a few exceptions, especially by the fourteenth century, and these coped with scores if not hundreds of the sick and needy: places like the great Roman papal hospitals (for instance, Santo Spirito in Sassia), those managed by a confraternity (such as Sant' Angelo, today San Giovanni), or Florence's Santa Maria Nova.[52]

Although they did not play a main role, women had a part in all these hospitals. The founders of such institutions were almost invariably men, because it was men who generally had the necessary capital and were able to dispose of it freely. But women had an active role in their foundation: many women's wills, especially widows', bequeathed their property to a hospital. When the woman was relatively poor these legacies may seem to modern eyes purely symbolic, but this was not so in medieval terms. Women bequeathed their own beds, with mattresses and linen.

Where a confraternity—like the Raccomandati del Salvatore in Rome—could offer masses in perpetuity on the anniversary of a benefactor's death, and in his or her church of choice, we can note hundreds of women who in the last two centuries of the Middle Ages put down no small sum (fifty florins) to have masses said for their own souls or for those of their husbands or children. This sort of donation provided an operating budget for the great hospital foundations, and here women, taking into account their lesser economic weight, were proportionately more active than men.[53]

Women were nearly always excluded from the management of these associations; indeed, only in a few cases were they full members of the confraternities. But they were often highly active in looking after the sick (particularly women and children) as *hospitalarie,* and as far as we can tell from the few surviving documents, practical hygiene and the preparation of food were their exclusive domain, much of the latter being done by wealthy women in their own homes and brought to the patients in hospital.[54] But women were especially strong among the Mendicant tertiaries. Among the Third Orders, women's participation was not always confined to active charity. Sometimes influenced by their confessors, sometimes conditioned by a society in which their freedom of action was relatively limited, the tertiaries with whom we make acquaintance in hagiographic texts were often praised for their strong emotional involvement and for forms of ardent piety and mysticism that had few parallels in the world of their male counterparts.

It is no easy matter to understand to what extent the stylized accounts offered by the hagiographers correspond to reality and how much is simply there to provide a model in the hope that it may be imitated.[55] But there is no doubt that at this time the official Church's saintly models did not diverge greatly between men and women. The undisputed success of the Mendicant orders during the thirteenth century translated itself into the canonizations of Francis of Assisi, Anthony of Padua, and Clare of Assisi.[56] The papacy demonstrated its approval of these new forms of religiosity by its choice of saints, seeking also in some way to "institutionalize" them.

Aside from their love of poverty, which was strongly accented in the cases of both Francis and Clare, their canonization bulls were expressed in fairly traditional terms, as was the even less "personalized" one for Anthony: Francis and Clare were sanctified more as initiators of a new form of religious life and as an exemplary abbess than as bearers of a new spirituality.[57] But it should not be thought that the Roman Church was any less interested in the Preachers: the canonization of Saint Dominic in 1233 by Gregory IX is a clear sign of approval for a family of religious that rendered indisputable services to the Holy See.

It is difficult to fit Dominic, Spanish by birth and for many years active in Provence, into a history of Italian sanctity, though his work was particularly important from an institutional standpoint in Italy. It would seem that Dominic personally obtained the first bulls approving his order in Rome and it was in Bologna in 1220 that the first general chapter of the order was held to approve the fundamental decision to live *sine proprio*.[58] Bolognese witnesses were certainly vital in the process of Dominic's canonization and his mortal remains in Bologna became the object of devout pilgrimage. The life of Benvenuta Bojani—one of the first women to testify to the strong relationship between the Order of Preachers and their devout women followers—was powerfully marked by her pilgrimage to the tomb of the saint.[59]

Beyond these official images painted by the Church, there is no doubt that the major saints of the Mendicant orders, especially the Franciscan saints, left a lasting effect on the religious life of medieval Italy. We should remember that it is to Francis that we owe the theme of the Nativity scene, "staged" by him for the first time in Greccio. The reevocation of the birth of the baby Jesus, displayed in all his poverty and original desolation, contributed greatly to the growth of devotion to the humanity of Christ. But even more important to medieval piety were Francis's stigmata. Received with great reserve, at least at the beginning, the stigmata confirmed his role as *alter Christus*, as the new Christ, perfect in his imitation of Christ's poverty, obedience, and humility, and made him the particular object of female piety.[60] From that moment dated the multiplication of pious women who bore on their bodies the mark of their love for Christ the man, of a "compassion," or shared passion, in the most powerful sense of the term; it would bring them to cover themselves with incurable wounds and ulcerations or even, like Clare of Montefalco, to bear on their hearts the instruments of his Passion.[61]

This Franciscan form of women's religiosity reveals a certain ambiguity. One could say that a love of Christ that became a perfect imitation of his sufferings made these women more faithful to the message of Saint Francis than many of his friars, stuffed with university doctrine and lacking in humility. At the same time one could argue that many of them seemed to have missed that part of Francis's teaching revealed in his "Canticle of the Creatures" or in his idea of perfect joy. Few or none managed to live in perfect unity with all of creation as Francis had; and it is hard to perceive among these women an attitude of inner joy. Their meditations on the suffering of Christ in fact led them to multiply ascetic practices, to fast to the point of losing all taste for food, to flog themselves mercilessly, to weep for days on end. Many years ago, André Vauchez observed this note of sorrow; within the narrow limits of female religiosity, these may have been the only forms of expression possible for the imitation of Christ.[62]

Vauchez's observation is only half true, however, for in the biographies of many holy women this phase of imitation through suffering is only the second stage in a journey to perfection that begins with active charity. This is an instance of precisely the difficulty in determining to what degree a spiritual path was the result of a woman's free choice, was molded by her confessor, or was simply a convention among hagiographers, confessors become biographers, to praise the spirituality of their devout clients.

Joy was a part of these women's religious experiences but it was a joy obtained by forswearing the things of this world; it was a mystical dimension that greatly impressed their contemporaries and still causes argument among contemporary historians.

Mystical phenomena are an integral part of the model of female sanctity that takes over in Europe from the twelfth century onward. During the 1200s, Italy lacked figures such as the Beguines, women who lived out their choice of a religious life in the secular world. Certainly there were none of fame comparable to that of a Mary of Oignies, much of whose celebrity is due to her having had, in Cardinal Jacques de Vitry, an exceptional hagiographer, notwithstanding which she was never recognized as a saint by the official Church.[63] Still, one cannot say that mysticism was wholly absent in Italy. It is difficult to evaluate very late testimony, such as that concerning the Blessed Elena Enselmini, who lived in the first half of the thirteenth century—as difficult as it is to separate out mysticism narrowly defined from a general visionary attitude.[64] In the religious experience of Umiliana de' Cerchi, for instance, diabolical appearances seem to play a greater role than union with Christ.[65]

While again underlining the high risk involved in analyzing female religiosity on the basis of tales, accounts of visions, and indications of mystical experiences related by men, from the middle of the thirteenth century there is no lack of Italian sources on mystical experiences in the strict sense.

At first, accounts are sporadic. Women seemed to be reluctant to tell of their own encounters with Christ, and these have to be intuited from outside. In the case of Clare of Montefalco, for instance, her sisters in religion who testified at her canonization spoke of long periods of ecstasy—they could last for several days—of the expression of joy that illuminated her face, of her unawareness of the world about her: all phenomena they knew far more about than they did about the actual content of her visions. When we do find out something about that content, it seems more heavily saturated with doctrinal matter than with the stuff of emotions. In one of her visions, Clare comes to realize that she has been chosen by God and that the human will should never deviate from the divine, so that the two might be confounded. This stance led to her being accused of quietism *ante litteram* or of being able to know the future.[66] Spousal mysticism would seem to have been totally absent in her.

A particularly striking mystic is Clare of Assisi. It is not that we have many attested visions of hers—on the contrary. But one vision is justly celebrated for its uniqueness and has brought her to the attention of contemporary scholars. In this vision she reports having an extremely intense relationship, not with Christ but with Francis, from whose breast she suckled a milk of ineffable sweetness.[67]

Beyond the restraint and modesty that may have led some of these women not to reveal their visionary gifts, there was certainly a language problem for those who had to write down these visions. There were authors who, if the vision was of any complexity, had great difficulty understanding what was told them. This, for instance, is the case with Senator Giovanni Colonna, biographer and hagiographer of his sister, the Blessed Margaret. Though he was far from being an uncultivated man and though he could write in near-ecclesiastical Latin, Giovanni showed his limitations as a hagiographer precisely when he undertook to recount his sister's visions. Somewhat more at ease in this area was her second biographer, the nun Stephania; though a mediocre narrator, she plainly was more familiar with devotional texts, and her long acquaintanceship with Margaret allowed her to make her accounts of the visions more intelligible to the reader.[68] To what degree this work of "explanation" risks becoming "interpretation" or outright "invention" will never be known.

Margaret Colonna, whose flesh bore the mark of the ring put on her finger by her divine Spouse, was the first of the mystics who felt themselves above all to be entirely the brides of Christ. The last quarter of the thirteenth century gives us at least two great Italian visionary figures, both laywomen, both secular wives or lovers and mothers, and both, certainly not perchance, unrecognized as saints by the medieval Church: Angela of Foligno and Margaret of Cortona.[69] Though reasonably well known at the time (her *Rivelazioni* were scrutinized for orthodoxy by Cardinal Giacomo Colonna), Angela has yet to be canonized; it took a papal decision in the eighteenth century, by which time the religious mind had undergone radical changes, to make Margaret a saint.

The story of Margaret of Cortona is an example of the new way in which women lived out their religious experience. After a youth not beyond reproach (she fled from an unloving family into the arms of a young aristocrat by whom she bore a son), the future saint was converted: not by a long, internal process of repentance but as the result of an external trauma. The violent death of her lover, which left her bereft of support was, even in the hagiographic report, the determining element in her subsequent search for perfection. After a failed attempt to return to her family, Margaret devoted herself to a life of penance in Cortona. Her son, separated from his mother— she seemed to regard him less as an object of affection than as living proof of her sinful life—was directed toward a life in religion. At first, Margaret lived in the secular world, keeping herself alive with what she earned by caring for the sick, particularly for mothers in confinement; then she detached herself little by little from the world. She ended up a recluse attached to the Church of Saint Basil. As she lost her links to the secular world, her mystical experience deepened. She was a nuptial mystic, enjoying the joys of her union and constantly fearing that her lover would prefer another. Her mystical Life, narrated by Giunta Bevegnate, a Franciscan who was for many years her confessor, cannot be entirely trusted. His use of Margaret's visions and her privileged relationship with Christ to advance himself is all too evident.[70]

Margaret's relationship with her own body is a good instance of this historical phase. The early Christian Middle Ages had in some ways abolished the physical. A gnostic vision had turned the flesh into something intrinsically inferior to the spirit, making any physical description of a person not only useless but potentially harmful. His biographer gives us no clue as to what Saint Benedict looked like, nor Clovis. It is only in those circles particularly sensitive to the values of aristocratic culture, in which the writings of the ancients had not been entirely forgotten, that physical beauty continued to be considered the expression of an inner beauty: for instance the striking Colombano in Giona di Bobbio's *vita,* and the portrait of the saintly queen Matilda, with her grace and her coloring of lily and rose.

From the thirteenth century onward, interest in the physical world, as rediscovered in ancient philosophy, brought to the fore the old problem of the physical body in which the human soul is contained. But the body, no longer a matter of indifference, became the "enemy of the soul." The idea of the beauty of a saint disappeared entirely from hagiography. Early witnesses to Francis spoke only of his insignificant looks, his olive coloring. Women of some beauty, like Margaret of Cortona or Clare of Montefalco, did all they could to destroy the attractions of their own bodies. Margaret saw her beauty as the very reason for her sinful life; nothing could stop her from annihilating it, and had not her confessor forbidden it, she would have cut off her nose to deform herself. This desire for self-destruction could not have been approved of by the Church, for the Church preached that one should love one's fellow beings as one loves oneself, and condemned any excessive devaluing of the flesh among the Cathars. Thus a Clara of Montefalco, who ate practically nothing, slept but a few hours a night, and sought to deny any form of physical feeling, preserved a body that showed no signs whatever of her extraordinary abstinence.

Family Life and the Desire for Perfection

The theme of the "saint in the family" is now well recognized, thanks to the work of Alessandro Barbero.[71] His book, however, is concerned almost exclusively with the relationship between those who aspired to perfection and their families of origin, especially the parents who often opposed their children's choice of a religious life. Indeed, family resistance was, according to the Gospels, almost mandatory to prove that one loved God more than one loved one's father and mother. Between husbands and wives, the matter was stated differently when a religious vocation made its appearance after marriage or a vocation was kept secret despite one's being forced into marriage by one's family. Marriage was a stronger tie than that which bound a woman to her parents or brothers and sisters: the Gospels made it, unless there was adultery on the part of the wife, an indissoluble link. Saint Paul clearly stated that with marriage each of the partners gives up the ownership of his or her body, which subsequently belongs to the other.

The early medieval Church fought a long, and largely futile, battle to impose fidelity and indissolubility as fundamental values of the Christian marriage. But for centuries, too, a religious vocation was seen as superior to marriage. Radegunda, queen of the Franks, became a saint even though she abandoned her husband; Alexis, who slipped away on his wedding night, was recognized as a saint after his death, thanks to the ring that only his virgin bride could remove from his finger. With the triumph of the Gregorian reform and the development of marital theology in the twelfth century, and with the ever clearer emergence of the sacramental value of marriage (not definitively ratified until the Council of Trent), aspirants to perfection could no longer so easily escape marriage—unless, of course, the partner was going through an analogous conversion, as was the case with the imperial couple of Henry II and Cunegund, both canonized, perhaps principally because of their virginal union.[72]

Many might see the reaction to this new vision of marriage as excessive and not very Christian. Consider, for instance, Angela of Foligno, who in her spiritual biography welcomed with relief the death of her whole family, including her husband and children, which at last allowed her to be fully herself. In a world in which mothers were ever more frequently called upon to instruct their children, even these could be felt as a burden. Consider, too, the extreme example of Elizabeth of Hungary, a tender and loving wife and mother: widowed, she hesitated not at all to abandon her children, though still very young, because to love them would be seen as conflicting with the love owed to God and her neighbors.[73] Paradoxically, the social success of the model of the Christian family seems to have rendered even more acute the need to keep one's own liberty intact through the radical choice of virginity.

Sainthood and Culture

In the wake of Vauchez's studies it seems clear that among the attributes of female (largely uncanonized) sanctity privileged by the Roman Church at the end of the thirteenth century the *illicterata* model predominated.[74] That is understandable. Most of the women to whom we refer had not received even that minimum of education which nuns received; they lived out in the world, and at most they had gained some form of literacy in the vernacular. Normally, they were unable to write (even Catherine of Siena dictated her letters)—hence the interposition, in nearly all cases, of men between their religious experiences and ourselves—and had but a superficial knowledge of Latin.

Near illiteracy made for a great difference between the Italian mystical tradition and that of so many Cistercians in the north, some of whom were highly educated and in many cases could set down accounts of their own experiences.[75] There was certainly in Italy a public among devout women capable of reading devotional texts in the vernacular. This was specifically remarked on, and without surprise, in the case of Francesca of Rome, and one can suppose that texts like the *Ordinazioni,* written in Italian for Francesca's community at Tor de' Specchi, or the vernacular version of her *vita* addressed the needs of that audience.[76] One can also presume a certain ability to write in women who, like Umiliana de' Cerchi, belonged to the Florentine aristocracy, in which the ability to read, at least in Boccaccio's time (the *Decameron* was written for ladies, not gentlemen), was fairly widespread. We cannot, therefore, hypothesize for Italy, as H. Grundmann did for Germany, a widespread diffusion of sacred or devotional texts translated into Italian or a consequent growth of the vernacular, which was already fully mature in Italy.

What is striking about many of these women is their capacity to understand even the most abstruse passages in Scripture and to resolve deep theological problems. They were able to do so thanks to a *sapientia* that owed nothing to the *scientia* of this world, the latter being the exclusive property of males who ever more frequently studied theology and law at the universities spreading throughout Europe or at the many *studia* of the Mendicant friars, present in any important Italian city. Certainly Clare of Montefalco reveals deep understanding and a refined dialectic, and the same is true of Catherine of Siena, the one medieval example of an artisan's daughter the profundity of whose religious visions was recognized by the official Church.

Saints and the City

Practically from the beginning, Mendicants had preached peace. The attempts of religious orders to influence society directly had nearly all been condemned to ephemeral or deceptive success.[77] Early on, they abandoned any attempt at specific political action and devoted themselves to producing tracts. The role of mediator, peacemaker, and protector against foreign enemies, by contrast, was taken up with some success by many women. As Vauchez points out, this function often resulted in their being chosen, even in their lifetime or immediately after their death, as the patron saint of their city, thus exercising an important influence on the self-definition of many urban communities in central Italy.[78] Thanks to this role, they long enjoyed the devotion of their fellow citizens—a devotion that, while often ignoring much of the saints' precise historical traits, survived right up to the modern age (as in the case of Rose of Viterbo, Rita of Cascia, and others).

Sainthood and Female Religiosity in a Period of Crisis

If there has been much discussion in recent years about whether the last one hundred and fifty years of the Middle Ages can be described in economic and social terms as a period of crisis, it is indisputable that in religious history the period 1300–1450 is one of great uncertainty and tragic wounds.

At the death of Benedict XI (1304) began the papacy's long exile from Rome. Without ever explicitly threatening to move the papal see, the pontiffs were absent from the eternal city for over seventy years. When Gregory XI returned from Avignon in 1377, rather than improving, the situation degenerated further. When Gregory died, the College of Cardinals proceeded to two successive elections, and thus there were two popes simultaneously: the Neapolitan Bartolomeo Prignani (Urban VI) and the Savoyard Robert of Geneva (Clement VII). From that point until 1417 the Church enjoyed not one guide but always two, and at some stages three, popes. Even after the election of the Roman Oddone Colonna in 1417 (Martin V) the internal situation of the Church remained extremely troubled: the pope and the council, the assembly of the universal Church that finally and after many labors healed the schism, continued to fight for the leadership of Christendom.

The popes' absence from Rome produced for Italy a distinct "marginalization": Italians were ever less numerous in the College of Cardinals; the political situation grew ever more anarchic, with a French pope seeking, generally without success, to impose his political leadership on Italy. Less money flowed into Rome, for the curial administration was transferred to Avignon, and the major issues of Christendom were all decided by the Curia. The Italian crisis was visible even in the canonization process: ever fewer investigations of Italian candidates for sainthood were authorized by the pope, and very few came to a successful conclusion. The major exceptions were Thomas of Aquinas, canonized by John XXII in 1323—according to Vauchez, John saw in Thomism *the* answer to the religious disquiet of the period and to the pauperistic yearnings of the Franciscan movement[79]—and Celestinus V, whose sanctity, for political reasons, was recognized by Clement V in 1311.

When one refers to the schism, it is difficult to grasp just how deeply it wounded Christendom. To give but one example, consider the fact that the Mendicant orders, those pillars of orthodoxy in the previous hundred and fifty years, were themselves split into two obediences. The University of Paris, mother of all the sciences, *parens scientiarum*—and of theology first and foremost—according to the celebrated formulation of a bull of Gregory IX in 1231, was now in full crisis: having first chosen to obey the pope in Avignon, then continuously wavering thereafter, it was no longer the single, authoritative voice on European theology. The universities that sprang up throughout east-central Europe after the middle of the fourteenth century took some pleasure in the eclipse of Paris, but in this delicate area likewise Europe was without leadership.

As though this were not enough, Europe also suffered from a century-old conflict—with a truce now and then, but no lasting peace—between its two principal Catholic powers, France and England. The political disorder, economic misery, and social conflicts attendant on war translated themselves into an exasperation of religious feeling, an anxious search for certainties that often found an outlet in apocalyptic expectation and faith in the many prophets whose *parola ispirita* made itself heard throughout Europe.[80]

Meanwhile the great plagues ravaged Europe, from the first and most notorious, the Black Death of 1348, which forms a tragic counterpoint to the diverting stories of the *Decameron,* to the many other plagues that followed in the succeeding decades. These decimated the population of Europe and made all Christians even more aware of the fragility of human life.

These circumstances form more or less the background against which European religiosity developed at the waning of the Middle Ages. According to Charles de la Roncière, in Italy the expectation of the end of the world, the sense of the precariousness of life, and the need for new forms of solidarity to replace the traditional but plague-destroyed bonds of family and neighborhood were the main reasons for the birth, or growing success, of confraternities in the Tuscan region.[81] In Rome, too—at least as far as scanty records allow us to see—membership in the confraternities grew, as (more important) did the bequests on which their flourishing economies depended. Above all, urban hospital institutions multiplied and organized themselves better.[82]

The pope's absence from Rome was naturally felt in Italy as a sort of mutilation. It should not therefore surprise us to hear the voices of the great female mystics of the period, whether Italian or Italianized, loudly invoking the return of the pontiff to his chosen city. Women as different as Catherine of Siena, the daughter of a modest artisan, or the Swedish Bridget, related to the royal family of Sweden and received in all the great houses of the Roman aristocracy, were persuaded that it was God's will that the papacy return to Rome.

Vauchez has noted how the mysticism of Bridget and Catherine, in so many ways similar to that of countless other women who preceded them, was approvingly heard and later officially recognized as divinely inspired, and thus sanctioned with canonization, because their visions were in perfect accord with the ecclesiastical hierarchy and buttressed the Church's wavering institutions.[83] To this characteristic Catherine, in part thanks to her biographer Raymond of Capua, added that of serving as a perfect example of the charity demanded of a *mantellata,* that is, a penitent under the spiritual direction of the Dominicans. Her fame during her lifetime, her extraordinary gifts, the richness and originality of her mystical experience, the language in which she expressed herself (mediated by those who took down her accounts) all guaranteed her tremendous success. At the end of the Middle Ages and the beginning of the modern era, imitations of Catherine became as common as imitations of Francis were a few centuries before. For the first time, however, the model was a woman.

Women like Bridget and Catherine did not limit themselves to describing their own experiences of communion with Christ; they acted in a concrete fashion on reality in a deeply and complexly "political" way. They were not isolated cases. Vauchez has studied the French mystics at the time of the schism, locating voices of simple Christians who were disturbed by the unheard-of divisions they faced and at the same time were instruments of people who used the mystics' prophetic gifts on behalf of their own cause.[84] In France the most celebrated case of a political mystic is Joan of Arc. But her political attitudes were far from unique: in the Rome of Eugene IV, Francesca of Rome sought to intervene to reconcile the pope with the Council of Basel;[85] in the years that followed Italy had many female court prophets who put their charisma at the service of politics.[86]

In Search of an "Ordained" Sainthood

As we have just seen, plagues and disorders led to new and extreme forms of religiosity in the last centuries of the Middle Ages. Where on the one hand mystics and prophets satisfied the need of individual Christians for some form of certainty obtained only by direct communication with God, on the other phenomena like the flagellants were symptomatic of a widespread need for collective expiation.

The flagellants made their first appearance in 1260, and it is not yet quite clear why: was it in some way connected to the Joachimite expectation that the world was coming to an end, the date of which some had set for 1260?[87] The movement broke out again with particular virulence throughout east-central Europe in the wake of the great plague of 1348, which many interpreted as a sign of God's wrath. Though these particular penitents were looked upon with suspicion and condemned by the papacy, a ritualized form of the practice of the "discipline," itself an old form of monastic ascesis, spread far and wide. Most confraternities in fact provided for self-flagellation, at least on the occasion of major liturgical celebrations, especially during Holy Week. In 1399, flagellants were at the heart of the movement of the Bianchi, who went all over Italy, sometimes accepted with enthusiasm, sometimes repressed by the authorities, as happened in Venice.[88]

The Church sought to respond to these extremist and uncontrolled devotional movements by regularizing and disciplining them, by transforming tertiaries into nuns living in communities and subject to enclosure (the regular Third Order was created at the end of the fourteenth century). Not very successful attempts were made to bring those *gruppi bizzocali* still living in the world under control. Another measure was to offer "imitable" models of sanctity that responded to the needs of a tormented society in search of order.

As examples of these new hagiographic proposals, some years ago Fernanda Sorelli suggested Thomas of Siena's *vita* of Mary of Venice. This Thomas was the same Dominican friar who was one of the most ardent advocates of sainthood for his fellow Sienese, Catherine, who had to wait until the middle of the fifteenth century, and for a Sienese pope, before being canonized. In Catherine, Thomas eulogized above all her exceptional charisms (her visions, her mystical marriage, her exchanging of her heart with Christ's); elsewhere, in the vulgarization of the lives of other Dominican tertiaries, he emphasized the mystical and thaumaturgic (Vanna of Orvieto, Margaret of Città di Castello). When it came to Mary of Venice, however, he praised her modesty, her chastity, her perfect obedience to her spiritual guide (Thomas himself), her charity toward others. Mary of Venice, the imitator of the inimitable Catherine of Siena, became in her turn an imitable model.[89]

The preaching of Bernardino of Siena and the treatise of the Dominican Giovanni Dominici contained instructions for pious if not saintly behavior and were governed by an acute understanding of the needs of society. The good wife need not aim to be a saint; she should be modest and reserved, a housewife skilled in the wise management of family property, and, though married, chaste. Dominici emphasized that she should guard her husband against temptation and be obedient and attentive so that she would not be asked, in the normal way of things, to do anything that might damage her chances of personal salvation. A loving mother, Dominici's ideal woman was to bring up her children in emulation of the saints, having them play with dolls representing saintly figures and build household altars. She was also to direct them toward activities in which they could be helpful to others, and for this reason would not be compelled to go into trades or professions contrary to their natural inclinations.[90]

If these were the characteristics of late medieval female devotion—on the one hand mysticism and the search for the absolute, and on the other religious practices carried out in a thousand daily activities, each insignificant but together constituting a form of sainthood that pleased the hierarchy— then Francesca of Rome deserves to conclude this study of sainthood and of women's religious experience in the Middle Ages. She combined—indeed they merged together without conflict—the mystic who cradled the infant Jesus in her arms, the prophet who was capable of predicting the difficulties of her beloved city; the counselor to so many troubled souls, both male and female, religious and lay; the wife solicitous of her husband's needs; the mother watching over the only son who remained to her; and the housekeeper who served also as a spiritual guide for all her servants.

Each sought out, in Francesca, that part of her that interested him or her most: the confessor looked to her visionary side; her sisters to a superior who was both strong and humble; her neighbors to a model of womanly modesty, heedless of pomp and vanity; those she healed saw her as a great thaumaturge; the official Church, which formulated the articles under which witnesses to her eventual canonization were questioned, by contrast, found in her the long-sought-for model for an exemplary Christian woman—devout, obedient, and charitable.[91]

Her sainthood was be recognized very late: not until 1608 did Paul V offer his fellow Romans a saint born in their city, the first since the martyrs of the first centuries.[92] And with her, before the storms of the Reformation and Counter-Reformation proposed new and different forms of life for female religiosity, a whole era came to an end.

Translated from the Italian by Keith Botsford

CHAPTER 4

Women, Faith, and Image in the Late Middle Ages

DOMINIQUE RIGAUX

The Sienese painter Sano di Pietro devoted a panel to the preaching of his fellow townsman Saint Bernardino (fig. 1) in their native city. Split into two parts, men and women, by a barrier covered with red cloth, a crowd kneels, avid for the words of this man of God.[1] Images of heaven, such as the *Coronation of the Virgin* or *The Last Judgment,* reproduce this separation of the sexes. All listen to the same words and contemplate the same image: the "tavola" with Christ's monogram brandished by the saint. But do they all receive this image in the same way? In this medieval world in which the words of churchmen allot women a predestined role and their writings imbed women's lives within a screen of hagiographic *topoi,* images are often the only available document with which we can "pass to the other side of the barrier."

Following the example of Countess Matilda, a great promoter of artistic renewal on her lands, women, and not just women of the highest rank, were ever more frequent investors in sacred art.[2] Works of art were a means to salvation for those who commissioned them. Did not the offer of a decorated chapel, an altarpiece, or a statue to a church or monastery mean that one's body and soul were assured of perpetual prayer and intercession?[3] And when the iconography was chosen, or even created, by women for other women— as is the case with the Last Judgment in the Vatican collection, whose dating is controversial but could go back to the second half of the eleventh century—the image reveals their fears and religious longings.[4]

These painted or sculpted images are witnesses to the religious life of their times; they are also widely welcomed proselytizers, for many a vocation came about through an iconic representation. Catherine of Alexandria, whom medieval art transformed into a sort of allegory of conversion—because the strength of her arguments had, according to the legend that developed at the end of the fourteenth century, been able to convince the emperor and phi-losophers—experienced this personally. While still very young, she went with her mother to visit a hermit who handed her an icon of a Virgin and child, her future spouse. The saint's iconography repeats the episode many times, un-derlining both the importance of images in transmitting the faith and the role of men, who remain the masters of this cleverly orchestrated form of instruction.[5]

Such images are closely linked to the cults of these women saints; they favor the spread of the cults and transform them. Once the figuration is widely distributed, the cult of that saint is no longer limited to specific shrines like the tomb or the saint's remains; the image takes up where the relic leaves off. The cult avoids the custodians of the saint's body, whoever they are, and enters the heart, penetrating the home, the young woman's bedroom. Better yet, in the absence of a written source, the image is the oldest known witness, the only one from the Middle Ages. Such, for instance, are the five scenes that form the predella of the altarpiece dedicated to the Blessed Julia of Certaldo (d. 1367) (fig. 11) of whose life we have nothing written down before the seventeenth century. Other accounts, from an even later date, only paraphrase this one.[6]

Before the end of the eleventh century, however, our remaining iconog-raphic sources are insufficient to allow us to build a significant general picture of female religiosity in Italy. Any image building done on behalf of those few women who died in the odor of sanctity between the eighth and twelfth centuries came very much later and was generally associated with efforts to obtain their canonization.[7] It is only from the twelfth century onward that we begin to see a rising number of female saints in a domain until then almost totally dominated by men. Even the rise of Marian devotion, whose iconogra-phy is an inexhaustible source of inspiration for representing women saints, or the anonymous female figures representing individual souls seen ascending to heaven like the glorified Mother of God, cannot be considered as a valoriza-tion of women. For Mary was, and remains, perceived as the impossible model: "alone, unique, virgin and mother."[8]

In a period in which the visual arts—most notably picture production relayed by wood engraving—take an unprecedented leap forward, whose importance we have yet to measure, it is several female figures whom the clergy propose as models of behavior to other women.[9] It is part of a peda-gogy refined by the Mendicant orders in which images play a major part: a woman for women and, if possible, a local woman, the local saint. In the Collegiate Church of San Gimignano, Saint Fina is depicted standing by the door through which women enter (fig. 2), her hand lying protectively on the head of a standing white-veiled figure; on the opposite side, by the men's door, that universally venerated saint, Catherine of Alexandria, repeats the same gesture on a kneeling man.[10]

Model Images, Models of Images

After the middle of the thirteenth century, together with the fresco, the altarpiece, vertical or horizontal, is the main source of the diffusion of saints' images.[11] The women who from this time begin to draw the public's attention by occupying the central panels are most often "people in the news": recently canonized saints, such as Clare of Assisi or Margaret of Cortona, whose images are a stimulus to their cult.[12] The reredos of Saint Clare (fig. 3) painted between 1281 and 1285 is one of the first examples of this new prominence accorded to women.[13] Its precedent, however, is masculine, for the panel in fact follows the formula used for the altarpieces devoted to Saint Francis some forty years before.[14] The various stages of her life, from her conversion to her death, are distributed according to an organizing structure used equally for freshly canonized saints and for those long venerated and familiar. These narrative structures rewrite the *vita* in a way that says far more about the cult than about the life of the woman herself, which is literally re-presented, by making the absent present. The need to make Clare fit known hagiographic structures is obvious. No allusion of any sort is made to the miracles for which she was celebrated, most notable among them the intervention that saved Assisi from sack by the Saracens in 1240. In compensation, Francis's presence punctuates the various episodes of her life, and a "horizontal reading" of the panel emphasizes the parallels: the welcome at Porziuncula is a pendant to the apparition of the Virgin and the women saints on her deathbed, who legitimize the holy nature of her choices and her life.

Making a Saint

The image of a woman saint is always a "symbolic construction." Even when painted shortly after her death, as in the fresco of Saint Catherine of Siena painted by her disciple Andrea Vanni in the Church of Saint Dominic (fig. 4), the image is no portrait, for the idealizing intent remains present.[15] The first official image is hugely important: it is the one that offers the "canonical version," the one her disciples want to promote. In the Assisi reredos, for instance, every element comes together to show Clare as the *alter Franciscus,* another Francis, and to such a degree that there is no reference to her rule, despite the fact that it was the only monastic rule written by a woman to have been approved by the papacy.[16] The choice of the various fragments of her life, four out of eight of which are devoted to her vocation, reveal this woman's extraordinary determination in turning her back on everything to follow in Francis's footsteps.

In the thaumaturgic scenes, gestures are reduced to the barest essentials: her blessing is barely sketched in with the imposition of her hands and a slight bow of her head. Showing the holiness of a woman in a narrative sequence of images necessarily demands a suitable *gestus* that will reflect a holy soul. The saint's body, most often tightly wrapped in her habit, is reduced to two elements: in most cases, to hands and face. We are not allowed to forget that, as a result of Eve's sin, a woman's body, however saintly, is always a source of desire—as is illustrated by the scene of Susanna surprised in her bath by two concupiscent elders on the southern wall of the main chapel of the Cathedral of Spilimbergo in Udine (fig. 5), where it is accompanied by an evocation of Adam and Eve being exiled from the earthly paradise.[17]

Like the faces, stories do not properly belong to only one woman saint: hagiographic *topoi* allow all sorts of materials to be shifted about, and many wonders are miracles in the art of borrowing. An iconographic pun on the saint's name often serves as a prop, and by onomastic contamination to Rose of Viterbo (d. 1251) is attributed the miracle of the roses, which after the last decades of the thirteenth century had become one of the favorite themes in the "Lives" and iconography of Saint Elizabeth of Thuringia in Italy.[18] In that tale of marvels, it is midwinter and the food destined for the poor is transformed into perfumed flowers to conceal from her jealous husband the prodigalities of the saintly princess. Thus in the convent of the Poor Clares in Viterbo, who declined to admit her to their community in her lifetime, Rose's name has been simply painted over the fresco created by Benozzo di Lese, known as Gozzoli, which showed Elizabeth standing, her head crowned, holding a basket of flowers in the skirt of her gown (fig. 6).[19]

Agnes's lamb, Catherine of Alexandria's wheel: it is their attributes that make saints immediately recognizable and sum up the very essence of their sanctity. Hence the importance of a judicious choice of symbol. In Lorenzo Vecchietta's fresco of 1461 in the Mappamundo room of the Palazzo Pubblico in Siena representing Catherine of Siena (1461), it is the addition of the book of doctrine to the virgin's lilies and the stigmata (which already figured in Vanni's painting, fig. 4) that give a new dimension to what could be considered the "official" version of Catherine on the eve of her canonization. In Catherine's iconography, the insistence on her doctrinal attributes—the book and above all the triple crown, which confer on her the anticipatory title of "doctor"—become the significant proof for the recognition of her teaching and her proclamation as a Doctor of the Church by Paul VI on October 4, 1970.

Canonization by Image

The golden nimbus that surrounds the heads of female saints contributes to their exaltation; it shows them in their heavenly glory.[20] The papacy's attempt, in the fourteenth century, to create a hierarchical distinction between canonized saints and the blessed—the former might have a halo, the latter had to content themselves with rays—was not always followed in practice, as shown in the panel painted by the Master of the Dominican Effigies.[21] Despite the protestations of a few humanists like the Florentine Franco Sacchetti, who deplored this evolution, many of the *beate* needed no more than the stroke of a brush to become *sante*. This happened to the Blessed Umiliana de' Cerchi, who died in Florence in 1246.[22] There are several cycles of frescoes dedicated to uncanonized saints in Italy, of which the most important is that executed in the Church of Saint Basil in Cortona in the first half of the fourteenth century in honor of Margaret (d. 1297) (fig. 9).[23] The main cycle of this kind still visible *in situ* is that painted in honor of the Blessed Joan of Signa (d. 1307) by the Bicci workshop in the parish church of her native village outside Florence: left wall in 1441 and right wall in 1462.[24]

To the degree in which, with the complicity of the local clergy, it contributes to the establishment of cults that have not been sanctioned by the ecclesiastical authorities, the image—as ever the mainstay and instrument for the diffusion of a cult—also becomes one of the best ways to propagandize a candidate for sainthood. The case of Catherine of Siena is a good example. Her biographer, Tommaso of Siena, known as *il Caffarini,* admitted that at the beginning of the fifteenth century there was a whole workshop in Venice devoted to producing a series of "publicity" images of the "Mamma." Painted on paper by the thousands, they were meant to be hung up in churches on her feast day. They could even be taken home, thus allowing individuals to venerate her privately.[25]

The Assassinated Shepherd-Lass

Direct contact through an image brings with it a new relationship between the devotee and "his" or "her" saint. No longer just a model, she is now a privileged intercessor. Alongside the Virgin, who continues to be the human race's advocate together with her son, as we see from the innumerable Virgins with a mantle, which flourished in the art of the fourteenth and fifteenth centuries (fig. 7), women saints offer a help all the more efficacious for being personal. This is the case with Saint Deliberata, whose cult springs up in Bolzano Novarese. Protector of childbirths, she holds her two sucklings wrapped in swaddling clothes, enameled according to the traditional iconography of Charity.[26]

1. Sano di Pietro. *Women Listen to Saint Bernardino Preach,* ca. 1450. Siena, Duomo, Chapter Library.

2. Attributed to Memmi di Filippuccio. *Saint Fina and Donatrix,* early fourteenth century. San Gimignano (Siena), Collegiate Church.

3. *Saint Clare and the Story of Her Life,* 1281–1285. Assisi, Basilica of Saint Clare.

4. Andrea Vanni. *Saint Catherine of Siena and Donatrix*, 1380–1390. Siena, Basilica of Saint Dominic.

5. Master of Spilimbergo. *Susanna Bathing,* second half of
fourteenth century. Spilimbergo (Udine), Duomo, Main Chapel.

6. Benozzo Gozzoli. *Saint Rose,* fifteenth
century. Viterbo, Convent of the Sisters of
Saint Clare.

7. Anon. Piedmontese. *Our Lady of Mercy,* 1478. Casalvolone (Novara), Saint Peter's Church.

8. Giovanni de Campis. *Translation of the Blessed Panacea,* 1476. Boccioleto, hamlet of Oro (Vercelli), Chapel of Saint Pantaleon.

9. *Stories of Saint Margaret of Cortona,* anonymous seventeenth-century drawings after the frescoes of Buffalmacco (ca. 1336), which decorated Saint Basil's Church in Cortona. Cortona (Arezzo), Town Library.

10. Niccolò Gerini. *Altarpiece of Saint Fina*, 1402. San Gimignano (Siena), Civic Museum (Scala, Florence).

11. *Stories of the Blessed Julia of Certaldo,* mid-fifteenth century. Certaldo (Florence), Church of Saints James and Phillip.

12. Pietro Lorenzetti. *Stories of the Blessed Humility: Humility Reading in the Refectory,* 1341. Florence, Uffizi.

13. Master of the Blessed Clare of Rimini. *Vision of Clare*, ca. 1330.
Ajaccio (Corsica), Fesch Museum. (Photo R.M.N., Paris)

14. First Master of Saint Clare of Montefalco. *Saint Clare and Christ,* 1333. Montefalco (Perugia), Church of Saint Clare.

15. Giovanni di Corraduccio. *An Angel Appearing to a Praying Woman Saint*, 1420–1430. Foligno (Perugia), Monastery of Saint Anne.

16. *Martha in Her Kitchen*, ca. 1431. Foligno (Perugia), Monastery of Saint Anne.

Christians remained attached to the identification of sainthood with martyrdom. The cult of the young shepherdess of Valsesia, Panacea Muzio, struck
and killed by her stepmother's distaff in the fourteenth century, is known only
through her iconography, by images that preceded by more than a century
her first official biography, written by Bernardino Lancia, parish priest of
Quarona (1598).[27] In 1446 the communal statutes of her native village of
Quarona required that her feast day be observed on the first Friday in May.
The frescoes of Giovanni de Campis, painted in the Chapel of Saint Pantaleon
at Boccioleto, show both the rural nature of her cult—she can cure epilepsy—
and the involvement of the whole community, with the clergy leading, which
solemnly parades her mortal remains (fig. 8).

The Patron Saint

Frenetic searching for a patron is not just an isolated or individual phenomenon. In northern and central Italy, where the communal movement began
early and vigorously, a whole town would seek out a patron saint.[28] The
funeral monument of Margaret of Cortona, a Sienese work from the early
fourteenth century, marks a turning point. It was the first time that a saintly
woman was interred not below ground but, like her most influential fellow
townspeople, in her own catafalque. Thus began a civic recognition best
exemplified by the now lost frescoes in the Church of Saint Basil, known to us
through several seventeenth-century copies (fig. 9).[29] Where the Sienese altarpiece in the diocesan museum of Cortona, which dates from the second
half of the fourteenth century, exalts Margaret's penitential role—she is portrayed in a long, narrow, checkered habit without a belt—the Saint Basil
frescoes emphasize her miracle work.[30]

Several years later, another local saint, Fina of Gimignano, replaced a
bishop as the local patron saint: a panel by Niccolò Gerini (1402) shows her,
as the bishop had been shown, at the center of the altarpiece, bearing a model
of the city in her arms (fig. 10). From the fourteenth century onward, there
are many examples of women as protectresses of cities, the city itself being
thought of as a woman.[31]

Spaces of "Reflection"

A place is both the instrument and the object of sainthood. Images show us
more than models of behavior; they reveal to us the spaces of sainthood,
privileged places where the elect exercises her power: tomb, reclusory (or
eremitic cell), and refectory. These were the places of reflection and meditation suggested by the Mendicants, most notably in the *Meditationes vitae
Christi,* one of the books most read in the Middle Ages and indeed written for

a woman, a Poor Clare.[32] There is nothing spontaneous about this phenomenon. Confessors and spiritual directors encouraged their flocks, religious or laywomen, to undertake a whole process of visualization as described in the prayer manuals of the day, such as the *Zardino de oration,* written for young women in 1454 and printed in Venice forty years later.[33]

The Tomb

Iconography does not get it wrong: the saint is born in her tomb and the death scene is ever the choice moment in medieval works. As the Saint Clare reredos shows (fig. 3), there are many new departures in these portrayals, and in these images increasingly the saint becomes the link between heaven, to which an angel conducts her soul, and earth, where beggars and the sick press about her mortal remains. The tomb is not just a figured representation, a symbol of Christ's tomb in Jerusalem, but a concrete space that, by drawing crowds, creates wealth and fame for a city or a monastery. The saint's dead body inflames the fervor of the faithful; they have to "touch to see." Starting in the thirteenth century, the tomb is often compared to the sacred host, which is venerated as a relic of Christ, particularly in women's cults.[34] Are not the saint's relics kept in tabernacles? The best known of these is that which contains the relics of Saint Catherine of Siena in the Church of Saint Dominic (end of the fourteenth century).[35]

From the fourteenth century onward, however, these physical links with the sanctuary and direct contact with relics begin to loosen. Increasingly they are seen from a distance and vows are made before an image of the saint, which becomes the relay for her intercession. Still, the tomb is where the mystery is revealed; it is there that these saintly women heard the Resurrection of Christ announced.

The Cell Revisited

The cell, that typically female space, frequently empty and a sort of nonspace, is not a place for rest. Verdiana of Castelfiorentino's cell is regularly visited by serpents. Crowds of all kind pressed up around the hermitage, for this symbolic space attracted the anonymous crowd as much as the bishop. In the altarpiece devoted to the recluse Julia of Certaldo (fig. 11) placed on the altar dedicated to her in the Church of Saints James and Phillip in Certaldo, the second scene shows us the Blessed Verdiana in her urban cell. Children pass her food through a little window, and in exchange she offers them flowers. In the medieval tradition, the painter cut away one wall of the hermitage, the one facing the viewer, so that the saint should be visible. In a single glance we can take in both interior and exterior. The most astonishing element is the portrait of the holy woman herself. Julia's long hair is depicted flowing freely on her shoulders—a sign of eroticism subject to condemnation—and she wears a short-sleeved tunic that contrasts with the monastic habit she wears in the first panel (the miracle) and the third (her death). This iconographical transgression expresses the marginal status of the recluse.[36] The transgression is even greater in the final panel, where she appears—in what is, to be sure, a posthumous miracle—dressed as a man, her hair uncovered and tied in a chignon.[37] Two wide black bands, however, run across her robe at the level of her hips, making a break just where the picture becomes provocative.[38]

Alongside Julia, the traditional recluse, the frescoes devoted to Joan of Signa, also from the fifteenth century, offer a portrait of the hermit outside the cell. The two images are the Italian iconographic poles of a like appetite for the eremitic life.[39] Meanwhile, the Margaret of Cortona altarpiece in the diocesan museum, in which the saint, a second Mary Magdalene, is seen receiving the host in her cell—unless this represents the ordeal of the unconsecrated host—reminds us the cell is also a place of communion.[40]

The Refectory

If any space reveals what a consecrated religious life meant to each and every woman in her time, such is the space in which the sisters broke bread while listening to the word of God, such as we see the Blessed Humility doing as she reads to her sisters in Pietro Lorenzetti's panel (fig. 12). A place of daily charity, the refectory is also a place of miracles: as one can see in the panels and frescoes of Clare of Assisi's altarpiece (fig. 3) or Antoniazzo Romano's frescoes showing Saint Francesca of Rome in the convent of Tor de' Specchi (1468). As the miracle of feeding follows the *topos* of Christ's miracle, so the saints' refectory table is wed to the Lord's own table.[41]

Before the refectory table ever was the "good place for reflection" painters were so fond of depicting, it was also a "living," geometrical space for which, in order to instruct their sisters, certain women chose a bold iconography. Was it not for the nuns of Saint Appollonia in Florence that Andrea del Castagno executed one of the most original representations of the *Cena*, or Last Supper, of his age?[42] It was again women, the Cistercian nuns of the convent of Saint Juliana of Perugia (today transformed into a military hospital), who around 1280 to 1290 commissioned the earliest refectory *Cena* in Italy of which any trace survives.[43] For the Lord's supper is not like any other. Perfectly adapted to its surroundings, it is simultaneously an edifying mirror for both the sisters who contemplate it and the painters who are inspired by the theme, and the reflection of the growing importance in the later Middle

Ages of eucharistic devotion in religious life, as well as one of the criteria for canonization.

Forms and Colors in Women's Devotion

A diagonal that starts at the kneeling nun and ends in the huge figure of Christ showing his wounds in the little panel depicting the vision of the Blessed Clare of Rimini, painted around 1330 (fig. 13), is a perfect illustration of the meditation that leads to the contemplation of Christ's wounds proper to saintly women, especially among Franciscan nuns, at the end of the thirteenth century.[44] Here, Clare wears a gray habit tied with a cord with three knots under a white mantle; her dress assimilates her to the Franciscan tertiaries, though it would seem she never belonged officially to any order. The picture goes well beyond the story of her vision, but the visions of mystic woman saints, all of them loaded with iconographical notations, not to speak of quotations from familiar works, testify to a constant coming and going between figurative and mental representations. Each suggests the other.[45] Together, they offer a form of devotion with three aspects: Christocentric, eucharistic, and charitable.

A Cross in the Heart

The development of feminine mysticism, which can be considered one of the major spiritual innovations of the thirteenth century, only reached Italy at the very end of the century and was not recognized by the Church until the fourteenth. From then on, iconographic images—such as the Umbrian frescoes devoted to Clare of Montefalco in her chapel—seized upon female figures who bore Christ's cross in their hearts (fig. 14). No popular art this: mystical sainthood, like its images, preferred rarer air and took pleasure in it.

One theme in Italian iconography, however, met with great success, especially in late-fourteenth-century Florence. This was the mystical marriage of Saint Catherine of Alexandria, which first appeared in hagiographic literature after 1337. Women saints, ancient and modern, throng around the Virgin's throne and guide Catherine's hand toward the ring the Holy Child offers her. The subject is well ingrained in the spiritual itinerary that women made from mystical marriage to the exchange of hearts and sheds light on the Christocentric piety of the period. In the altarpiece of Dominican female saints attributed to a late follower of Pietro Lorenzetti, the Master of the Dominican Effigies, Margaret of Città di Castello, praying before the altar, offers her heart to Christ on the cross. But it is the iconography of Catherine of Siena that offers the theme in its richest form. Her heart is the real attribute of the saint's first statue, a polychromed wood carving from the fifteenth century (these are rare at that period), today preserved in the oratory of the Contrada dell'Oca.[46]

Eucharistic Piety

From the fourteenth century onward, and especially after 1350, there was an upsurge in saintly mysticism and a recognition by the Church of that essentially feminine phenomenon. From that point on, eucharistic piety was central, precisely because it was communing with the body and blood of Christ that often brought on the saints' ecstasy or ravishment.[47] Communion was ardently sought after because it gave direct contact with Jesus, and from that derived the loving fusion of their wills, that of the servant-bride and that of Christ. In that perspective, the whole eucharistic theme was renewed, and it acquired in iconography, as in hagiographic literature, a new importance.

The most frequently recurring of these themes in the illustration of the lives of the female saints in the fourteenth and fifteenth centuries was that of the miraculous Communion, most notably, Catherine of Siena's. Any imperious desire for Communion was, in fact, forbidden by the Church, basically hostile to frequent Communion; therefore, to satisfy his bride's hunger, Jesus had to come to her in person, or send his angels. In the Giovanni di Corraduccio painting in the oratory of Saint Anne in Foligno, the angel who comes to satisfy the appetites of the lovely kneeling saint bears a small jug, and three little round loaves can be discerned swelling under a cloth (fig. 15). Because this eucharistic hunger went with an excessive abstinence and fasting that contributed to the saint's reputation, her very survival must have been miraculous.

To communicate with his bride and give himself to her, Jesus took a number of forms. First, there was the child in the sacred host: Catherine of Siena frequently saw him, offering himself as a child who treated her as a son would treat his mother. But most often there was blood—the blood that in the fifteenth century flowed unstoppably from altar and cross. Eucharistic realism reached new depths of atrocity with Catherine of Siena, as in certain images illustrating devotion to the Sacred Blood of Jesus. The images were neither simple nor single, and sometimes one image was superimposed on another: for instance, a little child flowing with blood. With its ferocious reddening, the period gave birth to a sacramental marvel that took over from the thaumaturgic.

The Choice of Martha

The way in which the artists of the fifteenth century concerned themselves with realism and verisimilitude in their details was a response to new aesthetic laws, according to which a holy image must first be convincing before it can be effective.[48] The murals that decorate the refectory of the *bizzoche,* or Beguines, of the Blessed Angelina of Montegiove in Foligno, bear precious witness to this, for they were commissioned by and for women.[49] All four lunettes are meal scenes: *The Marriage at Cana, The Last Supper, Meal at Martha and Mary,* and *Martha in Her Kitchen* (fig. 16). The first two subjects are not unique in a refectory, but the other two, both extremely rare in Italian painting of the time, display the parallel between the active and the contemplative life that lay at the heart of Beguine spirituality. By the relationship between food and women, the scenes indicate a choice of life. This Last Supper scene, compared to the highly unusual nature of the others, shows no original characteristics. But for the *bizzoche,* the model was feminine. To judge by the astonishing *Martha in Her Kitchen,* which occupies the whole lunette over the mother superior's table, while Martha and Mary face each other from opposite ends of the refectory, it is toward Martha that the sisters look. The same commitment to an active life based on charity is shown by the choice of episodes in the life of Francesca of Rome painted by Antoniazzo Romano at Tor de' Specchi.[50]

Sometimes, this choice leads medieval woman to find her own voice and speak. When she does that, it is not just in our eye, but in deeds, that she passes to the other side of the barrier, addressing her brothers, as Mary Magdalene does in the frescoes in the apse of Cusiano in the Trentino.[51]

Translated from the French by Keith Botsford

CHAPTER 5

From Prophecy to Discipline, 1450–1650

GABRIELLA ZARRI

Female Sanctity and Male Religion

When in 1506 the prince of Saxony commissioned Lucas Cranach the Elder to paint a panel for the altar of the Church of Saint Catherine of Wittemberg, he could have no idea that soon afterward that panel would become an emblem of the end on an era. Put up to celebrate the superiority of theology, as personified by the female saint who conducted virtuous debates with learned doctors about the trivium and quadrivium, the painting became a point of departure for a protest against sacred images and superstition.[1] The protest was not merely a moral revolt against disorderly and simoniacal devotions, but also a sign—parallel to Martin Luther's rejection of canon law as an intellectual instrument of Roman Catholic oppression—of radical opposition to the very idea that ecclesiastical knowledge was superior to other sciences. Cranach's Catherine, royally robed alongside the instrument of her martyrdom, towers triumphantly over her opponents, whom Cranach depicted in the likenesses of professors of the newly founded University of Wittemberg, Luther's colleagues.

The Alexandrian martyr, whose legend spread like wildfire throughout Europe in the late Middle Ages—both in the unadorned version of the ninth-century *passio* and in the ensuing corrupt forms that dominated in French-speaking and Anglo-Saxon areas—was an apt emblem of the revolt against the saints. As the woman who converted the scholars the emperor Maxentius sent to dissuade her from her perseverance in the Christian faith, Catherine represented the triumph of theology over the other sciences, and for that reason had been recognized as patron saint of the doctors of the University of Paris; as a woman of royal descent who refused marriage to devote herself to Christ (who blessed her vow by giving her a ring), the Alexandrian princess became the figure for the marital union between Christ and Church, and the type of the consecrated virgin. To refuse the cult of Catherine was symbolically to join Lutheran opposition to the Church hierarchy and the distinction between clergy and laity, and to sanction a radical rejection of monastic vows.

What is singular in this case is that the revolt which sought to abolish the hierarchical order of the Church ended up denying female sanctity; just at the time when, toward the end of the fifteenth century, female saints had reached the apogee of their power and were recognized on both the historical and symbolic levels. As Catherine had been raised to the patronage of the Sorbonne's doctors, so Ursula, the "captain" of a company of eleven thousand virgins, had become the patron saint of students at the University of Paris.[2] These instances of recognition did not directly involve the intellectual capacities of women, much debated by contemporary humanists, but they definitely did allow a now indisputable role to women in the science and prophetic knowledge of divine mysteries.[3]

A position such as Luther's, long considered "progressive," in fact turned out to be the opposite: it powerfully inhibited women's power in both real and symbolic terms. There were, in fact, some moments in the fifteenth century that marked the high point in the Church's official recognition of women's power and knowledge, though these were not institutionally approved until the twentieth century, when Saints Catherine of Siena and Teresa of Avila were proclaimed Doctors of the Church.

One such moment at the end of the fourteenth century was the University of Paris debate about whether or not to recognize the charismatic gifts of Bridget of Sweden. This was the first authoritative debate on female prophecy. On that occasion Jean Gerson, the university's chancellor, wrote his treatise on the *discretio spirituum*. Gerson there laid out the issues that for three centuries had given rise to attempts to rationalize, through subtle distinctions, the origin, nature, and effects of phenomena that could not be classified according to the theological and medical knowledge of the day—and indeed escaped the normal laws of sensory experience.[4] The distinguishing of spirits in extrasensorial phenomena called for *discretio*, in the etymological sense of the word; it required doctrine and practical examination of observed phenomena. The attention, even obsession, with the discernment of spirits not only involved events ascribable to what was already institutionally sacred, such as prophecy, levitation, stigmata, or prolonged fasting, but also inevitably involved phenomena of another nature, such as those classed as demoniacal. Religious manifestations that did not conform to the norm attracted the intense attention of religious and intellectuals, who closely observed, deduced, judged, and classified good or evil "spirits," using the familiar, traditional categories of "angels" and "demons" derived from the Neo-platonist Renaissance culture.

The "scientific" attention Gerson gave Bridget's prophecies must not have differed greatly from that which the inquisitors of Rouen gave Joan of Arc's "voices," no more than the way the interests of the German inquisitors James Sprenger and Heinrich Krämer in the witches they observed differed from Gianfrancesco Pico della Mirandola's when faced with Catherine of Racconigi's visions and struggles with the Devil.[5]

Because they were linked with prophecy and affected the body, charismatic religious experiences largely concerned women. As a result, a considerable number of theologians and inquisitors followed and observed the behavior of women thought to be saintly, to evaluate the orthodoxy of their devotions and revelations but primarily to gather and circulate experiences and doctrines. Whence rose that male figure later institutionalized under the name of "spiritual director." At this point, he had a rather different role. He was witness and observer, rarely judge; he was inclined to sudden shifts of position, to assuming the posture of disciple, son, and guarantor of charismatic and prophetic gifts, which he rarely questioned.

Because he was a well-known preacher, the interrogation to which Pietro of Lucca, a regular Lateran canon, was subjected by a commission of cardinals caused a great stir. He was alleged to support heretical doctrines because he had argued—on the basis of the revelations of the penitent, Chiara Bugni—that the Son of God had been conceived when three drops of blood were deposited in the Virgin's heart. Pietro, a much-quoted author of works of spirituality and a reckless disseminator of suspect female revelations, was absolved of the charge. The case, well known to scholars because it is cited in a famous essay by Delio Cantimori, was probably not unique.[6] Nonetheless, it revealed an unconditional consensus in which the prophecies of charismatic women prevailed in Catholic Europe throughout the fifteenth century and the first decades of the sixteenth. It can better be understood in the context of new information about late-medieval female religiosity provided by Caroline Bynum.[7]

Demographic expansion and economic growth in the latter part of the fifteenth century, and an overall crisis at the beginning of the sixteenth, played a role in the expansion of monastic institutions, now favoring the rise of new forms of religious communities, now causing a certain rigidification in the traditional monastic orders. The slow and varied processes that led to the formation of the "modern state," whether the size of the ancient Italian states or the size of the great "national" European states, had a considerable influence on the organization of the various churches that arose from the Protestant Reformation and the restructuring of the Roman Church. They accentuated aspects of rationalization and social discipline already at work in the new religious confessions and in the post-Tridentine Catholic Church.

A long process of secularization in politics gave a new and different dimension to religion, as we can see in the taking of oaths, which by the sixteenth century had reached new theoretical and practical heights.[8] However, a determining factor in the evolution of models of sanctity, and in the transformations of women's movements and monastic communities, was the cultural impact of debates about the cult of saints, sacred images, and monastic vows. These discussions, which took place in the intellectual milieu of Italian and European humanists in the latter part of the fifteenth century, expressed themselves in new theological foundations and renewed cultural practices in both the reformed churches and post-Tridentine Catholicism.

Certain factors brought about a major shift in sixteenth-century religion: a rejection of the "bodily" religiosity typical of the late Middle Ages in favor of an internalized concept of religion; a like rejection of the legendary and mythical aspects of religious belief in the name of the "historicity" of saintly phenomena;[9] a different role played by marriage and the family in relation to religious education, largely ordained by Protestantism's abolition of monastic institutions.

A direct and immediate consequence of these cultural shifts was the progressive eclipse of the "leadership" roles achieved by women between the thirteenth and sixteenth centuries and the establishment of a "male religion" characterized by the internalization and rationalization of religious phenomena—the direction of which was officially recognized by the Church as resting on the authority of Fathers, be these pastors, spiritual directors, inquisitors, or the male heads of families.

Even at a purely theological level, Protestantism was a religion of the Father; there was no woman to weigh in the balance. It was not that the centrality of the mystery of Redemption achieved by the vicarious death of Christ crucified was lessened by the eclipse of the veneration of the Virgin Mary from the cult, but that the Incarnation was no longer the definitive moment in the saving mission of the Son of God. The Father was the only actor in the act of mercy that forgave sins and justified the believer. The same Lutheran concept of "imputed" justice shifted to God, and it was now God who, in virtue of the merits of Christ, covered the transgressions of the faithful with his mantle, that iconographic attribute of Our Lady of Mercy which in the late Middle Ages had been applied not only to the Madonna but also to mythical saintly woman figures such as the Virgin Ursula.

Dressing the Father in maternal attributes did not mean recapturing in "female" form those traits which up to that moment had characterized the religion of the Roman Church. Lutheran and Reformed rejection of purgatory resulted in a further distancing of characteristic elements of female saints, whose role as intermediaries with the world of the dead had taken on many different and popular shapes of a kind that could both stimulate orthodox cults and fuel belief in witchcraft.[10]

Over the period in which these institutional and cultural shifts took place, a period now seen as one of imposed confessionalism and social discipline, there were stages that mark clear and significant breaks in the progressive definition of the historical process described above.[11]

Nuns and *Bizzoche,* Saints and Witches

When in 1456 Caterina Vigri, a Poor Clare educated at the court of Ferrara and fairly well known in her day for her culture and holy life, was asked by her superiors in the order to found a new Strict Observance Poor Clare convent in Bologna, Borso d'Este began diplomatic initiatives at the court in Rome to keep the nun in his own city. These negotiations failed and the prince wrote disdainfully to his agent, Ludovico Casella, that it was a great setback to the city to lose "a saintly woman."[12]

Caterina Vigri, the author of a book of devotions frequently reprinted between the end of the fifteenth and the middle of the sixteenth centuries, founded a convent in Bologna that drew support and protection from the lordship of Bentivoglio. Throughout the modern era it was considered the most observant in the city.[13] Caterina died in Bologna, performed miracles, and was the object of a considerable popular cult. Exceptional for the times, the city authorities set in motion the procedures for her canonization at the end of the sixteenth century, and finally, in 1712, she was proclaimed a saint.[14]

Protected and sought after by princes, the founder of convents, the author of a book that revealed tendencies toward a "modern devotion" well beyond mystical excesses addressed to the men and women of her time, Vigri can be considered an exemplary figure of female sainthood in the fifteenth century. It was not by chance that her deeds and miracles were immediately included in the manuscript of the lives of illustrious women written by the Bologna humanist Giovanni Sabadino degli Arienti; moreover, unlike many other of his biographical profiles, this one was published a few decades later.[15] A model of sanctity for the Poor Clares and for the noblewomen at court who chose Franciscan convents when they founded monasteries or took the veil, the devout and illuminated spirituality of Caterina was an alternative to the more prophetic models of sanctity of the Dominicans.

In the wake of the example offered by Catherine of Siena and under the sway of the fiery preaching of Girolamo Savonarola, Dominican women were distinguished by their active commitment to society and their times, dedicating themselves to the care of young women and to work in open convents, taking on the tasks of spiritual guides to the feudal lords and princes who turned to them for political advice, and directing their concerns and prophetic messages toward the urgent need for reform in the Church.[16]

A middle path between these two, living in obscurity in a single district of one city but immediately accessible because she offered an easily imitable model, was the Roman Olivetan Francesca de' Ponziani, founder of religious communities that led to the extension of the Beguine movement in many central and southern Italian cities.[17] That model of an active life, of commitment to reforming society and the Church, which distinguishes the holy women of the fifteenth and early sixteenth centuries, also holds true for the most innovative aspect of women's religious movements in the same period.

Between 1450 and 1520, in common with developments in the male religious orders, there was an unusual expansion of those monastic communities that drew their inspiration from the Observant movements. Reform of the older houses and the founding of new convents multiplied the number of convents in major rural centers and in the cities, in turn leading to the creation of new orders and various Observances.[18] Among female orders, the Franciscan Observants led the way in reforming and founding convents, but the truly innovative element in the religious movements of the fifteenth century was the extension of the Third Orders and the rapid expansion of the *pinzochere* communities. These were unenclosed religious communities in which women could live either in their own homes with an ecclesiastically approved rule and habit or autonomously in little groups of three or four "sisters."

During the fifteenth century, alongside the expansion of the tertiaries and "open," uncloistered convents, there was—as is attested to by the discovery of many statutory charters or *modus vivendi*—a marked expansion in the numbers of *pinzochere* living in their own houses.

The growth of tertiary communities, especially among Franciscans and Dominicans, was promoted, respectively, by Angelina of Montegiove[19] and Colomba of Rieti.[20] The process culminated in 1517 with papal approval of the constitution of the Regular Third Orders, based on those of cloistered convents, thus allowing many Third Order convents to be promoted to the Second Order; under the Tridentine decisions, this transferral was to become obligatory.

The expansion of the Third Order in its double form—secular (tertiaries living in their own homes but subject to a rule) or regular (tertiaries in an "open" convent)—was an original expression of the women's religious movement in the fifteenth century. The new institutional development here (it was to be followed a few decades later by the Ursulines and Angelics) was the affirmation and the approval of a form of religious (or "semireligious," as it is sometimes wrongly called) life without solemn vows, a foretaste of the congregations in simple vows that appeared in Italy at the end of the seventeenth century and reached their apogee in the nineteenth.

As André Vauchez writes in his introduction to *The Laity in the Middle Ages,* women (as a religious movement, as prophets) came to the fore in periods marked by an opening to the laity or a crisis in the Church.[21] The lay spirituality of the *devotio moderna,* the Italian humanist philosophers' restatement of the ideal of an active life, and the imitation of an "apostolic life" all led to the choice of a religious life in which Christian perfection was to be achieved in the world and in history, one primarily interested in charity, assistance, and generosity.

The Third Orders were originally limited to married women, widows, or converts living at home; unmarried young women could not join, for their charity needed better protection. The foundation of secular tertiary institutes in the fifteenth century (such as Valentini's in Udine) or of regular ones (such as the Florentine Dominicans of Saint Catherine of Siena) was the work of widows and members of noble or rich families. Living in a community and offering their own means to support their less well-endowed fellow sisters, or girls unable to marry for want of a dowry, became an alternative for many widows who remained without protection and were often harassed, by either their own or their husbands' families seeking restitution and the use of their dotal property. To found a conventional institution or to manage a *bizzocaggio* of small dimensions was to give widows a way of continuing, as per custom, to handle their own money and determine their own way of life. Demographic historical studies have shown that in the latter part of the fifteenth century and in some cities, such as Florence, there was a high rate of widowhood, due to a notable disparity of age in marriage.[22] Anthony Molho has suggested that this was caused by structural factors: the concept of honor; the preference of older men, often widowers, for marrying young women; the requirement of virginity for family honor even in second marriages, thus creating couples bound to be dissolved by the early death of the head of the family.[23]

The various tendencies described above clearly do not account for geographical variants in these situations or different evolutions in time. It remains important to consider the amplitude and multiplicity of these institutions, some of which lasted briefly and most of which were closely related to purely local economic and political conditions, which could determine both their creation and their extinction. Lucia Sebastiani has given us a significant example of the variety of women's institutions in Milan in the latter half of the fifteenth century. Most of them were, typologically and in terms of their aims, connected to most innovative forms of religious life in the early 1500s, and Milan and Venetia were where they particularly flourished.[24]

To add another piece to the variegated mosaic in religious life in the second half of the fifteenth century, it should be noted that a few years after the official establishment of the feast of Mary's Visitation to Saint Elizabeth, which Nicholas V added to the liturgical calendar of the Western Church in 1475, Pope Innocent VIII promulgated his bull *Summis desiderantes affectibus* (1484), which gave rise to the great witch-hunt. The contiguity of these events, which cannot be explained by the obviously ambiguous position of the Church toward women, should surprise no one. The Church's duplicity in this regard existed and historically manifested itself in proposing to the faithful a double, and opposed, choice of female models: the one evil and the other good, and both traceable back to the old opposition of Eve to Mary. Beyond any possible misogynist interpretation, this opposition was the cardinal element in any positive evaluation of women by the Church, and it was based on the theological proposition of a co-redemptory role for Mary, the New Eve, mother of the living.

For centuries, especially in Italy, the Madonna—summed up in a few characteristic traits—served as a role model for women. The main points of the model were: virginity confirmed as the highest state of perfection; humility as the foundation of virtue; and consistent obedience toward authority. This is readily verifiable in the fifteenth century, as we can see from the proliferation of devotions, iconography, and literature centered on Mary's life, together with an ever greater emphasis on the social value of female "honor" as reflected in virginity.

It is in this context that we have to view the officially sanctioned belief in the "new" sorcery, as codified by the German inquisitors Krämer and Sprenger in their *Malleus maleficarum* (1487). The work had powerful analogies, though in reverse, with the Marian model. The basic configuration of relations with devils was a pact with the Devil followed by carnal relations, a denial of conception, and the practice of abortion—in a kind of "extraordinary" marriage consummated with unearthly powers. The orgiastic banquet, complete with the preparation of food and the abuse of consecrated hosts, tied in with the heretical practices of the Cathars, already present in the thirteenth century, and became a sort of anti-mass whose sacred rituals were celebrated by women.[25]

Carrying recent scientific information on the origins of the witches' Sabbath and its social and cultural connections further,[26] one could make a suggestive reading of the witch-hunt terror authorized by the *Malleus maleficarum* as an expression of the fear inspired by women's power in the Low Countries and Germany at the end of the Middle Ages.[27] Women being more entrepreneurial and self-managing, and thus being described as more independent of if not indeed rebellious to marital authority, their power in the territories of the empire also seemed greater on the symbolic level. Devotion to Anna Selbdritt, (as well as Anne, Mary, and the infant Jesus) and Marian images with a matriarchal conception of the family were typical of the context on the other side of the Alps.[28]

Pope Joan, another mythical figure, was also an example of how witchcraft could be thought of as the reverse image of the saintly Virgin and the witches' Sabbath as a profane celebration of a sacramental reality from which women were excluded. The thirteenth- century myth of Joan, supposedly a tenth-century pontiff, had given rise to a number of ceremonials aimed at testing the virility of newly elected pontiffs. The myth was still alive in the fifteenth and sixteenth centuries and, according to Alain Boureau, fueled the perennial controversy over the legitimacy of papal power: in this case because a female priesthood was prohibited and the rule of ecclesiastical celibacy denied the sexuality of the ministers of God.[29]

Though they had a different level of self-determination throughout Europe between the fifteenth and sixteenth centuries, women had great symbolic value. Mary, the New Eve, became by right a part of the saving mystery of Redemption, and her imitators on the path to sainthood were seen as guides for the Church. Bridget, Catherine of Siena, and a large group of their disciples worked toward a reform of the papacy; the mythical Saint Ursula induced a pope to give up his tiara and follow her on a pilgrimage that ended in martyrdom; the myth of Pope Joan, for all its political undertones, was interpreted at the end of the fifteenth century as a glory of the female sex.[30]

But in this cultural milieu, what was presented as different from the model bore a negative charge. The witch figured as the counterexample of female sainthood and became a sort of anti-saint. What comes out of both hagiography and inquisitorial trials in the fifteenth and sixteenth centuries is a significant parallel between the female of saint and witch.[31]

The Care of Virgins and Spiritual Motherhood

After the recognition of the statutes of the regular Third Orders, new foundations marked time. The steady growth of the tertiaries and the *bizzoche* came to a halt. There were wars in Italy, the first news of rebellion in the Church drifted in from the empire, with it came preachers bearing a flood of new ideas. A crisis in the traditional religious orders—accentuated by the Franciscans' split into two branches, the Observants and the Conventuals (1517), and soon afterward by a massive apostasy by monks and friars secretly or openly adhering to the reformed doctrine—induced the faithful to experiment with different forms of religious groupings.

Political upheavals ensued in Italy as the first incursion of the French king

Charles VIII and the usual scourges that follow war brought on a mood of collective fear, which was then accentuated in the first three decades of the century by an unbridled campaign of apocalyptic preaching. Famines and epidemics resulted from bloody sieges; a hitherto unknown disease, syphilis, was proclaimed divine retribution for the extravagant immorality of the times; the poor, orphans, and girls without dowries or protection attracted the growing attention of the city authorities, which from the second half of the fifteenth century had been experimenting with new forms of centralized assistance.

In the general cultural disorientation and social unease, with one drama after another, many new forms of action opened up for women. In the first three decades of the century, following in the footsteps of Catherine of Siena, mystics and prophets found a vast popular consensus in the world of the cities and courts. Women could balance out the apocalyptic fears stirred by itinerant street preachers; holy women did this by offering themselves up as sacrificial victims to God for the salvation of the people and the protection of their cities.[32] Rich noblewomen or virgins could offer money and time healing the sick and protecting orphan girls. Cultivated princesses and ladies at court could breathe life into intellectual circles, and they tended to practice their religion in a way that was in part derived from Reformation doctrine. Between 1530 and 1560 charismatic women whose saintliness was widely recognized ventured into new forms of religious experience.

The reputation of sainthood that attached to one such noblewoman, Caterina Fieschi Adorno (d. 1510), Saint Catherine of Genoa, came from her care of lepers and syphilitics and the foundation of a large hospital for the incurable. Hers was a complex and varied spiritual itinerary, which included marriage and a period of libertinism; a conversion that also affected her husband; and, finally, a complete dedication to charitable works, which became the prototype of similar initiatives created by the devout members of the Spiritual Company or the Oratory of Divine Love in Genoa (1497), her native city. Her mystical gifts brought her recognition as a spiritual mother by a large number of priests and religious and lay persons; they gathered her revelations and doctrine in a *corpus* of her writings first printed in 1551.[33] Catherine was particularly remembered as the creator of a movement that spread rapidly in the twenty years after her death. Her disciple, the notary Ettore Vernazza, founded the Oratory of Divine Love in Rome in 1517 and probably also the hospitals for incurables in Bologna and Savona (1513 and 1514).

His co-founder, Gaetano de Thiene (Saint Cajetan), was mainly responsible for the spread of this officially recognized society of gentlemen and ecclesiastics, whose names were kept secret, in Vicenza (Cajetan's birthplace)

(1519), Verona (1520) and Venice (1522), which were among the first cities to have hospitals for incurables; they were quickly joined by Brescia (1521), where Bartolomeo Stella, a member of the Roman oratory, worked, and then by Padua (1526). Naples and Florence (1519 and 1520), and later Lucca (1540), Pavia (1556), and Bergamo (1572), also saw the rise of a secret society, followed by the organization of institutes for charitable works.[34]

Among the society's charitable works in Genoa were two institutions devoted to helping women in need: the convent of Santa Maria Maddalena for *convertite* (that is, the reborn to God) and the Refuge of San Giuseppe for poor young women. Both institutions confirmed—even in the socially disruptive period of the wars in Italy—a widespread and growing concern for the recovery and support of feminine honor, which was considered a fundamental requisite for the honor of the family and of the city itself. Used as we are to seeing this support system as the prototype of institutions that sociologists call "total institutions," with all the negative connotations of constraint and forced labor, it is worthwhile to take a glance at some of the historical conditions in which such institutions were founded and developed.

The concept of family honor from the latter half of the fifteenth century on was closely linked to virginity. We have already seen an example of this in the preference shown by widowers for marrying young virgin women. Further indirect proof of this social investment in virginity was provided by the growing cult of Saint Joseph, to whom the Genoese refuge for poor girls was dedicated.

While it is true that family honor and the guarding of virgins is an eminently masculine and urban problem, it was mothers and other female benefactors to whom their care was delegated.[35] After the building of the "Opera" of Saint Joseph in Genoa, other cities followed and provided their own institutions for the protection of orphan children and girls "in danger" of losing their honor, such as the daughters of prostitutes or of other "poor wretches." These shelters—a significant example was the college of Santa Maria del Baraccano in Bologna, founded around 1530—gave rise to many additional *conservatori*.[36] With different statutes but the same aim these spread through numerous cities of Italy for the next 150 years. Their aim was to preserve the virginity of the girls in their charge, not only by having them supervised by laywomen and women affiliated with unenclosed religious orders, but also by setting them to work so that they could earn a sufficient dowry to marry or join a convent. These shelters were a typical expression of a new urban charity policy designed to limit the social unease caused by pauperization and the spread of begging.

In many cases, however, the shelters remained isolated from the centralizing policy of public providential institutions. They maintained their own character as charities built and managed by private individuals who, at different times and in different ways, drew substantial economic advantage from them.[37] Because they were private foundations, mainly built on bequests from men and women who set aside a part of their own property for this purpose, they did not adopt as characteristics the compulsory internment and unpaid labor that marked the hospitals for the poor established in a number of Italian cities in the second part of the sixteenth century or in the seventeenth.[38]

Unsurprisingly, institutions devoted to the preservation of female honor, with the aim of providing dowries for the marriage market, statutorily required an examination of physical virginity, and thus were more severe than monastic institutions, in which proof of virginity was not required for entry. Although from the end of the patristic period theologians and casuists had distinguished between physical and mental virginity, and Thomas Aquinas himself had asserted that the former was not necessary to the monastic state but only a complement to it, it remained true that religious profession required a vow of chastity, which of itself did not necessarily mean physical virginity. The Church's monastic tradition had always accepted widows and *convertite*, not to speak of wives and husbands when these agreed to share a "spiritual marriage" within the cloister. It could therefore be said that monastic vows conferred the *status* of virginity symbolically, and could likewise restore the honor of virginity to those who had lost it, thus becoming the guarantor of conversion and protection.

As part of the humanist debate on education in general, the idea that intellectual and cultural education for women could contribute to safeguarding virginity had a long and painful development in the first half of the sixteenth century, as the first schools for the education of the children of noble families were established.[39] There is an emblem by the Bolognese jurist Andrea Alciati, entitled *Custodiendas virgines,* first printed in 1531, which was to become the forerunner of a whole new literature and the most important "mass media" form of the period. That emblem assigns Pallas, the goddess of wisdom, the task of safeguarding women's honor.[40] The recognition that instruction, especially religious instruction, should be part of the education of girls, even if they were poor, was an original idea. It led to the formation of the most significant institute created in the first half of the sixteenth century, the Company of Saint Ursula, founded in Brescia by Angela Merici in 1535. This institution came about in response to the new religious and social demands of young women who, for want of a dowry, could not enter convents and dedicate themselves to the contemplative life or receive at least rudimentary instruction.

Powerfully innovative both in its internal organization and in its religious and social aims, the Company of Saint Ursula,[41] shows how original the feminine contribution to the renewal of religious life in the early sixteenth century was.[42] Here, religious education was a priority in educating girls from the middle and lower classes.

A more articulated form of instruction and of fostering the behavioral models of the aristocratic class became available in another institution that took shape a few decades later, Guastalla College, founded in Milan in 1555 by Ludovica Torelli, countess of Guastalla, who in the words of her biographer "combed the city for girls rich in natural ability but poor in worldly fortune who ran the risk of going astray."[43]

Throughout the modern period, the guiding principle behind institutes founded for women had been protecting feminine honor. In the early sixteenth century, "conservatories," colleges, and shelters for *convertite* were created to face social problems that had been made more acute by economic and religious upheavals consequent to war and the spread of Protestant ideas. In time, these institutions acquired a more distinct character. The first became places primarily devoted to female labor; the second offered instruction; and the third grew into enclosed monasteries, yielding to others the role of welcoming and converting prostitutes who had "repented." As one might expect and as Sherill Cohen pointed out in her analysis of the refuges for the *convertite* in modern Tuscany, the concept of honor changed over the centuries.[44] But by the early sixteenth century Sabba da Castiglione, an acute observer of his time who addressed a sort of manual of comportment, called *Ricordi* ("Souvenirs"), to his nephew, had already noted the incongruity of a custom that had been honorable a century earlier, the remarriage of elderly widowers to young women.[45]

Living in Religion

Many groups wanted to lead an apostolic life. That is, they wanted to respond to the ideal of the early Church, which they now saw respected in the apostolic communities and realized in the age of the Church fathers, especially among the women who followed Saint Jerome. Widows and virgins in fact regularly accompanied Jerome, for whom Renaissance humanists had shown great veneration and who furnished them with the teachings necessary for a life of perfection.

Knowledge of the corruption of a large part of the monastic world was widespread. Now that environment, long undermined by the indiscriminate recruitment of young men and women whose families had destined them to the monasteries, had been infiltrated by innovative ideas from beyond the Alps, especially in those establishments with a greater commitment to the religious life. We have no way of knowing to what extent the Lutheran rejection of monastic vows influenced individual consciences, nor to what degree it acted as an agent of apostasy among monks or lack of discipline among nuns. But the idea that perfection need no longer be sought in the monastic life made headway even in spiritual circles not particularly inclined to heterodox ideas, such as those close to the Savonarolian reforms.

The prophetic tension that had aimed at Church reform had exhausted itself between 1530 and 1560 and given way to a consolidation of that welfare system—directed toward the recuperation and protection of women's honor—whose foundations had been laid by the Oratory of Divine Love. After the trauma of the sack of Rome (1527) and the reorganization of the Italian states that ensued after the temporary peace between the king of France and the emperor and the solemn coronation of Charles V (1530), religious life definitively turned its back on expressions of its burning mysticism and prophecy and took up new forms of spirituality. This new spirituality aimed to reproduce, in compact and restricted circles, the characteristics of the Church of the Apostles, that "true" Church which transalpine reformers opposed to the Roman Church and which they intended to bring back to life through their new ecclesiastical structures.

Aspirations to personal salvation, accomplished by pursuing a spiritual quest shared with others of a like mind, brought together individuals and groups with a wide and sometimes divergent variety of postures toward religious dissent, which bit by bit was defining itself organizationally and theologically. The initial aspirations of that apostolic pilgrim Ignatius of Loyola and his early companions, and of those spiritual circles that gathered round the Dominicans Battista da Crema in Milan or Vincenzo Arnolfini in Lucca,[46] did not differ greatly from those which moved the followers of Juan de Valdés in Naples or Angela Merici in Brescia.[47] What they had in common was a desire to build an *ecclesia*, a church whose authority no longer derived from the ecclesiastical hierarchy, but came from a "teacher," a spiritual "father" or "mother," whose charismatic qualities were recognizably such as led to perfection.

Events connected with the diffusion of Calvinistic and Anabaptist ideas in Italy—which gave rise among Sienese merchants[48] or Venetian Anabaptists[49] to the formation of *ecclesiae*, or churches, inspired by theological principles, moral practices, and organizational criteria now well defined—made it impossible to continue to ignore the problem of ecclesiastical authority. All the "spirituals" who for twenty years had been able to organize themselves into little groups in imitation of the apostolic life now had to choose whether to obey the authority of the pope or that of the charismatic leaders, whether these were the reformers or the mystics who led their "churches." Between 1542, the year in which the Roman Inquisition was created, and the period 1555–1559, under popes Marcellus II (Cervini) and Paul IV (Carafa), they had to choose which authority to obey: the Roman Church or the reformed churches. It was a difficult decision, both for men, who were the most frequently engaged in organizational tasks and in the management of the different *ecclesiae,* and for women, who often were not merely followers, collaborators, or patrons of the organizers of these churches, but their charismatic guides. In truth, women's role in Italian religious life in the first half of the sixteenth century was no less significant than it had been during the livelier and more gratifying period of the "living saints."

The first clear shift occurred at court. The close links between the princes and the Mendicant orders gradually came to an end. The ladies of the court continued to frequent monasteries where their relatives had made their professions or where they might find hospitality on a journey or if they were widowed, but increasingly their religious and cultural interests turned to spiritual guides chosen from outside the cloister. Princess Eleanora d'Este, a Poor Clare at the convent of Corpus Domini in Ferrara, took the learned physician Antonio Musa Brasavola as her spiritual mentor; Victoria Colonna lived in a convent but took her spiritual guidance from Juan Valdés and Cardinal Pole; Ludovica Torelli declined to found a convent and instead preferred to join a group of women in a form of religious life with a rule of their own choosing. Examples could be multiplied, but the essential factor is a radical shift, in a few decades, among aristocrats. They were now directly interested in joining the reform movement, as was the case with the Calvinist duchess of Ferrara, Renata di Francia, who not only protected religious dissenters but favored the rise of reformist groups with financial support.

While there were adherents to the Protestant Reformation among individual Italian women, it is hard to discern any group physiognomy. The actual state of research makes clear, however, that the women who kept up contacts with Italian reformers came primarily from the princely courts and the urban aristocracy. They were women who had been able to avail themselves of a cultural education superior to that of other classes, who often chose as spiritual guides their own "teachers" of grammar or the humanities but did not take active propaganda or leadership roles in any organized form of religious dissent. Nor did they seek original forms of self-expression *as women* within a movement that presented itself as "new" and involved a risky refusal of the traditional and the normal. Indeed, the most self-aware adherents to reform doctrine, like the Ferrarese humanist Olimpia Morata, thought that by professing the new Calvinist religion they were making a choice which aligned them with men:

> I, born a woman, have set aside women's things,
> Loom and spindle, threads and sewing-boxes.
> Now my pleasure lies where the Muses bloom,

And the joyful songs of twin-peaked Parnassus.
Other women may relish other delights,
But this is now my trade,
And here lie my joys.[50]

Beyond street debates about justification through faith or reading Beneficio di Cristo's "sweet" doctrine in common, it would appear that taking up
pro-Protestant ideas about the female sex was limited to those women who by
aristocratic birth or social position frequented cultural circles and social networks that permitted them to entertain relations, sometimes protective, with
exponents of religious dissidence.[51] Adhering to the Reformation, however,
meant an awareness of their negation as women: this was a religion of the
spirit, not the body, and not only a refusal of the "everyday."

Much more decisive was the female contribution to the dynamic of those
groups which, though identifying themselves as searching for new forms of
religious expression, continued to operate within the structures they themselves created for the protection and succor of women.

The main areas for these new religious movements involving women continued to be Lombardy and Venetia, though imperial and Spanish Naples was
an outstanding exception. Their common characteristic was that they did not
identify themselves as specifically female but instead acted in solidarity with
laymen and religious men, many of whom recognized in women their charismatic counselors. The cases of Mère Jeanne, venerated in Venice by the
cabalist theologian Guillaume Postel, and of the Angelic Paola Antonia Negri, are fairly well known.[52]

In post-Waldensian Naples the female religious movement that had vital-
ized the circle about the mystical reformer did not fade away but broke up
into many groups and grouplets. Functioning primarily among local and
Spanish aristocratic women, it welcomed the preaching of the Theatines
founded by the powerful Carafa family and the "new" religious, full of converting zeal, who came to Naples from other cities. Bonsignore Cacciaguerra,
a Sienese who preached the reform of religious life based on frequent recourse to the sacraments, was, for instance, well received and appreciated by
the Neapolitan aristocracy.[53]

New Images of Sanctity

The Tridentine decree "On the Invocation, Veneration, and Relics of Saints
and Holy Images" put an end to a long-lasting controversy. The subject had
first been raised during the great debates of the Council of Nicaea in the
eighth century, which noted the differences between the Eastern and Western

churches in relation to sacred images; it resurfaced in the debates surrounding the condemnation of the fifteenth-century reformers Jan Hus and John Wycliffe; and it had become a pressing issue by the early sixteenth century. Rome reconfirmed the legitimacy of the cult of saints and the veneration of their images and relics but also recognized the need to extirpate abuses, eliminate superstition, control the traffic in all objects connected to the cult, and reform the usages connected with the feasts of patron saints and local sanctuaries.

In short, before defining a doctrine and any new relationship with holy images, the council wished to arm itself against possible criticism by a radical purging of matters connected to the image of sanctity. Its first concern was to ask local bishops to undertake a real "cleanup" in sacred art and architecture. Externally, the result was cleaning, repainting, and new building; provincial councils were authorized to legislate on this score, and some more cultivated bishops, like Carlo Borromeo in Milan and Gabriel Paleotti in Bologna, entered into dialogues with trustworthy painters and technicians about the council's new dispositions on sacred art.[54]

The impact of those conciliar decrees and of the theories that derived from them was enormous. In fact, they influenced the whole development of art in that difficult period of transition between Mannerism and the Baroque; they reinforced naturalism in painting and created a specific form of Counter-Reformation art, which Federico Zeri has called "timeless art." Deviations had to be supervised and the new legislation on holy images enforced, but more important, the legitimacy, indeed the necessity, of a didactic use of images as "books for the simple" or the illiterate was reconfirmed.[55] This was a traditional doctrine of the Church and had never been denied even among Protestants, by whom the figurative arts were soon transformed into "moralities," as engraved sheets or books used emblems and historical tales to convey those behavioral norms which the Catholic Church continued to deliver through sacred images.

By the time the Council of Trent solemnly pronounced its doctrine and reform on the cult of saints and holy images, the Church had already issued a number of cautions concerning the approval and diffusion of new cults. The Church's reservations on this score were effectively a sort of response to the criticisms of superstition raised by Erasmus and to the iconoclasm of some of the more radical exponents of reform. If there was any one point on which Catholicism showed its awareness of the reformers' arguments, it was in the area that for centuries was to mark the difference between the two confessions: the veneration of saints, the Virgin, and relics.

After the succession of triumphal canonizations and beatifications of the preachers of the Observance, and of mystical women engaged in Church reform in the late Middle Ages, the Roman calendar now showed a vast empty space. For over half a century, the pope and his consistory approved not a single canonization. After a flourishing in the lives and legends of the saints, which had shifted from manuscript circulation to the printed book, nothing new was produced between the third decade and the last quarter of the sixteenth century.

The eclipse of the saints was accompanied by a revision of the cult of the Virgin: saintly episodes during her lifetime, most of which derived from the apocryphal Gospels, were downplayed, while a new emphasis was put on those "mysteries" of her cult linked to established tradition and on new theological concepts, such as her Assumption, Coronation, and Immaculate Conception. The more recent cult commemorating Mary's Visitation to Saint Elizabeth, though this had an undisputed scriptural basis and was among the mysteries of the rosary, was liturgically downgraded. From a feast celebrated with a vigil, the reform of the liturgical calendar undertaken by Cardinal Quiñones had already reduced it to a simple feast before the Council of Trent ended. A similar fate befell Saint Joseph: from having played a subordinate but highly significant moral and social role as Mary's husband, he was now declassified as an anonymous "confessor."

While there was a serious attempt to stem new devotions, it basically failed. The intent was to reduce the number of tales and hagiographic legends pertaining to the tradition of the martyrologies, which the culture of preaching had transmitted into late medieval culture—those endless vulgarizations and hugely successful lives of saints such as *The Golden Legend,* Domenico Cavalca's *Lives of the Holy Fathers,* and the countless "histories" and "legends" printed on a few sheets and widely sold. At the beginning of the sixteenth century, however, it became clear that there was an urgent need to anchor the cult of saints solidly in ancient tradition: hence the publishing success of *The Lives of the Most Holy Virgins,* which first appeared in 1511 and was then reprinted in 1525 and 1535 and several times more before the century's close.[56]

The success of this collection owed something to the contemporary orientation of the countries of the Lutheran and Anglican reformations, the only Protestant places where the cult of the saints was not totally rejected and where an effort was made to recover—within a context of bloody religious wars—the deeds of the Fathers of the Church and the martyrs and see them as heroic and exemplary figures. The first collection of the lives of the Fathers, the work of Hermannus Bonnus, was published in Germany in 1539: he included among his subjects a few popular Christian martyrs and even Mary Magdalene. In 1544 Georg Major produced another such collection. Both authors produced their texts at the solicitation and with the approval of Luther; their intention was to furnish preachers with exempla that could replace those of *The Golden Legend,* hence the use of Latin. Contemporary with these works was that of Georg Spalatino on the lives of the saints and other important figures. This collection had a more pious objective and was aimed directly at the faithful. Nonetheless, like the others, his text was printed in Latin. Finally there came (in the years 1554–1558) the celebrated illustrated collection of the lives of the martyrs ancient and modern written by the Strasbourg pastor Ludwig Rabus, who included the legends of the female Christian martyrs and of a number of women who had met their deaths during the Wars of Religion.[57]

The success of the Italian collection of female martyrs' lives—printed in the vernacular and illustrated with minuscule linecuts based on the woodcuts in Malerbi's translation of *The Golden Legend*—paralleled that of the Lutheran work. Yet by the end of the century, this Italian collection had all but disappeared. We can only speculate why this reversal occurred, but one obvious factor was that the tales and legends for which it drew on Jacobus da Voragine no longer fulfilled the new requirement for greater historical accuracy, a requirement that was becoming all-important in establishing "true" sainthood. Although even before the Council of Trent the Church had begun to regard the tricky question of the cult of saints with an eye to reform and rationality, it was not until the latter half of the sixteenth century that it drew the necessary conclusions from a developing process of great historical and cultural consequence.

The council's decisions on sacred art demanded that images be faithful to Scripture. The immediate effect was to eliminate all Apocrypha as a basis for the *inventio* of events and places connected with the life of Christ and the Virgin. Images of miracles whose historical truth was not properly authenticated were also banned. A single example should suffice: the decline in the cult of Saint Ursula, whose figure nonetheless remained closely linked throughout the modern period with all the welfare and educational institutions that bore her name.

Bringing naturalism and historicity back to sacred art and to the cult of the saints had a profound impact on culture in two ways: first, it acted as a powerful rational influence on the imaginary; and second, it excluded from what was approved and confirmed in the cults anything that could not be proven historically.[58] By so doing, it was a decisive factor in the decline of magic in Western Christianity.

Mental prayer, widespread in Europe from the fifteenth century on, and especially the spiritual exercises of Saint Ignatius, had channeled the religious imagination into a precise composition of the time and space in which the object of meditation had taken place. That is, it linked the imagination to an episode or event that could be, even when supernatural or metahistorical, circumscribed in a specific space and time. By contrast, other forms of prayer, proposed or imposed on the faithful in a massive way—such as the recital of the rosary—constrained the imagination into preestablished forms, leaving little room for individual experiences and reducing the creative space of visions. The erection of the "Holy Mounts" in Lombardy gave an urban dimension to the sacred space of the traditional sanctuary, transforming the ritual pilgrimages into a sort of realistic identification with the time and place of the crucified Christ's Passion and death.

The Marian cult was not exempt from an analogous transformation. It too was ever more closely tied to a uniform image and a concrete place, one which recalled not so much the real space in which Mary had lived but rather the sacred space that circumscribed the event of a miracle, itself recalled by the building of a sanctuary. The Marian miracles linked to extraordinary events had increased in number in the fifteenth century, but it was not until the end of the next century that the cult of the Virgin began to rival that of the saints, which now faced doubt and were being purged of their more obviously marvelous and magical characteristics. Quantitative studies have shown that the majority of sanctuaries devoted to Mary were built in Italy during the sixteenth and seventeenth centuries.[59]

There is no doubt that the Protestant challenge to the Marian cult and the iconoclasm associated with the Reformation led, in the Roman Church, to a reaction most readily perceptible in the increase in the number of Marian miracles and of sacred places dedicated to her. This phenomenon looks like the rise of a new form of devotion, but we should really ask ourselves what actually changed with this linking of extraordinary events and repetitive rituals. Was the image of the Virgin offered to the faithful a constant one, or was it the vehicle for a different cultural and symbolic content?

Two relevant aspects should be emphasized: the progressive dehumanization of the image of Mary and the progressive hieraticization of her person, increasingly freighted with titles and allegorical symbols that define her function as mediatrix between God and the faithful, between heaven and earth. The Virgin was still present among ordinary men and women, visibly accessible in special places dedicated to her, but she had lost her role as a woman among women, which had made of her an imitable subject.

Monastic Discipline and Urban Discipline

The reorganization engendered by the Tridentine Church had an immediate effect on women's convents. It returned them to that regular discipline which had been the chief aim of the reform movements of the fifteenth and early sixteenth centuries. The process of extirpating abuses and rebuilding a connective tissue that would give women's collegial institutions at least a minimum of community life was a long one and not entirely successful. Effective efforts, however, were made to transform women's monasteries into places of protection, isolated from the external world with bars and bolts and made ever more agreeable in their interiors by enlarging the buildings and extending their courtyards and gardens. To compensate for the rigorous enclosure, the new amenities sought to create convents in which the monastic and urban imagination would find a counterpart on earth of the Garden of Eden or the heavenly Jerusalem.

The transformation was a "success" for the fathers. The nuns, either openly or in secret, rebelled against the imposition of norms that had been no part of the orders in which they had taken their vows. Internal quarrels often took the place of that emulation which now had no means to express itself in the outside world. The nuns invested in fastuousness of display and in the prestige of their convents that loss of power in the life of religion and the city which they had often been able to exercise in the Middle Ages and the Renaissance. After the defections of the male orders and the public scandals of the female ones in the early 1500s, both society and the Church had decided to restore discipline to the monastic orders and they prevailed over the discontent of the nuns. Fidelity to their religious professions and obedience to the authority of the fathers became the bases of the new discipline, and bishops took over responsibility for the governance of the nuns.

The bishops undertook reform with zeal. To the fathers of families, often themselves relatives of the nuns, they delegated the task of putting monastic finances back in good order and administering their property; by granting and revoking confessional authority, they controlled the nuns' confessors; they dismissed from governance of the monasteries (the turnover was nearly total) the superiors of the traditional orders; they sent in preachers whom they trusted; they visited religious establishments with unexpected frequency, subjecting nuns to individual interrogation and inspecting the validity of monastic voting and elections; in short, they did all that was in their power to do to confer a new dignity on an institution that had been first challenged and then rejected by the transalpine reformers.

Two measures in the Tridentine reform particularly enabled the Church to gauge the institutional solidity on which its reform was based: the episcopal decision to inquire of every nun as to whether her "vocation" had been freely decided and the presence of the bishop or his delegate at the ceremony in which nuns made their final professions.

True, this cautionary conversation with the bishop was insufficient to unmask all forced enclosures or to undo family strategies, but it did make novices aware of the solemnity and legally binding nature of the vow they were about to make. The presence of a bishop at solemn professions forced respect for the rule; no longer could the rule be confused with any customary norm learned living and boarding in a monastery with an aunt or some other relative. Just how conscientiously this obligation to respect the rule implicit in a monastic profession was undertaken by nuns we can see from an interesting interrogatory conducted by the patriarch of Udine, Francesco Barbaro, on the occasion of his visit to the nuns of Santa Chiara on September 11, 1601.

The case is well known to historians because eleven years earlier the same Barbaro, then coadjutor to the patriarch Grimani, had submitted the Poor Clares to a trial for heresy, which had begun with a few nuns and eventually involved the whole convent.[60] Less well known are the circumstances and reasons for the Santa Chiara nuns' heresy. Consider, for instance, the testimony of Sister Theodora Antonini:

> My profession was not voluntary. My father forced me, for family reasons. But I hold that I promised nothing to God, because though I spoke with my mouth, my will did not consent . . . This I say because nothing more happened than that the veil was put on me and my hair cut as I knelt before the altar. The veil was put on by a friar, our chaplain, and I said nothing, nor did he make me promise anything. No wonder, then if the rigors of the rule seem confining and impossible, because we are accustomed to our freedom without any obligation of conscience, and so many times I went out in the time of the friars and the Bishop of Caorli.[61]

The knowledge that monastic discipline was henceforward unequivocally tied to the observance of a rule and fidelity to the vows of profession had, by the end of the sixteenth century, reached even those monasteries, like the one in Udine, most openly rebellious to hierarchical authority. By then it had become impossible to ignore what that authority was.

Even the more original female religious movements of the early 1500s were now subjected to reforms that strongly reduced their distinctive self-government. The Tridentine decree aimed at reforming nuns dusted off an old prohibition against women living in common without having made a solemn profession including enclosure. The regular Third Orders were thus compelled to become nuns of the Second Order, or their convents were suppressed. Congregations with a clearly religious mission, such as Torelli's, were transformed into monastic communities under one of the traditional rules.

The Company of Saint Ursula was allowed to retain its lay statutes but had to accept a hierarchical structure that subjected it directly to episcopal authority and fundamentally changed its character from that of the educational and providential institution it had been at its origins. The Ursulines, however, did retain, even in the second half of the century, an important institutional role, the only one that could act as a mediator in the new compact between Church and society. For this compact aimed to recreate a clear line of demarcation between the male and female religious experience—between organizational and managerial tasks, clearly controlled by the authority of men, and the pure patronage or the ordinary cooperation given to women. The way in which Carlo Borromeo reformed the Ursuline rule in Brescia and introduced it in Milan showed the passage from a form of institutional direction based on the typology of familial and maternal relations to an organizational structure dependent on the bishop.[62]

Though transformed in respect to its original structure and inspiration, the Company of Saint Ursula was allowed to spread beyond the confines of the diocese and to become the ideological base on which different institutions, still bearing the original name, were founded. Borromeo went even further. In Milan he founded the first colleges under the aegis of congregational Ursulines—that is, those living in a community—thus enabling them, thanks to their lay statute, to avoid the Tridentine prohibition of unenclosed female religious institutions. As both a spiritual company and colleges, the Ursulines spread quickly throughout Lombardy and the Po Valley. In the early 1600s they reached France and thence, transformed into a cloistered order, established themselves in Canada, where they became the first women's missionary order.

In Italy those Ursulines attracted to the monastic vocation preferred to conform to one of the traditional rules. Either in homage to Angela Merici's original religious choice, or through their rigorous spirituality, they chose the Poor Clares. An example is the transformation of the Ursuline college in Lodi into a Second Order Franciscan Capuchin convent.[63]

The normalization of monasteries, regular Third Orders, and female congregations greatly limited religious women's century-old freedom of association outside convents and the houses of their fathers. But the social and religious motives that had formerly inspired them gave no sign of flagging. Secular ecclesiastical authorities, and especially those bishops close to Borromeo's pastoral policy, became the interpreters of these demands. For example, there was fervid creation of women's communities such as the one known as the Dimesse, or the Humble, created by the Franciscan Antonio Pagani during the Tridentine and post-Tridentine period in Vicenza. Here again, young widows established institutions in which women of different social classes lived in community.

The Tridentine decree may have intended to bring discipline back to the cloister by imposing enclosure, but it was unable to extinguish altogether women's desire for freedom and the lively movement that had, in the first half of the century, led to the creation of innovative religious groups such as the Ursulines and the Angelics.[64]

The suppression of convents in reformed nations and the rediscovery of the family as fundamental to evangelism caused a marked change in the ecclesiastical hierarchy's attitude toward women and the female condition. In Italy the father's prerogatives as head of family and master to his wife and children were left untouched, but the Church now offered greater openings to women in the fields of education and evangelization. Although there seems to have been no major change in traditional sexual morality or relations in general between husband and wife in Italy during the sixteenth century, there is little doubt that regularizing marriage and publishing banns became a key target for ecclesiastical action and that the Church's attitudes on the family underwent a major shift.

Agostino Valier, bishop of Verona, who had approved Pagani's Company of the Dimesse,[65] addressed all categories of women in spiritual notices published in 1575. These revealed the Church's new way of looking at the condition of women. Not only were they to collaborate with their husbands in the education of their young, but they were to be directly involved in the honor and prestige of the city: "Because good mothers of families are the solid base of discipline in the city, and from discipline comes obedience, the good order and tranquillity of peoples, to the honor and glory of God."[66]

Restoring the city's discipline was also a task for cloistered virgins: their well-ordered and honored convents could provide a bulwark against the power of evil. Widows could contribute to discipline by dressing with humility, by devoting themselves to help young women "in danger," and by teaching Christian doctrine. Uncloistered virgins living at home could also offer much to family and Church.

Valier's treatises to women of many different conditions may, by their moral and expository weight, be considered the high point in the theoretical development of Church ideology toward the condition of women. As texts, they were parenetic and normative; their emphases and motivations were vastly different from previous texts of this kind. The supposed submission of women to their husbands and fathers gave way to a higher status, in which women cooperated in family and city discipline. Valier also added a new status to the traditional categories of virgins, widows, and married women, and the novelty was underlined by his calling them a "fourth state": the Humble virgins living at home.

As they responded to the Tridentine injunction to clean up monastic discipline, the bishops neither could, nor sought, to eradicate the social problem of forced "vocations," but they did raise an obstacle to it by legitimizing female celibacy. By the last quarter of the century, it had become impossible, unlike a few decades earlier, for anyone to be scandalized that a young woman over twenty-five should choose to live at home with her mother rather than be consigned to marriage or the cloister. The same prelates who had fostered the rise of Ursuline institutions in various cities now convinced the fathers of families of the advantage of this new status for women. A brief *excursus* on the rules of the first Ursuline foundations—those of Ferrara in 1587, Bologna in 1608, and Modena in 1620—made clear the decision to back these foundations, not merely for their spiritual value but also for their social utility. Paolo Leoni, the bishop of Ferrara, in his preface to the rules of 1587, defended the company he created against those who held it impossible for women alone to safeguard their honor in the secular world and thought it unseemly for them to continue to live in their paternal homes. He insisted that the institution in fact renewed an ancient spirit in the Church and put his seal of approval on this admirable, new "third state." He did not use the category of "fourth state" as had Valier, and appears to have assimilated the Ursulines to the widowed state, in which young women could serve God at home.[67]

The bishop of Bologna, Alfonso Paleotti, emphasized the double desirability to families—dignity and economic advantage—of founding and encouraging such institutions. He addressed fathers thus:

> for, freed of the need to marry them off, or find a convent for them, with the dowry and heavy expense involved, they will see their daughters become brides of the Heavenly King . . . They will feel secure due to their good governance of the honesty of their families and their own goods, and finally, with cordial affection, they will be cared for, served, consoled, and helped by them until death.[68]

Being forced into a convent or being destined to look after their parents and nephews and nieces may have been an equally painful fate for individual women, but there is no doubt that the new option of female celibacy, heretofore frowned upon by society, opened up a legitimate role for such women, thus in the future permitting forms of cohabitation based on purely economic or social considerations.

Professionalism and Virtue

Tightening monastic discipline was not just a matter of putting up bars and walls, of imposing a rigorous enclosure; it also involved a slow and assiduous process of education and persuasion, a professionalization of nuns who, up to that time, had based their knowledge on the transmission of customary norms. The bishops' inquiry into the free taking of vows and the control of monastic recruitment, which now required respect of a minimum age for novices, were the first steps taken by the council towards' ensuring that nuns knew what duties their monastic vows involved.[69] At the same time, the bishops and superiors of the orders saw to the printing and vernacular translation of the rules and constitutions meant to become the chief instrument in introducing and making monastic discipline uniform. Within a few decades there appeared—sometimes just the text, sometimes with commentaries—not only many editions and reeditions of the rules, but also ever more specific texts designed to make religious aware of the prerogatives and obligations of monastic life. These new texts were not merely exhortatory; they were what one might call professional in nature.

The imposition of a uniform habit and the restoration of the monastic offices foreseen in the constitutions helped to reduce the power of the abbesses and prioresses and their vicars; likewise, they involved a greater number of women in sharing the responsibility for the welfare of the community. Discharging the tasks incumbent on the various monastic offices also required renewed efforts in the fundamental instruction of the nuns. It was no longer sufficient to know the breviary by heart; nuns actually had to be able to read and write. Monastic libraries were enriched with devout works and texts to be read in common.[70] Reciting sacred dramas offered nuns archaic models of sanctity, while the comedies the nuns themselves sometimes produced reveal how professed nuns learned to convert love stories, such as Giovanni Boccaccio's *Filocolo,* into spiritual terms.[71]

Women's writing was refined and enriched by new literary genres at the end of the 1500s and in the following century: the requirement that the administration of the convent be accounted for led to an enlargement of the traditional book of Records and accounts of expenses; noting down the facts of daily life and contemporary events was accompanied by a desire to record the history of the institution in aulic terms.[72] Reports on spiritual direction were transformed into written notations of thoughts, inspirations, and visions, which in turn gave rise to autobiographical forms of mystical writing.[73]

The Renaissance involved the world of women; it enlarged their culture and their writing. While in the first half of the sixteenth century a few noblewomen in direct contact with humanists and intellectuals were able to join literary society as highly praised authors of poems, those women enclosed in convents read profane authors and cultivated writing for a long time thereafter, as a part of teaching. In the 1600s, as Benedetto Croce acutely observed, female culture existed exclusively within the cloister.[74]

Regular observance in monasteries was meant to contribute to the honor of the city. Convents were "bulwarks" against the work of the devil: it would seem convents discharged specific social obligations. But exactly what sort of profession was being a nun?

There were in fact two major specializations for monasteries: music, which added dignity to the liturgy and to the religious celebration of the patron saint's feast, and the education of young women of the nobility. Nuns were especially attracted to the former; they dedicated much of their time and energy, and internal conflicts, to questions of singing and the use of instruments.[75] Music was a way of presenting themselves to the outside world as professionals in an art that was an integral part of the education of young ladies and one of the openings through which they could advance the prestige of their convent and the honor of the city. It was no different with education. They lavished care on their tasks and increased the numbers of their educational institutes, which now had to compete with the colleges in the education they gave.

In the latter part of the sixteenth century, the college was the experimental and innovative part of the system of instruction, which, though numerically it involved fewer students than male institutions, was vital to women. After the founding of Guastalla College, specialized institutions for the education of girls from the upper classes spread through the cities of northern and central Italy. As secular institutions, most of them were run by Ursuline or Dimesse communities whose professionalism focused on teaching.

Centered on teaching how to behave in a disciplined fashion with an eye to passing this knowledge on to future generations, women's educational institutions reflect a profound change in the models of perfection and sanctity. Women had played an active, historical role in their prophetic calls for reform of society and Church; now the exercise of charity and virtue became the high road for religious activity. The caution with which everything associated with saints and the veneration of living saints had been regarded from the 1530s onward turned into open suspicion. The fight against superstition intensified in the last two decades of the century, and the first two inquisitorial trials of women accused of feigning sanctity took place in the kingdom of Naples.

Distinctions between "true" and "false" sanctity—given the apparent similarities between the extraordinary events connected with extrasensorial phenomena, mostly among devout women—became increasingly difficult to make. The involvement of confessors and spiritual directors in episodes deemed to be expressions of sanctity fell under suspicion and were no longer tolerated. The hint of heresy was the foundation that permitted the Inquisition to move with broad powers in examining cases related not so much to doctrinal deviations as to matters of religious behavior.[76] Confessors were supervised by inquisitors and sometimes undertook inquisitorial duties among women subject to mystical and visionary experiences when they themselves were directing. These moves were made easier by the crisis in models of sanctity of the period, models that awaited official redefinition by the Church.

After all the doctrinal controversies over the cult of saints and the institutional crisis that overtook the religious orders, the ecclesiastical hierarchy's main efforts were devoted to reaffirming the value of sainthood and the constitution of a "new" hagiography that purged marvelous and magical elements from the lives of the saints.

Starting in the mid 1500s, imposing and carefully researched histories of the religious orders were written. They contained accounts of the deeds of members marked by sanctity and aimed to reconfirm the loyalty to the Church of the earliest foundations. The traditional image of sanctity, which permitted miracles and extraordinary charismatic events, was reaffirmed. But official Church sanctioning of a new model of holiness after the doctrinal struggles and the disciplining of the cults was bound to come with the first canonizations after nearly a century of silence.

Between 1608 and 1610 the papacy gave a first clear indication of the image of perfection it proposed for the faithful. Church reform, charity, and virtue triumphed over mysticism and prophecy. The saints canonized (Francesca de' Ponziani and Carlo Borromeo) or beatified (Ignatius of Loyola, Isidore the Husbandman, Teresa of Avila, Philip Neri, and Francis Xavier), by Paul V, the latter confirmed as saints during the next pontificate, that of Gregory XV (1622), reveal the Church's desire to sacralize a broad spectrum of human conditions, characterized by type of conduct and status of life. Women were not left out. In her canonization bull, Francesca de' Ponziani (Saint Francesca of Rome), a noble Roman wife and mother, was singled out for her humility, her piety toward her fellow creatures, her renunciation of the prerogatives due her lofty status, and her work in founding religious communities.[77] The Counter-Reformation may be said to have transformed her into a figure not unlike her Humbled contemporaries. Teresa of Avila, whose fame was due above all to her contemplative life and her mysticism, was now exalted as a reformer of women's religious orders.

There were also the champions of male sainthood, destined to provide ideal models for the clergy: the holy pastor, the founder of an order, the apostle of the Roman periphery, the missionary. Laypeople, too, figured in this new geography of paradise, but its most eminent summits were reserved for those who had proven their loyalty to the Roman Church, those who persisted in their religion and fought to reconquer the world for Catholicism.

Women canonized in the succeeding centuries, with the exception of those nuns who followed Teresa's example and became reformers, mainly belong to the fertile, pre-Tridentine period. In the last quarter of the sixteenth century, however, one Italian nun who followed in the footsteps of the great Spanish saint was immediately celebrated for her sanctity: the Florentine Maria Maddalena de' Pazzi. Diffusion of the Life and writings of Saint Teresa went hand-in-hand with the cult of Maria Maddalena. The first Italian translations of the Spanish mystic's autobiography were published in Rome in 1599, at the time of her beatification process; but a translation of the *Way of Perfection* and the *Interior Castle*, by the Florentine canon Cosimo Gaci, was issued by the publisher Giunti in 1605.[78]

A mere seven years later the first steps toward canonizing Maria Maddalena were taken, and she was beatified in 1626. Shortly thereafter the Romagnolo painter Guido Cagnacci created a painting of great artistic and religious significance: the apotheosis of the two Carmelite saints—facing one another, the transverberated Teresa, struck through her heart by a fiery dart, and Maria Maddalena, heart in hand.[79] A mystic and a visionary, but a tenacious advocate of monastic and church reform, the Florentine *beata* seems to be the Italian incarnation of Teresan sanctity. The Carmelite reform that began in Spain was extended to Italy, and the ecclesiastical hierarchy's insistent pressure for a radical reform of monastic institutions led to the rapid recognition of their cults and by the promotion of the two Carmelite sisters as models of reform.

As documented in Baroque iconography, the Teresan model remained a vehicle for the sort of mysticism, delicately balanced between sanctity and demonic possession, that had survived in early-seventeenth-century convents and had been under particular attack in the middle levels of religious society, among the Dimesse and *bizocche*. Whether living in communities (like the Venetian Cecilia Ferrazzi) or at home (like the Bolognese Angela Mellini), they traveled the road to perfection in close collaboration with their spiritual directors, and were suspect and challenged as fictitious.[80] Indeed, abandoned in favor of a model of sanctity focused on behavior and virtue, mysticism in the early seventeenth century went through a sort of diffused and underground period. The generation after the Tridentine bishops studied it with interest, and mysticism was highly regarded in circles around Federico Borromeo in Milan and Alfonso Paleotti in Bologna, but it was also reduced to a more personal and intimate dimension and showed up mainly in private connections and writings, in the family or among adepts, seldom being institutionally recognized.

There is little doubt that the Congregation of Sacred Rites and Ceremonies, created in 1588 to study problems inherent in the saint cults and new standards governing canonization procedures (approved by Urban VIII between 1625 and 1634), prevailed over the residual manifestations of sanctity based on visions and prophecy.[81] A body disciplined by the hair shirt and the self-administered punishments of the Baroque Capuchin nuns was part of a conception of sanctity that made heroism and disdain for life an ideal form of modern religiosity obedient to the canonical standard of "heroic virtue."[82]

Nonetheless, a massive unfolding of female devotion took place during the Baroque era. The home became a monastic cell. Growing privacy in the house allowed private spaces for middle-class women, and they had an ever greater opportunity to practice mental prayer and contemplation at home. Similarly, literacy spread beyond the confines of cloistered nuns. The Italian model of sanctity grew closer to the French idea of "devotion" and flowered in the second half of the seventeenth century.[83] Baroque Italy and Spain seemed, in the first part of the century, to identify with the great Teresa of Avila, but nuns living at home and the Dimesse found their ideal in French religious practice.

In the mid 1600s there came from France the book that was to serve as a mirror for generations of devout Italian women, Paul de Barry's *Solitude of Philagia*. There they could read the following words:

> Because you are alone in the tiny desert of your room, perhaps you will allow me some small praise of the solitary life . . . The time to go out into the desert is past, no one speaks of that sort of solitude any more. I want to make you enamored of an easy and agreeable solitude, that of your little Bedroom, your Cabinet or a Room in your House, to which you can withdraw on occasion and speak only to God and your good Guardian Angel.[84]

The severe ascetic practices of Baroque nuns in the seventeenth century and the domestic devotions of aristocratic matrons and *bizzoche* confirmed the success of the disciplining of religious behavior demanded by the post-Tridentine Church's reorganizations. But the triumph of the religion of the Fathers, based on rationality and the word, thus less open to specifically female values such as prophecy and images, failed to include in its fine chains that new status of celibate women legitimized by the Catholic pastors at the close of the sixteenth century.

Translated from the Italian by Keith Botsford

❧ CHAPTER 6 ❧

Spiritual Letters

ADRIANO PROSPERI

> Everybody allows that the talent of writing agreeable letters is peculiarly female.
> Nature may have done something, but I am sure it must be essentially assisted
> by the practice of keeping a journal.
>
> JANE AUSTEN, *NORTHANGER ABBEY*

Visions of Love

Is letter-writing a feminine rather than a masculine genre? Looking back on
their own tradition, Italian readers might well answer affirmatively, perhaps
citing names from an obligatory list of great women letter-writers: Saint
Catherine of Siena, for one, or Alessandra Macinghi Strozzi. Those whose
training and sympathies are more directed toward the humanistic tradition or
certain heretical movements might think of Isotta Nogarole, Julia Gonzaga,
or Olympia Morata. Each set of letters differs greatly from the others,
whether by their content, by the way they came to be circulated, or by the
way in which they became (or failed to become) significant literary facts.

Right away, we can note two recurrent elements in the examples offered:
these are letters that came to be circulated, or were printed, through the
intervention of men and for nonliterary reasons. It was men who collected
and edited these correspondences, and they did so because they gave the
letters an importance and a value that had to do with life, not literature. In
Macinghi Strozzi's letters, Cesare Guasti found a model for the Christian
mother. The fact that she expressed herself in an elegant Florentine style may
have been greatly appreciated in the all-conquering age of Manzoni, but
much more important than her style was the religious world of the Florentine
lady, which lent itself to confuting the pagan image of the Italian renaissance.
Long before Guasti, Celio Secondo Curione, a religious exile from Italy,
undertook to edit the letters of Olympia, the learned daughter of the Ferrarese humanist Pellegrino Morato, with the intent of giving a concrete example of the fruits of an education founded on the Gospels and the classics of
literature. In short, had there not been men willing to become editors and

publishers, those letters would have stayed forever in family coffers, in the archives of convents or the Inquisition, or in other storing places.

Consider the most famous and oldest case, the only one from which a whole literary tradition might have been born: that of Saint Catherine of Siena. Her letters have been the intimate companions of generations of readers, and they have long been enshrined high in the canon of our Italian literary and linguistic tradition. Indeed, the century of printing opens with the letters of Catherine of Siena.[1] And still, that edition, over which Aldus Manutius spent years of attentive and passionate research, did not carry the Sienese saint into the world of literature; rather, Manutius's enterprise was a message of "religious and moral reform addressed to the Italian Church and to Italy."[2]

In other words, the edition of Catherine's letters was not conceived of as a document of that literary tradition or as an example of that Italian language which was then coming into being as the specific endeavor of Italian literary society. Furthermore, these letters, seen in their genesis, have some specific characteristics. First, the author did not know how to write, and therefore her letters were dictated to secretaries, so they may be considered "authentic" but not autographed letters. The secretaries clearly worked as filters and mediators—be it in matters linguistic, by eliminating vernacular forms, or when they had to take letters dictated by the saint in her ecstasies.[3] Second, the letters "were not collected by the saint herself; nor, would it seem, during her lifetime, but rather by her disciples and after her death, and for purposes that were neither biographical nor documentary, but exclusively edifying."[4]

This confronts us with a quite special critical problem, though one "not unique for the genre."[5] In fact, these characteristics can be found throughout the field of women's letters and spiritual writing and to such an extent that they might well be considered as part of the original nature of the genre. Endless examples are available. Consider some random instances: that of Angela of Foligno—"Not a single text of hers was written by her, they all result from transcription";[6] or that of Maria Maddalena de' Pazzi—"She wrote very little, two dozen letters . . . The rest are texts not written by her, but transcribed by her sisters in religion; dictated yes, but not dictated by her, because the author completely separated herself from the transcription of the words she uttered."[7] Between these two cases, and both before and after, there are innumerable analogous examples.

One could say, then, that there is little familiarity between women and writing, and that mystics seem uninterested in the fate of their words. Others transcribed them, conserved them, collected them, and printed them: with enormous effort and years of work, as was the case with Aldus and his edition of Catherine's letters. The argument usually offered—that there is an inherent opposition between a mystical experience and writing (together with all its variants, opposition between the truth of the experience and the lie of the word, between nature and writing, between the divine and the human)— does not correspond to the truth. We find exactly the same characteristics in a case whose protagonist was not a canonized saint but a woman who, having enjoyed a wide reputation for sanctity, was tried and condemned: that of the Angelic Paola Antonia Negri.

Paola Negri was the most celebrated author of spiritual letters in the Italy of the sixteenth century and almost achieved the first printed edition of such letters after those of Catherine of Siena. Her *Lettere spirituali* were readied for the press in 1563 (the Jesuit general Lainez' approval was dated June 30) and therefore came before the public, and with the same title, at the same time as those of the Sienese mystic Bonsignore Cacciaguerra. Both obscure and unlucky, the edition of Cacciaguerra's letters only just made it into safe harbor, finally doing so in 1563, despite the many money problems of its printer, Giovanni Maria Viotti.[8] Cacciaguerra was well known for his other writings, and his collection managed to become the first with that title only because the printing of Paola Negri's letters was interrupted by the Inquisition on January 13, 1564.[9] The apparent race between author and authoress of spiritual letters indicated by the publication dates is a totally unequal one: the male author personally supervised his own work, whereas Paola Negri was dead, and her letters were published by spiritual disciples devoted to her memory.

Something similar had already occurred with the Bolognese Elena Duglioli. A woman might "dictate" spiritual advice, but others wrote that advice down and decided, after her death, whether to make public use of it. Compared to the case of Duglioli, that of the famous "divine mother" of the Barnabites is even more complicated. No one ever challenged, then or since, Cacciaguerra's authorship of the letters published by him; Paola Negri was less fortunate. One of her devotees, the Barnabite Pietro Besozzi, rebelling against his mentor, opened up a controversy that quickly spread and then dragged on through the courts, claiming that he had written the letters and Negri had only signed them.[10] The case is exemplary: an "unlettered" woman could not lay claim to writing and publishing. De facto, a man had written those letters; it was his business to act as guide and director.

At stake was a woman's power to be an autonomous spiritual guide without passing through a male mediation. The argument was not settled then: a whole religious order, that of the Barnabites, was at stake. The Barnabites' origins were stamped with the figure of their divine mother, and from then on, they were periodically constrained to reenter the fray. But Negri's disciples and spiritual heirs showed themselves quite capable of defending her memory, as a later and more complete collection was printed in 1576. This time the letters were prefaced with a Life, in accordance with custom, which demanded that the value of women's writing be subordinated to the verification of her life. In her *vita,* its author, the Milanese scholar Giovan Battista Fontana de' Conti, made due reference to the 1564 trials and to the testimonies collected about the saintly nature of Negri's life; he also said that "no one doubted that she had written the letters disseminated under her name." A new issue, that of auctorial rights, now joined the old one of her saintly life. The material compiled from those letters by her one-time protégé and later enemy, Pietro Besozzi, soon enough produced documents showing he could write "spiritual letters" without needing the dictation of a woman.[11]

For women, however, the outcome led to a later and greater exclusion. The lesson had been learned. On the editorial market, the genre of spiritual letters was now entrusted to male supervision: in 1593 those of Juan de Avila were published in Florence by Giunti under the editorship of Timoteo Bottonio; and shortly before, a *Prattica spirituale,* or set of spiritual exercises, attributed to an anonymous nun was published with the authoritative presentation of Niccolò Sfondrati. When wholly exceptional circumstances brought onto the market letters that revived the tradition of Catherine—such as the letters of Teresa of Avila—the title page made it clear that these were texts verified or translated by members of the Holy Office.[12]

A new tradition arose, of "spiritual letters" written by men. These were obviously of a different nature: letters of spiritual direction, didactic and theologically sophisticated letters. They were written by men who had ideas and methods to offer, carefully elaborated systems for arriving at perfection, and they bear a closer resemblance to the work of the Dominican Battista da Crema, Paola Negri's teacher, than to that of his pupil. Passing through a large number of lesser-known spiritual breviaries of the same kind, they run from the letters of Bonsignore Cacciaguerra to those of Monsignor Giovanni Visconti.[13] The theological debate against Pascal and his *Lettres provinciales* was conducted in the genre of "spiritual letters."[14] Beyond the often complicated stories that lie behind these correspondences, and that specifically deal with the relationship between men and women in search of perfection, what is most striking is the male dominance being established.[15]

What would have brought this about? The answer is probably to be found in a negative definition offered by Negri's adversary, Besozzi. Writing to Fontana, he said, "Sanctity lies not in miracles, in prophecies, ecstasies, raptures and revelations." The statement has all the marks of a change of direction. What Besozzi meant was that sainthood *no longer* consisted of ecstasies and revelations, prophecies and miracles. The change is visible in the sudden loss of meaning in that which, until that time, had a real meaning. To Besozzi,

Paola Negri's experiences had suddenly lost all value. Ecstasies and raptures were now called "mental aberrations"; to build "on ecstasies, prophecies and women's revelations" seemed utterly senseless. Still, he recognized that he himself, first and to a greater degree than others, had based himself on them. Now, however, with his greater experience, he admitted to having changed his mind and to seeing matters in another light: "I perceive in ways I did not formerly perceive, and so I also speak in another manner than I once spoke."[16]

What Besozzi now saw was a whole series of risky extravaganzas, quite possibly heretical:

> During these mental aberrations, some have seen her with their own eyes making the sign of the cross and saying only *"In nomine patris et filii"* and not wanting to add the Holy Ghost . . . She would raise her hands on high, as though proffering the host; with a finger she demonstrated that she wanted what men had so that she could say mass . . . At times she vested herself as though for mass and feigned to celebrate it.[17]

To look at these odd and senseless gestures in another way, however, one must realize that they were duly written in contemporary Barnabite chapter records as the visible fragments of the divine mother's dialogue with the invisible. What her contemporaries saw was not just a series of gestures, but also the corresponding gestures of her divine interlocutor. It was a "way of seeing" with a long history.

We have an outstanding example of what one might call an "integral vision" of the behavior of a living saint: that drawn up by a notary and attested to by twenty-one persons present at the ecstasy of Sister Stefana Quinzani in Crema in 1497. The witnesses declared that they had "seen" many things at various times during the day: at dawn they had witnessed the saint's struggle with the Devil. "In an ecstatic state, her spirit raptured, she spoke intelligibly, replying to each argument and temptation of the Devil, and with divine grace she prevailed against him." Next, the saint was bound to the column like Christ. The bonds were, of course, invisible, and the flagellation was also *invisibiliter,* but everything that was going on "could be understood through visible and outward movements, which moved her body a whole half-hour: except for her hands and feet, which remained immobile as though bound with rope to a column." The body moved, therefore, according to a precise code; its language is understood without the slightest difficulty and in such a way that the viewers could decipher perfectly what was being done and said by invisible presences: the Devil, the executioners at the Passion, Christ himself. When "Jesus Christ appeared to her," a dialogue took place: Jesus "comforted her and exhorted her to bear the suffering, and offered her his most holy passion." This, too, was deduced from her movements: "as one could grasp through the devout gestures and saintly words of this sister." When Jesus offered her his crown of thorns, the witnesses understood this because Sister Stefana made the gesture of receiving it "with such pain, anguish and torment that neither by quill nor by human words could these sufferings, sweatings and movements of her body be fathomed." Her dialogue with Christ persisted right to the Crucifixion: the holy woman's body expressed exactly the various stages and writhings of the body nailed and then unnailed. Even the detaching of the members from the cross was shown in a series of gestures that lent themselves to the same form of reading. Then came the last apparition of Christ and the saint's dialogue with him, with thanks and calls for graces: for the clergy, for her order, for the other orders, and for the whole Church, at which point she prayed "for the state of Italy" and right afterward for the state (that is, the condition and well-being) of the city in which she lived, for her protectors and benefactors. Finally, she returned to herself and reassumed her normal gestures.

It was a dialogue made of words and movement, portrayed "with great modesty, devotion and joy." The grammar of her gestures was perfectly legible to her spectators. In those years and in those circles, it is true that people were very familiar with the meanings of gestures and images. We know, for instance, of an edifying game described in a letter from a friar of that area which consisted of deciphering the meaning of a "painted paper" with a series of figures representing a "morality" that had to be guessed at.[18] Besides, the scene experienced and played out by Sister Stefana was that of the stigmata, the "matrix of all mystical gestures."[19]

It is on this central mystical experience linked to Saint Francis that the "live saints" graft a display of dominance by which they put themselves forward as mediators between those they protect—their intimate circle, princely families, native cities, Italy—and the power of God.[20] From this foundation springs the unmistakable tone of their spiritual correspondence, and here, too, lies its explanation. These women have a power, and they know it. Their letters use a tone of instruction and are replete with threatening words addressed to the powerful. This is because they are in daily dialogue with heaven, because through heaven they have foresight, they can advise and protect. These dialogues of theirs are public acts. People attend their visions; the content is broadcast; they acquire fame for their exceptional powers. When Sister Stefana Quinzani writes to the mighty Mantuan marquis, Gianfrancesco Gonzaga, she allows herself to take a commanding tone; her authority is superhuman, her tone like that of Catherine of Siena.

This example should suffice to show that in the real social relations of the period, the model of spiritual maternity had deep roots and its fruit multiplied. The letters written by the divine mothers in their nunneries offered messages, comfort, advice, and even direct orders on concrete matters. If one wondered whether to endow or marry off children and grandchildren, whether or not to buy offices at the Curia, live in one city rather than another, or even if one was simply suffering from a momentary discouragement or depression, one wrote to the spiritual mother and obtained what one needed. The correspondence between Saint Gaetano da Thiene and Stefana Quinzani is replete with the minute, daily problems of a man full of doubt, a worried man who asks himself what he should do in a situation fraught with personal and collective drama, such as Italians lived through in the early 1500s.

Monasteries traditionally had a protective function for their communities and for individuals. They were places of prayer, dedicated to a constant rapport with God based on a division of labor that was both ancient and deeply rooted. They allowed and fostered networks of relationships between individual religious of exceptional spirituality and the faithful with greater spiritual needs and greater social importance. The correspondences of the princely families of Italy retain many traces of this sort of relationship: the convents were endowed and protected by the prince's family, and were thus the natural recipients of requests for prayers and advice for individual family members or the whole family.

Friars, too, took part in this exchange. Still, anyone reading such correspondences and comparing the letters written by friars to those written by nuns will immediately notice differences of tone and content. A good example is the series of letters in 1496 between the Dominican Thomas of Brescia and Countess Lucrezia of the powerful Gambara family. It is essentially a social conversation between a teacher and his pupil, full of hints about style and suggestions for reading. By contrast, the spiritual mothers addressed themselves to other matters. Their authority derived from direct contact with God, evidenced, as Sister Stefana's example shows, by numerous notarial documents that duly register stigmata, ecstasies, and revelations.

This form did not suddenly disappear; it was slowly transformed. Holy women continued to have visions and to enjoy the gift of prophecy. Owing to their powers, the curiosity and devotion of many, and sometimes fear, still attended them. Philip II of Spain himself, touched by the dreams and predictions of Milanese and Madrid visionaries, paid them considerable heed. But the attitude of the ecclesiastical hierarchy rapidly changed, the direction indicated by Cardinal Federico Borromeo in a treatise significantly entitled *De Vera et occulta sanctitate*. Borromeo was greatly interested in the phenomenona of female saintliness and corresponded with a number of holy women, but his treatise invited them, if they wished to be seen as "true" saints, to desist from public displays of sanctity and become instead secret saints.[21]

Where Besozzi had suffered from deceit and delusion, Borromeo, with a curiosity and passion fit for an entomologist, made a close study of the behavior of mystics, devout women, and visionaries now freed from popular curiosity. The phenomena the cardinal discussed belonged to raptures, visions, and revelations; the visionaries' behavior was described, along with the strange and unheard-of chants they listened to in their convents, which supposedly reproduced the music of heaven. But Borromeo's religion was one of silence. Saintly women should remain enclosed in their convents and their visions should be supervised with care by designated ecclesiastical authorities, he thought. The attention now paid to such phenomena differed greatly from that given by Stefana Quinzani's devotees in Crema. The change did not merely reflect Borromeo's views. Many people felt the same loss of meaning in the gestures of the visions and in the crisis provoked in a woman's heart by the divine presence. The more common scene became that of a woman alone melting with a love whose object the spectator could no longer understand. It was a tormenting and upsetting thing to see; it touched women of all kinds; and judges now had to distinguish the saint from the possessed or the witch.

Their lives, their letters and visions, the entirety of these holy women's literature, all express the sentiment of love in varied ways. The Man-God to whom they address themselves is the absent Beloved to whom they direct a dialogue that is really a love monologue. It was this latter aspect that worried the ecclesiastical authorities. So many women panting for a mystical union with a God of love caused uncertainty, embarrassment, and suspicion. The love of the mystics was like the reverse face of the eroticism of magic rituals and witchcraft. In both, love was always absent. Whether procured or imagined in Sabbath rites, it was, despite its face-to-face descriptions, described as a love that was disappointing—when it wasn't frankly admitted that the magic rites did not work. For mystics, however, their visions enabled them to enjoy it as something present and abundant, and they seemed much happier. Notwithstanding this supposed presence, the observer's eye perforce registered the disquieting behavior and words of lonely women absorbed in a love that could not be seen by others.

It must also be said that out of the convents streamed letters which spoke of secret loves, tempestuous events, and the frustrated feelings of women who felt abandoned and disabused. The ecclesiastics who were to judge the authenticity of mystical visions also had the task of repressing a much vaster and more violent explosion of affection. Theirs was a delicate undertaking, because they were also personally involved in the torrent of feeling emerging from convents; it affected them not only as judges (of the authenticity of saintliness) but as men. Bound to the defense of its honor and prerogatives, the hierarchy tried to stem this religion of the heart, whose power threatened the male bulwark of its organization. The creation of the inquisitorial offense of "soliciting for lewd purposes" shows with how great a determination the clergy sought to reestablish its distance from the feminine world, to which the Church offered openings and occasions for compensation that did not exist within the family or secular society. The ecclesiastical tribunals' archives over-flowed with testimony about love set alight in convents by preachers, confessors, and spiritual directors. The image of a transfixed heart marked and conjoined the devotions of the mystics and the earthly loves of the nuns. Evidence is there in the most successful visions and devotions and is laid out in love letters, as in those a Florentine sister wrote to a friar, begging for his return (because even in the convents, those residual laboratories of society, women expect the man to return).[22]

Such emotions are sufficient to explain why the authorities reacted with coldness and diffidence, with discord, rejection, and condemnation, and also why they chose to conceal rather than publicize. But it is insufficient to explain why visionary sanctity became meaningless, or why such a crisis arose, necessitating the disappearance of that grammar of gestures which, like some sacred dance, regulated the movements of the mystics. In the eyes of the authorities, it was the disorderly involvement of these possessed women that was progressively consuming all the space available for the collective consumption of the sacred.

This was neither a rapid nor a simple process. For many years society's experience of sanctity continued to refer to the same phenomena of the now suspect and banned world of visionaries and mystics, and holy women continued to be asked to decipher the will of God. In short, these women continued to be the most direct way to communicate with heaven. Their visions were spied on and written down, they were debated in the light of the methods and criteria for "discerning spirits." But the dominant criteria laid down by the official culture were now of a different kind.

To understand the extent of the change, one might consider a great masterwork of Baroque sculpture, Bernini's *Saint Teresa*. Bernini's eye saw only the visible. He saw not the ecstasy of a saint but the amorous swoon of a woman (a nun). Banished the visible marks of sanctity, gone the images that she claimed to see but the artist did not reproduce, all that remained to be seen was what confessors, spiritual directors, exorcists, and inquisitors saw: the spectacle of a woman in amorous rapture, represented in the ancient symbol of the arrow of Eros.

Women's Lives, Men's Writing

As we have seen, the century of the printing press opened in Italy with the edition of Saint Catherine's letters. Female imitators—and they were not lacking—worried less about meeting the norms of a literary genre than about reliving a particular experience of life. Catherine's imprint in this area is the deepest. Her letters, addressed to the most powerful authorities in the Christian world by a woman whose saintliness allowed her to employ an imperial tone, left behind a wake of female followers and imitators.

It was to her model that saintly women, like Caterina de' Ricci, referred in their work as letter writers and advisers to the mighty. Men were fascinated by them; they showed their devotion in a thousand ways; and some (the best known of whom was Lancellotto Politi, better known as Caterino) wanted to adopt their names. Caterina brought women's careers to their maximum, and she offered herself for emulation with all the prestige of a religious cult. As Silvano Razzi's book sought to show, women could be illustrious for their sanctity, and in that way aspire to become famous and be imitated.[23]

Lives counted for far more than letters as far as women were concerned. The former were their proving grounds, and in this they had a different point of departure from men. Women might also write, but it was not generally recommended. The career of sainthood and that of worldly fame were two very different paths, though perhaps not as divergent as the paths the myth of Hercules set for men. If a woman with a reputation for saintliness left written records, these would be at most texts dictated to others, part of a living relationship in teaching, a transmitting of experience; they were not writings conceived for publication.

Men took over the epistolary genre. The new literary tradition was inaugurated not by the saint of Siena but by Pietro Aretino, her neighbor, who was certainly not known for saintliness. But if the father of the genre had something less than a sterling reputation, this did not prevent letters written for publication from becoming a vehicle for religious ideas or feelings—on the contrary.

Still, the epistolary genre in the first half of the sixteenth century began with one dominating characteristic, which was not spiritual. The first century of printing was characterized by a considerable production of letters in the vernacular: the letters of "illustrious men," of "great men of clear genius," of "noble minds"; "letters from princes," business letters, and "love letters," nearly all of them from men, and mainly with the purpose of training their readers to write their own letters, whether for business purposes or out of friendship. The outcome, or one of the outcomes, was the rise of the "secretary," first for political and public affairs and then, as men of letters found it increasingly difficult to deal with matters of state, for private and amorous purposes. It was, however, their ingenious nature, their inventiveness, that brought a public to such letters; and inventiveness, with few exceptions, remained a masculine domain. Men could play both roles; they could be themselves and they could play the woman's role. A man (Ortensio Lando), under various women's names, published epistolary collections "by many distinguished women," in which he sought to demonstrate that "women were in no way inferior to men in either eloquence or doctrine."[24]

In the competition that subsequently arose in this area, men fought with different arguments and within a far greater field of social opportunity. That is, to become illustrious, men could invest in different sorts of lives and letters. A man's life was wide open to fortune, and it seemed to Machiavelli a "thing to wonder at, that all, or the greater part, of those who have achieved great things in this world . . . began their lives in a low or obscure fashion, or from fortune of an unusual kind."[25] Men did not renounce the field of biography as appropriate to the description of heroic sanctity or exceptional experiences. On the contrary, to recount their own lives became a normal way in which to feed curiosity and devotion. The biographies of holy men, told out of their own mouths, are frequent in the writings of the great orders (from the *Pilgrim's Tale* dictated by Ignatius of Loyola to the work of Gonçalves da Camara and onward). If many of these biographies, written with devotional purposes in mind, circulated only in manuscript form or in a limited group, there was no lack of weighty candidates whose careers were fostered on the printed page by men.

One need only reflect on the fact that the sixteenth-century version of *The Golden Legend* was written by Giorgio Vasari. This is no extravagant claim. Both Vasari and his readers understood that biographies were not just about the works of the mind but about celebrating a particular kind of man. The golden age that began with Giotto ended, in Vasari's eyes, with Michelangelo, not just a perfect artist but, as the implicit hagiography of Vasari's panegyric demonstrates, a perfect man. It was a question of relating the life of a man so exceptional in his work and his way of life as to impose an infraction of the rules of the literary genre. His life is described "in his lifetime," thus not so differently from the biographies of the "living saints."[26] The word of Properzia de' Rossi, a "Bolognese sculptress," with her sprightly and hasty praise of the excellence of women, was evidently insufficient to conceal from Vasari and his public the unequal condition of women. Canonized sanctity was clearly another matter: but even in that area the masters of the spiritual life showed that they had meditated on the example of Michelangelo and had taken seriously the model offered by Vasari. The proof lies in the first "spiritual letters" to go to press, those written by the Sienese pilgrim-mystic Bonsignore Cacciaguerra.

What use are spiritual letters? According to Bonsignore Cacciaguerra, their purpose was to "ripen and fructify in the Lord." The fruit and the utility of these "little works" was so vital that the Devil sought to prevent their being published.[27] The fruit derived from proposing the model of a Christian life; the spiritual existed because the model existed; and his letters transferred that model into text. Life entered the page. But even as an appeal to life was made, art remained present. Cacciaguerra, for instance, used arguments drawn from debates about the arts to show the link between the "spiritual" and the "worldly." The spiritual, the true Christian, is superior to the worldly as the sculptor is superior to the painter; one becomes a true Christian "through taking away the excess," while the worldly, like the painter, think only of adding to what they already possess.[28]

Cacciaguerra was plainly aware of the debate in the arts and sided with Michelangelo. The subject is of interest for two reasons: first, because these male writers chose to speak in the language of the cultivated elite; and second, because the Michelangelo model adopted by Cacciaguerra was taken almost textually from the *vita* by Vasari, an ideal model of artist and man that culminated in Michelangelo. The interweaving of biographies and model lives transmitted by letter might be said to have reached the highest point of which the Italian culture of the time was capable. At that level, writers felt they were qualified to teach something even in the specific area of Christian sanctity. A book served to transmit an image of saintliness and Christian perfection as a form of intellectual mastery, a secret mental exercise, and one relatively easy to accomplish, without any need of spectacular penances and physical acrobatics.

The dialogue between Juan de Valdés and Julia Gonzaga, offered to readers as a Christian "alphabet," proposed "a royal, lordly path," one that would permit even the court elite to approach sanctity. Something of the sort had indeed been proposed in the opuscule of Elena Duglioli.[29] The same concept is present in many spiritual breviaries printed in the sixteenth century: they offer easy access to Christian perfection. The significance of this "easier" path is only evident if one takes into account the ways in which sanctity was still pursued in many religious communities, lay confraternities, and hermitages. The old, ascetic model of the eremitic life still had a lasting resonance. In 1572 John of the Cross was still able to observe religious who exhibited themselves publicly, hanging by their feet and eating food from the ground below them.[30] Anyone reading the depositions of the first Barnabite congregations will find evidenced not too dissimilar ways of seeking perfection.

Literature underpins the history of sainthood and its bifurcation into male and female. The written page, which offered distance and reflection, was also a part of the history of how female prophetic and visionary sanctity was faced and domesticated. The Catholic Church continued to guarantee women a place of their own, as compensation for, or alternative to, marriage. In this open space, there was a double reason for the written letter and the autobiography as a means of communication: first, they kept the clergy at a distance from the perils of close contact with women; and second, they facilitated judgments of sanctity, which in this period became similar to those of the Inquisition. For both these reasons there was often a need to teach women to write, and the ecclesiastical archives are filled with letters, diaries, tales, and thoughts penned in shaky, uncertain feminine hands. Spiritual directors provided the paper, collected it, marked whatever was notable, and sometimes remarked on the extraordinary speed with which women learned to write.[31]

How many such documents there are in the ecclesiastical archives is difficult to say. There are enough to show that the cooling-off and interiorization of sanctity as an exceptional experience passed through the medium of writing. To be sure, the autobiographies of the holy women of Catholicism are not private or secret documents written for introspective purposes.[32] They were written under ecclesiastical control and form a genre whose high point is the *Libro de la vida* ("The Book of Life"), written by Teresa of Avila, but for the most part they remain buried in the archives. What emerged in this period was a form of authorized and authoritative writing by men, who published lives after lives of female candidates for sainthood. To do so they had to have recourse to the autobiographical materials deposited by women. But that is a history that is still mostly unwritten.

"Foreign Islands"

Letters bring what is far away close; one of their intrinsic qualities is that they come from a distant country. What printed letters most obviously offer is exoticism, and the more a letter tells about the unusual, the distant, the marvelous, the more likely it is to attract the reader. From how far away could letters be sent? One need only consider the range of books published in the 1500s to note that prior to the Manutius edition of Saint Catherine's letters, others had captured a vast readership: Christopher Columbus's account of the "new found islands," or Amerigo Vespucci's on the "New World."

Long before modern journeys into the remote regions of the self victoriously entered into competition with tales from exotic voyages, autobiographical writing was both attracted to and challenged by descriptions of new places and people. It was not by accident that Montaigne, to draw his reader's attention to the sincerity with which he intended to describe himself and to the novelty of that landscape the reader would discover, stated that his aim was to depict himself "naked and whole," as though he found himself among "those peoples of whom it is said that they still live in the sweet liberty of the first laws of nature."[33] Both genres were exploration journeys: the autobiographical borrowed from the geographic its connotations of the new and the guarantee implicit in an "eye-witness report." The mutual attraction between the world of the spirit and that beyond the ocean was based on such profound links that the geographic model almost inevitably emerged among those who wrote about the extraterrestrial world discovered by female saints and visionaries. The translator of Saint Teresa's letters offers a good example, pointing up the parallel between Isabel of Castille and the saint: "The one . . . made possible Columbus's discovery and conquest of the New; the other dove [*colomba*], even as he set foot there, flew to conquer the other."[34] It was not just rhetorical necessity that made for such inflation and such heroic examples.

It is not difficult to see why there should be a deep solidarity between the accounts of newly discovered worlds across the ocean and the accounts of adventures of the spirit. More than any terra incognita, the world of the dead—that "unexplored country from which no traveler ever returned"—fueled curiosity, a sense of distance, a need for news. Spiritual writing had precisely that as one of its purposes. To reveal the secrets of the spirit for an edifying purpose meant offering a mix of moral admonitions, on the one hand, and miracles, prophecies, and other marvels on the other. The unity of these disparate materials lay in the function assigned to "spiritual" people, and it should not be forgotten that the term (defined by a monk who understood such matters, Serafino da Fermo) superseded the old "spirited," or "inspirited."

"Spiritual" persons could and did act as mediators to the world of the divine; they listened to the voices of angels and the dead; and from God (or the Madonna) they received revelations on matters of great collective or individual importance. In the surrounding world the presence of the invisible was taken for granted; the problem was only how to decipher what it had to say. For this purpose exceptional people, endowed with their own merit or provided by an inscrutable providence with the antennae required to detect what escaped others, were needed as mediators. Precisely because of their knowledge and exceptional capacities, it was their duty to warn others of what God desired from them: Some "go to someone or other to ask something quite unnecessary, as, for instance, how fare their dead, whether they are in purgatory or in hell or paradise, or want to know what's become of their children or their friends . . . others whether there's to be war or peace, famine or flood."[35] These services were available but not peacefully accepted, for as Battista da Crema (quoted above) pointed out, the ordinary Church hierarchy felt itself trapped by forms of mediation with the dead that rested not on regular authority but on personal charismatic gifts. Hence there arose scandal and conflict, the horrified reactions of spiritual directors who felt their function was to fight these "wonders" and magic powers and replace them with a form of sanctity or spirituality based on moral values imparted by a constant and painstaking education.

Letters and other spiritual writings were consciously employed in this area of training for sanctity. Precepts, warnings, and true and proper "spiritual exercises" (in the happy formulation of Ignatius of Loyola) were addressed specifically to this major battleground in the struggle against the miraculous and for moral perfection. But they were insufficient and could not arouse the same curiosity as travel tales. The issue was resolved by "inventing" something that would be in direct competition with the exoticism of the latter. Thus it was that Jesuit headquarters produced letters from the Indies that assembled the ingredients necessary to create new heroes, new masters of the spirit. The letters came from as far away as those of Columbus and Vespucci, but they reported on extraordinary events in the life of the spirit. Conversions, visions, and miracles freely blended with descriptions of unknown and exotic animals, landscapes, and peoples. Enthusiastic readers grasped the point immediately, referring to the missionaries who wrote these letters as angels sent miraculously by God.

The whole genre was to be precisely defined by the title of the celebrated eighteenth-century collection *Lettres édifiantes et curieuses,* but it was already in place before the volumes printed by the Jesuits began to appear. Consider that curious proto-Jesuit visionary Guillaume Postel, with his eloquently titled work *Le prime nuove del altro mondo, cioè l'admirabile historia intitulata la Vergine venetiana* (The first news from the other world, that is, the admirable story called "The Venetian Virgin").[36] This was a perfect example: a female visionary, a prophet writing the message down, the resounding announcement of "the latest news from the other world." In fact, the opportunity to cross the other world with the New World had already attracted the man who discovered it: in his *Book of Prophesies,* he had superimposed the mysterious isles mentioned in the Bible on the islands in the Ocean Sea.

The deep link between exploration of the celestial world by spiritual women and that of the non-European world was often confirmed in the published literature. But I would like to limit myself to one aspect derived from archival documents I stumbled across by chance during this research, for it came to confirm the correctness of my original hypothesis. The document in question relates the vision of a "living saint" in eighteenth century Tuscany, Barbera Fivoli. Born in Leghorn in 1714 of a Florentine father, this lady was handed over to the spiritual direction of a confessor who daily gave her paper on which to set down her visions and thoughts. In her diary for 1762, two years before her death in Pisa, Fivoli noted the following vision:

A great, clear light penetrated me, and I came to understand why the marvelous novelties and strangeness of tidings—far from any ordinary understanding—which the soul sees in God, are called foreign islands.

Nor do I marvel that He is foreign to men who have never seen Him, because He remains strange even to angels and saints who have seen Him, because they can't finish seeing in Him—nor ever will be able to, until this world comes to an end on the Day of Judgment—these many novelties of His, as are his acts of mercy and justice, to the marvel of all, so that all angels and all men can call them "foreign islands."[37]

Translated from the Italian by Keith Botsford

CHAPTER 7

The Convent Muses: The Secular Writing of Italian Nuns, 1450–1650

ELISSA B. WEAVER

In the final pages of the diary of Fiammetta Frescobaldi, a Dominican nun of the convent of San Jacopo di Ripoli in Florence, there are several loose, folded sheets of miscellaneous texts, all written in the nun's own hand. One of the texts is a Spanish phrase book for convent use. It begins with a long list of Spanish words and phrases and their Italian translations, which the compiler has labeled "unordered" but which begins "Dios, hombre, rey, muger, hijo, hija," and then continues with a mix of words and phrases that are indeed without order—nouns, adjectives, verbs, and idiomatic expressions. The selection has been excerpted from a manual that was not originally intended for convent use, as is clear from some of the examples with secular references little suited to a convent setting, such as, "Soy por no entrar mas en su casa," and "Vieron unos hombres y tomoron por la mano unas mugeres y los unos y los otros se fueron a passear," glossed respectively as "I would never want to enter your house again" and "Some gentlemen came and took some ladies by the hand and they all went for a walk."[1]

Fiammetta Frescobaldi had many interests and, since she was an invalid who could not perform normal convent tasks, had the time to collect and translate texts for her own edification and that of her convent sisters. Besides the phrase book and devotional works, she took up history; she wrote an abridged version of Francesco Guicciardini's *History of Italy,* which has been lost, and, especially interested in natural history, she filled many volumes with descriptions of the entire known world.[2] Between 1561 and 1580 she wrote the *Sphere of the Universe (Sfera dell'universo),* a cosmography in multiple volumes, which begins with a description of the heavens and from there descends to continents, countries, cities, castles, villages, mountains, islands, and the variety and customs of their inhabitants. She traveled throughout the world with her imagination, from the Western to the Eastern Indies, and she brought her discoveries home to her Florentine convent.

Fiammetta Frescobaldi also wrote a *Chronicle of the Holy Order of Saint Dominic* (*Cronaca del sacro ordine di san Domenico,* 1576) and the above-mentioned *Diary (Diario),* which covers the years 1576 through 1586, the year of her death. In short, she expressed herself in various literary and historical genres that we generally consider "secular," ones whose aim is not the spiritual enlightenment but rather the entertainment of her convent sisters, the furthering of their knowledge of the world outside the convent, and the preservation in historical memory of their house, their religious order, and their times. She wrote the *Marvelous and Calamitous Things in This World (Cose prodigiose e calamitose del mondo),* as she explains, for "the consolation of those who don't have many books."[3] and the *Field of Flowers (Prato fiorito)* in order that the present and future nuns of her convent "might occasionally have the pleasure of reading it together" and in the hope that through it she could be of benefit to her "mothers and sisters in Christ." She writes that they "are so busy that they have no time to look for such things in so many books that are not so easily understood by everyone, since they are written in Latin; so out of love for them I have taken various authors and translated them, if not as I should have, at least as I knew how, in order to fulfill in some way my obligation to them."[4]

Fiammetta Frescobaldi was for the most part self-taught, as were convent writers generally in her time. In female religious houses the education of young women was entrusted to the older nuns and limited to teaching them to read the breviary and other devotional books, usually in the vernacular, and to training them to do the so-called women's work of spinning, sewing, embroidering, and the like. Frescobaldi's case was to a certain extent exceptional, since she had access to a wide range of information (her relatives and friends brought her books), and she had knowledge of languages that was rare for a nun at the time. The convent recorder who wrote her brief biography in San Jacopo's obituary book says she was a woman of "great intelligence and excellent memory,"[5] who had translated texts for the use of the other nuns "without ever having had a teacher."[6] But other nuns too, many others in this period, with only a convent education, continued their studies on their own and wrote out of duty, for the amusement and enlightenment of their convent sisters, and to leave a record of their lives for their successors.

For earlier periods, that is, before the sixteenth century, we can speak of women's writing in Italy but only in the limited sense of the writing of individual, exceptional women. There are cases of women whose humanistic education enabled them to write not only in Italian but also in Latin, and some of them in Greek. There were erudite religious women who wrote chronicles, devotional literature, and letters; and some secular, merchant-class women participated in the composition of family and business account books and carried on personal correspondence. These are, however, isolated examples, and we cannot for that period yet speak of a tradition in which entire classes of women participated.

The processes that would lead to a high degree of literacy for increasing numbers of women, and that would make it possible for more and more women to engage in some form of literary activity, began to take effect in Italian cities perhaps as early as the fourteenth century; they became more clearly defined in the fifteenth century with the establishment of a few public schools for girls and with the increase in the practice of sending daughters of the upper and the upwardly mobile classes for their education to the female convents, the numbers and populations of which began to grow dramatically from the end of the fifteenth century on.[7] Humanist educators began to defend the utility and appropriateness of education for women, ideas that were already in the air. Men like Leonardo Bruni recommended *studia humanitatis* also for women, and educators like Vittorino da Feltre accepted students of both sexes; certain families hired preceptors to teach their male and female children in their homes. Contributing to these changes—if not serving as the principal catalyst—was the old practice of entrusting mothers with the earliest education of their children. This custom led over time to the gradual extension of female literacy, yet the ability of women to read and write was not enough to create a class of female writers. Women had to have a reason to write, and they needed time and the necessary materials to do so.

Women humanists, as we know, wrote as long as they were encouraged in their endeavors by their families or their teachers; but they belonged to no other milieu that gave them support in their intellectual activities, and marriage tended to put an end to their brief adventures in the literary realm. It was the spread of the printing industry in the sixteenth century that created a public for women's writing, encouraging women to compose and publish lyric poetry and to experiment in other literary genres. Following upon the success of Vittoria Colonna's *Rime* (1538), many other women published books of verse. An extraordinary example was that of Laura Terracina, who published eight volumes of lyric poetry, several in more than one edition. Women writers were proclaimed new Corinnas, new Sapphos, yet another rediscovery of the Renaissance. But this favorable climate did not last long, and in the second half of the century books written by women began to lose their popularity and soon ceased almost entirely to appear in print.[8] Women did not, however, cease to write just because the market for their work was no longer favorable and they no longer had an interested public of readers. Indeed, it is precisely in this period that the writing of convent women can be seen continually to increase. The results of the progressive extension of education to women were felt especially in the convents, where the choir nuns, women of the higher social ranks, received instruction, limited though it was, and where they had the time, means, and motivation to write.[9]

Women's writing flourished in a context that not only made it possible but that authorized and motivated it. Nuns were encouraged by their communities to keep record books and to write works that were historical, spiritual, and even entertaining. If the writing of secular women poets enjoyed for a short time the support of court and city society and of the book market, that of women religious was supported by their convents for reasons of lasting importance that were not subject to changes in literary taste. Toward the end of the sixteenth century the fashion of Petrarchist verse subsided, and the Church and post-Tridentine society silenced the marginal groups who had for various decades enjoyed editorial successes writing such poetry. Yet it was in large part the same Tridentine prelates and those who carried out their reforms who promoted the practice of writing in female convents, precisely in those years that for so many scholars signal the end of the Renaissance phenomenon of literary women.

Convent Record Books

In many women's religious houses before Trent, and in all of them afterward, in conformity with the new regime set in motion by the decrees of the council and their interpreters, the nuns were required to keep their own books: the account books of income and expenditures, the records of professions and deaths of the nuns, and the succession of prioresses. To do so, convent women had to know how to write.[10] These books, which might appear superficially to be uninteresting, are eloquent documents of the rapid and progressive acquisition of literacy on the part of the nuns; and the obligation to keep such books seems to have contributed not a little to that process. Beginning in the late fifteenth century, throughout the sixteenth, and amply in the seventeenth, the convent books show that literacy was no longer exceptional and that a majority of choir nuns were fully capable of exercising the duties of the office of convent recorder.

At the simplest and most spontaneous level, as they filled in the registers, convent bookkeepers elaborated their entries, not satisfied with saying only the essential, but adding brief accounts of events they felt it important to "record" (which means, literally, "remember" in Italian). They not only entered a bill to pay or a new postulant accepted into the community, but also recorded events that had strongly impressed them, such as episodes of plague, of war, or some other calamity.[11] For example, in a book of *Ricordi* (1522–

1564) of the convent of the Murate (literally, "walled women," the Benedictine nuns of Santissima Annunziata in Florence) we find interspersed, with notations of expenses, accounts of the disputes between the friars of San Marco and Cosimo de' Medici and mention of a flood of the Arno River that had threatened the convent.[12] In the ledgers kept by the Franciscan sisters of San Girolamo of the same city, we find more or less extensive accounts of the plague of 1630, of a serious fire in the convent, and of a difference of opinion between the nuns and the grand duke.[13]

Convent record books took on some of the characteristics of the chronicle or diary, whereas the necrologies, that is, the registers that gave essential information about the deceased nuns—acceptance into the monastery, veiling, profession, and death—became collections of brief biographies, more or less informative and expressive depending upon the inspiration or the rhetorical ability of the convent scribe. The necrology of San Jacopo di Ripoli offers the reader brief narratives that are at times amusing, at times moving. The ability and the desire to narrate comes through sometimes in the choice of an allusion, or in the expressiveness of a turn of the phrase, as in the account of the death of Sister Michelangela Cioni on February 19, 1557:

> Sister Michelangela Cioni died on the 19th of said month. She received all the sacraments. This nun was very charitable. She died with great desire for Jesus. She said she saw her cute little curly-headed angel. She was 72 and worked harder than the young women. So great was her charity she took care of a madwoman. She combed and bathed her and received nothing but insults in return. She now reaps what she sowed.[14]

History Books

Another literary genre frequently associated with the convents is the chronicle or diary, also called annals, *memoriale, ricordanza,* and the like, without the difference in terms indicating any real difference in form or subject matter. It is not easy to distinguish this genre from that of some of the *Ricordi* that are replete with narrative interpolations. However, if they are similar in form, the *Ricordi* and the chronicles are quite different in their aims, since the former have as their primary purpose to document administrative expenses and actions, while the latter are designed to transmit to posterity the collective memory of the community, to affirm its rights, and to publicize its prestige.[15]

I would like once more to use the writing of Fiammetta Frescobaldi as illustration. Frescobaldi's *Chronicle* and *Diary* are two separate volumes but they are substantially a single work in two rather different parts. The first part, the *Chronicle,* narrates the history of the Dominican order, adding to the

information it gives about the men of the order other information of a historical, geographic, social, and political nature. Sometimes Frescobaldi's writing
reflects the influence of the great Florentine historian Francesco Guicciardini;
at other times, it is closer to the chroniclers, as, for example, when she
indulges in descriptions of natural phenomena.

In the *Diary* she continues to follow events of the world outside the convent, but, perhaps because she was writing it during the last ten years of her
life, she begins to look more and more to life inside her convent. She lists the
professions and the deaths of her convent sisters, the elections of new prioresses, and the progressive implementation of the Tridentine reforms (new
walls, expulsion of the confessors from the convents, and so on). Especially in
her last years she gives a careful account of the sermons preached to the nuns,
detailing their content and evaluating the preacher's competence. In this final
phase of her work and of her life Frescobaldi becomes more introspective in
her observations. She records cases of personal tragedy that have moved her,
like the deaths of members of the grand duke's family or the story of the wife
of Giovanni Strozzi, who was forced to withdraw to a convent because "she
gave no sign of producing children."[16] Here as elsewhere Frescobaldi shows
herself to be quite an effective writer. She says of the rejected wife that
"changing her clothes and life, she changed her name";[17] and she ends the
account with a meteorological observation that serves to symbolize the experience of the woman who after great sentimental tribulations finds peace in a
monastic retreat from life:

> that same day there was bad weather; lightning struck twice, without,
> however, doing any damage that we know of. The rain was light but it
> provided some relief from the great heat of this summer.[18]

The Modenese nun Lucia Pioppi has much in common with her Florentine
counterpart. Her *Diary* (*Diario*, 1541–1612), like Frescobaldi's, is primarily
concerned with events in the world beyond the convent, and she too was
sensitive to the personal tragedies of other women. In 1594 the Modenese
nun wrote in her breviary,

> On the 28th of May, a Saturday, at the first hour of the night, they took
> sister Serena Pazzana out of San Paulo; she had taken the veil there
> against her will in January of 1594. She was brought to her father's
> house and imprisoned in a room up high, all by herself. God help the
> poor thing.[19]

The monastic chronicles that we have for this rather extensive period are
formally quite heterogeneous. Some, like those of Pioppi and Frescobaldi,
have a single author, while others are collective works; and they vary widely

also in the breadth of their historical purview. In general they tell the story of a community from the time of its founding, although some versions place the moment of foundation in a larger history, while others narrate only the events of a specific moment in their history. The fifteenth-century Venetian *Chronicle of Corpus Domini*, written by the Dominican Bartolomea Riccoboni, deals with a brief period from the end of the fourteenth century through 1418. It begins with the divinely ordained founding of the community, made known to the founders through dreams and miraculous signs, and it ends with a long and detailed history of the schism in the Western Church, a saga in which the convent chronicler takes the side of her fellow Venetian, Angelo Correr, Pope Gregory XII.[20] The *Chronicle of the Convent of the "Vergini" in Venice (Cronica del monastero delle Vergini di Venetia)*, written at the beginning of the sixteenth century by several anonymous nuns, situates the founding of their famous convent in a universal history beginning with the Creation, and it narrates the story of their community up to the difficult time of their reform in 1519.[21] Another chronicle, an enormous one, written in many hands and carried on for centuries by a succession of convent chroniclers, the *Memoriale of Monteluce*, of the Clarissas of the convent of Monteluce near Perugia, covers four centuries of the internal history of the community, from 1448 to 1838. This book begins, not at the time of the founding of the house, but at that of its reform, when the convent passed from the governance of the Conventual Franciscans to that of the Observants.[22]

The convent chroniclers seem all, however, to have worked in a similar way: they declare that they have done careful research, consulting their convent's archival documents and interviewing the oldest nuns. At the end of the sixteenth century the chronicles reflect the influence of the most famous examples of Renaissance historiography, and they clearly try to follow in that tradition. Fiammetta Frescobaldi uses a variety of sources that allow her to situate the history of her house and of the Dominican order in Florence in the context of European and even world history (she discusses the colonization of the New World and especially the role played there by the religious orders). Both Frescobaldi and Giustina Niccolini, the author of the *Chronicles of the Most Venerable Convent of Santa Maria Annunziata of the "Murate" in Florence (Cronache del v[enerabilissimo] monastero di Santa Maria Annuntiata de le Murate di Fiorenza*, 1598), discuss their aims and methodologies in the dedication and preface to their works; Niccolini prides herself on how carefully she has checked all her data.[23]

Occasionally the personality of the chronicler will imprint itself strongly on the narrated events, as in the case of the *Book of the History of the Convent of San Cosimato*, written by Orsola Formicini.[24] Formicini becomes a character in her own chronicle: in the early history of the convent she is there as a researcher reading and rereading the early documents in order to bring back to light a lost history; and she is still in her story when she reconstructs more recent events, interviewing the oldest convent women and recollecting what she herself has witnessed.[25] The sack of Rome, which took place before her birth, in her telling of the story, becomes connected to her life. It is given as the reason for her monachization:

> And . . . the war between signor Marcantonio Colonna and the Pope, that is, Paul IV Caraffa, began, and because of it Rome was turned upside down . . . And my father, to protect his own from the misery he saw befall the children of others at that time [the sack of Rome], decided to make me a nun.[26]

Formicini had no inhibitions about making herself the protagonist of her story.

It was common for chroniclers of cities and institutions to create foundation myths based on glorious founders, saints, and heroes. Convent chroniclers, too, chose to follow this practice. They often begin by telling of a distant event, a legendary one characterized by miracles, the details of which cannot be fully reconstructed, but which serves generally to define the community and to enhance its image. The anonymous Venetian chroniclers of Santa Maria Nova in Gerusalemme, known as the Vergini, begin their providential history *ab origine mundi*. Their name is taken from that of the ancient convent in the Holy Land, Santa Maria in Gerusalemme, which had recently been occupied by Saracens, and of which the Venetian nuns considered themselves the continuation. They also give their origins a political and civic meaning by dating them to the time of the peace treaty brokered by the Venetian doge between the pope and the emperor Frederick Barbarossa (a date and event disputed by historians).[27] The nobility of the nuns is reflected in that of their founders, one of whom they claim was Julia, the daughter of the emperor and the convent's first abbess, another, Sicambria, a descendent of Priam of Troy! They sketch the history of the privileges the convent enjoyed, and in the ceremony of the installation of each new abbess they celebrate their most important and unusual privilege, that of the symbolic marriage of the abbess with the doge of Venice. The chronicle of the Vergini breaks off in the year 1519, when the patriarch of Venice sends his vicar to reform the convent, initiating a difficult period of negotiations between the Venetian Church and the nuns. Up to that point the style of the chronicle is elegant, the language a mixture of Latin and literary Italian, with some Venetian dialect elements;[28] but the chronicle concludes with a polemical tirade launched by the last convent chronicler against the authorities, aimed especially at the patriarch's vicar (whom she calls, for example, a "traitor who rides on an ass with its tail in his hands," 61r), a diatribe of insults in a language that is heavily Venetian.

Leaving aside the individual characteristics imposed on the narrations by the personality of the writers and the different chronologies adopted, the material treated in those chronicles that turn their attention to the internal life of the convents is rather uniform, as was the life of the nuns. In an overall structure that gives in succession the names of the abbesses and prioresses, the progressive building and rebuilding of the houses, the episodes of plague, the flooding of local rivers, and the fight against reform in the fifteenth and especially sixteenth centuries, we find inserted the biographies of exceptional nuns, visits of convent authorities, lists of privileges, relics, prayers, rules, and miracles. The interpersonal relations among the convent women appear too in these texts, but sporadically and in rare moments of the author's personal reflections; convent scribes generally write as the official chronicler of their community and they, therefore, abstain from openly expressing their private opinions. There are, however, occasional outbursts of anger, words of compassion, expressions of class pride, and everywhere affirmations of faith, all of which offer the modern reader a glimpse, albeit from a great distance, of life in the convent and of the feelings and the spirituality of the nuns of the time.

The chronicles may tell little about everyday life in the convents, but they are eloquent documents of the culture and especially of the high level of literacy of convent women. Writing skills, both in the literal sense of forming letters on a page and in the general meaning of the term, that is, of the ability to carry on a discourse, was by this time characteristic of the majority of the choir nuns (not, however, of the servant nuns, who did not receive the same convent education). Some of the chronicles that have survived, for example, those we have discussed of the Murate in Florence and of the Vergini in Venice, demonstrate a remarkable level of artistic achievement, both in the hand that copied them and in their ornamented pages and illustrations. And the works of Fiammetta Frescobaldi, written in a clear and regular, if not elegant, hand, show the Florentine nun's familiarity with formats of the printed page, which she imitates even in her formation of letters and in her placement on the page of paratextual materials, the title, dedication, and colophon. So too certain pages of the chronicle of Orsola Formicini follow the model of a printed book, and the holy pictures that she colored and glued to the sheets reproduce the effect of engraved book illustrations.

Theater

Besides the chronicles, the other literary genre of a "secular" nature that flourished in Italian convents was drama. Throughout Italy (but also in Spain and probably in all of the Catholic world)[29] the nuns, beginning certainly by the end of the fifteenth century, but probably even much earlier, at Carnival time and on other festive occasions staged *sacre rappresentazioni* (miracle and mystery plays) and comedies in the cloister. Performances have been documented in the convent of San Gaggio near Florence during the Carnival of 1496, 1497, and 1498;[30] and from the 1530s on one finds continued and abundant notice of this activity everywhere.[31]

The nuns used plays that were in circulation and were available to them, they commissioned new ones, and they wrote plays themselves; and plays seem to have been exchanged among the convents.[32] The prologues to the plays address a public of women religious and claim for convent theater the double aim of "spiritual fun" *(spasso spirituale)* and "learning" *(documento)*.[33] Ecclesiastical authorities generally gave their approval but with certain explicit restrictions, and they reserved the right to review a text before its performance. Not all the authorities, however, were in favor of this activity, and even those who sometimes approved did not do so always; at times the nuns got into trouble for not having entirely followed the rules laid down for them. The problem especially regarded the audience. The nuns were not to admit laypersons to the performances, but secular women, relatives, and benefactors often came, and even men were known to have attended—usually it was a relative, an old man or a child, but it was not unheard of that uninvited spectators came out of curiosity or for some other unacceptable motive. In Prato, for example, the carpenters, who had constructed the stage for a convent performance, stayed to see the play.[34] The theatrical nuns incurred the wrath of the authorities also when they borrowed secular clothes to use as costumes, especially when these were men's clothes; such costumes were prohibited by authorities, who considered them dangerous intrusions into the convents of the secular world.

In the sixteenth century the repertoire of convent theater grew to include, alongside the *sacre rappresentazioni,* comedies especially, but tragedies as well,[35] developments that followed closely those in the secular tradition. The comedies generally had a double plot, one that was religious and serious, the other secular and comic, and they employed music often in the *intermedi* and sometimes in the plays themselves to accompany the action. In the seventeenth century the traditional forms continued, but other more complex forms developed, plays with three intertwined plots, often plots that made no pretense of being religious. The productions were more or less elaborate depending on the convent's means or the importance of the occasion; and the texts that have come down to us, almost all of them manuscripts, richly document, through stage directions and marginalia, the occasions of the performance, the set, music, costumes, and even names of the actresses.

It is possible that every convent had its own dramatist. They were often the novice mistresses who wrote plays for performance by their charges; the recitation was part of the young women's education, and it also served as entertainment for all of the women in the convent. A collection of farces that belonged to the Franciscan convent of Santa Chiara in Pistoia contains the following notation on its title page: "Comedies of the nuns of Santa Chiara, written for the novices by sister Annalena when she was novice mistress."[36] The obituary notice, dated 1613, for Sister Pautilla della Casa of San Jacopo di Ripoli in Florence states that "when she was novice mistress she began to write comedies in a most elegant style . . . and she wrote a lot and did so up until her last days."[37]

One of the most accomplished texts of the monastic tradition in this period is the *Love of Virtue (Amor di virtú),* a spiritual comedy in verse, written by Beatrice del Sera (1515–1585), a Dominican nun in the convent of San Niccolò in Prato.[38] The play is based on Giovanni Boccaccio's early prose romance, the *Filocolo,* which is read in a spiritual key, as Boccaccio himself had suggested. The playwright introduces, also in the spirit of Boccaccio, an autobiographical allegory, representing herself through the figure of the female protagonist. Beatrice del Sera claims to have read not only Boccaccio's *Filocolo,* but his *Genealogy of the Gentile Gods (Genealogia deorum gentilium)* as well, and she seems to have gotten her knowledge of literary theory from these works. She owned a copy of Petrarch's lyric poetry, and the language of her play strongly reflects the influence of these two great fourteenth-century authors. Dante is there too, but not in the language, rather in the play's symbolic system: the female protagonist, Biancifiore in Boccaccio's romance, is rebaptized Aurabeatrice in the comedy, where she represents the writer's existential, poetic, and spiritual aspirations.

The author calls *Love of Virtue* a work "for stage performance," but the play is more lyric than dramatic in nature. Its most impressive moments are those in which the protagonists engage in introspection and the author is able convincingly to portray their state of mind and at the same time reflect through them her own personality and feelings. The action of the play places the protagonists, especially the female protagonist, in a series of confining and distressful spaces; these spaces and the desire to escape from them always clearly refer to the existential condition of the writer, who is an enclosed nun.

Escape through one's dreams and the power of the imagination are among the comedy's most important themes. It is made clear in the play and stressed in the accompanying metatextual materials (especially in the second *intermedio*) that the text is to be read on various levels and that it is self-referential.[39] The protagonists are separated again and again in the plot and reunited only at the end of the play, but through all their trials they overcome their solitude and the pain of their separation, finding union in their thoughts and in their dreams. The *intermedi,* especially, claim that the poet overcomes her isolation similarly, through her literary creation, transforming her dreams and her thoughts into the reality of a theatrical piece. The enclosed nun, in a sense, frees herself from her confinement by vicariously living the life of her protagonist; and the Christian longs for the liberation from her mortal shell that will come only with her death, in her "future life": "Reap [now], if you can, the rewards of your labors / whereas I, poor and alone in the rock / put my hopes in the good of my future life," the author writes, in the final tercet of a sonnet.[40]

Beatrice del Sera tells us in a brief prose autobiography appended to the comedy that she wrote other plays and that she enjoyed a small measure of fame in her lifetime.[41] She expresses surprise that persons living in the world outside the convent know and appreciate her work. Her plays must have circulated in manuscripts that are now lost; we have no record that she ever published anything, and that would have been very unusual at the time for a nun. In Italy the only sixteenth-century example that has come to light is the *Play of Moses (Rappresentazione di Moisè)* by Raffaella de' Sernigi, an Augustinian in the convent of Santa Maria della Disciplina, just outside Florence; this play had at least two editions, the first in 1550 or 1560 and the second in 1578. In the seventeenth century the situation changed. Cherubina Venturelli, a Benedictine in the convent of Santa Caterina in the Umbrian town of Amelia, wrote a prose comedy in five "parts," the *Play of Saint Cecilia Virgin and Martyr (Rappresentazione di Santa Cecilia vergine e martire),* which had at least six editions.[42] And in 1637 Maria Clemente Ruoti, a Franciscan at San Girolamo sulla Costa in Florence, published *Jacob the Patriarch (Giacob patriarca);* she was also granted permission by the governors of her order to publish her *Birth of Christ (Natal di Cristo)* in 1657, but to date only the manuscript version is known.[43]

Cherubina Venturelli and Maria Clemente Ruoti belonged to a generation of convent playwrights who were not only accomplished in drama but were also well versed in contemporary theory. The dedications and prologues of their plays are, or at least include, meditations on their art. Venturelli, in the prologue to her *Rappresentazione di Santa Cecilia vergine e martire,* discusses the terms *commedia* and *rappresentazione,* terms that initially referred to plays of different form and content, but that in the sixteenth and seventeenth centuries were often used interchangeably. Venturelli rejects *commedia* since, she argues, this term denotes a play about "pleasures and fun"; she prefers to indicate with the term *rappresentazione* that her play "represents," that is, portrays a holy life, and to avoid any confusion of her play with comedy, she calls its five divisions "parts" rather than "acts." In the appeal "To the courteous reader" with which Maria Clemente Ruoti opens the *Birth of Christ,* she defends her play's transgressions of certain "rules" of the theater: not following Aristotle's *Poetics* and creating instead characters and situations that were not at all verisimilar, and going against current theatrical practice in regard to the order of their entries on stage. She also complains that, having spent all of her life enclosed in the convent, she has not had much exposure to contemporary theater and she lacks the money necessary to build the elaborate stage machinery, then so widely in use in the secular world.

Ruoti is familiar with the literature and practice of theater, more so than one would expect in the closed world of her religious house. Indeed, she seems to have had an important connection to the Florentine literary world: she is listed among the members of an important Florentine literary academy, the Academy of the Apatisti, the first woman and the only nun to receive this distinction.[44] It was perhaps because of Ruoti's fame that in 1679 the Florentine playwright Gian Andrea Moniglia placed his daughter in the convent of San Girolamo, where she took vows and the religious name of Vittoria Felice, the name taken by Maria Clemente's sister, a nun in the same convent, who had died just a few years earlier.[45]

In this literary genre, more than in the chronicles, the nuns reflect on their own lives. They speak clearly, if indirectly, of their feelings and of the joys and the difficulties of communal life. Ruoti's *Jacob the Patriarch* is not so much the story of Jacob as it is that of the difficulty the women of his family encounter living together; and her *Birth of Christ* is a story of the victory of chaste, virtuous women over sinful, powerful men. The *Play of Saint Catherine of Köln,* the work of an anonymous sixteenth-century Florentine Dominican nun, is about a women who has a strong religious vocation, who has fought with her family in order to enter the convent, and who, nevertheless, suffers because of the separation from her family that a life of enclosure required. Often convent plays reflect the psychological suffering caused by the practice of forced monachizations. Beatrice del Sera makes it one of the recurrent themes of her play the *Love of Virtue,* and she puts words of protest in the mouth of one of her characters: "you lock up the body and not the heart" ("serrate il corpo e non il cuore," 4.613) and "they are women and not pictures to hang on the wall" ("le son donne e non pitture / d'appicarle ad un muro," 4.630–631).

Other Genres

The theme of forced monachization brings readily to mind the Venetian nun Arcangela Tarabotti, who made it her life's work to protest this practice. Arcangela Tarabotti (1604–1652), born Elena Cassandra Tarabotti, became a nun in the convent of Sant'Anna, which was in her own neighborhood in the district of Venice called Castello.[46] She did not have a religious vocation and this was both the cause of great spiritual anguish for her and the reason she became a writer. She dedicated herself especially to writing polemical treatises in defense of the dignity of women and against forced vocations, and she wrote letters.

Tarabotti carried on a correspondence with many important intellectuals of her time, among them Gianfrancesco Loredano, a Venetian nobleman, who in 1650 helped her publish her collected letters *(Lettere familiari e di compli-mento)*.[47] The letters testify to the importance of literary activity in her life; they are about her, her unhappiness, her illnesses, certain of her friendships, but most often they regard the genesis and the fate of her writing. To Vittoria della Rovere, the grand duchess of Tuscany, Tarabotti wrote that, at the request of certain gentlewomen, she had written a response to a satire of women's fashions entitled *Contro il lusso donnesco, satira menippea (Against the Extravagance of Women, a Menippean Satire)* by Francesco Buoninsegni.[48] Her response, entitled the *Antisatira,* which defended women and accused men (and society), was published together with Buoninsegni's satire in Venice in 1644, and there followed a series of polemical responses to Tarabotti to which her letters frequently refer. Her correspondents included Cardinal Mazarin's librarian, Gabriel Naudé, and Tarabotti had the courage to send a letter to the cardinal himself, asking him to promote the publication of one of her works in Paris (the cardinal is not known to have responded).[49]

Tarabotti's writing is eloquent; she is clever, her reasoning is sound, her language is highly figurative, and her works are replete with erudite allusions. While she complains in her letters that books are hard to come by in the convent, her literary allusions and the high linguistic register in which she writes indicate that she has read widely in both religious and secular literature. One could almost call her a professional writer, since literary activity was clearly foremost in her life. She published four books in her lifetime and left many others to be published posthumously. In a letter to her dear friend Betta Polani she says:

> It is impossible for me to stop writing. In these prisons and in my illness there is nothing else that gives me pleasure . . . if I hadn't had this diversion I would already be dead . . . only a tempered pen [a writing pen] can temper my pain. It doesn't frighten me to hear that my studies will kill me, since I wouldn't mind changing my surroundings, varying my torments, conversing with different angels and dealing with different demons.[50]

Although it has been said many times, it is still worth repeating that, however unjust and painful were the lives of so many women living in convents without religious vocation, convent life offered women of the *ancien régime* an access to literacy and writing that was unthinkable in the secular world. Clemenza Ninci, an Benedictine nun at San Michele in Prato, toward the middle of the seventeenth century wrote a comedy about a dilemma that had been a favorite of fifteenth-century humanists: whether to study or to marry.[51] Her play, the *Marriage of Hyparchia, Lady Philosopher (Sposalitio d'Iparchia filosofa)*,[52] demonstrates the importance the subject had for her and her convent sisters, and it shows, through the opposition the comedy postulates of study and marriage, that nuns were aware of the advantage that the convent offered and that marriage almost always precluded, the opportunity to study. The protagonist Hyparchia resolves the dilemma without having to renounce either: she decides to marry her teacher, a clever solution, but one that, at the time, was possible only in fiction.

A more thorough review of nonreligious convent literature (1450–1650) should include, besides the genres discussed here, the exemplary biographies (the *vitae*),[53] and especially the letters written by nuns. There are many published collections of letters available (Tarabotti's, which she published herself, Maria Celeste Galileo's, and those of numerous saints and *beatae*), and the archives hold many more in manuscript (for example the letters, almost all of them autographic and written in beautiful calligraphic hands, written by the nuns of Ferrara and Mantua to Isabella d'Este).[54] A study of the letters would give a better indication of the level of literacy and of the general level of culture in the convents, since this genre was not practiced exclusively by the better-educated nuns. Moreover, the large quantity of letters available, even though they contain conventional epistolary formulas, would speak more directly of the daily life of that multitude of women who knew how to write and wrote and who are still little known to us or completely forgotten.

While they are less well known and appreciated than the spiritual and mystical writings of nuns, the nonreligious or secular writings of convent women of the *ancien régime* represents a large part of their literary production and reveals aspects of the life and culture of women's religious communities that have been forgotten with the passage of time. All of their writing, sacred and profane, shows how women have responded in a positive and creative way to their isolation, making of their surroundings vital and culturally valid communities. And convent theater, some of the chronicles, and other secular genres (the Spanish phrase book of Fiammetta Frescobaldi, for example) make us aware of the closeness, despite formidable dividing walls, of the secular world and the world of women religious, even at times when enclosure was most strictly observed.

CHAPTER 8

Little Women, Great Heroines:
Simulated and Genuine Female Holiness
in Early Modern Italy

ANNE JACOBSON SCHUTTE

From the late summer of 1622 until the spring of 1623, the Capuchins Lorenzo Geri da Pistoia and Michelangelo da Soragna conducted a delicate special assignment in the small Tuscan town of Pescia, halfway between Pistoia and Lucca in the Valdinievole. Alfonso Giglioli, papal nuncio to the grand duke of Tuscany, had ordered them to investigate the suspicious behavior of one Benedetta Carlini, abbess of the recently founded but not yet officially sanctioned Congregation of the Mother of God, loosely affiliated with the Theatine order. The friars had to determine whether the revelations and special privileges that Carlini claimed to have received from on high—most notoriously, authorization for a spiritual marriage with Christ that had been celebrated publicly in the convent chapel—were in fact of divine origin. Since no clear, authoritative set of guidelines for arriving at such a judgment was available to them, the two investigators had to pore over a wide variety of works on theology, spirituality, and canon law bearing directly or tangentially on discernment of spirits, the science of distinguishing between genuine and false revelations. Their research led to the conclusion that, either deluded by the devil or misled by her own imagination, Carlini had fabricated evidence of her holiness.[1]

The learned tomes consulted by these ad hoc investigators, however, did not prescribe punishments for transgressions of the sort allegedly committed by Carlini. Hence the ecclesiastical authorities and Carlini's sisters in religion were forced to improvise a solution. Drawing most likely on disciplinary provisions in the rules of established female orders, they confined the errant nun to lifetime imprisonment in her convent. There, silenced and presumably penitent, she languished until her death in 1661. During Carlini's thirty-eight years of incarceration, according to the nun who recorded her demise in the

144

convent annals, the laity of Pescia had not forgotten the flamboyant pretender to holiness. Until her body was interred, therefore, the nuns prudently barred the church door, no doubt to prevent outsiders from snatching mementos, relics from their point of view, of a woman whom they persisted in considering a living saint.

It was no coincidence that the condemnation of Benedetta Carlini occurred at exactly the same moment as the canonization of the Spanish Discalced Carmelite Teresa of Avila, who was elevated to sainthood in 1622 along with three male paladins of the reoriented and increasingly militant Catholic Church (Ignatius of Loyola, Filippo Neri, and Francis Xavier). Indeed, the third and fourth decades of the seventeenth century stand at the end of a conjuncture in Catholic sainthood—a conjuncture not only in the ordinary meaning of that word but also in the technical connotation given it by scholars affiliated with the *Annales* school. Over a period of *moyenne durée* beginning in the 1580s and concluding in the 1630s, a transformation in the Church's formulations of holiness and nonholiness, accompanied by new methods of enforcing the distinction between the two, took place. As we shall see, this paradigm shift—prompted, particularly on the second front, by developments on the Iberian peninsula—had decisive consequences for women aspiring to holiness.

In the late sixteenth and early seventeenth centuries, while the processes of redefining the criteria for sainthood and modernizing the mechanism for applying them were under way, the concept of pretense of sanctity was being articulated and procedures for punishing perpetrators were being devised. That, broadly speaking, the discourses of "genuine" and "false" sanctity ran on parallel tracks appears evident in hindsight. They formed part of a massive effort conducted by the post-Tridentine Church, and by Protestant ecclesiastical establishments as well, subsumed in recent historical writing under the rubrics "forced confessionalization" and "discipline."[2] Only recently have historians concerned with holiness begun to inquire whether there were more direct connections, and whether contemporaries consciously and explicitly made them. In this essay I shall argue that the links not only existed but were fundamental to both processes.

At this point some general observations are in order. Recent scholarship has made clear that sainthood is an eminently social phenomenon: saints are made, not born. Holy people in all times, places, and religions are products of historically specific milieus in which certain models of behavior, out of a much larger repertoire theoretically available in their religious tradition, recommend themselves for imitation. As Pierre Delooz has put it, they become "saints for others," that is, they achieve positive recognition from their contemporaries, if they are perceived to incarnate the religious and social values considered most important at that moment and to meet urgent needs.[3] Conversely, if they appear to pose some challenge or threat to these values and needs, they are accorded negative recognition, frequently expressed in exemplary punishment. To employ the suggestive parlance of Peter Burke, particularly useful for our purposes, "it is impossible to explain the achievement of sanctity entirely in terms of the qualities of the individual, or even by the qualities which witnesses saw in each individual. The imputation of sainthood, like its converse, the imputation of heresy or witchcraft, should be seen as a process of interaction or 'negotiation' between centre and periphery, each with its own definition of the situation."[4]

True Holiness: A New Definition

Let us look first at the emergence of the Counter-Reformation definition of true holiness. In January 1588, after a hiatus of sixty-five years during which not a single dead holy person was elevated to the highest rank, official saint making resumed with the canonization of Diego de Alcalá. A few months earlier Pope Sixtus V, in the course of his major reorganization and modernization of the papal Curia, had assigned responsibility for canonizations to a new commission of cardinals, the Congregation of Sacred Rites and Ceremonies. As Romeo De Maio has shown,[5] the establishment of this congregation was not accompanied by an immediate change in the standards for canonization. Until the early years of the seventeenth century, saint makers continued to apply rather elastic criteria, "excellence of virtues" and "multiple excellence of life," prime evidence for which was miracles. In 1602, however, theologians of Salamanca who were preparing a case for the elevation of Teresa of Avila introduced a quite different standard: "heroic virtue," a concept strongly influenced by Renaissance humanism.

"Heroic virtue" involves, in the first place, "the glory of grace," which makes possible undertakings surpassing normal human capabilities. Significantly, the prime example is not the kind of miracle so highly prized under the previous system (the performance of cures, levitation, and the like), but rather such full participation in Christ's Passion as to receive physical marks identical to his wounds. Strong candidates for sainthood bear the excruciating pains that ensue, as well as the torments of final illness, with "heroic endurance." They counter well-intentioned advisers' disapproval of excessively severe penitential practices and extravagant vows with "heroic resistance." Prospective saints exhibit heroism not only in the struggle against their own human nature but also in combats with the devil and other adversaries of the Church, including heretics and infidels. On foreign missions and in service to victims of the plague, they sacrifice themselves for others and joyfully embrace martyrdom. Their main goal is "the glory of the Church," manifested above all in unquestioning obedience to the pope and their immediate superiors.

The concept of heroic virtue, which rapidly gained currency, was first applied in the *processi* (trials) of the Counter-Reformation figures canonized in 1622. It was articulated officially in 1629, when interim sanction of a cult for Gaetano da Thiene, founder of the Theatine order, was publicly announced by Urban VIII. This pope also implemented a series of major reforms in the procedures of canonization, promulgated between 1625 and 1634. For holy people who survived initial scrutiny by the Congregation of Rites, he introduced a new category, "blessed," which permitted devotees in the region, city, or religious order from which they came to honor them within explicitly stated limits pending further investigation and promotion to full sainthood. In the interest of rendering cases historically solid, he ordered that investigators rigorously verify the heroic exploits of prospective saints, making certain that they were neither perpetrated by the protagonists nor invented or embroidered by their promoters. To prevent informal saint making, he prohibited the initiation of local cults without explicit papal authorization. Finally, to circumvent the danger that political and personal pressure and temporary waves of enthusiasm for certain charismatic figures might result in imprudent elevations to sainthood, he ruled that while gathering of evidence might commence immediately following a holy person's death, half a century must pass before he or she was canonized.[6]

By the mid-1630s, then, the "center," Rome, had definitively assumed control over the making of saints by drastically circumscribing efforts launched on the "periphery" by clerics or layfolk to construct and promote models of true holiness. Consonant with other initiatives of the early modern papal monarchy, the mechanism chosen for accomplishing this objective was juridical: a carefully calibrated succession of *processi*. Given that a growing proportion of cardinals and therefore of popes (some of whom had previously served as inquisitors) were canon lawyers, a move in a legalistic direction was inevitable.[7] The means of identifying and punishing "false saints" would eventually assume almost identical form, but devising and putting it into practice proved considerably more difficult.

Discernment of Spirits and Pretense of Sanctity between Hard Covers

The friars charged with investigating Benedetta Carlini were able to draw on a body of literature addressing directly or in passing the problem of distinguishing true from invented or diabolically inspired revelations. Although theorists of discernment of spirits located the birth of their art in the New Testament era by citing two proof texts, 2 Corinthians 11:13–15 and 1 John 4:1,[8] its family tree branches out significantly in the early modern period. Illustrating their discussions with concrete examples, writers on discernment of spirits concurred that the overwhelming majority of self-proclaimed holy people were to be found in a single sector of the population: "little women" *(mulierculae),* uneducated laywomen of low socioeconomic status old enough to be sexually active. In describing and drawing conclusions about these women, clerical analysts utilized the entire repertoire of current assumptions about the inferiority of the female sex. On account of their mental incapacity, gullibility, and voracious sexual appetites, theologians argued, "little women" are prime candidates for diabolical suggestion. Because of their moral weakness, they are prone to perpetrating frauds. Voluble and superficially plausible, they easily attract support, particularly from women and men of the same ilk but also, all too often, from those who should be their spiritual guides: unwary, ill-prepared priests and members of the regular clergy. Even when a visionary is a nun of respectable social origin with some education leading an apparently impeccable life, like Bridget of Sweden, the inherent disabilities of her gender require that she be viewed with suspicion and thoroughly tested by experienced and competent authorities before her revelations are accepted as genuine.

Toward the end of the sixteenth century this discourse of "little women" began to extend beyond the Latin volumes lining the shelves of theologians' studies into vernacular manuals designed for spiritual directors and their penitents. The earliest of such works was Diego Pérez de Valdivia's *Aviso de gente recogida* (Barcelona, 1585), subsequently issued at least five times in Italian.[9] The readers to whom he directed his lengthy, turgid treatise were *beatae:* unmarried women and widows who committed themselves to a life of meditation, penitence, and chastity either in their own homes or in houses shared with other women because they did not choose—or more likely could not afford—to become nuns.[10] Although he recognized and sympathized with their difficult situation as "quasi-religious" living in an anomalous and therefore perilous liminal zone, Pérez was primarily concerned with alerting them to the insidious traps of spirituality and the dire consequences certain to ensue for those who fell into them.

That it was a Spaniard who inaugurated this new type of spiritual handbook comes as no surprise. In the Iberian world, distinctive features of the social and religious landscape contributed to early stigmatization of certain religious attitudes and behaviors as not merely deviant but formally heretical and subject to prosecution by the Inquisition. One was the presence of *beatae,* who were more loosely organized and thus less susceptible to clerical supervision—and probably also more numerous—than their closest Italian counterparts, tertiaries. Another was the widespread phenomenon of *alumbradismo* (the belief that salvation came primarily through direct communication with the divine, rather than being merited by performance of good works and mediated via the sacraments of the Church), of which there was no widely disseminated Italian analogue until the eruption of Quietism in the late seventeenth century.

Italian writers motivated by concerns similar to Pérez's soon turned their hand to the composition of manuals for spiritually inclined laypeople and quasi-religious. In 1587, two years after the first edition of the *Aviso* appeared in Spanish, the Italian Observant Franciscan Antonio Pagani issued four such guides. Addressing the Dimesse ("secular companies" of women living in common, which he himself had founded in several cities of the Veneto, who went out into their communities to do charitable work and provide catechetical instruction), Pagani cautioned the female reader not "to do anything according to her own opinion or inclination or for some temporal or spiritual gratification."[11] In a work aimed at a more general audience, he equated simulation, the "third daughter of pride," with hypocrisy, "the covering of hidden vice with a certain art and simulation of virtue."[12] Two decades later, the Milanese priest Marc'Aurelio Grattarola, who may well have intended to improve on Pérez's treatise, composed a briefer, better organized work of the same kind, *Prattica della vita spirituale* (1609), which was reissued three times in a revised edition. Unlike Pérez, who concentrated on dire warnings, but similar to Pagani, Grattarola emphasized the positive: he provided concrete practical advice on reading and meditation, as well as on translating into action the insight and energy gained by these means[13]—suggestions recalling those furnished by Ignatius of Loyola in his *Spiritual Exercises*.

In the latter part of the sixteenth century, exemplary tales of female pretenders to holiness (nuns as well as *beatae*) prosecuted by the Spanish Inquisition entered into international circulation, primarily through publications by Jesuits. José de Acosta's account of God's actions in the New World, for instance, disseminated the sad story of Francisco de la Cruz, a learned and pious professor of theology in Peru duped by a "little woman" who feigned raptures during which, she alleged, an angel instructed her. Acosta was less concerned with the woman, whom he did not name, than with the power of her wiles, which so corrupted the judgment of her male supporter that he publicized her politically oriented revelations. Brought to trial by the Inquisition in Lima, De la Cruz stubbornly refused to acknowledge and repent of his error and was burned at the stake.[14] Another Jesuit, the Louvain theologian Martin Del Rio, retold this story in his influential scholastic treatise on paranormal phenomena, locating it in the section "By what means can prophecy or divine revelation be determined to be of diabolical origin?" under the subheading "Concerning the revelations of laywomen."[15] Since Del Rio helpfully provided a detailed table of contents, readers who needed to deal with lay female ecstatics could easily locate the information they required.

Pretense of Sanctity: Procedural Uncertainty

From the fifteenth to the early seventeenth century, then, a succession of clerics, operating not only in their studies but also in confessional and nonsacramental encounters with spiritually inclined women, struggled to distinguish between legitimate and illegitimate claims to special status with God. It is possible to discern some signs of "progress" in the intellectual inquiry: writers in the late sixteenth and early seventeenth centuries seem somewhat more inclined than their predecessors to expatiate on "natural" causes and dismiss diabolical illusion. In operational terms, however, two centuries of discussion did not produce very much. We have seen that by the early 1620s, Rome had decided how to reward "real" saints once they had gone on to a better life. But as the case of Benedetta Carlini vividly illustrates, what to do about a woman whose inspiration was evidently not from heaven remained unclear, at least in Italy.

Ecclesiastical subjects of the Spanish rulers had long since solved this problem: put the woman on trial in an Inquisition tribunal. Why did Italian inquisitors not follow their example? One part of the answer to this question is that, despite ample dissemination of the Spanish solution in several genres of theological literature, it had not made its way into juridical literature. Of the many inquisitorial manuals issued and reissued in the sixteenth and early seventeenth centuries, only one, *De catholicis institutionibus* (Valladolid, 1552), by the Spanish bishop and canonist Diego de Simancas, even mentioned the subject. Toward the end of a section devoted primarily to sorcerers, Simancas spends two pages on those "who affirm or pretend that they have divine revelations." He cites a single instance: "that girl from Cordoba" (almost certainly the nun Magdalena de la Cruz), whose simulation of sanctity, inspired by the devil, came to light by chance during an illness, whereupon the Inquisition transferred her to another convent. Coming abruptly to a conclusion, he states that inquisitors must examine and punish those who report frequent revelations. Yet he offers no concrete suggestions about exactly how they are to conduct inquiries and proceed to trial and sentencing.[16]

Lack of attention to dubious claims of holiness in inquisitorial manuals no doubt contributed to the uncertainty and inconsistency with which Italian ecclesiastical authorities handled cases that came to their attention. As the treatment of Benedetta Carlini shows, it was by no means inevitable that a case would come before the ordinary, let alone the Holy Office—unless the alleged perpetrator was a "little woman" bereft of support from her betters. In 1581 the well-born Neapolitan visionary and convent founder Ursula Benincasa was deemed worthy of attention from a papal commission in Rome.[17] At the very same time, however, Alfonsina Rispola, a humbler inhabitant of the same city who had reported visions and claimed to have received the stigmata, was arrested by order of the vicar general of Naples and confined in a convent. After she had languished there for over a decade, the Congregation of the Holy Office ruled that although the vicar general's investigation, improperly conducted, provided no grounds for an inquisitorial prosecution, Rispola's internment should continue.[18] Several decades later, again in Naples, the bizarre amalgam of spirituality and sexual libertinism promoted by the Franciscan tertiary Giulia Di Marco and her two accomplices, the priest Aniello Arciero and the attorney Giuseppe de Vicariis, came to light. Because the trio had recruited numerous followers, some of them in the upper social strata, and because their activities evoked a bitter dispute between receptive Jesuits and hostile Theatines, this case took local inquisitors and the Holy Office eight years to resolve. Finally the chief perpetrators and several of their disciples were extradited to Rome, where on July 12, 1615, Di Marco, Arciero, and de Vicariis were sentenced to life imprisonment.[19] Hence, even when an inquisitor exchanged information with colleagues elsewhere or consulted his employers on the Congregation of the Holy Office, he was unlikely to obtain guidance applicable to more than a single case.

Pretense of Sanctity: The Emergence of Procedural Guidelines

Case law, on the contrary, drove the process of clarification in a sector of heresy related in some respects to pretense of sanctity—witchcraft, a subject that had generated considerable heat and some light not only in theological treatises but also in inquisitorial manuals. Giovanni Romeo has shown that in the 1580s, numerous witchcraft cases forwarded from provincial tribunals precipitated a struggle within the Congregation of the Holy Office between true believers in the devil-centered paradigm of witchcraft and moderates skeptical about it. Around 1588 this conflict ended in a compromise: the virtual exclusion of torture as an instrument for obtaining confessions, a ban on prosecuting alleged accomplices named by those on trial, and an approach toward sentencing that treated convicted witches as deluded souls capable of rehabilitation rather than apostates meriting harsh punishment. Although many years would pass before this new position—"a partial depenalization of the sabbath," to use Romeo's felicitous term—was promulgated in explicit, authoritative form, it was promptly implemented through the congregation's supervision of inquisitors in the field.[20]

The development of a coherent procedural model for handling witchcraft is almost certainly related to the otherwise inexplicable appearance in the mid-1630s of clear, detailed, and authoritative directives for handling cases that the inquisitors and their masters in Rome were soon tendentiously categorizing as "assumed," "feigned," "claimed," or "simulated" holiness. While the precise details of the process are difficult to trace, the emergence of a full-fledged paradigm capable of application in inquisitorial tribunals seems to relate to a "Cremonese connection." Early in 1636 the first edition of a new manual of inquisitorial procedure that would be reissued several times, Cesare Carena's *Tractatus de Officio Sanctissimae Inquisitionis et modo procedendi in causis fidei*, was published in Cremona. Its author, a young Cremonese jurist whose father divided his time between that city and Milan, had taken a law degree from the University of Pavia and studied theology at Padua. After serving as consultant to the Cremonese Inquisition, he was appointed its *avvocato fiscale* (prosecutor). Carena's rapid rise in his chosen career was due in large part to the support of a powerful patron, Pietro Cardinal Campori, who had served on the Congregation of the Holy Office before being appointed bishop of Cremona.[21] Unlike previous authors of inquisitorial manuals, Carena prescribes two precise judicial routings for cases of "women who purport to have revelations from God, the saints, and angels." Those whose revelations contain "nothing superstitious, erroneous, rash or heretical" are to be dealt with in episcopal courts. If such revelations seem in the least suspicious, however, "without a doubt such women fall under the jurisdiction of the inquisitor."[22]

That Carena's succinctly stated but explicit recommendations reflected something other than his own opinion on the matter is suggested by the almost simultaneous appearance of another work, Desiderio Cardinal Scaglia's *Prattica per procedere nelle cause del S. Offizio* (ca. 1635). Scaglia, a Dominican from Brescia, had pursued the career of inquisitor in Pavia, Cremona, and Milan before being appointed commissioner of the Holy Office in Rome and then raised to the cardinalate in 1621 by Paul V.[23] He and Carena's patron, Campori, both protégés of the pope and his family, the Borghese, were in Rome in Inquisition circles during a period when Carena was perhaps present in the Holy City as well. Almost certainly, therefore, Scaglia and Carena knew each other; very probably their works were shaped by a common mindset; perhaps they consulted and came to agreement on a strategy for coordinated dissemination of their works.

Scaglia's handbook, unpublished until much later but disseminated widely in manuscript among inquisitors, freed them from undertaking a review of the literature every time the specter of false holiness arose and provided them with even more explicit instructions on the disposition of such cases. Since Albano Biondi has recently published and analyzed the two sections of the *Prattica* bearing on the identification and prosecution of "false saints,"[24] an extensive summary is not required here. Suffice it to say that without wasting much space reiterating age-old misogynistic stereotypes, Scaglia succinctly describes the social and psychological pressures driving "little women" and nuns toward delusions or pretensions of sanctity. In contrast to practically all previous commentators on the subject, he pays attention also to male pretenders to holiness in quest of attention, money, and sexual gratification. With pungent sarcasm, he reveals how ineptly such cases are usually handled by spiritual directors and ecclesiastical superiors. When he turns to punishment, he prescribes differential treatment for men, laywomen, and nuns. Finally, he insists that prevention is the best cure for the problem. If pretense of sanctity is to be nipped in the bud, he argues, those on the front lines, all confessors and spiritual directors, must be thoroughly instructed in discernment of spirits. Therefore he concludes by distilling received wisdom on the subject.

At long last the "center" had declared itself on pretense of sanctity. With Carena's manual and Scaglia's *Prattica* in their libraries (shelved, perhaps, next to Urban VIII's directives, promulgated in the same years, on investigating and promoting genuine holy people), inquisitors and bishops—the latter responsible in the first instance for nuns, as well as for overseeing the initial stages of canonization *processi*—were reasonably well equipped to diagnose and manage cases of both genuine and false sanctity. Further out on the periphery, however, stood priests, friars, and their female clients in and outside convents. Even an increasingly centralized and efficient ecclesiastical bureaucracy could not guarantee that clerics in the lower ranks would promptly receive, understand, and take to heart Rome's messages.

A "Little Woman" and a "Great Heroine"

Let us conclude with two examples. No single case of pretense of sanctity can adequately represent an entire territory that has not yet been thoroughly explored and mapped. The trial of Antonia Pesenti by the Inquisition of Venice in 1668–69, however, presents an opportunity to identify some characteristic features of the phenomenon.[25]

Like a number of other women charged with this offense, Pesenti, the thirty-four-year-old daughter of an artisan resident in the parish of San Polo, did not stand trial alone. She had a co-defendant: Francesco Vincenzi, *pievano* (rector) of Santa Ternita, aged fifty-seven. Pesenti and Vincenzi were denounced to the Holy Office on June 19, 1668, by Giovanni Daviano, a canon from Cyprus who said mass in Vincenzi's church. According to the accuser, some months earlier Pesenti had left her parents' home on the other side of the city and taken up residence in a hermitage adjoining the priest's residence. Following her suggestion, allegedly inspired by the Virgin Mary, Vincenzi had moved a *Madonna alla greca,* a painting of the Virgin in Byzantine style, to a prominent location in the church, where, he claimed, it worked miracles. Pesenti frequently went into what appeared to be ecstasy in front of the painting; only Vincenzi could bring her out of these trances. With other young women she participated in ceremonies choreographed by the *pievano,* which in Daviano's view were at the very least superstitious. Worst of all, Vincenzi's aggressive promotion of Pesenti as a living saint was drawing crowds of credulous visitors to Santa Ternita, where Vincenzi was distributing "relics," pieces of cloth soaked with the sweat that poured from the woman's brow during her ecstasies.

Under interrogation to confirm his written denunciation, the canon furnished other incriminating details about Pesenti's behavior, including strange fits of paralysis and abstention from eating, and Vincenzi's involvement in it. Once this information had been corroborated and supplemented by numerous witnesses from the parish, the Holy Office ordered that the two suspects be apprehended. Brought in for questioning, Vincenzi cooperated enthusiastically, seeing the proceedings as an opportunity to elucidate the miraculous occurrences with which he and his church had been favored. In her initial appearance before the tribunal, by contrast, Pesenti responded only with stuttered syllables, sobs, and gestures, leading the Holy Office to suspect that she was possessed. Following an examination by the experienced Reformed Franciscan exorcist fra Candido Brugnoli, who succeeded in getting her to talk about the sexually charged fantasies she experienced at night, she was able to speak up in the presence of the inquisitor and his colleagues.

Many further interrogations of the two defendants brought to light a circumstantial account of their relationship, which had culminated in an improvised ceremony of spiritual marriage complete with a white gown and flowers for the bride and the placing of a ring, an *anello di San Carlo* borrowed from the groom's aunt, on her finger. Given the opportunity to consult attorneys, neither Pesenti nor Vincenzi opted to present a defense and threw themselves on the mercy of the Holy Office. On March 14, 1669, they were convicted as vehemently suspect of heresy. Pesenti was sentenced to a place and term of imprisonment to be determined by the Inquisition and was prohibited from further contact with her co-defendant, at which point she disappears from the records. Although Vincenzi's sentence was identical, he was not destined to historical oblivion. A petition from the parish council of Santa Ternita was instrumental in bringing about his early release and rehabilitation; he died in office as *pievano* on September 6, 1676. An eighteenth-century historian of Venetian churches lauded him as an exemplary pastor.[26]

Without a doubt, Antonia Pesenti was a "little woman." Her parents could not afford to finance her dream of entering a convent. Even if she had been able to do so, since she was illiterate, she could only have served as a *conversa* (lay sister) who performed menial chores for the professed nuns. Nor would her family have been able to furnish much of a dowry had she wished to marry. By the mid-1600s a woman of her class bent on dedicating herself to God had practically no option other than living as devoutly as she could in the world, for in Venice female Third Orders had practically evaporated and even the Dimesse demanded dowries.

Her mentor, Vincenzi, was no ignorant backwoods priest. Yet, just as many writers had previously warned, he proved susceptible to influence from and infatuation with a devout woman apparently favored by God who was young enough to be his daughter. That they ever consummated their spiritual marriage was never alleged and seems most unlikely. That he should have known better than to enter it and to promote Pesenti as a living saint constituted the inquisitor's chief reason for assigning him a relatively harsh punishment. The rapid reversal of his sentence but not Pesenti's identical one, however, illustrates the degree to which rank and membership in the male gender conveyed privilege, even in an Inquisition tribunal.

In almost every respect the story of Angela Maria Pasqualigo is different from Pesenti's—not only because Pasqualigo succeeded in gaining recognition as a "great heroine" (the term used by her biographer, the Veronese Theatine Giovanni Bonifacio Bagatta) but also because she is fully typical of women who passed muster as genuinely holy.[27] Their *vitae,* composed by men anxious to promote *processi* in their favor and well aware of what constituted heroic virtue, resemble one another so closely in both general outlines and details that they appear to be following a common script. These are tales of dedication from infancy to prayer and penitential practices, precocious vocation to celibacy, obstacles surmounted, special privileges amply demonstrated, and exemplary deaths, followed by posthumous occurrences that the writers prudently refrain from calling miracles.

Born in Venice on September 29, 1562, Angela Maria, daughter of a patrician, was set on the right path by her pious wet nurse, who prayed that if her charges were not destined to become good Christians, God would take them before they lost their innocence. As soon as she reached the age of reason, the girl began to pray often and eschew vanities; by the age of nine, she was fasting three days a week. Naturally the devil soon took notice of her and insinuated that she should weep over the pains of the damned rather than those of the crucified Christ, a suggestion she resisted. One day during Lent, when she stayed away from the dinner table to pray, she fell headfirst into a fireplace. Much to the surprise of everyone in the household, she emerged without a single singed hair—exactly like Catherine of Siena, her biographer points out. From then on, it was clear to all that she was destined for great things.

Orphaned at an early age, Angela Maria passed an eventful adolescence and early adulthood in Cyprus. Having overcome pressures from her uncle and others to marry, around 1588 she made her way back to Venice and took up the work that God had in mind for her: helping unfortunate girls whose poverty put them in danger of attacks on their virginity. This project required funds far beyond Pasqualigo's modest means. With help from her spiritual director, she undertook a long, difficult legal battle against her paternal relatives to recover her and her sister Lucia's inheritance. Even before the suit was decided in their favor, she approached the Provveditori sopra Monasteri (the lay magistrates in charge of convents) and the Theatine general in Rome for permission to found a convent affiliated with that order, which she intended to dedicate to Jesus and Mary. Surmounting a long series of obstacles through astutely conducted negotiations with authorities in Venice and Rome and assistance from on high, she eventually achieved her objective. In July 1647, shortly after she was stricken by the illness to which she would succumb five years later, the nuns of Gesù Maria received papal authorization to go into full enclosure.

While working to achieve this objective, Pasqualigo undertook a personal regimen resembling that of many other female aspirants to holiness in this period.[28] Consulting with her confessor, she increased her fasting until in 1605 she was able to survive the entire forty days of Lent on Communion alone and a single modest meal on Sundays, a practice she continued for the rest of her life. Since many Venetians interpreted this prodigy as some sort of fraud suggested and abetted by the devil, a substitute confessor decided to put her to the test. He ordered her to abstain from food during other holy seasons, which she managed to do even when the papal interdict of 1605 prevented her from taking Communion. Her fasts were soon rewarded: every Friday, for the three hours of Christ's Passion, she suffered acute pain in various parts of her body. These divine torments, as well as frequent assaults by the devil, she bore with a smile, emerging from them with renewed energy to do God's will.

Of the many trials and tribulations in the life of Angela Maria Pasqualigo adduced by Bagatta in support of her heroic virtues and extraordinary powers, two are particularly significant. The first is an experiment in the discernment of spirits, again involving food, in which she was the guinea pig. While she was struggling to establish the convent, opponents approached Patriarch Federico Corner to express doubts about the source of her ability to undertake prolonged fasts. When Corner shared this problem with the Congregation of the Religious in Rome, he was ordered to undertake a thorough investigation, which he entrusted to Giorgio Polacco, the vicar responsible for female religious in the diocese.[29] Pasqualigo was examined several times by competent theologians, the inquisitor, and Polacco. Her humility and obedience impressed everyone but Polacco, who in order to ascertain whether her fasting was a diabolical trick, deprived her of both normal food and Communion for a week. Though she survived this ordeal, Polacco was determined to seek further proof. In a preemptive strike, Pasqualigo called on the inquisitor. Thoroughly persuaded that her abstention from food was no fraud, he lobbied successfully with Patriarch Corner and the papal nuncio to exempt her from further tests. These three men put pressure on Urban VIII to let the regularization of her foundation proceed.[30]

Second, Pasqualigo herself proved capable of penetrating the disguise of the devil masquerading as an angel of light. In 1637 all Venice was enthralled with a young woman who seemed to have reached a precocious state of perfection. She often went into what appeared to be ecstasy, said that she was given Communion by Christ in person, claimed to have fasted totally during Lent, and showed marks on her hands that looked like the stigmata. Since Bagatta gives her first name, there is no question that this seeming prodigy was Cecilia Ferrazzi, who would be convicted of pretense of sanctity in the mid-1660s.[31] To remove Ferrazzi from the public eye "until her spirit was discovered," Patriarch Corner confined her in a convent. With considerable reluctance, Pasqualigo obeyed vicar Polacco's order to visit Ferrazzi there. One look at the self-proclaimed holy woman, attired in an all too attractive Carmelite habit and suspiciously vivacious, was enough to confirm Pasqualigo's worst fears. In the acrimonious interview that followed, Ferrazzi further manifested her pride and insolence. When Pasqualigo reported her negative findings to Polacco, the vicar complimented her for successfully completing an assignment that had daunted the most learned, experienced confessors and theologians in Venice.[32]

The differences between Angela Maria Pasqualigo's story and Antonia Pesenti's demonstrate clearly what was required in this era for gaining recognition as a "great heroine," a plausible candidate for canonization. Pasqualigo's high birth, the fact that she was literate, and her experience gained early in life in dealing with powerful people—along with some financial resources and the social connections needed to accumulate more—equipped her to persuade the civil and ecclesiastical authorities that her project of establishing a convent was appropriate and feasible. Although she attained the status of full-fledged nun in a properly enclosed convent only toward the end of her life, she enjoyed from infancy a degree of credibility that spiritual free-lancers like Pesenti could never hope to attain.

Pasqualigo's assets, automatically accruing from the social rank into which she was born, inclined ecclesiastical authorities to give her the benefit of the doubt, almost never accorded to "little women," when she undertook prodigious fasting. As brutal as the two tests of her ability to survive on Communion alone may appear to us, at least she was allowed to undergo them. On trial in Venice in the 1660s for pretense of sanctity, the priest-collaborator of another "holy anorectic," the "little woman" Maria Janis, urged that she be subjected to such an experiment; the inquisitor ignored his suggestion.[33] Pasqualigo, furthermore, was given credit for and allowed to demonstrate her theological expertise. Like many advisers of females aspiring to holiness, Pérez had warned "little women" not to "make a profession of being a *teologa* or *dottoressa*."[34] On at least one occasion, the discernment of Cecilia Ferrazzi's spirit, the "great heroine" Pasqualigo was actually invited to do so. Perhaps most important, she left behind a tangible monument, the convent of Gesù Maria. This durable reminder of her exemplary life may well have spoken louder than the reports of visions and revelations and the somatic "miracles" that were the sole means by which the "false saints" communicated their claims to holiness.[35]

CHAPTER 9

Models of Female Sanctity in Renaissance and Counter-Reformation Italy

SARA F. MATTHEWS GRIECO

Sacred Imagery before and after Trent

In terms of the representation of female sanctity, the most important single document of the period 1450–1650 was the Tridentine decree *Della invocazione, della venerazione e delle reliquie dei santi e delle sacre immagini* (December 3–4, 1563), which established the Church's official stance with respect to the Protestant Reformation and its iconoclastic critiques of sacred images, as well as the Catholic establishment's own desire to reform a number of superstitious, magical, and commercial abuses of religious imagery. Ultimately, however, the suggestions of stringent catholic reformers bent on expurgating the visual arts were never systematically applied by the Church. In fact, the Church demonstrated a relative tolerance with respect to the profane and "naturalistic" innovations of the Renaissance, as well as a grudging forbearance when faced with the survival of anecdotal hagiographic representations and borderline devotional traditions inherited from the Middle Ages.[1]

Simultaneously functioning as pedagogical texts and sacred objects, the religious images produced in Italy between 1450 and 1650 multiplied exponentially under the dual stimulus of a militant response to the threat of Protestantism and a growing commercial market for pictures (especially etchings and engravings). Didactic and devotional pictures were to be found in all households and public buildings, and at all levels of society. From the richly colored canvases commissioned by religious orders for the edification of the faithful (and the order's own greater glory) to the crude woodcut nailed above the laborer's humble pallet, these images conveyed models of male and female sanctity whose purpose, perception, and ultimate use were not always in harmony with the evolution of authorized religious practice.[2]

One of the new criteria for the representation of sanctity was historical

159

accuracy. Under the combined impetus of Renaissance naturalism, humanist scholarship, and religious reform, artists ceased representing the Virgin and female saints in the rich brocades and regal gowns that had characterized the altarpieces of the fourteenth and the first half of the fifteenth centuries. Humility, faith, and obedience were the trio of virtues expected of women in Counter-Reformation Italy, be they married to God or to an earthly husband, and these virtues were expected to be transmitted in the plastic arts, although sometimes they reached a level of literal representation considered excessive by the Church itself.

Caravaggio's almost hyperrealist paintings representing a barefoot Madonna consorting with humble peasants or lying, ghastly and bloated, on her deathbed convey a vision of the Mother of God that emphasizes the Christian values of *humanitas* and *humilitas*. In the case of the *Death of the Virgin,* however, the *humanitas* element was deemed unseemly, and the painting was ultimately rejected by the Church of Santa Maria della Scala in Trastevere on the grounds that Caravaggio had made the Virgin look more like a common whore (with bare legs and dirty feet) than the Immaculate Mother of Christ.[3]

All devotional imagery did not follow the path of historical "realism." Despite discredit by the Catholic reform, both popular and provincial art testify to a lasting taste for anecdotal and marvelous tales derived from literature such as the Apocrypha, *The Golden Legend,* and the *Meditations on the Life of Jesus Christ.* As late as the 1580s for example, a fresco by Pellegrino da Modena depicting the Funeral, Assumption, and Incoronation of the Virgin also features a prominent reference to the tale of the "impious Jew": having tried to impede the Virgin's burial by overturning her bier,[4] the offender is represented struck down by a sword-wielding angel. In the Pellegrino da Modena picture the narrative details are rendered with anecdotal relish; the transgressor lies dramatically prone in the foreground, his severed hands still clutching the Virgin's bier in a macabre but effective demonstration of the punishment reserved for anyone—Jew, Protestant, or infidel alike—who would be guilty of the crime of *lèse divinité.*

The Virgin Mary and the Holy Family: Dynastic and Domestic Models for Women

If one of the consequences of sixteenth-century religious reform was to reduce the number of saints whose lives were considered historically verifiable (and therefore valid for iconographic representation), another consequence was to increase representations of those models of female sanctity considered desirable by the dominant institutions of the time: the Church, the state, and the family.

The first of these models, and the one that was by far the most often represented, was that of the Virgin Mary.[5] Both human and divine, virgin and mother, she could hardly be a literal model for women, although girls, wives, widows, and nuns continued to identify themselves with her and emulate her devotion to the infant Christ. At the same time, Counter-Reformation artists took up arms in reaction to Protestant denials of the virginity and divinity of the Madonna. Whereas fifteenth- and early-sixteenth-century Annunciations had emphasized the elite humanity of the Mother of God, placing her in elegant contemporary settings and surrounding her with the latest in Renaissance interior decoration,[6] post-Tridentine art set the scene in a timeless, abstract space where beams of blinding light, hovering angels, and fluffy clouds bridge the gap between heaven and earth, elevating the Virgin into a celestial sphere far removed from that of daily experience.[7]

Despite post-Tridentine concerns for historical orthodoxy and the tendency to bodily remove the Virgin Mary from earth to heaven, where she is crowned and seated on the right hand of Christ,[8] the most frequent representation of the Mother of Christ remained that of mother and intercessor, especially in the domestic sphere and in terms of popular devotional practice, where her example spoke as much to wives and mothers as to women who had adopted the religious life. While Holy Family imagery, including depictions of the Virgin and Child in the company of Saint Anne (whose grandmotherly presence established a human dynastic lineage for the infant Jesus), reflected late medieval and Renaissance concern with lineage, household, and family,[9] images of a powerful mother and grandmother provided models of spiritual guidance that echoed the strong directive roles held by the spiritual "mothers" of Renaissance courts and religious communities. Such matriarchal and dynastic readings of the Holy Family are especially noticeable in paintings where Saint Anne is represented standing behind the Virgin, as in the Florentine altarpiece attributed to Giovanni Maria Butteri (fig. 1), which implicitly allies the Medici dynasty with that of Christ.

The Holy Family from Matriarchy to Patriarchy

As the later Middle Ages had focused more on Christ's humanity than on his divinity, it seemed natural that he should be part of a large, multigenerational family. This focus on the human lineage of Christ is most apparent in northern art,[10] where the Holy Kinship often takes on the appearance of a matriarchal family reunion, with Saint Anne presiding over a bevy of daughters, sons-in-law, and grandchildren. In Italy this theme is usually restricted to representations of Saint Anne or Saint Elizabeth (they are often interchangeable as representatives of the older generation), with the Virgin and the infants Christ and Saint John the Baptist. Joseph is generally absent or, if present, decidedly marginal with respect to the group of women and children.

Holy Family images of the multigenerational type date largely from the fifteenth and first half of the sixteenth centuries. An unusually late version of this maternal and quasi-matriarchal vision of female sanctity is to be found in an etching by Elisabetta Sirani, a seventeenth-century Bolognese painter who died at the age of twenty-seven, having produced a prodigious number of paintings and virtually supported her entire family since the age of sixteen (fig. 2). Perhaps it was her strong sense of family responsibility and disappointment with a weak and exploitative father that caused her to favor the old *Sacra Famiglia* model, wherein Mary and Saint Elizabeth care for the infant Christ and John the Baptist while Joseph wields the tools of his carpenter's trade in the shadowy background, his back to the women's world of infant feeding and care.

By the second half of the sixteenth century, however, most Holy Family imagery had embraced the nuclear family model, which not only downplayed the maternal bloodline of Jesus but also placed Saint Joseph in the protective, paternal role that has dominated his cult up to the present day. Changes in gender roles and the structure of families also contributed to the evolution of Holy Family imagery, where husbands (especially Joseph and Joachim, the husband of Saint Anne) not only take place next to their wives but even assume a dominant position. A good example of this is a print etched by Annibale Carracci in 1590 in which, seated in an elevated and protective position, Saint Joseph reads to his family from the Scriptures (fig. 3). No longer represented as a humble carpenter, Joseph is here promoted to the status of artisan of the soul. He is the *pater familias,* the protector and provider who is firmly ensconced, like God the Father, at the head of a family he has taken for his own.

The patriarchal trinity of Joseph, Mary, and Jesus tended to replace the matriarchal trinity of Saint Anne or Saint Elizabeth, the Virgin, and Christ in a period when both Church and state were in the process of promoting a "viricentric" reorganization of religion and society. In the process of this reorganization, women's lives became increasingly confined to house or convent and their reputation for virtue or "sanctity" depended increasingly on accepting—with humility, faith, and obedience—the subordinate domestic or religious roles allotted to them.

Pious Pedagogy

To what extent did women identify with and accept (or reject) the models of sanctity daily presented to their eyes, either at home or in the Church, at the printer's market stall, at a wayside shrine, or among a peddler's wares? The didactic function of religious imagery, which was supposed to inculcate desirable behavioral models in women and children, was stressed by fifteenth- and sixteenth-century moralists writing on the importance of visual "texts" for the edification of the illiterate, women, and the young.[11] In the sixteenth and seventeenth centuries, for example, images representing Saint Anne teaching the Virgin to read reinforced "approved" models of pious and charitable activity for women, not only in the home but also in institutions and religious or lay orders that provided instruction for needy young ladies. Reading, however, was not the only activity considered useful for mothers (be they biological or spiritual) to teach their "daughters." Sewing and needlework were universal female accomplishments and generally taught in the home. Thus the multiplication of pictures representing Saint Anne teaching the Virgin to sew (fig. 4) reflected both a social reality as well as an economic necessity for the majority of women whose skill provided clothing for the members of their household or community.[12] For the poor, spinning, weaving, and sewing might constitute their very means of sustenance.

Maternal Imprinting

Inventories of household objects reveal that from the fifteenth through the seventeenth century the most frequently found sacred object in the houses of middle- and upper-class urban dwellers was the image of the Virgin and Child. Most often placed in the bedroom, and even to be found in every room of the house, the Virgin and Child watched over the members of the household, inspired mothers to bear beautiful baby boys (the contemplation of a beautiful image during pregnancy was supposed to imprint itself upon the fetus), and provided a focus for domestic piety and prayers.[13]

Contemporary pictures representing domestic interiors also testify to the omnipresence of the Virgin and Child in urban households,[14] as well as to the model of female behavior considered most desirable in wives: that of prolific maternity.[15] Birth scenes represented by fifteenth- and sixteenth-century painters put special emphasis on the identification between the maternal model represented on the wall and its fulfillment in the domestic context. In the Duomo of Turin, for example, a picture of the birth of Saints Crispin and Crispinian (fig. 5) shows the newly delivered mother nursing one of the brothers in bed while a wet nurse tends the other in front of the fireplace. Above the bed (and at the focal center of the image) is a painting of the Virgin holding the Christ Child in close embrace, a domestic deity whose example and patronage has ensured the household a dual blessing.

Another means of inculcating the maternal and devotional model of the Mother of Christ was through play. Household and dowry inventories often mention a *putto* or *bambino Gesù*, a painted doll made of wax, plaster, or wood representing the infant Christ, whose often elaborate wardrobe implies that it could serve the purposes of both piety and play. Found as often in the trousseaux of young brides as in that of nuns entering the convent, these dolls doubtless served a variety of purposes: from a directive, ludic pastime considered suitable for young girls to the "impression" of a gestating fetus or, in the case of spiritual mothers, a compensatory and devotional function wherein the nun could identify herself with the Mother of God.[16]

A third but equally important representation of the Virgin Mary as a domestic deity is to be found on ex-votos, wherein a miraculous image of the Virgin and Child "appears" in a contemporary home, surrounded by celestial light or a garland of clouds, at the crucial moment in which the prayers or vows of the faithful have obtained her divine aid in the healing of an afflicted family member.[17] Ex-votos from Naples to Venice show both men and women beseeching the Virgin to heal their loved ones—in general, parents, spouses, or children—but the vast majority of images place women in the role of supplicant. Like the Virgin, who intercedes with Christ for humanity, women act as the principal intercessors between their families and heavenly helpers.[18]

Popular images such as these were reinforced by the elegant tabernacles found in well-to-do homes as much as by the rough woodcuts representing the Virgin and Child that graced more humble abodes.[19] Viewed daily, both in the home and on regular visits to the parish church, they provided contemporary women with sacred models that illustrated, reinforced, and justified widespread social expectations with respect to their domestic and religious responsibilities. All women, however, were not to be found living in secular households.

Mary Magdalene from Prophetess to "Convertita"

A second important model of female sanctity promoted by both the Renaissance and the Catholic Reformation was that of the penitent Magdalene, whose conversion from a life of voluptuous pleasure and subsequent ascetic devotions gave artists a variety of themes to exploit as a function of developments in female religious practice.[20] Thus the fifteenth and early sixteenth centuries (when women's religious authority was widely acknowledged by the Church) favored the emaciated prophetess, whereas the late sixteenth and early seventeenth centuries (at odds with problems of public morality) were to privilege the repentant courtesan.

Like a number of other highly popular saints, Mary Magdalene was a hybrid figure, made up from a variety of biblical and apocryphal texts as well as a wealth of medieval legends. By and large, however, she represented the

sinful woman—the prostitute—who was nonetheless the first of Christ's followers to recognize him after his Resurrection. Repenting of her life of sin,
she rose from the depths of depravity to become an apostle, a penitent ascetic,
and ultimately a saint. Mary Magdalene thus embodied the principle of Christian repentance and constituted a living example of the promise of redemption through faith that was offered to each and every sinner.

The Maddalena Orante

In the second half of the fifteenth century, a growing concern with Church
reform, penitential movements within the Dominican and Franciscan orders,
and a multiplication of female spiritual leaders motivated an increase in the
number of representations of Mary Magdalene as a penitent ascetic. Some of
the most striking of these are the polychrome statues made by Tuscan artists.[21] The most famous is, of course, Donatello's haggard anchorite.[22] Naked
under a mantle of once gilded (now faded) hair, her body is hidden enough to
preserve her modesty but not enough to dissimulate the gnarled limbs and
ravaged features of the fasting ascetic. This formerly golden Magdalene represents the figure that Saint Maximin of *The Golden Legend* saw in the "desert"
and described as so "radiant that one might more easily have looked into the
rays of the sun than into her face."

Donatello's well-known Magdalene is, however, but one of a series of
similar wooden sculptures produced in the fifteenth and early sixteenth centuries. All of these statues share the same emphasis on the Magdalene's wasted
limbs, long hair, and inward or otherworldly gaze as she extends her hands in
prayer. Redeemed through her ascetic practices, this is the preaching *Maddalena,* a conflation of her role as an "apostle" who announced Christ's
resurrection and preached alongside her male counterparts and her role as a
penitent anchorite who lived many years in the wilderness, naked and refusing
all earthly food. But the preaching Magdalene was to have a relatively brief
career. Initially nourished by the importance accorded to female ascetic spirituality in the fifteenth and early sixteenth centuries, when convents and courts
competed for the honor of housing "living saints" renowned for their prophetic and visionary gifts, this representation disappeared under the influence
of the Counter-Reformation, which clamped down on female prophecy and
shifted the emphasis to other episodes of the Magdalene's life.

There were, nonetheless, certain events in Mary Magdalene's spiritual career that were consistently represented from the Renaissance through the
Baroque period. One of these episodes is the Magdalene's colloquy with the
angels. According to legend, Mary Magdalene's penitential meditations in
the desert were rewarded by the visitation seven times a day of angels, who

not only elevated her up to the sky, but also nourished her with the divine Host. Thus Antonio Pollaiolo's *Saint Mary Magdalene in Conversation with the Angels* (fig. 6) shows the Magdalene as a ravaged hermit, levitated by four small angels while a fifth brings her the heavenly food that was to sustain her to the end of her life. Later representations of the angelic levitations of the Magdalene dispensed with the Host, a "food" increasingly abused by female ascetics whose spiritual and physical hunger for the consecrated body of Christ caused much debate on the use and abuse of the Eucharist, and whose voracious spiritual appetite tended to disregard the fact that the Council of Trent had clarified Church policy with respect to the sacraments and established the principle of monthly (as opposed to daily) Communion.

Images of the Magdalene's colloquy with the angels remained, for the most part, in the domain of "official" art, that is, paintings or sculpture groups commissioned for churches and other relatively "public" places, and could hardly be said to have any direct applicability as a role model for contemporary women other than visionary nuns who, in the footsteps of Saint Catherine of Siena and Teresa of Avila, aspired to similar, ecstatic transports. It was thus in the more private domain of individual commissions that the figure of Mary Magdalene took on a new guise and a new significance.

A Redeemed Sinner

Given her identity as a sinner redeemed through repentance and elevated via penance to sainthood, Mary Magdalene constituted a model of sanctity that could appeal to both men and women from a variety of social backgrounds. Whereas fifteenth-century visual chronicles of the life of the Magdalene tended to downplay the ethical errors she was supposed to have committed before her conversion and repentance (denying that they could have been so severe as to have included sexual promiscuity and extending them to include, instead, generically all the sins of the flesh),[23] sixteenth- and early-seventeenth-century representations of this saint reflected current social and moral campaigns for the moral reform of prostitutes by portraying her, above all, as a conscience-stricken courtesan or a still voluptuous *pentita*. This *topos* had a wide success in court circles, where the one feature required of the penitent was that she be *bellissima*.[24] However, although male patrons might have found the appeal of "beautiful" Magdalene paintings to be more carnal than spiritual (and there was a flourishing market for sensualized religious paintings of this sort), convents for converted prostitutes, which routinely housed images of the Magdalene as penitent, certainly would have put more emphasis on the spiritual dimension of this saint's mystical career.

Women of the aristocracy had yet another, specific interest in this saint. For these ladies, brought up in the Neoplatonic court culture of the Renaissance,

1. Giovanni Maria Butteri. *Altarpiece of Saint Anne and the Saints* (Medici portraits), 1575. Florence, Uffizi.

2. Elisabetta Sirani. *The Holy Family with Saint Elizabeth and Saint John the Baptist*. Engraving. Bologna, ca. 1650. Washington, D.C., National Gallery of Art.

3. Annibale Carracci. *The Holy Family with Joseph Reading.*
Engraving. Bologna, 1590. Gift of Mrs. Thomas Hockley. Courtesy
Museum of Fine Arts, Boston.

4. Attributed to Giovanni Antonio Galli, "The Swordsmith."
The Education of the Virgin, early seventeenth century. Rome, Spada
Gallery.

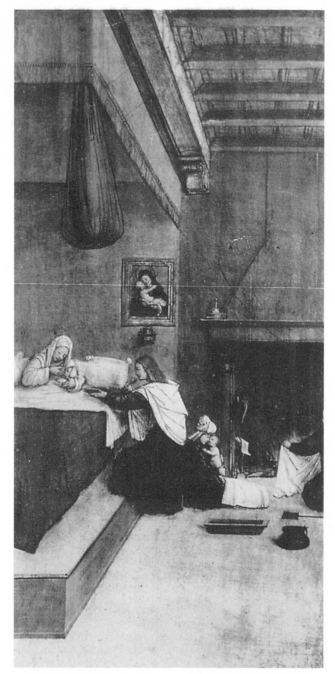

5. Giovanni Martino Spanzotti. *Birth of Saints Crispin and Crispinian,* late fifteenth century. Turin, Duomo.

6. Antonio Pollaiolo. *Saint Mary Magdalene in Conversation with the Angels*, second half of the fifteenth century. Staggia (Siena), Parish Church of Santa Maria Assunta.

7. Artemisia Gentileschi. *The Penitent Magdalene,* 1617–1620. Florence, Pitti Palace.

8. Florentine manufacturer, wax figure representing the penitent Magdalene, early seventeenth century. Florence, Pitti Palace.

9. *Saint Catherine of Siena and Four Scenes from Her Life.* Woodcut. Florence, 1460–1465. London, British Museum, Department of Prints and Drawings.

10. Benvenuto di Giovanni. *Saint Catherine Leads Gregory XI Back to Rome*. Siena, Ospedale di Santa Maria della Scala. Florence, Scala.

11. *Saint Catherine in Ecstasy Dictates Her Visions.* Woodcut, in *Dialogo de la seraphica vergine sancta Caterina di Siena dela divina providentia.* Venice, 1494.

12. Giovanni Antonio Bazzi, "The Sodomite." *The Ecstasy of Saint Catherine of Siena*, 1526. Siena, Basilica of Saint Dominic.

13. Crescenzio Gambarelli. *Saint Catherine Recites the Holy Office with Christ,* ca. 1607. Siena, Basilica of Saint Dominic.

14. Francesco Curradi. *Sister Maria Maddalena in a Posture of Great Humility.* Sanguine, in *Vita della Santa Madre in Disegno di Matita Rossa,* 1610. Florence, Archive of the Carmelite Monastery of Careggi.

15. Francesco Curradi. *Santa Maria Maddelena de' Pazzi Receives the Stigmata,* 1610. Florence, Monastery of Careggi.

16. Andrea Camassei. *Mystical Marriage of Maria Maddalena de' Pazzi in the Presence of Saint Augustine and Saint Catherine of Siena,* ca. 1637. Florence, Monastery of Careggi.

the beauty of Mary Magdalene was an outward and visible condition of her inner and invisible, but ultimately triumphant, virtue. Her costly clothes, elegant accoutrements, and many jewels all identified her with the privileged world of the high-class courtesan, as well as with that of the respectable court lady or *Dama di Corte*. Thus *The Penitent Magdalene* painted by Artemisia Gentileschi (fig. 7), depicted in the very moment of her conversion, wears a gown worthy of a court lady, although its golden color would have obliquely reminded the viewer of the identifying clothing prostitutes were obliged to wear (generally yellow ribbons or sleeves).

The fact of the matter is that many women of the elite found in the Magdalene a model of sanctity that promised them an eventual pardon for the ostentatious consumption and parade of worldly wealth they were obliged to adopt in order to maintain their husbands' rank and social prestige as well as their own.[25] Fully cognizant of contradiction between their worldly ways and the otherworldly ideals of the Church, these women doubtless saw in the Magdalene a promise of future redemption, which would account for the special interest that many female patrons and owners of Magdalene paintings had in the saint.[26]

A Sensuous Penitent

Although episodes from the evangelical biography of the Magdalene have a place in sixteenth- and seventeenth-century art (episodes such as the anointing of Christ's feet at the house of the Pharisee, Christ at the house of Martha and Mary, or the *Noli me tangere*), the most frequent representations of the Magdalene in this period remain those derived from the medieval legends relative to her life as a penitent in the wilderness. Far from evoking the haggard features of the fifteenth-century orating Magdalenes, these figures display the fetching physiognomy of a beautiful woman. An early seventeenth-century wax figure of the repentant saint from the Museo degli Argenti, for example, creates a three-dimensional grotto where the youthful saint reclines, reading a sacred text. Despite all the traditional accoutrements of the saint's contemplative existence (the cross, the skull, and the flail to mortify her flesh), she looks more like a precocious adolescent bent over a gripping romance than a repentant ascetic (fig. 8).

The erotic potential of Magdalene iconography was responsible for a steady stream of *pentita* pictures, which were always sure to bring a good price. Elisabetta Sirani, for example, always in need of funds for her family, painted no less than seven Magdalenes, most of them in the erotic mode. The dewy-eyed beauty of the penitent Magdalene was not, however, solely an excuse for erotic display or an indirect homage to the aristocratic women who identified with her cult. Beauty was also considered a guarantee of the depth and sincerity of her repentance, for an ugly Magdalene would be suspected of having "changed careers," as it were, for lack of better employ. This prejudice in favor of beauty is evident in the recruiting policies for *convertite* (repentant prostitutes). In Rome, for example, the Charity of Saint Jerome had precise standards for admission to the convents it directed: "We will give admission neither to the infirm nor to those encumbered with old age, since the art of sinning has abandoned them, and not they the art."[27]

A Visionary Ascetic

A last variant on the Magdalene as a behavioral model for contemporary women addressed itself more to the aspiring saints of post-Tridentine convents and tertiary orders than to the milieus of converted courtesans or aristocratic court ladies.

A good example of this is Sigismondo Coccapani's *Saint Mary Magdalene in Ecstasy* (ca. 1635), where a wealth of signifying objects and hovering cherubim define the penitential program considered most fruitful in Counter-Reformation practice.[28] Abandoned in a quasi-swoon, her eyes rolled up to heaven, this highly carnal Magdalene holds a metal flail that refers to a form of physical discipline practiced (often to excess) in contemporary convents. On the ground beside her, a skull and serpent refer to the Original Sin (as well as to all sins of the flesh) and constitute the inevitable *memento mori* upon which all devout—be they secular or religious—were encouraged to meditate on a regular basis.[29] Finally, a book of Scriptures and an inkwell refer to her pious meditations as well as to the exercise of recording ecstatic visions, an exercise widely encouraged—and closely controlled—by both confessors and inquisitors in a period increasingly alert to the danger of false or "affected" sanctity.[30]

The success of Magdalene ecstatic iconography in the early seventeenth century, was responsible for the reappearance of an iconographic theme that had last been popular in the fourteenth and fifteenth centuries: the Last Communion of Mary Magdalene. According to *The Golden Legend*, Saint Maximin was summoned to administer the last rites to the Magdalene after her thirty years in the wilderness. She was said to have appeared miraculously in his oratory, having been transported by angels in order to receive from his hands the Body of Christ. After this rite she expired, leaving behind a suave odor *(la sainte baume)*, which persisted for seven days. The new importance of this theme after Trent lay in the figure of Saint Maximin and in the fact that the Magdalene received the host from his hands as opposed to those of hovering angels, as can be seen in Counter-Reformation renditions of the "Last Communion of Saint Mary Magdalene" by Francesco Vanni and

Domenico Pugliani. Access to the Eucharist was increasingly controlled after Trent, especially as "holy anorexics" had a tendency to try and live on a diet of consecrated wafers and water, having manipulated their confessors into giving them overly frequent Communion.[31] Although the Magdalene might have partaken of the host seven times a day while levitating in the desert, Counter-Reformation nuns and tertiaries were hardly encouraged to follow her example.

Over and above the issue of the ecstatic's menu, the second, and perhaps most important, issue addressed by representations of the Magdalene's Last Communion was that of male ecclesiastical mediation with respect to female visionary experience. Although religious women still continued to have a privileged relationship with divinity through their assiduous fasting, physical mortification, and ecstatic visions, post-Tridentine concerns regarding the propriety of conventual behavior (not to speak of the orthodoxy of religious experience) moved men as arbiters into the religious arena. Thus Saint Maximin, a secondary but important figure in the legendary biography of Mary Magdalene, takes on a new significance in the context of Counter-Reformation concern with female religious life, especially as regards the management of religious rites and the administration of the sacraments. The message of Vanni's painting could not be more clear: women may faint with ecstasy and be succored by angels, but the Host is held by male hands, which also firmly hold the reins of religious authority as God's representative on earth.

Catherine of Siena: A Curriculum Vitae in Pictures

With the iconography of Saint Catherine of Siena, the representation of female sanctity moves out of the secular arena where wives and mothers, court ladies and repentant courtesans could find a saintly model for their social identity.[32] Yet Saint Catherine was not a conventual figure but rather a saint "in the world," a Dominican tertiary whose life furnished an example of active involvement in the major religious issues of her day as well as a model of visionary sainthood whose ecstatic career was to furnish a precedent for a plethora of charismatic nuns, from the *sante vive* of the Renaissance courts to the mystic reformers of the Counter-Reformation. The importance of the life and example of Saint Catherine of Siena cannot be underestimated. She is one of the most consistently represented saints in all of the plastic arts and easily rivals the Magdalene in terms of the sheer number of images produced in central and northern Italy between 1450 and 1650.

It was the relatively new art of printmaking that most contributed to the cult of Caterina Benincasa from her death in 1380 to her canonization in 1461. In Siena and Venice, for example, small paper effigies of the saint were bought by the faithful, who created shrines of branches and garlands of flowers in their homes in annual commemoration of her death.[33] Even the most remote centers bought and circulated gaudily colored images of the saint, which represented her surrounded by her many attributes or by key episodes from her life (fig. 9). Similarly, altarpieces and frescoes multiplied in the churches of the Dominican order, where the only difference between the *beata* and the *santa* lay in the halo of luminous rays (which indicated the blessed tertiary) as opposed to the circular halo, prerogative of the canonized saint. By the middle of the fifteenth century, therefore, the iconography of Saint Catherine was well established, to the extent that, even after her canonization, it underwent essentially no changes until the early decades of the sixteenth century.

Catherine as a Dominican Heroine

In the late fifteenth and early sixteenth centuries, Saint Catherine's pictorial persona proposed an active and heroic model of female sanctity, putting as much emphasis on her writings and contribution to the spiritual library of the Catholic Church as on her historical and political role in bringing the papacy back to Rome.[34] Several fifteenth-century editions of her works contain woodcuts that represent the saint dictating her visions and thus communicating divine will to a group of scribes hard-pressed to keep up with her inspired utterings. In this same period (although she did not actually accompany the pope on the journey from Avignon) she is also represented as being a prominent member of the papal suite, actually preceding his holiness on the road to Rome (figs. 10 and 11). Images of Catherine dictating God's will or traveling with the pope provided religious women with a strong precedent that was actively followed by nuns attached to Renaissance courts. As Gabriella Zarri has demonstrated, these "living saints" modeled their religious lifestyles and political careers on their illustrious and relatively contemporary forebear Catherine of Siena.[35] It is therefore hardly a coincidence that art should have chosen Caterina Benincasa as an exemplum of female sanctity at its best, not withdrawn from the world, as was the case with the haggard, penitent Magdalene favored by the *piagnoni* movement in central and northern Italy, but actively in the world, as was the case with women in both the courts and a growing number of increasingly influential tertiary orders.

The Triumph of the Ecstatic Mode

The "active" model enjoyed a singularly brief career in the visual arts. With the decline of the *sante vive* in the early decades of the sixteenth century came the decline of Saint Catherine's political persona and a new emphasis on her mystical identity. Despite the fact that Caterina Benincasa's example continued to inspire female reformers, founders of orders, and tertiaries dedicated to charitable work, it was her career as a visionary that received expansive treatment in the imagery of the sixteenth and seventeenth centuries. Paintings such as the Bazzi frescoes in the Church of Saint Dominic in Siena place her in a timeless context, surrounded by hovering angels as she meditates, like the Magdalene, on sacred writ, her book propped on a skull, next to a crucifix and a lily (the one attribute, over and above her nun's garb, not shared by the Magdalene). The book here represented is not hers, but rather the fount of her religious revelations, and as such subtly shifts the emphasis from her role as a spiritual leader to that of a penitent mystic (fig. 12). Visions such as these accurately transmit the new tone set by religious women who, under increasingly strict enclosure and a hothouse atmosphere of asceticism, contemplation, and religious reform, tended to compensate a greater separation from the world with an increase in visionary escapism.[36]

Although never as numerous as the representations of Saint Catherine rapt in ecstasy, images of the mystical marriage of Catherine of Siena multiply in the course of the sixteenth and seventeenth centuries in direct ratio to Tridentine rulings on the sanctity of marriage and the contemporary development of "nuns in the house."[37] Marriage to Christ became more than an imitative religious mode, however; it also became a means of asserting a woman's relative autonomy with respect to both Church and family. As brides of Christ, women in both secondary and tertiary orders could attempt to circumvent priestly authority by embracing their "Husband's" spiritual authority (and that of his kin) according to a long-standing concept of conjugal relations gaining increasing weight under the elaboration of patriarchal ideology. Thus Crescenzio Gambarelli's representation of Saint Catherine reciting the Divine Office with her spiritual spouse takes place under an assembled company of saints—the "brothers" and "sisters" of Christ—presided over by the Virgin, who blesses their union, and the Holy Ghost (fig. 13). Cemented by the presence of the Heavenly Kinship, Catherine's "marriage" relaunched a socially acceptable model for religious women that could be interpreted in a variety of ways.

Despite the development of a mystical and ahistorical iconography, Saint Catherine of Siena remained a figure of primary importance for the Counter-Reformation. Ignatius of Loyola, Teresa of Avila, and Carlo Borromeo looked to her example as well as to her doctrine in their concern for the Reformation of the Church and their foundation of new religious communities. In post-Tridentine Italy, however, the most renowned female follower in Catherine's footsteps was a Florentine Carmelite nun, Maria Maddalena de'

Pazzi, whose personal and iconographic trajectories demonstrate the increasing gap between individual religious experience and official iconographic representation throughout the Counter-Reformation period.

Maria Maddalena de' Pazzi, or, How to be a Counter-Reformation Saint

The iconographic campaign in favor of the beatification and ultimate canonization of Maria Maddalena de' Pazzi provides a prime example of the visual reconstruction of a saint's biography according to the criteria of female sanctity current after the Council of Trent. Neither entirely fact nor entirely fiction, the eighty-seven sanguine sketches representing the life of Caterina de' Pazzi (in religion Maria Maddalena) attributed to Francesco Curradi and bearing the date October 4, 1610,[38] constitute a culturally stereotyped account of the life of a holy woman. Inspired by a biography of the saint written by her last confessor, Vincenzo Puccini, this remarkable series of pictures illustrates events in the saint's life that point to her "irrefutable" sanctity. Commissioned by Puccini himself as part of a campaign waged by the Florentine ecclesiastical community in tandem with the Medici and Pazzi families in view of the beatification of Florence's most recent and widely acclaimed "saint," this series of pictures nonetheless presents a noticeable difference from the more official and more public commissions executed in honor of the Carmelite nun.

A Cloistered Echo of the Active Life

In addition to the ecstatic experiences that make up the bulk of this visual biography, Maria Maddalena de' Pazzi is also represented as excelling in the ascetic practices that are indissociable from the mystical model of sanctity. Thus she aspires to humility by lying across a convent threshold and having the nuns walk on her (Fig. 14), she licks the putrescent sores of an infected nun to cure her of her affliction, and she even apes the mendicant privileges of her masculine peers by begging bread from her fellow nuns, which she then proceeds to eat on the refectory floor. Finally, as the true "proof" of sanctity is the ability of a saint to intervene in favor of the faithful after death,[39] Maria Maddalena de' Pazzi's demise is accompanied by a number of postmortem miracles: her cadaver turns its head away from a sinner "whose angelic aspect had almost fooled the Blessed Virgin," and flowers that had touched her dead body free a possessed woman from a host of malignant spirits. Implicit in her postmortem imagery are also the criteria of popular acclaim and public honor that were to weigh so heavily in favor of her beatification and canonization:

crowds are represented worshiping at her bier, and both the archbishop of Florence and the grand duke of Tuscany are depicted paying homage to her sepulcher three years after her death.

Only one of the Curradi sketches represents Maria Maddalena de' Pazzi engaged in an activity that derives more from the late-medieval and early-Renaissance model of female sanctity than from the post-Tridentine norm. Sketch number 36 shows Cardinal Alessandro de' Medici, the archbishop of Florence, with his suite, in the convent *parloir.* Behind the grille Maria Maddalena de' Medici is shown in ecstasy as she prophesies his elevation to the papacy (he was to become Pope Leo XI). This contact with the greater world and implied intervention of a nun in the affairs of the ecclesiastical state refers back to the prophetic model of female sanctity that was encouraged in the late fifteenth and early sixteenth centuries, only to be actively discouraged by the post-Tridentine institution.

Yet, as Karen-edis Barzman has pointed out, Maria Maddalena de' Pazzi actually saw herself in the role of prophet and director of Church affairs. She declared herself commanded, in a vision, to undertake a role similar to that of Catherine of Siena, and even attempted to communicate with ecclesiastical officials, the pope, and political personages within the Medici state in imitation of her model's voluminous epistolary correspondence.[40] The irony of the matter is that her letters were seldom (if ever) sent, and that both her official biography and iconographic *vita* decline any mention of career aspirations out of consonance with approved models of feminine sanctity.

"Official" Art: The Mystical Melting Pot and the Nun's Gaze

If the Curradi sketches were destined for multiple reproduction as prints with the aim of promoting the cult and prestige of Maria Maddalena de' Pazzi, they were, as such, also meant for relatively private consumption and devotional practice. Pazzi's supporters were, however, equally if not more active in the public domain, where paintings of her greater mystical moments were commissioned for the Carmelite Church of Santa Maria degli Angeli in the San Frediano district of Florence and, when the good sisters were moved to more salubrious quarters in Borgo Pinti, for their new convent, later to be dedicated to Saint Maria Maddalena de' Pazzi.

In these "official" commissions, whose purpose was to keep the popular cult of Maria Maddalena de' Pazzi active as well as maintain a high saintly profile in expectation of her beatification, Pazzi's voice and identity were further obscured by the mystical melting pot of post-Tridentine iconography and its *passe-partout* recipe for female sanctity. Thus a Curradi painting of Maria Maddalena de' Pazzi receiving the stigmata (fig. 15) shows the saint in a cloud-rimmed and timeless space. Only her personalized physiognomy and Carmelite habit distinguish her from numerous contemporary representations of Catherine of Siena, although the composure with which she receives the stigmata may seem excessively calm. This decorum, a necessary virtue in a nun whose beatification had not as yet been confirmed, was not exceptional in a period that laid as much emphasis on the need for feminine self-control as on the glorification of the mystic's inner spirituality.

The Florentines were not the only group interested in the promotion of Maria Maddalena de' Pazzi to sainthood. Urban VIII had two nieces in the Carmelite convent whose intervention in favor of their "saint" was a key factor in the Barberini family's commitment to her beatification and ultimate canonization. Barberini support also took the shape of gifts and pictures, including a significant iconographic donation in the year 1637: eight paintings destined for the convent in Borgo Pinti where the Carmelite nuns now resided.[41]

Whereas previous decorative programs in honor of Maria Maddalena de' Pazzi were oriented primarily toward the public,[42] the 1637 pictorial cycle was intended for the nun's eyes only. The original pictorial program (of which only part has survived) constituted a predominantly mystical biography of the saint. In the various lunettes, Maria Maddalena de' Pazzi is shown receiving the stigmata, receiving the crown of thorns, receiving the veil of purity from the Virgin, receiving a marriage ring from Christ (fig. 16), and so on. What is striking in this group of pictures is the fact that the saint is uniformly represented as being the passive recipient of divine honors. Absent from this cycle are any references to the saint's convent career, to her ascetic practices (she is always represented in the pink of health), or to any of her pre- or postmortem miracles, all of which had been so painstakingly recounted in the lengthy visual biography sketched by Francesco Curradi.

Was it the pope who was responsible for commissioning a mystical program for the most important room in the nun's part of the convent? Or did the nuns themselves express a wish for this sequence of saintly "events," which both explicitly and implicitly identified their *beata* with her most illustrious model and fellow Tuscan, Saint Catherine of Siena, who appears in almost every picture? The question of intention is as pertinent here as the question of a more monothematic model of saintly behavior.

Gendered and Institutional Motives for the Mystical Model

There are two primary reasons for the selective iconographic program in the cycle of eight paintings donated to the nuns, and these are the same two primary reasons that account for the predominance of mystical representations of female sanctity in the Counter-Reformation period. The first lies in there being a need for "compensations" for the contemplative life women were restricted to in post-Tridentine convents. Mystical marriage, vicarious motherhood, symbiosis with Christ, and intimate colloquies with the saintly population of heaven were all rewards that cloistered women could aspire to in their imaginative lives, not only compensating them for emotions theoretically restricted to the secular world, but also widening their potential for experience far beyond the convent walls.[43] The second reason for the mystical orientation of the Barberini donation can be attributed to the more general phenomenon of a female "specialization" in mysticism. As much as the post-Tridentine Church tried to impose on female religious orders a model lifestyle based on contemplation and prayer, unquestioning obedience, subordination to hierarchy, and charitable activity, this ideal was hardly equivalent to the male religious dichotomy between an active apostolate and the contemplative life. Furthermore, women tended to express their devotion through ascetic practices based on the denial of the body (with which they were culturally more identified than men),[44] and to reap, through these practices, a visionary reward. Add to this factor of cultural and religious conditioning the fact that the Tridentine enforcement of ecclesiastical hierarchy and strict enclosure gave an impetus to the practice of ecstatic evasion, and the causes behind the post-Tridentine multiplication of mystical nuns and tertiaries becomes self-evident.

Over and above these considerations, the humble and obedient model of female sanctity promoted in the post-Tridentine period hardly had the pictorial power of the mystical union, in which the invisible became visible, and living and breathing nuns reached intimacy with God. Visionary iconography thus continued to serve both the aspirations of enclosed female religious and the didactic concerns of the Tridentine decree of 1563 by demonstrating the privileged relationship of saints with divinity. Nevertheless, mystical iconography was doubtless intended to serve this pedagogical and devotional purpose far more than it was intended to serve as a literal model for female behavior.

Whatever the purposes (avowed and disavowed) of the mystical model may have been, it remained one of the most consistently dominant models in the religious imagination of women from the fifteenth through the seventeenth century, and that which gave them the most notoriety, be it empowering and authoritative, as with Saint Catherine of Siena, the *sante vive,* and Maria Maddalena de' Pazzi,[45] or be it ultimately scandalous and disempowering, as with the much more numerous "failed" visionaries of the Counter-Reformation.[46]

CHAPTER 10

From the Late Baroque Mystical Explosion to the Social Apostolate, 1650–1850

MARINA CAFFIERO

"In February, my aunt commissioned a miniature portrait of Luisina from a Spanish lady called Leona Darro. The poor child sat for hours with truly angelic patience. My aunt wanted us to dress her up as a nun, because she thought the habit matched the sweet expression on the child's face. But Matilda and I felt a deep sadness to see her dressed up as a miniature Saint Teresa with her eyes looking up to heaven . . . Our melancholy feelings, however, increased when we saw that the artist had painted a saint's halo around the little nun's head."[1]

Thus wrote Vittoria Giorgini Manzoni in her *Memorie* in 1851. The language is full of references to hagiographic stereotypes that derived from a long tradition, and it powerfully evokes the legend destined to grow up about the little girl, the "prodigious" Luisina. In fact, the premature death of the child, not long afterward, surrounded her with an aura of precocious saintliness, as foreshadowed in her portrait. Still, beyond any forebodings, the melancholy that affected the Manzoni sisters, Vittoria and Matilda, when they saw the little girl dressed up as a nun, reflected a decisive change of mentality and perception that occurred toward the middle of the nineteenth century, thus concluding one phase in the history of sanctity and women's religious life in the modern world and introducing a new one.

The timespan of this chapter, which runs from 1650 to 1850, signals two significant turning points. At one extremity, with the end of the Thirty Years' War and with worsening economic conditions—even as the regulatory process concerning sainthood and canonizations set in motion by Urban VIII was arriving at its full definition—there was a reinforcement of, but also the first signs of cracks in, the social, cultural, and Counter-Reformational order.[2] At the other, and besides the obvious importance of the date 1870, when Italy completed its unification, the very first years of Pius IX's pontificate marked a watershed in the relationship between Church and society—the triumph of intransigent ideological attitudes toward the modern world and a clearly defined vision of sanctity and the religious life.[3]

Within this long period, which hardly coincides with that which historiography traditionally assigns to the "modern era," there are internal subdivisions. In defining the history of sanctity and women's religious life—normatively, institutionally, and on the level of representations and behavior—three phases were decisive, and each contains a further specific chronology. First, there are the years from the mid-seventeenth century to the beginning of the eighteenth; second, from the first decades of the eighteenth century until the 1770s; and, finally, the period between 1770 and the mid-nineteenth century. All of these mark further steps in the complex path along which the female model of Christian perfection was opened up to the acceptance of the lay condition, while the image of the nun underwent a deep and definitive transformation.

Un-Quiet Women: Crisis of the Counter-Reformation

The Monastic Model

In the mid-seventeenth century, little girls dressed as nuns would have aroused no embarrassment among their relatives. The monastic model was by far the dominant one proposed by ecclesiastical institutions for women seeking Christian perfection. Among the "Christian people," convents retained their reputation at a fairly high level and were well regarded. Indeed, halfway through the century, when the dread effects of the plague of 1656–57, which struck various Italian regions, began to pass, some areas actually saw an increase in women's monastic vocations, as well as a renewed impulse toward new foundations.[4] Evidence for a correspondence between this demographic point (a rising population) and the concrete reality of this life choice for women comes not only from the obvious, given that in the second half of the seventeenth century the rare canonizations involved only nuns and not laywomen, but also from clear indications that in the alternatives for women's conditions—as wives or widows—the models of a perfect and saintly life were based on the cloister.[5]

Humility, obedience, dependence on the confessor, intense devotions, a concealment of the eventual signs of sanctity: all these were the characteristics that show up in the period's treatises on the "saintly nun." The principal concern was to keep mystical urges—which in the early seventeenth century had again taken a strong hold in women's convents—under strict control and to divert these urges into safe institutional channels.[6] The second half of the century was deeply marked by tensions between the institutional version of sanctity—papal teaching, now firmly grounded on the criterion of the heroic nature of moral virtues and a parallel downgrading of the extraordinary manifestations and charismatic gifts that characterized the mystical model of the Middle Ages—and concrete social practice, specifically, the various models that escaped the behavioral norm and the Counter-Reformational codes that regulated the discipline of monastic life.[7]

Treatises addressed to nuns contained an image of the "perfect nun," increasingly that rational, peaceful image, free of excess (whether of penance or of mysticism), favoring devotion rather than contemplation, which was to prevail in the next century. Despite institutional diffidence toward women's mystical experiences, the convents pullulated with ecstatics, and women's social experience was governed by a religious model in which visionary and charismatic experiences played a dominant role.

The expressions of amorous possession that accompanied the penitential and expiatory longing for suffering (in memory and in imitation of Christ's suffering) were alike in all the mystics. To love was to suffer. Love and a longing for suffering were declined together in the mystical discourse of the cloistered women, most of whom were inspired by the Franciscan model and especially the Spanish Carmelite model. The latter, diluting Teresa's apostolic activity and exalting her ecstatic experience instead, was the dominant female example in the late Baroque period. The voluptuousness of "pure suffering" was obsessively sought out by the Capuchin nun from Città di Castello, Veronica Giuliani (1660–1727), and divided between her stigmata and her many celestial "marriages," each duly noted with accurate care. Quietist influences and the unitive spirituality of pure love, by contrast, informed the penitential anxiety of the Benedictine nun from Bassano, Giovanna Maria Bonomo (1606–1670), and the aristocratic Poor Clare Capuchin from Brescia, Maria Maddalena Martinengo di Barco (1687–1737).[8]

As is indicated by their names in religion, these women all shared a harsh self-mortification of the body that led them to a form of spirituality centered on the humanity of Jesus and his suffering, wounded body and to devotional practices closely linked to the Passion. They made a cult of Christ's wounds, the cross, and his Sacred Heart, the last recently introduced through the visions of the French Visitation sister Margaret-Mary Alacoque. From the end of the seventeenth century through the next century and beyond, such forms of piety—with their expiatory meaning, but also with the easy emotional and affective external manifestations of their amorous raptures and their victim sublimations—were destined to become, in and out of the cloister, a stable aspect of female devotion. Marian devotions grew in tandem. Here, too, alongside the human aspects of the Virgin, such as Mary's role in the Passion (the *Mater Dolorosa*) and her bodily or sexual features—virginity, motherhood, childbirth, suckling—the age-old controversy over her Immaculate Conception brought about a parallel shift toward her divinization and dehumanization.[9]

Sanctity and Aristocracy: A "Symbolic" Capital

The veritable implosion of mysticism within the cloister walls may be considered the reverse side of the better-known phenomenon of forced vocations, which at the halfway mark of the seventeenth century found their bitterest criticism in the writings of the Venetian Benedictine nun Arcangela Tarabotti. Her *Inferno monacale*, or *Monastic Hell*, unmasked the various familial and patrimonial strategies employed by the upper classes: in obedience to the system of patrilinear inheritance, young women who fell outside the restricted marriage market were immediately packed off to a convent.[10]

Not all monastic vocations, however, were forced, just as not all nuns were simply pawns in the hands of others. Hagiographic literature offers many examples of early vocations, some manifest even in early childhood. Such was the case, for instance, with Veronica Giuliani, whose first visions dated from when she was three and who, at age four, was giving milk to the Holy Child; or with Giovanna Maria Bonomo, who made her vow of virginity at ten. Other accounts tell us of pregnancies and deliveries of the mothers of future saints rich in indications of a monastic vocation, as in the case of Isabella (Maria Crocifissa) Tomasi. Indeed, if childhood is the time in which sainthood is first revealed, then that state of being but a "little child," and of maintaining a constant spiritual childhood in conversations with Jesus, becomes among the mystics one of the preferred forms of body language through which to express surrender and union. The nexus that bound together childhood and sanctity seems to have reflected the contemporary transformation in the perception of childhood into a positive period in life.[11]

Beyond what might seem to be the usual and repetitive stereotypes of hagiography, determined to show the precocity of divine election, it is interesting to note that saintly nuns actively engaged in the choices they had made fitted within the selfsame social and cultural logic as their sisters forced into the religious life. This followed logically on the process of aristocratization and the closing down of the upper classes that took place in Italian society under Spanish rule in the Baroque period. The mystics who crowded the monasteries corresponded to the aristocratic cloistered nuns in general, as the former did to the latter's social motivations as well: affirming or raising family prestige. Both the older and the more recent nobility founded new convents into which the women of their families could be introduced, because these created a "symbolic" capital every bit as relevant as patrimonial capital.[12]

The path of family sanctity was an effective means of legitimization and ennoblement, especially for the new nobility. But young women from the aristocracy or the upper bourgeoisie, who entered convents bearing the behavior, values, and cultural baggage of their upper-class world, found in mystical spirituality an exceptional way in which to express themselves as individuals: first and foremost through writing. Even in the rhetorical guises of convent culture, imposed by the stereotypes of feminine sanctity, and despite being subjected to the control and interference of spiritual directors— this was another of those relationships in which the clash between theological knowledge and mystical science was played out in the clash between male and female—the edifice of writing built within the world of the cloister in this period was gigantic and reflected its learned and aristocratic nature. Equally vast was the tapestry of reading, which often extended even to prohibited Quietist texts.[13]

Chiara della Passione Colonna: An Aristocratic Nun in Baroque Rome

Among the biographies of the founding saints one would expect a tone somewhat less steeped in the contemplative experience. In reality, however, because it was still the example of Saint Teresa that largely conditioned the direction of new monastic foundations, one often finds among female founders a fusion of mystical vocation and active life, the latter being vital for the organization and guidance of new communities. An exemplar of this fusion, Chiara della Passione (1610–1675), whose name in the world was Vittoria Colonna, is a particularly illuminating instance of the aristocratic model of convent sanctity. A perfection of life and ardent devotion were in her united, as her biographer wrote, to a great lady's capacity "to sanctify the manners of the time" into a sort of code of Christian good manners, in which the Christianization of the cream of the nobility was seen as an essential component of sanctity itself.[14]

Her *vita,* published in 1681 and revised and reprinted in 1708 by the priest Ignazio Orsolini, located the figure of Chiara within a dense web of relationships with aristocratic power, enriched by an equally rich latticework of sanctity. Even through the mediation of Orsolini in his role as hagiographer, Chiara's progress from noblewoman to austere penitent, embellished with mystical gifts, intensely devoted to charity and to the founding of religious establishments, was interwoven with the analogous lives of two other important figures of the Roman nobility, Livia Vipereschi and Camilla Orsini Borghese. But it was chiefly within her own pious and illustrious lineage that

Chiara found solid signs of sanctity: within her own family in the distant figure of the Blessed Margaret Colonna (d. 1280), in her blood relative Carlo Borromeo, her father's uncle; and in her spiritual adviser Philip Neri. In the daughter of Philip, duke of Paliano and high constable of the kingdom of Naples, and in Lucrezia Tomacelli, all related to her, she found an austere and penitential spirituality flourishing within an ancient family from the feudal aristocracy. The family found itself, however, in some difficulties and it sought on the one hand a fresh symbolical legitimation and on the other solid matrimonial alliances with the more recently formed pontifical elite, which would permit the family to recover its former standing.

The family's two daughters, Vittoria and Anna—the one with a reputation for saintliness that reflected well on the family, not to speak of the influence she exercised on the spiritual life and the popes of her time, the other, the future wife of Taddeo Barberini, the nephew of Urban VIII—were knowing participants in a double project. Her illustrious birth and her powerful family connections and patronage ran through Chiara's life and that of her foundation, in which these aristocratic relations were solidly established. It was Urban VIII himself who helped the young woman overcome her family's objections to her monastic vocation and to her proposing to enter the oldest, the poorest, and the most rigid Carmelite convent in Rome, that of Saint Egidis.

The life of the new monastery of Regina Coeli, founded by Chiara in 1654, developed under the same aristocratic and then royal auspices, constantly given material help and protective guidance by the now widowed Anna. It soon became a lodestar for religious life in Rome and was chosen as a refuge by Christina of Sweden. And while Chiara's sanctity powerfully infected her nearest relations—her two sisters and her father, but also her erstwhile betrothed and his parents, who themselves took up the religious life—it was the theme of nobility, now concealed and therefore all the more meritorious and praiseworthy, that was evoked by her hagiographer, even regarding her professed name in religion. That name in fact united two things: a total disregard of the splendor of her rich and noble lineage, and a total annihilation of the self through her participation in Christ's Passion, the painful signs of which she bore on her own body.

Nevertheless, the *vita* put great weight on her rigid observance of the monastic rule and the way she imposed it even when faced with the traditional pressures of her family or those of the highly placed who sought to restrict the autonomy of the convents. Thus Chiara's firmness seemed to run counter to the evolution of a century in which, to face the growing economic difficulties of the convents, the search for dowries had limited recruitment to the better-off families, inducing many convents to yield to a certain loosening of the harshness of the rule.[15] In contrast to the other major Carmelite convent in Rome, that of the Incarnation, sponsored by Urban VIII and well enmeshed in the patronage of the Barberinis, in which the aristocratic nature of the nuns was openly displayed, the apparent concealment of the noble character of Regina Coeli and its pursuit·of sanctity made it possible for private mystical experience, when well supported by its aristocratic origins and relations, to become a reforming and "politically active" force, capable of solid and autonomous government.

Monopolies of Sanctity and Sanctity "Unmasked"

The rise of individualism and the subjective element in the religious experience of the latter half of the seventeenth century can hardly be said to have been confined to the cloister. The general context was one of serious troubles, of instability caused by war and the plague of 1656–57, which struck a large part of the peninsula, and of a deep recession in the economy. All of these factors favored the spread of various forms of religious enthusiasm and popular mysticism: genuine nests of subversion of the prevailing ethical and political models. They came into being as expressions of unrest and unease toward both the ecclesiastical order that emerged from the Counter-Reformation and the very social structure which sanctioned it.

Within that larger context which Paul Hazard called "the Crisis of the European conscience," the process of breaking with and challenging the rigid centralizing and disciplinary codes imposed by the post-Tridentine period also involved sainthood. On the one hand, the persistence of the Pelagini sect and its eventual merging with Quietism, even after the repression of the 1650s, was one aspect of the flowering of "spiritual" movements led by laypersons and especially women, which assumed a strongly confrontational position toward the doctrinal and normative institutional definitions. On the other hand, precisely because of the widespread participation of women in these movements (as visionaries, ecstatics, and even "theologians")—participation that eventually led to the formation of the innumerable women's conventicles, both cloistered and otherwise, which flourished around the Quietist Miguel de Molinos (1640–1697) and his followers—the problem of women's "excessive" devotion was a troublesome one, for it was capable of subverting the Tridentine male monopoly of the sacred.[16]

Even before the great anti-Quietist repression of the end of the century, the gradual harshening of the techniques of control over individual and autonomous expressions of religiosity and the increasing polarization between positive and negative models of sanctity showed that behavior perceived as suspect by the religious and political authorities was widespread in the fabric of society and was far from fitting the approved paradigm of Christian perfection. A strong light on the tensions of the period is provided by recent studies on the conflict between real and "feigned" sanctity.[17] During the crisis of the Counter-Reformation, women's religiosity and the demand for female sainthood, spilling out of the controlled cloister and institutional security, sought to break the monastic, educated, aristocratic monopoly of Christian perfection as well as the mediation of male authority.

In the many surviving inquisitorial *processi* (trials) of pretended sanctity—most of them affecting women, for pretense was considered a specifically feminine quality—the criteria employed to determine "true" sanctity seem quite the contrary of the official norms. The cases concerned prophetic and charismatic powers and marked a renewal of the sainthood model offered by Catherine of Siena. Again, they revealed the presence and support offered by ecclesiastical disciples, but it was above all the social provenance of the women accused of feigned sanctity or rejected in their desire to find a free, autonomous road to sainthood that was revealing. Through them we can understand the unease and tension these cases expressed as well as the reasons why they were repressed. The fact that most of these women were laywomen or tertiaries, that they were relatively uneducated and mostly belonged to the lower middle classes, that they were therefore not grouped under the protection and legitimation of a religious institution or of a good lineage, is a clear sign of social conflict.

The visionary and prophetic mysticism of these "irregulars," often frustrated in their desire to become nuns, expressed both protest and dissent but also new religious expectations that threw the rigid, global order of the Counter-Reformation into crisis. Simulation, in this context as in the political, became the secret language in which resistance to the abstract rules imposed by the authorities expressed.[18] The conflict brings us back to the aristocratic nature of convents and to the mystique of birth and blood that justified social but also symbolic hierarchies. Only within the convent could exceptional and charismatic spirituality be anointed with orthodoxy; the filter of institutional control had to be present.

The "Virile" Woman: Model of the Devout Wife

In the end, the prevailing monastic ideal also conditioned the behavior demanded of laywomen: wives, widows, and the unmarried. The high praise accorded the monastic state, if it brought about a substantial devaluation of marriage, accentuating its more painful and burdensome aspects (as was evident from the devotional literature and preaching manuals),[19] obviously did not stop ecclesiastical teaching and morality from paying close heed to married life. In these decades, the role of the wife was slowly being outlined: she was "the Church's emissary to her husband and a transmitter of virtue," thus anticipating the definitive line that was to prevail in the ensuing centuries and right up to the twentieth century.[20] As the Jesuit Paul Segneri wrote in 1679: "The sanctity of women, I don't know how, has such power that it is often transmitted to the husband, even the wicked."[21] Still, in harmony with the strongly patriarchal and patrilinear restructuring of the family and relations between the sexes under way during the Counter-Reformation, the virtues held out to the ideal wife—humility, silence, modesty, purity to the point of chastity, devotion, respect, and above all total submission to her husband—form a constellation of wifely qualities that differed little from the virtues specific to monastics. This version of wifely virtue was again vigorously re-stated at the beginning of the seventeenth century.

The biography published in 1716 by the Jesuit father Antonio Maria Bonucci, the *Istoria della vita di Bianca Teresa Massei Buonvisi,* was a significant event on a number of levels. Bonucci was a prominent Jesuit hagiographer of the late Baroque and his work is a perfect example of the "devout" and Jesuit model of female sanctity. Alien to any form of mysticism and tormented religiosity, rather ascetic and partial to good works and charity, he argued that genuinely virtuous behavior was to be found in concealing signs of sanctity.[22] He called for a dissimulated sanctity, a sort of simulation of nonsanctity, which again confirms, even in the positive example offered by its exemplum, the identification of a language and rhetoric of pretense with women.

The "servant of God" Bianca Teresa Massei Buonvisi (1657–1714), a wealthy and aristocratic lady from Lucca, who converted after many years of the pomp and worldliness associated with one of her rank to a life of withdrawal and austerity, was a perfect example of sainthood sought out in the world by an "illustrious woman," one marked by her absolute retirement from the world, from luxury as from her personal affections, and even from her family duties. Her refusal of the rules of a worldly, aristocratic life, and her choice of an austere and near-monastic life did not, however, make her refuse or feel embarrassed by her patrimony or by the relation of money and saint-hood, nor did it equate sanctity with poverty, a nexus that would reappear later.[23] The positive value of money used by aristocrats for religious and charitable purposes is fundamental to nearly all portrayals of lay, aristocratic sanctity and highlights a difference from the monastic ideal.

The explicit models in this instance, in addition to the saintly, noble, married women of the Middle Ages—as noted by the references to Francesca of Rome, the two queens Elizabeth, of Hungary and Portugal, and Bridget of Sweden—are above all the rich and patrician Roman women clustered around

Saint Jerome. Pride of place here went to Saint Paula, on whose life Massei's is based. Such *exampla* show other women reading her story the outlines of a form of sanctity for noblewomen, one directed either toward an active life, full of charity and welfare, or toward the assiduous practice of the Marian or Eucharistic devotions so dear to the Jesuits. The Jesuit model had broad and symbolic significance, by means of which such women could distance themselves from the external and profane emblems of rank but not from rank itself and its social responsibilities.

When it comes to the relations between Massei and her husband, her biographer is evasive. He refers to their harmony and mutual respect but flinches at accepting sexuality. The old model of the chaste marriage resurfaced. The fleeting appearance of her nonetheless numerous children and the total irrelevance of her duties to her household and house offered an ambiguous picture. In one way, as contemporary devotional literature pointed out, the invasive ecclesiastical guide and the excessive religiosity of such women risked subverting the proper family hierarchy and weakened their womanly subordination to their husbands; in another way, family ties, and the double role as wife and mother, seemed quite secondary, for the notion of spiritual motherhood outweighed that of the biological. Through constant recall of the classical model of the widowed matrons of antiquity, it was the virtue of widows rather than of wives that seemed to offer the best chance of accepting female sainthood outside the monastic and virginal status.

"Architects" of the Public Good: The Widows

According to the writers of moral treatises, widows had a greater disposition for spiritual matters than wives, for the latter were worldly, and the "precious" liberty that the former acquired on the deaths of their husbands allowed them to become "teachers of Christian virtues to the female sex." In a curious late-seventeenth-century manual addressed to widows, Abbot Carlo Bartolomeo Piazza, the well-known author of many books of ethical maxims, went so far as to affirm that "the true widow thinks of Godly matters . . . while a wife thinks how to please her husband."[24]

In the second half of the century, widows of recognized sanctity, such as Ludovica Albertoni (1473–1533), beatified in 1671 by Clement X (Altieri) as part of a politicoreligious operation to raise the prestige of the families of the Roman civic nobility, or living women with a reputation of sanctity, such as Camilla Orsini Borghese (1603–1685), contributed to the glorification of the authority, credit, and power of their original families or of those into which they had married.[25] The political and symbolic enterprise within which the founding of monasteries or conservatories was justified was not modified. On the whole, the ideal life to which widows aspired was still largely monastic, and many of them in fact did make their vows.

Piazza's little work, published in Rome in 1708, does seem, however, to open up a new direction in the Catholic world, and it offers some interesting insights on the complex marriage between the old and the new. Both the dedication to Maria Casimira, the widow of the Polish king Jan Sobieski, the heroic liberator of a Vienna from the Turks in 1683, and the examples it offers of saints and "true" widows—from the illustrious disciples of Jerome and the Roman patrician Galla down to more recent queens, princesses, and noblewomen—almost all of them carefully chosen from the narrow circles of the highest nobility, once again reinforced the customary elitist conception of feminine sanctity. Virtuous nobility merely confirmed noble blood; dynastic or noble sanctity, as tradition required, was conjoined with widowhood. While the saintly queen and consort remained a rare figure, for royal and noble widows the decision not to remarry was essential to achieving sainthood. This in turn reflected not just the rigid social requirements that succession and the patrimonial strategies of families—to ensure the recovery of dowries—imposed on widows, but also that ideal of feminine perfection which put so high a value on chastity and virginity.[26] The "true" widow, the one who refused a second, and frowned-upon, marriage, might as well have been kept to the standard of virginity.

Nonetheless, there are other elements in Piazza's writings that seem to go beyond the traditional formulation and open out onto an image of female sanctity more compatible with the lay and married state. Once he moved past his ritual homage to the established model of widowhood, the freedom and autonomy of the widow was no longer to be feared, as in the past, because it might lead to the break-up of a family's patrimony, but could instead be praised and valued for its positive potential for religion and ecclesiastical institutions, even outside the cloister. Often in contrast to classical devotional literature, and more in keeping with the ever greater value assigned to a woman's role as the moral guide of her family, the trend in the post-Tridentine Church was to conceive of widowhood as an autonomous road to sainthood. Where once the image of the widow was that of a woman who, having earned her sanctity by patiently suffering the intemperies and ill-treatment of her husband, was finally able to flee behind the high walls of a convent, the "active" widow who acquired merit by her autonomous conduct of domestic life and by rearing and educating her children came increasingly to the fore.

The sign of this shift was a new insistence in behavior manuals on the social role of widows, on their expertise as "architects" of the public good through the "civil, moral and Christian education of their children."[27] "Strong, virile" widows became teachers and guides, in family life as in public affairs. Most important, they took the places of their deceased husbands in that all-important paternal prerogative, the moral and religious instruction of children and the transmission of a precise code of good Christian manners. Catholic morality now increasingly extended this role to mothers as well. Almost a symbol of this slow shift of roles, a foretaste of the definitive transfer of the educational task from fathers to mothers that came to fulfillment between the eighteenth and nineteenth centuries, Piazza's treatise closes with a synthesis of the advice offered to fathers drawn from the most important of all Counter-Reformation treatises on education—the *Tre libri dell'educazione christiana de i figliuoli* by Cardinal Silvio Antoniano (1584)—which Piazza addressed directly to "the practical use of those saintly, wise women, and virtuous Widows," the mothers.

The Age of Lights and the Antimystical Revolution

Stopping Women's Fantasies

The new valuation of a woman's role outside convent walls was part of a broader movement of changes and adjustments that, from the end of the seventeenth century to the early years of the eighteenth, involved both Italy and Europe as a whole, leading to new demands, a new sensibility, and a fresh climate. As the era of the Counter-Reformation drew to a close and the long Spanish hegemony over Italy was replaced by a new territorial and political order in an Italy ever more open to the circulation of European ideas, new critical attitudes, free to roam in every domain of knowledge, new cultural and religious anxieties, and a restless desire for change began to break down the old, established order.

In the world of religion, the Quietist phenomenon was the most obvious expression of ferment; and the condemnations of the Quietist leader Molinos in 1687, and then of François de Fénelon's *Maxims of the Saints* in 1699, symbolized a turning point, marking the defeat of mysticism and of the late Baroque contemplative life. The transition from the Counter-Reformation to the Enlightenment was marked by the renewal and consolidation of the new juridical definition of sainthood and of canonization proceedings set in motion by Urban VIII and culminating in the well-known work of Cardinal Prospero Lambertini (the future Benedict XIV), *De servorum Dei beatificatione et beatorum canonizatione*.[28] The need for more effective institutional control over every form of religious manifestation, especially those of a mystical-visionary character, fundamentally feminine, was combined with a will to impose once and for all a conception of sainthood anchored to the objective and verifiable criterion of heroic virtue. It was an altogether ascetic, rational, sober, and active vision of religious experience, and it corresponded fully to the idea of "regulated devotion" imposed by the new cultural climate.

The antimystical triumph of the early eighteenth century went in tandem with the evolution of hagiographic literature. The rational, critical, and scientific requirements that underpinned the erudition and philological research in the fields of ecclesiastical history and hagiography of the Maurist school and the Bollandist *Acta sanctorum* rapidly reached Italy.[29] There they were echoed not only by the work of Cardinal Lambertini but by much of the work of Ludovico Antonio Muratori and the whole rigorist-Jansenist school of scholarship. The battle over hagiography and hagiographic method, finally won by those who favored a "regulated" religiosity—one purged, that is, of excessive devotion and simple beliefs—was one of the pivots on which turned the projected reform of the Church and the return to the purity of its Christian origins initiated by Catholic reform groups.

This shift in religion and culture imposed greater caution and verification on hagiography and created rigorous new criteria for identifying sainthood. Women's religiosity and the mystical and visionary style they favored, now singled out as the fruit of unsettled fantasies, was naturally the most affected.[30] An antifemale distrust was part and parcel of erudite and scientific ecclesiastical reaction to Baroque piety in general and to the religious and devotional choices of the Franciscans and Jesuits in particular. After long debates during the first half of the eighteenth century, it found expression in condemnations of various female visionary experiences, all powerfully backed by the Jesuits and all with specific devotional implications. First to be condemned were the revelations of the French Visitation nun Margaret-Mary Alacoque, fundamental to the cult of the Sacred Heart of Jesus; then came the turns of the Bavarian Franciscan Crescentia of Kaufbeuren, who had a particular, feminine devotion to the Holy Ghost, and the Spanish Franciscan Maria de Agreda, whose celebrated treatise *Mystica Ciudad de Dios* (1670) contained revelations of the Virgin that were used to push the disputed devotion to the Immaculate Conception.[31] Muratori had harshly attacked the "indiscreet cult" of Mary, inveighing against the "abusive" attribution to Mary of the role of indispensable mediatrix of graces and the current practice of the "bloody vow" made by the faithful in defense of the belief in the Immaculate Conception, which was not yet established dogma—attacks that attracted a polemical reply from Alphonsus Liguori.[32]

In this new climate, the battle against female saintly excess was also waged to block suspect canonizations. In 1745 Cardinal Angelo Maria Querini, bishop of Brescia, turned down the urgent solicitations of the abbess of the local Capuchin convent, who sought to advance the beatification of the mystic Mary Magdalene Martinengo.[33] In fact, she was recognized officially only in 1900 in a vastly different cultural and religious context. But antifeminism and critical revision wasted not much time before launching an attack on older cults and far more firmly established sainthood.

A Hagiographic Battle: The Legend of Blessed Clare of Rimini

The hagiographic debate, as we have seen, played a major role in the cultural shift of the eighteenth century. This emerged powerfully in the work the Rimini scholar Count Giuseppe Garampi, destined for a brilliant Curia career culminating in a cardinal's hat, wrote about the Blessed Clare of Rimini. This work was one of the finest fruits of the revisionist criticohistorical erudition in ecclesiastical history and hagiography that ensued from the Muratorian school.[34] Garampi's *Memorie ecclesiastiche appartenenti all'istoria e al culto della Beata Chiara di Rimini,* published in Rome in 1755 and not by chance dedicated to the Lambertini pope, is a good example of the systematic destruction of a doubtful hagiographic tradition, one that when seen through the eyes of "healthy criticism" of sources and "solid piety" was both "popular" and "monkish" in origin and historically uncertain.

Clare Agolanti (1280–1326), a rich young noblewoman, was widowed early.[35] Converted after a period of worldly dissipation, she dedicated herself to a life of extremely severe penance, which was rewarded by considerable mystical gifts. She had long been the object of a local cult. In the latter part of the seventeenth century her saintly fame was given a fresh impetus by miracles and several published Lives. Her cult had been officially sanctioned by what was called "equipollent" beatification: that is, one equivalent to a beatification. When in 1751 Clare's intercession worked a new miracle, this offered a chance to repropose the definitive recognition of her sanctity, but Garampi's book, though not hostile to the cult, eventually denied her this status.

What in fact happened was that Garampi, basing himself quite explicitly on Muratori, set out to publish, together with a scrupulous philological and historical commentary, an anonymous fourteenth-century manuscript that contained the earliest *vita* of the Blessed Clare, had served as the keystone of the cult, and had been the basis for all of the numerous seventeenth- to eighteenth-century biographies. By providing an exact interpretation of certain facts contained in the codex and rejecting others as untrue Garampi managed to finish off the old belief that Clare had been a Franciscan tertiary, had then joined the Poor Clares, and eventually had founded the monastery of Santa Maria degli Angeli in Rimini. He argued that she had been no more than a Beguine or *pinzochera* and therefore a laywoman who, though she wore a religious habit and devoted her life to penitence, poverty, and devotion, was bound by neither rule nor vows.

He scrupulously added that Clare had kept her distance from the "dangerous heresies" common to Beguines in those times; and in homage to the antipauperistic and utilitarian sensibilities of his own time, Garampi also emphasized the fact that Clare's poverty had led her neither to deplorable idleness nor to begging, but rather to earn her own bread by hard work. Nonetheless, it was obvious from her irregular, nonmonastic status, from the risk of heresy she courted, and from the denial of the prestigious role of founder that a blow had been dealt to her claim to sanctity. Indeed, even the extreme physical penances she inflicted on herself were the subject of veiled criticism: they had been exhibited in public rather than in the privacy of a convent cell. No reference was made to the prophecies, visions, or miracles on which the manuscript spent so many of its pages. Even her status as a member of the noble Agolanti family was called into question and no importance was ascribed to her life before her conversion or to her relations with her husband, even though these were extensively described in the codex.

An indication of just how aware the author was of his contentiousness was the harsh criticism he meted out to previous hagiographers of Clare at the close of his book. Of them he said that he had taken no account of their works because the facts they reported had not "been examined with sufficiently critical an attitude."[36] Among the authors scolded by Garampi was the Jesuit Antonio Maria Bonucci, a prolific biographer of saintly women who in 1718 had published in Rome an *Istoria dell'ammirabile Vita della Beata Chiara degli Agolanti*. It is by comparing and contrasting the Baroque fantasy of Bonucci with the austere and rigorous work of Garampi—which reflected both Rome's clear determination to control canonizations and revisionist historians' ambition to transform religious models and forms of piety, to make them less "easy" and "feeling"—that we can get a full understanding of the extent of the cultural and religious shift of the eighteenth century.

From its very title, Bonucci's *Istoria* unhesitatingly repeated all those bits of information about Clare that Garampi was later to challenge. Accentuating his stereotypical account of her worldly, dissolute life and her ensuing turnabout due to her conversion, described with a surfeit of detail not to be found in the fourteenth-century codex, and thus totally invented, Bonucci built up a sort of sacred narrative. In its own way attractive to a large public, it focused on the conversion of a sinful woman into a virile example of Christian virtues. Her obedience to her husband after her conversion; her chaste marriage; the loathsome penances and mortifications of the flesh, such as swallowing a live toad; the apparitions of the Virgin and Jesus; the ecstasies that followed after six months without food; levitations and miracles—these made up a sort of devout romance of Clara's sanctity. Bonucci's tale was rhetorical, fantastic, and exaggerated, and the power of his narrative and his imaginative religiosity, which undoubtedly made his book more attractive and enjoyable than

Garampi's elitist and rigorous approach, tended to emphasize precisely the legendary, charismatic, and visionary aspects of the Baroque saint that the new hagiography sought to set aside or refute.[37]

A Jansenist Collection of Saints' Lives

This new, Italian, eighteenth-century, rationalist, and anti-Baroque world created a void in hagiography, one of the literary genres most read in convents and by laywomen, even the less literate. It fell to philo-Jansenist hagiographers to fill the gap. The educated clergy and the intellectual elites felt a growing dissatisfaction with the hagiography of the previous centuries, with its background of prodigies and legends that now seemed so fragile and unreliable as to be useless. We owe to the Oratorian Carlo Ignazio Massini—author of two important *Raccolte di vite de'santi,* published in Rome in 1763 and 1767 with a success that lasted through the nineteenth century—a curious and little-known *Raccolta* in a specialized genre, dedicated exclusively to women saints and addressed to a precise female audience: that of nuns, still identified as belonging to the most privileged state on the path to perfection. Starting with its presentation, the *Vite di sante vergini e di alcune ss. fondatrici di monasterj e congregazioni di religiose,* drawn from his two earlier works and published in Rome in 1768, laid down the scientific criteria that governed the author's work.[38] The most startling thing in this collection is the massive presence of hagiographic profiles of virgin martyrs, many of them not well known, from the early centuries of Christianity. Of 161 biographies, 73 in fact deal with virgin martyrs. This Jansenist exaltation of the early Church—a time when the presence of women and their role had been vital, and a mythical golden age to which it behooved the Church to return through an institutional and disciplinary reform—showed a clear Jansenist concern for women's sanctity but also a limited interest in the female presence in less remote times. In fact, from the fifteenth century to the eighteenth, this book included only 15 women saints, chosen among the best known and most important.

The antimystical stance of this work—its insistence on the austerity of the saints' behavior, far removed from any penitential excess; its emphasis on constant prayer not pervaded by contemplative anxieties, on work, on charitable action on behalf of the poor, on tending the sick, on teaching girls and founding new female religious institutions in which the founders showed an energetic capacity to manage and organize—revealed a new concept of the nun, now directed toward the choice of an active life, an external apostolate, and an involvement in society. This new tendency was to grow parallel to the old cloistered model.

Alongside its virgins, the collection also contained mothers and widows, which suggests that though the celibate life was superior to the married, sainthood could be achieved by women of all conditions; it sketched a new vision, already outlined in Catholic treatises, of a more tender and affectionate conjugal society.[39] Thus, within a still strongly elitist and noble picture of feminine sanctity, two images were being formed: that of the new nun, and that of the "saintly" mother, the latter eventually a keystone of Catholic ideology.

Out of the Convent: The Maestre Pie and the New Forms of Religious Life

By the late 1700s there was a widespread conviction that perfection could be achieved in all conditions of life. This belief, if on the one hand it opened up accessible paths to sainthood, enabling the ambit of female sanctity to extend beyond the cloister, on the other drew a different picture and offered a different role for the monastic condition. Enlightened Catholicism, the rigorist, philo-Jansenist tendency, and a "benignist" theology inclined to benevolence combined, during the eighteenth century, in a redefinition of the ideal nun. The "Spanish" model, based on contemplation, was replaced by the "French," one, deeply committed to an active life. Even in the tractarian literature, the picture of the perfect nun freed itself of its seventeenth-century typology to reach its high point in the well-received image depicted in 1760 by Alphonsus de' Ligouri in *La vera sposa di Gesù Cristo cioè la monaca santa*.[40] External devotion, sometimes simple, Marian piety, moderate penance, mental prayer, daily Communion, spiritual readings, all of this indicates a level, calm life as far removed from rigoristic scruples as from mystical anxiety, one that could be led not just by nuns but by "all kinds of persons."

In reality, the very idea of the excellence of the cloistered state—the convent as "paradise on earth," as manuals addressed to nuns would have it—though it had not yet disappeared, was being chipped away. Enlightenment and jurisdictionalist attacks on a "useless" regular clergy had their effect.[41] Before the suppression of convents and before nuns were permitted to secularize themselves, these attacks focused on the violent debate over monastic dowries, which was sweeping the peninsula. In response to this crisis in traditional female monasticism, expressed in the general eighteenth-century decline in vocations, a new form of religious organization, involving the founding of new institutes and uncloistered women's communities, came into being. With its social apostolate and its activity in the outside world, this new movement, though somewhat later than analogous experiments in France, constituted a break with Counter-Reformation logic. Indeed, it could be said that by responding better to the religious aspirations and social needs caused by the profound transformations of the modern world, it strikingly anticipated the characteristics of women's religious congregations dedicated to teaching and various forms of social service, which flourished with the Restoration.

The lay congregation of the Maestre Pie, or "Pious Schoolmistresses," was born on the cusp of the eighteenth century in little communes in the upper Lazio countryside and quickly extended to Rome and the rest of the region, spreading in the next hundred years to most of the adjacent regions. The Maestre Pie Filippini e Venerini, called thus after the founders of the two branches, Lucia Filippini (1672–1732) and Rosa Venerini (1656–1728), were a new form of women's congregation that broke with the past in terms of the presence and position of women in the church and in society and moved well past the post-Tridentine model of a cloistered religious life for women. The Maestre Pie were tiny nuclei, often only two or three lay teachers, who ran free, popular schools for girls. By their activity and their significant freedom of movement in the countryside and in town outside the enclosed and controlled places destined for females, these schoolmistresses challenged the social prohibitions against spatial and social mobility for "single" women, a group to whom these new communities offered a social outlet and an alternative to the traditional wife-mother or nun roles, but one also officially recognized by the ecclesiastical hierarchy.[42]

The rapid growth of this new institution reflected a significant, new attentiveness to the concerns of women on the part of the Church. With the primary task of forming future mothers the Maestre Pie were to have a capillary influence on the social fabric. The ecclesiastical hierarchy now flanked the older religious communities with groups of women who did not take vows but who had approved "rules" and lived a communal life under the supervision, in most cases, of local bishops.[43] As with other institutions of a local character, the evolution of the Maestre Pie led them to fit smoothly into new nineteenth-century congregations, no longer dependent on a male order but governed by a female superior general.

In the eighteenth-century transitional phase between old and new forms of religious life, the relationship between these institutes and the male religious orders, especially the more recent ones, remained quite close, at least as far as their spiritual typology and their devotional behavior was concerned. Thus, if the Filippini Maestre Pie remained under the spiritual direction of the Pii Operai, from whom they absorbed their intensive asceticism and penitentialism, and their apostolate on behalf of poor young rural girls, their Venerini counterparts, under Jesuit direction, were less austere, and their educational activity was addressed more to urban girls. In this manner a rapport was established between male pastoral activity and an active presence in society by women. Among the new, male, religious orders, and generally those which

specialized in mission activity, this relationship introduced a legitimizing effect: the prestige of the "saintly" female founder of the new congregations
was now, in fact, invested and transferred to the male religious institute that
had undertaken to provide her with spiritual guidance or with whom she had
been in close relations. An outstanding instance was the link between Maria
Celeste Crostarosa (1696–1755) and the Redemptorists.

Toward a Feminization of Religion

The juridical ambiguity of the Maestre Pie and other new female institutions—lay congregations but with rules, a habit, a common life, and often
simple vows—is reminiscent of that older ambiguity that affected the tertiaries and the *bizzoche,* women's groups in constant growth between 1650 and
1750.[44] These women, who lived in the world but wore the habits of the most
varied sorts of orders with whom they had preferential relations, which allowed them to bypass episcopal control, had been a troubling and suspect
presence for a long time. They had become involved in the Quietist movement, in mystical episodes, and (as we have seen) in "feigned" sanctity and in
the abuses and disorder ascribed to them. By the end of the seventeenth
century and the beginning of the eighteenth, there had been numerous disciplinary interventions against them by local bishops and even by popes. Most
went unheeded and did not affect the generally positive social view of the
movement. Its members were especially numerous in the south, but the
movement had a presence throughout the peninsula. These women, living
either alone or in small communities, testified to a widespread religious aspi-
ration in the lower classes. Unable to find an institutional outlet in convents,
they fell back on a sort of domestic monasticism that, as the century progressed, was less and less unfavorably perceived, and indeed was encouraged
by such charismatic figures as Saint Alphonsus. The latter, as though putting
a seal of approval on the institutional shift the movement had produced,
praised—in the *Discorso alle zitelle devote,* which appeared in the same year
(1760) as his book devoted to the "saintly nun"—the opportunity for a
saintly life which the *bizzoche* could pursue within the confines of their own
homes.

Furthermore, the tertiaries and *bizzoche* by avoiding the social separation
imposed by enclosure, and by the work they did, which ranged from manual
labor to social work and teaching, had laid claim to new social and religious
spaces for women and enjoyed freedom of behavior and movement. Their
growing presence not only anticipated the progressive feminization of Catholicism, ever more evident between the eighteenth and nineteenth centuries, but also took on an active role and had considerable influence in what is

termed popular religion. Simple, devout people turned toward charismatic figures such as the Neapolitan Maria Francesca of the Five Wounds (1715–1791) and Maria Crocifissa of the Wounds of Our Lord Jesus Christ (1782–1846) as guides, protectors, and readily accessible intermediaries to the sacred.[45]

Still, the ambiguous status of these women, who bridged the traditional gulf between the religious and the lay state, who lived in a sort of middle way, reverberated too on their ambiguous role in society. The free and autonomous model of their religiosity was in fact accompanied by a spirituality with a powerful mystical and visionary component. Their growing role in society worked its way into forms of religious behavior, beliefs, and external devotional practices that were emotional, gentle and womanly, vastly different from the regulated devotions pursued by the enlightened culture of the century. Influenced by Alphonsine religiosity and by Jesuit and Franciscan contributions—Italian sanctity in the 1700s is Franciscan and southern[46]—they brought with them a feminization of the whole tone of a devotional life, one that would have a great outlet in the nineteenth century. Their frequent Communion, their forty-hour devotion to the Blessed Sacrament, their cult of the saints and guardian angels, their enthusiasm for Marian piety in all its most emotional and consoling forms, their particular fervor for the Passion (the Sacred Heart, the Way of the Cross), and their symbology, centered on suffering as reparation and the salvific power of sacrifice—virtues seen as eminently female—outlined a religious practice whose ideological connotations were all antirationalist, anti-Jansenist, and, later, also counterrevolutionary. They were, in fact, a genuine challenge to the Enlightenment spirit.

The Feminization of Religion and the Christian Reconquest

The Return of Mysticism and the Crisis of Reason

The charismatic character of the *bizzoche* saints and the late-eighteenth-century renewal of a mystical and visionary sensibility overturned the rigorist and rational religious outlook of the Enlightenment, pointing out the gaps between cultural proposals, the realities of social practice, and changes in institutional strategies. The gaps were made evident not merely by the fact that many charismatic women of the preceding centuries were promoted to sainthood during the eighteenth, nor by the constant presence throughout the century of numerous "live saints" who were mystics and ecstatics, nor even by the enormous popularity and editorial success of such as a work as the Jesuit G. B. Scaramelli's *Direttorio mistico*. These were but signals. By the 1770s, however, a whole series of events demonstrated the recovery of a visionary dimension and revealed the early signs of a real crisis of reason—a crisis induced in the society of the ancien regime by a series of political and religious crises whose causes lay in their sovereigns' attempts to secularize and their jurisdictionalist reformism. These events differed from one another but had many elements—including their absolute feminine leadership—in common. Among these events were the accusations of Quietism and libertine behavior made against the Dominican sisters of Prato in 1774–75 and the analogous charges made at roughly the same time in the duchy of Modena. Both showed the progress of this latest transformation of religious culture in directions still more remote from a rational faith.[47]

The notorious case of the "prophetesses" of Valentano in the Papal States, led by a Dominican nun and a *bizzocha* of humble origins who prophesied calamity and disaster for the Church as a result of its banning of the Society of Jesus in 1773, was a further instance of the extraordinary recovery, late in the eighteenth century, of the mystical-visionary line and its close connection to the mental and cultural traumas caused by its contemporaries' political and religious decisions.[48] Special note should be taken of the way in which the political and propaganda function of this line—taking up the defense of the Jesuits, the papacy, and the Church against the attacks of the Enlightenment and of jurisdictionalism, thus bringing concrete support to the counterrevolutionary struggle—contributed to the reinforcement of the ecclesiastical establishment's project to reconquer society for Catholicism, a project in which a leading role was planned for women.

In close relation with a strategy to popularize the Catholic religion and—as a result of the defection of the educated elite—to give a privileged status to the lower classes, renewed attention was now paid to the role of women and the reality of their situation, whether lay or religious. Women were to be a vital factor in the re-Christianization and the reconversion of men lukewarm to Catholicism. The increasing number of canonizations of women signaled a shift in the perception of female sanctity. In another sense, the revival, with the full consent and guidance of the hierarchy, of the mystical and prophetic mode was well suited to the new myth of medieval Christianity, which shaped Catholicism and the papacy's attitude in its conflict with the modern world. The role of certain religious orders, especially the ex-Jesuits who, in these troubled decades, were rediscovering a visionary and apocalyptic line and increasing their already well-established missionary work among women, was particularly significant in this process.

Still, new characteristics and functions differentiated this recuperation of the mystical dimension, destined to continue throughout the nineteenth century, from its previous incarnations. The political dimension of the feminization of religion, which sought to take a fresh grip on society by the Church through attention to various social "subjects"—in the instance, women and the lower classes—adds a definite social and cultural connotation to the participants. Female saints and seers no longer, as in the past, came exclusively from the privileged classes and from the world of the cloister. As in the cases of the most famous Neapolitan *bizzocha,* Maria Francesca of the Five Wounds. an artisan's daughter, and of the Montefiascone Benedictine sister Maria Cecilia Baj (1697–1766), a bricklayer's daughter, a new sanctity-poverty equation took over from the old one of sanctity and aristocracy.

This shows to how great an extent the Church's renewed insistence on poverty functioned as a riposte to the "bourgeois" values of a modern society in which culture and wealth had ceased to be Christian. In social terms, this equation corresponded to a genuine "democratization." A decline in religious professions led to the opening up of convents to women of a humbler class. Affirming lay, popular sanctity, no longer suspect but rather on the rise, led to further modifications of the social model by a new nexus, the freshly established equation of sanctity and ignorance. No longer confined to the privileged world of the convent, visions, prophecies, and revelations become the appanage of a simple, popular world of laywomen: ignorant and therefore candid and close to God, they were incapable of affirming through the medium of educated writing that they, too, had a right to a biography, like their mystical sisters in the preceding century.[49]

The alliance between the Church, the lower classes, and women was based on identifying these two new subjects with the naturalness and innocence of children, so it is not surprising that the seers were now from among the people, often young, and sometimes children. In contrast to the pride of the learned, this new compact exalted an ideal simplicity linked to humility and submissive obedience to the guidance of the Church and its dictates. It was a reciprocal relationship, for God's greater closeness to the humble, to women and girls, was testified to by miracles and visions, and thereby the authority of the Church and the truth of its dogma was enhanced.

The Queen and the Bizzocha: *Popular Sanctity and Royal Sanctity in the Restoration*

The ideological and "political" content of a privileged relationship between women and the Church was not confined to giving a greater value to "the people," it also mirrored what was happening on the political plane. There, the events of the revolutionary age had drawn "the people" to the cause of legitimizing monarchy. Leaping to the extreme opposite of the social scale, this new ideological mixture exalted a sainthood tied to the political system of the *ancien régime* and absolute monarchy. The relationship between the saintly and the royal was both an old and a traditional one; it had lasted for centuries and become specifically tied to the House of Savoy. Specific to the Savoy dynasty was the centuries-old link between female sanctity and the legitimation and sacralization of the dynasty's political power—as exemplified by the angelic women of the House of Savoy, starting with the Blessed Margaret (1382–1464) and extending down to the nineteenth-century figures of Maria Cristina, Maria Adelaide, and Maria Clotilde.[50]

However, as revolution gave way to restoration, the political significance of royal sanctity and its link with the most prevalent expressions of popular religiosity found their greatest prominence and their greatest symbolic expression in the person of another, though less well known Savoyard "saint": Maria Clotilde Adelaide de Bourbon (1759–1802), wife as of 1775 to the future king of Sardinia, Vittorio Emanuele IV, daughter of the dauphin of France, and niece of Louis XV. The fact that she was the sister of the "martyred" princes, of Louis XVI and especially Madame Elizabeth—who had soon become, even more than her kingly brother, a symbol of Bourbon and Catholic restoration as well as of royal martyrdom—invested Maria Clotilde with a double dynastic heritage, that of France and that of Savoy, just as both monarchies were being "persecuted." Thanks to her equally devout and ascetic husband—both were in Third Orders, and after her death Vittorio Emanuele entered the restored Jesuit order—the old model of a chaste marriage was restored and, during their years of exile in Naples, the life of the royal couple incarnated the religious ideals of the Restoration, dedicated to the reestablishment of the Society of Jesus and the incessant practice of "popular" devotions.

The great popularizer of the Marian devotion to the Divine Shepherdess in Naples had been Maria Francesca of the Five Wounds, and the humble and uneducated woman of the people and the queen, her admirer, now seemed to unite in a battle for the faith and the traditional religious and political order.[51] Thus, on the one hand, the saintliness of Maria Clotilde reminded Restoration sovereigns of both the need for and the indissolubility of the marriage of two institutions, throne and altar, made triumphant by the glory of martyrdom, and their indispensable need for popular support; on the other, Maria Clotilde's saintliness gave rise to a series of dynastic celebrations through the saintliness of their queens, which lasted right through the Risorgimento, celebrations constructed not just by Catholics but by Savoyard memorialists and historians. This symbolic conjuncture reached its climax with the exaltation of Maria Adelaide, the wife of Vittorio Emanuele II, a model of the "Christian wife," the "true saint," who died early, as "a resigned victim of conjugal love."[52]

The Mother, the Church, and the Pope: Anna Maria Taigi

At all levels of society the powerful, emergent image of the wife-mother as the incarnation of the Catholic feminine ideal, the object of ever-increasing interest in the devotional literature of the nineteenth century, was informed by the spirituality of resignation.[53] The mission and leadership of women as emissaries of the Church and as mediators of values and of a Christian education to their children concentrated expectations of salvation and general redemption on the figure of the mother. United with the powerful revival of the cult of Mary, women fused—in a wheel of mutual meanings turning around the theme of suffering and expiatory sacrifice—the images of Church, Madonna, and Motherhood.

By the end of the process of emancipation of women's roles within marriage, and within a general process of feminization of family education, primary responsibility for the rearing of children, including boys, had passed from fathers to mothers. (This trend was recognized by Catholic morality despite the sudden rigidifying of the juridical condition of women by which, in European society, the Restoration had canceled out the incomplete concessions of the Revolution.) It was within the world of the family, an institution greatly favored by ecclesiastical strategy, that the greater "informal" power and autonomy of women, their self-knowledge and the recognition by the outside world of their value, made themselves evident. The family became the source of power, of leadership, of autonomous female strategies. These may have taken place concurrently with a clearly defined task, that of mediating ecclesiastical values, but they could easily be translated into an institutional role for mothers, even in social terms, as elements of stability, order, and discipline. As in other areas of female religious leadership during those decades, there now arose a contradictory tendency that wavered ambiguously between constructing a new and more autonomous social identity for women and cooperating with the intransigent party's grand project for an ideological and cultural restoration, and the reconstruction of Catholic hegemony within society.[54]

Typical of the insistence on the power of the maternal role in the family was the exemplum constructed around the "Roman" Blessed Anna Maria Taigi (1769–1837). Her role as "a model of perfect married life" was exactly reproduced in that of another holy Roman mother of the same period: Elisabetta Canori Mora (1774–1825).[55] In her biography, firmly centered on her "political" influence, Taigi's saintliness assumed the mystical and visionary characteristics that contemporary religious sensibility greatly valued and now accorded to poor and ignorant laywomen (Taigi could read but not write). On the model of Saint Catherine, who was often invoked by analogy for "the influence ordinary women could have on the political events of their time,"[56] to Taigi and Canori, both living in a papal Rome subjected to the upheavals of an age of revolution and liberalism, were attributed apocalyptic and reassuring prophecies dealing with the persecutions endured by Church and papacy between Pius VII and Pius IX and with the final triumph that would reaffirm ecclesiastical mastery of society.

Offering herself up as a sacrificial victim to the impiety of "revolutionary sects," the maternal figure of Taigi was a pillar of Church, papacy, and faith. But alongside this public, political, and apologetic role—and it is no accident that Taigi had a particular devotion to Saint Philomena, that "warrior for the faith"[57] so beloved by the Sanfedisti[58] and intransigents—her biography was centered also on her role as a saint in the family. Taigi became the model for a new kind of mystic, one common in humdrum daily life, the affectionate and respectful wife, the perfect housekeeper. Within the family, her saintliness lay in being a good mother; her relationship to her children was more important than that to her spouse. Tender and able to show an affection she had until recently been told to repress, the saintly mother looked after her children's bodies but especially their souls; she taught them religious and moral principles; she watched attentively what they did outside the home or at work; when it came time for them to be married, she instructed them in their duties; she watched over them all their lives. Submissiveness, obedience, passivity, and sacrifice concealed her self-consciousness, and her control over every aspect of family life was anything but passive. On the one hand, her maternal power as mediator between fathers and children, between laypeople and ecclesiastics, was nearly priestly power and came to resemble that of the Church itself. On the other hand, the virtues of self-giving, of dedication and generosity without hope of return, which shaped the nineteenth-century model of femininity, neither merely maternal nor Catholic, referred to the model that all women were to pursue, that of Mary.[59]

From the Marian Miracles to the Mariophanic Explosion of the Nineteenth Century: A Weapon?

While the eighteenth-century shift toward a less popular form of religiosity may—in relation to its huge expansion in the previous century—seem to have brought with it a momentary pause in the cult of Mary, the century of Enlightenment in fact powerfully affirmed the cult.[60] The old figuration of Mary as an allegorical figure of the Church was vigorously rejuvenated: Mary was now associated with the Church as a powerful ally in the epic battle against the menace of the modern world and secularization. Many of the most important stages in the development of Marian piety took place in the eighteenth century, specifically at a time when Muratori's defeat in the debate over the intercessional powers of the Virgin made Saint Alphonsus Liguori's *Glories of Mary* (which ran to numberless editions) not just a keystone of Mariology but the main symbol of the absolute triumph and centrality of devotion to the Virgin.

A solution to the long controversy over the Immaculate Conception, which began in the eighteenth century, was found in 1854 with Pius IX's proclamation of the dogma and with the ratification of the apparitions of Lourdes. This Marian triumph showed just how closely Marian devotion was linked to the vicissitudes of the Church and just how powerful was its apologetic role in defense of religion within a symbolic scheme that read current events as a cosmic struggle between good and evil. As in the past Catholic victories over Turks or Protestants had been placed under the banner of a victorious Mary, so now the battle against the new heresies that had steadily emerged during the rationalist century and likewise against the upheavals of the French Revolution and liberalism was fought under her flag. The late-eighteenth-century Sanfedista and counterrevolutionary reaction in Italy, with its war cry of "Viva Maria!" was, by that very rallying cry, linked to the great flood of "miracles," the fruit of Marian images produced in Rome and in the Papal States in 1796 in response to the threatening invasion of the French. In the ecclesiastics' interpretation, these Marian "prodigies," many of them involving or attested to by women of the people, were incontrovertible proof of heavenly support and of the legitimacy of the cause of Catholicism and papal authority. Thus, if the language of miracle and vision, both threatening and reassuring, had become, between the eighteenth and nineteenth centuries, the official language of institutional religion, it was above all the expectation of miracles mediated by Mary on behalf of the Church that profoundly penetrated Catholic consciousness and theological wisdom.[61]

Yet the ever more widespread diffusion of images of the Immaculate Conception—with Mary standing on the moon crushing the serpent, her head surrounded by an aureole of stars, in evident recall of Genesis and the Apocalypse—showed the increasing emphasis placed on the eschatological role of Mary and her Immaculate Conception. The devotion announced the age of Mary as precursor of the coming of Christ.[62] The fusion of eschatological vision, Christian restoration, and legitimist political aspirations fashioned Marian devotion into a formidable cultural weapon. In its aggressive and "militant" form, marked by warlike language and military metaphors, during these decades it became the weapon of choice in the campaign of Catholic reconquest.[63]

During the age of Restoration there were a number of specific papal statements that referred to Mary as the savior of the Church, the papacy, and

Rome, and their combined triumph over their infernal enemies. As a result, a kind of meaningful historical symmetry was established, which included both the persecutions suffered by Pius VII and Pius IX and their theological arguments, forming a link between the two popes' Marian proclamations, the former's *Maria Auxilium Christianorum* and the latter's proclamation of the dogma of the Immaculate Conception. Compared to the French Marian *ensemble,* which was centered on the Virgin's apparitions,[64] the Italian Mariophany was created specifically so that collective witnesses would prevail over individual visionaries. The Italian "system," rather than creating a powerful national identity, focused on the language, unspoken but decipherable, of miraculous images, on the doctrinal significance of Marian definitions, and on symbolism tied to Church teaching. Nonetheless, in the context of the religious and political anxieties that followed on the events of 1848, the system had a constant, coherent line of development: it was the system of prodigious images that took on new life with their ambiguous meanings, still both threatening and reassuring but also with an unmistakable ideological and political message.

The consoling, maternal, but also warlike image of Mary contributed in a decisive fashion to the feminization of religious practice. New "feminine" devotions were inaugurated—feminine by their gentle, sentimental tone, through the object to which they were directed, and through the prevalence of the sex applied to them. Growing devotion to the Sacred Heart, which had long offered a feminized image of Christ, was now joined by new forms of Marian piety such as the Marian month of May. This particular practice, which in part thanks to the efforts of Don Bosco became widespread in the nineteenth century, originated in Jesuit circles a century earlier. A little work published in Ferrara in 1785 by the former Jesuit A. Muzzarelli, one of the leaders of the Catholic ultras, *Il Mese di Maria o sia il Mese di Maggio consegrato a Maria Santissima,* went through thirty editions between 1815 and 1850, denouncing the link between the pronounced Roman and papal connotations of the Marian month and the more "aggressive" historical phase of modern Catholicism.[65] Marian May months, spiritual flowers, "Mary gardens," rosaries, and crowns of flowers not only became devotional practices especially directed toward the education of girls and young women,[66] but through their communitarian and social character they contributed a recruiting point for a new form of feminine association.

"A Vast Machine Almost Entirely Set in Motion by the Hand of a Woman": *The New Women's Congregations*

Numerous laypeople's, women's, and youth groups, devoted to Mary and directed toward the new leaders of religious life, women, and the young, now took the place of the old and long-abandoned confraternities in which these elements had had little weight. There were Associations of Christian Mothers, Companies and Pious Unions of the Daughters of Mary, and congregations devoted to the Immaculate Heart of Mary. They spread through Italy with great rapidity in the first half of the nineteenth century.[67] Impelled by a powerful need for community and solidarity, and brought together by collective prayer and devotions, these community networks were likewise active in society, particularly in welfare and the education of poor girls. Most of these sodalities were founded by laywomen with a specific aim in mind; but they were eventually transformed into active, new religious communities devoted to the social apostolate. They were at the origins of the Servants of Charity in Brescia (1844), the Daughters of the Sacred Heart of Jesus in Bergamo (1831), and the Canossian Daughters of Charity in Verona (1808).

The central role of the Marian model in women's education and in the nexus between Marian spirituality and a modern active apostolate brought about a deep change in the figure of the nun. This was another important aspect of the nineteenth-century model of a Catholic woman, for nuns had a leading role, equal to that of mothers within the family, in that one of their principal tasks was to form good, Christian mothers. The new religious congregations created a new kind of "sister." On the one hand, she had to meet the internal needs of the Catholic world and face changing times with a freer and more incisive role in society; on the other, she had to be responsive to external pressures and face the distrust of secular governments for the cloistered and contemplative orders, which culminated in the suppression of convents begun by eighteenth-century reformer sovereigns and continued under their revolutionary and Napoleonic successors. As a consequence, the new foundations—basing themselves on the collective experience of the houses and schools of oblates, on tertiaries, Maestre Pie, and the women's "conservatories"—accentuated their social functions and activities, for these made them acceptable and even necessary, thus guaranteeing their survival.

This second aspect of what has been called Feminine Catholicism, as defined by Charles Langlois, was reflected quantitatively in an unprecedented flowering of new female religious congregations.[68] Between 1800 and 1860 no fewer than 127 new foundations were approved in Italy, most of them in the center and the north, confining the more traditional orders to the south. The history of women's religious life now showed a clear division between the two Italies.

Within this bigger frame, it is worth noting that the new foundations were no longer cloistered monasteries. Their social, educational, and welfare activities actually pushed the surviving or reformed cloistered convents to open educational institutions and schools for girls, so that the new model also involved older orders and new institutes.[69] But the juridical status of the

204 • *Women and Faith*

latter, in which new and more precisely defined and codified religious obligations accompanied the greater liberty enjoyed by traditional congregations of oblates or tertiaries, reflected the major religious and mental changes that had supervened. These new "sisters" were made up part of a centralized system of governance in which the figure of the superior general, who de facto freed these institutions from the traditional authority of the local ordinaries, constituted an absolute novelty in women's ecclesiastical organization.

The post of superior general not only guaranteed the autonomy of the foundation, but also offered ample managerial powers over major institutions to a single woman without the male guidance of an ecclesiastical superior. "A vast machine almost entirely set in motion by the hand of a woman": that is how the powers of the superior general of the Maestre di Santa Dorothea were described halfway through the century.[70] In short order, the difficulties raised by many sectors of the Church concerning the "weakness of their sex," their lack of the necessary authority to manage such complex organizations, the indecorousness inherent in their need to travel and move from one house to another all fell, reflecting obvious societal change in regard to female roles.

The new religious congregations, therefore, seemed to configure a shift toward autonomy, internal authority, and emancipation. In a society as antifeminist as that of the nineteenth century, it was these religious groups, lay or not, which guaranteed the survival of female community networks that were not merely informal but organized and recognized. They offered women a way to establish their individuality, a genuine democratization of access, ample space, hitherto unknown, in which to make effective, responsible interventions; they offered perhaps the only means to escape from subordination within their families, by assuring them also respectability and social protection.

Besides spreading the lingering notion that there were typical female tasks and missions, such as education, health, and charitable works, this sort of feminine sociability, developing within a society itself undergoing transformation, exercised a role that was not without ambiguities and contradictions. By analogy to the power of mothers within the family, the power of these new religious congregations, forming future mothers in their schools, did double service. On the one hand, as a new female social identity was being created, they marked a break with the old order; on the other, they provided a stabilizing and disciplining influence, one which could control and transmit cultural and ideological models. "Holy" mothers and new "sisters" formed on the Marian model, they acted in harness with the strategy of religious reconquest and Catholic restoration that marked the Church's antimodern struggle in the first half of the nineteenth century.

Translated from the Italian by Keith Botsford

CHAPTER 11

Mystical Writing

MARILENA MODICA VASTA

"Experience through Silent Mirrors"

Recalling the beginnings of her own spiritual life, Sister Maria Celeste Crostarosa (of the Most Holy Redeemer) (1696–1755), the inspirer of the female and contemplative branch of the Liguorian Congregation of the Most Holy Redeemer, reevoked in ecstatic terms God's call to the monastic state. In the autobiography she penned at her confessor's orders after 1750, she wrote:

> Being then twenty, you, my Lord, ordained, without my cooperation, that I should be brought to visit a servant of God in Marigliano, nine miles from the city of Naples, where this servant of God had founded a convent of nuns of the reformed congregation of Mother Serafina of Capri.

On the way to the convent, she saw herself as having become "like a little girl," without memory, her mind bathed "in a most pure, divine clarity" and her will "in the purest love of the Lord."

Almost like Paul of Tarsus on the road to Damascus, she was lightning-struck by God's summons: until she reached that "place . . . chosen" by the Lord, the home of the future servant of God, "She saw as one who does not see, she heard as one who does not hear . . . She spoke as one who is moved by another." In her words, "[my] soul was rapt and annihilated by your divine doing . . . and thus united, you filled it as you would have it, without the intervention of man, within or without, save for the most simple consent of the soul by your doing, moved by you and drawn to you, my beloved."[1]

In her description of that far-off event—in which the interplay of distance and memory arranged the events of an earthly life that was already near

205

hagiography—her language heralds the full ripeness of a path in whose development the inner experience of the nun had been shaped in the rich tapestry of the mystical tradition. They were "words of ecstasy" that Sister Maria Celeste had learned, or learned to recognize, on her own personal path to perfection, in that often hard-to-reconstruct coming together of subjective, spiritual tension with the models, the codes, and the language elaborated by the Christian mystical tradition and culture.

The themes of that long and authoritative tradition, which had found such a deep and shattering resonance among women in the seventeenth century, are present in her writing, in a form so concentrated that this is a sign they have already been integrated. The margins of the risk that had always been present within mysticism and had now been brought to light—by the Quietist crisis of the end of the century and by the condemnation of the theories of Molinos (1687) and, later, of the *Maxims* of Fénelon (1699)—were now reset.[2]

It is not by accident that this essay opens with the writing of Sister Maria Celeste Crostarosa. Rich in contrasts and tensions, the path taken by this "great eighteenth-century mystic"—to use the words applied to her by a biographer whose 1936 work, despite its inevitable apologetic tone, is the richest and most detailed[3]—lay at the crossroads of an intense process of cultural and spiritual transformations, of changes in conditions, which between the end of the seventeenth century and the beginning of the century of the Enlightenment affected the religious world of women.

Sister Celeste is invoked here as an emblematic figure of a fervid seventeenth-century spirituality being drawn into the more sober ideals of an eighteenth century both rational and devout. Although one can find in her traces of the later Liguorian Holy Nun, her links with the post-Tridentine feminine mystical ideal remain both visible and tenacious. The changes in this latter ideal in fact took place so slowly as to be almost imperceptible; furthermore, in the context of women's spiritual lives, though the mystical experience was being somewhat tendentiously reshaped, it had not altogether lost its prestige.

The themes of contemplation and of total fusion with God, of the self being annihilated and dispossessed, of that *anéantissement* which Mino Bergamo defined as a true "catastrophe of identity," were the fulcrum of eighteenth-century spiritual experience and among the signs that best portrayed the crisis of the century and the arduous labor of the European religious conscience in its difficult passage toward modernity.[4] They had already come sharply to the fore in the second half of the sixteenth century, slowly grafting themselves, often in a conflictual manner, on the Tridentine reforms. They were the fundamental themes of a complex spiritual culture—the expression, as Michel de Certeau put it, of the difficulty some marginal social groups found in integrating themselves into the new political and religious order.[5] By writing, the anxiety of the *cupio dissolvi*, of the "smashing of one's own identity," both longed-for and feared, of the fugitive nature of the dividing line between reason and delirium, was consigned to the framework of an anxiety-ridden literature. And that literature itself introduced a new tension within the unvarying linguistic code of the spiritual and contemplative tradition.

"Annihilationes, expropriationes, resignationes, indifferentias": this lexical and symbolic register played so insistently on the dispersion of the "ego" and yet rested on medieval exegesis and the thinking of the Church fathers. It relied, therefore, on the very tradition that had fixed the essential conditions and the original definition of the contemplative experience.[6] But it represented the crushing nature of eighteenth-century mysticism in such a way as to suggest to contemporaries that it had assumed a new and different posture. Some clearly saw, in the experiences of those who were significantly called the "new spirituals," a need for a subjectivity that could make the very words of the tradition into something new. This need was reinforced by the return of themes connected to the pseudo-Dionysian "negative way" (themselves derived from the Rhenish-Flemish mysticism of Meister Eckhart and Johann Tauler, and reconstructed with its own specific characteristics in the fertile cultural ground of Spain and the spirituality of John of the Cross).

A "new" mysticism, a new language to express religious experience, grew up in the climate of spiritual regeneration and normative discipline that accompanied, though not in any linear fashion, the early Tridentine period and then the whole seventeenth century with its complex crises. This new element significantly altered the religious world of women, which at the time was undergoing profound institutional reforms, especially as regards the sometimes traumatic return of enclosure and the tighter definition—through the drafting of written constitutions and the much more rigid attribution of jurisdictional responsibilities—of the diverse characteristics of monastic orders and the rules of community life.[7]

Having been returned to the care of the ecclesiastical hierarchies, nuns were progressively restricted in the exercise of their contemplative spirituality: solidly tied to the conventual organization, that spirituality gave stability to the feminization of the mystical model by subordinating it to the ideal of monastic perfection.

The paths women's mysticism had taken—beyond those interpretations that had made it meaningful in the linguistic or psychoanalytic sense— seemed inseparable from the ensemble of reforming and normative directions of the Tridentine Church.[8] The Church had seen in the cloistered life and the rules that marked its material and spiritual rhythms a potent vehicle for the moral regeneration of Christian society and assigned to this cloistered life a privileged place for the expression of the contemplative experience. But that place was both privileged and controlled. Within it the peculiar individualistic tension of mysticism, the extraordinary character of a way of life marked by union with the divine and by elusive secrecy and ineffability—so promptly claimed by the "new" contemplatives—could more readily be accommodated if it were channeled into an orthodox mysticism, in line with the spirit of the Counter-Reformation.

The fulfillment of knowledge, beginning with the senses and then shaped by intellectual abstraction, arriving finally at contemplation, mysticism was in the end principally seen as an experience of God. The experience was direct, dazzling, and mysterious; it ravished the soul, as Saint Bonaventure put it, *ad supermentales excessus,* "in excess beyond the mind."[9]

But a breach had been opened in the apparent simplicity and essentialism of this scheme: by excluding human agency in the impetus toward union—the fundamental moment in an ecstatic love relationship—there was a risk of muffling the theological reasons for its existence and nullifying the distinctions between the different stages of the experience. This was precisely the crucial reason the theologians and inquisitors gave for the heterodox character of *alumbrado* mysticism and late-seventeenth-century Quietism. All the negative perceptions—of a spirituality without reason or control and of the exercise of harsh ascetic practices—gathered almost obsessively around these two movements: for under pain of exclusion for heresy there could be no loss of human reason in a mystical union.

As codified by the theologians of the New Scholasticism,[10] riding the wave of sixteenth-century diffusion of mental prayer and the mysticism of *dejamiento,*[11] or "abandonment," these various distinguishing stages, this scansion by intimately connected and inseparable phases—all of them aiming to maintain a level of rationality centered on "discursive" meditation rather than on the unpredictable flow of the contemplative—disappeared into the "methodical and ordered" practice into which confessors and spiritual directors sought to inscribe women's experience.

Tridentine mysticism had two aspects: one, "the dark night of the soul" of Saint John of the Cross; the other, marked by Thomism, which Ignatian spirituality made its own. There were these two different itineraries and practices in contemplative life, and an attempt was made to harmonize them, either through disciplinary control or through subtler and more persuasive processes of interiorization.

The ambivalent, side-by-side placing of these two images in the Tridentine system created an obstacle to the development of a form of sanctity that would be, at one and the same time, the fruit of method and of "feeling devotion," of mystical fervor and of prudent and regulated contemplative discipline. In the solitude of those cloisters in which the spiritual lives of sisters marked by the convulsions of ecstatic love were often consumed between doubt and the dazzling certainties of the divine encounter, the one seemed to exclude the other.

For the Sicilian Benedictine nun Maria Crocifissa Tomasi (1645–1699), this alternation between "sweet and supernatural invitations" and the "penalty of conscience" transformed the "bread of life" into "morsels of hell . . . and for every morsel I swallow, I die of fear, or I go weary and famished to procure it, so that were you to see me, you'd find an Ethiopian woman in hell, for the bread which keeps me alive is being baked here, and it makes suffer such an ache in my jaws that I can make neither sign nor word."[12]

The "common enemy" ever lurks, depriving mystics even of their moment of peace in confession. Tomasi tells how "diabolical pretension" had often prevented her from going to confession: "In my heart [that pretension] a terrible heat is kindled; . . . in this fire, the use of reason is entirely extinguished, so that I must resist, and, dissolved as I am, the transport spills the blood from my veins."[13]

The great success of eighteenth-century hagiography—in which the equilibrium between Christian virtues and extraordinary manifestations seemed nearly always to come down on the latter side—was based on the visionary marvels of female saints and servants of God, on physical miracles and women's words inspired by God's presence.

How to define the undefinable, how to grasp the ungraspable? Despite the diversity of their perspectives and conditions, and given the distance that inevitably separated an experience that had been lived and the models offered by the standard, normative literature, in treatises, and in theoretical speculation, this question remained the chief preoccupation of mystics and theologians. Contemplatives—more concerned with the "experimental science of the love of God" than with theological knowledge—often pointed to this gulf; the gap seemed congruous mainly for the unlettered *illuminati*, perhaps aided by an *indocta sapientia* (an untaught wisdom), and for the uneducated *mulierculae*, (little women), who had neither knowledge nor doctrine.

For both of these groups, the distance between mystical theology and scholastic theology, instead of evoking a possible harmonious synthesis, suggested rather a proud affirmation of spiritual superiority of the spiritual. As Tomasi wrote: "In the Academy of my Cross, we do not offer scholastic propositions, but mystical and divine ones; we do not teach knowledge but experience understood through silent observation, not through words . . . Remove theory, one arrives at practice . . . My Lord calls me to [feel] the pain of my sins, not to theological discourses."[14]

While this experience "understood through silent observation," this "holy training which can only be learned in silent words and infinite terms," constituted the great laboratory of theological speculation, the living material that the latter sought to reach, the fact is that the mistrust of centuries continued to circumscribe women's mysticism with ever narrower standards, with references to the "natural" weakness of women, to the physical makeup and humors that rendered them incapable of taking the correct path toward a life of divine union.

The task of correcting a prejudice rooted in the collective consciousness and in religious culture was left to the few great ecstatics; in a culture lacking any intimation of a possible diversity in women's experience in the formation of the contemplative tradition, women remained protagonists almost totally scripted into a standard and unaltered line. It was with that obsessive repetition of stereotyped concepts and formulas of their "weak nature" that the dubious role of the female in the imaginary symbolic world of Christianity and her troubled contiguity with the male returned in force. The fact that she was classed in that fashion—as corroded by vainglory, by gossip mongering and curiosity, which traditionally implied hypocrisy and diabolical deceits— and was shrewdly kept as far as possible from "carnal and worldly knowledge" was no impediment to women being the essential designers of eighteenth-century spiritual experience.

The years of conflict that followed, caught between continuity and interruption, with mysticism seeking its footing in the Enlightenment, were marked by ever stricter and more regulated forms of contemplative devotion. The aim was to contain the more morbid aspects of female experience, which the devotional literature of the day ascribed to the peculiar, cold, and melancholy nature of women, and to enclose within the "withdrawal of the heart" the extraordinary rhythms of mystical union.

Physical excesses;[15] the ecstatic and visionary models pursued and cultivated in convents as a mark of the superiority of cloistered sanctity; the radical innovations in the language of mysticism, which by transforming its meaning had unhinged the normal sense of words—"Habet mystica Theologia suas voces" (mystical theology has its own voices), said Cardinal Giovanni Bona[16]—all these underwent a slow process of regulation that gradually transformed the contemplative model into a more practicable ideal of monastic asceticism.

Order, moderation, sobriety; a spiritual and material life that softened the darker corners of the cloister: in the midst of Enlightenment polemics against the monastic condition, this was Alphonsus Liguori's reply to a cultural and religious climate already greatly modified by increasing secularization, one in which the female condition was rapidly moving away from its traditional models of reference.

Sister Maria Celeste Crostarosa—who was far from such bodily excess, from overwhelming ecstasies, and from Quietist contemplative experience and who was probably more attracted to the model of active mysticism incarnated in Teresa of Avila—like a number of other nuns turned her own visionary language and writing toward an ambitious project, that of replenishing, indeed refounding, the community to which they belonged. This was a climate in which ecstasies, visions, and women's revelations were being minimized. A complete rethinking of the mystical experience was taking place—one that was about to widen and consolidate the ample, established course of the *discretio spirituum* as described in Benedict XV's *De servorum Dei beatificatione et beatorum canonizatione*. Hence Sister Maria's was a road all the more difficult to take.[17]

Consider the mode of her inspired writing, the development of a traditional representation of mystical experience. Convents were subjected to discipline and contemplative practice; and for religious mystics writing interwoven with many other tasks and tribulations took on a prophetic dimension. A divine revelation had taken the simple and obscure nun that Sister Maria Celeste had been right out of the anonymity of the community, out of that silence and "withdrawal of the heart" in which she had begun to cultivate her contemplative experience, and had entrusted her with the project of a new foundation.

Her revelation had been surrounded by extraordinary circumstances, for Sister Maria Celeste felt she had united with the Lord through wounds in her hands, feet, and side; in a bright, white light she had seen him dip his finger in his own blood and write out in her heart his life and his will that a new institution be founded. Thus, as had been the case with Ursula Benincasa, founder of the Eremitic Theatines of the Most Holy Conception, to whom the Lord had made known "in the mind, and with great certainty and clarity,"[18] their constitution, so to Sister Maria Celeste he gave full and whole consciousness of all that the rule should contain. He then ordered her to write it all down and prepare herself for the task of writing by fasting on bread and water, by silence and prayer. Maria Celeste obeyed, and wrote with such dexterity that her hand seemed to fly on the sheets of paper.

The ritual manner in which the divine word unfolded, the impact that broke through Sister Celeste's writing block as the words flowed quickly and almost unbeknownst to her from her hand (which recalls that of Tomasi's "usual mode" of writing), were part of a frame of reference already well established in seventeenth-century women's spiritual biographies, a form of writing by nuns that proliferated in a double register of obedience: obedience to the confessor and to *indocta sapientia*. Her spiritual director thought Maria Crocifissa Tomasi's capacity to write "a wonderful work of God, and all the more splendid the less able the writer."[19]

Blind obedience to superiors was necessary in the monastic condition. It was designed to impose an exercise in humility linking a "conditional" credit to those autonomous female spaces created by an extraordinary path to perfection. As intuitively understood by Alphonsus Liguori, Crostarosa's autonomy was not born merely of the intensity of her spiritual life, nor from mystic and penitential fervor, but from a capacity for reflection with which writing under the direction of her confessor had a good deal to do, and which, escaping from the routines of "spiritual reports," rose to the superior form of knowledge, "dilatatione et illuminatione mentis (by the "broadening and illumination of the mind").[20] This was a certainty that Sister Celeste felt in her heart; it gave her the courage—the same displayed in her time by Teresa of Ahumada—to renounce her spiritual director, Father Falcoia.

"I Write Everything with Pure Obedience and Great Repugnance"

A "withdrawal of the heart," linked to Maria Celeste Crostarosa's indefatigable labors as an organizer of convents, marked the difference between herself and the experience of female mystics of the Counter-Reformation and the seventeenth century. Her writing, nevertheless, showed a visible continuity with that experience. The clear drafting of her autobiography, her account of her inner life, was achieved only after a long apprenticeship that began when she was but fifteen and her first confessor noted that the girl "had things to tell."

Like many young women, Giulia Crostarosa could read but not write. Only girls of an exalted station were taught and allowed the "modest practice in writing" required for family prestige and social decorum. Women of a "middling station," such as Crostarosa, were not denied reading, but those of "humble and poor estate" were almost without exception excluded.[21]

Only the monastic condition permitted this rule to be breached and, given the poverty of culture to which most women could aspire, the religious life was the one way in which they might arrive at even a limited form of knowledge. Convents and religious communities were, in fact, the refuges of a suppressed female knowledge; it was there that women could reach a level of literacy which, while it permitted them to exercise monastic "good management," also brought them into contact with the practice of reading, which was so essential a part of the preparation for religious perfection. Bit by bit, as the means and arrangements governing access to reading and the organization of the convent libraries recommended by abbesses, advisers, and monastic tutors were clarified, the practice of reading became central to the religious life of post-Tridentine communities.[22]

Saints' biographies, devotional texts, and the classics of spiritual literature marked the communal rhythm of the enclosure, but a slower form of assimilating these texts took place in the cell and in the silent labor of intelligence and memory in the thoughts and imagination of the nuns. Food for the soul, reading favored—as a sort of preparation for the written word—the sharpening of concentration and sensibility; it shifted the borderline between learning and experience; it could act as the privileged instrument of sanctity, even taking the place of mortifying the body. "Chains! Hair shirts!" wrote Alphonsus Liguori to a community of nuns in 1731, "I'm sending you a good supply of books. They'll be better than chains in helping you become saints!"[23] Even in the discipline of voice production, communal readings brought out the order and moderation that were supposed to regulate convent life and behavior. For as the saint went on: "And when you're reading at table, beware (as I warned the Scala convent, and they obeyed me) . . . that you do not read breathlessly or colourlessly at the end, for then you will not be heard and the desire to listen will be gone."

With the tumultuous proliferation of female mysticism, the reasons for controlling writing shifted from forbidding women's access to words to emphasizing the incentive to write and promoting a learning process in the theoretical foundations of experience, reaching an ever wider audience among nuns and opening up for them further, unforeseen paths. How much more tormented did the itineraries of writing become!

For instance, the illiterate Bolognese hosier Angela Mellini (ca. 1664–ca. 1707), into whose hands her confessor had put "a pen and a sheet of paper with the letters written out" so that she might, by learning to write, succeed in giving him a full accounting of her spiritual profit, was one of those women "of poor and humble station."[24] Modeling itself on expectations of a holiness in charismatic form, the same coercive masculine power that brought out women's writing could also lead—as was the case with Mellini, her Sicilian contemporary the Melinist Sister Teresa of San Geronimo, and many others—to an unexpected and dangerous reversal of roles. In that exchange of knowledge and experience which, in reality and beyond institutionalized hierarchies, governed the nun-confessor relationship, the latter became "the spiritual son" while the mystic nun recaptured the old image and symbolic power of the "divine mothers."[25] By the end of the seventeenth century, when the Quietist crisis was in full flow and the theme of passive contemplation took on an extreme tonality that pushed spiritual experience into the worrisome and heterodox realm of the "free spirit" and the idea of the "faultless" nature of the perfect, heavy clouds gathered over excessively intimate relations between confessors and their women penitents—especially when the latter lived in the world as *bizzoche*.

Like Mellini and many other nuns, Giulia Crostarosa wrote—indeed, learned to write—under obedience. And if through her laborious exercises in mastering grammar the Bolognese *pinzochera* eventually discovered the joys of writing—a pleasure of which the judges who examined her for Quietism deprived her in the same peremptory fashion her confessor had used to oblige her to write—the fact is that Giulia Crostarosa learned prodigiously and quickly. She was part of that tenacious tradition in which the anomaly of women's knowledge could be justified only by divine command or that of a confessor, a tradition which, by assimilation to the exceptional gifts of mystical experience, transformed writing into an indication of sanctity.[26]

By the way in which it came up against the very threshold of the divine mystery, by being the instrument of the word of God that was installed in the insignificance, in the "nullity" of women, mystical writing—even when it did not challenge the major devotional and theological themes, such as those discussed in the *Mistica Ciudad de Dios* by the Spanish Maria de Agreda or the revelation on the cult of the Sacred Heart of Jesus to Margaret-Mary Alacoque, which generally infused women's visions and revelations[27]—bore the marks of an exceptionality that required verification and certification through the established techniques of the "discernment of spirits." Only the sacred nature implied by these writings transformed the virtues of humility and secrecy on which the writings had to be based into a pressing demand for communication, one that would break the seal of silence that stood as a guarantee of the "true female mystic" and dissolved the links of subjection which bound her to her spiritual father. God's "command to speak" was of greater import than a human requirement. In the general climate of distrust with which her revelations met, Crostarosa implied that that command was what allowed her to defend the revelations God had made to her before Father Falcoia and a divided community. "Write about me," the Lord had said. "What I have told you in secret you must now tell in public."[28]

The sacred nature of writing was reinforced when the edifying biographies of women assigned a healing power to women's written words. For instance, by laying the rule written by Sister Maria Celeste Crostarosa on the head of a nun "affected by folly," she was immediately cured; another nun who suffered from "an extremely fierce inflammation of the throat" swallowed "a fragment of a letter" written by Sister Mary of the Crucifixion Satellico and "felt her throat clear and the pain cease."[29]

Not without risk to themselves and often sowing confusion in a theological science that had managed to confine within a single methodical, regulatory scheme the ineffable material of the *via unitiva,* women pursued their itineraries of mystical writing, thus putting themselves at the heart of an experience that by its very nature tended to push them beyond the limits of human rationality and, consequently, of the human body. It was an intellectual and practical whole, and the mystical experience had to convert those points at which it could break through those frontiers into writing and into writing's unvarying codes and order; it had to make body and mind, reason and ec-static delirium, divine and human language coexist; it had to unite the organized scansion of the path to union with the irruption of the divine presence.

The task was wearying and burdensome, tormented by "disputes with hellish enemies." The image that fixed the relationship between women and writing in their spiritual biographies and the lives of saints allows one to observe how women trained themselves to conform to the conceptual and rhetorical apparatus that governed mystical writing and to observe the skill with which they had learned to manage its required guarantees. Sister Mary of the Crucifixion Satellico wrote of "various impediments and diabolical insolences . . . Sometimes they have prevented me from taking up paper and ink, and on such days I have not been able to write."[30]

Symbolic of a rather more human kind of effort, this imagined devilry filled the exiguous space of the cell or fell on the instruments of writing, sometimes leaving lasting and troublesome traces of its passage. Among Tomasi's writings, there is a sheet written by the devil, scrawled with obscure and indecipherable characters; it sums up her tormented relationship with writing and the anxiety caused by her confessor's "order."[31]

The practice of writing, which was the fulcrum of the mystical life of nuns, was thus traditionally regulated by an initial impulse external to a woman's freedom of choice. Whether the command came from God or from her confessor, it was this initial stimulus that circumscribed one of the possible ways to sanctity. The obligation to write—which Veronica Giuliani (1660–1727) felt as a "death penalty," as something "so repugnant that I felt unable to produce a single line"—molded the spiritual experience of nuns in a manner that would have differed greatly had they been allowed free access to theological knowledge and culture.[32] For many the pain caused by the obligation to write was part of that world of "suffering" which is the special mark of women's mystical experience.

To the sufferings of the body caused by hair shirts and "disciplines," by the mortification of fasts and vigils, to the pain of the soul's "exile" and the "abyss of personal nothingness"—to which consoling visions brought only temporary relief—were added the suffering of writing. The suffering was made more acute by the rigor of the confessors themselves, who—as in the case of Chiara Isabella Fornari (1697–1744), briefly guided by the selfsame Jesuit, Giovanni Maria Crivelli, who for so long "tortured" Veronica Giuliani—pushed their coercive powers to the point of insisting that these mystical writings be improvised on the spur of the moment and before their own eyes.[33]

Both loathed and loved, spiritual directors verified the nuns' "accounts," but "spiritual writings" did not fully placate the mystics' fear and anxiety, their dread of having written down "falsehoods and contrivances." As they did to Sister Mary of the Crucifixion, these seemed "infernal materials, and myself a demon"; her self-hatred made her want to throw herself "over any precipice, including the convent wall." Later, in 1763, the Benedictine nun Maria Cecilia Baj (1694–1766), whose life in the cloister was thrown into turmoil by myriad obsessions, was to write her own confessor: "I had to struggle again over those books [probably the six Colloqui she wrote between 1731 and 1735] which Your Reverence has in his possession: that they might be lunacies, disorders of my own mind, and sometimes this puts me in a frenzy. Why can't I have them in my hands and burn them?"

This fearfulness was a persistent trait in the spiritual experiences of female mystics and reflected, in a grossly exaggerated form, the endless distrust the ecclesiastical hierarchy felt for the "inner words" of women. "I've heard it said," writes Baj, "that women's fantasy becomes corrupted, so that they think that the things they see and hear are true, when in fact they are not true. I fear this might be true of me, and I would not wish to be guilty of such things before God and cause my soul to be damned."[34] Doubts and scruples of all sorts besieged the legitimacy of feminine discourse. In typical Baroque style their doubts ended in a typology of rhetorical artifice, which sought to conceal the very liberty and intellectual autonomy they had acquired by identifying women's knowledge with the art of dissimulation. Few confessed to how laborious a process it was to absorb devotional texts or to heighten their sensibility so that they could become receptive to the language and images of spiritual experience. Tomasi judged that she had been educated only in the School of Divine Grace, and Mary Magdalene Martinengo (1687–1737), though admitting to having looked for doctrinal solutions in books, confessed that she had derived no advantage from them.[35] The "self" being dead, all form of self-awareness having been expropriated, only God nurtured their knowledge.

Writing meant submitting to mental and physical discipline, but what liberated writing from human constraints and subjected it—by a mechanism in which the "rational level of the soul" arrived at a point beyond discourse through "the revealed word of God"[36]—to the direct intervention of God was extreme humility and obedience. As he had entered their lacerated bodies, God took up his abode in the writings of mystics, in order to confound their confessors and reveal to them the sanctity of their penitents.

Whether a displacement of the self or a divine possession, both yearned for and feared, the experience changed their identity and confounded it with the divine. If there is a "feminine" modality to be found in mystical writing, it lies precisely in the paradox of an intellectual and cultural conquest (for such was the access to writing for women) based on the experience of losing the self. It is not by chance that the tormented relationship between nuns and their own bodies, almost always reduced to a theater for the imitation of Christ, should have organized their writing around the themes of passivity and the mysticism of nothingness—the "think nothing," *no pensar nada* of the saint from Avila.

In the interstice "between Earth and the Cross, as between humility and suffering," Sister Maria Crocifissa Tomasi felt herself to be "but a little wind, a nothing, a nullity dwelling here without memory of myself, in that God renewed my first calling, which was always for total annihilation."[37]

Thought of as the "mirror of an angelic mind," as noted by her biographer Giovanni Batista Scaramelli, Satellico's writing was also the mirror of a well-ordered reasoning: "She put her material in good order, without creating confusion . . . She expressed her feelings, even in difficult matters, with great economy and equal clarity, something that is not easy even for an educated mind."[38]

This "clarity" and "economy," used as a criterion for discerning the divine word within a soul oppressed by the darkness and confusion of the diabolical, defined a rational way of writing. An orderly and methodical disposition was the prerequisite for that experience of God which the tradition of seventeenth-century mysticism, as contained in the Salesian *Traité de l'amour de Dieu,* had placed in the soul's highest sphere, the "pointe suprème de l'esprit."[39]

In line with the Ignatian tradition and Jesuit writings, which had made the rigid disposition of the various "parts" and the method of prayer into an embankment against a fall into an "abyss of nothingness," in which human will and reason risked disappearing, Scaramelli placed the gift of "infused" contemplation received by Satellico at the very summit of an ideal road to perfection, one in which she had never abandoned the carefully regulated exercise of prayer and had heroically resisted every sort of tribulation: "a brief contemplation, of the sort that God infuses into the soul with his own hands . . . which left her rich in affection, in a profound annihilation of her self, a destruction through love."[40]

Not nearly so clear and well ordered as in the hagiographical portraits—which, to create a more trustworthy reconstruction, intertwined the sister's "document" with the apologetic intent of the author—were the paths of female experience: especially when these paths were entrusted to the endless "spiritual reports" that accumulated with the passing of the years and the orders of their confessors. In this domain, the formation of the experience, the hard work of constructing the cognitive processes and learning the right and proper rules of writing—alongside which lay another and perhaps more difficult "spiritual grammar" and a lexicon peculiar to mystical writing—were neither linear nor orderly; rather these steps simply accumulated what Cardinal Giuseppe Tomasi, referring to the "spiritual reports" of his sister, Crocifissa, defined as "a great quantity of writings."[41]

This practice, the resounding outcome of ecclesiastical control over the female mystical experiences of the seventeenth century—which decisively affected the interweaving of theory and practice (for the former did not always coincide with the knowledge of the theologians and confessors)—was for many years to accompany the slow modification of the female religious condition, marked by an ever-increasing secularization. The counterpoint to the loss of effectiveness of the prophetic-visionary model was a return of the mystical experience to a more internalized and less visible dimension, about the supervision of which confessors still felt no uncertainties.

As the monastic condition lost its centrality, female experiences in the eighteenth and early nineteenth centuries concealed the exuberance of unitive mysticism and contemplation in the "withdrawal of the heart," already practiced by Crostarosa. While the experience of Maria Gaetana Agnesi (1718–1799)—Carlo Emilio Gadda's "mathematicessa e filosofa"—took an elitist dimension, stamped as it was with the extraordinary intellectual temper revealed not only in the *Istituzioni analitiche ad uso della gioventù italiana* but in the dry style of her *Cielo mistico*,[42] Rosa Teresa Brenti (1790–1872), who survived the Napoleonic suppressions and the Restoration, experienced dramatically a stubborn attempt to conceal a mystical path based on the traditional paradigm of the imitation of Christ.[43]

Brenti's life combined the two poles of the condition of religious women in those crucial years: marked on the one hand by the educational activity through which women's religious institutions proved their social utility and on the other by a mystical sensibility not without physical and penitential excesses, which linked her to medieval and Counter-Reformational female mystics.

The words of female mystics, voices of their bodies and souls, yielded in time to the body as narrative, and the medical language of the nineteenth century reaffirmed the old stereotype of female weakness, adding to it fresh discoveries from the medical science of the late eighteenth century, whose most systematic observer was France's Pierre Roussel (1742–1802).[44]

The lack of any word, not to speak of writing, from the two nineteenth-century "stigmatized Tyroleans," Maria de Moerl and Domenica Lazzari,[45] whose ecstatic experience consisted wholly in uninterrupted bodily suffering, would seem to underline the separation of the body sanctified by divine gifts, from whatever form, even when coerced, of self-awareness. This separation consigned the physical phenomena of ecstasy to the hegemony of science and nineteenth-century positivism, and anticipated the more complex operations performed by Charcot when, at the end of the century, he outlined the signs of hysteria to be found among eighteenth-century ecstatics, female saints, and women possessed by the Devil.[46]

Translated from the Italian by Keith Botsford

CHAPTER 12

Female Dynastic Sanctity, 1650–1850

SARA CABIBBO

The Earthly Court and the Court of Heaven

"Daughter, orphan, wife, sovereign, widow, nun, ever spotless and pure, Louise brought honor to the most difficult conditions of life that any princess could face."[1]

Monsignor Paolo Durio was domestic prelate to Gregory XVI, and when he wrote those lines, at the urging of the prince Carlo Alberto of Piedmont, he brought up from the remote past of the House of Savoy the figure of the Blessed Louise (1463–1503) on whom the pope, on August 3, 1839, had just conferred the decree "super confirmatione cultus ab immemoriabili," in recognition of the cult accorded her since time immemorial. By so doing, in a century marked by the "foolish presumption" and the "immorality of many," Durio was proposing to his readers a biography of a servant of God and a sovereign, one worthy to inspire pages by Manzoni, Chateaubriand, or Montalambert.

Durio was making his contribution as a churchman to a moderate neo-Guelph concept and placing the events of long ago in the political and idealistic context that increasingly animated the destinies of modern nation-states. He had concentrated his attention on an "area beloved of heaven, where peace and virtue prosper in the shadow of a modest, but no less glorious for that, throne." In this instance, a country located between Italy and France in which "a people, hard-working and peaceful, behaved like a well-ordered family under the rule of Amadeus IX, the Blessed, third duke of Savoy."

It was there, between those alps which "naturally" predisposed the early flowering of the idea of nationhood, that Louise had been born. Here her pious parents had brought her up to works of charity and devotion; later, after

219

her father's death and the brief, weak regency of her mother, Violante, she experienced the need to seek for herself "a husband in whose custody her virtue would remain intact and through whose firm help the pressures on the duchy would come to an end." And it was here, too, though she hated the idea of a marriage that would take her away from her cherished devotions, that the young woman, "humble but not base, kind but not womanishly yielding, demure but not affected," had chosen as her spouse Hugo of Châlon-Arlay, thus becoming the sovereign of a tiny earthly court that, molded to her exemplary life, was soon transformed into a "court of heaven."

In reconstructing the life of his heroine, Durio used the manuscript evidence of an unknown Poor Clare who was a contemporary of Louise's.[2] Her biographer traced a portrait of female sanctity that based its case substantially on the duchess's chaste marriage, which provided no children after eleven years of wedlock; on her charitable works, both material and symbolic, on behalf of her subjects and her husband, which were such that "the more Louise and Hugo were prodigal with their treasures to the poor, the greater the treasure became"; and on her subsequent entry, despite the protests of the population, into the Franciscan convent of Orbe on the death of her husband and her ordering of the affairs of the state. The only slight digression from the typology of the sovereign-saint the prelate allowed himself, as homage to a romantic vision of conjugal love, was a description of the death of Louise, who, like the Blessed Ermengard, expired surrounded by her sisters in Christ.

If in describing the characteristics of women's dynastic sanctity between the second half of the seventeenth century and the first fifty years of the nineteenth I have begun with this biography of Louise of Savoy—which as an expression of the neo-Gothic tastes of the early nineteenth century is at the extreme limits of my period—it is because its dichronicity, that which separates the life and times of the duchess and of her first biographer from those of her later chronicler, permits me to show both what is permanent and what has not lasted in a model of sanctity that, perhaps more than any other, has immediate public and political connotations. What has lasted and what is lost shows not only in the edifying content of the biographies but also in the uses made of the sources, which reveal "through the sources that have been preserved what men of the Church, whether urged on by the faithful or by the reigning kings, wished to express when they raised a king to sanctity."[3]

This observation by Robert Folz, which catches the dichronicity of the many royal king-saints between the sixth and twelfth centuries, can aptly be applied to the hagiographic fortunes of Louise of Savoy and, more generally, to the phenomenon of female dynastic sanctity. First defined between the sixth and seventh centuries by the spare testimonies concerning the Merovingian queens Radegunda and Batilde and the Saxon Matilda, this kind of sanctity flourished particularly in the latter part of the thirteenth century when, "alongside the male ideals (founder of the nation, missionary, just king, knightly king, *athleta patriae*) personified in most cases by saintly princes and kings," queens and princesses presented themselves on the threshold of edification by becoming "the principal trustees of royalty within their dynasties."[4]

From that point on—from the varied vicissitudes of Elizabeth of Thuringia, Edwige of Silesia, Cunigond, Margaret of Scotland, and others—female dynastic sanctity, measuring itself against the changing realities of political and religious institutions or sociocultural demands, over the centuries took on the features of other queens. Occasionally, this process would point up the processes of affirmation or consolidation of this or that dynasty, the dynamics in play between the social and political components of a given country, the relative power held by the sacred or the profane, all involved in the progressive secularization of the modern state. It would also reveal, and the phenomenon is no less important, whether this sort of female sanctity was exportable in time and space. For women transposed the dynamics of "alliance" of which they, as queens, were the principal instruments, to the symbolic plane of heavenly kinship: this allowed one dynasty, especially in times of conflict, to recover the material and ideal heritage of a saintly queen who had belonged to another. Such, for instance, was the case with the relics of Margaret of Scotland (1046–1093), whose head, acquired by Philip II of Spain during the wars between Catholic Spain and Protestant England, was lodged in the royal place of the Escorial, thus guaranteeing the "prudent king" a symbolic link to the otherwise unattainable British throne.[5]

Returning to Louise of Savoy and the huge gap in time that separates her life as lived and related in the fifteenth century from that reconstructed in the nineteenth, one fact requires special attention: the existence of a biography written by her fellow nun. Authentic or not, well translated or not, it is a reminder of an element that often plays a part in authenticating female sanctity, for that authentication is often based on the existence of a first Life—in most cases written by a woman who knew the saint—and on a later, second biography written by a man.

Frequently—especially beginning with the years of the Counter-Reformation, when convents were filled with ecstasies and the edifying tales of the numerous servants of God, duly noted by their fellow nuns—this double register of authentication and publication of female sanctity was necessary, even in the case of a queen's authority. Durio, too, probably faced the specificity of a female language which, as the edition of the biography by Louise's fellow nun shows, skipped the facts of her life and her illustrious ancestors and ignored most of her charitable works and her marital relations with her husband in order to register those episodes that fell into the category of the "marvelous" as understood by a nun in the early sixteenth century, or at the very least those that seemed most likely to have an effect on her contemporaries: her ability to memorize holy sermons, her capacity to learn, superior to that of a man, and her distaste for the worldly life of the time.

The first Life places little emphasis on the duchess's ascetic practices or her charitable works, matters with which Durio fills many pages, but notes only Louise's preference for "the humblest fare" and her charity toward "poor lepers, widows, orphan children and poor pregnant women." The matrimonial chastity that so intrigued the later biographer finds no place in the earlier work, which becomes more circumstantial when the holy duchess, widowed, "gave away all she owned to poor churches and poor religious" and, with a few ladies of her court, sought refuge in the convent of Orbe. Here, no longer "my Lady" but simply Sister Louise, she died uttering the words "Maria mater gratiae" (Mary Mother of Grace).

The business of rereading and adapting a source to the tastes and mentality of the nineteenth century, the need to take a quiet, local cult and extend it to the needs for enhancement of the house of Savoy—which culminated in 1842 with the transferral of Louise's relics to the Royal Chapel—requires that we go more deeply into the variations in the typology of dynastic sanctity; within the period under study we must consider certain thematic and temporal points around which this changed perspective organized itself.

The Models of Dynastic Hagiography

An essay written a decade ago on the lives of the Merovingian saints Radegunda and Batilde pointed out how essential to their sainthood was the choice of the monastic life.[6] Though both queens demonstrated that in those days only sovereigns and bishops could "reconcile heaven and earth," they otherwise differed greatly, in the course of their lives and in how these lives were told. While the former, Radegunda, was a "queen who abandoned the world and a woman who turned her back on the marriage to enter into a convent while her husband was still alive,"[7] Batilde was tied by deep affection and solidarity to her husband, further demonstrating by her incessant activity "that the duty of every sovereign is to exercise her own power while respecting Christian morals and the advice of bishops."[8]

These two exempla, established in the sixth and seventh centuries, had a decisive influence on the subsequent, long history of female dynastic sanctity; they became a sort of litmus test by which to measure and qualify the behavior of other queens who, in other contexts, enjoyed the honors of the altar.

The biographer lies between these two typologies. The cultivated Fortunatus, a refined admirer of the constancy of the noble Roman ladies who had converted to Christianity, celebrated the Merovingian queen Radegunda as a *mulier virilis,* "manly woman." Overcoming the fragility of her sex and despising the things of this world, "she gained paradise." By contrast, Baldwina, a nun of the royal convent of the Holy Cross, who some twenty years later and on her abbess's orders wrote Radegunda's *vita,* glossed over her heroine's discomforts over her marriage and husband and placed her accent instead on the public role played by the ex-queen. Fortunatus and Baldwina look at the same thing in different ways, and even considering the observations made about the two biographies of Louise of Savoy, this suggests one ought to qualify the role the husband, the sovereign, played in the sainthood of his wife and to put into context the value that the two different biographies ascribed to the relationship between the sexes.

The relationship between the holy spouse and her husband was not fixed in time, but was rather greatly influenced by contemporary social and cultural practices. Generally, it oscillated between two poles. The first was focused on the gulf between the vulgarity and brutality of the man and the deep devotion of the woman, so that the latter's saintly reputation derived in part from the resignation with which she submitted to her wifely duties. The other focused on how the married pair complemented one another; it would linger on the woman's capacity to soften a male heart (itself often pious) and how she brought him to the summits of devotion, piety, and continence.

The first category would include Elizabeth of Portugal, canonized in 1625, who forced herself to "placere viro . . . sed magis Deo" (please her husband but God more), and who educated not just her children in Christian fashion but also those children who resulted from her kingly husband's lusts for other *mulierculae.*[9] The second would include Margaret of Scotland, celebrated during the seventeenth century for her marriage, for the influence she had on the good governance of Malcolm III, and its worthy epilogue: her death on learning that her husband and their firstborn had both perished on the field of battle.

As an example of a middle way, there are the troubles of Margaret of Savoy (1382–1464). Proclaimed Blessed Margaret in 1566, her sanctity was further confirmed by Clement X in 1670, when he authorized her cult throughout the domains of Savoy. The daughter of Amadeus of Savoy-Acaja and Louise's cousin, a disciple of Saint Vincent Ferrer, the young princess was given in marriage to Theodore II Paleologus as a means to end the contention between the two royal families. Theodore was fifteen years older than she, a rough, military man, and already the father of two children who were nearly of the same age as the young bride. She made great efforts to improve their thorny characters and dedicated herself wholeheartedly to the education of her stepchildren. "After fifteen years of most holy union," Margaret donned the habit of the Dominican tertiaries and founded the Augustinian convent of Saint Mary Magdalene in Alba. In the city hospital of Santa Maria degli Angeli, as recorded a nineteenth-century biographer, she was often seen "personally looking after the patients with admirable zeal," humbly "dressing their sores."[10]

The three women all have one thing in common: they were all canonized, or reached the height of their fame, in the seventeenth century—precisely at the time when the homogenizing and Romanizing impetus of the papacy (especially in Italy) intersected with the consolidation of Spanish power, and its elites as well as its political institutions were being "civilized." As no saintly queens lived in that period, but the female religious ideal promoting virginity and the monastic life flourished—many aristocrats, in deference to the strategies of their families, turned their backs on the world and took up the path of religious perfection—any attempt to sum up the particularity of female dynastic sanctity necessarily must be focused, between the 1600s and 1700s, on the edifying works written about the queens of an earlier age.

The renewed attention given these early sovereigns was much influenced by political events and by the dynamics of dynastic alliances that run through the nations involved in the wars of the so-called Iron Century. To a society of "Lords, patricians, and knights," which was that of Italy in the modern period, was conjoined an ethic of civil and religious behavior that took on a "prevailingly private character," one in which, to accompany the decline of the old, glorious ruling class, "less heroic, but no less taxing duties" became part of the game.[11]

The phenomenon of the "living saints"—the women prophets, the advisers to princes, the spiritual mothers who had given such a luster to Italian Renaissance courts—had faded into the past, and other traits among sovereigns that would exemplify the marriage of throne and altar so characteristic of the Restoration had not yet emerged. Hence the various exempla offered by the queens of the past, jostling within the pages of innumerable eighteenth-century works of hagiography, became the vehicle by means of which a decaying model of sanctity (one that claimed to "whisper into the ears and the hearts" of princes and their spouses, their children and sisters) could instill in them the devotional practices that had created the pasts of great dynasties and splendid courts.[12] As an appanage of the royal houses that created states, dynastic sanctity broke up during the irregular and contradictory conformity of the Baroque period into a polyfunctional model of seigneurial sanctity within whose coordinates were formed the various strategies, the "team games," of the variegated nobilities of Italy, which modeled themselves on court life.[13]

Women—daughters and sisters of noble houses both great and small—could indeed become saints. In the shadows of their cloisters and in the complex and all-inclusive mosaic of a family project destined to influence the history of men and the *historia salutis* they could display the credentials of their lives, made up of renunciation, of prayer, of bodily mortifications and supernatural gifts: so did Isabella Tomasi of the dukes of Palma di Montechiaro, in religion Maria Crocifissa, around whose ups and downs as a Benedictine nun and mystic the Sicilian ducal family built its prestige between the seventeenth and eighteenth centuries.

The many *principessae, ducissae, marchionessae,* and *comiissae*—the wives of magnates and often prolific mothers—could also become saints. Within the principles of marital law that emerged from the Council of Trent, and in the context of the pluralism of usages and customs of which the Church of the Counter-Reformation was well aware, they illustrated, by the variety of their lives and their points of reference, the enormous regional variations within Italy.[14]

Arbitrated by male authority, the saintliness of the sovereign woman was modeled on a set of various edifying and often contradictory experiences: those, for instance, of the pious and delicate Bridget of Sweden, who, having long lived a continent life with her husband, when he died had "divided half her worldly goods with her children" and founded the monastery of Vadstena;[15] or those of the warlike Adelaide of Susa (in the eleventh century), three times married and the mother of eight, who was included in Filippo Ferrario's 1625 catalog of saints "qui in Martyrologio non sunt,"[16] the latter being an instance of a saint who, despite her conflict with the Church's current tendency to discourage remarriages, nonetheless had the door to sainthood opened to her by reason of an unconstrained submission to the rules of social prestige.

This echo of a stereotype that in the remote Merovingian past had sanctioned the irreconcilable natures of heaven and earth, that had then kept in step with the affirmation of an urban, community dimension to royal female sanctity, and that included seclusion in a monastery or the founding of a convent (as performed by the sovereigns of yore) was now proposed to the descendents of these edifying Lives—whether secluded virgins or widowed laywomen—as a symbolic validation of that choice of a religious life.

It worked as a legitimation of the institutions of fideicommissum and primogeniture; it assured the return of dowries to the family. This "exile" from the secular world, as suggested in the hagiographic texts, also served in some ways to remove the noblewoman of the modern age from the contentious juridical struggle between the widow's family and her husband's that so often ensued on the nobleman's death.[17]

The Romantic Queen

When Maria Cristina of Savoy, queen of the Two Sicilies, died in 1836, the court encomiasts promptly celebrated the life of a queen who had remained in the world—of the court, that is—"barely three years and a brilliant fourth," brilliant because she had given the kingdom an heir, even if it cost her her life. In the grief that struck down both illustrious families, the Savoyards and the Bourbons of Naples, they saw a sign of divine will, which had rewarded the "immaculate religious behavior" of one of their own.[18]

A deeply religious woman, whose "angelic face was embellished by its modest dignity,' she had borne the tedium and pomp of her role only to satisfy the rituals of her marriage contract: "for a highly popular man," wrote Father Cagnazzi," is much moved by appearance." Maria Cristina was certainly the appropriate sort of female figure to blunt those "princely weapons" which had figured so powerfully in the destinies of the House of Savoy and to restore popularity to a Neapolitan dynasty that from the earliest days of its return to the kingdom had had to live with the incubi of the republic and revolutions.[19]

We can delineate—largely through Guglielmo De Cesare's imposing work, *Vita della venerabile serva di Dio Maria Cristina*[20]—the expression of a new form of royal female sanctity, which differed from older forms in that it had to confront a conscious dynastic ambition of the most extensive sort and the many problems bequeathed to the crown, from the age of reform and revolution to that of the Restoration.

The first distinction to which attention should be drawn is that, contrary to the biographical reconstructions with which we have so far been concerned, Maria Cristina's life, the *processi* of her beatification, and her hagiographic portrait are all confined to little more than twenty years. She died in 1836 and was beatified on July 9, 1859; De Cesare's *Vita* was published four years later, in 1863. Thus two contexts are brought together: first that of the frail and melancholy princess whom Rudolph Bell includes among his anorexic saints[21] and whom her biographer romanticizes; and second, that of a time-span which, by removing Maria Cristina from the hands of that "great sculptor," time, paradoxically consigns her to us as too greatly involved, indeed almost submerged, in the political, social, and cultural climate of the years that formed the backdrop to her life and its recounting.

The second difference is that in this case the sovereign, unlike other dynastic saints celebrated in the past, is "claimed" by her original Savoyard family, even though the link to the Neapolitan royal family appears in the biography and the various funeral eulogies. This was a sure sign of the successes already achieved or in preparation for the Savoy dynasty, but it was also probably a representation of a female identity—privileged, of course, as is fitting for a queen—that paid greater heed to her moral, psychological, and intellectual gifts than to her role as a wife, though as we shall see, the *topos* of the role to be played by a queen at her husband's court continued to carry considerable weight.

Having determined where within the model of female dynastic sanctity to place Maria Cristina—more Batilde than Radegunda, perhaps a new Edwige of Silesia, who in the thirteenth century personified the traits of "a queen who becomes a saint by making use of the influence provided by her high birth and her eminent place in society"[22]—De Cesaris painted his portrait of the sovereign using the overall forms that had emerged, not least through the decrees of Urban VIII, in hagiographic literature and in the beatification procedures: a virtuous and devout childhood in the company of affectionate, pious parents, enemies to any kind of social injustice; an overwhelming desire to enter a monastery; a life in the world that respected all the cardinal virtues; heroic virtue; an edifying death; and miracles postmortem. Such were the elements of a chaste and pious life that had emerged from the darkness which pervaded female sanctity during the Counter-Reformation, which had survived the practice of the eighteenth century's "regulated devotion," and was now interacting with the dynamics of the times.

In fact, as a child and after hours of prayer and devotion, Maria Cristina "would run joyfully to the waters of the fountains that adorned the royal delights of Turin and Cagliari, jumping in and out of the water, now spraying the plants . . . now picking flowers from the beds with which, when she had woven them into garlands, she would adorn the pictures of Jesus and Mary" (p. 9). Later, as a young woman, she would take pleasure in dancing, "but dancing for her was but an innocent exercise, a delight for her light legs, with no further thought: as proved by her choosing to dance with her sisters and her firm determination to enter a cloister" (p. 31).

To place the nineteenth-century sovereign in a well-established tradition, her biographer used another element along with the conventions of typical hagiography: he recalled the heavenly genealogy of the holy queens of the House of Savoy over the centuries. These, from the remote Adelaide of Susa through Louise and Margaret, had constantly renewed the dynasty's alliance between heaven and earth; and if Maria Clotilde, the daughter of Vittorio Emmanuele II, had not yet risen to sainthood, Abbot De Cesaris hardly undervalued the fact that the tribulations of that unhappy princess, for some years married to the libertine Jerome Bonaparte, could have created a new kind of saint for the Savoyards: a martyr who used kindness and charity against the new paganism of the nineteenth century.[23]

Even within the staid hagiographical tradition Maria Cristina represented all those hopes that, since the last decades of the eighteenth century and as a result of men's progressive abandonment of the religious life during the Enlightenment, the Church had placed in women.[24] Their influence on the morality and ideas of our time," wrote our biographer, "is extremely great and important in matters of religion and behavior."

Where the identifying status or condition came from models of imitation, the edifying message now became more explicit, and Abbot De Cesaris stated that writing a book on the Savoyard queen was "to demonstrate that there is no station in life in which a life of perfection, by which I mean a sober, just life which piously respects both God and man, may not be pursued."

Sobriety, justice, piety: these are the key words in a vocabulary that remains unchanged during the two centuries between 1650 and 1850 as definitions of the prerogatives of female dynastic sanctity. Because of the "grave" nature of the royal function it can no longer be measured by the "excesses" that marked the experiences of other women (the mystics, ecstatics, and prophets). Still, defining Christian perfection as a science showed the gulf between Maria Cristina's experience and that of the saintly sovereigns of previous centuries. It was no longer a matter of the "science of good management," the exclusive preserve of princes and men who had assigned to their wives a marginal role as agents of charity and of the gentling of manners; the "science of Christian perfection" was now in the hands of the queen and she became an instrument of government.

To satisfy her cousin Carlo Alberto, who wished her to ally her family with the Bourbons, Maria Cristina abandoned her desire to "preserve herself for a life devoted to God, for prayer and meditation at the foot of the cross, for mortification in a convent," and married Ferdinand. Like so many other princesses before her, she gave up her childhood home and became queen of a kingdom of which she knew nothing. There, much admired "for her mind, for the saintliness of her soul, her vivacious spirit and the gracefulness of her ways" (p. 130), the young woman proposed not only to model her court on monastic lines, but also to place her relations with her husband and people on a new basis.

In rereading Durio on Louise of Savoy we have seen how powerfully romantic love affected the royal dynamics between the sexes; and while it is unlikely that the holy union of the duke and duchess of Châlon-Arlay was consummated under its aegis, it is more believable that the union of Maria Cristina and Ferdinand—beyond their royal relationship—was reciprocally based on an image that had a powerful resonance in their sensibilities.

The background to this representation of their feelings was the court, the theater, the opera, and the ball, the arenas of sociability in the early 1800s. The queen, who was much given to visiting churches and sanctuaries, may well have been scandalized by the scanty garments worn by the dancers of San Carlo at the Neapolitan Opera House, but the king, reminding her that in Naples music was "practiced by many and loved by all" and that it was a monarch's duty to "promote the benefits of fame and fortune which many musicians derived from their art" (p. 183), sought to limit the blushes of his consort by introducing a number of restrictions which, De Desaris wrote, 'were so immediate and effective that they left a lasting mark on the long reign of Ferdinand II and were respected until a series of misadventures fell upon the area and put an end to such peaceful and happy times" (p. 184).

The bitter words of the Neapolitan abbot, the nostalgia with which throughout the biography of Maria Cristina he looks back to a recent past, bring up another matter that shows both the permanence and the cracks in the model of female dynastic sanctity between the seventeenth and nineteenth centuries: the queen's relationship with her kingdom and her people.

Ever present in medieval and early modern hagiographic texts, always sensitive to the beneficial interventions of the sovereign in the lives of the poor, the sick, widows, religious, and often a generic people oppressed by wars, famines, or epidemics, this stereotype of the relationship between a sovereign and her subjects continues to operate in the edifying biographies produced in the seventeenth and eighteenth centuries, which are rich in the often violent protests of a population that refused to give up its beloved queen when she had decided to enter a monastery.

As a prototype of royal relations, within which flourished the ferment of an easily guided *jacquerie,* this benevolent link between a queen and her subjects was also evidence of the fears and tensions that ran through royal behavior. The dynamic is made explicit in the biography of Maria Cristina: moderate Italy's view that "the people" might, led by ideologists, permanently destroy the social order, "despoil the temples, threaten religion, and seek to abolish throne and church," was what guided both biographer and subject. Memories of a baying crowd "assembled before the Palace" shouting the word "constitution," of the "tumultuous shouts" that had haunted the queen's dreams from childhood, now mingled with the grown-up queen's disputes with contemporary economists who sought some way in which "the mighty could give joy to all while at the same time respond to the lamentations of the poor."

So the queen "promoted work and Neapolitan industry"; she praised local manufacturers over foreign, and set the example to her court by buying cloth, fabrics, lace, and artificial flowers produced within the kingdom. Wishing to advance the Neapolitan silk industry, she increased the number of looms in the little village of San Leucio, buying more modern machinery and the latest fabrics abroad "to offer them as models" for the villagers. Invited to the

Universal Exhibition of 1834, she "carefully and with judgment examined what products might be most useful at home"; and their "manufactures' eyes shone with joy at her encouraging words . . . She asked to see silks from Catania and, as none were available, she expressed her displeasure that such fabrics, highly valued throughout Italy and abroad, were not part of the Exhibition. This alone was enough to give a great stimulus to the silk industry on the island" (pp. 197–198). What a miracle this nineteenth-century sovereign who cloaked protectionism under the protection she owed her subjects!

Exhausted by the fatigues of the journey, from a difficult pregnancy, and the birth of the heir, Maria Cristina died on January 31, 1836. Her biographer notes that before expiring, the queen called three times for Ferdinand; her maid, Clementina Aratore, summoned as a witness in her beatification, unable to bear her cries, "ran breathlessly to the King's rooms and spoke to his chamberlain, Cocle, who forbade that this last wish of the servant of God be referred to the King, and suggested that she tell the dying woman that the King was in council with his ministers" (p. 264).

With the weakening of her voice, in that dumb insensibility of the palace, a shadow was cast over a function that for centuries had helped to found dynasties that linked heaven and earth.

Translated from the Italian by Keith Botsford

CHAPTER 13

Sacred Imagery and the Religious Lives of Women, 1650–1850

KAREN-EDIS BARZMAN

The Relation of Art to the World of Social Exchange: The Case of Maria Maddalena de' Pazzi

The year 1669 marked the canonization of the Carmelite Maria Maddalena de' Pazzi (1566–1607) and the beginning of a campaign to deploy her image in art. In the Florentine church named for her, painters and sculptors depicted her mystical encounters with Jesus and Mary, as well as miracles approved at the time of her canonization.[1] Their canvases, frescoes, and sculptures constitute a visual analogue to the authorized biography written by her confessor in 1609. For example, Luca Giordano's *Mary Magdalene with Mary and the Infant Jesus* of 1684 (fig. 1), which appears on the right wall of the reliquary chapel, illustrates this passage from the biography:

> Maria Maddalena had many times desired to see the infant Jesus as he had issued forth from Mary's womb. Whence, one time when she was rapt in ecstasy, the most holy Virgin appeared to her with the baby Jesus . . . and she not only showed him to [Maria Maddalena] but also placed him in her arms; and she tenderly held him to her heart . . . and appeared to melt completely with love.[2]

Giordano painted the mystic kneeling, with hands raised and face lifted, employing a language of the body that conveys a mixed expression of devotion and longing to hold the infant.

Having found a textual source for the painting's narrative, we could say that the demands of iconographic analysis have already been met. Yet the biography was composed to promote the mystic for sainthood; in its second printing by 1611, it conformed in every respect to the conventions of hagiographic writing, even in its assertions of Maria Maddalena's exceptionality.

231

What we are left to wonder about is the relationship of the painting and its text to the voice and lived experience of the historical woman.

Maria Maddalena lived in clausura throughout her adult life, which generally required restraint from speech. Yet we know that she did not live in silence. Transcriptions of her ecstatic professions literally fill volumes. Although these are the most authoritative sources for the mystic's speech and lived experiences, the transcriptions were not printed in their entirety until 1960. They record Maria Maddalena's union with the infant Jesus in different terms than those of the authorized biography informing Giordano's painting. In the transcriptions, the union is part of a twelve-hour ecstasy in which the mystic speaks through metaphor about the moral transgressions of religious life and the means to salvation. The ecstasy began in the novitiate, with many witnesses present as Maria Maddalena preached in rapture, condemning those who broke vows of obedience, chastity, and charity. We are told that she appeared to comprehend great things as she spoke and knelt in prayer, with eyes uplifted. Then she rose, indicating that Jesus was descending from the breast of God the Father. She called to the baby, gesturing that she cradled him in her arms, laughing and talking with joy and affection. Suddenly she fell silent, indicating through pantomime that the baby had departed, which prompted her to lament about the impurities of the world that had offended him. Finally, she lifted her face and said: "It is better for him to remain in the bosom of his Father."[3]

From the transcriptions, we learn that Maria Maddalena introduced an unconventional image of the infant Jesus at the breast of God the Father, with the baby descending of his own will. The union was part of an extended ecstasy through which the mystic gained knowledge and preached a larger discourse of reform. Indeed, the transcriptions go on to suggest that she attempted to institute a discalced reform in her cloistered chapter, on the model of Teresa of Avila, and to promote reform more broadly in the Church.[4]

Significantly, the authorized biography and Giordano's pictorial counterpart make no allusion to preaching. The painting reduces the mystic to a passive recipient rather than the active agent of narrative. Both text and picture refuse the coupling of the infant with the Father and substitute Mary, according to convention. Finally, they present the union as a discrete episode of devotion, cast in gendered terms of maternal love and completely removed from the context of reform. In effect, they neutralize the political tenor of Maria Maddalena's voice, which the transcriptions of her speech clearly reveal. Surely there is a gap between the mystic's utterances and these monuments to her sainthood, between her voice and the mythologized femininity she was made to represent.

The Function of Art as Social Technology

This gap takes on social significance once we acknowledge that images and objects can have a powerful effect in shaping identity and social practice. In fact, they often function as part of a larger social technology, conveying or reinforcing beliefs and codes of conduct promoted by the dominant institutions. Despite the diffusion of normalizing models of subjectivity in visual culture, social technologies sometimes fail within communities, or there may be significant nodal points of resistance. This is precisely what we find in Italy in the religious lives of women between 1650 and 1850. Many women conformed to the protocols of church, state, and family in piety and in devotional practice—protocols often promoted through pictures (with transgressions simply erased by the same pictorial means), as in Giordano's painting of Maria Maddalena de' Pazzi. Yet for others, a decisive gap existed between lived experience and the authorized terms of piety offered in their visual worlds.

The Council of Trent (1545–1563) affirmed the efficacy of images in devotional practice, among other things pointing to examples of piety and virtue in representations of saints. This institutional endorsement had a profound effect on the subsequent production and reception of art in Italy, with a veritable industry springing up to promote the representation of saints in two- and three-dimensional media, in "high" and "low" art. In the two-hundred-year period under consideration, biblical saints, with the exception of the Magdalene, did not figure significantly in sacred imagery, nor did early Christian or medieval martyrs. The saints most widely deployed were relative newcomers, generally from religious orders, whose stature was enhanced by the canonization of their members.[5] The constructed *vitae* of these saints could easily be used for specific pastoral purposes, according to the exigencies of the time, which made these figures into particularly attractive models for the faithful. The saints included the mystics Catherine of Siena (1347–1380, canonized 1461), a Dominican tertiary, and the Carmelites Teresa of Avila (1512–1582, canonized 1622) and Maria Maddalena de' Pazzi. These women, who lived before, during, and after Trent, respectively, fashioned themselves as recipients of divine knowledge through union with God, and used this knowledge to formulate discourses of reform. The first two moved with relative freedom and success compared to Maria Maddalena, who belonged entirely to an age of strict enclosure and increasing surveillance and supervision, in religious communities as well as in the secular world. Yet despite their apostolic activities, and the abundant primary material documenting their discourses (some of which was in wide circulation in the period under discussion), Catherine and Teresa were also refashioned in post-Tridentine art, reduced in representation, like Maria Maddalena, to acceptable feminine models of contemplation and devotion.

The following material addresses the circulation of these models in the complex world of social exchange. Of continuing interest are the disjunctions between the authorized images of sanctity and the lives of the female saints represented. But the primary focus is audience, reception, and the relative success or failure of imagery as part of a given social technology. As a consequence, this chapter deals for the most part with images and objects that belonged to authorized discourses on feminine sanctity and on women's spirituality (not surprisingly, these are the works that have been carefully preserved). The concluding sections deal with expressions of piety and devotion at a popular level, *outside* the sphere of institutional control with respect to production and iconography. This category includes work by women, primarily in the "minor arts" and in areas of "amateur production," as women were excluded institutionally from most professional forms of artistic practice.

Catherine of Siena

A selective survey of the imagery of Catherine of Siena is a good place to start.[6] An austere ascetic, a preacher and converter of souls, an adviser to popes—Catherine became the object of intense veneration after her death and was quickly embraced as patron saint of Italy. A small group of pictures from the mid-seventeenth through the mid-eighteenth centuries shows Catherine at a table with a crown of thorns on her head and a crucifix, both of which allude to the sacrifice of Jesus and, by extension, to the redemption of humanity (fig. 2). A skull might be included as a *memento mori,* providing a means for viewers to identify with the sanctified woman (for those initiated into this language of symbols) through the notion of shared mortality. The curious thing about these paintings is that Catherine is figured writing, even though it was well known that she was illiterate and dictated her treatises and correspondence to scribes. Here is another example of the distance between the representational construct and the historical evidence. Perhaps these pictures were not to be taken literally; the act of writing might have been intended as a trope for Catherine's theological wisdom and discursive acumen. We should note, though, that these qualities were considered uncharacteristic of the feminine and were not widely fostered among women in early modern Italy. It is true that writing by female religious increased during this period, but it was rigorously monitored by confessors, as a check to the women's mystical impulses, in an attempt to maintain a seamless orthodoxy within conventual walls. In this context, paintings of a woman freely putting pen to paper, without supervision, might seem discordant with prevailing gender protocols. Yet these pictures of Catherine are easily redeemed, for they do not refer to a woman's autonomous discourse. Divine inspiration is figured as her guide, with Catherine literally drawing ink from the bleeding wounds of Jesus.

A half-length figure of Catherine in ecstasy, or contemplating the Passion, was popular throughout the seventeenth century in paintings and prints. In addition to the skull, crown of thorns, and crucifix, lilies were usually included as a symbol of purity. In this age of *la monaca santa* (the saintly nun), when the institutions of church and family promoted the feminine ideal of self-discipline and the denial of carnal and other worldly pleasures, the lily as symbol was almost ubiquitous.

Starting in the 1720s a controversial iconography for Catherine was widely circulated in small, cheaply produced, and affordable prints later known as *santini*. Here a half-length Catherine with a crown of thorns gazes at a cross in one hand and raises the other in a gesture of acknowledgment and awe as she contemplates the Crucifixion (fig. 3). Central to its meaning are her stigmata. The number of such prints in circulation was impressive and might be taken as a reflection of popular investment in a new aspect of her cult. Yet the production of imagery often constitutes social practice rather than merely reflecting it, engendering new forms of reception and shifting patterns of devotion in ways that are determined hierarchically. In the eighteenth century this took place as part of a larger campaign to foster daily devotion among the laity, particularly among women whom the Church began to cultivate as "emissaries" of faith and of Christian virtue in the home. The origins and authenticity of Catherine's bodily wounds were questioned in earlier periods, with the dispute led by the Franciscans, who argued for the singularity of their founder's stigmata. Sixtus IV, a Franciscan himself, issued a papal bull in 1472 prohibiting stigmata in representations of Catherine. The ban was not universally observed, and images of Catherine displaying her wounds were not unknown. The mass production of this kind of imagery in prints, however, began in the 1720s and was surely prompted by Benedict XIII's authorization of the liturgical celebration of Catherine's stigmata in 1727, and by his papal concession in 1728, which granted indulgences for the veneration of her images. Many of the prints bear inscriptions explicitly connecting the stigmata imagery to Benedict's papal agenda. Small in size (approximately four and a half by three inches), and easily slipped between the pages of a book or tacked upon a wall, these prints were intended for close and regular inspection by individual viewers. With inscriptions in the vernacular, they were ideal for the promotion of directed forms of devotion in the daily routines of the laity.

In the mid-eighteenth century a simplified half-length image of Catherine was introduced, based on prototypes of contemplative female saints and of Jesus as Man of Sorrows *(Ecce Homo),* which were made popular in the seventeenth century by such artists as Guido Reni and Carlo Dolci. In an example by Gianbattista Tiepolo, Catherine's only attributes are the crown of thorns and the stigmata, as she turns in three-quarter view and crosses her hands on her breast, lifting her eyes and parting her lips in a languid expression of devotion (fig. 4). The type was widely disseminated through painted copies and prints. One of the most challenging tasks for artists after Trent was to give somatic expression to religious interiority; one of the results was a codified language of the body that became part of a gestural vocabulary of the beholder. The portrait of *la monachina,* described by Vittoria Giorgini Manzoni in 1851 in her *Memorie* (see Chapter 10), was clearly fashioned after this type of painting, with the somatic inflection of the little girl ("occhi rivolti al cielo," or "eyes upturned toward heaven") striking a similarly pathetic chord. Although Manzoni refers to the child as a "minuscola santa Teresa," the analogy with Catherine is relevant, since Teresa, Catherine, and even Maria Maddalena de' Pazzi had become virtually interchangeable as models of feminine piety by the late seventeenth century.

Aestheticized Ecstasy

Despite institutional attempts to regulate and restrain religiosity, in keeping with developing Enlightenment principles, late-seventeenth- and eighteenth-century Italy experienced the spread of religious "enthusiasm" and popular currents of mysticism, which is a good example of the breakdown of a social technology in the face of popular belief and practice. Women played a significant role in this popular mysticism, with many from the poorer classes leading paramonastic lives or moving freely in secular society (hence, without institutional protection or support). There are works of art from the early part of the period that celebrate female ecstasy; Gianlorenzo Bernini's figure of the Franciscan tertiary Ludovica Albertoni (1473–1533, beatified 1671) is a good example (fig. 5).[7] A recumbent Ludovica clutches her breast and throws back her head, her eyes rolled up and her lips parted in a perpetual gasp of ecstasy. Executed between 1672 and 1674 for the woman's mortuary chapel in San Francesco a Ripa in Rome, the sculpture renders visible the internal movements of her soul, aestheticizing her rapture in monumental and spectacular terms, despite its smaller-than-life size.

Undoubtedly Ludovica's noble blood, as well as her affiliation with one of the powerful Mendicant orders, led to the institutional validation of her mystical activity, to her beatification, and ultimately to approval of her public veneration. Indeed, Bernini was commissioned by Cardinal Paluzzi-Albertoni/Altieri, Ludovica's great-great grandson and Clement X Altieri's adopted nephew, to carve the figure of the mystic, whose commemoration surely enhanced the prestige of his family. Unlike Ludovica, most female mystics in this period spoke extrainstitutionally, in unauthorized voices, without the privileges accorded those from families of wealth and influence. They were often denounced by family and friends and discredited by inquisitorial courts.[8] These women did not figure in sacred monuments (public or private) that were comparable to Bernini's *Ludovica Albertoni;* indeed, a survey of authorized art from the period does not even hint at their existence.

Eroticized Ecstasy

Modern viewers have argued that Bernini intended to elide the sexual and the spiritual in his *Ludovica,* and in his even more renowned *Teresa of Avila,* which was executed for the Roman church of Santa Maria della Vittoria in the late 1640s. For seventeenth- and eighteenth-century audiences, however, more titillating images surely belonged to a group of paintings of Mary Magdalene, the quintessential sinner turned penitent, in which iconographic elisions of the sacred and the profane were intentional and primary in terms of the paintings' meaning.[9] Tridentine reformers had denounced the eroticizing of sacred imagery as indecent and inconsistent with the ends of Christian instruction and the presentation of models for imitation. But the control of the bishops, who were responsible for approving images for public devotion, did not extend to more private spheres of patronage. It was precisely within these spheres that the taste for sexually charged imagery played itself out. The Magdalene was an ideal vehicle—not a near-contemporary but a woman from the early Christian past whose antiquity and associations with prostitution provided temporal and social distance that rendered her eroticization licit. In sacred imagery of the seventeenth century, her ascetic virtue and religious devotion were often undercut by a sensuous rendering of her nude or semidraped body inscribed in ambiguous iconographic contexts. Livio Mehus's painting *The Magdalene in Ecstasy* from ca. 1665 is a prime example.[10] Reclining on a couch and gazing upward with a cross in her right hand between her open legs, this loosely draped Magdalene is based on famous paintings of *Danaë* by Correggio and Titian from the sixteenth century, which aestheticize the rape of a woman by a god in a shower of gold. Mehus painted other pictures of the Magdalene that invoked the "loves" of pagan gods for mortal women; the connections between his pictures and famous sixteenth-century paintings of similar subjects would have been obvious to cultured viewers, for whom the iconographic slippage would have intensified the erotic charge. Although the *Magdalene*'s original owner is not known, Grand Prince Ferdinando de' Medici had it in his private collection by 1701. Pictures like it were generally commissioned by men for personal delectation, but it is also possible that some were destined for the walls of brothels, where they would have belonged to the visual world of women.

The Ascetic Paradigm of Penitence

In addition to the market for erotic Magdalenes, there was also an audience for the Magdalene as penitent. In Giacomo Ceruti's painting of ca. 1740, the nudity of the Magdalene's body is discreetly covered by abundant hair and drapery, while feminine sensuality is undercut by the muscularity of her arm, reddened mouth, and swollen eyes.[11] More restrained in its gestural language than Bernini's *Ludovica,* Ceruti's *Magdalene* nonetheless offers a powerful image of female religiosity, in this instance, in the form of a woman gripped with remorse by the consequences of her wayward actions. Here the figure functions as a reminder, particularly for women, of the rewards that come from renouncing worldly vanities. The Magdalene cannot see the angels at her back, who offer assurance to the viewer of saving grace through the penitent's faith in Jesus as Redeemer and through her devotion to the Passion, which is signaled by the crucifix against which she rests her head.

The Age of Enlightenment and the Tempering of Models

The Church's ongoing concern after Trent with women's asceticism and excessive penitence suggests that these practices were difficult to eradicate. Problematic in this context were Baroque images that vividly rendered the suffering of Jesus and the *imitatio Christi* of female saints, which were particularly seductive for those linked by the dominant culture with the body and the emotions (the masculine in this period retained exclusive associations with the soul and the intellect). Not coincidentally, images of intense female ecstasy and penitence diminished in the eighteenth century, as religious models increasingly offered tempered expressions of devotion and virtuous behavior typically assigned to the feminine in the social world. Common examples are of female saints cuddling the infant Jesus. Catherine of Siena is only one of several mystics figured this way. Maria Maddalena de' Pazzi also belongs in this category, as do Rosa of Lima (1586–1617, canonized 1671), a Dominican tertiary from the "New World," and the Poor Clare Catherine of Bologna (1413–1463, canonized 1712). These women were also mystics whose unions with the divine were frequently cast in affective terms of maternal love. In Marc'Antonio Franceschini's *Catherine of Bologna with the Infant Jesus,* painted in 1710 as a gift from the Senate of Bologna to Clement XI, the emotive restraint of the figures was characteristic of the new age (fig. 6). The tender caress exchanged between woman and child displays traces of the sentimental that would soon develop as part of religious iconography. Based on this painting, one would hardly guess this woman's authorship of *Le sette armi spirituali,* a mystical treatise playing on the metaphor of war and a favorite among Catholic Reformation figures like Gabriele Paleotti, the archbishop of Bologna, in the late sixteenth century.[12] In his *Glory of Catherine in Heaven,* painted at the end of the preceding century in the cupola of the Poor Clares' church of Corpus Domini in Bologna, Franceschini had alluded to the treatise in the form of a generic book held open by an angel. As public affirmation of the woman's spiritual accomplishments, the fresco calls attention to "a text" that made her a favorite in Catholic-Reformation Rome. The allusion, however, is vague, as the book is almost lost in the larger pictorial field. Its complete suppression in the official gift of state intended for the pope was consonant with the prevailing ideals of Christian femininity.

Veneration of Catherine of Bologna (Caterina Vigri) was relatively local, centered in Bologna, where her body was preserved in the Corpus Domini, and in Ferrara, her birthplace and the site of other relics associated with her cult. Devotion to the Peruvian Rosa of Lima, by contrast, was promoted widely, as the Dominicans actively fostered the cults of newly canonized members of their community. Rosa led a life of austerity and self-mortification, a woman of reputed beauty, she practiced self-mutilation as a girl to discourage the attention of suitors and, after donning the habit, to eschew vanity. This constituted a kind of *imitatio Christi* embraced by other religious and lay women of the age. Evidence of severe asceticism, however, was omitted in imagery of Rosa. In Gregorio de Ferrari's painting of 1720 for the Church of Saint Dominic in the Ligurian town of Taggia, she is figured with the infant Jesus, kneeling between two Dominicans also canonized in 1671, the Spaniards Vincenzo Ferrer (1350–1419) and Luigi Bertrán (1526–1581) (fig. 7). Ferrer, a renowned evangelizer, dominates the left side of the picture as he gestures to a crucifix and looks out at the viewer. A missionary in the "New World" also famous for preaching, Bertrán is relegated to the right corner of the painting, rapt in an interior dialogue about the same Passion mysteries. The figure of Rosa presents a striking contrast. While the men are linked visually with a relatively abstract sign of the suffering of Jesus (the crucifix), Rosa's devotion is sentimentalized around the adorable infant in her arms, her expression of faith limited to a "feminine" practice. Moreover, her person is wholly constituted in paint in rosy and milky-white perfection, effecting the erasure of all signs of the asceticism that marked her body in life.

This is not a representation of Rosa in historical time, for she, Ferrer, and

Bertrán were not contemporaries. Indeed, it must be a heavenly space where the three reside with God as canonized saints. Thus, one could argue that her body is reconstituted in perfect form, as was the body of Jesus upon his Resurrection. Standard theology, however, implies that only the *souls* of saints reside in heaven, their bodies awaiting resurrection, along with those of other mortals, at the Final Judgment. And, indeed, the doctrine of the Assumption makes the mother of Jesus unique among mortals in the union of body and soul in heaven (explaining the lack of bodily relics in Mary's cult). But the Assumption was declared official dogma only in 1950, and the ontological status of saints in heaven remained murky in the early modern period, especially at the level of popular belief. The reconstitution of the bodies of ascetics was typical in sacred art, due as much to artistic protocols as to popular thought. The phenomenon was not limited to the imagery of Rosa, nor to women in general. Yet women seemed particularly susceptible to the allures of self-mortification (given their association with the body in culture), even when such bodily mortification was represented in the person of a man. And the erasure of its traces *on their bodies* in sacred art should be questioned in this context.

The Glorification of Mary

As in earlier periods, Mary embodied perfection and the ideal terms of Christian femininity: fully human, yet free from the stain of original sin, even at her own conception; virgin in perpetuity, yet mother of Jesus; obedient and humble, yet Queen of Heaven.[13] Clearly, Mary constituted a set of contradictions impossible for women to mirror, either in clausura or in the secular world. As a symbol of humility and obedience, she could function effectively as a model of feminine virtue. But in seventeenth- and eighteenth-century Italy, she was put into representation primarily as heavenly mediatrix and immaculate mother of God, interceding with her son on behalf of the pious and those worthy of her charity. These forms of glorification had their origins in the decades succeeding Trent, when the Church responded to the Protestant challenge to Mary's status and to her role in redemption. By the late seventeenth century, when Rome emerged from a period of internal reform, the renewed Church was already promulgating imagery that affirmed Mary's centrality in Catholic faith. It recognized the dangers of deifying the Mother of God, not least because the Incarnate Word derived his humanity from her; thus, Mary's humanity was essential to preserve. But in terms of the preeminence it assigned to members of the heavenly court, Mary was second only to Jesus; and, with respect to popular devotion, she often seemed to outstrip him.

Mary Mediatrix

The most spectacular affirmations of Mary's centrality were the canvases and frescoes on church ceilings featuring her Assumption or her dispensation of grace and direction of the sanctified in heaven. Painters of the early Baroque had produced classicized Madonnas of palpability and corpulence who defied gravity in their ascent to heaven or who sat enthroned in weighty repose, in rich, saturated colors. Succeeding generations of artists, however, tended toward airy, refined spectacles, in a range of pastels. Among these Rococo confections were the Venetian ceilings of Gianbattista Piazzetta and Gianbattista Tiepolo, which dissolved architecture in a dizzying array of nearly transparent figures and clouds in the recesses of ethereal space. In Piazzetta's ceiling canvas of 1724–1726 for the chapel of Saint Dominic in the Church of Saints John and Paul in Venice, the figures in his *Glory of Saint Dominic* are swept upward on a vortex of clouds—from the Dominicans to the lower right, directing the viewer's attention to Dominic above and left, to an ethereal Mary at right, bleached by divine light and knee-deep in clouds, waiting to present the saint to the trinitarian God at the apex of the composition (fig. 8). Mary is strategically placed on this explosive ceiling, with the illusionistic power of the spectacle impressing upon the viewer her importance in celestial affairs.

Mary was also conceived as protector and mediatrix for less prominent individuals than the founders of great orders, and even for entire communities. The people of Guardia Sanframondo, a Campanian town virtually leveled by the earthquake of 1688, was such a community. In the early eighteenth century, after the local church of San Sebastiano was reconstructed, Paolo de Matteis frescoed the vault of the nave with Mary interceding with the Trinity on behalf of Guardia Sanframondo.[14] An angel at the lower right bears a miniature model of the medieval towers by which the town was still identified. Here the mother of God beseeches on behalf of a people living in constant fear of natural disaster. The airborne spectacle opens a lofty space for a theater, within which Mary's intercession perpetually played itself out for those who frequented the church. Given social patterns of devotion at the time, when women attended church more than men (and sometimes daily), it surely played itself out in their visual fields.

Communal invocations of Mary took many forms. Ubiquitous in Faenza and neighboring towns were small ceramic plaques placed on building facades, which represented the "Beata Vergine delle Grazie," or "Blessed Virgin of Mercy," a form of Marian devotion dating back to the fifteenth century but particularly intense in this period. According to legend, when plague raged through Faenza in 1412, a noble laywoman venerated a painting of Mary, beseeching her to placate her son and liberate the town from the scourge. Mary appeared to the woman with broken arrows in her hands and assured her that the wrath of her son would also be broken.[15] The local bishop organized a penitential procession through the city upon hearing of the apparition and, three days later, the city was liberated from the plague. Believing Mary to have interceded, the Faentines began to promote her veneration as the Beata Virgine delle Grazie.

Paintings and frescoes of the subject survive from the fifteenth and sixteenth centuries, but production of ceramic plaques began around the plague of 1630 and increased in subsequent years. Mary was initially figured in isolation on these plaques, raising her arms with three broken arrows in each hand, which signified the cessation of God's wrath. The iconography remained constant until the second half of the eighteenth century, when the female suppliant was inserted (fig. 9). Significantly, this was when a domestic, lay model of piety for women began to replace that of *la monaca santa,* and it is surely not coincidental that the figure of the laywoman was concurrently inserted in the pictorial field.

A confraternity devoted to the Blessed Virgin delle Grazie fostered her public cult in Faenza by distributing plaques for display on local houses during times of adversity. Wider in circulation were prints with her image, which were intended for more personal and private forms of devotion. An example from the late eighteenth century represents Mary and the suppliant woman in the interior of a classical temple, wearing the attire of ancient Roman matrons and sharing the pictorial field with semidraped figures *all'antica* who personify the plague, its victims, and the ameliorating intervention of divine grace (fig. 10). The print bears an inscription identifying Mary as the mother of grace and as the patroness of Faenza, with an all-purpose invocation for protection against plague, earthquakes, and other forms of adversity. Relatively refined in its neoclassical style, with a text in Latin, this kind of print would probably have been framed on the walls of middle-class homes.

Immaculate Mary

The Immaculate Mary, free from the stain of original sin, was also part of the Church's campaign to glorify the mother of Jesus. By the eighteenth century, when this particular cult was building in intensity, images of the Immaculate Mary were widely circulated in paintings and prints ranging in refinement and artistic value. Theological debate concerning Mary's status at the time of her conception had a long history and continued well into this period; indeed, the doctrine was not declared official dogma until 1854. By the late eighteenth century, however, the Dominicans were virtually alone among Catholics in their opposition to the belief, and the sheer amount of Immaculate Conception imagery attests to popular investment in the doctrine. Images of the Immaculate Mary from the seventeenth and eighteenth centuries generally show her as a teenager in a white gown of purity and a blue cloak (her red dress in other iconographic contexts alluded to her suffering in the face of her son's Passion). The remaining iconographic details derive from imagery associated with the Woman of the Apocalypse, "clothed with the sun and the moon under her feet, and upon her head a crown of twelve stars . . . she brought forth a man child who was to rule all nations" (Revelations 12:1–12). This passage was easily construed as a reference to Mary. It asserts that the woman was present at the defeat of a great dragon or serpent, which was taken as the incarnation of evil. The serpent under Mary's feet is a symbol of her own triumph over original sin, which lies at the heart of Immaculate Conception imagery, even as it alludes to the ultimate triumph of Jesus over Satan.

This iconographic type was popular in prints, many as small as *santini* with didactic inscriptions necessitating close inspection. Although cheaply produced and inexpensive to purchase, they were not limited to those of modest means. In the 1740s, Anna Maria Louisa de' Medici (last of the Tuscan grand ducal descendants), had at least four *santini* of the Immaculate Mary in her possession.[16] In the nineteenth century, terra-cotta plaques and reliefs of the Immacolata appeared on building facades and roadside shrines, while wooden and gesso statues proliferated in churches and were acquired for personal devotion in the home. These statues were the objects of intense veneration, particularly by women.

The Mother as Spiritual Guide: Anne and the Education of Mary

The behaviors extolled in the Renaissance for the ideal wife and mother were charity, humility, and obedience, on the model of monastic virtue. Social distance was encouraged between parents of both sexes and their children, reinforcing power asymmetries in the home, with the role of spiritual guide assigned to the *pater familias.*

When more intimate relations developed in the eighteenth and nineteenth centuries between parents and their children, it was the mother who emerged in Italy as the upholder of Christian virtue in the home, encouraged to intervene directly in the spiritual education of her young as the Church extended its influence within the family via her agency. While in many contexts Mary still embodied maternal love, it was Mary's own mother, Anne, who emerged in sacred art as spiritual instructor in the domestic sphere. Anne had conceived Mary late in life, and examples from Italian Renaissance art portray her as an aged woman, with both the adult Mary and the infant Jesus on her lap. Virtually disappearing after Trent, when the council diminished Anne's theological importance, this iconography had constituted a matrilineal genealogy across generations, affirming the humanity of Jesus and emphasizing extended family ties.[17] Interestingly, in Italian Renaissance cities where this imagery predominated, the common family structure was nuclear. Only the urban elites and rural poor lived in extended families, while patrilineal ties dominated in nuclear and extended households. At any rate, neither household model featured intimate relations among family members until the eighteenth century, when even elite families became increasingly nuclear.[18] At this point, kin from more than one generation disappear from sacred art. Anne reemerges, but with her husband, Joachim, and their daughter, or with Mary alone, teaching the little girl to sew or read, with an air of intimacy generally absent in the earlier iconography. Marianna Pascoli-Angeli's *Saint Anne Teaching Mary to Read* in the Venetian church of San Felice takes its place in this iconographic tradition, reflecting on the merits of the mother who provides spiritual direction and a virtuous model of piety for the young in her nuclear family (fig. 11). It is worth noting that, like most women, Pascoli-Angeli did not have the benefit of a workshop education, and a good deal of her training was in provincial artistic centers. This is reflected in her relatively crude style of execution, compared to that of male contemporaries who were dignified with important commissions and generous payments. Indeed, Pascoli-Angeli's painting, signed and dated 1823, was a gift from the artist, for which she received no remuneration.

"La Piccola Bambina": Mary Dolls and the Virtues of Childhood

We know that holy dolls were given to young women in the fifteenth century upon marriage or upon taking religious vows.[19] While mostly of the infant Jesus, some were of adult female saints, including the Magdalene and Margaret, who was the patron saint of pregnant women. Dolls of the infant Mary became popular later, particularly in Lombardy, where they were made of wax or plaster, dressed in garments of expensive material, laid in silk-lined cribs, and enclosed in glass cases as gifts for brides. The inscription accompanying one of these dolls suggests that they were intended to augur the birth of children: "May your children be good and beautiful, like the little [doll of] Mary."[20] Even as an infant, Mary was made to embody the sweetness and obedience with which, as an older child, she would receive instruction from her mother. Clearly not meant to be handled, the enclosed effigies were likely set up as centerpieces of personal *altarini* (small altars).

1. Luca Giordano. *Mary Magdalene with Mary and the Infant Jesus,* 1684. Florence, Church of Santa Maria de' Pazzi.

2. N. Guarguagnini. *Saint Catherine Contemplating the Mysteries of the Passion*, ca. 1675. Volterra (Pisa), Duomo.

S. CATARINA DI SIENA V.ne del ORD.ne di S. DOM.a

Chi venererà qualunque Immagine di questa cara Santa
gran protetrice in Cielo a favore de suoi devoti acquistera
cento giorni d'Indulgenza concessa in perpetuo dalla S. M.
di P.P. Benedetto XIII. con Rescritto dei 9. Luglio 1728.

3. *Saint Catherine of Siena.* Engraving, ca. 1730. Rome, National Print Collection.

4. Gianbattista Tiepolo. *Saint Catherine of Siena,* ca. 1740–1745. Vienna, Kunsthistorisches Museum.

5. Gianlorenzo Bernini. *The Ecstasy of Ludovica Albertoni,* 1672–1674. Rome, Church of San Francesco a Ripa.

6. Marc'Antonio Franceschini. *Catherine of Bologna with the Infant Jesus,* 1710. Bologna, Museo Davia Bargellini.

7. Gregorio de Ferrari. *Saint Vincenzo Ferrer, Saint Rosa of Lima, and Saint Luigi Bertrán,* 1720. Taggia (Imperia), Church of Saint Dominic.

8. Gianbattista Piazzetta. *The Glory of Saint Dominic,* 1724–1726. Venice, Church of Saints John and Paul.

9. *The Virgin of the Graces Appears to a Female Suppliant.* Ceramic, seventeenth century. Brisighella (Ravenna), private collection.

10. Print of an engraving by Paolo Bernardi, Faenza (Ravenna), ca. 1790. Faenza, private collection.

11. Marianna Pascoli-Angeli. *Saint Anne Teaching Mary to Read,* 1823. Venice, Church of San Felice.

12. *Legend in the Founding of the Cult of the* **Madonna** *of the* **Bagni.** Polychromed ceramic, ca. 1685. Deruta (Perugia), Church of the Madonna dei Bagni.

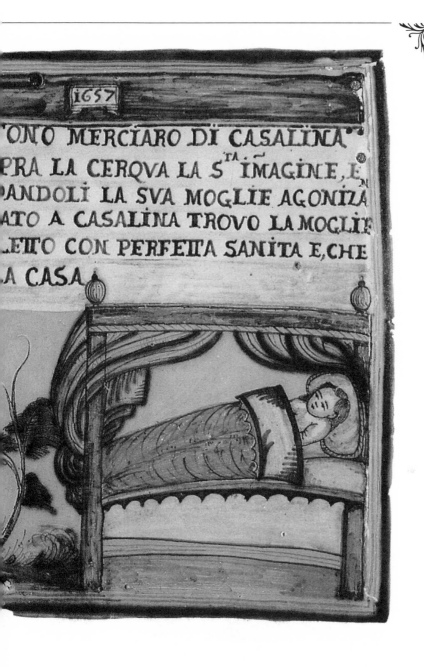

1657

...ONO MERCIARO DI CASALINA
...PRA LA CERQVA LA S.TA IMAGINE, E
...ANDOLI LA SVA MOGLIE AGONIZA
...ATO A CASALINA TROVO LA MOGLIE
...LETTO CON PERFETTA SANITA E, CHE
...A CASA

13. Ex-voto offered by a sick man, 1846.

14. *The Baby Jesus.* Intaglio on
perforated paper, nineteenth century.

Expressions of Lived Experience

The objects and images above belong to official or authorized discourses on feminine sanctity and on women's spirituality, despite their popular appeal and wide diffusion in copies and prints.[21] Even those cheaply produced fall within the category of legitimate "art," rendered in traditional media and formats, according to the conventions of professional artists and the specifications of sophisticated patrons or promoters (both individual and corporate, lay and ecclesiastical). Popular forms of expression, however, occurred alongside this institutionally sanctioned production and often give evidence of beliefs and practices outside those codified by the Church.

Ex-votos provide numerous such examples. They form part of a long tradition, dating back to pagan antiquity, of decorating icons and shrines that were thought to hold supernatural powers. They were commissioned by people of all classes to mark the dispensation of divine grace upon veneration of the icons during illness or subsequent to accidents. Made of materials from silver to terra-cotta and wax, they come in many forms and media, from found objects, to three-dimensional copies of healed limbs and organs, to articles of clothing worn at the time of the momentous events. Historiated ex-votos, typically painted in a naive style on panel, paper, and terra-cotta plaques, were generally anonymous in production or made by the untrained hands of the suppliants themselves. Above all, they were records of extraordinary lived experience and expressions of gratitude in the aftermath of divine intervention. Yet they also reveal much about the quotidian and the mundane, the sociology of religion, and caretaking (both physical and spiritual) among the poor, the middle class, and the wealthy.

An early example, ca. 1685, is the terra-cotta ex-voto in the Church of the Madonna dei Bagni in Deruta, illustrating the foundation of the cult of an icon of the same name. In 1657 a local merchant found the fragment of an image of Mary and the infant Jesus, which he reverently placed between the branches of an oak tree. According to legend, this act alone was deemed a gesture of great devotion, for which the man received divine grace: upon returning home, he found that his wife, whom he had left gravely ill in bed, was fully recovered and cleaning house. The event is charmingly illustrated in vivid colors (fig. 12), with an inscription above the woman's bed providing the essential details. The date of "1657," in the border around the scene, alludes to the year of the miraculous event, rather than to the piece's production, the plaque being a copy of the first ex-voto placed on the tree (where a church soon was erected).

Historiated ex-votos illustrate a rupture in the ordinary sequence of life, the distress that ensues, and appeals to higher powers for the resumption of an ordered life. The seventeenth century was a time when the social order was thought to mirror cosmic design, and in this ex-voto the restoration of order in human affairs is signaled by the wife's resumption of housekeeping. This cultural inscription of women in the family was effected by endless assertions that assumed its naturalness, in texts and images belonging to "high culture" as well as to "low."

Ex-votos suggest that women appealed to miraculous icons on behalf of family members with greater frequency than men, given that scenes of women beseeching in the interest of others are most common. Caring for the ill and the infirm was women's work, and, ideally, their nursing of the body was to be accompanied by frequent prayer for divine grace. An ex-voto of 1846 commemorating the grace received by an ailing man from the Blessed Virgin di Barbana, represents a doctor at the sickbed, unable to provide a cure (fig. 13). The doctor's gesture directs the attention of the viewer, along with that of the patient, to the Blessed Virgin di Barbana, a miraculous icon in a sanctuary on the laguna di Grado, which appears at the upper left in a burst of clouds; the infant and angels appear with Mary, as they do in the icon, crowning her head. While the patient joins his hands in devotion, it is the woman in the foreground who is the active agent, offering up the prayers that the man believed led to his cure. Only he is identified in the inscription ("P[er] G[razia] R[icevuta] dalla B[eata] V[ergine] di Barbana addì 3 aprile 1846. Francesco Bertossi di Malisana"); therefore, his relationship to the woman remains open to question. She was likely a member of his immediate family, for she is depicted assuming the responsibilities relegated to mothers or wives.

Women as Producers of Devotional Art

The concern of this chapter with the production of sacred art *for* women, rather than with *women's production* itself, reflects the institutionalized exclusion of women in the period from most professional forms of artistic practice. That they were engaged in "amateur production," making images and objects as expressions of piety or as remembrances of religious experience without monetary compensation, is beyond doubt. Generally, however, their work was not valued as highly as that of professional artists and does not survive. A little *Ecce Homo* painted by Caterina de' Ricci (1523–1590, canonized 1746) was prized by Carlo Borromeo, the Catholic Reformation bishop of Milan who received it as a gift. He framed it by his bed, but now it cannot be identified.[22] Catherine of Bologna, Maria Maddalena de' Pazzi, and Rosa of Lima all produced paintings or drawings in ecstatic rapture. Indeed, Catherine was named patron saint of the Bolognese *Accademia Clementina*, an institution promoting the figurative arts and formalized in 1710 under the patronage of Clement XI, who approved her canonization two years later. But despite the search for objects and relics associated with the persons of saints, only a few works by Ricci have been identified.

In addition to spontaneous mystical expressions, women produced works at the request of confessors, as records of ecstatic visions that were scrutinized for possible heterodoxy. Cloistered in a Capuchin convent near Modena, Diomira del Verbo Incarnato (1708–1768) was instructed by her confessor to embroider a likeness of Jesus as he had appeared to her in a vision. In her autobiography she wrote that she would be able to recall the vision of his bleeding body vividly until her final day, making it easy for her to reproduce it.[23]

Diomira was accomplished in embroidery and rendered the image deftly with needle and thread, but other women labored to produce such documents in amateurish style in various media. The quality of work, however, was ultimately unimportant, as the focus was on the signified rather than the sign itself—"Your Most Illustrious Lordship must not regard the badly painted figure, but [rather] he who has been figured," Caterina de' Ricci humbly reminded Borromeo upon sending him her gift.[24]

The sum of these mystical expressions was negligible compared to the vast amount of handiwork produced by women anonymously in the organized shops of convents and monasteries.[25] This kind of labor served a dual purpose—to help maintain the discipline of the *vita regolare,* and to enhance the communities' economic self-sufficiency. Sewing, embroidery, and lacework were the most common forms of work, but production ranged from stucco sculpture to the gilding of frames. Skills were perfected in the novitiate, while commissioned work was supervised in a common room where spiritual instruction kept the women's minds as occupied as their hands. Based on patterns, their products were primarily liturgical cloth and linens for *trousseaux;* but the women also produced *immaginette,* that is, miniature images of their own design, of paint, embroidery, and, increasingly in the nineteenth century, collage. These featured a variety of diminutive figures (the saints, Mary, the infant or child Jesus cuddling the lamb, his sacred heart or Mary's, both of which had become objects of devotion). In collage, these figures were made as cutouts from prints or chromolithographs, surrounded by elaborate lace borders or placed on decorative paper supports (fig. 14). These little objects were offered as gifts to friends and family members on onomastic and feast days, and were also given to children for their first Communion. Considered more precious than the mechanically produced *santini* that were used in catechism and were in wide circulation among adults, these gifts were cherished and often preserved in albums. The production of religious *immagi-nette* was also encouraged at convent schools, where girls received most of the formal education available to them outside the home through the nineteenth century. In these schools their creative impulses were channeled into practices that served as expressions of Christian piety, which they were supposed to internalize in the process of maturing into women. As in this case, the functioning of a social technology often depends on the contributing role of individuals to the visual and material culture that sets the stage for social transactions. Directed participation in production cannot *ensure* the internalizing of authorized models of subjectivity; however, the historical evidence suggests that many young women went on to embrace social roles (wife, mother) of selfless and pious virtue.

CHAPTER 14

"Christianity Has Liberated Her and Placed Her alongside Man in the Family": From 1850 to 1988 (Mulieris Dignitatem)

LUCETTA SCARAFFIA

An Alliance between Two Losers

As of the latter half of the nineteenth century, the Catholic Church faced not only a progressively more secular and modernizing world, one indifferent to the Church's condemnations and anathemas, but also the loss of its own territorial power. Its resistance had to be organized within a new Italian nation perceived as an adversary, having in some ways been founded "against" the Church itself. The situation was a new one, in which "the very movement of society became the major force opposed to the Church, which found itself challenged and conditioned by it."[1] After centuries in which the Church had been the guiding force in society and often the principal ally of the groups in power, a total displacement was now called for: the Church was in opposition and allied to the two "losers" in society, peasants and women.

In a first phase, rather than seeking to reinforce its potential allies, the Church concentrated all its energies on the struggle against the changes whose dangers had been pointed out by a series of popes. In 1864 Pius IX had set out his *Syllabus of Errors,* a collection of "the main errors of our time," which opposed an absolute, timeless religion to a historical "becoming" in a state of rapid transformation. The task facing Catholics was to return every aspect of a rapidly de-Christianizing society back to that old, immutable standard. The lost papal territory was to be compensated by the attempt to create an integrated Catholic movement that would recover for the Church all those sectors in society it was losing.

Although the Church saw itself as precluded from returning to its alliance with the ruling classes, it declined to withdraw into a "private" world and confine itself to a devotionalism heavily loaded with charitable works. To

249

restore its historical autonomy it chose an active form of social resistance, relying for this purpose on its base among the people.

The papal intransigence displayed by the *Syllabus of Errors,* and confirmed in 1891 by Leo XIII's encyclical *De Rerum Novarum,* had two simultaneous objectives. One was a strong condemnation of modernity—"This burning desire for the new which has long agitated the peoples of the world would naturally spread from the political to the social and economic spheres" and was given a profoundly negative twist; the other was an attempt to obtain Catholic participation in the social life of the secular states. That was the basis on which "social Catholicism," that is, "a firm reaction against the concept of the laicization of society," was built.[2]

In this difficult situation and in a church with misogynist tendencies and little desire to move away from its traditional alliances, the role of women was of unprecedented importance and brought about a church allied with the weakest element in society. The clergy adapted itself unwillingly to an audience of feminized churchgoers, and misogyny showed no signs of diminishing in the 1900s. Women were still spoken of with distrust; to them and to the ease with which they yielded to fashion and novelty was ascribed the current de-Christianization, and the Church undertook the task of controlling their dangerous nature: "She, the Church, well knew that all of us can succumb and that the weakest of all, because of her heart, is woman. Over the centuries there has been no lack of the necessary providential laws."[3]

The misogyny of the clergy was offset by the diffidence of the women's husbands. Faced with the privileged rapport between housewives and their priests, especially their confessors, they felt threatened by a relationship that seemed to detract from the authority of the husband or father. In Catholic countries—that is, in those where confessions were heard—this raised controversy over the practice, with the confessor being accused of prying with indiscreet questions into the intimacies of family life and the modesty of women. In France Jules Michelet met with considerable success when his book *Le prêtre, Le femme et la famille* was published in 1843, denouncing the deep influence confessors could have in the lives of women.[4] The debate had its echoes in Italy, where it found fertile ground in the anticlericalism of the Risorgimento, as demonstrated, for instance, in the numerous editions of a little book signed "P. Chiniquy" (probably a pseudonym), which attributed the "decadence" of Catholic countries to this very assault on the unity of the family and, more important, to this attack on the authority of husbands. He asked, "What do husbands know of the dark mysteries of the confessional . . . I ask, who is the real master in the house?"[5]

The fears were unjustified. Indeed, the highly successful Catholic manuals addressed to women in the nineteenth century hardly incited them to rebellion against the man of the family. The model proposed was that of a woman who from childhood onward "preferred the occupations proper to her sex to childish games," one "who needs to be restrained from her devotion to all sorts of womanly duties."[6] For this woman, what her "father wanted was . . . law";[7] "she did not intrigue to find herself a husband but disinterestedly waited to be placed according to the will of God and the prudence and affection of her parents."[8] She obeyed her husband and before all things concerned herself with the education of her children. Her constant preoccupation was to watch over their purity—"She would have them sleep nearly fully dressed with their hands crossed on their chests . . . and left their bedside only when they had fallen asleep"[9]—and she would heroically suffer their loss rather than see them fall into mortal sin:

> Death, O dear Jesus, death, sudden and unexpected, yes, a thousand times death first . . . And when she pronounced the word "death," her face lit up, her voice rose, her emphasis deepened, so that the children grew startled and fearful and anyone else present would be moved and edified by this scene.[10]

Her charity toward the "humble poor" made her a "holy lady."[11]

This model of daughter, wife, and mother was reinforced by the models of female sanctity in the late nineteenth century, by saints like Rita of Cascia, who begged God to take her children rather than allow them to commit a mortal sin by avenging themselves for the murder of their father.

There was no great difference for women between their religious and their secular culture: women were universally considered to be incapable of reflection, prey to emotion and sensation, and therefore

> . . . external to the innovative process, living in an unchanging world of weakness and fear . . . The origin of their segregation and inferiority lay not in that they worked less than men but in that they were shaped by principles that were the exact opposite of those society taught the stronger sex. The greater society's belief in science, reason and progress, the more women were pushed toward religion, irrationality and feeling.[12]

In a society such as Italy in the late 1800s, where tension between the lay world and the Church ran high, women's education was almost exclusively the province of religious institutions. Confirmation lies in the failure of the various projects for women's education advanced by the new kingdom and the success of private, mostly religious, educational institutions. Whereas in the first half of the century there were over one hundred private schools for women, mainly opened in the north and the center by religious institutions, that number doubled in the forty years after unification, while in 1900 the state could count on only eighty-six public schools (and these were partly staffed by religious congregations).

Religious institutions offered undeniable advantages. They had their own property and income; as they did not have to pay their staff, their fees were lower and accessible even to middle-class families; and they had long had a well-established reputation and were safe from the ill-natured gossip that in those days affected laywomen who dedicated themselves to education.[13] The sort of education these religious institutions provided seemed to offer greater guarantees for girls' education, for "even anticlericals felt that religion was necessary to regulate women's conduct."[14]

It is hardly surprising, then, to find that the heroines of the Risorgimento, even when they were courageous and nonconformist women such as Cristina di Belgioioso, cultivated substantial religious interests. Indeed, in 1842, while in exile in Paris, the Lombard princess published her *Essai sur la formation du Dogme Catholique,* in which she proposed that "theology be interpreted more through feeling than intellect, to make that which by its nature is only intelligible almost felt."[15]

Despite the fact that Risorgimento culture sought to renew the feminine examples offered to women readers by the publication of a series of lay Plutarchian Lives—which nonetheless contained some of the religious figures best loved by the Catholic tradition, such as the Countess Matilda and Catherine of Siena, both now refurbished as the glories of the nation—the influence of Catholic culture was insuperable: "the legitimation offered by Christian and domestic virtues was now necessary to enter the category of illustrious women."[16]

An extraordinary example of the similarities between the biographies of Risorgimento heroines and the Catholic hagiographic models of the time is the story of Maria Adelaide Cairoli, the mother of six children, five of whom fell fighting for Italian unity while the sixth, Benedetto, remained crippled by a wound. There grew up around Maria Adelaide, the exemplary mother who sacrificed her children on the altar of the nation and a fervent Christian dedicated, despite her excommunication by Pius IX, to charitable works, a true cult, as is shown by the memorial album dedicated to her by the emancipationist Mazzinian women, guided by Gualberta Beccari, on the death of Cairoli's fifth son and published on the occasion of her death in 1873.[17] In his introduction, Beccari wrote that "for this heroic woman we have not esteem, but veneration, not just affection but a cult . . . and through her writings and her image, which we often contemplate, we gain strength for our task and for our poor lives."[18]

The Social Revolutionary Anna Kuliscoff, imprisoned in 1898 during the antisocialist reaction, herself sent her daughter Andreana the *Imitation of*

Christ. The volume, thoroughly blue-penciled, had a powerful effect on her daughter. Many years later Andreana asked to be baptized; she thereafter lived an exemplary religious life, which was then carried on and perfected by her two sons, Guido, who became a Benedictine, and Anna, who under the name of Angela became a Carmelite mystic.[19]

Even in these lay, feminine models, a new factor came into play: a strong emphasis on maternity, on the mother as the figure who imparts the basics of education to her children and thus becomes indispensable to their scholastic and moral preparation.[20] Thanks to this reevaluation of the role of mothers, the Church began to realize that women were becoming a "strategic group for the defense of the Church and of Church rights against male secularization."[21] As they carried out their functions as educators to their children, it was women "who make the Christian character of our society and the clergy's role as spiritual guide a living, visible factor."[22]

What had begun as an alliance imposed by circumstance between two losers—women and the Church, both excluded from enlightened progress as symbols of those values which the new, industrial society was abandoning—now seemed to offer a point of departure for the reconquest of secular society. The alliance that started unwillingly and seemed to have been designed only to keep women safe from all the changes around them turned out instead in the long run to be a success. Certainly, from the 1930s onward, women became an essential part of the political success of the Catholic parties and of a sort of new Christianization of social life. Between 1945 and 1960, the Church harvested the fruit of the privileged rapport it had established with women: it is in these years that women were the most active and best-prepared element in Catholic organizations, and it is within those organizations that they found room to affirm their role in public life. The only crises in Italy that came to interrupt this relationship, fruitful to both, were the referenda on divorce (1974) and abortion (1978).

How was this passage from a negative to a positive vision of women brought about? Compared to lay feminist movements, which sought to oppose the traditional image of a woman as a weak and sentimental creature and to thrust her into a male political world, the Church movements began with those specific characteristics, valued them, considered them as positive factors, and interpreted them as a treasure trove of values being lost in modern society: altruism, sacrifice, attentiveness to the feelings of others. Thus, wrote Paola Gaiotti de Biase, "that culture of diversity which began in the lay world with Rousseau as an instrument by which women were excluded from competition . . . was translated into an attempt . . . to defend women against the allurements of secular culture . . . guaranteeing their survival as a reserve and a defense of the Church."[23]

But even Catholics, when they began to look with favor on greater participation by women in society, realized that attention should be paid to the education of their feelings, to their excess of sentimentalism, which in these years was much affected by somewhat childish and sugary forms of devotion, especially those present in the dominant forms of the Marian cult.

Founders and Mystics

The irruption of women into religious life, which characterizes the nineteenth century, had its repercussions on the beatification and canonization policy of the Church: the traditional misogyny of the ecclesiastical establishment began to lessen in the nineteenth century. Up to that time only 14 out of 125 saints created by papal authority were women, and of 981 saints chosen by various churches, only 209 women were saints.[24] But, between 1851 and 1950 the proportion of women saints showed a notable increase, both as regards saints who died in that period (of 51 saints, 16 were women) and those who had lived in the past.[25] This greater recognition of women saints became especially visible in the twentieth century, a period in which more than half of all female canonizations (30 out of 50) has taken place. Half of these were women who founded religious institutions, which can be explained by the fact that the congregations they created were financially able, and sufficiently stable, to pursue the necessary procedures to establish the recognition of sanctity. In almost all cases, women were advanced for sanctification by women's social groups, something that could only have come about in recent times, when women's institutions have had the necessary financial autonomy and enough initiative to follow such a long and costly path.

The same was true for beatifications. Prior to 1901, only 42 out of 413 beatifications, just about one-tenth, were of women; after 1901, 206 out of 796, better than a quarter, were women.[26]

Most of the new saints were nuns (27 nuns, of whom 19 were also founders, out of 31 female saints), understandable given the greater number of nuns compared to male religious. If during the *ancien régime* there were far fewer nuns than male religious, from the early nineteenth century onward this proportion was suddenly reversed, to the point that by 1956 there were twice as many women as men.[27] The increased number of saints did not derive solely from this change but also resulted from the greater attention paid by the clergy to a new set of devout women, to whom fresh examples of a Christian life, even if rescued from long oblivion, could be offered: of the 31 female saints canonized between 1900 and 1961, 8 died before the nineteenth century.

The most typical of these is without doubt Saint Rita of Cascia, who lived in the fifteenth century and was canonized in 1900 together with Saint Jean

Battiste de la Salle. They formed, as it were, an ideal couple for the next century. He was a priest who had lived in the second half of the seventeenth century and founded the Christian Brothers, an institution dedicated to the education of poor boys, itself anticipatory of the welfare institutions founded by religious of both sexes in the nineteenth century. She was both nun and mystic—her image, painfully and ecstatically gazing on the crucifix, circulated rapidly through the churches of Italy and in sanctuaries dedicated to her in the outlying areas of industrial towns—but also, in the earlier stages of her life, an obedient wife to a violent and faithless husband and a mother afflicted with children who failed to understand her.

Her success is particularly due to the devotion of women, spread by means of hagiographic propaganda that emphasized her unhappy family life, thus offering mothers and wives imprisoned in a burdensome role, poor in gratifications, a model of resignation with which to identify. Devotion to Saint Rita also had its thaumaturgic side (she was the "saint of the impossible"), which offered a model of a woman who helped and consoled those in distress and prayed for the conversion of her husband.[28]

Two other canonizations from the past were celebrated in 1920: those of Joan of Arc and of Margaret-Mary Alacoque. Both canonizations were signs of the growing importance of French Catholicism (an importance confirmed in the next few years by the canonization of no fewer than fourteen French female saints), but they could also be linked to contemporary events: the extraordinary success of devotion to the Sacred Heart for the latter and, for the former, the intervention in ideological struggles of experienced virgins grouped in associations, of which Joan of Arc became the protector.

To this panoply of saints actively engaged in the world was added a smaller group of female mystics and visionaries, such as Bernadette Soubirous, protagonist of the apparitions at Lourdes. But even these women, remarkable as they were in their continuity with the old mystical model—the control of a spiritual director and the nearly inevitable demand that their experiences be written down—show some novel characteristics.

To start with, they were mostly laywomen who lived at home because the convents had refused them, frightened by their paranormal incidents—hard to interpret in an age in which interest in spiritualism was increasing—and by their poor health. Unlike the older mystics, healthy women who sought out physical suffering by tormenting their flesh with lacerations, flagellation, or fasting, modern mystics suffered from an illness, almost always tuberculosis, from which they went early to their graves. Thérèse Martin, Gemma Galgani, Bernadette Soubirous, Bartolomea Capitanio, and Clelia Barbieri all died of tuberculosis.

For them, sickness was a sign of divine favor, a reply to their desire to expiate, through physical suffering, the ills of a world drifting away from God. As Thérèse de Lisieux wrote, "to live a life of perfect love, I offer myself as a sacrificial victim to your merciful love."[29]

To interpret illness as an instrument and as a sign of spiritual evolution was something that came from outside the culture of religion: it derived from the romanticism that had made of tuberculosis—the most widespread fatal disease of that period—a metaphor of a sickness of the soul. Tuberculosis "was celebrated as an illness with predestined victims, of the sensitive and passive who did not care sufficiently for life to survive."[30] Such people were "superior"; their illness promoted them to the status of individuals outside a society that both wounded and disgusted them. Mystics, and especially women mystics, took over this interpretation and gave it a religious connotation: as in the typical case of Gemma Galgani, born in Lucca into a middle-class family, who after a happy childhood was hard hit by deaths in the family and by economic distress. Consumptive, poor, refused by the convents to which she dreamed of retiring—"I can't go on any longer," she wrote, "No matter where I go, it's always the same: all I want is to be shut away and for no one to see me again. That's how badly off I am."[31]—she spent her youth as a domestic servant and as the guest, sickly and subject to mysterious psychic and physical manifestations, of a pious family in the city. Possibly under the influence of her confessor, the Passionist father Germano Ruoppolo, whom she called "Babbo" or "Daddy" in her letters, she chose as her model Gabriele dell'Addolorata, a young Passionist brother who died of tuberculosis at twenty-four, and Gabriele, together with Jesus and the Madonna, often appeared to her. In keeping with this model, in a vision Jesus pointed out to her a spiritual path that lent meaning to the physical sufferings her illness inflicted on her:

> Do as you can. I want to make use of you, because you are the poorest of the poor, the most sinful of my creatures; you merit no better than that I should consign you to hell, but instead I want you to be a victim and for you to suffer to placate the indignation my Father feels for sinners, I want you to offer yourself to Him as a victim of all sinners.[32]

In more recent times, the Jesuit preacher Father Lombardi—in the immediate postwar years, alongside the Christian Democratic party, he waged an anti-Communist war with frequent apocalyptic notes—was spiritually linked to young women mystics, not always nuns, but all of them sick, who said they offered their sufferings up to God to further his mission. He described how "two young women offered themselves in Brescia," a "young lady offered herself in Cremona," and "Mariolina Lanza died in the Maria Theresa Clinic in Rome on December 14, 1946, with the name of my apostolate on her heart."[33] By his own admission, the most important of these was Gilda Maggiorini, a member of a lay religious institute in Lucca, Regnum Christi, whom Father Lombardi caused to be transferred to his brother's house in Rome so that he could be near her. Always ill, she died in 1971 after having said to him on the telephone, "Courage! Don't despair!"[34]

This vindictive, offended God of the female mystics, and this seeking out of suffering and the expiation of the ills of a world that was more and more abandoning religion, would seem remote both from the positive God who intervenes in concrete fashion to foster the equally concrete projects of the saintly female founders, and from their love for joy, as demonstrated by the most exemplary among them, Francesca Cabrini.

Born in Sant'Angelo Lodigiano in 1850, Cabrini dreamed from her early childhood of serving as a missionary to China, thus feminizing a type of religious activity always considered exclusively male. After she had founded the Missionaries of the Sacred Heart, her superiors compelled her to change destination: her mission sent her first to the United States and then to other countries in Central and South America, wherever in fact there were Italian immigrants. To these she offered medical care, schools, and—more important—a way to restore their ties to their religion. Her organizing and financial skills, her courage in undertaking tiring and dangerous travels, her broad view of serving God—"The world is too small, I would like to embrace all of it"—was joined to a constant serenity. "I will always have a joyous face," she wrote; against ill humor there was but one remedy: work.

> When I go to certain of our houses and see long faces, and note that our people are downhearted, lacking in will and in a bad mood, rather than asking each what is the matter, I start up some fresh project, some work that involves movement, a more active life, which forces the Sisters to come out of themselves, and in a few days their faces are once again serene and the ill humor is gone.[35]

This contrast in models of sanctity probably derived in part from the different opinion groups that supported the canonization proceedings. Supporting the active and joyous models, which fought sickness with concrete activities, were the new women's congregations; and supporting the women's mystical or martyr model, which offered its suffering for the redemption of the world—as with Gemma Galgani or Maria Goretti, both laywomen—were the more traditional Catholic organizations, such as the Passionist fathers. The accent intransigent Catholics placed on martyrdom, always accompanied by virginity,[36] had, whether through renewed devotion to early Christian female martyrs like Saint Agnes—some "invented" as in the famous case of Saint Philomena[37]—or through the proposal to canonize girls who died during attempted rapes, marked the whole of the nineteenth century.[38] After various failed attempts, and with the explicit intervention of Pius XII, Maria Goretti, a twelve-year-old peasant girl from the Pontine Marshes killed by a young neighbor in an attempted rape, was finally canonized in 1950—thanks to a joint effort in proposing the canonization by the Passionists and by Armida Barelli's Female Catholic Youth, thus combining intransigent Catholicism and new forms of women's associations. The model Goretti offered was addressed to the younger generations and especially to the age group recently discovered by secular culture, adolescents. The younger generations were the most deeply involved in the transformation of the condition of women that characterized the period after the Second World War, for whom Goretti was "a girl from a poor, but honest and hard-working family, who died defending a 'common,' unconsecrated virginity—a value that every young woman should learn to defend."[39]

During this time of transformation of the female condition, the women saints the Church proposed as models for laypeople, Rita of Cascia and Maria Goretti, lacked any sort of biographical "depth"; they were more or less "invented" to provide rigid and traditional models of the female roles, then in a state of crisis—the roles of wife and mother for the first, and the role of adolescent girl for the second. After their early success, these models surely owed their persistence more to their miraculous capacities than to their moral standing. It remains true, however, that Rita and Maria are better known and more frequently invoked than the numerous saintly female founders, though the latter offered more modern and sometimes transgressive feminine models but had cults nearly always limited to members of their own congregations.

Contemporary models of female sainthood can be divided into three types: behavior models for the different phases of life, represented by figures "constructed" to this end (Saint Rita, Maria Goretti); symbolic saints, whose bodies were a figure of the Church's body martyred by secularization; and finally the new, founder-saint, an autonomous person who intervenes in the world and constantly widens her sphere of action until she comes close, as we shall see, to touching the altar.

From Nuns to Sisters

The transformation that had taken place in the behavior of the woman religious is well expressed in this remark of Francesca Cabrini about one of her sisters: "from childhood she did not dare look up or around with her eyes, and she was thirty before, finding herself heading an institute, she said, 'I realize now it is important to look about me, and now I keep my eyes wide open.'"[40]

Such an "opening up of the eyes" onto the real world, an effective image to indicate that the days of enclosure lay in the past, came about as a result of the demands made and sometimes imposed by the external world on women's religious institutions. The effects of the French Revolution and its abrupt interruption of the centuries-old continuity in the life of monasteries was most powerfully felt in the newer foundations. These were no longer based on the old convent scheme—especially in regard to enclosure and perpetual vows, which, given the social situation, now seemed unlikely to be accepted. Then, in Italy too, the suppression of religious institutions in the kingdom of Sardinia in 1855, extended to the rest of the country between 1866 and 1873, spared only those religious institutions that performed some useful function in society, thus pushing the nuns to a more active social role. It is estimated, in fact, that of the 527 women's houses suppressed, with their 9,700 nuns, almost all were cloistered monasteries.[41] This would explain the constant fall in the number of nuns after the beginning of the nineteenth century, excepting only the Kingdom of the Two Sicilies and the Papal States, where the transformation of the religious life of women was much slower and almost always took place through institutions imported from France or from northern Italy.

The new religious institution that imposed itself with increasing success in the nineteenth century was the congregation; between 1801 and 1973 almost 400 new institutes were founded, as many as 185 of which in the nineteenth century, and 162 more in the twentieth.[42] The greatest number of foundations occurred in the decade between 1830 and 1840, but new foundations were made throughout the century, without being at all affected by the 1866 laws. Indeed, the number of female religious entering these institutions, which was fairly modest until 1860, increased so rapidly that after 1870 the new institutes account for a majority of all Italian female religious.

Despite the success of these institutes for women, which continued to grow right up to the census of 1931, the overall number of female religious in relation to the whole population remained inferior to the number noted in the 1861 census, which was a sign that the laws of suppression and, more generally, the overall process of secularization had brought about an irrevocable diminution in religious vocations, even though among women these fell at a lower rate than male vocations.

The geographical distribution of these new foundations was irregular: Lombardy-Venetia and the kingdom of Savoy had a near monopoly of new foundations, so much so that if in 1861 the greatest number of female religious was to be found in the south, twenty years later, in 1881, the area most densely populated with female religious was Lombardy.[43] It was, however, these northern regions, the avant-garde of the foundations of new congregations, that experienced the most severe drop in vocations after 1931.

All these many foundations of a new type, designed for women of the upper middle class, full of initiative and organizational capacity, constituted an important novelty from several points of view. First, there was the vastness of the phenomenon. Founders had not been wanting in the past, but these had been exceptional women with charismatic gifts who obtained the approval of their institutions by relations, sometimes conflictual, with their spiritual directors or confessors. Now, however, the large number of women who set about creating new forms of religious life brought them into a complex and often difficult and contentious relationship with the ecclesiastical establishment as represented by the Sacred Congregation of Bishops and Regular Clergy, one that often had to be resolved without intermediaries. This may have been one of the reasons why the labors of the Sacred Congregation were rendered so difficult and laborious, for it was only in 1900 with the constitution *Conditae a Christo* and the standards set out in the *Norme* of 1901 that the ecclesiastical establishment managed to set the norms which defined the physiognomy and competence of women's congregations.

With varying elements of novelty the female founders projected life models that broke the "chains" of traditional monastic life: the end of enclosure; temporary vows that had to be regularly renewed, in some cases yearly; an active, social apostolate; the elimination of dowries and therefore of the distinction between choir nuns (endowed) and lay sisters (unendowed). Their institutions sought to define themselves in the same terms as male institutions: strongly centralized government offering the greatest possible freedom from even economic encroachment by the central or local institutions of the Church; the power to draw up their own constitutions; the free movement of the female religious; the possibility of engaging in multiple social activities, which might even change according to need.

The reactions of the ecclesiastical institution were ambivalent. On the one hand, the welfare work undertaken by the sisters was fundamental to giving the Church a renewed presence in society; on the other hand, this ever greater protagonistic role taken by women occasioned fear and perplexity. More and more often these women referred to their activity as an "apostolate," which brought them perilously close to the figure of the priest.

The new institutions were predominantly active in two fields: teaching, which extended from nursery schools right through to the secondary schools inaugurated by the Marcellines of Milan, and assistance to the sick, in hospitals or at home. Both raised problems that were not readily soluble. Traditionally, nuns had taught only girls; now their schools were opening up to boys too, at least up to the age of ten. This change met with powerful opposition from the Church authorities, on the grounds that it was contrary "to decency and decorum." Faced with competition from the new public schools, which offered a scientific curriculum for girls as well as boys (though until 1923 the curriculum for boys was different) plus a physical education requirement, teaching nuns had to obtain adequate professional preparation. Until the founding of the Catholic university such instruction had to be acquired in secular schools. Despite the fact that it was often viewed with suspicion by the Church, the drive toward education brought nuns into the vanguard of female education in Italy. And while most of the institutes limited the training of nuns to the *patente di maestre,* a teaching certificate, the Marcellines of Milan, the first to create secondary schools for girls, decided to send some sisters to take degrees at universities that had just opened their doors to women; it would seem that nine Marcellines, including their founder Marina Videmari, took the *laurea* degree in letters at the University of Genoa in 1889, and some certainly took specialized degrees at the University of Pavia in succeeding years.[44]

Though access to higher education for male religious involved in teaching monks was, without mentioning the women, reconfirmed by Pius X in 1907, in fact the practice of sending sisters to university had begun to spread to the south: the first degree in natural science granted in Catania in 1915 was conferred on a Dominican sister of the Sacred Heart of Jesus.[45]

The problems faced by the sisters who had chosen to help the sick were even more complex: as contact with human bodies was recognized as particularly dangerous, home visits were forbidden, as was care of male patients or midwifery. But, owing to the nature of their calling, nursing sisters often paid little heed to such orders and would not refuse their help to the sick, thus opening up a continual debate with the institution, one that is testified to by a general inquiry undertaken throughout the Catholic world by the Sacred Congregation of Religious in 1909 as a result of many protests over the established practice of religious women giving nursing help, at home as in hospitals, to men.[46]

The nursing sisters, too, soon felt the need for professional preparation. Aware of the demand, in 1905 Pius X created the first professional nursing school in Rome, and taking a degree in medicine began to be considered for missionary sisters. Often, especially in smaller towns, the congregations' activities included both education and care of the sick, or alternated between the two according to need.

Another new activity was providing help to working women, offered in factories by worker sisters or supervisor sisters, and especially the creation of boarding schools that lodged young women constrained to live away from home.

A new factor within the internal structure of the congregations was internal equality: that is, the suppression of divisions between the women religious.

Combined with an unheard-of access to education, this change had a powerful, positive effect in social promotion. An outstanding case is that of Maria Domenica Mazzarello, a peasant woman from Monferrato whom Don Bosco had met in 1864 while she was teaching catechism to the girls—grouped together in a Union of the Daughters of Mary, which she had founded with the approval of her parish priest—of her little town. The saint charged her with founding and directing the Daughters of Mary the Auxiliary, the women's branch of his own institute, and at thirty-five she learned to speak and write in Italian.

Toward the middle of the century, the autonomy of these institutions was guaranteed by the creation of the figure of superior general, who, though still deprived of spiritual jurisdiction, was the supreme internal authority over all the congregation's houses and reported only to her cardinal protector. This new figure of authority met with many obstacles in Italy. It was feared that she might find herself in conflict with representatives of the local Church; there was widespread concern over her need to travel, which until then had been unthinkable for a woman—"The decorum of the sex," wrote the Sacred Congregation of Bishops and Regular Clergy in 1848, "would suggest that women travel as little as possible in order that they not be exposed to the gaze of the profane."[47]

Bit by bit, a list of things that a superior general could do without prior authorization was drawn up, limiting the proposals of the most independent-minded of the founders, such as Teresa Eustochio Verzieri (who founded the Sisters of the Sacred Heart of Jesus) or Paola Frassinetti (the Sisters of Saint Dorothy). Drafting the constitution of her own institution for presentation to the ecclesiastical authorities in 1847, Verzieri spoke forcefully of the need for an autonomous superior general: "Our constitutions give our General complete liberty to make visitations without any obligation whatever to account for them to anyone else. This freedom is not only useful, it is necessary."[48] However, the Sacred Congregation's view, both toward her and toward other, analogous requests by founders of the period, was to delay these innovations for as long as possible. Behind its resistance lay an undoubted mistrust of female capacities. Evidence of this lies in the answer the congregation gave to the request for a superior general by the Lovere Sisters of Charity in 1855: "The weakness and volubility of the sex caused us to fear potential excessive power in the hands of the General, which could have serious consequences. To obviate this difficulty, we created as Ordinary a cardinal protector from whom the superior general depended."[49] Despite the Church's resistance, there did emerge, de facto, an ecclesial, managerial role for women.

The battle for autonomy also went through a radical transformation of the economic administration of women's institutions. Up to then, every monastery—whose subsistence was based on the capital offered by its nuns' dowries and by gifts and bequests—was administered by a "syndic" or manager, or by a procurator (the latter office was abolished in 1866). The new institutions, however, were established with a centralized administration directly under the superior. Furthermore, as the sisters were not canonically speaking nuns— they did not take perpetual vows—they could not accept bequests and dona- tions as had always been the practice in monasteries: hence they were com- pelled, and this was a great novelty, to base their survival no longer on the mortmain (a system opposed by the Italian government) but rather on the professional activities of the sisters themselves. However, as these new institu- tions no longer limited themselves to seeing to their members' survival, but rather—at least in their first years of existence—tended to expand, forming new houses and taking up fresh activities, often even missionary activity, it was essential that their superiors have financial ability of an entrepreneurial sort. Many superiors, like Don Bosco, could be considered "private entrepreneurs engaged in charitable and philanthropic initiatives."[50]

The woman manager was an absolute novelty: she held high office and moved from one house to another with ease, but she also administered assets of a certain importance that required courageous investment decisions and included indebtedness and risk.

The most successful female founder-entrepreneur was without a doubt Francesca Cabrini. When she died in Chicago in 1917, her congregation numbered 1,500 sisters scattered through eight countries, in Europe and in the Americas, and 67 institutes dedicated to education or to looking after orphans and the sick. Cabrini managed to raise money for her foundations and to invest it profitably in constructing schools and hospitals. She showed considerable financial acumen, and her ability to read and prepare contracts was legendary: she was able to avoid the pitfalls that in some cases had been laid by not particularly devout proprietors and lawyers.[51] She was sufficiently conscious of her managerial vocation to write to one of her sisters who complained of having too much work, "Without hard work and application, one never gets anywhere. What do businessmen do in the world for their business? And why shouldn't we do as much in the interest of our beloved Jesus? These are the talents we were given with which to bring our work to fruition; what else?"[52]

What the sister meant by talents to be fructified was real estate in which to found hospitals and schools and funds with which to maintain them, even if to do so meant "keeping one's head among deceitful men."[53] But Mother Cabrini was no exception. Many other women, perhaps with less conspicuous talents, took the same road and, after founding houses in their own regions of Italy, went on to expand into missionary territory. Costanza Troiani, who founded the Franciscan Missionary Sisters of the Immaculate Heart of Mary, died in Cairo in 1887 after she had established other houses in Egypt and

Palestine. Anna Maria Rubatto (beatified on October 10, 1993) went on from the Capuchin tertiaries of Loano, whose institution she had founded in 1885 to provide local assistance to Liguria and thence to Uruguay, Argentina, and Brazil. Maria Giuseppa Rossello, another Ligurian, who began with a small school for girls in Albisola in 1837, by the time of her death in 1880 supervised 65 houses in Liguria and Argentina.

Many other instances could be adduced to show that in the nineteenth century becoming a sister in one of the new congregations offered travel, social mobility, education, or at least a professional skill, the possibility of managing substantial capital, and above all an escape from the power of family and the opportunity to feel that being unmarried and working was not something inferior. As Giancarlo Rocca has pointed out, these religious women and the foundation of these congregations in Italy—a form of female emancipation not only in regard to the Church but also as far as secular society was concerned—anticipated lay feminism by at least a half-century. But like the latter, these religious institutions created their own sphere of action in women's philanthropy, the only way in which a woman could, "by a kind of displacement, intervene in collective history and exercise, with her support, the only political responsibility conceded her."[54]

The innovative thrust of these new institutions, however, thanks to the slow but constant reorganization imposed on them by the Sacred Congregation of Bishops and Regular Clergy, began to wane in the last years of the nineteenth century: when the sisters submitted their constitutions for ecclesiastical approval, in return they had to submit to rigid standards, against which they often opposed a lively resistance.

The Daughters of Saint Anne, founded in Piedmont by Rosa Gattorno, was a typical example of this conflict. The order provided only for temporary vows; it proposed to serve the sick of either sex, without excluding any disease, day and night, to teach in a school to which boys would be admitted up to the age of ten, and to admit widows.[55] In 1876 the Sacred Congregation returned the constitutions that had been sent for official approval, requesting that they be radically corrected: boys to the age of ten could not be admitted, "for this was quite dangerous," nor could widows be accepted; temporary vows could not be renewed indefinitely but should give way to final vows after a trial period; every convent should have at least six religious, and a minimal dowry should be required. After negotiations with the order, the Daughters of Saint Anne, meeting in general chapter in 1881, rejected the proposed modifications and faced a bitter outcome: the Sacred Congregation annulled the chapter's acts, prohibited the founding of new convents and the admission of new sisters, deprived the superiors of their office, and went so far as the threaten to deprive them of the sacraments. Only in 1892, having taken meeker counsel, did the Daughters of Saint Anne finally receive definitive approval of their constitution.

With the constitution *Conditae* in 1900 and more firmly still with the code of canon law promulgated in 1917, the innovative tendencies of these congregations were stemmed. Temporary vows were abolished and the women's liberties curtailed, with the result that there was once again a clear differentiation between male and female communities. The effect was not long in coming: in the first years of this century only two new female institutes were founded in Lombardy.

While, in 1919, the Italian state passed a law granting full juridical status to women independent of their husbands and allowed them full access to any profession, Church law moved in the opposite direction. As well as imposing uniformity and regularization on new congregations, other provisions revealed the alarm with which the Church viewed the way female religious were coming closer and closer to the traditional apostolates of the priests. In 1903 Pius X excluded women from sacred song, which he deemed a "liturgical" office. The sisters who by then frequently assisted priests in their parish duties were forbidden to sing with the church choirs. The assistance they gave in teaching the catechism was allowed only provisionally, "when there was no available priest."[56]

In 1883 Leo XIII had sought to compensate for this steady limitation on the social activity of sisters—which represented a weakening of their presence in lay society—by reforming the Franciscan Third Order, whose members were asked to be involved in social action. This empowered female tertiaries to undertake "male" activities such as religious instruction without competing, since they were laypersons, with the priest. The new tendency in the Church was, while looking with suspicion on any extension of the apostolate of religious women, to recognize it among laypersons, as Pius XI confirmed when he recognized the work of Catholic Action as a Church apostolate.

In the years that followed, new departures came from secular institutes. There were a few exceptions: Luigia Tincani sought in 1924 to found the School Missionaries, who would wear ordinary clothes and devote themselves to an intellectual apostolate; and the Daughters of Saint Paul of Alba, founded by Giacomo Alberione in 1929 and devoted to an apostolate in the press, was briefly entrusted with the editorship of the new, weekly *Famiglia cristiana;* but these exceptions served to prove the rule.

Not to Vote, But to Devote Oneself

The growing presence of women in the workplace and in Italian public life was in large part due to the feminist activity of Anna Maria Mozzoni, who in

1864 published *La donna e i suoi rapporti sociali (Woman and Her Social Relations)* and then in 1870 translated John Stuart Mill's *The Subjection of Women*, and to that of the women Mazzinians like Gualberta Beccari and the group that gravitated around the magazine she edited, *La Donna*. This trend somewhat belatedly pushed Catholics to accept some forms of public activity on the part of women. As Monsignor Radini Tedeschi, the future bishop of Bergamo, said clearly in 1900:

> No one can deny that in our times we have seen a great fear of so-called *feminism*, utterly un-Christian, with claims that not only are against Catholic doctrine but are a prostitution of body and soul, subjecting women to the infamy of a liberty which is a lie and a slavery which is all too true, but horrible. If, in normal times, women must indeed stay at home, today, in these abnormal circumstances, she should *leave the house* as the priest leaves his sacristy.[57]

These openings to social action for women met with powerful resistance within the Church, though it was otherwise highly attentive to the social ferment affecting women. Between 1906 and 1908, the Jesuit father Passivich published a long novel in serial form in *La Civiltà Cattolica* called *Donna vecchia e donna nuova: scene di domani* (The old and the new woman: scenes from the future), which dealt with contemporary Italian feminism, to which he opposed a last-ditch defense of the traditional role of women: "The Italian woman is queen of the hearth and as a consequence the Italian family is the most moral in the world. Here the sanctuary of the home has not yet been defiled by impiety and license, for the woman maintains her domain unchallenged and freely discharges her duties in the home."[58]

It was only in 1890 that an aristocratic Roman woman, Vincenzina de Felice Lancellotti, at the request of a priest, Father Zocchi, began publishing a fortnightly magazine for "educated young ladies and women," written entirely by women, called *Vittoria Colonna*.[59] The magazine contained at least one essay-article (political, social, or pedagogical) and biographies of the most important Catholics, plus a narrative section for the young added later.

Subscribers remained steady at about three hundred, but it circulated throughout the country, unlike other women's magazines—such as the Genoese *La Donna e la Famiglia*—which only circulated locally. Lancellotti's position on women's issues did not differ from the one maturing in intransigent Catholic circles: women should have a leading role in social life, not because of any suppositions of equality, but as subjects equal to and complementary to men. A feminine presence aimed to deal with the secular offensive on matters such as divorce (first proposed in parliament in 1892) and the defense of Christian values. Its tone was that of a crusade: *Vittoria Colonna* should be "a closed area in which women trained for the good fight can ready themselves for the commands of the Maximum Leader when He pleased to summon them."[60]

The first attempts to create a Catholic women's organization took place within intransigent circles and were built around the concept of "a call, an apostolate, a Christian duty," which would involve women in a battle on behalf of Christian values against modern society.[61] It differed from secular feminism, which fought for its rights, by seeing women's action as an exclusively religious social service.

That intellectual and social tasks were combined with a religious mission can be seen in the background of the protagonists of the new model: nearly all of them came from the Third Orders. Adelaide Coari, Salerno, and Antonietta Giacomelli were Franciscans; Cristina Giustiniani Bandini and Luigia Tincani were Dominicans; and only Luisa Anzoletti and Elena da Persico were not tertiaries. The last of these was the controversial founder of a secular institute, the Daughters of the Queen of the Apostles, which was devoted to an intellectual apostolate. This "third way" of religious activity had the double advantage of allowing young women a certain independence from their families while keeping them fully involved in a lay life.

The most thorough elaboration of a Christian feminist theory in those years came from Luisa Anzoletti, a Trentine poet and writer who, having moved to Milan and come into contact with the liberal-Catholic circles of the *Rassegna nazionale,* made her mark with a series of articles claiming women's right to a good education based on religious principles. Her polemic with lay feminists came out mainly in her book *La donna nel progresso cristiano,* which appeared in Milan in 1895, was subsequently translated into French, and enjoyed a noteworthy success. According to Anzoletti, only Christianity had broken down the servitude of women, giving them full dignity in their inner lives and offering widows and unmarried women a role in society. Conforming to intransigent thought, Anzoletti saw women as only the bearers of spiritual values and redemption, but her ideas were to evolve under the influence of modernist thinking. In fact, as her major biography of Maria Gaetana Agnesi shows, she came to propose ever broader tasks for Christian women in public life.[62] Through Agnesi, this exemplary eighteenth-century woman, devoted to scholarship—she was an important scientist—but also to prayer and social welfare, Anzoletti offered a model of the modern woman engaged in religious life but also in social and scientific questions, and one who, furthermore, had distinguished herself in scientific research, traditionally a "male" activity.

The Catholic movement taking shape within the Opera dei Congressi gave close attention to women's problems, especially those concerning the mass of unprotected young women entering the paid work force. The congresses held in Venice (1874), Bergamo (1877), and Modena (1879) all offered final resolutions supporting the formation of women's associations. At Lodi in 1892, the problem of female labor and equal pay were central to a debate that proposed the abolition of night work, a ten-hour maximum workday, time off before and after childbirth, and above all an end to the exploitation of women through the establishment of a "just" salary. *Rerum novarum* (1891) opened up new possibilities of social action and shifted discussion of women's issues from the theoretical and moral plane to a more realistic level, which took into account the social problems arising from industrialization and urbanization. As Decurtins said at the international congress in Zurich, demands for a "just" salary for women workers sought to make it less desirable for employ-ers to build a female work force and thus put an end to the exploitation of a section of the proletariat and to one of the main factors favoring the breakup of the family and the abandonment of childcare. Thus a more modern atti-tude in Christian social thinking toward defending the proletariat was indis-tinguishable from a nostalgic vision of family relations.

Monsignor Radini Tedeschi, vice president of the Opera, was well aware of the new importance of feminism in the first decade of the twentieth century, and it was thanks to him—at the 1900 congress in Rome—that we have the first expression in an official context of a project for a Catholic women's organization, a project that has been considered the Italian manifesto of Christian feminism. Its innovative character went unmatched until John XXIII's encyclical *Pacem in terris*. Radini Tedeschi's proposal, designed to "stem one of the great evils of the century," was the first theoretical legitima-tion of the public role of women and was immediately put into practice by a group of Catholic women in Milan grouped around a new magazine, *Azione muliebre*.[63]

The magazine had just been started by a Franciscan friar, Father Antonio da Trabaso. Linked to the Franciscan Third Order and directed by Maria Baldi, most of the editorial work was done by Adelaide Coari, a twenty-one-year-old Lombard schoolteacher. The magazine carried the first serious analysis of the condition of women and led in turn to a number of concrete social initiatives, such as the Catholic Women's League for the Regeneration of Labor (1901), led by Adele Colombo, who died of tuberculosis in 1904, and which a thou-sand working women immediately joined, and the Committee for the Protec-tion of the Young Woman, which offered succor to young female workers and young women coming to the cities to seek work. In response to feminist movements which claimed that the Church was in great part responsible for the subjection of women, Catholics rediscovered the modern and emancipa-tory features of the Christian tradition. The magazine made objective demands of a moral, educational sort about ending the "demeaning of female dignity" in modern society.[64] But while the editors argued strenuously against divorce, seeking signatures for a petition, the question of votes for women caused a break between Coari (pro) and Elena da Persico (contra), a Venetian aristocrat who had been promoted to the directorship of the magazine with the help of the ecclesiastical hierarchy.

Elena da Persico was in fact responding to the directives of Pius X, who had declared his opposition to the vote, while Coari defended the right to keep an open mind and favored fighting for the issue in alliance with lay feminists. In 1904 Coari left *Azione muliebre* and concentrated her efforts within the Christian Democratic Women's Fascio, a group officially founded in 1902, influenced by Murri and inspired by Father Carlo Grugni, a former assistant at *Azione muliebre* and chaplain to the labor movement. At the 1903 Bologna congress a women's section of the Opera was established and Coari, with six other women, was entrusted by Radini Tedeschi with the task of writing its statute. The Women's Fascio was extremely active in those years: it organized various workers' groups, set up schools for vocational training and home economics, established study groups, and promoted campaigns on behalf of the condition of girls and women and the right to vote. From 1904 until its suppression in 1908, Coari ran the Fascio's women's periodical, *Pensiero e azione*, the first issue of which appeared on December 8, 1904, the fiftieth anniversary of the proclamation of the dogma of the Immaculate Conception. The paper was addressed to women workers and sought to educate and prepare them for a strong women's labor association.

These interests in social issues did not, however, distract Coari from the heart of her mission, which was to promote increased religious knowledge among women so that they could pass from traditional adherence to a stage of true and complete involvement. She saw that religious education should go beyond mere mechanical learning and awaken women to a more intimate and powerful form of religiosity. That brought her into closer contact with a Christian intellectual, Antonietta Giacomelli, particularly active in religious and pedagogical renewal. Giacomelli had written highly successful teaching manuals, such as *The Mass: Liturgical Text and Prayers* (1905) and *The Christian Ritual* (1907), which were subsequently put on the Index (the list of prohibited books) for their "modernist" leanings.[65] Giacomelli had provoked many polemics, especially in *Civiltà Cattolica*, in which she was ironically called "the Christian Amazon." Though the theme of the Catholic "new woman," elaborated in the modernist culture of Giovanni Semeria and Antonio Fogazzaro, was close to her position, Coari and her review did not emphasize modernism. An intellectually modest woman, the feisty Lombard teacher seemed unaware of how close she was to modernist positions, which—while forever insisting on obedience to the Church hierarchy—she actually supported, mainly in concrete ways, indignant with Catholic "organizational sloth" as opposed to socialist commitment.

At a congress in 1905, *Pensiero e azione* gave rise to the Milanese Women's Federation, which quickly gained twenty thousand members in and around Milan. Coari seemed to cast off her moderate Christian feminist theories and be involved, on their own ground and often alongside them, with the secular and socialist feminist movements. This evolution, born of her concrete experience alongside women workers, was influenced by Father Grugni, who wrote her: "It's time an end was put to seeing the women's movement as purely a form of welfare countering human misery. It should be primarily a democratic movement designed to elevate its members."[66] This brought out into the open Coari's quarrel with the charitable works proposed by the "ladies" who now headed da Persico's *Azione muliebre*.

The crisis in the Christian Democratic movement, sanctioned by the dissolution of the Opera dei Congressi, indirectly hit all the women's organizations allied to it, a development confirmed by Cardinal Merry del Val's circular, which said that among the norms to be respected by Catholic congresses "women, however respectable and pious, should never be allowed to speak. If from time to time a bishop should consider it opportune to allow a meeting for women only, they will be allowed to speak only under the presidency and supervision of experienced ecclesiastics."[67] Coari wrote to Radini Tedeschi to express her deep disappointment but she did not give up, and the Women's Fascio joined the popular Catholic Action, the Opera's only surviving organization. *Pensiero e Azione's* support for the women's vote further widened the gulf between the review and da Persico's group, and the latter, in a meeting with Pius X in 1906, received his confirmation of the unfavorable position of the Holy See: a "woman should not vote [*votare*] but devote herself [*votarsi*] to an high ideal of human good."[68]

After having been sent by her Milanese committee to bring aid to the victims of the earthquake in Calabria, Coari extended the Catholic feminist sphere of action to the whole of Italy. To that end, she organized a national women's conference held in Milan in 1907, in which lay feminists were also invited to take part. The opening session was given over to a report by Luisa Anzoletti on civil goals and feminism, which acknowledged that the Christian feminist movement should be active on the social and political fronts. Coari's own speech, "A Minimal Feminist Program," dealt with more concrete matters such as equal pay, the administrative vote, double standards, and the regulation of prostitution.

Many of these themes had points in common with lay feminism, but Coari's conflict with da Persico now broke out into the open, leading to a deep division within Christian feminism. The *Pensiero e azione* group was now markedly isolated within the Catholic world. But the Church's perplexity did not stop Coari: alongside her secular allies, she continued to crusade for the abolition of prostitution and for public morality. She and Giacomelli were the only two Catholic feminists who took part in the First Women's Congress in Rome in 1908. Their participation was limited and strictly personal; they were unable to prevent the congress from declaring itself against obligatory religious instruction in the schools, thus bringing about a definitive break between the two groups. Coari defended her attendance at the Rome congress, writing that "the struggle should be taken to the enemy's territory."[69] This courageous stance, however, brought her review to an end. It was closed in 1908. Italian Catholicism pointed at the Milanese group to which *Pensiero e azione* referred, accusing it of "modernism."

Thus this bright but quickly consumed first phase of Catholic feminist organization, largely restricted to Milan, came to an end. Catholic interest in women's issues was somewhat backward compared to that of secular feminism derived from Mazzini (through Anna Maria Mozzoni and Gualberta Beccari), which was especially active in the cultural sphere and was a direct reaction to the initiatives of socialist feminism. In 1894 the socialist Linda Malnati founded the League for the Protection of Women's Interests. Ersilia Majno Bronzini's National Feminist Union dates from 1899, and in 1901 Bronzini opened the Mariuccia home for endangered or wayward young women.[70] The first trade union for women workers was founded in 1902. On this score, apart from the group around *Pensiero e azione,* Catholic women were less well prepared, less ready to fight, and above all less autonomous.

On the one hand, their obligatory obedience to the Church hierarchy brought them into constant conflict with an institution that was growing increasingly rigid in its defense of the "traditional" female model; on the other, every one of their initiatives derived from the support or stimulus of a more "modern" cleric who pushed them to act and supported them in relation to the hierarchy. The role of certain Franciscan friars, of Monsignor Radini Tedeschi, and of Father Grugni, was so imposing that it deprived the leaders of the feminist movement of many of the emancipating factors that characterized the equivalent secular movements.

Despite this situation, the leaders of the Catholic feminist movement did present a new model of womanhood: they went about alone, which was still forbidden; they took on public tasks, such as heading magazines and social organizations, previously considered "male" preserves; and they spoke in public. In objective terms, their behavior transgressed the traditional rules of Catholic culture. Adelaide Coari, who rose daily at dawn to travel, alone, on the train that took her to join striking women workers and speak out to defend their cause in public was creating a new form of behavior, yet one which was somehow seen as less dangerous than that of secular feminists. In fact, she blended the new and the old. The female Catholic leaders did not take responsibility for their own choices; rather their behavior was approved by at least some members of the clergy; this gave them respectability, while their religious militancy gave proof to their chastity, an aspect confirmed by their deliberately modest demeanor.

This new kind of emancipated woman did not oppose the male power of the Church hierarchy; she was its expression and its instrument. At the beginning of the movement, then, Catholic feminists had the road ahead smoothed for them by male protection, and in this respect their secular counterparts paid for their greater freedom with the difficulty they faced in being understood and accepted by society. This heavy debt to men should not, however, conceal the considerable contribution to emancipation made by Catholic women, which became more obvious in the immediate postwar period.

Both the secular and the Catholic feminist movements had one limit in common: they were restricted in their activities by their narrow geographical base. All of these associations were founded in Milan and were unable to spread beyond northern Italy. Their leaders, in both cases, were often born in Lombardy-Venetia (Mozzoni in Rescaldina, Majno and Coari in Milan, Giacomelli in Treviso, Anzoletti in Trent, and Beccari in Padua) to well-to-do families that had given them a relatively high level of education, and they all lived within a climate of vigorous social change. It took direct intervention by the Holy See—which in 1909 supported the founding of the National Catholic Women's Union—to involve the women of the rest of Italy.

Female Apostles of the Sacred Heart

A year after the Rome congress that led to the abrupt break between the Catholic and the secular feminist movements, and after *Pensiero e azione* had been shut down, Princess Cristina Giustiniani Bandini, charged with the task by Pius X himself, officially created a new association, the National Catholic Women's Union, over which she presided until 1918. Unlike its predecessors, the union was not federal in structure but was an institution of individuals, centrally controlled, with an exclusively religious program: "The women's problem," its constitution stated, "requires no radical innovations, but only a broader and more perfect application of Christian principles."[71] Its program called for a break in relations with non-Catholic women and a defense of the family and religious ideals, both under attack from ever-increasing secularization. The association's energies were primarily directed to the education of its members rather than social action, thus, in its founder's words, fostering "an apostolate of brains."[72]

The union succeeded in involving a considerable number of women, nearly thirty thousand throughout Italy, urging them to take up "public" issues including women's education, child rearing (with a special emphasis on fighting for religious instruction in school), the defense of the family against divorce, and professional instruction in certain areas, such as nursing. Though Giustiniana Bandini stuck to a strongly negative view of the female and social conquests of the first decade of the twentieth century, waging a real offensive against any emancipation outside the control and approval of the Church, the concrete accomplishments of the union were a determining factor in widening the traditional feminine role, extending the sphere of women's action to certain public sectors that had always been considered exclusively male.

But the real breakthrough to a modern mass-organization took place in the immediate postwar period thanks to Armida Barelli, a young Milanese woman, educated in Switzerland, who defied her non-Catholic family by entering the Franciscan Third Order and dedicating herself to promoting the devotion to the Sacred Heart of Jesus. Her lifelong association with the order's Father Gemelli began in 1910; she collaborated with him throughout her life, first during the war as secretary to the committee (Gemelli was its president) founded to persuade soldiers to dedicate themselves to the Sacred Heart; she then became treasurer of the drive to gather funds for the building of the Catholic University of the Sacred Heart founded by Gemelli right after the war. Her organizing and recruiting gifts led Cardinal Ferrari of Milan to choose her to found a Lombard young women's association. Its success was so great (it soon had five thousand members) that in 1918 Benedict XV gave her, as deputy secretary of the union, the youth portfolio.

Barelli offered young Catholic women a militant apostolate—"either apostles or apostates." She was convinced that women could pass from being weak allies of the Church to becoming the instrument of a Catholic reconquest of society. The Italian Catholic Young Women's Association, though it had spread throughout the rest of the nation, retained a strongly centralized structure owing to the creation of a compact group of particularly able leaders. They all belonged to the Pious Association of the Missionaries of the Kingship of Christ (directed by Barelli and Father Gemelli) and were chosen among the Franciscan tertiaries of the Social Realm of the Sacred Heart, whose new rule, approved in Assisi in 1919, called for consecration to God with vows of poverty, chastity, and obedience and required an apostolate in Catholic Action.

The leaders of this group were trained in the appropriate courses by Gemelli or his colleagues at Catholic University, where they learned to debate in public, organize conferences, and participate in a form of group therapy designed to master individual feelings: "Forget your selves . . . Speak as little as possible personally."[73] "To defend and spread religion," Gemelli told the members, "You have to know enough about it to do it." His technique was to propose an annual theme, a truth or a doctrine to be studied in depth, one "most useful for our inner life and our apostolate."[74]

Thousands of women participated in these courses, which were veritable cadre training for a mass movement; they were a vastly important element in the "modernization" of Italian women, weaning them from a lukewarm and sentimental traditional religiosity and involving them in general problems and new and collectively symbolic and pedagogical forms of devotion such as that of the Sacred Heart. The meetings and the retreats often took place in Assisi, where Barelli founded an Oasis of the Sacred Heart; to these were added regional and national meetings and pilgrimages (such as that to Palestine in 1930). Meetings gave the young women an opportunity to travel, to meet new people, to speak in public, to improve their own minds. These were strikingly original initiatives, but they were also carried out within an authoritarian structure and under the supervision of ecclesiastical assistants and parish priests. By 1922, the Italian Catholic Young Women's Association had over 220,000 members in 4,360 "circles" spread among 230 dioceses; by the end of the decade the number had doubled and spread throughout the peninsula.

During the 1930s, membership remained static because of competition from the Fascist youth movements, though the association was enlarged to take in new age-groups (the *piccolissime* and the *angioletti*). After the war, membership rose again, especially at the time of the 1948 elections, when its members were heavily engaged on behalf of the Christian Democrats. The organization and its leadership were deeply involved in postwar reconstruction and their contribution to the political victory of the Catholic party was decisive, for they were the largest, the most active and ideologically compact single group in Catholic Action. Barelli was well aware of the potential of her organization, as she wrote in the association's paper, *Squilli di resurrezione* (Sounds of resurrection):

> you know that women have been given the vote. It is a new form of political action for us: we must prepare ourselves, we must understand what the social principles of the Church are so that we can exercise our duties as citizens. We women are a power in Italy. Out of every hundred voters, forty-seven are men, fifty-three are women. If we can agree, we can put in power those who will defend our religion, the Church, the family, our schools, and our motherland.[75]

Women, by their political action and their prayers, were a bulwark against Communism: "only thus," wrote Paola di Cori, could "we become aware of the existence of many thousands of different Catholic women silently emancipating themselves in the shadow of the regime."[76]

Barelli, who called herself Older Sister, was also an admired and accepted example of the emancipated woman. For instance, in 1922, Sardinian association members thronged every station at which her train stopped to give her flowers, and this caused consternation among the other travelers: a woman, traveling alone, a recognized leader showered with flowers! For Barelli, the trip was a long victory. When Benedict XV had asked her to found the women's youth movement, she told him: "I have never traveled alone, I've never been without my mother, I've never spoken in public." But traveling alone became necessary for her apostolate, and it was to cause her quite a few discomforts and moments of dismay, such as when she spent a whole night in the waiting room of the train station at Civita Castellana alone with a drunken soldier.[77]

Barelli was a strong woman, then, one who had won out over every kind of sentimentality, one whom other women could imitate, said Giovanna Canuti, the head of the National Catholic Women's Union, by engaging oneself in serious study of the catechism, for the "religious fervor one wants from women is not based on 'sentimental' movements that come easily to feminine piety, but on the hard rock of the catechism, on doctrine, on the study of religion."[78] *Fiamma viva,* the magazine directed by Barelli and by Maria Sticco, professor at Catholic University, was even more explicit: "there are three things we must learn to acquire: control over our own feelings, which are always too impulsive; a reasonable seriousness in judgment; and knowledge of the conditions and historic needs of our country, of which women know very little, being more inclined toward literature than history or the social sciences."[79]

This line of teaching, which sought to correct what had always been considered the significant characteristics of female identity, was part of a broad-ranging project to create a "new woman," one who was modern but not emancipated in the feminist sense and one in whom nothing was left to individual decision. The association's papers set out a "ten commandments of fashion" and recommended behaviors that were carefully differentiated by the class to which their readers belonged. They gave advice on how to behave with members of the opposite sex, defined what was permissible (for a long time, dancing was considered a dangerous pastime), and praised purity and virginity.[80]

The women's organizations' principal contribution was to transform weak and sentimental women, devout in a way that was often childish and superficial, into well-prepared and combative "apostles" of Christianity in an increasingly secular world. As Dau Novelli has written, "Basically, the history of the Catholic women's movement can be read as a laborious attempt to take [women] out of the world of fantasies, dreams, and sensations into the world of rationality, judgment, and study, but without ever foreswearing the main characteristics of a woman's nature."[81]

A preliminary evaluation of the Catholic women's associations indicates that through an ideological acceptance of traditional roles—never debated but constantly offered as a model, an acceptance linked to intensive teaching and the creation of conditions which were de facto emancipated—there had come about a slow but radical transformation of both female and male culture. It was within that institution, the Church, which in an ideological sense seemed to contribute most to perpetuating female inferiority, that a vast and deep process of emancipation had taken place, whose fruit the Church harvested in the first decades after the Second World War.

Shifting the Boundaries

In October 1945 Pius XII, speaking to the women of the Italian Women's Center, declared himself favorable to giving the vote and equal rights to women. He asked how one might "maintain and reinforce the dignity of women, so important in the circumstances in which God has placed us."[82] This was a confirmation of women's personal dignity seen wholly from within tradition, discounting the effects of past and current social changes; it could be said, as Father Gaiotti de Biase argues, that "the Church entered the history of modern women's rights with a sort of superficial optimism, without taking into account the objective pressures toward change, without at all challenging the practice of centuries."[83] The opposition, by contrast, suspected that, given the clear dominance of women among the Catholics, giving the vote to women concealed an anti-Communist move.

The Church softened the new public role of women by its insistence on the figure of the mother, whose task it was to bring the men of the family back to the faith and protect the traditional institution of the family. The processions of Our Lady the Pilgrim that marked the immediate postwar period in Italy symbolized the "return" of men to the Church as part of their transformation into sons. "Can there be a human heart that hasn't felt the need for his own mother's love? Even the mature man, beset by the storms of life, becomes a child alongside his mother. In the same way, every woman that suffers is a mother."[84]

Society, meanwhile, was moving toward the emancipation of women, and bit by bit the Church was compelled to yield to women's insistent demand for freedom, including those in religious institutions. The new formula of the secular institutes, recognized in 1947 with the publication of *Provida mater,* did not play the same vastly renewing role in our century as the various congregations had played in monastic life in the previous century. The number of institutes grew slowly—there were thirty-five lay institutes in 1976 and forty-four by 1993—but the overall number of members diminished.

Renewal after the Second World War came mostly through the creation of new forms of religious life: communities seeking a normal life at work and in society through the possibility of collaboration between the sexes, the participation of husbands and wives, and sometimes whole families, and the commitment to political and labor union activities.

The first community of this sort was that of the Focolarini (the Hearth movement), founded in 1943 by Chiara Lubich, which in its founder's words offered a "fourth way"—different from marriage, the convent, or secular institutes. Many other such groups followed, some devoted to social activity (among the handicapped or drug addicts) and others to the contemplative life. Particularly important among the latter were the Student Youth (Gioventù Studentesca) of Father Giussani, the original nucleus of Comunione e Liberazione.[85] For the first time, both men and women who had not chosen to remain chaste could take part in a consecrated religious life.

Alongside these communities another old form of the solitary religious life revived: consecrated virgins and hermits. Vatican II in fact allowed consecrated virgins to live alone, unconnected to any institute, with no more than the approval of their bishop, and free to undertake any activity of their choice. Hermits were a further stage of this evolution. The new ability to live a solitary life consecrated to God, which marked the end of a conception of women, and especially religious women, as weak creatures in need of control and protection, has been embraced in the last few years even by women deeply involved in political life, such as the Christian Democrats Tina Anselmi and Rosy Bindi.

The life of women in monasteries, which had been slowest to change, also underwent a renewal: the outward constrictions of enclosure—grilles, prohibitions on leaving the convent and on hospitality—were abolished. The monastic life became a form of inner commitment, maintained without any material controls. Sisters have been especially active. They fought to obtain more specifically apostolic duties, clearly heading toward that "cure of souls" in parish life from which they were usually excluded. A major difficulty has been the question of serving at the altar, which was still decisively forbidden by a 1970 decree on the renewal of the liturgy. But as the need for women's help in these tasks made itself felt, owing to the crisis in vocations among men, in 1973 *Immensae caritatis* allowed women to distribute Communion; in 1980, women were allowed to read the Scriptures during mass; and in 1983 they were granted the authority, when necessary, to serve at mass; by

1998 altar girls were recognized. Rather than victories for emancipation obtained by the mobilization of women, these were adaptations to an increasingly secular society, with women filling in the voids left by the fall in the birthrate.

The transformations in women's religious life in the last few decades, though not yet all codified by the ecclesiastical authorities, are important: they tend to overcome the barriers between male and female institutions, for the first time proposing mixed organizations; they include married women and families—thus overcoming the traditional privilege accorded to unmarried and celibate women; and they accept an individual sort of religious vocation.

These recent changes should not be considered as gains made by nuns, who in Italy, unlike in other countries, were unaffected—with a few exceptions, such as the Daughters of Mary Auxiliatrix[86]—by feminist culture. They resulted from the opening up of the Church, especially in the 1970s during the pontificate of Paul VI, to modernity.[87] From 1965 onward the Catholic Church has shown a changed attitude toward the demands of women, as is revealed in the Council's Message to Women (December 8, 1965): "The hour is upon us, the hour has come, in which a woman's vocation is fully exercised, the hour in which women have acquired an influence in society, a power, a radiation never before seen. That is why, at a time when humanity is undergoing profound change, women illuminated by the evangelical spirit can do so much to keep humanity from decline."

This recognition of women's parity—confirmed by Paul VI's granting, for the first time in history, the title of Doctor of the Church to two women saints, Catherine of Siena and Teresa of Avila—came at the critical transition point in the relationship between women and the Church as configured in the nineteenth century. Women in the Church, whose presence was imposed on it by external circumstances such as the decrease in male vocations, took advantage of the opportunities for assertiveness that were available to them, using the force of their qualifications to challenge the resistance and refusals of the ecclesiastical establishment. All those prohibitions and refusals the Church had originally made against a new role for women were overcome by concrete facts that caused them to be overridden a few decades later. Both the enlargement of women's democratic liberties, which characterizes the evolution of the Italian state, and their numerical importance within the Church militated on behalf of women. As differentiated from secular women, Catholic women could count on the clergy's need—given the reduced male presence in religious life and in the lay apostolate—to depend on them to act in society.

This slow progress of women into the public world and into religious and secular life came about in close alliance with the Church, and hence it accepted its moral direction. In 1968, though, Paul VI's *Humanae vitae,* confirming the Church's condemnation of unnatural methods of birth control, opened an unbridgeable gulf between Church doctrine and the freer emotional and sexual behavior of the times. The polemics aroused by the encyclical, which were seen also as proof of the insensibility of the Church toward demographic problems, signaled a breakdown between the norms of the clerical establishment and the behavior of the faithful, especially women, who were the most affected. Then in Italy came the referendums on divorce (1974) and on abortion (1978), which revealed how a great number of women now demanded personal autonomy in their decisions as against the prescriptions of the Church, especially in regard to relations within marriage and sexual behavior.

So the new opening seemed to have come too late. Even the American feminist Betty Friedan, who visited Paul VI under the most cordial conditions, raised no great enthusiasm. Friedan, whose gift to the pope was a golden symbol of the feminist movement, declared that she had been much pleased by the attentiveness and kindness with which the pontiff addressed her, on her part recognizing that more had been done for women during his pontificate "than in the previous 1,900 years."[88] The Church, which seemed to have yielded on every point on which it had previously denied a social role for women, was in fact preparing itself to defend the last frontier toward which the current process seemed to lead: the priesthood.

In 1971 Paul VI set up an international study group, composed of seventeen experts, mainly theologians, including five women, to consider the women's problem. It was to conclude its work in 1975, which had been proclaimed Year of the Woman by UNESCO. The committee labored at its task with some difficulty and spent most of its time on the question of a female priesthood, in part because the pope had been asked by the archbishop of Canterbury (who was about to sanction female ordination, though not in the immediate future) to rule on the question. While admitting that Scripture offered no clear answer on the matter, the proposal for women's ordination was defeated by twelve to five, and a minority report, by the five women, lamented the fact that they had been treated with suspicion. The committee's response was a theological one, made on the basis of the Church's longstanding practice and due to the opposition of the clergy.[89]

While this exclusion has been repeatedly confirmed, practice continued to move in the opposite direction. Sisters who, after 1970, were allowed to assist priests in the parish, launched a protest to insist on their financial autonomy (originally they had been paid by the parish priest himself) and to demand that discussion of parish projects take place on a plane of equality.[90]

If the ordination of women has been raised officially only in Protestant churches, the sisters—mainly because of the critical state of male vocations—have undertaken tasks that have brought them ever closer to the altar. They teach in universities; they preach, sometimes even in Church (the only limit placed on them by the new code of canon law is that they may not give the homily during mass); and they have so settled into parish work that they have taken over the care of parishes that lack priests.[91]

The theoretical discussion indispensable to rooting these experiences in Catholic culture has been led in recent years by feminist theologians who have dug deeply into the Gospels to study the relationship between Christ and women and the later departure of Christian theology from that premise; it is laying the basis for a complete revision of the Christian message.[92] John Paul II's apostolic letter *Mulieris Dignitatem,* given out during the Marian Year on the feast of the Assumption (August 15), 1988, is not far from this rereading of theology.

John Paul II made a brave reinterpretation of Genesis, and particularly of the figure of Eve: "That original sin is Man's sin, who was created by God both male and female."[93] Discussing the attitude of Jesus toward women, he said, "It is universally admitted . . . that to his contemporaries, Christ promoted the true dignity of women and that of the vocations which correspond to that dignity."[94] He added an explicit recognition that women have shown toward Jesus "and his mystery a special sensibility that corresponds to a characteristic of her femininity."[95] The Church then has explicitly accepted an essential equality between man and woman, while at the same time defending women from "masculinization": "In freeing herself from the 'domination' of men, a woman may not seek to appropriate masculine characteristics against her own feminine 'originality.'"[96] This mission, which is specific and consubstantial to her nature is of a sentimental order: "Woman cannot find herself save by giving love to others."[97]

Her equality, then, accepts an equal value, but the gender roles are not interchangeable; on the institutional plane John Paul II's letter sanctions an asymmetric relationship between men and women within the Church. Thus women, who from being undervalued allies had become, by the middle of the twentieth century, the strong point through which the Church sought to reconquer a secularized society, have now become one of the gravest problems the Church faces. They have not only challenged the norms of sexual morality, but have come dangerously close to what constitutes the ultimate stronghold of Catholic tradition: the priesthood.

Translated from the Italian by Keith Botsford

CHAPTER 15

A Voyage to the Madonna

EMMA FATTORINI

The nineteenth century is rightly perceived as the century of the great revival of the Marian cult, which reached its climax in 1854 with the dogma of the Immaculate Conception, a dogma in some ways imposed, after centuries of theological-doctrinal argument, by constant popular pressure.

Marian spirituality has shown no signs of diminishing in the twentieth century:[1] data on true and false apparitions of the Virgin show a great number of these—between 1928 and 1958, for instance, 179 apparitions were recorded. It was in 1950 that Pius XII solemnly declared the dogma of the Assumption of the Blessed Virgin to heaven, long celebrated in both the East and the West. Carl Jung defined this dogma as "the most important event since the period of the Reformation," because for the first time in Western culture a woman had been made "divine." After the figures of Sophia (wisdom) and the goddess Isis, the valorization of the Madonna by Catholicism showed that even God needed a woman to become a man, through which the incarnation of Christ is humanized and the female conditions of virginity and maternity are divinized: "For our period it is psychologically significant that in 1950 the celestial bride was united to her beloved."[2]

According to many female scholars, the virginal motherhood of Mary should no longer be read as a deprivation and mortification of femininity, but rather as an opportunity to disjoin sexuality and procreation, "to accede to the son without passing through the father." Many different strands of contemporary feminism see Mary as incarnating the extraordinary symbolic power of the feminine.[3]

It remains that women have been the main protagonists and beneficiaries of the Marian cult, the apex of a romantic religiosity that marks the whole century. The feminization of Catholicism and the Marian cult have gone hand in hand. But how, and in what sense?

As we shall see, women's devotion to the Madonna is a constant over a long period; rather than constructing a high cultural and theological structure about her, women sought out Mary for her greater spiritual immediacy, one that often came close to superstition. Even the female mystics failed to express a specifically feminine Marian spirituality. It is the supreme feminine cult but, more than most, it has been transmitted by a "male theology."

In the Mariophany of the nineteenth and twentieth centuries, the Madonna appeared more frequently to women and girls, whereas, surprisingly, between the sixth and eleventh centuries male seers—at least those authenticated by tradition—were more numerous than female, and adults were more numerous than children.[4] But the criteria by which apparitions and seers were validated varied between those officially recognized by the Church and those bequeathed to us by tradition.[5] Historically, one can make a basic distinction between the apparitions of the Middle Ages, which were widespread, not exclusive to a few seers, and undifferentiatedly identified with the practices of a mass religion, and those of our own time, which have been far more circumscribed and recognized as surprising events.[6] The latter have become objects of spectacle, and mass communication has so broadened and so glorified their importance as to make them seem more relevant than in the past.

The feminization of Marian cults of the nineteenth century, as examined through the Church's official documents on the Madonna, provides another surprise. The documents almost wholly ignore any direct reference to what Marian devotion was supposed to do for women as such. This "disinterest" survived until the first Marian congress—such congresses have continued every four years up to the present—held at Livorno in 1895. At that congress, through Father Giovanni Battista Semeria, the Church finally revealed what the Madonna "wanted from women." Semeria, an important figure in the Christian Democratic movement, had in his earlier life been accused of "modernism" and been marginalized; he eventually became the indefatigable military chaplain alongside General Luigi Cadorna in 1915. In Livorno he started out by saying that, "taking into account that in God's wisdom Mary was established as the perfect Catholic woman," the aim of Marian spirituality was to encourage the new condition of modern women: "Even if a woman is tied to her home, she has energies sufficient to perform other tasks, to act in a wider sphere: the conditions of the times summon women to social action."[7]

He continued with a detailed description of those areas in which women should produce their positive effect, under the Madonna's inspiration: above all, the education of the young, but also works of charity with a social context increasingly marked by class conflict.

The Marian congregations became the centers for the new religious practices among women. Having matured in Rome in Jesuit colleges during the second half of the sixteenth century, the Marian congregations experienced a true boom in the 1800s and have continued to spread up to our day with a capillarity and variety such as to form a genuine and powerful Marian movement, one that because of its excessive charismatic outbursts the Church of Rome has not always found easy to control.

The congregations were associations without clerical connections. They often arose quite outside official religious organizations and were nourished by a communitarian, apostolic spirit, strongly international in nature and often dominated by women. One of the best known of these was the Focolarini movement, founded in 1943 by Chiara Lubich and a circle of her friends. Though they were not, strictly speaking, a Marian congregation, they were inspired by the type. In its aesthetic and liturgical symbolism and in its leadership and organization, the movement bore an unequivocal feminine stamp.[8]

The Marian movement offered women an opportunity for socialization, to express publicly a female apostolate. The pilgrimages Marian congregations offered allowed an extraordinary mobility, an unheard-of chance to travel for women who had never left the narrow circles of country parishes. The model of virginal maternity enabled women to live without insupportable guilt in their new space in the modern world.[9]

To understand the significance of the Marian cult between the nineteenth and twentieth centuries, one has to understand how the cult interacted with the processes of social modernization and the condition of women. Though they reprocessed traditional *topoi*—thus confirming that among popular religious manifestations, Marian devotion had been constant over a long period— the cults of the time faced the modern world, illuminating aspects that were important not just for religious history but for history itself.

For instance, even as national states and nationalist movements were being created, the national basis of the cult underwent a rapid universalization; it crossed borders without losing any of its power, its sense of local belonging. We see this shift in "the letters of emigrants from the south to the rectors of their own, local sanctuary, which reveal an interesting process of identification, not just with their own village but with their own sanctuary: for the villager in a faraway land, his country is his sanctuary, it is *his* Madonna."[10]

In the same way, the most important Mariophanies are responses to the threat of modernity. Lourdes (1858) offers the classic, medieval miracle—the body in all its physicality healed: the paralytic who walks, the blind man who sees—and seems to want to "use" the miraculous event against the omnipotent optimism of a positivist medical science.

Fatima (1917) expresses the apocalyptic prophecy common to all major historical turning points, and the cult of Fatima was "used" politically to face such enormous turbulences as the Great War and the Russian Revolution.

Medjugorje (1981), coming as it did at the end of the millennium and of a century that had seen the rise and fall of the great Communist heresy, further accentuates these millenarian traits. It seeks a pacification directed more at human consciences than at political powers; it cures the ills of the soul rather than those of the body, the soul being wounded and disillusioned by an era that, after raising high hopes of brotherhood and equality, miserably betrayed those hopes.

Our own times have seen a proliferation of apparitions and a recrudescence, in grand style, of the international Marian movement, decisively supported by John Paul II.

The Miracles of Lourdes: The Train and the Body

"Should you have reason one day to wander about Lourdes," laments the French railway magazine, "you will search in vain for a street or a square named after Colomès de Juillan. Ingratitude, indifference . . . that would be going too far. Rather let's just call it ignorance."[11] De Juillan was the engineer who had the good idea of making Lourdes the center of an important rail link in the Pyrenees. It was a practical, modern decision, and no less "providential" than the many miraculous events that succeeded one another in the plain around Lourdes. It was a good marriage, an example of admirable concord among technology, scientific progress and supernatural intervention. With justified pride, the magazine recalled the complex itinerary involved in opening the railway line on April 9, 1866, in time for the official consecration of the grotto on May 21: "The line ran right in front of the grotto along the opposite bank of the stream . . . The locomotive's efforts [seemed] to pay homage to Our Lady of Lourdes."[12] The *Journal de la Grotte* (collectively the *Annales de Lourdes*) followed the Lourdes phenomenon year by year: from its pages we can learn that in July 1867 the train transported 700 members of the Congregation of the Daughters of Mary, and a year later a special train, made up of twenty-four carriages, brought 923 "ladies" or *dames*—the ever more numerous women who in the succeeding decades, together with male stretcher-bearers, accompanied many millions of the sick to the grotto.[13] At this time began the great train pilgrimages that continued to multiply, especially after the Franco-Prussian War (1870), and reached their real, international boom years with the arrival of Portuguese, Swiss, Spanish, and Italian pilgrims starting in 1877.

Today the transportation links have become imposing: a major rail line links Lourdes to Paris, Bordeaux, and Toulouse; the Lourdes airport's runways can accommodate Boeing jets. After Rome, Lourdes is the goal of the greatest numbers of pilgrimages in the world; with its four to five million pilgrims annually, Lourdes is, after Paris, the city with the best-developed hotel industry in France. This sanctuary has the most copious literature in the world on its own history: it is the Marian shrine that breaks all records.

Why talk about trains, transports, trips, and pilgrimages? The success of a sanctuary depends not a little on its locality, on how easy it is to reach, on what housing is available locally, on its proximity to major lines of communication.[14] Lourdes is exceptional in that this whole complex of conditions was artificially created. We should not forget that the nineteenth was a century of great, solitary travelers and that travel was not yet common, certainly not a mass activity; it was restricted to an elite which was even more reduced in the case of women.[15] With Lourdes, pilgrimages, which had always been opportunities for travel and communication, were made available to all in highly organized structures that precluded discomfort and uncertainty; Lourdes may be said to have created its own mass travel industry.[16]

In seeking to understand the phenomenon, the information contained in the numerous manuals and guidebooks is far more useful than the rather dry sociological literature or the vast apologetic literature. Authentic little treatises on making a "good pilgrimage" contained a rigorous set of practical and spiritual rules. They were handed out to each and every pilgrim together with his or her number, and priced according to the class of train by which he or she arrived. They recommended, for instance, that women should dress "without vanity . . . [and] baggage should be in keeping, take no more than is strictly necessary"; men should "seek to perform the external acts of piety," and should feel no shame through what was once called "human modesty." Above all, the pleasures of travel should be measured, joy being properly contained.[17]

Even as these handbooks reminded pilgrims to behave with austerity, there was no lack of enticing tourist information about the climactic wonders and beauty of the surrounding towns: the south of France was lovely and Paris, after all, was not so very far. Thus useful advice and precise instructions were given so that even the most bewildered provincial from Lombardy or the Veneto who had never left home could profit from this great dawn of mass tourism. All the most modern means of transport were puffed: "The bicycle, that latest creation of industry, is not unknown in Lourdes; it appears there in all its forms and its latest perfections, not excluding the most recent, with a gas engine."[18]

"Modern" means of transport did not exclude traditional ones, and women especially renewed the tradition of pilgrimages on foot: for instance, two poor Polish women, one of them a miraculously cured blind woman, completely unfamiliar with the outside world, went on from Lourdes to Rome, where they were received by Leo XIII; more recently the Bolognese woman Egle Zoffoli wrote a rich diary of her encounters and inner experiences during the walk from Bologna to Lourdes—an account altogether exemplary for its simplicity, the naturalness of the trip, and the purity and sobriety with which she treated her deep and powerful emotions. This modern pilgrim began her account as follows: "Alone and old as I am, and not without physical problems, I left without a travel plan, without knowing in the morning where I would lay my head at night, and without any certainty that I would complete my journey."[19] Her travel diary is exquisitely feminine for its attention to even the most insignificant details. The practical information conveyed without emphasis is a signal of more important matters; it is a pilgrimage lived through the eyes of a woman, as when she gives touching thanks to the many sisters who gave her hospitality, in comfort or in poverty—unlike many parish priests who, despite her presenting a letter from her bishop, were suspicious, unwelcoming, or diffident concerning the extravagant nature of her enterprise.

Healing the Sick Body

The sick body is the real protagonist of Lourdes: the body in all its materiality, naked, immersed in great pools of holy water before the grotto. Interminable lines of stretchers and wheelchairs in torchlight processions recall the great mass rituals that, often inauspiciously, have so dominated the collective manifestations of the twentieth century. Communitarian liturgy occupies a special place. It is bodily, in the sense that one prays with outstretched arms, and itinerant, in that it takes place in the nighttime processions that emerged spontaneously as the collective expression of supplication and hope in a specific historical context: the turn of the century in which the masses enjoyed, in quite a different guise, a new central place.

The body is miraculously cured along classic medieval lines: as though winning a challenge, competing with the obvious, infinite resources of medical science.[20] In their various capacities, doctors too have been principals at these displays: either as evaluators of miracles performed (from 1890 to the present, 22,237 doctors' signatures have been deposited in the Bureau des Constatations, where any doctor may freely examine the records of all the doctors who have certified the authenticity of the healings) or as skeptics seeking to demolish such palpable superstition who were dumbstruck by their own sudden conversions.

For some time, and for many obvious reasons, there has been a decline in the number of traditional miracles at Lourdes: nineteenth-century, positivist medical standards of authentication have lost all credibility. Medical science, too, has changed; it is now less certain of the causes of illness and of its cure; and theology itself, which no longer feels threatened by science, is unwilling directly to attribute cures—many of which remain inexplicable but need not for such a reason be considered miraculous—to supernatural agency. There are far more links between science and theology than were thought possible a century ago: consider, for example, the psychological powers of subjectivity. Besides, as Goethe said, a "mystery is not yet a miracle."

It is in this intermediate zone between science and the supernatural that the special atmosphere, of which so many laypeople who have participated in the liturgy at Lourdes speak, is nourished. There now prevails neither an extenuated psychologism nor a sort of dumb stupor in the expectation of a single extraordinary miracle, such as always accompanies the early days of an apparition—when the public wills and begs for its famous proof, a sign from heaven that confirms the supernatural presence (the most famous of these took place at Fatima, when the sun pulsated and seemed to spill onto the earth, a prodigy that will be repeated in many contemporary apparitions)[21] No longer does expectation derive from the single cure; rather, it comes from the fact of living in a place, a space in which pain and suffering are represented in their very essence, as tragedy and hope, and these, without rhetoric, become metaphors for the human condition.

Visitors are often at first understandably put off by the consumerist aspects of Lourdes's only industry; subsequently many of the disenchanted are surprised to note the silence, the prayer, and the concentration all about them. Despite all the distractions, the town's central focus remains the solemn and sacred nature of sickness, lived with spiritual withdrawal into prayer and a hope that lies beyond any particular faith. In fact, Lourdes has an ecumenical breadth that has detached itself from the Marian cult in the strict sense and especially in the last thirty years has, more than any other shrine, resisted postconciliar secularization: "Everything is in decline except pilgrimages," said Cardinal Marty of the three to four million annual visitors to the grotto.

Lourdes paved the way for the Marian cult in its modern aspects, and it carries a meaning that extends beyond the cult to become the precipitate of Christian values against secularization; it is a shop window for those nonbelievers who find preserved there, beyond its vulgar commercialism and a vaguely superstitious devotion, some of the characteristics that might temper the hard edges of modernism, such as solidarity and openness and a sense of sharing with those who find themselves in the real harshness of life, which is suffering.

Fatima: The Virgin on the Ways of the World

Fatima, wrote Claudel, is the greatest religious event of the first half of the twentieth century, "the overwhelming explosion of the supernatural into this world imprisoned in matter." Fatima incarnates the values of tradition; it opposes the menacing advances of materialism and the seduction of the masses caught in the bright lights of history by the October Revolution and the Great War of 1914–1918.

The Madonna of Fatima is essentially a political Madonna—not merely in a propagandistic sense (though her image was put to widespread use during the Cold War) but in a broader, more modern, more twentieth-century sense. "The Virgin is involved in politics"; she takes part in history; she comes down among men and women; she herself makes her pilgrimage on the ways of the world. Unlike the Virgin of Lourdes she is not first and foremost the object of a pilgrimage. At Lourdes the Madonna bade Bernadette to build a chapel to which people would make a pilgrimage; but she asked the three little shepherd girls of Fatima to build two sedan chairs so that she could go on pilgrimage.

She appeared to them at Cova da Ria in May of 1917, at the very time of the two events that conditioned the history of our time: the Bolshevik Revolution and the Great War. It was the last year of the war and the Church was expending itself in exhausting and unsuccessful peace efforts; it had been the only force that had opposed the war with real conviction. Its most important statement, Benedict XV's *Nota sulla inutile straga* (Note on the useless slaughter), which he had sent in August 1917 to all the belligerents, coincided with the apparitions, six in all, which began on May 13 and ended on October 13. Cardinal Pacelli, named nuncio to Germany three days before the apparition of the Virgin, was to be an excellent mediator and to become so devoted to the apparitions as to want to be known, when he became Pius XII, as "the pope of Fatima."

The Church, too, was torn by internal conflict because of the nationalistic struggles in which Catholic nations were themselves taking part.[22] The Madonna was often "used" as a peacemaker. One of the more sensational instances was just before the plebiscite in Upper Silesia after the Great War, when the Poles gave their oath to their Black Virgin that they would remain faithful to Poland over the now defeated Germany: "It would seem that during pilgrimages, especially those to the famous sanctuary of the Black Virgin in Czestochowa, the Polish clergy, taking advantage of the great hold that priests have over this good and deeply religious people, made the pilgrims swear *en masse* that they would vote for Catholic Poland and not for Lutheran Germany." Thus the pope's special envoy to Upper Silesia wrote back to the Holy See during the difficult months leading up to the plebiscite.[23]

The Virgin, then, was a partisan who took sides, who protected one side against another, but was also a warm mother who gathered under her great cloak the sufferings of these troubled times. As Our Lady of Sorrows, she expressed the hopes and fears of women in a different form during the two world wars.[24]

At Fatima, the Virgin appeared under the sign of reparation and prophecy. In her message to the children she announced the end of the war and the consecration of atheist Russia to her Immaculate Heart. A third secret message was written down by Lucia, the oldest of the children and the only survivor, in 1943, and has been buried ever since in the Vatican archives. This secret message has over time attracted endless fantasies and elucubrations. Indeed, around Fatima have gathered, from time to time, accusations about the esoteric, catastrophic, and apocalyptic nature of the hidden secret. One should rather be asking what is the *prophetic nature* of the message of Fatima.

The culture represented at the Second Vatican Council was hostile to the Fatima cult because of Fatima's intransigently traditional character, with its elements of penitence, sin, hell, reparation, and rosary. In fact, woven through the much-discussed prophetism of Fatima, one could read the fundamental question posed by Vatican II: what should be the relations between the Church and the modern world, between the message of salvation and history?[25] The different ways in which the three last great popes expressed their otherwise common devotion to Fatima is emblematic of the way in which Church-history relations have been understood by different pontiffs.

It was Pius XII who gave Fatima its traditionalist imprint. Twenty-five years after the apparitions, and on the silver jubilee of his own consecration as a bishop, on October 31, 1942, he consecrated the world to the heart of Mary; on May 13, 1946, came the crowning of Mary Queen of Heaven; and in 1951 he concluded the Holy Year at Fatima. Throughout his pontificate, but especially during the years of the Cold War, Fatima was used as an instrument of anti-Communism and of opposition to the modern world. His means was the *peregrinatio,* or "voyage of marvels," as Pius XII called it after the fervor caused by the Virgin's passage as she traveled in every part of the world by every possible form of transportation.

The *peregrinatio* of Mary was part of a centuries-old tradition. Usually, holy images were moved about to ward off the plague or some other calamity and carried in solemn procession, as was the case with Saint Luke in Bologna. In more recent times, however, the *peregrinatio* became a proper cult of its own and not just a variation on the traditional procession: it was no longer restricted to a single day, as the image was taken from place to place and along the way gathered as many consecrations to the Virgin as possible. It took on the aspect of a mission to the modern world, for the churches were ever emptier and the Madonna was sent forth to find her lost sons.

There was behind this mission a new kind of missionary spirit that, instead of undertaking to convert the pagans of other continents, sought to bring the Word to the modern unbeliever, a prey to malevolent materialist ideologies that competed with and sought to replace religion. While Medjugorje was used to fight the skepticism and disenchantment of our times without any illusions, Fatima was used to halt the spread of new and heretical "forms of religions": materialism and Communism, satanic incarnations of evil.

The first *peregrinatio* took place in Milan between 1947 and 1949 and was repeated with increasing frequency during the Cold War and up to the present. In 1978 the statue of the Virgin circled the globe in forty days; in 1978–79 another *peregrinatio* was promoted by Father Pio's prayer groups (Father Pio himself having supposedly been vouchsafed the third revelation) and covered two thirds of all Italian dioceses. The longest and most intensive was when the Black Madonna of Czestochowa was carried about Poland for twenty-three years, between 1957 and 1980.

Paul VI, though maintaining Pius XII's devotion to Fatima, sought to tie the cult into the general climate of the Second Vatican Council: as though to confirm her importance and official status, when the third section of the council was over, he himself went on pilgrimage and presented himself to the vast throng, together with Lucia, on May 13, 1967, on the fiftieth anniversary of the apparitions. He was to say, with Saint Ambrose, that "Mary was the ideal image, the archetype, the model of the Church"; in that light, in a speech on December 5, 1962, he invited the fathers assembled in council "to place the Church at the center of their deliberations, to integrate Mary into the Church."[26]

After the council, however, the Fatima cult lost some of its impetus, which it did not recover until recently. One need only recall (and this is no spurious anecdote) that after the fall of Communism, not a few Russian ministers had statues of Our Lady of Fatima on their desks. Wounded on May 13, 1982, during an assassination attempt, John Paul II went to Portugal the following year to thank the Virgin of Fatima for his recovery and there decreed her absolute primacy among the cults of the century—a legacy that now falls to Medjugorje.

Medjugorje, the Virgin at the End of the Millennium

In the present period of deep and rapid changes, Marian apparitions have multiplied in surprising fashion and in the most disparate and unforeseen places: in the heart of black Africa, at Kibeho in Rwanda, where the Madonna first appeared in 1981—simultaneously with Medjugorje, with which it shares many traits[27]—and in more likely places, such as the Basque country[28] and the village of Oliveto Cistra in the Salernitano.[29]

Marian apparitions in Italy, especially in the south (such as the Weeping Madonna of Syracuse), have lately been studied in conjunction with other extraordinary phenomena in the popular cult of saints (San Gennaro's blood in Naples) in excessively psychodynamic or rigidly anthropological fashion: the role of the Mediterranean mother and a presumed "nature of the Italian family," which intensifies "sexual desire for the parent of the opposite sex," supposedly explain "the domination of Marian apparitions in Italy."[30]

Thanks to its content and the worldwide diffusion of its cult, the apparitions at Medjugorje in Herzegovina seem to me to bear a unifying significance to that proliferation of apocalyptic cults at the close of the millennium so dear to the actual pontiff. Standard-bearer of the predicted fall of Communism in the struggle against the spread of the so-called consumerist and hedonistic values of Western society, the Virgin of Medjugorje began her mission in 1981, when the war still lay far in the future. Quite unlike other Mariophanies, the Virgin has appeared without interruption every day since, pleading for prayer and fasts for peace.

Her mission has recently been made more specific, as reparation for "two great errors, Communism and pan-Slavism . . . emerging in the name of brotherhood and justice," but since revealed to be disastrous and inhuman. "The cosmic struggle between good and evil . . . is paralleled by the present conflict in Croatia and Bosnia-Herzegovina."[31] By these lights, our century will end under the sign of Satan; the Virgin of Medjugorje—through her strategic position and the kind of message she offers—has brought down on earth the apocalyptic struggle foreseen in Revelation between the "woman arrayed with the sun" and the "great red dragon."[32]

Such apocalyptic utterances are not too remote from the more radical versions of Our Lady of Fatima; but, in distinction to Fatima, the Virgin of Medjugorje seems much less punitive and threatening, less resentful of and offended by the world's brutalities. She is sorrowful and broken-hearted, yet also trusting; she turns to those who come to her and thanks them for listening, more as a patient mother than as an exacting and exigent mediator.

The manner of her appearing and the kind of miracle she performs also differ from those of Fatima. The Virgin's apparitions at Mejdugorje are more a matter of being there, of being seen, than of showing herself. They depend less on the subjective perception of the seer than on the objective reality of her presence. Unlike other apparitions, there is no question of true or false seers, but only weaker and stronger visions, in the sense that everyone is, potentially, a seer.[33] If trance and "transport" are reserved for the seven seers who have been designated for more than a decade, others among the faithful—probably through the customary nature of a daily apparition and thus in some way familiar and not limited to a single exceptional moment—feel and experience the presence of the Virgin with such intensity that many claim to see her and all seem to feel her presence.

Her presence is felt in a deep, general sense but also in a more specific and technological sense. On one level, the visitor can see how the pilgrims gathered around the seven seers who speak directly and personally to the Virgin live a form of intensely felt and participatory spirituality, so far exempt from the kind of exteriorization common in cults at the height of their success. On another level, this perception—the Virgin's "being seen" rather than "making herself visible"—can be translated into technology: that is, though in many cases the human eye does not discern the Virgin, cameras, whether sophisticated or simple Polaroids, seem able to capture her image.

In her messages, the Virgin denounces television as a diabolical instrument that, together with the other apparatuses of technologically advanced societies, reduce the available space for prayer, for concentration, for personal communication within the family. The apparent paradox is that it is through these very means that the Virgin's cult spreads. Furthermore, she herself, for her daily projection and serialization, prefers the open skies to a dark cave.[34]

The other great instrument of transmission of her cult is Radio Maria, the most widely heard Catholic station and, in Italy, the second-largest in terms of listenership. It has 520 retransmitters as against 700 for the Italian state system, RAI, and is heard by more than two million people. Completely self-financed, it transmits day and night and has direct links with its audience, relating personal histories, sorrows, conversions, miracles, and experiences of faith or religion, with strong input from simple people and women. Rosaries, masses, and easy-to-listen-to music, with a steady rhythm, quite without artistic pretension but very effective emotionally, make Radio Maria a true "Prayer Radio."

Finally, science and religion, at peace with each other, enjoy a sort of technologicalization of miracles. But the most interesting aspect of all is the completely novel quality of the miraculous event. Physical miracles, though these happen, cause no great fuss—they are broadcast discreetly and without triumphalism, whereas the less dramatic personal transformations become far more prominent. The Virgin stresses a form of psychological "freeing from guilt" of the faithful; she exhorts them to accept themselves according to the words of Saint Francis of Sales: "Be patient with all, but especially with yourselves; do not be discouraged by your own imperfections."[35]

The way we now live, we still have incurable illnesses, but we also suffer from a new kind of despair, unknown to those pleading for miracles in centuries past: depression, a lack of meaning, a weariness with life and hope. In the accounts constantly broadcast by the multimedia installations around Medjugorje, one often hears of this sort of great miracle: someone has been saved from "sadness," from the subtlest melancholy or the most desperate of the depressions that mark the ills of our century's end—as the paralytic who finally, miraculously, walked symbolically marked the end of the last century.

The Medjugorje cult has not yet been officially approved, but it is seen with ever less suspicion by the hierarchy, perhaps because of the prudence of its faithful, who propose prayer and fasting rather than triumphalist ecclesial exhibitions, or perhaps because of their number, their constancy, and the multiple effects of conversions. John Paul II seems to go beyond mere tolerance; indeed, he shows a protective indulgence and satisfaction toward similar phenomena throughout the world. His quiet encouragement is neither extemporaneous nor merely devotional, but is based on a powerful theological and geopolitical design.

In his encyclical on the Virgin, *Redemptoris Mater,* of 1987—delivered just before the fall of Communism—the object of Mary's intercession and its theological-political content was to prepare, with the arrival of the next millennium, a reconciliation with the Eastern Church. Mary, *ianua coeli,* Gate of Heaven, became the means of passage of access to the East, in the likeness of the splendid Vladimir Icon and its consuming melancholy, "which accompanied the long pilgrimage of the Russian people toward faith." The pope puts his faith in all the icons venerated in Ukraine, in Belarus, and in Russia, and appeals to the faraway and deeply rooted Marian traditions of the Syrian and Armenian churches, the Greek and the Byzantine, so that "the Church may again breathe with both its lungs," West and East. In his ambitious plan, which seeks the reconciliation of East and West in one great Christian Europe, the Madonna is the key, the new *ianua orientis.*

Translated from the Italian by Keith Botsford

CHAPTER 16

Sisters and Saints on the Screen

GIOVANNA GRIGNAFFINI

A Panoramic Look

Anyone seeking to chart sanctity and religious life, or for that matter anything sacred, in film cannot help being struck by the fact that the most Catholic of nations, Italy, is completely marginal in this regard. This is not just a matter of the supranational talents of the filmmakers (Carl Dreyer, Robert Bresson, and Ingmar Bergman have all produced masterpieces, and Luis Buñuel biting, desecrating satire). The truth is that even in perfectly ordinary or generic films, not to speak of big-budget productions (such as Hollywood's block-buster hagiographies in which stars like Jennifer Jones, Ingrid Bergman, Katherine Hepburn, Jean Seberg, and others have played saints or worn the habits of nuns), such themes are barely represented.

As a result, female figures of note, capable of fashioning themselves a real autonomy, are extremely rare. The blood and martyrdom of the early Christians has flowed in rivers from pulp scenarios; parish and bar life has animated the comic cycles of Peppone and Don Camillo films; the degeneration of power and of religious institutions has been a stock-in-trade of the comedies of the 1960s and 1970s; and Jesus, Mary, and the saints have been dressed in the picture-postcard prettiness of Franco Zeffirelli. But these are mostly back-ground pictures, a sort of backdrop landscape of the stereotypes of costume drama against which to project the big picture of "national life." They have provided a touch of "local color" on the screen without ever giving rise to a single, serious question or ever stating a single problem of a spiritual order; they have been monuments of the same kind as the archaeological monu-ments scattered all over the Italian countryside.

In many texts drawn from a higher inspiration, the "monumental" character assumed by religious life in the Italian cinema, while remaining anchored in a determined social and historical context, becomes more shaded and dialectical. It is as though the abstract treatment of strictly spiritual problems were a sort of limit: to be looked at but to be kept at a due distance. This is certainly true of the spare, poetic prose of Rossellini and Olmi (rich in lay sanctity and laboring innocence when not actually dealing with the phenomenology of a miracle); of the magnificent and grotesque imagination of Fellini and Avati, with their gallery of the humble and downtrodden, poor in spirit and pure of heart; of the earthly, fleshly religiosity, at the very boundary of "scandal," of Pier Paolo Pasolini's and Liliana Cavani's characters. Looked at from this point of view, all of Italian, postwar cinema seems, in much of its neorealism, to have undergone a radical process of "secularization," maintaining a strong tendency toward a revolutionary humanism built on a Christian matrix. Precisely that tendency led many critics and Catholic historians of the period to say that Italy did not need hagiographic films, or films directly derived from Christian values, for that kind of film already existed.

In this light, many of the positions taken by Catholics in the institutional politics of the cinema assume a different coloring. Catholics chose to favor the double axis of formation-promotion-distribution (control over cultural and professional institutions, preventive censorship, and the role of critics and information) and distribution-marketing (control of the distribution circuits, programming, and cinema management) over the whole production chain. By choice, they did not interfere in so delicate a sector, and these choices have always characterized the Catholic position in the film industry. This noninterventionism accounts for the exiguous number of productions in the sector to which I have referred.

There remains one other factor to identify. At least in Italy, films on sacred themes or religious life have shown no independence at all from the standard discourse of cinematography, as though in matters of faith the latter were also the only recognized authority. Of course films are specific and need to combine the entertainment and spiritual elevation of the masses, but that would take us far afield. Instead, let us look at the place of origin in which the first decisive relationship between cinematographic institutions and sacred representation took place.

The Passion of the Origins

Sacred themes were part of films from the very beginning and the life and Passion of Christ was the most important subject. Some productions going back to 1897 bear witness to this: especially the Passion directed by Kirchner-

Lear in Paris for Bonne-Presse; Georges Hatot's, likewise in Paris, for the Lumière Company; and the Vincent-Paley version made for Hallaman Production in New York. To these we can add the slightly later productions of Georges Méliés and Ferdinand Zecca for Gaumont and later still for Pathé, whose innumerable remakes testify to the great popular success of the genre.

The fact that at least thirty such biographies of Jesus Christ were brought to the screen within a decade cannot be explained just by the widespread plagiarism and remaking of those early days. In fact, such sacred subjects were entirely absent from the spectacles based on images (magic lanterns, panoramas, dioramas, new worlds, and so on) that preceded the birth of the cinema and fed its iconographic patrimony.

The central role occupied by sacred themes in the early years of cinema is based on the availability—and recognition by the masses—of a huge iconographic and theatrical repertory whose motifs were endlessly drawn on and inserted into this new form of popular spectacle. For religious themes were particularly adaptable to the two dominant genres in early cinema: reconstructed actuality and views of transformation. But the life and Passion of Christ contained another secret ingredient.

The two versions produced in France were far ahead of the standards of their period, and the Paley-Russell production, filmed on the terrace of a New York skyscraper with expensive costumes and professional actors, and lasting an unusually long half-hour, was the first, true "colossal" production. The reasons for this phenomenon, however, are to be found in the double structure of the Passion itself: a compositional structure dominated by the *tableau vivant* and a narrative structure dominated by a succession of independent but interconnected scenes. There is also a double linguistic effect along whose lines the representational system of early films developed: on the one hand, the theatricalization of the "view," the passage from the primacy of the unparticularized "moment" to the primacy of the significant one; and on the other, the linear nature of the narrative, the passage from the parataxic, or discontinuous, articulation of the scenes to the syntactic, to "showing" a story. It was a system that articulated figurations as well as story and narrative, and created from the materials of the "composed" scene its own unity of discourse.

It is hardly surprising then that the life of Christ should have become not only a powerful point of reference for the early film industry, but also an iconographic and narrative model central to its subsequent linguistic development. It was so central as to dominate films directly inspired by religion for the next three decades, symbolically closing the era of the silent film with Cecil B. De Mille's superproduction *The King of Kings* (1927); so central as to become the model of a whole series of profane stories, especially those tales of feminine suffering, passion, and "faith" in the film melodramas that found their long and tormented way into the hearts of a vast female public.

The Italian cinema inaugurated the theme of the sacred in 1908 with the great actor Amleto Novelli in the *Life, Passion, Death, and Resurrection of Jesus Christ,* produced for Cines. Its own Christological line then continued in 1917 with Giulio C. Antamoro's spectacular and grandiloquent *Christus,* also made for Cines, and continues up to the present with films by Pasolini, Rossellini, and Zeffirelli. Two other elements serve to render this line more complex. The first, to which reference has already been made, concerns the way in which religious themes were fitted into the historical-mythological genre (the best-known and often-repeated prototypes here being *Quo Vadis* and *Fabiola*), which ineluctably led to the depiction of the characters in these films in "legendary" rather than strictly hagiographic ways. The second, which is directly connected to the first, concerned the choice and prominence given to their heroic components and to an "active life" linked to sanctity. This is true, for instance, of the Don Bosco biography, staged by Goffredo Alessandrini, high priest of the deeds and heroic morality of the regime.

Given this picture of a cinema dominated by the Christ model, by an ideology of warlike and muscular defense of the values of the faith, and by the power of the heroes of gesture and action, the viewer would have been hard put to discern the more subtle note of a quite different phenomenology of grace: to be heard at all, its voice had to await the flowering of a new culture and a new historical time.

Female Martyrs, Saints, Virgins

Themes derived directly from a religious inspiration are rare enough in the first forty years of Italian cinema, but the women connected to such themes are almost totally missing. The only exceptions were the martyrdoms of Joan of Arc and Saint Cecilia. The first was the subject of no fewer than three films, all of them well financed and successful commercially: the Cines production (1909, directed by Mario Caserini, with Joan played by Maria Gasperini); the Savoy Film version (1913, directed by Ubaldo Maria Del Colle and Nino Oxilia, starring Maria Jacobini); and the Zannini Film production (1917, directed by Mario Zannini with Lina Pellegrini).

In contrast, the martyrdom of Saint Cecilia was given only marginal productions, with correspondingly less elaborate staging and spectacle. In a more markedly hagiographic form, Saint Cecilia was twice brought to the screen: in 1910 by Cines and in 1919 by Vitrix Film. The relative importance of these two different stories of feminine martyrdom in the Italian film economy is due to many factors and not just the fact that Joan of Arc occupied a central position in popular imagination.

First, there is the richness of the sources (not just iconographic, but literary, theatrical, and historical) on such a subject as Joan: a whole repertory of scenes, plots, and motives so great and widely available that it would have been hard for film to ignore them. Second, and related to the first, was the rapid consolidation of a "tradition," including a cinematographic tradition, around the legendary figure of the Maid of Orleans—as proof of which one need only consider the illustrious precedents set by Georges Méliés, Georges Hatot, Alberto Cappellani, and Cecil B. De Mille in his 1916 blockbuster. Finally, there was the complexity, and thus the variegated meanings, attached to the figure of Joan: warrior, charismatic leader, symbol of national unity, woman, heroine through her purity, her ingenuity, and her loyalty, a fighter both within and without, a heroine of anti-institutional resistance, martyr, and saint.

Such complexity (with all its infinite variations, gradations, and degradations) seduced the most diverse and important writers and filmmakers, so that up to the present her filmography contains some fifty productions. The Italian silent film versions, entrusted to two of its most famous stars, looked mainly to her role as triumphant warrior and martyr to the faith and perfectly reflected the historical-mythological genre.

It was thirty years before a completely new Joan made her appearance in the Italian cinema. This was Roberto Rossellini's 1954 *Joan of Arc at the Stake,* in which Joan figured as a martyr without armor or triumphalism, as disarmed as its star, Ingrid Bergman. Hers was a career made up of solitude, madness, and feminine opposition—a trajectory that Rossellini had already traced with her in his triptych, *Europa '51, Stromboli,* and *Viaggio in Italia,* films that offer three different forms of lay sanctity—and it was a long way from the glitter of Hollywood.

But by 1954, the path trodden by Ingrid Bergman's Joan was no longer so solitary, for other women, even during the war, had already begun to make their appearance in sacred subjects. Their presence, given the marginality of such themes and the long silence of the preceding period, was immediately relevant and full of significance, even if only in quantitative terms. For there was a flowering of women martyrs, saints, and virgins in Italian film between 1943 and 1960. Less markedly legendary, but thoroughly hagiographic, these films brought to the screen "exemplary" lives of women that fitted in with what was going on throughout the Italian film industry of the time.

Among these films were Antonio Leonviola's *Rita da Cascia* (1943); Aurelio Battistoni's medium-length *Vita e miracoli della Beata Madre Cabrini*

1. Ingrid Bergman in Victor Fleming's *Joan of Arc*, 1948.

2. Ingrid Bergman in Roberto Rosselini's *Joan of Arc at the Stake,* 1954.

3. Michèle Morgan in the Joan of Arc section, directed by Jean Delannoy, of *Destini di donne*, 1954. (AFE, Rome)

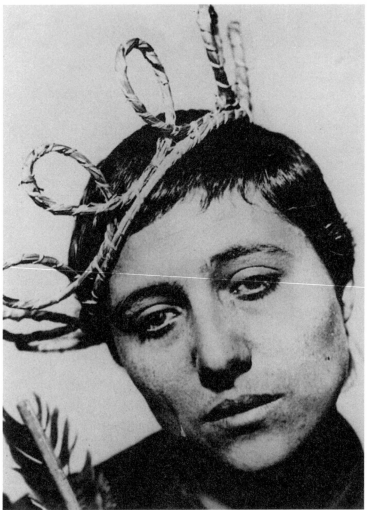

4. Renée Falconetti in Carl Theodor Dreyer's *The Passion of Joan of Arc,* 1928. (AFE, Rome)

5. Jean Seberg in Otto Preminger's *Saint Joan*, 1957. (AFE, Rome)

6. Ines Orsini playing Maria Goretti in *Cielo sulla palude*, by
Augusto Genina, 1949. (AFE, Rome)

7 and **8.** Pascale Petit (below with Massimo Goretti) in Alberto Lattuada's *Letters of a Novice,* 1960.

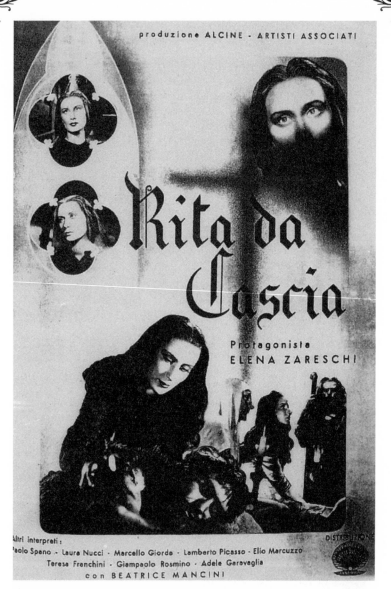

9. Original poster for Antonio Leonviola's film *Rita di Cascia*, 1943.

10. Original poster for *Il suo più grande amore,* by Antonio Leonviola, 1956.

11. Original poster for Oreste Palella's *Io, Caterina*, 1957.

12. Anna Magnani with director Mario Camerini on the set of *Sister Letizia*, 1956.

13. Anna Magnani in Mario Camerini's *Sister Letizia*, 1956.

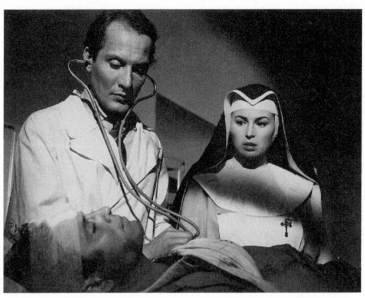

14. Silvana Mangano and Raf Vallone in Alberto Lattuada's *Anna*, 1952. (AFE, Rome)

(1946); Oreste Palella's *Catherine of Siena* (1947); Augusto Genina's *Cielo sulle palude* (1949); Arrigo Cinotti's court-metrage *Chiara d'Assisi* (1949); another short, by Piero Costa, *Santa Cecilia, regina delle armonie* (1949); Mario Bonnard's *Margaret of Cortona* (1950); Father Emilio Cordero's *Mater Dei* (1950); Dante Moccheggiani's documentary *La fanciulla di Corinaldo* (1950); Rossellini's *Joan of Arc at the Stake* (1954); Antonio Leonviola's *Il suo più grande amore* (1956); *Io, Caterina*, by Oreste Palella (1957); and Raffaello Pacini's *La tragica notte di Assisi (Chiara degli Scifi)* (1960).

No doubt there are contingent or institutional reasons that go some of the way toward explaining this sudden and never to be repeated domination of women in religious films (in the same period, only two documentaries and three features were devoted to males—Saint Benedict, Saint Francis, and Jesus Christ). For instance, a filmmaker like Oreste Palella was devoted to Saint Catherine, about whom he made two films; there was the beatification of Maria Goretti during the 1950s, which had, thanks to the coverage it received, a considerable popular impact; there were the multiple spin-offs from the Marian Year, which could explain the one and only film made about the life, passion, and Ascension of the Madonna, *Mater Dei*.

But there were also other reasons linked to the particular cultural project of the film industry in the postwar period and the 1950s, and the role of women within that project. That role was absolutely central—postwar cinema in Italy was skewed toward the feminine as far as its principals, its stars-models, and its scripts were concerned—but closely linked to three key concepts: the Italianization of cultural models, the idea of rebirth, and the indissoluble bond between women and landscape, understood as nature, but also in the anthropological, historical, and cultural sense of the word.

In this context the stories of Rita of Cascia, Margaret of Cortona, Maria Goretti, Catherine of Siena, and Clare degli Scifi show a rediscovery and reevaluation of an "Italian way" to sainthood, a way whose references, on the symbolic plane, are remote from the male and heroic model proposed by culture (not just film) during the fascist regime. They select from the more general process of economic, cultural, and moral rebirth to which the nation was summoned a specifically spiritual variable in the "new life" and "redemption" through faith.

Renewal and redemption from a dark personal and worldly past was explicit in the stories of Rita of Cascia and Margaret of Cortona, but there is no lack of examples of uncorrupted female heroism in public and social life (Catherine of Siena and Joan of Arc), or of references to women's ability to resist and their obstinate determination to maintain their purity (Rossellini's Joan again, but especially Maria Goretti). This "Italian and feminine way to sanctity" remained unconnected to any abstract or transhistorical Italian "character." It was concretely set in a "landscape" in the broadest sense of the word: the wild and menacing nature of *Cielo sulla palude,* the recall of religious iconography and of melodramatic structures in *Rita of Cascia, Il suo più grande amore,* and other films, which set out a landscape economy with characters capable of entering into reciprocal relations.

The most luminous image of this earthy female sanctity is perhaps *Cielo sulla palude,* the only film from which any reference to religious iconography is rigorously excluded. *Cielo sulla palude* is not a hagiography but a biography in which the life, passion, and death of a little peasant woman is screened from a phenomenological perspective. It does not choose predestination but finds in the purity of Maria Goretti a concrete model of being and of making human relationships: a state of the body and heart in addition to that of the mind. As the critic André Bazin pointed out, "Logically and theologically, the saint comes only afterward: when canonized."[1]

The Nun of Monza, Sister Addolorata, and Sister Letizia

The roles for female protagonists in Italian postwar film attack the boundaries of civil and religious society; they take the theme of the historical and symbolic rebirth of the nation and tell it differently: the heart of postwar cinema's representational system is the female body caught in a net of motives that far more explicitly bring out the conflicts between guilt and innocence, sexuality and maternity. Postwar heroines suffer from the same dark interweaving of sin and violent emotion as in the melodramas that were the staples of postwar film. Film plots were deeply rooted in a typically Italian culture (nineteenth-century opera, but also film in the first decade of the twentieth century), which made possible the recapture of a popular public. It is within this genre that we see sanctuaries, cult shrines, and sudden vocations; that convents open their doors to a swarm of unwed mothers; that the healing and caring tasks of a thousand anonymous "sisters" are carried out within prison and hospital walls. It is likewise within this genre that the "stars," at least once, take the monastic veil.

Seeing that their function is to hide the identical style of life and to reveal the identical model of expiation as those of the nun of Monza—brought back to the public mind by the 1942 Mario Camerini production of *I promessi Sposi*—these veils bear a heavy charge of Italian culture and history. Within the period covered in this essay, the first really successful model, locally and internationally, was Silvana Mangano (in Alberto Lattuada's *Anna,* 1952), and the last was Pascale Petit (in the same director's 1960 *Letters of a Novice,* adapted from the novel of the same name by Guido Piovene). Under its nun's white habit, austere and yet loaded with sensuality, Mangano's body remained ambiguously resplendent. So did her face, for she had a troubled past to redeem: that of a ballet dancer who had been involuntarily responsible for a crime of passion. But she also had to redeem her cinematographic past as the heroine of *Wild Rice*, in which the guilty apparition of the female body had found a first and provisional redemption in death.

In *Anna*, by taking her vows and devoting herself body and soul to curing the sick, Mangano was not only the femme fatale and ex-ballerina who found a new life (in the film, through flashbacks, the exhibition of her body and of her obscure past dominate the cleanliness of the present), she was also the ex–rice picker Silvana Meliga, who found her definitive redemption, allowing the posed body and womanly desire of the star Silvana Magano to be affirmed without mediation.

For the novice Pascale Petit, with her malicious face and body, ambiguous and charged with erotic tension, the convent represented no more than a temporary moment of peace, a refuge from the strains and intrigue of her passions. There was to be no redemption for her—just the court, in which the only justice is of this earth.

The case of Yvonne Sanson in Raffaello Matarazzo's 1955 film *The Angel in White* differs from both the others, not only because the "cultivated," literary frame of reference of the Lattuada films was entirely flattened out into one of cheap, romance novels (especially Vicki Baum's *Grand Hotel*), with a plot so complex that it was all but incomprehensible and full of unrealistic scenes, but because all eroticism and passion have been removed, replaced only by their effects and obvious symbolism—the illegitimate child, symbol of guilt. Sister Addolorata (Yvonne Sanson, who does not have a past as a ballerina but has a double in the film who was one) chooses the convent not for a vocation but out of necessity: it is a refuge from a world of misfortune and the vicissitudes of a destiny that is both absurd and inexplicably cruel. Rather, her destiny is only apparently inexplicable, given that it developed from her bearing a son out of wedlock, an original sin that must be expiated and that marks—like the stations of the cross—Sanson's interminable sufferings in *Tormento* and *I figli di nessuno*, the two films she made with Nazzari by Matarazzo in 1951, to which *The Angel in White* is the explicit sequel.

There are a thousand and one tales of ordinary illegitimacy and lost innocence (ones that cannot be redeemed by faith) around this powerful trilogy about redemption from an original sin, a box-office smash: the tales we find in movies like *Disonorata senza colpa* or *La colpa di une madre*, all of them attesting to the many faces of renewal and rebirth. For renewal is more than an idea; it is an obsession in postwar films: an obsession made flesh through motherhood in its multiple forms (biological, social, symbolic, linked to the mysteries of sexuality or the mystery of faith) and through the film history of the greatest and most popular star of Italian film, Anna Magnani.

A histrionic mother, full of life and devotion in Luchino Visconti's *Bellis-*

sima (1951), *mater dolorosa* in Pier Paolo Pasolini's 1962 *Mamma Rome,* a film whose deeply religious character is explicated through constant quotations from the paintings of Masaccio and Mantegna, Anna Magnani also faces the mystery of maternity in Mario Camerini's 1956 *Sister Letizia,* in which she gets caught up in an immaculate but socially guilty motherhood, in which redemption can be achieved only through the restitution of the beloved child to its true mother. A little-known and "minor" work, it shows, however subtly and backlit, a deep devotion to the cult of Mary, virgin and mother: an irreplaceable model of the life of every woman and every kind of sanctity because she is above all a creature of this world. Earthly, "placed," singular, but also suitable for generalization, Anna Magnani remains, in all her films, an actress who can carry the complex symbolism of the Italian mother in the postwar period, yet never become, in an abstract sense, the Mother.

Translated from the Italian by Keith Botsford

Notes

Introduction

1. Gal. 3:28. [All biblical texts in this translation, unless otherwise specified, are cited in the King James version. Trans.]
2. See, for instance, J. M. Soskice, "Can a Feminist Call God 'Father'?" in Teresa Elwes, ed., *Women's Voices: Essays in Contemporary Feminist Theology* (London: Marshall Pickering, 1992); and more generally, Joan Wallach Scott, "Women's History," in Peter Burke, ed., *New Perspectives on Historical Writing* (Cambridge, Eng.: Polity Press, 1991).
3. G. Charachidzé, *La mémoire indo-européenne du Caucase* (Paris: Hachette, 1987), p. 45.
4. Eyleen Edna Power, *Medieval Women* (Cambridge, Eng.: Cambridge University Press, 1975); Régine Pernoud, *La femme au temps des cathédrales* (Paris: Stock, 1980).
5. Romana Guarnieri, *Il movimento del Libero Spirito* (1965); Natalie Zemon Davis, "Gender and Genre, Women as Historical Writers, 1400–1820," in Patricia H. Labalme, ed., *Beyond Their Sex. Learned Women of the European Past* (New York: New York University Press, 1980).
6. Luisa Muraro Vaiani, *Giuglielma e Maifreda* (Milan: La Tartaruga, 1985).
7. Luce Irigaray, *Sexes and Genealogies,* trans. Gillian C. Gill (New York: Columbia University Press, 1993).
8. Ibid., p. 67.
9. Adriana Valerio, *Cristianesmo al femminile: donne protagoniste nella storia delle chiese* (Naples: M. D'Auria, 1990); Carla Ricci, *Mary Magdalene and Many Others,* trans. Paul Burns (Tunbridge Wells, Eng.: Burns and Oates, 1994); Kari Elizabeth Børresen and Kari Vogt, *Women's Studies of the Christian and Islamic Traditions: Ancient, Medieval, and Renaissance Foremothers* (Boston: Kluwer Academic, 1993).
10. L. Accati, "Simboli maschili a simboli femminili nella devozione alla Madonna della Contrariforma: appunti per una discussione," in Elisja Schulte van Kessel, ed., *Women and Men in Spiritual Culture, XIV–XVII Centuries: A Meeting of South and North* (The Hague: Netherlands Government Publications Office, 1986); Rosa Rossi, *Teresa d'Avila: biografia di una scrittrice* (Rome: 1983); Ida Magli, *Santa Teresa di Lisieux* (Milan, 1984). [See also Rosa Rossi, *Esperienza*

interiore nelle antiche autobiografie di Teresa d'Avila (Bari: Adriatica, 1977). Trans.]

11. Peter Brown, *Body and Society: Men, Women, and Sexual Renunciation in Early Christianity* (New York: Columbia University Press, 1988), p. 27.

12. Ibid., p. 54.

13. Joan Kelly, "Did Women Have a Renaissance?" in Joan Kelly, *Women, History, and Theory: The Essays of Joan Kelly* (Chicago: University of Chicago Press, 1984).

14. Reinhart Koselleck, *Futures Past: On the Semantics of Historical Time,* trans. Keith Tribe (Cambridge, Mass.: MIT Press, 1985).

15. Caroline Walker Bynum, *Holy Feast and Holy Fast: The Religious Significance of Food to Medieval Women* (Berkeley: University of California Press, 1987).

16. Birgitta of Sweden, *Revelations,* 7, 21, in Anthony Butkovich, *Revelations: Saint Birgitta of Sweden* (Los Angeles: Ecumenical Foundation of America, 1972). See also Chiara Frugoni, "La mistica femminile nell'iconografia delle visioni," in *Temi e problemi della mistica femminile trecentesca: atti del Convegno del Centro di studi sulla spiritualità medievale,* University of Perugia, October 14–17, 1979 (Todi, 1983).

17. Leo Steinberg, *The Sexuality of Christ in Renaissance Art and in Modern Oblivion* (New York: Pantheon, 1983).

1. Female Asceticism and Monasticism in Italy from the Fourth to the Eighth Centuries

1. On the "natural" inferiority of women in patristic thought, see Joyce E. Salisbury, *Church Fathers, Independent Virgins* (New York and London: Verso, 1991), pp. 49ff.

2. 1 Cor. 7:8–9, 34.

3. Acts 21:9. "And this man had four daughters, virgins, which did prophesy . . ."

4. Anthony, Epistle 6, 13, 1.

5. Phil. 4:3.

6. See Wilhelm Schneemelcher, ed., *Neutestamentliche Apokryphe* (Tübingen, 1989), pp. 200–202, 216–224, trans. and rev. R. McL. Wilson (Louisville, Ky.: John Knox Press, 1991–92); Mario Erbetta, *Gli Apocrifi del Nuovo Testamento,* vol. 2, *Atti e leggende* (Turin: Marietti, 1966–1969), pp. 245ff.

7. *De baptismo,* 17, 5.

8. Gilbert Dagron, *Vie et miracles de Sainte Thècle* (Brussels, 1978), pp. 31ff.

9. *Vita Macrinae,* ed. Maraval. On Thecla as model to Macrina and virgins in general, see Ruth Albrecht, *Das Leben der Heiligen Makrina auf dem Hintergrund der Thekla-Traditionen* (Göttingen: Wanderhoek u. Ruprecht, 1986).

10. Many of these are signaled in F. E. Consolino, "Il monachismo feminile nella tarda antichità," in "Segundo seminario sobre el Monacado: Monacado y sociedad," *Codex Aquilarensis,* 2 (1989), pp. 33ff.

11. [A "manly woman." Trans.]

12. [The Encratites were early Christian heretics who believed in abstinence from

all physical pleasures, including food, wine, and marriage. Their views figure largely in the apocryphal Acts. Trans.]

13. *De sancta virginitate*, 51:52.

14. 1 Tim. 5:14–15: "I desire therefore that the younger widows marry, bear children, rule the household, give no occasion to the adversary for reviling. For already some are turned aside after Satan."

15. *De virginibus*, 1: 59.

16. On the significance this growth in the ranks of virgins could have for the weight and prestige it afforded the bishop of Milan, see Rita Lizzi, "Una società esortata all'esceticismo: misure legislative e motivazioni economiche nel IV-V secolo d. C.," *Studi storici*, 30 (1989), pp. 129ff. On the Moorish slaves, p. 137.

17. *De virginibus*, 1:65ff.

18. *De virginitate*, 24–26.

19. *De virginibus*, 3:15ff.

20. ["Parent" and "author." Trans.]

21. *De virginibus*, 3:37ff.

22. Ibid., 3:38.

23. *De viduis*, 27, in *Patrologia Latina*, 16:243a. "Whose generosity lies not in her patrimony, but in the kindness of her love." *Patrologia Latina* hereafter cited *PL*.

24. *De viduis*, 53–54.

25. For a more detailed analysis, see F. E. Consolino, "Dagli 'exempla' ad un esempio di comportamento cristiano: il 'de exhortatione virginitatis' di Ambrogio," *Rivista storica italiana*, 94 (1982), pp. 455–477.

26. *De exhortatione virginitatis*, 55, in *PL*, 16:353B.

27. *Epistle*, 22, 16, 1, in vol. 54 of *Corpus Scriptorum Ecclesiasticorum Latinorum*, 54.

28. Jerome, Epistle 130, 6, 1; Pelagius, *Ad Demetriadem*, 14, in *PL*, 33:1108 = *PL*, 30:28C–D. For points of contact between the two, and on the aristocratic temperament shown by both, see F. E. Consolino, "Fra Pelagio e Claudiano: l'elogio degli Anicii nell'apistola di Girolamo a Demetriade," *Studi tardoantichi*, 3 (1992), pp. 65ff.

29. [Vettius Agorius Praetextatus, d. 384, was an ardent opponent of Christianity who sought a synthesis of pagan cults to oppose to the new religion. Trans.]

30. *Contra Ioh. Hieroselymam*, 8, in *PL*, 23:361C.

31. Epistle, 23, 3, 3, in *CSEL*, vol. 54, *quam unius cubiculi secreta vallabant*, "immured apart in a single room."

32. Epistle 39, 5, 5, in *CSEL*, vol. 54.

33. On Paula, see "Paula 1," pp. 674ff, in the first volume of A. H. M. Jones, J. R. Martindale, and J. Morris, *Prosopography of the Later Roman Empire*, 2 vols. (Cambridge, Eng.: Cambridge University Press, 1971–1980), hereafter cited *PLRE*.

34. This is also noted in two epigrams that Ambrose composed in her honor, in Epistle 108, 33, 2ff., on which see F. E. Consolino, "Girolamo poeta: gli epigrammi per Paola," in *Disiecti membra poetae*, vol. 3 (Foggia, 1988), pp. 226ff.

35. For Melania the Elder see *PLRE*, vol. 1, "Melania 1," pp. 592ff.

36. [Jerome broke with the theologian Rufinus over the question of Origen's orthodoxy. Rufinus was a close friend of Melania. Trans.]
37. One of the rare exceptions, as usual, is Augustine. See *De moribus ecclesiae catholicae*, 1:31, 68, 33, 70, in *CSEL*, vol. 90.
38. Epistle 130.
39. *PL*, 33:1099ff. = *PL*, 30:15ff.
40. Epistle 188.
41. "*Epistula ad Demetriadem de vera humilitate,*" ed. and trans. M. Kathryn Krabbe, in *Patristic Studies* (Washington, D.C.: Catholic University Press, 1965), vol. 97.
42. Peter Brown, *Religion and Society in the Age of Saint Augustine* (New York: Harper and Row, 1972), particularly the section on Pelagius and his followers, pp. 173ff.
43. Exod. 14:20.
44. *Corpus scriptorum Christianorum Orientalium* (Louvain, 1955), 151:64.
45. On the fortunes of this maiden in preaching on virginity, see the commentary by Michel Aubineau, in Gregory of Nyssa, *De virginitate,* ed. Aubineau, in *Sources chrétiennes,* vol. 119 (Paris, 1966), chap. 19, p. 486, n. 1. Compare the frequent recurrence of Moses' Miriam in C. W. Neumann, *The Virgin Mary in the Work of Saint Ambrose* (Fribourg, 1962).
46. For this reading of the Song of Songs, see Franca Ela Consolini, "Veni huc a libano: ad un esempio di comportamento cristiano: il 'De exhortatione virginitatis' di Ambrogio," *Athenaeum,* 62 (1984), pp. 399–415. Compare E. A. Clark, "Authority and Humility: A Conflict of Values in Fourth-Century Female Monasticism," *Byzantinische Forschungen,* 9 (1986), pp. 17ff., reprinted in Elizabeth Ann Clark, *Ascetic Piety and Women's Faith: Essays on Late Ancient Christianity* (Lewiston, N.Y.: E. Mellen Press, 1986), pp. 209ff.
47. Agnes's feast day was already being celebrated on January 21 in the liturgical calendar for 354. On Agnes, compare *Bibliotheca sanctorum*, 13 vols. (Rome, 1961–1970), vol. 1, col. 382ff.
48. *De virginibus,* 1:5.
49. Ibid., 1:9.
50. Respectively, *Epigrammata damasiana,* ed. Antonio Ferrua, *Sussidi allo studio delle antichità cristiane,* vol. 2 (Rome: Pontifical Institute of Christian Archaeology, 1942), epig. 37; Filippo Ermini, ed., *Peristephanon, studi prudenziani* (Rome: Ermanno Loeschi, 1914), 14; and the hymn "Agnes beatae virginis," *PL,* 17:1210.
51. *De virginibus,* 3:33–36.
52. Bernice, Prosdoce, and Domnina are exalted in a homily by Bishop Eusebius of Emesa, which has come down to us in a Latin translation. See *Analecta Bollandiana,* 38 (1924), pp. 241ff.; and *Patrologia Graeca,* 50:629–640, 641–644, by John Chrysostom. *Patrologia Graeca* hereafter cited *PG.* Pelagia of Antioch is commemorated in an authentic homily, *PG,* 50:579–584, and a spurious one, *PG,* 50:585ff. by Chrysostom. Ambrose alone makes Pelagia a sister of the other two.
53. *Civitatis Dei,* 1:26.

54. Ibid., 1:19.

55. Compare Franca Ela Consolino, "Modelli di santità femminile nelle più antiche Passioni romane," *Augustinianum,* 24 (1984), pp. 83–113.

56. "Mary," in *Dictionnaire de la spiritualité,* cols. 423–459.

57. *In Lucam,* frag. 12, in *Sources chrétiennes,* vol. 87 (Paris, 1962), pp. 472–474. On Origen's Mariology, see the introduction by F. Fournier.

58. *In Matthiam,* 10, 17, 22, in *Sources chrétiennes,* vol. 162 (Paris, 1970), p. 216.

59. *In Lucam* (in the translation by Rufinus), 6:7, p. 148.

60. *Corpus Scriptorum Christ. Orient.,* 151:59–61.

61. *De virginibus,* 2:6.

62. *In Lucam,* 2:8. *Corpus Christianorum Series Latina,* hereafter cited *CCSL,* vol. 14, pt. 4, pp. 33ff.

63. Compare, for instance, Gregory Naziansus, *Oratio* 38, 1, in *Sources chrétiennes* (Paris, 1990), 358:472–474: "Women, practice virginity to become mothers of Christ."

64. *PG,* 46:1140C–1141A.

65. *De sancta virginitate,* 4:4.

66. Ibid., 4:5–6.

67. See under "Vierge" and "Virginity" in the *Dictionnaire d'archéologie chrétienne et de la liturgie,* vol. 15, pt. 2, pp. 3103–3105.

68. Epistle 6, 2, 1, and 7, 4. *CSEL,* vol. 54.

69. Jerome, Epistle 7, 6.

70. Epistle 11.

71. *De virginibus,* 1:32: "virgo individuum pignus parentum, quae . . . non emigratione destituat" ("A virgin remains the inseparable child of her parents . . . not abandoned to leaving home").

72. *De virginibus,* 1:60.

73. *Carmina latina epigraphica,* 1434 = *Inscriptiones Lat. Christ. Veteres,* 2165 (quoted in vol. 3).

74. Epistle 130, 17.

75. Epistles 1, 10, and 2, 7 and 15.

76. Epistle 4.

77. In Epistle 22, 14, and Epistle 117.

78. *PG,* 47:495ff., 513ff., *Les cohabitations suspectes* and *Comment observer la virginité,* ed. Jean Dumortier (Paris: Les Belles Lettres, 1955).

79. "Liber ad Renatum monachum," ed. Salvatore Gennaro, in *CCSL,* vol. 85.

80. *De moribus ecclesiae catholicae,* 1:39, 68.

81. Epistle 127, 14, in *CSEL,* vol. 56.

82. Jerome, Epistle 127, 5. On Marcella, compare *PLRE,* 1:542, under "Marcella 2."

83. Epistle 24.

84. Epistle 23, 3.

85. Epistle 22.

86. Compare *PLRE,* 1:593, under "Melania 2."

87. For Fabiola, see *PLRE,* 1:323.

88. Jerome, Epistle 77, 10. On Pammachius, compare *PLRE,* 1:663.

89. The most authoritative list of Roman monasteries is still that of G. Ferrari, *Early Roman Monasteries: Notes for the History of the Monasteries and Convents of Rome from the Fifth through the Tenth Century* (Vatican City, 1957).

90. See Eligius Dekkers, "Saint Grégoire et les moniales," *Collectanea cistercensia,* 46 (1984), pp. 23ff.

91. Gregory, *Epistles,* ed. Norberg (Turnhout, 1982), Epistle 9, 115.

92. Epistle 9, 233.

93. Epistle 5, 4.

94. Compare Epistle 2, 46, 8, Epistle 3, 17, and Epistle 9, 138.

95. Epistle 7, 23, 86ff.

96. Epistle 9, 133.

97. Epistle 9, 54.

98. Epistle 4, 11, 42ff.

99. Epistle 4, 9, 10ff.

100. Compare Epistles 4, 6; 4, 9 and 26; 4, 24 and 29; 5, 19; 8, 9 and 9.

101. Epistle 5, 4, 25ff.

102. Epistle 9, 208.

103. Epistle 11, 13.

104. Epistle 14, 10.

105. Compare Epistle 4, 8, and Epistle 4, 10, on the foundation of a monastery in Cagliari; also Epistle 6, 44, and Epistle 9, 138.

106. Epistle 4, 6, 5–7, and Epistle 9, 198 (Abbess Sirica's will is not valid, because any person entering a convent forfeits the right to bequeath).

107. *Homily in Evangelium,* 38, 15. The youngest, Jordana, subsequently married her administrator.

108. Epistle 8, 14ff.

109. A list of royally founded monasteries, and the norms they obeyed, is to be found in Karl Voigt, *Die königlichen Eigenklöster im Langobardenreiche* (Gotha, 1909).

110. *Historia Langobardorum,* hereafter cited *HL,* 6:1.

111. Ibid., 4:48.

112. Ibid., 6:17.

113. Ibid., 6:35.

114. *Monumenta Germaniae historiam, Scriptores rerum Langobardorum,* ed. Bethmann-Waitz, pp. 189–191 = *Poetae Lat. Medii Aevi,* ed. Karl Strecker, vol. 4, no. 2, pp. 728–731.

115. *HL,* 5:35.

116. The monastery was still in existence during the lifetime of Opicinus of Canistris (1320–1330); compare Donald A. Bullough, "Urban Change in Early Medieval Italy: The Example of Pavia," *Papers of the British School at Rome,* 34 (1966), pp. 82–130 (p. 120).

117. *Carmina,* p. 727. Cuniperga's epitaph, dated between 750 and 760, is in N. Gray, "The Paleography of Latin Inscriptions in the Eighth, Ninth and Tenth Centuries in Italy," *Papers of the British School at Rome,* 16 (1948), pp. 38–167 (p. 76, no. 45, and plate 13, 3).

118. Between 672 and 688. Compare Gray, "The Paleography," p. 75. The event is noted by Paul the Deacon, in *HL,* 5:37.
119. *HL,* 5:37.
120. Diploma no. 27 of 899, in Luigi Schiaparelli, ed., "I diplomi di Berengario," in *Fonti per la storia d'Italia* (Rome: Senatorial Typography, 1903), no. 35, p. 81, 7.
121. Luigi Schiaparelli, ed., "I diplomi di Guido e Lamberto," in *Fonti per la storia d'Italia,* (Rome: Senatorial Typography, 1906), no. 36, 10, pp. 26 and 24ff.
122. See Strecker, *Poetae Lat. Medii Aevi,* pt. 2 (Berlin: 1914), 140, A, B, C, pp. 724ff. On the monastic complex itself, see A. Peroni, "Il monasterio medievale di Santa Maria 'Teodote' a Pavia," *Studi Mediaevali,* vol. 13, no. 1 (1972), pp. 1–93. The allusion to an unidentified indiction varies the dating from 705 to 720, 735, and 750 on a paleographic basis. Gray, "The Paleography," pp. 74–75, opts for one of the later dates.
123. *Carmina,* 140B, 4ff.
124. Ibid., Ludovico Antonio Muratori had no problem identifying her as Cunipertus's beloved. See L. A. Muratori, *Annali d'Italia dal principio dell'era volgare fino all'anno 1750* (Munich, 1761–1764), 4:197–200.
125. Luigi Schiaparelli, *Codice diplomatico longobardo,* vol. 1 (Rome, 1929), no. 18. Compare Lothario, Diploma 38, in Schieffer, ed., *Monumenta Germaniae historiam, Diploma Karol III* (Berlin and Zurich, 1966), p. 118, 35.
126. Bullough, *Urban Change,* pp. 103ff.
127. According to Bullough, "Urban Change," p. 123, who refers to the *Chronica de corporibus* (1236?).
128. Desiderius, Diploma 42 from 711, in Giulio Porro-Lambertenghi, *Codex diplomaticus langobardiaem, Historia Patriae monumenta* (Turin: 1848), vol. 13, cols. 80ff.
129. This right is already stated in Desiderius, Diploma 26, a bull of Paul I, from 711, though this would seem to be a forgery; nonetheless, the terms of the foundation are confirmed by an act of Bishop Sigualdus of Aquilea, dated October 13, 772. See Porro-Lambertenghi, *Codex,* vol. 48, cols. 90–92.
130. Diplomas 22 and 32; 25; 35; 36, 37 and 38; 43; 46.
131. Adelchis places the convent of Santa Maria in vado Alphiani under the jurisdiction of San Salvatore of Brescia. See Diploma 47, dated August 24, 772.
132. Elizabeth Ann Clark, *Ascetic Piety and Women's Faith. Essays on Late Ancient Christianity* (Lewiston, N.Y.: E. Mellen Press, 1986).
133. Jerome, Epistle 108, 20.
134. Jerome, Epistle 66, 13, 3.
135. *Vita Melaniae,* 40.
136. Epistle 130, 15.
137. There is a list of ancient rules in Elijius Dekker, "Clavis Patrum Latinorum," in *Sacris erudiri, Jaarboek van Gotsdienstweterschappen,* vol. 3 (Steebrugis: St. Peter's Abbey, 1951), pp. 312–320, nn. 1838–1876.
138. Largely thanks to L. M. Verheijen, *La règle de S. Augustin: I, Tradition manuscrite; II, Recherches historiques* (Paris, 1967).
139. [Cassian (ca. 360–435) founded two monasteries in Marseilles, a convent for

nuns and the Abbey of Saint Victor. His *De Institutione Cenobiorum,* in twelve books, though referring primarily to the East, is a detailed description of monastic life, including its dangers and how they may be overcome. See *PL,* vols. 49 and 50, and *CSEL,* ed. M. Petschenig (Vienna, 1886–1888). On Caesarius, see William E. Klingshern, *Caesarius of Arles* (Cambridge, Eng.: Cambridge University Press, 1995), which appeared after the publication of this essay. Trans.]

140. See Cyrille Lambot, "La règle de S. Augustin et S. Césaire," *Revue Bénédictine,.* 41 (1929), pp. 333–341; Sister Lazare de Seilhac, "L'utilization par S. Césaire d'Arles de la Règle de S. Augustin," *Studia Anselmiana,* 62 (1974).

141. Compare Gregorio Penco, "La prima diffusione della Regola di D. Benedetto: ricerche e osservazioni," *Studia Anselmiana,* 42 (1957), pp. 321–345.

142. Fernando Villegas, ed., in *Revue Bénédictine,* 84 (1974), pp. 7–65.

143. "Regula Columbani ad virgines," *Zeitschrift für Kirchengeschichte,* 16 (1896), pp. 465–470.

144. See Adalbertus de Vogüé, "La règle de Donat pour l'Abbesse Gauthsrude," *Benedictina,* 25 (1978), pp. 219–313.

145. Penco, "La prima diffusione."

146. The rule has the incipit *Psallendo pro sancta devotione;* its text was originally a sheet of codex Bruxell., 9964–9966, later set apart as Bruxell. 2, 7358. It was published by D. De Bruyne in *Revue Bénédictine,* 35 (1923), pp. 126–128, and later by François Masai in *Scriptorium,* 2 (1948), pp. 215–220, with notes appearing in *Scriptorium,* 5 (1941), pp. 123ff.

147. *PL,* 88: 1053–1070.

2. Mystical Marriage

1. A. E. Green, "The Song of Songs in Early Jewish Mysticism," in Harold Bloom, ed., *Modern Critical Interpretation: The Song of Songs* (New York: Chelsea House, 1988), pp. 141–153.

2. Rabbi Akiba's words are in *Mishna, Yadayim* 3, 5. Further commentary will be found in *Tosefta, Sanhedrin,* 12, 10, and in the *Babylonian Talmud, Sanhedrin,* 101a.

3. These texts will be found in H. Baehrens, *Origenes Werke,* 8, in *Die Griechischen christlichen Schriftsteller der ersten drei Jahrhunderte,* 33 (1925). The homilies are on pp. xiv–xx and 26–60; the commentary on pp. xx–xxviii and 61–241. The edition also reproduces the fragments of Origen's Greek text found in the *Catena* [i.e., a form of commentary in which extracts from the fathers are interspersed with elucidatory additions. Trans.] of Procopius. For a general survey, see E. Ann Matter, "Il 'Cantico dei Cantici' nel contesto del cristianesimo medievale: l'eredità di Origine," *Aevum,* 61, no. 2 (1987), pp. 303–312. For an English translation, see R. P. Lawson, trans., *Origen. The Song of Songs, Commentary, and Homilies,* Ancient Christian Writers Series 26 (New York: Newman Press, 1957).

4. Among the most important studies on Origen, see Jean Danielou, *Origène* (Paris: La Table Ronde, 1948), and Henri Crouzel, *Origène et la "Connaissance Mystique"* (Paris: Declée de Brouwer, 1961). For relations between Origen and

the Jews, see Ronald Reuven Kimelman, "Rabbi Yohanan and Origen on the Song of Songs. A Third-Century Jewish-Christian Disputation," *Harvard Theological Review,* 73 (1980), pp. 567–595; Efraim Elimalech Urbach, "The Homilectical Interpretations of the Sages and the Exposition of Origen on Canticles, and the Christian Disputation," *Scripta Hierosolymitana,* 22 (1971), pp. 248–275; and Nicholas R. M. De Lange, *Origen and the Jews* (Cambridge, Eng.: Cambridge University Press, 1976).

5. Origen, *Commentary,* "Prologue," in Baehrens, *Origenes,* 61. The homilies do not refer explicitly to the Beloved as the soul, but traces of this interpretation can be found in I, 6, pp. 35–36, and II, 4, pp. 47–48.

6. For the historical development of medieval exegeses of the Song of Songs, see E. Ann Matter, *The Voice of My Beloved: The Song of Songs in Western Medieval Christianity* (Philadelphia: University of Pennsylvania Press, 1990); Friedrich Ohly, *Hohelied-Studien: Grundzüge einer Geschichte der Hohenliedauslegung des Abendlandes bis um 1200* (Wiesbaden: Franz Steiner Verlag, 1958); and Helmut Riedlinger, "Die Makellosigkeit der Kirche in den Lateinischen Hoheliedkommentaren des Mittelalters," *Beitrage zur Geschichte der Philosophie und Theologie des Mittelalters,* 38, no. 3 (1958). On the "four senses" of scripture, see John Cassian, *Collationes,* 14, 8 (Paris: Sources chrétiennes, 1958). The four senses of Scripture, or four exegetical possibilities, as described by Cassian, are historical, allegorical (speaking in terms of Christ and the Church), tropological (moral) and anagogical (referring to the "last things").

7. Bernard's homilies are in J. Leclercq, Charles H. Talbot, and Henri Maria Rochais, eds., *Sancti Bernardi opera,* vol. 1 (Rome: Editiones Cisterciences, 1957). Bernard's works have been translated by Killian Walsh. See Cistercian Fathers Series 4 (Kalamazoo, Mich.: Cistercian Publications, 1976). For an account of their writing, see the introduction, especially pp. xvi–xvii.

8. *Sancti Bernardi opera,* vol. 1, I, 1, p. 3. "I fed you with milk, not with meat, for ye were not yet able to hear it." [Cor. I. 3. 2. Trans.]

9. Ibid., p. 14.

10. For a study of Bernard's poetic prose, see Christine Mohrmann, "Observations sur la langue et le style de Saint Bernard," introduction to ibid., vol. 2, pp. x–xxxiii.

11. Matter, *The Voice of My Beloved,* p. 127.

12. For the "marriage" of the doge and the sea, Andrea Mosto, *I dogi di Venezia: nella vita pubblica e privata* (Milan: A. Martello, 1966; repr. Florence, 1977).

13. Thomas of Celano, *Vita altera,* in College of Saint Bonaventure, ed., *Analecta franciscana* (Florence: Quaracchi, 1949), vol. 10, XXV, 55. See also the vision of Lady Poverty in L, 82. For an English translation, see Marion A. Habig, ed., *Saint Francis of Assisi: Writings and Early Biographies* (Chicago: Franciscan Herald Press, 1972), pp. 357–543.

14. Giovanni of Parma, *Sacrum Commercium Sancti Francisci cum Domina Paupertate,* ed. Stefano Brufani (Assisi: Porziuncula, 1990).

15. See the text as edited by Isidorus Hilberg, in *Corpus Scriptorum Ecclesiasticorum Latinorum,* vol. 54, 1 (1910), pp. 143–211.

16. Matter, *The Voice of My Beloved.* pp. 151–177.

17. Hermann Menhardt, ed., "Das St. Trudperter Höhe Lied," in *Rheinische Beiträge und Hülfsbücher zur germanischen Philologie und Volkskunde,* vol. 21 (Halle: Max Niemayer Verlag, 1934), no. 22, p. 180.

18. Jatta Seyfarth, ed., "Incipit epithalamium Christi virginum: alternatim," in *Speculum virginum,* in *Corpus Christianorum Continuatio Medievalis,* vol. 5 (Turnhout: Brepols, 1990), pp. 365–377. Matthäus Bernards, *Speculum virginum. Geistigkeit und Seelenleben der Frau im Hochmittelalter* (Cologne and Vienna: Bohlau Verlag, 1982).

19. Clare of Assisi, first letter to Agnes of Prague, in M. F. Becker, J.-F. Goder, and Theresa Matura, eds., *Claire d'Assise: Ecrits* (Paris: Sources chrétiennes, 1967), no. 325, p. 86. Regis A. Armstrong, Ignatius C. Brady, trans. *Francis and Clare: The Complete Works* (New York: Paulist Press, 1982), pp. 190–194.

20. Gertrude d'Helfta, *Exercitia spirituala: oeuvres spirituelles,* ed. Jacques Hourlier and A. Schmitt, pt. 1, "Les exercises" (Paris: Editions du Cerf, Sources chrétiennes, 1967), no. 127, p. 73. For an English translation, see Gertrud Jaron Lewis and Jack Lewis, *Gertrude the Great of Helfta: Spiritual Exercises,* Cistercian Fathers Series 49 (Kalamazoo, Mich.: Cistercian Publications, 1989).

21. Rudolph M. Bell, *Holy Anorexia* (Chicago: Chicago University Press, 1985).

22. Caroline Walker Bynum, *Holy Feast and Holy Fast: The Religious Significance of Food to Medieval Women* (Berkeley: University of California Press, 1987).

23. Ibid., pp. 246–249.

24. John Coakley, "Friars as Confidants of Holy Women in Medieval Dominican Hagiography," in Renata Blumenfeld-Kosinski and Timea Szell, eds., *Images of Sainthood in Medieval Europe* (Ithaca, N.Y.: Cornell University Press, 1991), pp. 222–246; and Coakley, "Gender and the Authority of the Friars: The Significance of Holy Women for the Thirteenth-Century Franciscans and Dominicans," *Church History,* 60 (1991), pp. 445–460.

25. Bella Millet and Jocelyn Wogan-Browne, eds., *Medieval English Prose for Women: Selections from Katherine Group and Ancrene Wisse]* (Oxford: Clarendon Press, 1990). See pp. 38–41 for a discussion of the nun as bride of Christ in "Haili Meidhad."

26. Karen Scott, "Saint Catherine of Siena, 'Apostola,'" in *Church History,* 61 (1992), pp. 34–46.

27. Raymond of Capua, "Legenda maior," *Acta sanctorum,* 3 (April 1863), pp. 861–967.

28. For the legend of Catherine of Alexandria, see René Coursault, *Sainte Catherine d'Alexandrie: le mythe et la tradition* (Paris, 1984).

29. In P. Misciatelli, ed., *Le lettere de S. Caterina da Siena, ridotte a miglior lezione, e in ordine nuovo disposte con note di Niccolò Tommaseo,* 6 vols. (Siena: Giuntini e Bentivoglio, 1913–1922), vol. 3, letter 221, p. 337. [See also Suzanne Noffke, trans., *The Letters of Saint Catherine of Siena* (Binghampton, N.Y.: Modern and Renaissance Texts and Studies). Trans.]

30. Misciatelli, *Lettere de S. Caterina,* vol. 1, letter 50, p. 236.

31. Ibid., vol. 4, letter 261, p. 146.

32. Bynum, *Holy Feast and Holy Fast,* pp. 174–175.

33. Katherine Gill, "Open Monasteries for Women in Late Medieval and Early Moden Italy: Two Roman Examples," in Craig A. Monson, ed., *The Crannied*

Wall: Women, Religion, and the Arts in Early Modern Europe (Ann Arbor: University of Michigan Press, 1992), pp. 15–47; Raymond Creytens, "La riforma dei monasteri femminili," in *Il Concilio di Trento e la Riforma Tridentina,* vol. 1 (Rome: Herder 1965), pp. 45–83.

34. Gabriella Zarri, "Pietà e profezia alle corte padane," in Zarri, *Le sante vive: cultura e religiosità femminile nella prima età moderna* (Turin: Rosenberg e Sellier, 1990), pp. 51–85; E. Ann Matter and John Coakley, eds., *Creative Women in Medieval and Early Modern Italy: A Religious and Artistic Renaissance* (Philadelphia: University of Pennsylvania Press, 1994).

35. Elissa Barbara Weaver, ed., *Beatrice del Sera, amor di virtù, commedia in cinque atti, 1548* (Ravenna: Longo Editore, 1990); Weaver, "The Convent Wall in Tuscan Drama," in Craig A. Monson, ed., *The Crannied Wall: Women, Religion, and the Arts in Early Modern Europe* (Ann Arbor: University Michigan Press, 1992), pp. 73–86; R. Kendrick, "The Traditions of Milanese Convent Music and the Sacred Dialogues of Chiara Margarita Cozzolani," in Monson, *The Crannied Wall,* pp. 311–233; and Kendrick, *Celestial Sirens: Nuns and Their Music in Early Modern Milan* (Oxford: Clarendon Press, 1996).

36. Teresa of Avila, *Libro de la vida* (1562–1565), ed. Damaso Chicharro (Madrid: Ediciones Cátedra, 1982), p. 117. For the history of its writing, see Chicharro's introduction, pp. 65–68. For an English translation, see J. M. Cohen, trans., *The Life of Saint Teresa. By Herself* (Harmondsworth, Middlesex: Penguin Books, 1957).

37. Teresa of Avila, *Libro de la vida,* 29, 13, pp. 352–353.

38. Teresa of Avila, *Relaciones espirituales,* no. 35 (November 1572), in Fr. Silvestro of Santa Teresa, ed., *Obras de Sta. Teresa de Jesus* (Burgos, 1915), vol. 2, pp. 63–65. See also Teresa of Avila, *Complete Works,* trans. E. Allison Peers (New York: Sheed and Ward, 1946).

39. Letter (1616), Milan, Biblioteca Ambrosiana, Ms. H. 91, *sussidio,* f. 218v. Interpreted in M. G. Bianchi, "Una 'Illuminata' del secolo XVII: Suor M. Domitilla Galluzzi, Capuccina a Pavia," *Bollettino della Società Pavese di Storia Patria,* n.s., 20–21 (1968–69), pp. 42–44.

40. Letter (May 10, 1634), Milan, Biblioteca Ambrosiana, Ms. G 97, *sussidio,* f. 413r; Ms. H 47, *sussidio,* ff. 177v to 178r.

41. E. Ann Matter, "The Personal and the Paradigm: The Book of Maria Domitilla Galluzzi," in C. A. Monson, ed., *The Crannied Wall: Women, Religion, and the Arts in Early Modern Europe* (Ann Arbor: University of Michigan Press, 1992), pp. 87–103.

3. Society and Women's Religiosity, 750–1450

1. Luigi Schiaparelli, ed., *Codice diplomatico longobardo,* vol. 1 (Rome, 1929), no. 18, pp. 53–59.

2. On relations between Lombards and the original Roman population, see the fine essay of Paolo Delogu, "Lombardi e Romani: altre congetture," in Paolo Commarosano and Stefano Gasperri, eds., *Langobardia* (Udine: Casamassima, 1990), pp. 111–167.

3. On Lombard monasticism as a whole, the only text remains the old essay by

Hans Grasshoff, *Langobardisch-fränkisches Klosterwesen in Italien* (Göttingen, 1909). On the foundation of the Tuscan monastery by Valafredus, see Karl Schmid, ed., *Vita Walfredi und Kloster Monteverdi: toskanischer Monchtum zwischen Langobardischen und fränkische Herrschaft* (Tübingen: Niemayer, 1991), Bibliothek des Deutschen Historisches Institut in Rom vol. 73, especially pp. 437–442.

4. [See H. Maine, *Ancient Law* (1876), 5: "All the Germanic immigrants seem to have recognized a corporate union of the family under the *mund* or authority of a patriarchal chief." The original version is retained here for purposes of clarity. Trans.]

5. Lombard legislation is rich in dispositions taken with regard to women. The best edition remains that of Franz Beyerle, ed., *Leges Langobardorum, 643–866* (Witzenhausen, 1962), revised as *The Lombard Laws,* trans. Katherine Fischer Drew (Philadelphia: University of Pennsylvania Press, 1973). On domestic nuns, see under "Liutprand."

6. Stefano Gasparri, "Grandi proprietari a sovrani nell'Italia Langobarda dell'VIII secolo," in *Atti del VI Congresso internazionale di studi sull'Alto Medioevo, "Langobardi e Lombardia: aspetti di civiltà Langobarda,"* Milan, October 21–25, 1978 (Spoleto, 1980), pp. 429–443, esp. pp. 437–442.

7. Joachim Fischer, *Königtum, Adel und Kirche im Königreich Italien, 774–875* (Ph.D. diss., Tübingen University, 1965, Bonn: R. Schwarzbold, 1965), esp. pp. 174, 188, 194.

8. Victor Fumagalli, "La nobiltà," in *Terra e società nell'Italia padana; i secoli IX e X* (Turin: G. Einaudi, 1976).

9. Schmid, *Vita Walfredi,* p. 175.

10. Wilhelm Kurze, *Monasteri e nobiltà nel Senese a nella Toscana medievale* (Siena: Ente provinciale per il turismo di Siena, 1984), "Monasteri e nobiltà nella Tuscia altomedievale," pp. 305–306.

11. Giles Constable, "Monasteries, Rural Churches and the 'Cura Animarum' in the Early Middle Ages," in *Il secolo di feroo: mito e realtà del secolo X* (Spoleto: Settimane di Spoleto, 1982), no. 28, pp. 362–364.

12. On the role of women belonging to important aristocratic families in the *Regnum Germaniae* and Lotharingia, see Patrick Corbet, *Les saints ottoniens, sainteté dynastique, sainteté royale et sainteté féminine autour de l'an mil"* (Sigmaringen, 1986), esp. pp. 191–200; Michel Parisse, "Les femmes au monastère dans le Nord de l'Allemagne du IXe au XIe siècle: conditions sociales et religieuses," in Werner Affeldt, ed., *Frauen in Spätantike und Frühmittelalter: Lebensbedingungen, Lebensnormen, Lebensformen* (Sigmaringen: J. Thornbecke, 1986), pp. 311–324; and Patrick Corbet, "'Pro anima sui senioris': la pastorale ottonienne du veuvage," in Michel Parisse, *Veuves et veuvages dans le Haut Moyen Age* (Paris: Picard, 1993), pp. 233–253. On the importance of liturgical commemoration for family consciousness, see Gerd Althoff, *Adels und Königsfamilien im Spiegel ihrer Memorialüberlieferung: Studien zum Totangedanken der Billunger und Ottonen: Bestandteil der Billunger Quellenwerkes, Societas et Fraternitas* (Munich: W. Fink, 1984). The Santa Giulia necrology is available in the old edition of Andrea Valentini, ed., *Codice necrologico-liturgico del monaste-*

rio di San Salvatore o Santa Giulia in Brescia (Brescia: Tipografia Apollonio, 1887). On the monastery itself, see Clara Stella and Gerardo Brentegani, *Santa Giulia di Brescia: archeologia, arte, storia di un monastero dai longobardi al Barbarossa* (Brescia: Grafo, 1992).

13. Kurze, *Monasteri e nobiltà*, 1989, p. 303.

14. C. Papa, "Radegonda e Batilde: modelli di santità femminile nel regno merovingio," *Benedictina*, 36 (1989), pp. 13–33; and particularly Robert Folz, "Les saintes reines du Moyen Age en Occident," in *Subsidia Hagiographica*, no. 76 (Brussels: Société des Bollandistes, 1992).

15. Paolo Delogu, "'Censors regni': un problema carolingio," *Bollettino dell'Instituto Storico Italiano*, 76 (1964), pp. 47–98.

16. For "Iron Age" Rome, see Girolamo Arnaldi, "Mito e realtà nel secolo X romano e papale," in *Il secolo di ferro: mito e realtà del secolo X* (Spoleto: Settimane di Spoleto, 1982), no. 28, pp. 27–56.

17. Joachim Wollasch, "Das Grabkloster der Kaiserin Adelheid in Selz am Rhein," *Frühmittelalterische Studien*, 2 (1968), pp. 135–143.

18. For Adelaide, see Corbet, *Les saints ottoniens*, pp. 59–72; Giulia Barone, "Une hagiographie sans miracles: observations en marge de quelques vies di X siècle," in *Les fonctions des saints dans le monde occidentale, IIIe, XIIIe siècle* (Rome, 1991), pp. 439, 445.

19. [In a number of versions, Adelaide was rescued by Otto the Great himself. Trans.]

20. Maïeul's Life has recently been published. See Dominique Iagno-Prat, *Agni immaculati: recherches sur les sources hagiographiques relatives à saint Maïeul de Cluny* (Paris: Editions du Cerf, 1988).

21. Odilo of Cluny, *Odilonis Cluniacensis abbatis Epitaphium domine Adelheide auguste*, in Herbert Paulhart, ed., *Die Lebensbeschreibung der Kaiserin Adelheid von Abt Odilo von Cluny (Mitteilungen des Instituts für Österreichische Geschichtsforschung)*, vol. 2 (Graz and Köln: H. Bohlaus, 1962), no. 20, pp. 27–45.

22. See under "Abbondanza," in *Bibliotheca sanctorum*, 13 vols. (Rome, 1961–1970), vol. 1, cols. 20–22.

23. For the Cluniac presence in Italy, see, among the many available sources, "Convegno storico celebrativo della fondazione del priorato cluniacense di Pontida," in *Cluny in Lombradia: atti del Convegno storico celebrativo del IX centenario della fondazione del priorato cluniacense di Pontida* April 22–25, 1977 (Cesena: Centro storico benedettino italiano, 1979); Simone Leone and Giovanni Vitolo, *Minima Cavensia* (Salerno, 1983), pp. 19–44.

24. Jean-Marie Sansterre, "Otton III et les saints ascètes de son temps," *Rivista di storia della Chiesa in Italia*, 43 (1989), pp. 377–412.

25. Cinzio Violante, "Alcune caratteristiche delle strutture familiari in Lombardia, Emilia e Toscana durante i secoli IX–XII," in Georges Duby and Jacques Le Goff, eds., *Famille et parenté dans l'Occident médiéval: actes du Colloque de Paris, 6–8 Juin, 1974* (Rome: Ecole française de Rome, 1977); Guiseppe Sergi, "Vescovi, monasteri, aristocrazia militare," in *Annali*, vol. 9 (Turin, 1986), pp. 75–98.

26. Paolo Golinelli, *Indiscreta sanctitas: studi sui rapporti tra culti, potere e società nel pieno Medioevo* (Rome: Istituto storico italiano per il Medio Evo, 1988), fasc. 197–198, pp. 76–77.

27. On this subject, see Giulia Barone, "La Riforma gregoriana," in G. de Rosa, André Vauchez, and Giulia Barone, eds., *Storia dell'Italia religiosa (storia e società)* (Rome and Bari: Laterza, 1993–), vol. 1, *L'antichità e il Medioevo,* pp. 243–270.

28. Georges Duby, *The Knight, the Lady, and the Priest: The Making of Modern Marriage in Medieval France* (Chicago: University of Chicago Press, 1993; orig. pub. New York: Pantheon Books, 1983).

29. J. Tibbets Schulenberg, "Sexism and the Ecclesiastical Gynaeceum from 500 to 1200," *Journal of Medieval History,* 4 (1978), pp. 125–126.

30. André Vauchez, *The Spirituality of the Medieval West: From the Eighth to the Twelfth Century* (Kalamazoo, Mich.: Cistercian Publications, 1993).

31. For both, see under their names in, respectively, the *Bibliotheca sanctorum,* vol. 1 (1961), col. 411; vol. 6 (1965), cols. 555–556.

32. There is an ample and recent bibliography of Matilda in Paolo Golinelli, *Mathilde e i Canossa nel cuore del medioevo* (Milan: Camunia, 1991); for a comparison with another interesting woman, see Vito Fumagalli, "Adelaide e Mathilde: due protagoniste del potere medievale," in "La Contessa Adelaide e la società del secolo XI," *Segusium,* 32 (1992), pp. 243–257.

33. There is an up-to-date bibliography about the Monteforte heretics in the *Lexicon des Mittelalters,* vol. 6 (1992), col. 793.

34. On the role of women in the spread of Catharism, see Michel Roquebert, "Le catharisme comme traditions dans la 'familia' languedocienne," in *Cahiers de Fanjeaux,* vol. 20, *Effacement du catharisme?* (Toulouse: Privat, 1985), pp. 233–234.

35. On the importance of the Mendicant friars in reabsorbing Cathars, see Marie-Humbert Vicaire, "L'action de l'enseignement et de la prédication des Mendicans vis-à-vis des Cathares," in *Cahiers de Fanjeaux,* vol. 20 (cited in previous note), pp. 277–340; in the same volume, see also R. Manselli, "La fin du Catharisme en Italie," pp. 116–118.

36. Gottfried Koch, *Frauenfrage und Ketzenturm in Mittelalter* (Berlin, 1962), pp. 30–34.

37. Manlio Bellomo, *Profili della famiglia italiana nell'età dei Comuni* (Catania: Giannotta, 1966).

38. On the diffusion of the Marian patrimony, see C. Peyer, *Stadt und Stadtpatron im mittelalterichen Italien* (Zürich, 1955), pp. 86–90.

39. Still fundamental on confraternities in general, and Marian ones in particular, is Gilles Gerard Meersseman and Gian Piero Pacini, *Ordo fraternitatis: confraternite e pietà dei laici nel medioevo* (Rome: Herder, 1977), "Italia sacra," nos. 24–26.

40. Jean Leclerq, *Monks and Love in Twelfth-Century France: Psycho-historical Essays* (New York: Oxford University Press, 1979).

41. Robert Fossier, "The Feudal Era," in Jack Goody and Martine Segalen, eds., *Storia universale della famiglia* (Milan, 1986–), vol. 1, *Antichità, medioevo, Oriente antico* (Milan, 1987), p. 392.

42. Georges Duby, "The Courtly Model," trans. Arthur Goldhammer, in Georges Duby and Michelle Perrot, eds., *A History of Women in the West*, vol. 2, *Silences of the Middle Ages*, ed. Christiane Klapisch-Zuber (Cambridge, Mass.: The Belknap Press of Harvard University Press, 1992).

43. On the nature and history of the Mendicant orders in the thirteenth and fourteenth centuries, see the synthesis by Giulia Barone, "Gli Ordini Mendicanti," in G. de Rosa, Angré Vauchez, and Giulia Barone, eds., *Storia dell'Italia religiosa (storia e società)* (Rome and Bari: Laterza, 1993–), vol. 1, *L'antichità e il Medioevo*, pp. 347–373.

44. Among the most recent publications on Clare are the papers, and ample bibliography, delivered in Assisi, October 15–17, 1992, collected as *Chiara d'Assisi* (Spoleto, 1993).

45. On the Poor Clares in the early stage of their history, see Anna Benvenuti Papi, "La fortuna del movimento damianita in Italia (sec. XIII): propositi per un censimento da fare," in *Assisi*, pp. 57–106.

46. See Herbert Grundmann, *Religious Movements in the Middle Ages: The Historical Links between Heresy, the Mendicant Orders, and the Women's Religious Movement in the Twelfth and Thirteenth Century, with the Foundations of German Mysticism* (Notre Dame, Ind.: University of Notre Dame Press, 1994).

47. For double monasteries, see Kaspar Elm and Michel Parisse, eds., *Doppelkloster und andere Formen der Symbiose männlicher und weiblicher Religiosen in Mittelalter* (Berlin: Duncker und Humboldt, 1992).

48. On the failure of the Italian experiments, see Georg Jenal, "Döppelkloster und monastische Gesetzgebung im Italien des frühen und hohen Mittelalters," in Elm and Parisse, *Doppelklöster*, pp. 25–55.

49. Many facets of the spread of charitable activity in Italy are to be found in *La conversione alla povertà nell'Italia dei secoli XII–XIV*, conference papers presented in Todi, October 14–17, 1990 (Spoleto, 1991).

50. On the increase in the number of travelers and pilgrims from the end of the eleventh century on, see Hans Conrad Peyer and Elizabeth Müller-Lückner, eds., "Gastfreundschaft, Taverne und Gasthaus im Mittelalter," in *Schriften des Historischen Kollegs: Kolloquien*, vol. 3 (Munich: R. Oldenbourg, 1983); and H. C. Peyer, *Von de Gastfreundschaft zum Gasthaus: Studien zur Gastlichkeit im Mittelalter, Monumenta Germaniae historiam*, vol. 31 (Hanover: Hahnsche Buchhandlung, 1987).

51. A tale of an "experienced" poverty is related in Michel Mollat, *The Poor in the Middle Ages: An Essay in Social History* (New Haven, Conn.: Yale University Press, 1986).

52. On the Roman confraternities and their relationships to the hospitals, see *Richerche per la storia religiosa di Roma*, vol. 5, *Le confraternite romane: esperienza religiosa, società, commitenza artistica* (Rome: Edizione di storia e letteratura, 1984); in the same volume see Paola Pavan, "I raccommandati del Salvatore e la società romana del tre-quattrocento," pp. 81–90, on the Salvational management of the Sant'Angelo hospital; the organization of Florentine welfare is reconstructed in Charles M. de la Roncière, "Poveri e povertà a Firenze nel XIV secolo," in *Tra preghiera e rivolta: le folle toscane nel XIV secolo* (Rome: Jouvence, 1993), pp. 197–281.

53. The fraternity's memorial book is in Pietro Egidi, "Liber Anniversariorum dei Raccommandata del SS. Salvatore ad Sancta Sanctorum," in *Necrologi e libri affini della provincia romana* (Rome: Forzani, 1908), vol. 1, *Fonti per la storia d'Italia,* bk. 44, pp. 310–541.

54. Charitable attitudes of this sort are to be found in Umiliana de' Cerchi, for whom see Anna Benvenuti Papi, "Umiliana dei Cerchi," *Studi francescani,* 77 (1980), pp. 87–111; for Francesca of Rome, see Giorgio Picasso, ed., *Una santa tutta Romana* (Monte Oliveto Maggiore, 1984).

55. Our difficulty in reconstructing a faithful portrait of a woman saint known to us only through a male filter has recently been emphasized by Jacques Dalarun, "Parole di 'simplices': Da Celestino V alle sante donne italiane tra Duecento e Trecento," in *Aspetti della spiritualità ai tempi di Celestino V* (Casamari, 1993).

56. On the triumph of the Mendicant saints, see the fine pages devoted to them in André Vauchez, *La sainteté en Occident aux derniers siècles du Moyen Age: d'après les proces de canonisation et les documentes hagiographiques* (Rome: Ecole française de Rome, Boccard, 1988).

57. Giulia Barone, "Ideali di santità fra XII et XIII secolo," in *Assisi,* pp. 37, 39–41.

58. Marie-Humbert Vicaire, "Les origines de la pauvreté mendiante des Precheurs," in *Dominique et ses precheurs, Studia Friburgensia,* n.s., vol. 55 (Freiburg: Editions universitaires, Paris: Editions du Cerf, 1977), pp. 237–241.

59. The Life of Benvenuta Bojani is in *Acta sanctorum,* 3 (October 1969).

60. André Vauchez, "Les stigmates de S. François et leurs détracteurs aux derniers siècles du Moyen Age," *Mélanges de l'Ecole française de Rome, Moyen Age,* 80 (1968), pp. 595–625. On the role played by stigmata in building the sanctity of Francis, see Chiara Frugoni, *Francesco e l'invenzione delle stimmate: une storia per parole e imagini fino a Bonaventura e Giotto* (Turin: G. Einaudi, 1993).

61. The bibliography on Clare of Montefalco is now extensive. See my entry in *Dizionario biografico degli Italiani* (Rome: Istituto della Enciclopedia italiana, 1960–), vol. 24, 1980, pp. 508–512; C. Leonardi and Enrico Menestò, eds., *S. Chiara da Montefalco e il suo tempo* (Florence and Perugia, 1984); and Giulia Barone, "Probleme um Klara von Montefalco," in Peter Dinzelbacher and Dieter R. Bauer, eds., *Religiöse Frauenbewegung und mystische Frommigkeit im Mittelalter, Beihefte zum Archiv für Kulturgeschichte,* vol. 28 (Cologne: Bohlau, 1988).

62. André Vauchez, "L'idéal de sainteté dans le mouvement féminin franciscain," in *Movimento religioso femminile e francescanismo nel secolo XIII,* paper delivered in Assisi, October 11–13, 1979, (Assisi, 1980).

63. M. Lauwers, "Expérience béguinale et récit hagiographique: a propos de la Vita Mariae Oigniacensis de Jacques de Vitry (vers 1215)," *Le journal des savants* (1989), pp. 61–103.

64. For the Life of Enselmini, see *Acta sanctorum,* 2 (November 1894), pp. 512–517. For an idea of mysticism as an almost universal phenomenon, see Peter Dinzelbacher, *Wörterbuch der Mystik* (Stuttgart: Kroner, 1989).

65. For the Life of Umiliana, see *Acta sanctorum,* 4 (May 1865), pp. 386–413.

66. Barone, "Probleme," pp. 256–257.

67. See Marco Bartoli, *Clare of Assisi* (Quincy, Ill.: Franciscan Press, 1993).

68. Giulia Barone, "Le due vite di Margherita Colonna," in M. Modica Vasta, ed., *Esperienza religiosa e scritture femminile tra medioevo ed età moderna* (Acireale, 1992).

69. A critical edition of Angela's visions is L. Their and A. Caluffetti, eds., *Il libro della beata Angela da Foligno* (Grottaferrata, 1985); the *vita* of Margaret, which contains many visions, is in *Acta sanctorum*, 3 (February 1985), pp. 300–357.

70. On Margaret see Anna Benvenuti Papi, *"In castro poenitentiae": santità e società femminile nell'Italia medivale* (Rome: Herder, 1990), pp. 141–168.

71. Alessandro Barbero, *Un santo in famiglia: vocazione religiosa e resistenze sociali nell'agiografia latina medievale* (Turin: Rosenberg e Sellier, 1991).

72. On the canonization of Henry and Cunegund, see Renate Neumüllers-Klauser, *Der Heinrichs- und Kunigundenkult im mittelalterischen Bistum Bamberg* (Bamberg: Historischer Verein für die Pflege der Geschichte des ehemaligen Furstbistums Bamberg, 1957).

73. Direct accounts of Elizabeth of Hungary are collected in Albert Huyskens, ed., *Der sogennante Libellus di dictis IV ancillarum* (Kempten and Munich, 1911).

74. André Vauchez, "Culture et sainteté d'après les procès de canonisation des XIIIe et XIVe siècles," in *Le scuole degli Ordini Mendicanti (secoli XIII–XIV)*, paper given in Todi, October 11–14, 1976 (Todi, 1978), pp. 151–172.

75. Such, for instance, was the case with Beatrice of Nazareth and Gertrude of Helfta, for whom see their entries in Dinzelbacher, *Wörterbuch*.

76. The *Ordinazioni* can be found in Picasso, *Una santa*.

77. On this subject, see Barone, "Gli Ordini Mendicanti," pp. 365–370.

78. André Vauchez, *The Laity in the Middle Ages: Religious Beliefs and Devotional Practices* (Notre Dame, Ind.: University of Notre Dame Press, 1993).

79. André Vauchez, "Le canonizzazioni di san Tommaso e di San Bonaventura: perché due secoli di scarto?" in *Ordini Mendicanti e società italiana (XIII–XIV secolo)* (Milan: Saggiatore, 1990), pp. 257–273.

80. "Parole inspirée et pouvoirs charismatiques," *Mélanges de l'Ecole française de Rome, Moyen Age,* 98 (1986), pp. 7–327; *Les textes prophétiques et la prophétie en Occident (XII–XVI siècle)* (Rome, 1991).

81. Charles de la Roncière, "Il ruolo delle confraternitate nell'inquadramento religioso del contado fiorentinno (il caso della Veldelsa)," in *Tra preghiera e rivolta: le folle toscane nel XIV secolo* (Rome: Jouvence, 1993), pp. 89–134.

82. Giulia Barone and Ambrogio Piazzoni, "Le più antiche carte dell'archivio del Gonfalone," in *Le chiavi della memoria* (Vatican City, 1984), p. 20, n. 14 Giulia Barone, "Les confréries romaines de dévotion à la fin du Moyen-Age," in Françoise Thelamon, ed., *Sociabilité, pouvoirs et société: Actes du Colloque de Rouen* (Rouen: Publications de l'Université de Rouen, 1987, no. 110), p. 302.

83. André Vauchez, *La sainteté en Occident;* also in *Bibliothèque des écoles françaises d'Athènes et de Rome,* fasc. 241, pp. 366–368 and 399–405.

84. This kind of saint is the subject of all the essays in the fifth section of Vauchez, *The Laity in the Middle Ages.*

85. Giulia Barone, "Processi di canonizzazione e modelli si santità nel Basso Medio-

evo," in Deutsches historisches Institut, *Quellen und Forschungen aus italienischen Archiven und Bibliotheken*, vol. 68 (Tübingen, 1982), p. 349.

86. Gabriella Zarri, "Les prophètes de cour dans l'Italie de la Renaissance," *Mélanges de l'Ecole française de Rome, Moyen Age*, 102 (1990), pp. 649–675.

87. Ludovico Scaramucci, ed., *Il movimento dei Disciplinati nel settimocentenario dal suo inizio a Perugia (1260)*, proceedings of the international convention in Perugia, September 25–28, 1960 (Perugia: Deputazione di storia patria per l'Umbria, 1962). [Joachimites were followers of Joachim of Fiore, a Franciscan, whose interpretation of the Apocalypse, casting Islam as the Beast from the Sea and heretical sects as the False Prophet, led to widespread millennial expectations. Trans.]

88. Arsenio Frugoni, "La devozione dei Bianchi del 1399," in *Incontri nel Medioevo* (Bologna: Il Mulino, 1979), pp. 203–214. [See, more recently, Daniel Ethan Bornstein, *The Bianchi of 1399: Popular Devotion in Late Medieval Italy* (Ithaca, N.Y.: Cornell University Press, 1993). The Bianchi, or "Whites," grew out of the Franciscan penitential movement, and by the middle of the thirteenth century, flagellant confraternities existed all over Italy. Trans.]

89. Fernanda Sorelli, "La produzione agiografica del domenicano Tommaso d'Antonio da Siena: esempi di santità ed intenti di propaganda," in Daniel Ethan Bornstein and Roberto Rusconi, eds., *Mistiche e devote nell'Italia tardomedievale*, vol. 40 (Naples: Liguori, 1992), pp. 157–169.

90. On Dominici, see D. Salvi, ed., *Regola del governo di cura familiare compilato del B, Giovanni Dominici* (Florence: A. Garinei, 1860); for treatises on "the good wife," see Silvana Vecchio, "The Good Wife," trans. Clarissa Botsford, in Duby and Perrot, *History of Women*, vol. 2, *Silences of the Middle Ages*, ed. Kalpisch-Zuber.

91. Giulia Barone, "L'immagine di Santa Francesca Romana nei processi di canonizzazione e nella 'Vita' in volgare," in Picasso, *Una santa*, pp. 57–70.

92. Giulia Barone, "La canonizzazione di Francesca Romana (1608): la riproposta di un modello agiografico medievale," in Gabriella Zarri, ed., *Finzione e santità tra medioeve ed eta moderna* (Turin: Rosenberg e Sellier, 1991).

4. Women, Faith, and Image in the Late Middle Ages

1. George Kaftal, *Iconography of the Saints in Tuscan Painting*, 4 vols. (Florence: Sansoni, 1952–1985), vol. 1, fig. 210, col. 198.

2. See Arturo Carlo Quintavalle, *Wiligelmo e Matilde: l'officina romanica* (Milan: Electa, 1991). Catalog of an exhibition held by the Centro internazionale d'arte e di cultura at the Palazzo Te-Fruttiera, Mantua, June 15–September 30, 1991.

3. Herbert L. Kessler, "On the State of Medieval Art History," *Art Bulletin*, 70 (1988), p. 177.

4. Chiara Frugoni, "The Imagined Woman," trans. Clarissa Botsford, in Georges Duby and Michelle Perrot, eds., *A History of Women in the West*, vol. 2, *Silences of the Middle Ages*, ed. Christine Klapisch-Zuber (Cambridge, Mass.: Harvard University Press, 1992), pp. 354–355 and fig. 11.

5. For the iconography of Catherine and of Italian saints in general, see Kaftal,

Iconography of the Saints. On the role of images in the transmission of faith, see Dominique Rigaud, "Dire la foi avec des images, une affaire de femmes?" in J. Delumeau, *La religion de ma mère* (Paris, 1992), pp. 71–90.

6. This predella was described many times in the seventeenth century: L. Torelli, *Opere de' Secoli Agostiniani* (Bologna, 1680), vol. 6, year 1372, pp. 131–135; Andrea Arrighi, *La chiesa dei santi Michele a Jacobo di Certaldo e sue filiali* (1692), ed. D[omenico?] Tordi (Orvieto, 1913), pp. 20–21; F. Soldani, *Ragguaglio istorico della Beata Giovanna da Signa romita vallombrosana* (Florence, 1741), pp. 134–137.

7. For instance, the cult of Chelidonia at Subiaco. See Sofia Boesch Gajano, "Monastero, città, campagna: il culto di santa Chelidonia a Subiaco tra XII et XIV secolo," in Boesch Cajano and Lucia Sebastiani, eds., *Culto dei santi, istituzioni e classi sociali in età preindustriale* (L'Aquila and Rome: L. U. Japadre Editore, 1984).

8. Marina Warner, *Alone of All Her Sex: The Myth and Cult of the Virgin Mary* (New York: Random House, 1976).

9. Edward B. Garrison, "Note on the Survival of Thirteenth-Century Panel Paintings in Italy," *Art Bulletin,* 54 (1972), p. 140.

10. Enzo Carli and Jole Vichi Imberciadori, *San Gimignano* (English ed., Milan: Electa, 1987).

11. On the evolution of the altarpiece, or reredos, see Claudie Ressort, ed., *Rétables italiens: du XIIIe au XVe siècle,* exhibition at the Louvre, Paris, October 14, 1977–January 15, 1978 (Paris: Editions de le Réunion des musées nationaux, 1978).

12. André Vauchez, *La sainteté en Occident aux derniers siècles du Moyen Age: d'après les proces de canonisation et les documentes hagiographiques* (Rome: Ecole française de Rome, Boccard, 1988).

13. Jeryldene Wood, "Perceptions of Holiness in Thirteenth-Century Italian Painting: Clare of Assisi," *Art History,*" 14 (1991), pp. 301–328.

14. These are the reredos painted by Bonaventura Berlingheri in 1235, preserved in Pescia, for which see Alastair Smart, *The Dawn of Italian Painting, 1250–1400* (Ithaca, N.Y.: Cornell University Press, 1978), fig. 1; and the Bardi panel in the chapel of the same name in the Church of Santa Croce in Florence, which Chiara Frugoni dates as ca. 1240, for which see Frugoni, *Francesco un'altra storia* (Genoa, 1988).

15. Robert Fawtier, "Le portrait de sainte Catherine de Sienne," *Mélanges d'archaeologie et d'histoire de l'Ecole française de Rome,* 1912, pp. 233–244.

16. Marco Bartoli, *Clare of Assisi* (Quincy, Ill.: Franciscan Press, 1993), pp. 171–198.

17. Caterina Furtal and Italo Zannier, *Il duomo di Spilimbergo, 1284–1984* (Spilimbergo: Commune of Spilimbergo, 1985), pp. 117–142.

18. Kaftal, *Iconography of the Saints,* vol. 1, cols. 380–398. On the appearance of this theme in the literature about Elizabeth, see André Vauchez, ed., *Histoire des saints et de la sainteté chrétienne,* vol. 6 (Paris, 1986), the chapter by Vauchez entitled "Elizabeth de Thuringe," p. 132.

19. Kaftal, *Iconography of the Saints,* vol. 2, col. 975, fig. 1144.

20. For the use of the halo, see Edwin Hall and Ulrich Horst, "'Aureola super Auream': Crowns and Related Symbols for Saints in Late Gothic and Renaissance Iconography," *Art Bulletin,* 67 (1985), pp. 567–603; A. Volpato, "Il tema agiografico della triplice aureola nei secoli XIII–XIV," in Sofia Boesch Gajano and Lucia Sebastiani, eds., *Culto dei santi, istituzioni e classi sociali in età preindustriale* (L'Aquila and Rome: L. U. Japadre Editore, 1984), pp. 509–526.

21. Vauchez, *La sainteté en Occident.*

22. Ibid.

23. Anna Benvenuti Papi, "Marguerite de Cortone," in Vauchez, *Histoire des saints,* vol. 7, pp. 178–183.

24. Daniel Russo, "Jeanne de Signa ou l'iconographie au féminin: etude sur les fresques de l'église paroissale de Signa, milieu XVe siècle," *Mélanges de l'Ecole française de Rome, Moyen Age,* 98 (1986), pp. 201–218.

25. Vauchez, *La sainteté en Occident,* on the canonization of Saint Catherine of Siena.

26. For instance, on the frescoes by Tommaso and Matteo Biazaci da Busca in Montegrazie, in the Church of Santa Maria delle Grazie. Kaftal, *Iconography of the Saints,* vol. 4, cols. 669–672.

27. R. Andorno and Mario Perotti, *Beata Panacea* (Ghemme: 1983).

28. For a recent update on this subject, see André Vauchez, ed., "La religion civique à l'époque médiévale at moderne," proceedings of the conference at the University of Paris X at Nanterre, June 21–23, 1993.

29. Codex Castogro 429, Communal Library, Cortona. Several reproductions are in Benvenuti Papi, "Marguerite de Cortone," pp. 179–183.

30. Kaftal, *Iconography of the Saints,* vol. 2, cols. 667–671.

31. There are many examples in Frugoni, "Imagined Woman," in Duby and Perrot, *History of Women in the West,* vol. 2, *Silences of the Middle Ages,* ed. Klapisch-Zuber, pp. 420–422.

32. E. Simi Varanelli, "Le Meditationes Vitae Nostri Domini Jesu Christi," *Arte medievale,* 2d ser., 6 (1992), pp. 137–148.

33. Michael Baxandall, *Painting and Experience in Fifteenth-Century Italy: A Primer in the Social History of Pictorial Style* (Oxford and New York: Oxford University Press, 1988).

34. Caroline Walker Bynum, *Holy Feast and Holy Fast: The Religious Significance of Food to Medieval Women* (Berkeley: University of California Press, 1987), p. 255.

35. Doris Karl, "Der Fina-Altar von Benedetto da Maianon in der Collegiata zu San Gimignano: zu seiner datierung und Rekonstruktion," in *Mitteilungen des Kunsthistorischen Instituts in Florenz,* vol. 22 (Florence, 1978), pt. 3, pp. 265–586.

36. Anna Benvenuti Papi, "'Velut in Sepuchro': cellane e recluse nella tradizione agiografica italiana," in Sofia Boesch Gajano and Lucia Sebastiani, eds., *Culto dei santi, institutzioni e classe sociali in età preindustriale* (L'Aquila and Rome: L. U. Japadre Editore, 1984), pp. 509–526.

37. On women dressed as men before Joan of Arc, see the tale of Marina dressed as

a monk and many variants among the *exempla* in Jacques Berlioz and Marie Anne Polo de Beaulieu, eds., *Les exempla médievaux: introduction à la recherche* (Carcassonne, France: GARAE/Hésiode, 1992); Jacques Berlioz in J.-Claude Schmitt, ed., *Prêchez d'example* (Paris: 1985), pp. 173–178. The most extreme example is Pope Joan. See Alain Boureau, *La Papesse Jeanne* (Paris: Aubier, 1988).

38. Kaftal, *Iconography of the Saints,* vol. 1, cols. 591–592, fig. 680. Julia saves two horsemen crossing the River Elsa.

39. Jacques Dalarun, "Jeanne de Signa, ermite toscane du XIVe siècle, ou la sainteté ordinaire," *Mélanges de l'Ecole française de Rome, Moyen Age,* 98 (1986), pp. 161–199. On the iconography of eremiticism in Italy, see D. Russo, "L'iconographie de l'érimitisme en Italie de la fin du Moyen Age (XIIIe-XVe siècle)," in *Eremetismo nel Francescanesimo medievale* (Assisi, 1991).

40. Anna Benvenuti Papi, *"In castro poenitentiae": santità e società femminile nell'Italia medievale* (Rome: Herder, 1990).

41. Dominique Rigaux, *A la table du Seigneur: l'Eucharistie chez les primitifs italiens, 1250–1497* (Paris: Editions du Cerf, 1989), pp. 248–253.

42. Ibid., p. 164 and fig 89.

43. Ibid., p. 195 and fig. 78.

44. School of Rimini, ca. 1330, painting on a gold background, from the Convent degli Angeli in Rimini. Dominique Thiébaut, *Ajaccio, musée Fesch: les primitifs italiens* (Paris: Ministère de la culture et de la communication, Editions de la Réunion des musées nationaux, 1987). *Inventaires des collections publiques françaises,* cat. 40, pp. 144–153.

45. Chiara Frugoni, "La mistica femminile nell'iconografia delle visioni," in *Temi e problemi della mistica femminile trecentesca: atti del Convegno del Centro di Studi sulla spiritualità medievale,* University of Perugia, October 14–17, 1979 (Todi, 1983).

46. M. Flusin, "Art, société et dévotion: les Dominicains et la première statue de Sainte Catherine de Sienne," in *Symboles de la Renaissance* (Paris: Presse de l'école normale supérieure, 1982), pp. 151–167.

47. André Vauchez, *The Laity in the Middle Ages: Religious Beliefs and Devotional Practices* (Notre Dame, Ind.: University of Notre Dame Press, 1993).

48. Daniel Arasse, "Entre dévotion et culture: fonctions de l'image religieuse au XVe siècle," in *Faire croire: modalités de la diffusion et de la réception des messages religieux du XIIe au XVe siècle* (Rome: Ecole française de Rome, 1981), pp. 131–146.

49. Dominique Rigaux, "The Franciscan Tertiaries at Folligno," *Gesta,* 31–32 (1992), pp. 92–98; Rigaux, "Dire la foi," in J. Delumeau, *La religion* (Paris, 1992), pp. 87–90.

50. Gian Paolo Brizzi, "Contributo all'iconografia di Santa Francesca Romana," in Giorgo Picasso, *Una santa tutta Romana* (Monte Oliveto Maggiore, 1984), pp. 272–289.

51. Generally attributed to the Baschenis. See Quirino Bezzi, "Gli affreschi di Giovanni e Battista Baschenis di Averaria nella chiesa di S. Maria Maddalena di Cusiano," *Studi Trentini,* 49 (1970), pp. 358–372; Bruno Bronzini, Domenica

Primerano, and Piera Ventrini, *Arte e devozione nelle chiese della Val di Sole* (Trent: Publilux, 1983), pp. 243–244.

5. From Prophecy to Discipline, 1450–1650

1. *Gemäldegalerie Dresden, alte Meister: Katalog der ausgestellten Werke* (Dresden: Staatliche Kunstsammlungen Dresden, 1992), pp. 155–156; Max J. Friedlander and Jakob Rosenberg, *The Paintings of Lucas Cranach* (London: Sotheby Parke-Bernet, 1978), pp. 68–69.

2. P. Perdizet, *Le calendrier parisien à la fin du Moyen Age d'après les Bréviaires et les Livres d'Heures* (Paris, 1933), p. 262.

3. Margaret L. King, *Women of the Renaissance* (Chicago: University of Chicago Press, 1991); Patricia H. Labalme, *Beyond Their Sex: Learned Women of the European Past* (New York: New York University Press, 1980).

4. André Vauchez, "La nascita del sospetto," in Gabriella Zarri, ed., *Finzione e santità tra medioevo ed età moderna* (Turin: Rosenberg e Sellier, 1991), pp. 39–51; Jean-Michel Sallmann, ed., *Visions indiennes, visions baroques: les métissages de l'inconscient* (Paris: Presses universitaires de France, 1992), pp. 91–116.

5. Givanfrancesco Pico della Mirandola and Pietro Martire Morelli, *Compendio delle cose mirabili della venerabil serva di Dio Catterina di Raconisio Vergine integerrima del Sacro Ordine della Penitenza di san Domenico, distinto in Dieci Libri e composto dall'Ill.mo Sig Giovanni Francesco Pico . . . et ultimato dall'umile servo di Gesù Cristo Fr. Pietro Martire Morelli de Garessio dell'ordine de'predicatori* (Bologna, ca. 1680).

6. Delio Cantimori, *Eretici italiani del cinquecento e altri scritti* (Turin: G. Einaudi, 1992), pp. 591–594; Gabriella Zarri, *Le sante vive: cultura e religiosità femminile nella prima età moderna* (Turin: Rosenberg e Sellier, 1990), pp. 168–169. On the relationship between confessors and penitent women, see John Wayland Coakley, "Friars as Confidants of Holy Women in Medieval Dominican Hagiography," in Renate Blumenfeld-Kosinski and Timea Klara Szell, eds., *Images of Sainthood in Medieval Europe* (Ithaca, N.Y.: Cornell University Press, 1991), pp. 222–246, and Coakley, "Gender and Authority of the Friars: The Significance of Holy Women for the Thirteenth-Century Franciscans and Dominicans," *Church History,* 60 (1991), pp. 445–460.

7. Caroline Walker Bynum, *Jesus as Mother: Studies in the Spirituality of the High Middle Ages* (Berkeley, Calif.: University of California Press, 1982); Bynum, *Holy Feast and Holy Fast: The Religious Significance of Food to Medieval Women* (Berkeley, Calif.: University of California Press, 1987; and Bynum, *Fragmentation and Redemption: Essays on Gender and the Human Body in the High Middle Ages* (New York: Zone Books, 1991).

8. Paolo Prodi, *Il sacramento del potere: il giuramento politico nella storia costituzionale dell'Occidente* (Bologna: Il Mulino, 1992). [It is in this period, in both law and politics, that the nature of oaths, heretofore sworn only before God and often presided over by the Church, began to take on a more secular aspect and be enforced in different ways. Trans.]

9. Adriano Prosperi, "L'elemento storico nelle polemiche sulla santità." in

Gabriella Zarri, ed., *Finzione e santità tra medioevo ed età moderna* (Turin: Rosenberg e Sellier, 1991), pp. 88–118.

10. Carlo Ginzburg, *The Night Battles: Witchcraft and Agrarian Cults in the Sixteenth and Seventeenth Centuries* (Baltimore: Johns Hopkins University Press, 1983).

11. Wolfgang Reinhard, "Confessionalizzazione forzata? prologomeni ad una teoria dell'età confessionale," *Annali dell'Istituto Storico italo-germanico in Trento,* 8 (1982), pp. 13–37; Pierangelo Schiera, "Lo stato moderno e il rapporto disciplinamento/legittimazione," *Problemi del socialismo,* 5 (1985), pp. 115–135.

12. Gabriella Zarri, "Monache e sante alla corte estense (XV-XVI secolo)," in Francesca Bocchi, Diego Cavallina, and Angela Ghinato, eds., *Storia illustrata di Ferrara* (Rep. di San Marino: AIEP, 1987–1989, vols. 1–2; Milan: AIEP, vols. 3–4).

13. Caterina Vigri's book is reprinted in Catherine of Bologna, *Le sette armi spirituali,* ed. Cecilia Foletti (Padua: Antenore, 1985).

14. S. Spanò Martinelli, "La canonizzazione di Caterina Vigri: un problema cittadino nella Bologna del Seicento," in Sofia Boesch Gajano, ed., *Raccolte di vite di santi dal XIII al XVIII secolo: strutture, messaggi, fruizioni* (Fasano di Brindisi: Schena, 1990).

15. Arienti's lives of illustrious women were published in the nineteenth century: Giovanni Sabadino degli Arienti, *Gynevera de le clare donne,* ed. Corrado Ricci and A. Bacchi della Lega (Bologna: Presso Romagnoli-dall'Acqua, 1888). The *vita* of Caterina Vigri first appeared in printed form in 1502 with no indication of authorship.

16. Zarri, *Le sante vive,* and "Les prophètes de cour dans l'Italie de la Renaissance," *Mélanges de l'Ecole française de Rome, Moyen Age,* 102 (1990), pp. 649–675.

17. A. Esposito, "Santa Francesca e le comunità religiose femminili a Roma nel secolo XV," in Sofia Boesch Gajano and Lucia Sebastiani, eds., *Culto dei santi, istituzioni e classi sociali in età preindustriale* (L'Aquila and Rome: L. U. Japadre Editore, 1984), pp. 537–562; K. Gill, "Open Monasteries for Women in Late Medieval and Early Modern Italy: Two Roman Examples," in Craig A. Monson, ed., *The Crannied Wall: Women, Religion, and the Arts in Early Modern Europe* (Ann Arbor. University of Michigan Press, 1992), pp. 15–47.

18. Gabriella Zarri, "Aspetti dello sviluppo degli ordini religiosi in Italia tra Quatro e Cinquecento: Studi e problemi," in Paolo Prodi and Peter Johanek, eds., *Strutture ecclesiastiche in Italia e in Germania prima della Riforma* (Bologna: Il Mulino, 1984). [The Observants were founded in 1415 under the Franciscan rule; they were part of a reforming (and closely supervised) movement within monasticism that included the Hieronymites (1375), under the Augustinian rule, and the Minims (founded by Saint Francis of Paola ca. 1460). Trans.]

19. Raffaele Pazzelli and Mario Sensi, "Le Beata Angelina da Montegiove e il movimento del Terz'Ordine Regolare francescano femminile," in *Atti del Convegno di studi francescani,* Foligno, September 22–24, 1983 (Rome: Analecta TOR, 1984). [The Blessed Angelina is more generally known as Angelina of Marsciano. Trans.]

20. Giovanna Casagrande and Ernesto Menestò, eds., *Una santa, una città: atti del*

convegno storico nel V centenario della venuta a Perugia di Colomba da Rieti, Perugia, November 10–12, 1989 (Spoleto: Centro italiano di studi sull'alto Medioevo, 1991).

21. André Vauchez, *The Laity in the Middle Ages: Religious Beliefs and Devotional Practices* (Notre Dame: University of Notre Dame Press, 1993).

22. David Herlihy and Christiane Klapisch-Zuber, *Tuscans and Their Families: A Study of the Florentine Catasto of 1427* (New Haven, Conn.: Yale University Press, 1985). [This edition is substantially abridged, and the reader is referred to the original French, *Les Toscans et leurs familles,* or the Italian, *I Toscani e le loro famiglie,* where the reference is to pp. 832–833. Trans.] See also Giulia Calvi, *Il contratto morale: madri e figli nella Toscana moderna* (Rome: Laterza, 1994).

23. Anthony Molho, "'Tamquam vere mortua': le professioni religiose femminile nella Firenze del tardo Medioevo," *Società e storia,* 43 (1989), pp. 1–44; and Molho, *Marriage Alliance in Late Medieval Florence* (Cambridge, Mass.: Harvard University Press, 1994).

24. Lucia Sebastiani, "Monasteri femminili milanesi tra medioevo e età moderna," in Craig Hugh Smyth and Gian Carlo Garfagnini, eds., *Florence and Milan: Comparisons and Relations* (Florence: La Nuova Editrice Italiana, 1989), pp. 3–15.

25. G. Biondi, *Benvenuta e l'inquisitore: un destino di donna nella Modena del Trecento* (Modena, 1993).

26. Carlo Ginzburg, *Ecstasies: Deciphering the Witches' Sabbath* (New York: Pantheon, 1991).

27. Lene Dresen-Coenders and Petty Bange, eds., *Saints and She-devils: Images of Women in the Fifteenth and Sixteenth Centuries* (London and Portland, Oreg.: Rubicon Press, 1987), trans. of *Tussen heks en heilige.* exhibition cataloge, Commanderie van St. Jan, Nijmegen, November–January, 1986, and Rijksmuseum Catharinjeconvent, Utrecht, March–June 1988.

28. J. Held, "Marienbild und Volkfrommigkeit: Zur Function der Marienverherung im Hoch- und Spätmittelalter," in Ilsebill Barta, ed., *Frauen, Bilder, Männer, Mythen: kunsthistorische Beitrage* (Berlin: D. Reimer, 1987). See the contributions of I. Barta, Z. Breu, D. Hammer-Tugendhat, U. Jenni, I. Nierhaus, and J. Schlobel.

29. Alain Boureau, *La Papesse Jeanne* (Paris: Aubier, 1988).

30. Jacobus Philippus Bergomensis, *De claris selectisque mulieribus* (Ferrara: Rossi, 1497).

31. Marcello Craveri, *Sante e streghe: biografie e documenti dal XIV al XVII secolo* (Milan: Feltrinelli economica, 1981).

32. Ottavia Niccoli, *Prophecy and People in Renaissance Italy* (Princeton, N.J.: Princeton University Press, 1990).

33. [There are several published translations of her work. See Catherine of Genoa, *Treatise of Purgatory: The Dialogue,* trans. Helen Douglas Irvine and Charlotte Balfour (London: Sheed and Ward, 1946). Trans.]

34. S. Solfaroli Camillocci, "Le confraternite del Divino Amore: interpretazioni storiografiche e proposte attuali di ricerca," *Rivista di storia e letteratura religiosa,* 27 (1991), pp. 315–332.

35. Lucia Ferrante, "L'onore ritrovato: donne nella Casa del Soccorso di San Paolo a Bologna (sec. XVI–XVII)," *Quaderni storici,* 53 (1983), pp. 499–527.

36. Luisa Ciammitti, "Quanto costa essere normali: la dote nel conservatorio femminile di Santa Maria del Baraccano (1630–1680)," *Quaderni storici,* 53 (1983), pp. 469–498.

37. Luisa Ciammitti, "La dote come rendita: note sull'assistenza a Bologna nei secoli XVI–XVIII," in *Forme e soggetti dell'intervento assistenziale in una città d'antico regime: atti del IV Colloquio,* Bologna, January 20–21, 1984 (Bologna: Istituto per la storia di Bologna, 1986). See also A. Groppi, *I conservatori della virtù: donne recluse nella Roma dei Papi* (Rome: Laterza, 1994).

38. Daniela Lombardi, *Povertà maschile, povertà femminile: l'ospedale dei Mendicanti nella Firenze dei Medici* (Bologna: Il Mulino, 1988).

39. Cecilia Asso, *La teologia e la grammatica: la controversia tra Erasmo ed Edward Lee* (Florence: Leo S. Olschki, 1993).

40. Illustrated in Sara F. Matthews Grieco, *Ange ou diablesse: la représantation de la femme au XVIe siècle* (Paris: Flammarion, 1991), pp. 111–113.

41. Luciana Mariani, Elisa Tarolli, and Marie Seynaeve, *Angela Merici: contributo per una biografia* (Milan: Ancora Milano, 1986).

42. Gabriella Zarri, "Ursula and Catherine: The Marriage of Virgins in the Sixteenth Century," in E. Ann Matter and John Wayland Coakley, eds., *Creative Women in Medieval and Early Modern Italy* (Philadelphia: University of Pennsylvania Press, 1994).

43. Compare Aldo Zagni, *La Contessa di Guastalla* (Reggiolo: Como d'Oro, 1987).

44. Sherill Cohen, *The Evolution of Women's Asylums since 1500: From Refuges for Ex-Prostitutes to Shelters for Battered Women* (Oxford and New York: Oxford University Press, 1992).

45. Sabba da Castiglione, *Ricordi, ovvero Ammaestramenti* (1555).

46. Gabriella Zarri, "Ginevra Gozzadini dell'Armi, gentildonna bolognese (1520/27–1567)," in Elizabeth Storr Cohen and Ottavia Niccoli, eds., *Rinascimento al femminile* (Rome: Laterza, 1991), pp. 117–142.

47. Massimo Firpo, *Tra alumbrados e "spirituali": studi su Juan de Valdés e il valdesianesimo nella crisi religiosa del cinquecento italiano* (Florence: L. S. Olschki, 1990).

48. Valerio Marchetti, *Gruppi ereticali senesi del cinquecento* (Florence: La nuova Italia, 1975).

49. Pietro Manelfi, *I costituti di don Pietro Manelfi,* ed. Carlo Ginzburg (Florence: G. C. Sansoni, and Chicago: Newberry Library, 1970).

50. Roland Herbert Bainton, *Women of the Reformation in Germany and Italy* (Minneapolis, Minn.: Augsburg Publishing House, 1971). See the introduction to the Italian translation by Susanna Peyronel Rambaldi, in *Per una storia delle donne nella Riforma* (Turin: Claudiana, 1993).

51. Carlo Ginzburg and Adriano Prosperi, *Giochi di pazienza: un seminario sul Beneficio di Cristo* (Turin: G. Einaudi, 1975).

52. Marion L. Kuntz (Marion Leathers), ed., *Postello, Venezia e il suo mondo* (Florence: L. S. Olschki, 1988). See also Massimo Firpo, "Paolo Antonia Negri

da 'divina madre maestra' a 'spirito diabolico,'" *Barnabiti studi*, 7 (1992), pp. 7–66.

53. Romeo de Maio, *Bonsignore Cacciaguerra: un mistico senese nella Napoli del cinquecento* (Milan: R. Ricciardi, 1965).

54. Paolo Prodi, *Ricerca sulla teorica delle arti figurative nella Riforma Cattolica* (Bologna: Nuova Alfa, 1984).

55. Adriano Prosperi, "Teologi e pittura: la questione delle immagini nel cinquecento," in *La pittura in Italia: il cinquecento,* vol. 2 (Milan, 1988), pp. 581–592.

56. *Legendario delle santissime vergine* (Venice, 1525).

57. Robert Kolb, *For All the Saints: Changing Perceptions of Martyrdom and Sainthood in the Lutheran Reformation* (Macon, Ga.: Mercer University Press, 1987).

58. Prosperi, "L'elemento storico nelle polemiche sulla santità," pp. 88–118.

59. Giuseppe Maria Besutti, "Motivi del sorgere a dello sviluppo dei santuari," in *Nuovo dizionario di Mariologia* (Cinisello Balsamo, 1986), pp. 1268–1272.

60. Luigi De Biasio, "L'eresia protestante in Friuli nella seconda metà del secolo XVI," *Memorie storiche forogiuliesi,* 52 (1972), pp. 116–130; Giovanna Paolin, "L'eterodossia nel monastero delle clarisse di Udine nella seconda metà del cinquecento," *Collectanea franciscana,* 50 (1980) pp. 106167.

61. Document transcribed in Alessandra Ballico, "Istituzioni ecclesiastiche della città di Udine nelle visite del patriarca Francesco Barbara (dal 1593 al 1601)" (Bacc. diss., Udine, 1990–91), pp. 505–506.

62. Luigi Rinaldini, ed., *Regola della Compagnia di S. Orsola di Brescia, ora detta di S. Angela: versione critica secondo lo spirito di S. Angela e la tradizione alla luce dei documenti nella ed. anastatica della Regola del 1538–1581* (Brescia: Edizioni S. Orsola, 1971), repr. of *Regola della Compagnia di sant'Orsola fatta per quelle giovani che desiderano servire a Dio nello stato verginale, stando nel secolo, e per quelle, le quali per povertà, o per altri impedimenti non possono entrare in Monasteri: aggiuntovi i capitoli del Governo, che hanno di avere i Governatori e Governatrice di essa Compagnia* (Milan, 1567).

63. M. Bascapè, "'Ut perpetuo veritas appareat': l'origine del monastero delle cappucine di Lodi," *Archivio storico lombardo,* 9th ser., 3, no. 112 (1987), pp. 53–138.

64. Cf. Renée Baernstein, in *Sixteenth Century Journal,* 25, no. 14 (1994), pp. 787–807. [The use of the term "Angelics"—that is, of the congregation of women founded by Ludorica Torelli, under the direction of Saint Antony Zaccaria—here and elsewhere in this volume is left standing, though in fact "Angelicals" is the term for the women's congregations. Trans.]

65. [For further information on the Dimesse, see the *Dizionario istituti di perfezione,* vol. 3, cols. 503–505. Trans.]

66. Agostino Valier, *Instruttione delle donne maritate* . . . (Venice, 1577), Prologue.

67. *Regole della Compagnia delle Vergini di Santa Orsola stampate per ordine del molto Ill. e R.mo Mons. Paolo Leone vescovo di Ferrara* (Ferrara, 1587), intro.

68. *Regole della Compagnia di S. Orsola eretta in Bologna da Mons. ill.mo e rev.mo Alfonso Paleotti* . . .(Bologna, 1608), chap. 1.

69. Giuseppe Aberigo, ed., *Decisioni dei concili ecumenici* (Turin: Unione tipografica-editrice torinese, 1978), pp. 722 and 724.

70. Danilo Zardin, "Mercato librario e letture devote nella svolta del cinquecento tridentino: note in margine ad un inventario milanese di libri di monache," in Nicola Raponi and Angelo Turchini, eds., *Stampa, libri e letture a Milano nell'età di Carlo Borromeo* (Milan: Vita e pensiero, 1992), pp. 135–246.

71. Beatrice Del Sera, ed., *"Amor di virtù": commedia in cinque atti* (1548), reprinted under the same title in Elissa Weaver, ed. (Ravenna: Longo, 1990).

72. Silvia Evangelisti, "Angelica Bartelli, la storica," in Giulia Calvi, *Barocco al femminile* (Rome and Bari: Laterza, 1992), pp. 71–95.

73. Sara Cabibbo and Marilena Modica Vasta, *La santa dei Tomasi: storia di suor Maria Crocifissa (1645–1699)* (Turin: G. Einaudi, 1989).

74. Benedetto Croce, *Storia della età barocca in Italia: pensiero-poesia e letteratura vita morale* (Bari: Laterza, 1929), pp. 489–490.

75. Craig A. Monson, "Disembodied Voices. Music in the Nunneries of Bologna in the Midst of the Counter-Reformation," in Monson, ed., *The Crannied Wall: Women, Religion, and the Arts in Early Modern Europe* (Ann Arbor: University of Michigan Press, 1992), pp. 191–209; H. Robert Kendrick, "The Traditions of Milanese Convent Music and the Sacred Dialogues of Chiara Margarita Cozzolani," in Monson, *The Crannied Wall*, pp. 211–233. See also Danilo Zardin, *Donna e religiosa di rara eccellenza. Prospera Corona Bascapè, i libri e la cultura nei monasteri milanesi del cinque e seicento* (Florence, 1992).

76. Gabriella Zarri, ed., *Finzione e santità tra medioevo ed età moderna* (Turia: Rosenberg e Sellier, 1991).

77. Giulia Barone, "La canonizzazione di Francesca Romana (1608): la riproposta di un modello agiografico medievale," in Zarri, *Finzione e santità*, pp. 264–279. [First known as Oblates of Mary, Francesca's order was later known as the Oblates of Tor de' Specchi after their mother house. Trans.]

78. Teresa of Avila, *Il cammino di perfezione: el castello interiore . . .* (Florence, 1605).

79. Daniele Benati and Marco Bona Castellotti, eds., *Guido Cagnacci* (Milan: Electa, 1993). Catalog of the exhibition in the City Museum, Rimini, August 21 to November 28, 1993.

80. For Cecilia Ferrazzi, see her autobiography: *Autobiografia di una santa mancata*, ed. Anne Jacobson Schutte (Bergamo: Pierluigi Lubrina, 1990), English trans. *Autobiography of an Aspiring Saint* (Chicago: University of Chicago Press, 1996). For Angela Mellini, see Luisa Ciammitti, "Una santa di meno: storia di Angela Mellini, cucitrice bolognese (1667–17..)," *Quaderni storici*, 41 (1979), pp. 603–639.

81. Giuseppe Dalla Torre, "Santità ed economia processuale: l'esperienza giuridica da Urbano VIII a Benedetto XIV," in Zarri, *Finzione e santità*, pp. 231–263.

82. Mario Rosa, "The Nun," in Rosario Villari, ed., *Baroque Personae* (Chicago: University of Chicago Press, 1995).

83. Elizabeth Rapley, *The Dévotes: Women and Church in Seventeenth-century France* (Montreal and Buffalo: McGill-Queen's University Press, 1990).

84. Paul de Barry, *Solitudine di Filagia, overo indirizzo dell'anima amante della*

santità . . . (Rome, 1659). [The most recent edition (the twentieth) is Paul de Barry, *Le paradis ouvert à Philagie par cent dévotions à la Mère de Dieu* (Paris: Martin-Beaupré frères, 1868). Trans.]

6. Spiritual Letters

1. Catherine of Siena, *Epistole,* ed. Bartolomeo da Alzano and Aldus Manutius (Venice, 1500). [For an English translation, see Catherine of Siena, *The Letters of Saint Catherine of Siena,* trans. Suzanne Noffke (Binghampton, N.Y.: Medieval and Renaissance Texts and Studies, 1988). Trans.]

2. Carlo Dionisotti, *Gli umanisti e il volgare tra quattro e cinquecento* (Florence: F. Le Monnier, 1968).

3. Catherine of Siena, *Epistolario di santa Caterina da Siena,* ed. Eugenio Dupré Theseider (Rome: Tipografia del Senato, 1940). Sources for the History of Italy: Letters, Fourteenth Century, no. 82, intro., p. xv.

4. Ibid., p. xiv.

5. Ibid. See also the same author's study, "Il problema critico delle lettere di santa Caterina da Siena," *Bullettino dell'Istituto storico italiano e archivio muratoriano,* 49 (1933).

6. Angela da Foligno, *Il libro dell'esperienza,* ed. Giovanni Pozzi (Milan, 1992), p. 22. [For an English version, see Angela of Foligno, *Complete Works* (New York: Paulist Press, 1993). Trans.]

7. Maria Maddalena de' Pazzi, *Le parole dell'estasi,* ed. Giovanni Pozzi (Milan, 1992), p. 22.

8. See Romeo de Maio, *Bonsignore Cacciaguerra: un mistico senese nella Napoli del cinquecento, con un' appendice sulla sua fortuna letteraria fuori d'Italia* (Milan: R. Ricciardi, 1965).

9. See Massimo Firpo, "Paola Antonia Negri da 'divina madre maestra' a 'spirito diabolico,'" *Barnabiti studi,* 7 (1992), esp. p. 12.

10. See the documentation studied by Giuseppe Maria Cagni, "Negri o Besozzi: come nacque la 'vexatia quaestio' della paternità delle 'lettere spirituali' dell'Angelica Paola Antonia Negri," *Barnabiti studi,* 6 (1989), pp. 177–217. On Elena Duglioli, see Gabriella Zarri, *Le sante vive: cultura e religiosità femminile nella prima età moderna* (Turin: Rosenberg e Sellier, 1990), pp. 165–196.

11. The collection *Lettere spirituali sopra alcune feste et sacri tempi dell'anno,* by Besozzi, was printed in Milan by Paolo Gottardo [Antonio Giorgio?] Ponzio in 1578.

12. *Lettere della serafica madre S. Teresa di Gisù fondatrice delle monache e Padri Carmelitani scalzi . . . tradotte da don Oratio Quaranta consultore della Sacra Congregatione dell'Indice* (Venice: Iseppo Prodocimo, 1685), cod. A 2 verso. The *Prattica spirituale* was published in Venice, by Giacomo Cornetti, in 1592.

13. Monsignor Giovanni Visconti, *Lettere ed instruzioni spirituali con altre devote materie* (Florence, 1716).

14. For instance, the anonymous *Lettere di un direttore ad un suo penitente intorno al libro intitolato letteres provinciali* (Venice, 1698).

15. On the relationship between Giovanni Visconti and a visionary "false saint," I

have been able to read an early draft of the work by Adelisa Malena, whom I thank. Another collection of letters that concerns a relationship of spiritual filiation is that published in the second part of *Strada di salute breve, facile e sicura insegnata nuovamente da un religioso scalzo eremitano agostiniano ad una sua penitente* . . . (Bologna). The inquisitorial approval dates from 1679 and the letters date from 1677 to 1678, pp. 343ff. In this second example, it was the penitent who became the editor of the letters written to her.

16. The quotations are taken from a long letter to Fontana, which survives under the title of *Apologia,* preserved in the Archive of San Carlo a'Catinari, Rome, ms. Lb. 6.

17. Ibid. The fragment is quoted in Firpo, "Paola Antonia Negri," p. 62.

18. Letter from the friar Onorio Pezzi of Brescia, written on March 3, 1497, to Countess Lucrezia Gambara, in Antonio Cistellini, *Figure della riforma pretri-dentina: Stefana Quinzani, Angela Merici, Laura Mignani, Bartolomeo Stella, Frencesco Cabrini e Francesco Santabona* (Brescia: Morcelliana, 1948), pp. 257–258; ibid., pp. 194–197, for the notarial act concerning the Blessed Stefana Quinzani. On the grammar of gesture, see Michael Baxandall, *Painting and Experience in Fifteenth Century Italy: A Primer in the Social History of Pictorial Style* (Oxford and New York, Oxford University Press, 1988).

19. Jean-Claude Schmitt, *La raison des gestes dans l'Occident medieval* (Paris: Galli-mard, 1990), pp. 291–292. See also Chiara Frugoni, *Francesco e l'invenzione delle stimate: una storia per parole e immagini fino a Bonaventura e Giotto* (Turin: G. Einaudi, 1993).

20. The obvious reference on this subject is Gabriella Zarri, especially the studies collected in *Sante vive.*

21. Federico Borromeo, *De vera et occulta sanctitate libri tres* (Milan, 1650).

22. The letters, from Sister Beatrice of San Casciano of the Florentine convent of San Jacopo to Brother Dominic "de Ianellis" in 1567, are kept in the file devoted to the trial held by the nuncio of Florence in 1578 (Florentine State Archives, Nunziatura, Criminal Complaints, f. 851, cc, unnumbered). For the figure of the transfixed heart, see Luisa Ciamitti, "Una santa di meno: storia di Angela Mellini, cucitrice bolognese," *Quaderni storici,* 41 (1979), pp. 603–639.

23. *Delle vite delle donne illustri per santità* (Florence: Heirs of I. Giunti, 1597).

24. Venice: Giolito, 1549. See Anne Jacobson Schutte, "The 'Lettere volgari' and the Crisis of Evangelism in Italy," *Renaissance Quarterly,* 28 (1975), pp. 639–683.

25. Niccolò Machiavelli, *La vita di Castruccio Castracani,* in *Istorie fiorentine* (Mi-lan: Feltrinelli, 1962), p. 9.

26. Giorgio Vasari, *Le vite de' più eccellenti architetti, pittori, et scultori italiani, da Cimabue a' tempi nostri* (Florence: Torrentino, 1550). The citations come from Vasari, *Le vite* (Turin: G. Einaudi, 1986), p. 914.

27. The citations from Cacciaguerra's *Autobiografia* are taken from de Maio, *Bon-signore Cacciaguerra,* pp. 160–161.

28. Bonsignore Cacciaguerra, *Lettere spirituali* (Venice: 1575) ("As the true Chris-tian resembles the sculptor, who always takes away the excess, and the worldly

man resembles the painter, who colors, puts in, and adds"), p. 266. The Bolognese Ginevra Gozzadini used an image closer to the artisan's workshop in corresponding with her spiritual father: a spiritual steeping, as with wood before the cabinetmaker works it. See Gabriella Zarri, "Ginevra Gozzadini dall'Armi, gentildonna bolognese (1520/27–1567)," in Ottavia Niccoli, ed., *Rinascimento al femminile* (Rome and Bari: Laterza, 1991), p. 132.

29. I mention this significant connection in my Italian edition of Juan Valdés, *Alfabeto cristiano* (Rome: Istituto storico italiano per l'età moderna e contemporanea, 1988), pp. 11–12.

30. For the relationship between early asceticism and the Carmelite reform, see I. Poutrin, "Ascèse et desert en Espagne (1560–1600): autour de la réforme carmélitaine," *Mélanges de la casa de Velásquez,* 25 (1989), pp. 145–149.

31. Such is the meaning of an annotation made by her spiritual director on the first page of the "diary" of Barbera Fivoli, a candidate for sainthood in eighteenth-century Tuscany (Archdiocesal Archives of Pisa, "Beatification proceedings," letters of B. Fivoli, *Diario, 1762,* p. 1).

32. In this regard, see Kaspar von Greyerz, "Religion in the Life of German and Swiss Autobiographers (Sixteenth and Early Seventeenth Centuries)," in Greyerz, ed., *Religion and Society in Early Modern Europe, 1500–1800* (London: German Historical Institute, Allen and Unwin, 1984), pp. 223–241. A comparison of the effects on the condition of women of the Protestant Reformation and the Counter-Reformation can be found in Natalie Zemon Davis, *Society and Culture in Early Modern France: Eight Essays* (London: Duckworth, 1975), pp. 91–129. More schematic is the reconstruction in Bonnie S. Anderson and Judith P. Zinsser, *A History of Their Own: Women in Europe from Prehistory to the Present* (New York: Harper and Row, 1988). The authors limit themselves to saying that "groups which worked to grant women's rights in the eighteenth and nineteenth centuries enjoyed greater success in Protestant countries."

33. Montaigne, *Essais,* 1:1.

34. *Lettere della serafica madre S. Teresa di Gisù fondatrice delle monache e Padri Carmelitani scalzi . . . tradotte da don Oratio Quaranta consultore della Sacra Congregatione dell'Indice* (Venice: I. Prodocimo, 1685), p. 12v.

35. Battista da Crema, *Specchio interiore, opera divina per la cui lettione ciascuno devoto potrà facilmente ascendere al colmo della perfettione* (Milano: Calvo, 1540), col. 86r. On these functions of spiritual people, the reader is referred to the observations and sources in Elisja Schulte van Kessel, ed., *Women and Men in Spiritual Culture, XIV–XVII Centuries: A Meeting of North and South* (The Hague: Netherlands Government Publications Office, 1986), pp. 71–90. On Battista da Crema, see Paul E. Grendler, "Man Is Almost a God: Fra Battista Carioni between Renaissance and Reformation," in Charles Edward Trinkaus, John W. O'Malley, and Thomas Izbicki, eds., *Humanity and Divinity in Renaissance and Reformation: Essays in Honor of Charles Trinkaus* (Leiden and New York: E. J. Brill, 1993), pp. 227–249.

36. Venice, 1555.

37. Archdiocesan Archives, Pisa, "Beatification Proceedings," letters from B. Fivoli, *Diario,* 1762, p. 152.

7. The Convent Muses

1. "Non vorria mai piú intrare in casa sua"; and "Vennono alquanti huomini e pigliaron per la mano alquante donne e tutti insieme se ne andorno a spasso."

2. Most of Frescobaldi's works are in the Frescobaldi Archives (Poggio a Remole, just outside Florence). The location of her résumé of Guicciardini's history is unknown, but other works can be found in Florence at the National Library and in the archives of Santa Maria Novella. G. Pierattini has studied her life and works in "Suor Fiammetta Frescobaldi cronista del monastero domenicano di San Iacopo a Ripoli in Firenze (1523–1586)," in *Memorie domenicane*, 56 (1939), pp. 101–116, 233–240; 57 (1940), pp. 106–111, 260–269; 58 (1941), pp. 28–38, 74–84, 226–234, 258–268. See also my entry on her in Katharina Wilson, ed., *An Encyclopedia of Continental Women Writers*, 2 vols. (New York and London: Garland Publishing, 1991).

3. "A consolazione di chi non ha copia di libri," Frescobaldi Archives, autograph manuscript, vol. 1, p. 154.

4. ". . . solo per giovare alle mie in Christo madre e sorelle che son tanto ochupate che non resta loro tempo da cercare di tali cose in tanti libri i quali per essere latini non cosí da tutte con facilità sono intesi, però li ò adunati da varii autori per amor loro et fattogli vulgari, se non come dovevo almeno come ò saputo, per mostrare in qualche parte lo obrigo che io tengo con loro," this and previous passage from *Prato fiorito*, Biblioteca Nazionale di Firenze (hereafter BNF), *Conventi soppressi*, C. 2.504, pp. iii verso and ix verso (modern page numbers, in pencil).

5. The phrase is "grande ingenio e acutissia memoria," *Chroniche* (or *Chronicle Books*), Florence, Archivio di Stato (hereafter ASF), *San Jacopo di Ripoli*, 23, 137v. The three *Chroniche,* respectively, list the professed nuns, the prioresses, and the record of deaths, which for each entry provides, along with the time and cause of death, a biography of the nun, in some cases amply narrated.

6. "Senza avere mai hauto precettore," ibid.

7. On the education of women, see Paul Grendler, *Schooling in Renaissance Italy* (Baltimore and London: Johns Hopkins University Press, 1989), esp. pp. 87–102; Margaret King, *Women of the Renaissance* (Chicago: University of Chicago Press, 1991), chap. 3, pp. 157–239; Christiane Klapisch-Zuber, "Le chiavi fiorentine di Barbablú: l'apprendimento della lettura a Firenze nel XV secolo," *Quaderni storici*, 57 (1984), pp. 765–792; Anthony Grafton and Lisa Jardine, *From Humanism to the Humanities* (Cambridge, Mass.: Harvard University Press, 1986); and Gian Ludovico Masetti Zannini, *Motivi storici dell'educazione femminile (1500–1560)*, vol. 1, *Morale, religione, lettere, arte musica* (Bari: Editorialbari, 1980), and vol. 2, *Scienza, lavoro, giuochi* (Naples: M. D'Auria Editore, 1981). On the convents in general, see Gabriella Zarri, "Monasteri femminili e città (secoli XV–XVIII)," in G. Chittolini and G. Miccoli, eds., *Storia d'Italia, annali IX: la Chiesa e il potere politico dal Medioevo all'età contemporanea* (Turin: G. Einaudi, 1986), pp. 357–429.

8. See Carlo Dionisotti, "La letteratura italiana nell'età del Concilio di Trento," in *Il Concilio di Trento e la Riforma Tridentina*, vol. 1 (Rome: Herder, 1965),

pp. 317–343, reprinted in Carlo Dionisotti, *Geografia e storia della letteratura italiana* (Turin: G. Einaudi, 1967), pp. 227–254.

9. It is possible, too, that another class of women, the *commedia dell'arte* actresses, were enabled and encouraged to write at this time. The published work of actresses such as Isabella Andreini, Maddalena Campiglia, Margherita Costa, and Valeria Miani Negri would seem to support such a hypothesis.

10. See Carlo Borromeo, *Acta ecclesiae mediolanensis,* vol. 1 (1754), pp. 38–41, where, pursuant to the reforms undertaken by the Council of Trent, it is stated that each convent should elect a convent recorder, and her duties and term of office are specified.

11. Such a mix of information was characteristic of the genre of record books in the secular world as well.

12. *Ricordi* (1522–1564), ASF, *Carte Strozziane,* ser. 1, 103, *passim.*

13. ASF, *Corporazioni religiose soppresse,* 96, f. 12, 129r–130r, 13, 181v–182r, 197v, and 14, 180v–201r.

14. "Suor Michelangela Cioni morì addì 19 di detto. Ebbe tutti e sagramenti. Era questa suora molto caritativa. Morì con gran ghusto di Iesú. Disse che vedeva il suo angelino tanto bello ricciutino. Avea anni 72 e durava faticha più che le giovani. Tanto era la sua carità governava una paza. Spazzava e lavavala e da quella riceveva molte ingiurie. Adesso miete la sementa." *Chroniche,* ASF, *San Jacopo di Ripoli,* 23, 126r.

15. On the forms and uses of the historical genres in Italian convents, see S. Evangelisti, "Memoria di antiche madri: i generi della storiografia monastica femminile in Italia (sece. XV–XVIII)," in C. Segura, ed., *La voz del silencio: fuentes directas para la historia de las mujeres, siglos III al XVI* (Madrid, 1992), pp. 221–249. Evangelisti discusses biographies, accounts of miracles, and chronicles; she does not consider record books. On women's historiography, see also G. Pomata, "Storia particolare e storia universale: in margine ad alcuni manuali di storia delle donne, *Quaderni storici,* 74 (1990), pp. 341–385, and Natalie Zemon Davis, "Gender and Genre: Women as Historical Writers, 1400–1820," in Patricia H. Labalme, ed., *Beyond Their Sex: Learned Women of the European Past* (New York: New York University Press, 1980), pp. 153–182.

16. "Non ebbe mai segno di figliuoli," *Diario,* Archive of Santa Maria Novella, Florence, 41v.

17. "Mutando panni e vita, mutò nome." Ibid.

18. "Lo stesso dí fu assai maltempo; cascò dua saette, non però fecion danno che si sia saputo. La pioggia non fu molta ma refrigerò alquanto il grande ardore di questa state." Ibid.

19. "Il dí 28 maggio sabbato ad hore una di notte levorono fuor di San Paulo suor Serena Pazzana, qual fu vestita da suora di gennaio 1594 contra sua voglia; fu condotta nella casa paterna et subito posta ad alto in prigione, sola soletta. Dio l'aiuta la poverina." Suor Lucia Pioppi, *Diario (1541–1612),* ed. R. Bussi (Panini: Modena, 1982), p. 117. Pioppi's diary is also divided into two parts, the second of which is written in the margins of her breviary.

20. Bartolomea Riccoboni, *Cronaca del Corpus Domini,* ed. Maria Teresa Casella and Giovanni Pozzi, published in the appendix to their edition of B. Giovanni

Dominici, O. P., *Lettere spirituali* (Freiburg, Switzerland: Edizioni Universitarie Friburgo Svizzera, 1969), pp. 257–294.

21. *Cronica del monastero delle Vergini di Venetia* (written between 1519 and 1523), Venice, Biblioteca del Museo Correr, Correr codex 317, Classe 1.

22. *Memoriale di Monteluce cronaca del monastero delle clarisse di Perugia dal 1448 al 1838*, ed. Ugolino Nicolini (Santa Maria degli Angeli [Assisi]: Edizioni Porziuncola, 1983).

23. Giustina Niccolini, *Cronache del v[enerabilissimo] monastero di Santa Maria Annuntiata de le Murate di Fiorenza . . .*, BNF, Fondo nazionale, II.II.509. On this chronicle see K. J. P. Lowe, "Female Strategies for Success in a Male-ordered World: The Benedictine Convent of Le Murate in Florence," *Studies in Church History*, 27 (1990), pp. 209–221.

24. Orsola Formicini, *Libro de l'antichità del monasterio di San Cosimato . . .*, Rome, Biblioteca Nazionale Vittorio Emanuele, Varia 5 and Varia 6, two autograph redactions. See the comments of Amadeo Quondam in "Lanzichenecchi in convento: Suor Orsola e la storia tra archivio e devozione," *Schifanoia*, 6 (1988), pp. 46–47.

25. Quondam, "Lanzichenecchi," pp. 54–60.

26. "Et . . . cominciò la guerra del sig. Marcantonio Colonna et il papa, cioè, Paulo 4 Charrafa, per il che tutta Roma andava sotto sopra . . . Et mio padre, per non veder in sé la miseria qual vide allora [al tempo del Sacco di Roma] nelli figlioli altrui si deliberò farmi religiosa." Formicini, *Libro*, Varia 5 (the second autograph redaction), 240v, published in Quondam, "Lanzichenecchi," p. 58; and on pp. 88–125, Quondam transcribes the part of the *Libro* that narrates the sack of Rome, which was reconstructed by Formicini on the basis of the recollections of the oldest nuns of San Cosimato.

27. See, for example, Flaminio Corner, *Notizie storiche delle chiese e monasteri di Venezia e di Torcello . . .* (Padua: Giovanni Manfrè, 1778), p. 93.

28. Many of the women of the convent of the Vergini were accomplished Latinists. On the occasion of the election of each new abbess the Correr codex presents a Latin oration said to have been delivered by an "erudite" nun. In his report on four abbesses of unreformed houses, who in 1521 argued against their reform in person before the doge, Marin Sanudo claims that the abbess of the Vergini, Clara Donado, spoke in Latin, giving something of a speech: "quella di le verzene parloe *latine,* facendo quasi una orazione . . ." (M. Sanudo, *Diari,* Venice: Fratelli Visentini Editori, 1879–1903; repr. Bologna: Forni, 1969–70, xxxi, col. 176).

29. For convent theater in Spain, see Electa Arenal and Stacey Schlau, *Untold Sisters: Hispanic Nuns in Their Own Works,* Eng. translations by Amanda Powell (Albuquerque: University of New Mexico Press, 1989), and the edition of the works (dramatic and poetic) of the daughter of Lope de Vega, Marcela de San Felix, *Obra completa,* ed. Electa Arenal and G. Sabat de Rivers (Barcelona: Producciones y promociones universitarias, 1988).

30. Richard Trexler, "Florentine Theater, 1280–1500: A Checklist of Performances and Institutions," *Forum italicum,* 14 (1980), p. 471.

31. See the introduction to my edition of Beatrice del Sera, *Amor di virtú* (Ra-

venna: Longo, 1990), pp. 20–31. My study of convent theater, *Spiritual Fun (Cambridge: Cambridge University Press, 1997), provides more extensive documentation of the tradition.*

32. Maria Maddalena de' Pazzi, a Florentine nun (and future saint) in Santa Maria degli Angeli, wrote to her friend Carità Rucellai in another Florentine house, San Giovannino delle Cavalieresse di Malta, on September 1, 1592, to thank her for having lent her a play, which she had copied and was returning with the letter (transcribed in the *Memorie* of San Giovannino delle Cavalieresse di Malta of Sister Maria Esaltata Ridolfi, ASF, *Corporazioni religiose soppresse*, 130, filza 60, 207–209, now published in M. M. de' Pazzi, *Tutte le opere*, vol. 7, *Rinovatione della Chiesa*, ed. Mons. F. Vallainc [Florence: Centro internazionale del libro di Bruno Nardini, 1960], p. 145). For texts commissioned by the nuns from religious and secular playwrights, see my article "Spasso spirituale, ovvero il gioco delle monache," in *Passare il tempo: la letteratura del gioco e dell'intrattenimento dal XII al XVI secolo* (Rome: Salerno Editrice, 1993), pp. 351–371.

33. See, for example, Giovan Maria Cecchi, prologue to the *Acquisto di Giacobbe* (1580–1587), written for convent performance, ll. 70–77. The *Acquisto* is published in Raffaello Rocchi, ed., *Drammi spirituali inediti*, vol. 1 (Florence: Successori Le Monnier, 1895), pp. 93–169, the prologue, pp. 95–98.

34. Weaver, "Spasso spirituale," pp. 359–360. There, too, see documentation of other restrictions, most of which are found in the correspondence of the *Sacra congregazione vescovi e regolari* at the Archivio Segreto Vaticano.

35. The term *rappresentazione* is used for the typical one-act plays and also for comedies divided into acts, while *commedia* in almost all of the plays belonging to this repertoire denotes a theatrical work divided into acts.

36. "Chommedie delle monache di santa Chiara conposte da suor Annalena quando l'era maestra per le sue novitie," Florence, Biblioteca Riccardiana, Riccardian codex 2976, vol. 6. See my article "Convent Comedy and the World: The Farces of Suor Annalena Odaldi (1572–1638)," in Rebecca West and Dino Cervigni, eds., "Women's Voices in Italian Literature," *Annali d'Italianistica*, 7 (1989), pp. 182–192.

37. "Quando fu maestra di novitie cominciò a comporre comedie con stile elegantissimo . . . e nel detto esercizio si affatichò assai fino che era all'ultima età sua." ASF, *San Jacopo di Ripoli*, 23, 150v–151r.

38. Beatrice del Sera was the daughter of Andrea di Neri del Sera and first cousin of Michelangelo Buonarroti, whose mother was Andrea's sister. At two years of age she was taken to the convent of San Niccolò, where she spent her life. The manuscript of her play, partly autograph, is Riccardian codex 2932. My quotations are taken from the modern edition, cited above in n. 31. The play was first studied by Angelo Emanuele in *Virtú d'amore di suor Beatrice del Sera* (Catania: F. Tropea, 1903).

39. Weaver, intro., in *Amor di virtú*.

40. "Miete chi n'ha di sue fatiche onori, / ond'io che pover' son, sol' dentr' al sasso, / spero nel ben della vita futura," from *Quant'amor fusse mai contant' e forte*, ll. 12–14, ibid., p. 91.

41. Ibid., p. 267.

42. Five editions were published in Macerata—by Pietro Salvioni and Agostino Grisei in 1612 and 1631, by Agostino Grisei in 1640 and 1651, and by Giuseppe Piccini in 1685; there was a Roman edition as well, published by Angelo Bernabò in 1668.

43. *Giacob patriarca* (Pisa: Francesco delle Dote, 1637); *Natal di Cristo,* Riccardian codex 2783, vol. 7.

44. Anton Francesco Gori, *Memorie dell'Accademia degli Apatisti,* Florence, Biblioteca Marucelliana, codex A, 36, on page 58r lists "suor M. Clemente Ruoti, monaca in S. Girolamo di S. Giorgio" among those members inducted into the academy during the period 1649–1650. This manuscript was published in part in Alessandro Lazzeri, *Intellettuali e consenso nella Toscana del Seicento: l'Accademia degli Apatisti* (Milan: Dott. A. Giuffré Editore, 1983), pp. 57–121; the reference to "suor M. Clemente Ruoti" is on p. 82.

45. ASF, *Corp. rel. sopp.* 96, f. 15, 182r.

46. A number of scholars have studied Tarabotti: Emilio Zanette wrote a biography of the nun, which is still useful for its copious documentation, though the material is not presented in the most logical fashion and the author never seems to understand or sympathize with the issues that were so important to her: Emilio Zanette, *Suor Arcangela monaca del Seicento veneziano* (Rome, 1960). Others who have written about Tarabotti are Patricia H. Labalme, "Women's Roles in Early Modern Venice: An Exceptional Case," in Labalme, ed., *Beyond Their Sex: Learned Women of the European Past* (New York: New York University Press, 1980), pp. 135–139, 149; E. Biga, "Una polemica antifemminista del Seicento: la maschera scoperta di Angelico Aprosio," *Quaderno dell'Aprosiano,* 4 (1989); M. Rosa, "La religiosa," in R. Villari, ed., *L'uomo barocco* (Rome, 1991), pp. 233–234; King, *Women of the Renaissance,* pp. 89–91, 176; and F. Medioli, *L' "Inferno monacale" di Arcangela Tarabotti* (Turin, 1990).

47. Arcangela Tarabotti, *Lettere familiari e di complimento* (Venice: Guerigli, 1650). The letters are not dated, and often the name of the correspondent is omitted.

48. Ibid, pp. 55–57. Vittoria della Rovere was an important patron of female religious houses. Maria Clemente Ruoti, like Tarabotti, dedicated one of her works, *Jacob the Patriarch,* to the grand duchess.

49. Ibid, pp. 186–188.

50. "Ch'io resti di scrivere m'è impossibile il farlo. In queste carceri, e nei miei mali non ho altro di che contentarmi . . . se non havessi questo trattenimento sarei di già morta . . . solo una penna temperata ha valore di temperare le mie pene. Non m'atterrisse punto il sentire che gli studi mi causeranno la morte; perché non mi spiacerà il mutar aria, variar tormenti, conversar con altri angeli e praticar altri demoni." Ibid, p. 75.

51. On this theme in the writing of the humanists, see Margaret King, "Isotta Nogarola, umanista e devota (1418–1466)," in O Niccoli, ed., *Rinascimento al femminile* (Rome, 1991), pp. 3–33, esp. p. 16.

52. Cesare Guasti studied this play and published an abridged version of it in the *Calendario pratese del 1850,* vol. 5 (Prato, 1849), pp. 53–101.

53. S. Evangelisti, "Memoria di antiche madri," in C. Segura, ed., *La voz del Silencio* (Madrid, 1992), pp. 221–249. These are not biographies in the modern sense of the term but accounts of the exemplary lives of saints, *beatae,* and venerated founders of convents, model lives to be imitated and, therefore, devotional works rather than conventional historiography.

54. On the relationship of the Ferrarese nuns with the Este and Gonzaga families, see Gabriella Zarri, "Monache e sante alla corte estense (XV–XVI secolo)," in F. Bocchi, ed., *Storia illustrata di Ferrar* (Milan, 1987), pp. 417–432; on the nuns' letters (now in the Gonzaga Archive at the Archivio di Stato di Montova), see pp. 425 and 429.

8. Little Women, Great Heroines

1. On Benedetta Carlini, see Judith C. Brown, *Immodest Acts: The Life of a Lesbian Nun in Renaissance Italy* (New York and Oxford: Oxford University Press, 1986); and Rudolph M. Bell and Judith C. Brown, "Renaissance Sexuality in the Archives: An Exchange," *Renaissance Quarterly,* 40 (1987), pp. 485–511. Two documents from the Carlini case concerning discernment of spirits, "Segni delle vere visioni et revelationi" and "Modo di conoscere le divine dalle diaboliche revelazioni" (not utilized by Brown and mentioned only in passing by Bell), may be found in Florence, Archivio di Stato, Miscellanea Medicea, 376, insert 28.

2. On "forced confessionalization" and "discipline," see Peter Burke, "The Triumph of Lent," in *Popular Culture in Early Modern Europe* (New York: Harper and Row, 1978), pp. 207–244; Wolfgang Reinhard, "Confessionalizzazione forzata? prolegomeni ad una teoria dell'età confessionale," *Annali dell'Istituto storico italo-germanico in Trento,* 8 (1982), pp. 13–38; Reinhard, "Disciplinamento sociale, confessionalizzazione, modernizzazione: un discorso storico," in Paolo Prodi, ed., *Disciplina dell'anima, disciplina del corpo e disciplina della società tra medioevo ed età moderna* (Bologna: Il Mulino, 1994), pp. 101–123; Pierangelo Schiera, "Lo stato moderno e il rapporto disciplinamento/legittimazione," *Problemi del socialismo,* 5 (1985), pp. 111–135; Schiera, "Disciplina, Stato moderno, disciplinamento: considerazioni a cavallo fra lo sociologia del potere e la storia costituzionale," in Prodi, ed., *Disciplina,* pp. 21–46; and Heinz Schilling, "Chiese confessionali e disciplinamento sociale: un bilancio provvisorio della ricerca storica," in Prodi, ed., *Disciplina,* pp. 125–160.

3. Pierre Delooz, "Per uno studio sociologico della santità," in Sofia Boesch Gajano, ed., *Agiografia altomedioevale* (Bologna: Il Mulino, 1976), esp. pp. 233–239. On the social construction of holiness, see also Delooz, *Sociologie et canonisations* (The Hague: Martinus Nijhoff, 1969); André Vauchez, *La sainteté en Occident aux derniers siècles du Moyen Age d'après les procès de canonisation et les documents hagiographiques* (Rome: Ecole française de Rome, 1981); Donald Weinstein and Rudolph M. Bell, *Saints and Society: The Two Worlds of Western Christendom, 1100–1700* (Chicago and London: University of Chicago Press, 1982); and the essays in Sofia Boesch Gajano and Lucia Sebastiani, eds., *Culto dei santi, istituzioni e classi sociali in età preindustriale* (L'Aquila and Rome: L. U. Japadre Editore, 1984).

4. Peter Burke, "How to Be a Counter-Reformation Saint," in *The Historical Anthropology of Early Modern Europe: Essays on Perception and Communication* (Cambridge: Cambridge University Press, 1987), p. 59.

5. Romeo De Maio, "L'ideale eroico nei processi di canonizzazione della Controriforma," in *Riforme e miti nella Chiesa del cinquecento* (Naples: Guida, 1973), pp. 257–278.

6. On the new criteria for sainthood and procedures for canonization, see also Burke, "How to Be a Counter-Reformation Saint"; and Giuseppe Dalla Torre, "Santità ed economia processulae: l'esperienza giuridica da Urbano VIII a Benedetto XIV," in Gabriella Zarri, ed., *Finzione e santità tra medioevo ed età moderna* (Turin: Rosenberg e Sellier, 1991), pp. 231–263.

7. Paolo Prodi, *The Papal Prince, One Body and Two Souls: The Papal Monarchy in Early Modern Europe,* trans. Susan Haskins (Cambridge: Cambridge University Press, 1988).

8. 2 Cor. 11:13–15: "For such boasters are false apostles, deceitful workers, disguising themselves as apostles of Christ. And no wonder! Even Satan disguises himself as an angel of light. So it is not strange if his ministers also disguise themselves as ministers of righteousness. Their end will match their deeds." 1 John 4:1: "Beloved, do not believe every spirit, but test the spirits to see whether they are from God; for many false prophets have gone out into the world." (Translations from the New Revised Standard Version.)

9. The most easily accessible version of Pérez's treatise is the modern edition: *Aviso de gente recogida,* ed. Alvaro Huerga and Juan Esquerda Bifet (Madrid: Universidad Pontificia di Salamanca, Fundación Universitaria Española, 1977). The Italian translation by unidentified Dominicans, *Avvertimenti spirituali per quelli che specialmente si sono dedicati al servitio di Dio,* was issued in Florence in 1590 and 1592, in Brescia in 1602, and in Venice in 1610 and 1650. On Pérez, see Alison Weber, "Between Ecstasy and Exorcism: Religious Negotiation in Sixteenth-Century Spain," *Journal of Medieval and Renaissance Studies,* 23 (1993), pp. 221–234.

10. On the Spanish *beatae,* see Claire Guilhem, "L'Inquisition et la dévaluation des discours féminins," in Bartolomé Bennassar, ed., *L'Inquisition espagnole XVe–XIXe siècle* (Paris: Hachette, 1979), pp. 197–240; Mary Elizabeth Perry, "Beatas and the Inquisition in Early Modern Spain," in Stephen Haliczer, ed., *Inquisition and Society in Early Modern Europe* (London and Sydney: Croom Helm, and New York: Barnes and Noble, 1987), pp. 147–168; and Perry, *Gender and Disorder in Early Modern Seville* (Princeton: Princeton University Press, 1990), pp. 97–117.

11. Antonio Pagani, *Gli Ordini della divota Compagnia delle Dimesse che vivono sotto il nome e la protettione della purissima Madre di Dio Maria Vergine* (Venice: Domenico Nicolini, 1587), pp. 45–46.

12. Antonio Pagani, *La breve somma delli essercitii de' penitenti per la profittevole riforma dell'huomo interiore* (Venice: Giovanni Varisco Paganino Paganini, 1587), pp. 203–207.

13. Marc'Aurelio Grattarola, *Pratica della vita spirituale per ogni stato di persone desiderose di far progresso nella christiana perfettione* (Venice: Giovanni Battista Combi, 1609, ca. 1614, 1621; Como: Giovanni Angelo Turato, 1617). I thank

Adriano Prosperi for calling my attention to this work and Gabriella Zarri for allowing me to consult her copy of it. The *Pratica* is discussed briefly by Prosperi, "L'elemento storico nelle polemiche sulla santità," in Zarri, ed., *Finzione e santità tra medioevo ed età moderna* (Turin: Rosenberg e Sellier, 1991), pp. 112–113.

14. José de Acosta, *De temporibus novissimis libri quatuor* (Rome: Giuseppe Tornerio, 1590), 2.11 ("De quodam insanissimae superbiae exemplo, digressio"), pp. 54–56. On Acosta (ca. 1539–1600), see Prosperi, "L'elemento storico," pp. 107–108, 113; and Prosperi, "America e Apocalisse: Note sulla 'conquista spirituale' del Nuovo Mondo," *Critica storica*, 13 (1976), pp. 1–61.

15. Martin Antoine Del Rio, *Disquisitionum magicarum libri sex* (Venice: Vincenzo Florini, 1616), pp. 503–504. The first edition of this work appeared in 1599–1600.

16. Diego de Simancas, *De catholicis institutionibus ad praecaudendas et extirpandas haereses admodum necessarius,* 3d ed. (Rome: In aedibus Populi Romani, 1575), pp. 148–149.

17. On Benincasa, see *Dizionario biografico degli Italiani,* s.v. "Benincasa, Orsola," by Silvana Menchi, 8:528–530; and Jean-Michel Sallmann, "La sainteté mystique féminine à Naples au tournant des XVIe e XVIIe siècles," in Boesch Gajano and Sebastiani, *Culto dei santi,* pp. 684–687. Although the president of the nine-member commission was Cardinal Giulio Antonio Santoro, head of the Congregation of the Holy Office, Sallmann is mistaken in calling it "certainly a tribunal of the Holy Office of the Roman Inquisition" (p. 685).

18. Giovanni Romeo, "Una 'simulatrice di santita' a Napoli nel '500: Alfonsina Rispola," *Campania sacra,* 8–9 (1977–78), pp. 159–218.

19. On this case, see Luigi Amabile, *Il Santo Officio della Inquisizione in Napoli* (Città di Castello: S. Lapi, 1892; repr., Soveria Mannelli: Rubbettino, 1987), 2:22–30; *Dizionario biografico degli Italiani,* s.v. "Di Marco, Giulia," by Jean-Michel Sallmann, 40:78–81.

20. Giovanni Romeo, *Inquisitori, esorcisti e streghe nell'Italia della Controriforma* (Florence: Sansoni, 1993), chaps. 1–3, 8 (pp. 3–108, 247–274); quoted phrase on p. 54.

21. On Carena, see Gabriele Cornaggia Medici, "Cesare Carena, giurista cremonese del secolo XVII," *Archivio storico lombardo,* 6th ser., 57 (1930), pp. 297–330.

22. Cesare Carena, *Tractatus de modo procedendi in causis Sancti Officii* (Cremona: Marc'Antonio Belpieri, 1636), pp. 371–372.

23. On Scaglia, see John Tedeschi, "The Roman Inquisition and Witchcraft: An Early Seventeenth-Century 'Instruction' on Correct Trial Procedure" and "The Question of Magic and Witchcraft in Two Inquisitorial Manuals of the Seventeenth Century," in *The Prosecution of Heresy: Collected Studies on the Inquisition in Early Modern Italy* (Binghamton, N.Y.: Medieval and Renaissance Texts and Studies, 1991), pp. 205–227, 229–258. Fifty years later, Giovanni Battista Neri issued under his own name a pirated edition, *De iudice S. Inquisitionis opusculum* (Florence, 1685), to which he added a chapter on tobacco. Tedeschi, *Prosecution of Heresy,* p. 244n, pp. 259–272.

24. Albano Biondi, "L''inordinata devozione' nella *Prattica* del Cardinale Scaglia

(ca. 1635)," in Gabrielle Zarri, ed., *Finzione e santità tra medioevo ed età moderna* (Turin: Rosenberg e Sellier, 1991), pp. 306–325.

25. Venice, Archivio di Stato, Sant'Ufficio, busta 112, trial of Antonia Pesenti and Francesco Vincenzi.

26. Emmanuele Antonio Cicogna, *Delle inscrizioni veneziane,* vol. 5 (Venice, 1842), pp. 156, 256.

27. Giovanni Bonifacio Bagatta, *Vita della serva di Dio Madre Angela Maria Pasqualiga nobile venetiana, institutrice delle Vergini regolari di Giesù e Maria* (Venice: Giovanni Francesco Valvasense, 1680).

28. Two influential and conflicting treatments of religious inedia are Rudolph M. Bell, *Holy Anorexia* (Chicago and London: University of Chicago Press, 1985); and Caroline Walker Bynum, *Holy Feast and Holy Fast: The Religious Significance of Food to Medieval Women* (Berkeley: University of California Press, 1987).

29. On this figure, see Anne Jacobson Schutte, "Tra Scilla e Cariddi: Giorgio Polacco, donne e disciplina nella Venezia del Seicento," in Gabriella Zarri, ed., *Donna, disciplina, creanza cristiana dal XV al XVII secolo: studi e testi a stampa* (Rome: Edizioni di Storia e Letteratura, 1996), pp. 215–236 (English version: "Discernment and Discipline: Giorgio Polacco and Religious Women in Early Modern Italy," in William J. Connell, ed., *Culture and Self in Renaissance Europe* [Berkeley: University of California Press, forthcoming]).

30. Bagatta, *Pasqualiga,* pp. 73–76.

31. On this "false saint," see Anne Jacobson Schutte, "'Questo non è il ritratto che ho fatto io': Painters, the Inquisition, and the Shape of Sanctity in Seventeenth-Century Venice," in Peter Denley and Caroline Elam, eds., *Florence and Italy: Studies in Honour of Nicolai Rubinstein* (London: Westfield College, 1988), pp. 419–431; Schutte, "Inquisition and Female Autobiography: The Case of Cecilia Ferrazzi," in Craig Monson, ed., *The Crannied Wall: Women, Religion, and the Arts in Early Modern Europe* (Ann Arbor: University of Michigan Press, 1992), pp. 105–118; and Cecilia Ferrazzi, *Autobiography of an Aspiring Saint,* ed. Anne Jacobson Schutte (Chicago: University of Chicago Press, 1996).

32. Bagatta, *Pasqualiga,* pp. 76–80.

33. Fulvio Tomizza, *Heavenly Supper: The Story of Maria Janis,* trans. Anne Jacobson Schutte (Chicago and London: University of Chicago Press, 1991), p. 146.

34. Pérez, *Avvertimenti spirituali* (Florence: Filippo Giunti, 1592), pp. 567–568.

35. On this point, see Tomizza, *Heavenly Supper,* p. 104, and Anne Jacobson Schutte, *"Per speculum in enigmate:* Failed Saints, Artists, and Self-Construction of the Female Body in Early Modern Italy," in John Coakley and E. Ann Matter, eds., *Creative Women in Medieval and Renaissance Italy* (Philadelphia: University of Pennsylvania Press, 1994), pp. 188–200.

9. Models of Female Sanctity in Renaissance and Counter-Reformation Italy

1. On the Council of Trent and the more general impact of the Counter-Reformation on religious iconography, see Enrico Cattaneo, *Arte e liturgia dalle origini*

al Vaticano II (Milano: Università Cattolica del Sacro Cuore, 1982), chap. 6 (esp. the text of the Tridentine decree of 1563, pp. 170–174); Emile Male, *L'art religieux après le Concile de Trente* (Paris: Armand Colin, 1932); and Paolo Prodi, *Ricerca sulla teorica delle arti figurative nella Riforma Cattolica* (Bologna: Nuova Alfa Editoriale, 1984).

2. On the orthodox and less orthodox uses and perception of sacred art, see Peter Burke, *The Italian Renaissance: Culture and Society in Italy* (Princeton, N.J.: Princeton University Press, 1986), chap. 5, "The Uses of Works of Art: Religion and Magic," pp. 124–130; David Freedberg, *The Power of Images: Studies in the History and Theory of Response* (Chicago and London: University of Chicago Press, 1989), chap. 11, "Live Images," pp. 283–344; Pieroberto Scaramella, *Le Madonne del Purgatorio: iconografiae religione in Campania tra rinascimento e controriforma* (Genoa: Casa Editrice Marietti, 1991), chap. 4, "Il potere dell'immagine sacra," and chap. 5, "L'immagine devota: declino delle immagini miracolose ed emmergenza di nuovi modelli devozionali"; and Richard Trexler, "Florentine Religious Experience: The Sacred Image," in *Church and Community, 1200–1600: Studies in the History of Florence and New Spain* (Rome: Edizioni di Storia e Letteratura 168, 1987), pp. 37–74.

3. Pamela Askew, *Caravaggio's Death of the Virgin* (Princeton, N.J.: Princeton University Press, 1990), pp. 13–83.

4. Ibid., p. 32.

5. The major work on the cult and iconography of the Virgin Mary remains that of Marina Warner, *Alone of All Her Sex: The Myth and the Cult of the Virgin Mary* (New York: Vintage Books, 1983).

6. For example, the Annunciation painted by Ludovico Carracci (ca. 1583–84) now in the Pinacoteca of Bologna.

7. For example, the Annunciation painted by Guido Reni (1620–21) in the Church of San Pietro in Valle, Fano.

8. The Assumption and Coronation of the Virgin Mary are an important theme in "official" post-Tridentine art. See Else Staedel, *Ikonographie der Himmelfahrt Mariens* (Strasbourg: Heitz, 1935); and Elaine G. Tulanowski, *The Iconography of the Assumption of the Virgin in Italian Paintings: 1480–1580* (Ph.D. diss., Ohio State University 1986) (Ann Arbor, Mich.: University Microfilms International, 1986).

9. Pamela Sheingorn, "Appropriating the Holy Kinship: Gender and Family History," in Kathleen Ashley and Pamela Sheingorn, eds., *Interpreting Cultural Symbols: Saint Anne in Late Medieval Society* (Athens: University of Georgia Press, 1990), pp. 169–198. On medieval and Renaissance concern for lineage, see, for example, Marzio Barbagli, *Sotto lo stesso tetto: mutamenti della famiglia in Italia dal XV al XX secolo* (Bologna: Il Mulino, 1988); David Herlihy, *Medieval Households* (Cambridge, Mass.: Harvard University Press, 1985); Christiane Klapisch-Zuber, "Les généologies florentines du XIVe et du XVe siècle," in *Le modèle familial européen: normes, déviances, contrôle du pouvoir* (Rome: Ecole française de Rome, 1986); and Christiane Klapisch-Zuber, *Women, the Family, and Ritual in Renaissance Italy* (Chicago: University of Chicago Press, 1985).

10. Ton Brandenbarg, "St. Anne and Her Family: The Veneration of St. Anne in Connection with Concepts of Marriage and the Family in the Early-Modern Period," in Lène Dresen-Coenders, ed., *Saints and She-Devils: Images of Women in the 15th and 16th Centuries* (London: Rubicon Press, 1987), pp. 101–129; and Sheingorn, "Holy Kinship."

11. Freedberg, *Power of Images,* chap. 1, "The Power of Images: Response and Repression," pp. 1–26.

12. For example, a charming painting by a follower of Caravaggio now in the Galleria Borghese of Rome.

13. On the role of domestic art in maternal imprinting, see Jacqueline Marie Musacchio, "Imaginative Conceptions in Renaissance Italy," in Sara Matthews Grieco and Geraldine Johnson, eds., *Picturing Women in Renaissance and Baroque Italy* (Cambridge: Cambridge University Press, 1997).

14. On tabernacles of the Madonna in fifteenth- and sixteenth-century domestic interiors, see Ronald G. Kecks *Madonna und Kind: Das haüsliche Andachts bild in Florenz des 15. Jahrhunderts* (Berlin: Gebr. Mann Verlag, 1988); and Peter Thornton, *The Italian Renaissance Interior (1400–1600)* (London: Weidenfeld and Nicolson, 1991).

15. On the the ideology of Christian motherhood, see Clarissa W. Atkinson, "Your Servant, My Mother: The Figure of Saint Monica in the Ideology of Christian Motherhood," in Clarissa W. Atkinson, Constance H. Buchanan, and Margaret R. Miles, eds., *Immaculate and Powerful: The Female in Sacred Image and Social Reality* (Boston: Beacon Press, 1985), pp. 139–172. On the lactating Madonna as a model for Renaissance mothers, see Megan Holmes, "Disrobing the Virgin: The 'Madonna Lactans" in Fifteenth-century Florentine Art," in Sara Matthews Grieco and Geraldine Johnson, eds., *Picturing Women in Renaissance and Baroque Italy* (Cambridge: Cambridge University Press, 1997). On the natalist imperative of the fifteenth through seventeenth centuries, see Sara Matthews Grieco, "Breastfeeding, Wet Nursing, and Infant Mortality in Europe (1400–1800)," in *Historical Perspectives on Breastfeeding: Two Essays by Sara F. Matthews Grieco and Carlo A. Corsini* (Florence: Istituto degli Innocenti/Unicef International Child Development Center, 1991).

16. See Musacchio, "Imaginative Conceptions," and Klapisch-Zuber, *Women, the Family, and Ritual,* chap. 14, "Holy Dolls: Play and Piety in Florence in the Quattrocento," pp. 310–330.

17. On ex-votos from the fifteenth through the seventeenth centuries, see Salvatore Abita, Lucia Bellodi Casanova, Luigi Lombardi Satirani, and Antonio Niero, *Immagini di devozione popolare: ex-voto del Santuario napoletano della Madonna dell'Arco e del litorale veneziano, secoli XVI–XIX* (Venice: Fondazione Querini Stampalia, 1982); Antonio Ermanno Giardino, and Michele Rak, *Per Grazia Ricevuta: le tavolette dipinte ex voto per la Madonna dell'Arco, il cinquecento* (Naples, 1983); Maria Pia Mannini, ed., *Immagini di devozione: ceramiche votive nell'area fiorentina dal XVI al XIX secolo* (Florence: Electa Editore, 1981); P. Toschi and R. Penna, *Le tavolette votive della Madonna dell'Arco a Napoli* (Naples: Del Mauro Ed., 1971).

18. See Luisa Accati, "Simboli maschili e simboli femminili nelle devozione alla

Madonna della Contyroriforma," in Elisja Schulte van Kessel, ed., *Women and Men in Spiritual Culture, XIV–XVII Centuries* (The Hague: Netherlands Government Publication Office, 1986), pp. 35–46, on the role of intercessor adopted by women in sixteenth- and seventeenth-century Italy.

19. On popular religious prints and their use, see, for example, Lorenzo Baldacchini, *Bibliografia delle stampe popolari religiose del XVI–XVII secolo: Biblioteche Vaticana, Alessandrina, Estense* (Florence: Olschki Editore, 1980); Giuseppina Benassati and Antonio Savoli, eds., *Incisori Faentini di immagini mariane dei secoli XVI–XIX in fogli sciolti da collezioni private: catalogo della Mostra a Faenza, 7–9 maggio 1988* (Faenza, Biblioteca Card. G. Cicognani, 1988); David Kunzle, *The Early Comic Strip. Narrative Strips and Picture Stories in the European Broadsheet from c. 1450 to 1825*, vol. 1 (Berkeley: University of California Press, 1973); and Alberto Vecchi, *Il culto delle immagini nelle stampe popolari* (Florence: Leo S. Olschki Editore, 1968).

20. The most important publications on the Magdalene remain those of Susan Haskins, *Mary Magdalen: Truth and Untruth in the Making of a Christian Icon* (London: Harper Collins, 1993), and Marilena Mosco, *La Maddalena tra sacro e profano: catalogo della mostra a Palazzo Pitti, Firenze, 24 maggio–7 settembre 1986* (Florence: La Casa Uscher, and Milan: A. Mondadori Editore, 1986). On the cult and iconography of specific saints, consult George Kaftal, *Iconography of the Saints*, 4 vols. (Florence: Casa Ed. Sansoni, 1952–1985); Louis Reau, *Iconographie de l'art chrétien*, vol. 3, *L'iconographie des saints* (Paris, Presses Universitaires de France, 1958); the *Bibliotheca sanctorum*, 13 vols. (Rome, 1961—1970); and the *Enciclopedia Cattolica*, 12 vols. (Florence: Casa Editrice Sansoni, 1948–1954).

21. On the fifteenth-century Magdalene in Tuscany, see Sarah Wilk, "The Cult of Mary Magdalen in Fifteenth Century Florence and Its Iconography," *Studi medievali*, 3d ser., Anno year 26, fasc. 2 (1985), pp. 685–698.

22. Dated 1455, now in the Museo dell'Opera del Duomo, Florence.

23. This was the opinion of Saint Antonino, for example (see Wilk, "The Cult of Mary Magdalen").

24. Anne-Christine Junkerman, *"Bellissima Donna": An Interdisciplinary Study of Venetian Sensuous Half-Length Images of the Early Sixteenth-Century* (Ph.D. diss., University of California at Berkeley, 1988) (Ann Arbor, Mich.: University Microfilms, 1989), pp. 409–411.

25. On the obligation of ostentatious consumption for women of the aristocracy, see Junkerman, *"Bellissima Donna,"* part 2, "Women as Image in Sixteenth Century Venice"; and Diane Owen Hughes, "Sumptuary Law and Social Relations in Renaissance Italy," in John Bossy, ed., *Disputes and Settlements: Law and Human Relations in the West* (Cambridge: Cambridge University Press, 1983), pp. 69–100.

26. This was the case, for example, with Vittoria Colonna, Isabella d'Este, and Maria Maddalena d'Austria, wife of Cosimo II (see Mosco, *La Maddalena tra sacro e profano*).

27. Junkerman, *"Bellissima Donna,"* p. 421. On these refuges for women, see Sherill Cohen, "Asylums for Women in Counter-Reformation Italy," in Sherrin Marshall, ed., *Women in Reformation and Counter-Reformation Europe* (Bloom-

ington: University of Indiana Press, 1989), pp. 120–139; Cohen, "Convertite e malmaritate: donne 'irregolari' e ordini religiosi nella Firenze rinascimentale," *Memoria: rivista di storia delle donne,* 5 (1982), pp. 46–63; Cohen, *The Evolution of Women's Asylums since 1500: From Refuges for Ex-Prostitutes to Shelters for Battered Women* (Oxford: Oxford University Press, 1992); and Lucia Ferrante, 'L'Onore ritrovato: donne nella casa di soccorso di S. Paolo a Bologna (sec. XVI–XVII)," *Quaderni storici* 53 (1983), pp. 499–527.

28. Deposito di Palazzo Pitti, Florence. Reproduced in Mosco, *La Maddalena tra sacro e profano,* p. 171.

29. On this sort of *memento mori* before and after Trent, see Scaramello, *Le Madonne del Purgatorio,* "Il Purgatorio ed il gusto macabro," pp. 234–246.

30. Gabriella Zarri, ed., *Finzione e santità tra medioevo e età moderna* (Turin: Rosenberg e Sellier, 1991), *passim.* Judith C. Brown's well-known book on a "lesbian nun," *Immodest Acts: The Life of a Lesbian Nun in Renaissance Italy* (New York and Oxford: Oxford University Press, 1986), is based on trial records dealing with the issue of false sanctity.

31. See Rudolph M. Bell, *Holy Anorexia* (Chicago: University of Chicago Press, 1985), on the phenomenon of "holy anorexia."

32. The most authoritative studies of the cult and iconography of Saint Catherine of Siena are the Avignon catalog *Catherine de Sienne: catalogue de l'exposition au Musée du Palais des Papes* (Avignon, 1992), and the impressive catalog edited by Lidia Bianchi and Diega Giunta, *Iconografia di S. Caterina di Siena,* vol. 1, *L'immagine* (Rome: Città Nuova Editore, 1988).

33. Bianchi and Giunta, *Iconografia,* pp. 68–69.

34. On the fashioning of Catherine as a saintly *claris mulieribus,* see Sofia Boesch Gajano and Odile Redon, "La *Legenda Maior* di Raimondo da Capua, costruzione di una santa," in Domenico Maffei and Paolo Nardi, eds., *Atti del Simposio Internazionale Cateriniano-Bernardiniano, Siena 17–20 Aprile 1980* (Siena: Accademia Senese degli Intronati, 1982), pp. 15–36; and Antonio Volpato, "Tra sante profetesse e santi dottori: Caterina da Siena," in Elisja Schulte Van Kessel, *Women and Men in Spiritual Culture, XIV–XVII Centuries: A Meeting of South and North* (The Hague: Netherlands Government Publications Office, 1986), pp. 149–162.

35. Gabriella Zarri, *Le sante vive: cultura e religiosità femminile nella prima età moderna* (Turin: Rosenberg e Sellier, 1990).

36. On the diversification in male and female modes of sanctity, see Adriano Prosperi, "Dalle 'divine madri' ai 'padri spirituali,'" in Elisja Schulte Van Kessel, *Women and Men in Spiritual Culture, XIV–XVII Centuries: A Meeting of South and North* (The Hague: Netherlands Government Publications Office, 1986), pp. 71–92; and Donale Weinstein and Rudolph M. Bell, *Saints and Society: Christendom, 1000–1700* (Chicago: University of Chicago Press, 1982), chap. 8, "Men and Women," pp. 220–228.

37. Gabriella Zarri, "Ursula and Catherine: The Marriage of Virgins in the Sixteenth Century," in John Croakley and E. Ann Matter, eds., *Creative Women in Medieval and Early Modern Italy: A Religious and Artistic Renaissance* (Philadelphia: University of Pennsylvania Press, 1994), pp. 237–278.

38. The entire series of sketches is reproduced in Piero Pacini, "Contributi per

l'iconografia di Santa Maria Maddalena de'Pazzi; una 'vita' inedita di Francesco Curradi," *Mitteilungen des Kunsthistorisches Institutes in Florenz,* 28 (1984), pp. 279–350.

39. On post-Tridentine models of sanctity, see Sofia Boesch Gajano, ed., *Raccolte di Vite di Santi dal XIII al XVIII secolo: strutture, messaggi, fruizioni,* (Brindisi and Rome: Schena Editore, 1990); chap. 5, "How to Be a Counter-Reformation Saint," pp. 48–62; and Jean-Michel Sallmann, "Il santo e le rappresentazioni della santità: problemi di metodo," *Quaderni Storici,* 41 (1979), pp. 584–602.

40. On the erasure of Maria Maddalena's political persona, see Karen-edis Barzman, "Devotion and Desire: The Reliquary Chapel of Maria Maddalena de' Pazzi," *Art History,* 15, no. 2, (1992), pp. 171–196.

41. For documentation on this cycle, see Piero Pacini, "I 'Depositi' di Santa Maria Maddalena de'Pazzi e la diffusione delle sue immagini (1607–1668)," *Mitteilungen des Kunsthistorisches Institutes in Florenz,* 32 (1988), pp. 173–252.

42. For example, the iconographic program for Pazzi's beatification in 1626, described in ibid.

43. As Elissa Weaver also points out with respect to convent theater; see "Spiritual Fun: A Study of Sixteenth-Century Tuscan Convent Theatre," in Mary Beth Rose, ed., *Women in the Middle Ages and the Renaissance: Literary and Historical Perspectives* (Syracuse, N.Y.: Syracuse University Press, 1986), pp. 173–206.

44. On women's cultural identification with the body and food, see Caroline Walker Bynum, *Fragmentation and Redemption: Essays on Gender and the Human Body in Medieval Religion* (New York: Zone Books, 1991); and Bynum, *Holy Feast and Holy Fast: The Religious Significance of Food to Medieval Women* (Berkeley: University of California Press, 1987).

45. For another example of this sort of self-fashioning, see E. Ann Matter, "The Personal and the Paradigm: The Book of Maria Domitilla Galluzzi" in Craig A. Monson, ed., *The Crannied Wall: Women, Religion, and the Arts in Early Modern Europe* (Ann Arbor: University of Michigan Press, 1992), pp. 87–104.

46. Over and above Zarri, *Finzione e santità,* see Luisa Ciammitti, "Una santa di meno: storia di Angela Mellini, cucitrice bolognese (1667–17..)," *Quaderni storici,* 41 (1979), pp. 603–639; and Anne Jacobsen Schutte, "Inquisition and Female Autobiography: The Case of Cecilia Ferrazzi" in Craig A. Monson, ed., *The Crannied Wall: Women, Religion, and the Arts in Early Modern Europe* (Ann Arbor: University of Michigan Press, 1992), pp. 105–118.

10. From the Late Baroque Mystical Explosion to the Social Apostolate, 1650–1850

1. Michele Scherillo, ed., *Manzoni intimo,* vol. 1, *Vittoria e Matilde Manzoni: Memorie di Vittoria Giorgini Manzoni* (Milan: U. Hoepli, 1923), p. 113; repr., Matilde Manzoni, *Journal,* ed. Cesare Garboli (Milan: Adelphi, 1992), p. 133.

2. Compare Giuseppe Dalla Torre, "Processo di beatificazione e canonizzazione," in *Enciclopedia del diritto* (Milan: Giuffre, 1958–1995), vol. 36, p. 935; and Dalla Torre, "Santità ed economia processuale: l'esperienza giuridica da Urbano VIII a Benedetto XIV," in Gabriela Zarri, ed., *Finzione e santità, tra medioeve ed età moderna* (Turin: Rosenberg e Sellier, 1991), pp. 231–263.

3. Giulio Battelli, "Santa Sede e vescovi nello Stato unitario: dal secondo otto-cento ai primi anni della Repubblica," in Giorgio Chittolini and Giovanni Mic-coli, eds., *Le Chiesa e il potere politico dal Medioevo all'età contemporanea* (Turin: G. Einaudi, 1986), pp. 809–810.

4. For Naples, see Carla Russo, *I monasteri femminile di clausura a Napoli nel secolo XVIII* (Naples, 1970), pp. 40ff.; for Rome, see Luigi Fiorani, "Monache e monasteri romani all'età del quietismo," in *Richerche per la storia religiosa di Roma,* vol. 1 (Rome: Edizione di storia e letteratura, 1977), pp. 63–111.

5. The two canonizations were those of Maria Maddalena de' Pazzi (1669) and Rose of Lima (1671).

6. Mario Rosa, "La religiosa," in Rosario Villari, ed., *Baroque Personae* (Chicago: University of Chicago Press, 1995). Translation of *L'uomo barocco* (Rome: Laterza, 1991), pp. 219–267. See pp. 227 and 241ff.

7. Compare Gabriella Zarri, *Le sante vive: cultura e religiosità femminile nella prima età moderna* (Turin: Rosenberg e Sellier, 1990), pp. 129ff, and Zarri, "'Vera' santità, 'simulata' santità," in *Finzione e santità*, pp. 9–17; Romeo De Maio, "L'ideale eroico nei processi di canonnizzazione della Controriforma," in De Maio, *Riformi e miti nella Chiesa del cinquecento,* 2d ed. (Naples: Guida, 1992), pp. 257–278.

8. On Giuliani and Martinengo, see Giovanni Pozzi and Claudio Leonardi, eds., *Scrittrici mistiche italiane* (Genoa: Marietti, 1988), pp. 505–542, 552–563; and Rosa, "La religiosa," pp. 256–261.

9. For devotion to the Sacred Heart, see Mario Rosa, "Regalità e 'douceur' nell'Europa del settecento: la contrasta devozione al Sacro Cuore," in Francesco Traniello, ed., *Dai Quaccheri a Gandhi: studi di storia religiosa in onore di Ettore Passerin d'Entrèves* (Bologna: Il Mulino, 1988), pp. 71–98. On Marian devo-tion in this period, see Marina Warner, *Alone of All Her Sex: The Myth and Cult of the Virgin Mary* (New York: Random House, 1976).

10. Francesca Medioli, *"L'Inferno monacale" di Arcangela Tarabotti* (Turin: Rosen-berg e Sellier, 1990).

11. On the "little child" as regards Maria Crocifissa Tomasi, see Sara Cabibbo and Marilena Modica Vasta, *La santa dei Tomasi: storia di suor Maria Crocifissa (1645–1699)* (Turin: G. Einaudi, 1989), pp. 133ff. The analagous experiences of M. A. Biondini and Martinengo are described in Pozzi and Leonardi, *Scrit-trici mistiche,* pp. 495 and 558–559. For the new perception of childhood, the basic text remains Philippe Ariès, *Centuries of Childhood: A Social History of Family Life* (New York: Vintage, 1962), trans. R. Baldick of *L'enfant et la vie familiale sous l'Ancien Régime* (Paris: Plon, 1960).

12. On Tomasi, who came from a recently ennobled family, see Cabibbo and Modica Vasta, *La santa dei Tomasi;* compare Marie Antoinette Visceglia, "San-tità e strategie nobiliari: i Tomasi," *Quaderni storici,* 76 (1991), pp. 285–293.

13. On culture and writing in seventeenth-century convents, see Sara Cabibbo, "La capra, il sale e il sacco: per uno studio della vedovanza femminile tra cinque e seicento," *Archivio storico per la Sicilia Orientale,* 85, fasc. 1–3, pp. 117–167. On mystical culture, see Pozzi and Leonardi, *Scrittrici mistiche.* On the spread of Quietist books in Roman convents, see Fiorani, "Monache e monasteri," pp. 63–111. For the relationship between religious experience and women's

writing, compare Marilena Modica Vasta, ed., *Esperienza religiosa e scritture femminile tra medioevo ed età moderna* (Acireale, 1992) and her essay in the present volume. See also, G. Calvi, *Barocco al femminile*, 1992.

14. Ignazio Orsolini, *Vita della Venerabil Madre suor Chiara Maria della Passione Carmelita Scalza, fondatrice del Monastero di Regina Coeli di Roma, nel secolo Donna Vittoria Colonna, figlia di Don Filippo Gran Conestabile del Regno di Napoli . . .* (Rome: Francesco Gonzaga, 1708), p. 68. For Clare, see Fiorani, "Monache e monasteri," pp. 94–98.

15. On these aspects, see Gabriella Zarri, "Monasteri femminili e città (secoli XV–XVIII)," in G. Chittolini and G. Miccoli, eds., *Storia d'Italia, annali IX: la Chiesa e il potere politico dal Medioevo all'età contemporanea* (Turin: G. Einaudi, 1986), pp. 415 and 420, and Fiorani, "Monache e monasteri," p. 82.

16. On the Pelagini sect and her "theologesse," see Gianvittorio Signorotto, *Inquisitori e mistici nel seicento italiano: l'eresia di Santa Pelagia* (Bologna: Il Mulino, 1989). On female Quietist groups, see Massimo Petrocchi, *Il quietismo italiano del seicento* (Rome: Edizione di Storia e letteratura, 1948), pp. 107ff. and 178–192; also R. Guarnieri, "Pinzochere," in *Dizionario degli istituti di perfezione*, vol. 6 (Rome, 1980), cols. 1721–1749.

17. See the various contributions in Gabriella Zarri, ed., *Finzione e santità tra medioeve ed età moderna* (Turin: Rosenberg e Sellier, 1991). On "feigned" sanctity, see Anne Jacobson Schutte in this volume, and Cecilia Ferrazzi: *Autobiography of an Aspiring Saint*, ed. Schutte (Chicago: University of Chicago Press, 1996).

18. Rosario Villari, *Elogio della dissimulazione: la lotta politica nel seicento* (Rome and Bari: Laterza, 1987), pp. 25ff.

19. E. Novi Chavarria, "Ideologia a comportamenti familiari nei predicatori italiani tra cinque e settecento: tematiche e modelli," *Rivista storica italiana*, 100, no. 3 (1988), pp. 679–773, esp. p. 692.

20. Jean-Louis Flandrin, *Families in Former Times: Kinship, Household, and Sexuality* (New York: Cambridge University Press, 1979).

21. Chavarria, "Ideologia e comportamenti," p. 684.

22. Zarri, "'Vera' santità," pp. 28–29.

23. On the relationship between money and religiosity, see Marilena Modica Vasta, "La santità femminile nelle 'Vitae sanctorum Siculorum' di Ottavio Gaetani," in Sofia Boesch Gajano, ed., *Raccolte di vite dei santi dal XIII al XVIII secolo: strutture, messaggi, fruizioni* (Brindisi: Schena, 1990), pp. 208–209.

24. Carlo Bartolomeo Piazza, *Cherosilogio overo Discorso dello stato vedovile spiegato con le Memorie illustri di S, Galla Patrizia Vedova Romana . . .* (Rome: Stamperia del Bernabò, 1708), pp. 191 and 195. On widowhood in the modern period, see S. Cabibbo, "La Capra, il sale e il sacco" and "Modelli culturali, modelli istituzionali. Marcella romana, vedova, nell'età della Controriforma," in G. Barone, M. Caffiero, and F. Scorza Barcellona, eds., *Modelli di comportamento, modelli di santità: intersezioni, complementarietà* (Turin: 1994).

25. On the way in which the cult of Ludovica was built up by the patrician Albertoni and Altieri families to whom she was related, see Laurie Nussdorfer, *Civic Politics in the Rome of Urban VIII* (Princeton, N.J.: Princeton University Press, 1992), pp. 169–171.

26. Chavarria, "Ideologia e comportamenti," p. 693; Cabibbo, "La Capra," p. 148.

27. Piazza, *Cherosilogio,* p. 225.

28. Rome, 1734–1738. On Lambertini's work, see Mario Rosa, "Prospero Lambertini tra 'regolata devozione' e mistica visionaria," in Zarri, *Finzione e santità,* pp. 521–550; and in the same volume, G. Dalla Torre, "Santità ed economia processuale: l'esperienza giuridica da Urbano VIII a Benedetto XIV," pp. 231–263.

29. [The Maurists were a French Benedictine congregation noted for their superior scholarship and scrupulous critical editions in patristics, ecclesiastic and monastic antiquities, and other works of erudition; the Bollandists were Belgian Jesuits, similarly erudite, but especially devoted to hagiography. Trans.]

30. Ludovico Antonio Muratori, *Della forza della fantasia umana* (Venice, 1745); repr. in G. Falcone and F. Forti, eds., *Opere di L. A. Muratori* (Milan: R. Ricciardi, 1964), p. 915.

31. On Alacoque, see Rosa, "Regalità e 'douceur'"; on Crescentia of Kaufbeuren, see François Boespflug, *Dio nell'arte: "Sollecitudini Nostrae" di Benedetto XIV (1745) e il caso di Crescenzia di Kaufbeuren* (1984), and Rosa, "Prospero Lambertini," pp. 532–534; on Maria de Agreda, see Sara Cabibbo, "'Ignorantia Scripturarum, ignorantia Christi est'; tradizione e pratica delle Scritture nei testi monastici femminili del XVII secolo," *Rivista storica italiana,* 101, no. 1 (1989), pp. 85–124, and Rosa, "Prospero Lambertini," pp. 536–545.

32. L. A. Muratori, *De superstitione vitanda sive censura voti sanguinarii* (Milan, 1740). After Muratori's death, Saint Alphonsus published *Le glorie di Maria* (1750).

33. Alberto Vecchi, *Correnti religiose nel sei-settecento veneto* (Venice and Rome, 1962), p. 202.

34. Compare Mario Rosa, "L''età muratoriana' nell'Italia del settecento," in Rosa, *Riformatori a ribelli nel settecente religioso italiano* (Bari: Dedalo, 1969), pp. 30–31.

35. [Alban Butler gives her date of death as 1346. Trans.]

36. Giuseppe Garampi, *Memorie ecclesiastiche appartenenti all'istoria e al culto della Beata Chiara di Rimini* (Rome: Pagliarini, 1755), p. 467.

37. Compare Anton Maria Bonucci, *Istoria dell'amirabile Vita della Beata Chiara degli Agolanti, Monaca del P. S. Francesco, e fondatrice del Monastero di S. Maria degli Angeli in Rimini . . .* (Rome: Rocco Bernabò, 1718). Maria de Agreda's *Mystica Ciudad de Dios* is called a "devout romance" by Muratori.

38. Carlo Ignazio Massini, *Vite di sante vergine e di alcuni ss. fondatrici di monasterj e congregazioni di religiose . . .* (Rome: Marco Pagliarini, 1768), p. x. I thank Stefania Nanni for having pointed out and obtained this book for me. On Massini and Jansenist hagiography, see Pietro Stella, "Giansenismo e agiografia in Italia tra settecento e ottocento," *Salesiasnum,* 42 (1980), pp. 835–853, and Stella, "Le 'Vies des saints' di A. Baillet: diffusione e recezione in area italiana," in Sofia Boesch Gajano, ed., *Raccolte di vite dei santi dal XIII al XVIII secolo: strutture, messaggi, fruizioni* (Brindisi: Schena, 1990), pp. 231–232.

39. On this new vision of the relations among married people, see C. Gentile, "La società coniugale nella trattatistica italiana del settecento: appunti per una ricerca," *Rivista di storia della Chiesa in Italia,* 40 (1986), pp. 92–102.

40. On the evolution of the model of the nun, see Rosa, "La religiosa," pp. 261–266.

41. ["Jurisdictionalism": a contemporary movement that sought to put Church administration under state control. Trans.]

42. On the Maestre Pie, see Giancarlo Rocca under the relevant entries in G. Rocca and Guerrino Pelliccia, eds., *Dizionario degli istituti di perfezione* (Rome, Edizioni paoline, 1974–), cols. 828–831 and 835–840; M. Rocca, *Una luce nella Chiesa. Santa Lucia Filippini (1672–1732) fondatrice delle Maestre Pie Filippini* (Rome: 1969); M. Caffiero, "Un santo per le donne: Benedetto Giuseppe Labre e la femminilizzazione del cattolicesimo tra settecento a ottocento," *Memoria*, 30, no. 3 (1990), pp. 89–106.

43. *Regole per le Maestre delle Scuole Pie dirette da' Padri Pii Operari approvate dalla Santità di N.S. Clemente Papa XIII* (Rome: Stamperia della R.C.A., 1760).

44. On this increase, see Zarri, "Monasteri femminili," pp. 403 and 423; Romana Guarnieri, under "Pinzochere" in *Dizionario degli istituti*, cols. 1735–1736. For Naples, see the essays in *La santa dei quartieri: aspetti della vita religiosa a Napoli nel settecento* (Naples: Centro studi storici della pontifica facolta teologica dell'Italia meridionale, 1991). On the tertiaries, see Jean-Marie Sallmann, "Eremitismo e Terzi Ordini dalla fine del secolo XV alla metà del secolo XIX," in Mario Rosa, ed., *Clero e società nell'Italia moderna* (Bari: Laterza, 1992).

45. On Maria Francesca of the Five Wounds (delle Cinque Piaghe) and the phenomenon of the *bizzoche* in eighteenth-century Naples, see *La santa dei quartieri*.

46. J. de la Viguerie, "La sainteté au XVIIIe siècle," in *Histoire et sainteté* (Angers: Publications du Centre de recherche d'histoire religieuse et d'histoire des idées, 1982), p. 121.

47. Basilio Petrà, "Quietismo a incredulità nel tardo settecento pratese," *Archivio storico Pratese*, 64 (1988); Giuseppe Orlandi, *Le fede al vaglio: quietismo, satanismo, e massoneria nel Ducato di Modena fra sette e ottocento* (Modena: Aedes Muratoriana, 1988); and Orlandi, "Vera e falsa santità in alcuni predicatori popolari e direttori di spirito del sei e settecento," in Zarri, *Finzione e santità*, pp. 435–463.

48. M. Caffiero, "Le profetesse di Valentano," in Zarri, *Finzione e santità*, pp. 493–517; Caffiero, *La nuova era: miti e profezie dell'Italia in Rivoluzione* (Genoa: Marietti, 1991).

49. On the exaltation of poverty and ignorance and their relationship with the world of women, see Caffiero, "Un santo per le donne." 1990.

50. Compare Sara Cabibbo's essay in the present volume.

51. The main *vita* of Francesca was dedicated to Vittorio Emmanuele, who sought her beatification. On Maria Clotilde, see L. Bottiglia, *Vita della venerabile Serve di Dio Maria Clotilde Adelaide Saveria di Francia Regina di Sardegna dedicataalla Santità di N. S. Papa Pio VIII* (Rome, 1816).

52. P. G. Camaiani, "La donna, la morte e il giovane Vittorio Emanuele," in Francesco Traniello, ed., *Dai Quaccheri a Gandhi: studi di storia religiosa in*

onore di Ettore Passerin d'Entrèves (Bologna: Il Mulino, 1988), pp. 151–179, esp. p. 166.

53. Compare M. L. Trebiliani, "Modello mariano e immagine della donna nell'esperienza educativa di Don Bosco nella cultura popolare," in Francesco Traniello, ed., *Don Bosco nella storia della cultura popolare* (Turin: Società editrice internazionale, 1987), pp. 187–207.

54. On this ambiguity, see Caffiero, "Un santo per le donne," pp. 103–104.

55. On Taigi, beatified in 1920, see the first biography: J.-F. O. Luquet, *Notizia sulla vita e sulle virtù dell'umile serva di Dio Anna Maria Antonietta Gesualda Taigi nata Giannetti . . .* (Rome: Tipografia della eredi Paternò, 1851).

56. Ibid, p. 72.

57. S. La Salvia, "L'invenzione di un culto. Santa Philomena da taumaturga a guerriera della fede," in Sofia Boesch Gajani and Lucia Sebastiani, eds., *Culto dei santi, istituzioni e classi sociali in età* preindustriale (L'Aquila and Rome: L. U. Japadre Editore, 1984), pp. 873–956.

58. [The Sanfedisti were members of the armed bands organized by Cardinal Ruffo at the end of the eighteenth century to fight against the radical Neapolitan republic: thus, by extension, they were members of the many "reactionary" sects that proliferated in Enlightenment Italy. Trans.]

59. On the model nineteenth-century Catholic woman, see Trebiliani, "Modello mariano"; M. De Giorgio, "Il modello cattolico," in G. Duby and M. Perrot, *Storia delle Donne in Occidente,* vol. 4, *L'ottocento,* ed. G. Fraisse and M. Perrot (Rome and Bari, 1991). On women's role as mediators in conflicts, see Luigi Accati, "Il padre naturale: tra simboli dominanti e categorie scientifiche," *Memoria,* 21 (1987), pp. 79–106; and Accati, "La sposa in prestito: soggetto collettivo, soggetto individuale e conflitto (1566–1759)," in Maura Palazzi and Anna Scattigno, eds., *Discutendo di storia: soggettività, ricerca, biografia* (Turin: Rosenberg e Sellier, 1990), pp. 77–101.

60. On the spread of popular seventeenth-century Marian devotion to the rosary, linked to the victory over the Turks at Lepanto, see Mario Rosa, *Religione e società nel Mezzogiorno tra cinque e settecento* (Bari: De Donato, 1976); Warner, *Alone of All Her Sex,* pp. 305–314.

61. Pietro Stella, "Per una storia del profetismo apocaliptico cattolico ottocentesco," *Rivista di storia e letteratura religiosa,* 4 (1968), p. 457; Thomas Albert Kselman, *Miracles and Prophecies in Nineteenth-Century France* (New Brunswick, N.J.: Rutgers University Press, 1983).

62. On the eschatological significance of the Marian cult, and especially the Immaculate Conception, see Warner, *Alone of All Her Sex,* pp. 258ff.; Paolo Apolito, *Il cielo in terra: costruzioni simboliche di un'apparizione mariana* (Bologna, 1992), pp. 153–168. On the role of the eschatological vision in the creation of new Marian religious congregations, see J. Coste, "Marie dans l'Eglise naissante et à la fin des temps," *Acta Societatis Mariae,* 27 (1959), pp. 418–451, and Coste, "Maristes et eschatologie," *Recherches et documents du Centre Thomas More,* 36 (1982), pp. 25–37; Jean Séguy, "Ordres religieux et Troisième Age du monde," *Recherches et documents du Centre Thomas More,* 29 (1981), pp. 1–15.

63. On the relationship between the Virgin and war, see Warner, *Alone of All Her Sex,* pp. 299–314; for a more recent period, see T. A. Kselman and Steven M. Avella, "Marian Piety and the Cold War in the United States," *Catholic Historical Review,* 72 (1986), pp. 403–424.

64. Claude Savart, "Cent ans après: les apparitions mariales en France au XIXe siècle, un ensemble?" *Revue d'histoire de la spiritualité,* 48, no. 190 (1972), pp. 205–220; Claude Langlois, "La conjonction miraculaire à la fin de la Restauration: migné, miracle oublié," *Revue d'histoire de la spiritualité,* 49 (1973), pp. 227–242. On miraculous apparitions in general, see Sylvie Barnay, *Les apparitions de la Vierge* (Paris: Cerf; and Montreal: Fides, 1992).

65. Pietro Stella, "I tempi e gli scritti che prepararono il 'mese di maggio' di Don Bosco," *Salesianum,* 14 (1958), pp. 648–693,

66. De Giorgio, *Il modello cattolico,* pp. 173–177; A. Scattigno, "Letture devote," in Ilaria Porciani, ed., *Le donne a scuola: l'educazione femminile nell'Italia dell'Ottocento* (Florence: Il Sedicesimo, 1987). Documentary and Iconographic Exhibition, Palazzo Publico of Siena, February 14–April 26, 1987.

67. Stella, "I tempi e gli scritti," pp. 664–665; Trebiliani, "Modello mariano," p. 197.

68. Claude Langlois, *Le catholicisme au féminin: les congrégations françaises à supérieure générale au XIXe siècle* (Paris: Cerf, 1984).

69. Cosimo Semeraro, *Restaurazione, Chiesa e società: la "seconda ricupera" e la rinascita degli ordini religiosi nello Stato pontifice (Marche e legazioni, 1815–1823)* (Rome: L.A.S., 1982), pp. 245–247. On Italian religious women's congregations in the early nineteenth century, see Giancarlo Rocca, "Le nuove fondazioni religiose femminili in Italia dal 1800 al 1860," in *Problemi di storia della Chiesa: dalla restaurazione all'unità d'Italia* (Naples: Edizioni Deohaniane, 1985), pp. 107–192; and Rocca, "Istituti religiosi in Italia tra otto e novecento," in *Clero e società nell'Italia contemporanea* (Rome and Bari: Laterza, 1992), pp. 207–256.

70. Rocca, "Le nuove fondazioni," p. 158; on superiors general, see pp. 152ff. For France, see Langlois, *Le catholicisme au féminin.*

11. Mystical Writing

1. This quotation, and the preceding one, are drawn from the anthology put together by Giovanni Pozzi and Claudio Leonardi, eds., *Scrittrici mistiche italiane* (Genoa: Marietti, 1988), p. 58. They come from the eighth chapter and the third soliloquy of Crostarosa's "Autobiography."

2. The literature on Quietism, as is known, is ample if somewhat dated. I will limit myself here to citing a few fundamental studies. On Molinos, see Paul Dudon, *Le quiétiste espagnol Michel Molinos (1628–1696)* (Paris: Gabriel Beauchesne, 1921); on Italian Quietism, see the classic text, Massimo Petrocchi, *Il quietismo italiano nel seicento* (Rome: Edizioni di storie e letteratura, 1948), and Romana Guarnieri, "Il quietismo in otto manoscritti chigiani," *Rivista di storia della Chiesa in Italia,* 5 (1951), pp. 381ff.; on the polemic between Bossuet and Fénelon, see Jacques Le Brun, *La spiritualité de Bossuet* (Paris: Klincksieck,

1972). An up-to-date and deeper analysis of Italian midcentury Quietism and the alarm it aroused in the ecclesiastical hierarchy can be found in Gianvittorio Signorotto, *Inquisitori e mistici nel seicento italiano: l'eresia di Santa Pelagia*, (Bologna: Il Mulino, 1989).

3. J. Favre, *Une grande mystique au XVIIIe siècle: la vénérable Maria Celeste Crostarosa* (Paris, 1936). See also, *Bibliotheca sanctorum*, 13 vols. (Rome, 1961–1970), vol. 4 (1964), cols. 378ff.; *Dizionario biografico degli italiani* (Rome: Istituto della Enciclopedia italiana, 1985), pp. 243ff.; *Dictionnaire de spiritualité ascétique et mystique, doctrine et histoire*, vol. 2 (Paris: G. Beauchesne, 1949), col. 2627.

4. The first systematic work on the language of eighteenth-century mysticism, seen as being in sharp conflict with contemporary culture, is Mino Bergamo, *La scienza dei santi: studi sul misticismo secentesco* (Florence: Sansoni, 1984).

5. Among the many works of the French scholar, see Michel de Certeau, "Crisi sociale e riformismo spirituale all'inizio del XVII secolo: una nuova spiritualità tra i gesuiti francesi," in *Politica e mistica* (Milan, 1975). See also, de Certeau, *The Mystic Fable* (Chicago: University of Chicago Press, 1992).

6. Henri de Lubac, *Exégèse médiévale: les quatre sens de l'ecriture* (Paris: Aubier, 1959–1964). There is a thorough reflection on the elaboration of mysticism in the Church fathers as related to the unfolding of eighteenth-century mystical language in Carlo Ossola, "Apoteosi ed ossimoro: retorica della 'traslazone' e retorica dell'"unione' nel viaggio mistico a Dio, Testi italiani dei secoli XVI–XVII," in Franco Bolgiani, ed., *Mistica e retorica: studi* (Florence: L. S. Olschki, 1977).

7. A general but scrupulous account of this process is to be found in Mario Rosa, "La religiosa," in Rosario Villari, ed., *L'uomo barocco* (Rome: Laterza, 1991); trans. *Baroque Personae* (Chicago: University of Chicago Press, 1995).

8. Besides the works of M. de Certeau and M. Bergamo previously cited, see Giovanni Pozzi, "Patire e non potere nel discorso dei santi," *Studi medievali, 26 (1985), pp. 1ff.*; M. Macola, *Il castello interiore: il percorso soggettivo nell'esperienza mistica di Giovanni della Croce e Teresa d'Avila* (Pordenone, 1987).

9. Bonaventure, "Itinerarum mentis in Deum," in *Opera Omnia*, vol. 5 (Florence, 1991), p. 298. See the English translation, *The Journey of the Mind to God* (Indianapolis: Hackett Publishing, 1993).

10. See Alvaro Huerga, "Un problema de la segunda escolastica: la oración mistica," *Angelicum*, 44 (1967), pp. 10ff.

11. For the centrality of the Spanish context in *dejamiento* mysticism, see the classic 1937 work of Maurice Bataillon, *Erasme at l'Espagne* (Geneva: Droz, 1991).

12. Manuscript report by Suor Maria Crocifissa della Concezione, dated February 15, 1677. Archive of the Monastery of the Most Holy Rosary in Palma Montechiaro, henceforth AMMHR.

13. Manuscript report of Tomasi, March 3, 1676, in AMMHR.

14. Tomasi, manuscript report, November 5, 1677, in AMMHR.

15. On the relationship between the female body and spirituality in seventeenth-century biographies, see Jacques Le Brun, "A corps perdu: les biographies

spirituelles féminines du XVIIe siècle," *Les temps de la réflexion*, 7 (1986), pp. 389ff.

16. Giovanni Bona, *De discretione spirituum in vita spirituali deducendorum* (Rome, 1872), p. 193.

17. The discernment of spirits *(discretio spirituum)* was a fundamental notion in mystical theology; it was a way of finding out the origin and the quality of the forces that were acting on the human will. This "discerning" was the decisive instrument through which directors of conscience were able to distinguish whether their penitents were inspired by God or by the Devil, or just by their own temperament. This theme has so far not received much historical attention, but see the recent work in Jean-Michel Sallman, ed., *Visions indiennes, visions baroques: les métissages de l'inconscient* (Paris: Presses universitaires de France, 1992). On "discerning" marked by Lambertini's reflection, as part of the long tradition of female ecstatic phenomena, see the careful analysis in Rosa, "La religiosa."

18. Francesco Maria Maggio, *Compendioso ragguaglio della vita, morte e monisteri della Madre Orsola Benincasa* (Naples, 1669), p. 186.

19. Marginal note by her confessor to a report of Tomasi's, June 1 and 2, 1673, AMMHR.

20. Bona, *De discretione,* p. 146.

21. Silvio Antoniano, *Tre libri dell'educatione christiana de i figlivoli* (Verona: Sebastiano delle Donne e Girolamo Stringari, 1584).

22. On monasteries as privileged places of learning, see G. Zarri, "Le istituzioni dell'educazione femminile," in G. Chittollini and G. Miccoli, eds., *Storia d'Italia: Annali IX, la Chiesa e il potere politco dal Medioevo all'età contemporanea* (Turin, 1986), pp. 357–429. On the creation of an exemplary monastic library in the post-Tridentine period, see Sara Cabibbo and Marilena Modica Vasta, *La Santa dei Tomasi: storia di suor Maria Crocifissa (1645–1699)* (Turin: G. Einaudi, 1989).

23. Alphonsus Liguori, letter to an unspecified religious community of nuns, 1731, in *Corrispondenza generale,* vol. 1 (Rome, 1887), p. 8.

24. On Angela Mellini, see Luisa Ciamitti, "Una santa di meno: storia di Angela Mellini, cucitrice bolognese," *Quaderni storici*, 41 (1979), pp. 603–679; and fragments of Mellini's diary in Pozzi and Leonardi, *Scrittrici mistiche,* pp. 554ff.

25. On this theme, see Gabriella Zarri, "'Vera' santità, 'simulata' santità," in Zarri, ed., *Finzione e santità tra medioevo ed età moderna* (Turin: Rosenberg e Sellier, 1991; A. Prosperi, "Dalle 'divine madri,'" in Elisja Schulte van Kessel, ed., *Women and Men in Spiritual Culture, XIV–XVII Centuries: A Meeting of North and South* (The Hague: Netherlands Government Publications Office, 1986).

26. In the long tradition of feminine writing, the Medieval mystic Hildegard of Bingen is the most significant example of divinely commanded writing. See Michele Pereira, "Profezia e scrittura in Ildegarda di Bingen," in Marilena Modica Vasta, ed., *Esperienza religiosa e scritture femminile tra medioeva ed età moderna* (Acireale, 1992), pp. 15ff.

27. On the debate over the works of the Spanish Franciscan nun, see J. Le Brun, *La*

spiritualité; Sara Cabibbo, "'Ignorantia Scripturarum, ignorantia Christi est': tradizione e pratica delle Scritture nei tesh monastici femminili del XVII secolo," *Rivista storica italiana,* 101, no. 1 (1989), pp. 85–124; and Rosa, "La religiosa."

28. Favre, *Une grande mystique,* p. 336.

29. Giovanni Batista Scaramelli, *Vita della ven. serva di Dio suor Maria Crocifissa Satellico: monaca francescana nel monastero di Monte Novo* (Venice, 1750), p. 338. New, corrected ed., Rome: Vincenzo Poggioli, 1819.

30. Ibid., p. 3.

31. On the mystical writings of Tomasi, see Cabibbo and Modica Vasta, *La santa dei Tomasi.*

32. Ample extracts from Giuliani's diary are given in Filippo Maria Salvatori, *Vita della beata Veronica Giuliani badessa delle cappuccine in S. Chiara di Città di Castello* (Rome, 1803), p. 189. On Giuliani, who was one of the most disturbing figures of seventeenth-century female mysticism, see also, *Canonizationis ven servae dei sororis Veronicae de Iulianis* (Rome, 1745). [Salvatori is widely considered an unsatisfactory source, but was translated into English in 1874. Her diary was edited in ten volumes by Father Pizzicaria and a wide selection is in Father Desiré des Planches, ed., *Le journal de Ste. Véronique Giuliani,* 1931, with medical comment by J. F. Gentili. See also Father L. Veuthey, *Vita Cristiana,* vol. 15, 1943, pp. 481–489 and 566–589. Trans.]

33. On Fornari, see Pozzi and Leonardi, *Scrittrici mistiche,* pp. 593ff. See also the relevant entry in *Bibliotheca sanctorum,* vol. 5 (1964), pp. 969ff. and in *Dictionnaire de spiritualité,* vol. 5, cols. 716ff.

34. See under the relevant entry in *Dictionnaire de la spiritualité,* vol. 1, 1937, col. 1192.

35. On Martinengo, see Pozzi and Leonardi, *Scrittrici mistiche,* pp. 552ff., and the relevant entry in *Bibliotheca sanctorum,* vol. 8 (1966), pp. 1223ff, and *Dictionnaire de spiritualité,* vol. 10, 1980, cols. 575ff.

36. It was in seventeenth-century mysticism and contemplation that the mechanisms of the soul were most profoundly analyzed. This analysis was characterized by the consolidation of the image of the soul as an interior, liberated space in which the mystic could meet the divine. As Mino Bergamo wrote, the seventeenth century represents the culmination of the "history of interiority, characterized by the opening up of interior, limitless space to a transcendental force field." On this subject, see the extremely close study of Mino Bergamo, *L'anatomia dell'anima: da François de Sales a Fénelon* (Bologna: Il Mulino, 1991).

37. Manuscript report, February 20, 1680, in AMMHR.

38. Scaramelli, *Vita,* p. 312.

39. An analysis of the soul's structure according to Saint Francis of Sales and his innovations within the Thomist tradition is in Bergamo, *L'anatomia dell'anima.*

40. Scaramelli, *Vita,* p. 291.

41. See Cabibbo and Modica Vasta, *La santa dei Tomasi.*

42. On Agnesi, see the entry on her in the *Dizionario Biografico degli italiani,*

1960, pp. 1141ff.; Maria Luisa Altieri Biagi and B. Basile, eds., *Scienziati del settecento* (Milan and Naples: Rizzoli, 1983); Pozzi and Leonardi, *Scrittrici mistiche,* pp. 610ff.

43. On Brenti, see the entry in the *Enciclopedia cattolica,* 12 vols. (Florence: Casa Editrice Sansoni, 1948–1954), vol. 3 (1949), pp. 447ff.; Pozzi and Leonardi, *Scrittrici mistiche,* pp. 623ff.

44. Pierre Roussel, *Système physique et moral de la femme, ou, Tableau philosophique de la constitution de l'état organique, du tempérament, des moeurs, et des fonctions propres au sexe* (Paris: Vincent, 1775).

45. M. L. Boré, *Les stigmatisées du Tyrol* (Paris, 1846). On the general theme of mortification in the monastic life of women in the nineteenth century, see O. Arnold, *Le corps et l'ame: la vie des religieuses au XIXe siècle* (Paris, 1984).

46. Jean Martin Charcot and Paul Marie Louis Richer, *Les démoniaques dans l'art* (Paris: Macula, 1984); original title: *Foi qui guerit.* See the Postface to the last edition of this work: G. Didi-Huberman, 1984.

12. Female Dynastic Sanctity, 1650–1850

1. Paolo Durio, *Vita della beata Ludovica di Savoia* (Rome, 1840), p. 6.

2. The *Vita di Ludovica di Savoia, scritta in francese da una monaca clarissa del Monastero di Orbe coetanea della Santa,* was preserved for centuries in the convent of Orbe and was translated and published in 1840. A biography of Louise included in an eighteenth-century collection of Lives of Savoyard saints makes no reference to the Poor Clare's manuscript and asserts that Louise probably spent no more than a year in the convent (Giuseppe Gallizia, *Atti dei santi che fiorirono nei domini della Real Casa di Savoia,* vol. 3 (Turin, 1757), pp. 346–361.

3. Robert Folz, "Les saints rois du moyen âge en Occident (VI–XIIe siècles)," *Subsidia hagiographica,* 68 (1984), p. 5.

4. Gabòr Klaniczay, "Il Monte di S. Gherardo e l'isola di S. Margherita a Buda nel Medio Evo," in Sofia Boesch Gajano and Lucetta Scaraffia, eds., *Luoghi sacri e spazi della santità* (Turin: Rosenberg e Sellier, 1990), p. 271. On dynastic sanctity in the Middle Ages, the period densest with historiographical interpretations, see also G. Klaniczay, *The Uses of Supernatural Power: The Transformation of Popular Religion in Medieval and Early-Modern Europe* (Cambridge: Polity, in association with Basil Blackwell, 1990); André Vauchez, "Beata stirps: sainteté et lignage en Occident aux XIIIe et XIVe siècles," in G. Duby and J. Le Goff, eds., *Famille et parenté dans l'Occident médiéval* (Rome, 1977); P. Corbet, *Les saints ottoniens, sainteté dynastique, sainteté royale et sainteté féminine autour de l'an mil* (Sigmaringen, 1986); V. Graus, "La sanctification du souverain dans l'Europe centrale des Xe et XIe siècles," in Evelyne Patlagean and P. Riché, eds., *Hagiographie, cultures et sociétés, IVe–XIIe siècles* (Paris: Etudes augustiniennes, 1981); and A. Barbero, *Un santo in famiglia: vocazione religiosa e resistenze sociali nell'agiografia latina medievale* (Turin: Rosenberg e Sellier, 1991).

5. *Acta sanctorum,* 2 (June 1867), pp. 315–335. On Margaret, who became very

well known in Italy at the time of the Penal Laws through the propaganda issued by the Scottish community in Rome and was to be the patron saint of Scotland, compare W. A. Leslie, *L'idée d'une reine parfaite en la vie de S. Marguerite, reine d'Ecosse* (Rome, 1660).

6. C. Papa, "Radegonda e Batilde: modelli di santità femminile nel regno merovingio," *Benedictina*, 36 (1989), pp. 13–33.

7. F. E. Consolino, "Due agiografi per una regina: Radegonda di Turingia fra Fortunato e Baudonivia," *Studi storici*, 29 (1988), p. 144.

8. Papa, Radegonda e Batilde," p. 28.

9. "Relatio facta in Consistorio secreto coram S. D. N. Urbano VIII a Francisco Maria Episcopo ostiense, S. R. E. card. a Monte, die XIII Januarii 1625 supervista, sanctitate, actis Canonizationis et miraculis piae memoriae Beatae Elisabethae Lusitanae Reginae," *Acta sanctorum*, 2 (June 1867), p. 203.

10. J. Frezet, *Histoire de la maison de Savoie*, vol. 1 (Turin, 1826), p. 44. For Margaret's life, essentially limited to the sphere of action of the friars and influenced by Catherine of Siena, see her biography in the *Bibliotheca sanctorum*, 13 vols. (Rome, 1961–1970), vol. 8 (1966), pp. 793–795.

11. Sergio Marchisio, "Ideologia e problemi dell'economia familiare nelle lettere della nobiltà piemontese," *Bollettino storico-bibliografico subalpino*, 83 (1985), p. 68. The words in quotation marks refer to the title of the collection, Maria Antonietta Visceglia, ed., *Signori, patrizi, cavalieri in Italia centro-meridionale nell'età moderna* (Bari: Laterza, 1992), which has recently shed light on the peculiarities and differences among the various Italian aristocracies within the *ancien régime*.

12. The reference in "ears and hearts" is to the work of the Jesuit G. Arata, *La bocca della verità all'orecchio e ai cuori dei Principi studiosi della clemenza* (Rome, 1669), which was part of that strand in religious literature between the seventeenth and eighteenth centuries that sought to Christianize the manners of the court and thence other classes in society.

13. On the "structural and internal contradictions which the Baroque era gave of itself" and their respective historiographical interpretations, compare Rosario Villari, ed., *Baroque Personae* (Chicago: University of Chicago Press, 1995), introduction. On family strategies in the seventeenth century and their references to court life, see Renata Ago, "Giochi di squadra: uomini e donne nelle famiglie nobili del XVII secolo," in Visceglia, *Signori*, pp. 279–308.

14. On Isabella, as interpreted in the light of the strategies employed for the social promotion of the family, see Sara Cabibbo and Marilena Modica Vasta, *La santa dei Tomasi: storia di suor Maria Crocifissa (1645–1699)* (Turina: G. Einandi, 1989). For the validity of the wedded saint as refurbished in the seventeenth century, see the analysis in Giulia Barone, "La canonizzazione di Francesa Romana (1608): la riproposta di un modella agiografico medievale," in Gabriella Zarri, ed., *Finzione e santità tra medioeve ed età moderna* (Turin: Rosenberg e Sellier, 1991), pp. 264–279.

15. Giovanni Felice Astolfi, *Nuovo leggendario di sante vergini, vedove, maritate, penitenti . . . scelte dalle vite de'santi dello Lippomano e del Surio, autori dottissimi e gravi* (Venice, 1625), p. 176.

16. Filippo Ferrario, *Catalogus generalis sanctorum qui in Martyrologio Romano non sunt* (Venice, 1625), p. 176.

17. On this subject, see Sara Cabibbo, "La capra, il sale e il sacco: per uno studio della vedovanza femminile tra cinque e seicento," *Archive* storico per la Sicilia Orientale, 85 (1989), fasc. I–III, pp. 117–167.

18. *All'augusta memoria di Maria Cristina di Savoia, regine delle due Sicilie: elogio letto ne'solenni funerali celebrati della Real Compagnia dei Biachi de'SS Michele e Raffaele nella Chiesa di S. Tomaso d'Aquino in Napoli dall'arcidiacono Luca De Samuele Cagnazzi* (Naples, 1856). [Maria Cristina's death is the subject of a remarkable set piece in Harold Acton, *The Last Bourbons of Naples (1825–1861)* (London: Methuen, 1961), pp. 84–89. Trans.]

19. On the warlike nature of the Savoyards from the reorganization of the state after the peace of Cateau-Cambrésis to the wars of the eighteenth century, see Walter Barberis, *Le armi del principe: la tradizione militare sabauda* (Turin: G. Einaudi, 1988).

20. *Vita della venerabile serva di Dio Maria Cristina di Savoia regina delle Due Sicilie, cavata da'processi per la beatificazione e canonizzazione da D. Guglielmo De Cesare, abate generale ed ordinario di Montevergine postulatore della causa* (Rome, 1863).

21. Rudolph M. Bell, *Holy Anorexia* (Chicago: University of Chicago Press, 1985). Maria Cristina is included in his list: see p. 267.

22. André Vauchez, *La sainteté en Occident aux derniers siècles du Moyen Age d'après les procès de canonisation et les documents hagiographiques* (Rome: Ecole français de Rome, 1981).

23. On the heroic virtue of Maria Clotilde, who suffered a life of tormented resignation with her "impious" husband, "violently opposed to both Church and Papacy," see the hagiographic biography of P. L. Fanfani, *La principessa Clotilde* (Grottaferrata, 1913).

24. On men's abandonment of religious vocations and the feminization of the Church between the end of the eighteenth century and the beginning of the nineteenth, see Edith Saurer, "Donne e preti: colloqui in confessionale agli inizi dell'Ottocento," in Lucia Ferrante, Maura Palazzi, and Gianna Pomata, eds., *Ragnatele di rapporti: patronage e reti di relazioni nella storia delle donne* (Turin: Rosenberg e Sellier, 1988); Lucetta Scaraffia, *La santa degli impossibili: vicende e significati della devozione a santa Rita* (Turin: Rosenberg e Sellier, 1990); M. De Giorgio, "Il modello cattolico," in G. Duby and M. Perrot, *Storia delle Donne in Occidente*, vol. 4, *L'ottocento*, ed. G. Fraisse and M. Perrot (Rome and Bari, 1991).

13. Sacred Imagery and the Religious Lives of Women, 1650–1850

1. For basic information on the saints discussed in this chapter, see *Bibliotheca sanctorum*, 13 vols. (Rome, 1961–1970), and *Enciclopedia cattolica*, 12 vols. (Florence: Casa Editrice Sansoni, 1948–1954). For discussions of the works

occasioned by the canonization of Maria Maddalena de' Pazzi, see Piero Pacini, "Firenze 1669: un teatro sacro per Santa Maria Maddalena de' Pazzi," *Mitteilungen des kunsthistorischen Instituts in Florenz*, 33, no. 1 (1992), pp. 129–202; Karen-edis Barzman, "Devotion and Desire: The Reliquary Chapel of Maria Maddalena de' Pazzi," *Art History*, 15, no. 2 (1992), pp. 171–196; Edward Goldberg, *Patterns in Late Medici Art Patronage* (Princeton, N.J.: Princeton University Press, 1983), pp. 191–226.

2. Vincenzo Puccini, *La vita di Santa Maria Maddalena de' Pazzi nobile Fiorentina* (Florence, 1609), chap. 48.

3. *Tutte le opere di Santa Maria Maddalena de' Pazzi dai manoscritti originali*, vol. 3, ed. Fulvio Nardoni (Florence, 1960), pp. 182–183.

4. For Maria Maddalena's reform, see Barzman, "Devotion and Desire."

5. On the fifty-five individuals newly canonized between 1588 and 1767, thirty-eight of whom were from religious orders, see Peter Burke, "How to Be a Counter-Reformation Saint," in *The Historical Anthropology of Early Modern Italy: Essays on Perception and Communication* (Cambridge: Cambridge University Press, 1987), pp. 48–62.

6. For a comprehensive survey of the imagery of Catherine of Siena, documenting shifts in iconography from her death in 1380 through the twentieth century and including multifigural scenes that are not addressed here, see Lidia Bianchi and Diega Giunta, *Iconografia di Santa Caterina da Siena: l'immagine* (Rome: Città Nuova Editrice, 1988).

7. For a comprehensive treatment of the Albertoni monument, see Shelley Karen Perlove, *Bernini and the Idealization of Death: The Blessed Ludovica Albertoni and the Altieri Chapel* (University Park: Pennsylvania State University Press, 1990). See also Giovanni Careri, *Bernini: Flights of Love, the Art of Devotion* (Chicago, University of Chicago Press, 1995), pp. 51–86.

8. On the inquisitorial processes intended to curtail the "simulation" of sanctity, a phenomenon associated with women in particular, see Gabriella Zarri, ed., *Finzione e santità tra medioevo ed età moderna* (Turin: Rosenberg e Sellier, 1991).

9. For a survey of representations of the Magdelene tending toward the erotic, see Marilena Mosco, ed., *La Maddalena tra sacro e profano* (Milan: Arnoldo Mondadori Editore, 1986).

10. For a reproduction of the painting by Mehus, see Karen-edis Barzman, "Cultural Production, Relgious Devotion, and Subjectivity in Early Modern Italy: The Case Study of Maria Maddalena del Pazzi," *Annali d'Italianistica: Women Writers*, 13 (1995), p. 303.

11. For a reproduction of Ceruti's painting, see Mina Gregori, *Giacomo Ceruti* (Milan: Credito Bergamasco, 1982), fig. 152.

12. On Catherine of Bologna's spiritual treatise, see Santa Caterina Vegri, *Le sette armi spirituali*, ed. Cecilia Foletti (Padua: Editrice Antenore, 1985).

13. Still a classic on Marian imagery, in text as well as pictures, is Marina Warner, *Alone of All Her Sex: The Myth and Cult of the Virgin Mary* (New York: Knopf and Random House, 1976).

14. For a reproduction of the fresco, see Riccardo Lattuada, *Il barocco a Napoli e in Campania* (Naples: Società Editrice Napoletana, 1988), fig. 88.

15. From a 1531 redaction quoted by Antonio Savioli, *L'immagine della B.V. delle Grazie di Faenza e le sue derivazioni: prima parte—l'iconografia ceramica* (Faenza: Stabilimento Grafico Fratelli Lega, 1962), pp. 14–16.

16. The *santini* are among Anna Maria Louisa's papers in Florence, Archivio di Stato, Miscellanea Medicea, no. 1, insert 3.

17. On the iconography of Anne, see Kathleen Ashley and Pamela Sheingorn, eds., *Interpreting Cultural Symbols: Saint Anne in Late Medieval Society* (Athens: University of Georgia Press, 1990).

18. See M. Barbagli, *Sotto lo stesso tetto: Mutamenti della famiglia in Italia dal xv al xx secolo* (Bologna, 1984), in particular pp. 31–137.

19. The classic essay on the topic is Christiane Klapisch-Zuber, "Holy Dolls: Play and Piety in Florence in the Quattrocento," in *Women, Family, and Ritual in Renaissance Italy* (Chicago: University of Chicago Press, 1985), pp. 310–329.

20. Laura Borello, *Devozione pubblica e privata* (Turin, 1984), p. 39.

21. "The feminine," of course, takes on import only in relation to its opposite, "the masculine," both of which are unstable terms whose meaning(s) shift in time and place. To reconstruct the context within which images of Mary and female saints circulated in early modern Italy, it would be necessary to examine the field of representation more broadly, to include the figuration of Jesus, Joseph, and male saints, along with their reception by male *and* female viewers. Such an undertaking, unfortunately, is beyond the scope of this anthology.

22. On Caterina de' Ricci's production, see Alberto Vecchi and E. Gulli Grigioni, *Con mano devota: mostra delle immaginette spirituali manufatte* (Padua: Edizioni Messagero, 1985), pp. 12ff.

23. Ibid., on the embroidery of Diomira del Verbo Incarnato, as well as her autobiography; in particular, pp. 16, 21, and 30.

24. Ibid., p. 13.

25. Ibid., on organized labor in female monasteries; in particular, pp. 12–21.

14. "Christianity Has Liberated Her and Placed Her alongside Man in the Family"

1. Emile Poulat, *Eglise contre bourgeoisie: introduction au devoir du Catholicisme actuel* (Tournai: Casterman, 1977).

2. Ibid. See also Giovanni Miccoli, "Chiesa e società in Italia fra ottocento e novecento," in Miccoli, ed., *Fra mito della christianità a secolarizzazione: studi sul rapporto Chiesa-società nell'età contemporanea* (Casale Monferrato: Marietti, 1985); Giuseppe Alberigo and Andrea Riccardi, eds., *Chiesa e papato nel mondo contemporaneo* (Rome and Bari: Laterza, 1990); Daniele Menozzi, *La Chiesa cattolica e la secolarizzazione* (Turin: G. Eindaudi, 1993).

3. Cecilia Dau Novelli, "I vescovi e la questione femminile (1900–1917)," *Rivista di storia e letteratura religiosa*, 30 (1984), pp. 439–440.

4. Edith Saurer, "Donne e preti: colloqui in confessionale agli inizi dell'ottocento,"

in L. Ferrante, M. Palazzi, and G. Pomata, eds., *Ragnatela di rapporti: patronage e reti di relazione nella storia delle donne* (Turin: 1988), pp. 253–281. [Michelet's journals are rich sources for a quasi-erotic view of this relationship. Trans.]

5. "Father Chiniquy," Charles Pascal Telesphore Chiniquy (1809–1899), *The Priest, the Woman, and the Confessional* (Chicago: A. Craig, 1880).

6. Gioiacchino Ventura, *La donna cristiana* (Milan, 1867), p. 42. Father Venturi created a model that was highly influential in nineteenth-century Catholic thought well past his own death. On this subject, see I. Porciani, "Il Plutarco femminile," in Simonetta Soldani, ed., *L'educazione delle donne: scuole e modelli di vota femminile nell'Italia del ottocento* (Milan: L. Angeli, 1989), pp. 253–281. Soldani's book contains several essays of interest, cited below.

7. Ventura, *La donna*, p. 99.

8. Ibid, p. 16.

9. Ibid, p. 91.

10. Ibid, p. 89.

11. Ibid., p. 102.

12. Dau Novelli, "I vescovi," p. 3.

13. G. Bini, "La maestra nella letteratura: un specchio della realtà," in Soldani, *L'educazione della donne*, pp. 331–362.

14. Silvia Franchini, "Gli educanti nell'Italia post-unitaria," in Soldani, *L'educazione delle donne*, p. 72.

15. Marchese Aldobrandino Malvezzi de' Medici, *La principessa Cristina di Belgiojoso*, 2d ed., vol. 2 (Milan: Fratelli Treves, 1936), p. 375.

16. Porciani, "Il Plutarco femminile," p. 302.

17. On this subject see Adelaide Cairoli (Boni), *Adelaide Cairoli e is suoi figli: lettere inedite dal 1847 al 1871,* ed. Erminia Ghiglione Giulietti (Milan: Gastaldi, 1952, repr., Cortina: Pavia, 1960).

18. Gualberta Aloide Beccari, intro. to *Ad Adelaide Cairoli le donne italiane* (Padua, 1873). See also M. Scwegman, *Feminisme als boetdaming: biografie van de Italiaause schijfster en feministe Gualberta Aloide Beccari (1842–1906)* (The Hague, 1989).

19. See under Angela Gavazza (1907–1975) in Giovanni Pozzi and Claudio Leonardi, eds., *Scrittrici mistiche italiane* (Genoa: Marietta, 1988), pp. 676–683.

20. Carmela Covato, "Educata ad educare: ruolo materno ed itinerari formativi," in Soldani, *L'educazione delle donne*, pp. 131–147; M. D'Amelia, "Figli," in P. Melograni, ed., *La famiglia italiana dall'ottocento ad oggi* (Rome and Bari: Laterza, 1988), pp. 465–524; M. L. Trebiliani, "Modello mariano e immagine della donna nell'esperienza educativa di don Bosco," in F. Traniello, ed., *Don Bosco nella cultura popolare* (Turin: SEI, 1987), pp. 187–207.

21. Paola Gaiotti de Biase, "Da una cittadinanza all'altra: il duplice protagonismo della donne cattoliche," in Giovanni Bonacchi and Angela Groppi, eds., *Il dilemma della cittadinanza* (Rome and Bari: Laterza, 1993).

22. Ibid.

23. Ibid.

24. Pierre Delooz, *Sociologie et canonisations* (Liège: Faculté de Droit, 1969), p. 255.

25. Ibid., p. 285.

26. Ibid., p. 288.

27. Ibid., p. 289.

28. Lucetta Scaraffia, *La santa degli impossibili: vicende e significati della devozione a santa Rita* (Turin, 1990).

29. Quoted in Ida Magli, *Santa Teresa di Lisieux* (Milian, 1984).

30. Susan Sontag, *Illness as Metaphor* (New York: Farrar, Strauss and Giroux, 1978), p. 21.

31. Giovanna Galgani, *Lettere: postulazione dei passionisti* (Rome, 1941); on Gemma and the Luccan context, see M. L. Trebiliani, "Santità femminile e società a Lucca nell'ottocento," in Sofia Boesch Gajano and Lucia Sebastiani, eds., *Culto dei santi, istituzioni e classi sociali in età preindustriale* (L'Aquila and Rome: L. U. Japadre Editore, 1984).

32. Ibid., p. 268.

33. Giancarlo Zizola, *Il microfono di Dio: Pio XII, padre Lombardi e i cattolici italiani* (Milan: Mondadori, 1990), p. 92.

34. Ibid., p. 516.

35. Quoted in Giuseppe De Luca, ed., *Parole sparse della Beata Cabrini* (Rome, 1938), p. 298.

36. Monica Turi, "Modena 1827: una vergine martyre," *Quaderni storici*, 75 (1990), p. 847.

37. In this connection see Philippe Boutry, "Les saints des catacombes: itinéraire français d'une pieté ultramontaine (1800–1881)," *Mélanges de l'Ecole française de Rome, Moyen Age*, 91 (1979); S. La Salvia, "L'invenzione di un culto: Santa Filomena da taumaturga a guerriera della fede," in Sofia Boesch Gajano and Lucia Sebastiani, eds., *Culto dei santi, istituzioni e classi sociali in età preindustriale* (L'Aquila and Rome: L. U. Japadre Editore, 1984), pp. 873–956.

38. Turi, "Modena 1827."

39. Monica Turi, "Il 'brutto peccato': adolescenza e controllo sessuale nel modello agiografico di Maria Goretti," in A. Benvenuto Papi and E. Giannarelli, eds., *Bambini santi* (Turin, 1991), p. 131.

40. Quoted in De Luca, *Parole sparse*, p. 76.

41. Giancarlo Rocca, *Donne religiose: contributo a una storia della condizione femminile in Italia nei secoli XIX–XX* (Rome: Paoline, 1992), p. 43.

42. Ibid., p. 47.

43. Ibid., p. 54.

44. Ibid., pp. 176–177. It should be recalled that at the beginning of the twentieth century there were only 233 women registered in the royal (state) lyceums (as against 12,605 men) and 84 (out of 10,004) in the technical institutes; women's university degrees granted between 1877 and 1900 numbered 257.

45. Ibid., p. 220.

46. Ibid., p. 244.

47. Quoted in ibid., p. 88.

48. Quoted in ibid., p. 80.

49. Quoted in ibid., p. 81.

50. Piero Bairati, "Cultura salesiana e società industriale," in F. Traniello, ed., *Don Bosco nella cultura popolare* (Turin: SEI, 1987), p. 334.

51. Giuseppe Dall'Ongaro, *Francesca Cabrini: la suora che conquistò l'America* (Milan: Rusconi, 1982).

52. Quoted in De Luca, *Parole sparse*, p. 258.

53. Ibid.

54. Gaiotti de Biase, "Da una cittadinanza," p. 150.

55. Rocca, *Donne religiose*, p. 43.

56. Ibid., p. 232.

57. Quoted in Dau Novelli, "I vescovi," p. 68.

58. Passivich, quoted in Michela De Giorgio and Paola Di Cori, "Politica e sentimenti: le organizzazioni femminili cattoliche dall'età giolittiana al fascismo," *Rivista si storia contemporanea,*" 3 (1980).

59. M. A. Colomba Fonzi, "Vincenzina De Felice Lancellotti e la rivista *Vittoria Colonna,*" in *Dimensioni e problemi della ricerca storica,* 2 (1991).

60. Quoted in ibid., p. 165.

61. Gaiotti de Biase, "Da una cittadinanza," p. 141.

62. Luisa Anzoletti, *Maria Gaetana Agnesi* (Milan: L. F. Cogliani, 1900).

63. Gaiotti de Biase, "Da una cittadinanza."

64. Ibid., p. 39.

65. See Camillo Brezzi, under "A. Giacomelli," in Francesco Traniello and Giorgio Campanini, eds., *Dizionario storico del movimento cattolico in Italia,* 3 vols. in 5 (Turin: Marietti, 1981–1984), vol. 1; A. Scatttigno, "L'educazione della donna nella cultura moderna: Antonietta Giacomelli," in Simonetta Soldani, *L'educazione delle donne: scuole e modelli di vita femminile nell'Italia dell'ottocento* (Milan: Angeli, 1989).

66. Gaiotto de Biase, "Da una cittadinanza," p. 89.

67. Quoted in ibid., p. 74.

68. Ibid., p. 100.

69. Quoted in ibid., p. 152.

70. Annarita Buttafuoco, *Le Mariuccine: storia di un'istituzione laica, l'Asilo Mariuccia* (Milan: F. Angeli, 1985).

71. Quoted in Gaiotti di Biase, "Da una cittadinanza," p. 167.

72. Cecilia Dau Novelli, *Società, chiesa e associazionismo femminile* (Rome, 1988).

73. Gemelli, quoted in Paola di Cori, "Rosso e bianco: la devozione al Sacro Cuore di Gesù nel primo dopoguerra," *Memoria,* 5 (1982), p. 89.

74. Quoted in A. Barelli, "La 'nostra' storia," manuscript, pp. 136–137.

75. Quoted by L. Rozza, under "Armida Barelli," in *Dizionario storico* (see n. 65), p. 32.

76. Di Cori, "Rosso e bianco," p. 102.

77. Giovanna Canuti, *Cinquant'anni di vita* (Rome: Sales, 1959), p. 24.

78. Ibid., p. 32.

79. Quoted in Michela De Giorgio, "Metodi e tempi di una educazione sentimentale: la gioventù femminile cattolica italiana negli anni venti," *Nuova DWF,* 10–11 (1979).

80. Monica Turi, "La costruzione di un nuovo modello di comportamento fem-

minile, Maria Goretti tra cronaca nera e agiografia," *Movimento operaio e socialista*, 3 (1987).

81. Dau Novelli, *Società*, p. 6.

82. Pius XII, "Dal discorso alle donne sulla dignità e missione delle donne," in Raimondo M. Spiazzi and O. P. Massimo, eds., *Documenti sociali della Chiesa da Pio IX a Giovanni Paolo II (1864–1982)*, vol. 1 (Milan: Massimo, 1983), pp. 524ff.

83. Gaiotti de Biase, "Da una cittadinanza," p. 155.

84. Lucetta Scaraffia, "Devozioni di guerra: identità femminile e simboli religiosi negli anni quaranta," in Anna Bravo, ed., *Donne e uomini nelle guerre mondiali* (Rome: Laterza, 1991), pp. 159–160.

85. Rocca, *Donne religiose*, p. 281.

86. Ibid., p. 283.

87. See Alberigo and Riccardi, *Chiesa e papato*; Menozzi, *La Chiesa cattolica*.

88. Peter Hebblethwaite, *Paul VI: The First Modern Pope* (London: Harper-Collins, 1993), p. 649.

89. Ibid., pp. 650ff.

90. Rocca, *Donne religiose*, p. 281.

91. C. Bonicelli, "La presenza pastorale a tempo pieno delle religiose in Italia," *Orientamenti pastorali*, 35 (1987).

92. In this connection, see Raffaele Piazza, *Adamo, Eva e il serpente* (Palermo, 1988); Adriana Valerio, *Cristianesimo al femminile: donne protagoniste nella storia delle Chiese* (Naples: M. D'Auria, 1990); Carla Ricci, *Mary Magdalene and Many Others: Women Who Followed Jesus* (Tunbridge Wells, Kent: Burns and Oates, 1994); Kari Elizabeth Borresen, *Women's Studies of the Christian and Islamic Traditions: Ancient, Medieval, and Renaissance Foremothers* (Dordrecht, Netherlands, and Boston: Kluwer Academic, 1993). [Since this book was written, Grace M. Jantzen, *Power, Gender, and Christian Mysticism* (Cambridge: Cambridge University Press, 1995), has been published. Trans.]

93. *Mulieris Dignitatem*, p. 23.

94. Ibid., p. 33.

95. Ibid., p. 43.

96. Ibid., pp. 27–28.

97. Ibid., p. 76.

15. A Voyage to the Madonna

1. "The first serious studies on the choice of Christian baptismal names prove the durability of the name Mary at the beginning of the twentieth century, in spite of growing diversification and an ever more rapid shift in fashions." Etienne Fouilloux, "Le due vie della pietà cattolica nel XX secolo," in Giuseppe Alberigo and Andrea Riccardi, eds., *Chiesa e papato nel mondo contemporaneo* (Rome: Laterza, 1990), p. 308.

2. Carl Gustav Jung, *Answer to Job* (Cleveland, Ohio: World Publishing, 1963), p. 442.

3. According to Luce Irigaray, *Sexes and Genealogies* (New York: Columbia Uni-

versity Press, 1993), she confers power on women; by contrast, for Luisa Accati, "Il furto del desiderio, relazioni sociale nell'Europa cattolica del XVII secolo: alcune ipotesi," *Memoria,* 7 (1983), pp. 7–16, she became a source of regression and repression for women.

4. P. G. Besutti, "Saggio di ricerca sull'origine dei santuari mariani in Italia," in *De cultu mariano saeculis VI–XI: acta congressus mariologici-mariani internationalis in Croatia anno 1971 celebrati,* vol. 5 (Rome, 1972).

5. Bernard Billet, "Le fait des apparitions non reconnues par l'Eglise," in Billet and René Laurentin, eds., *Vraies at fausses apparitions dans l'Eglise* (Paris, 1973).

6. Sylvie Barnay, *Les apparitions de la Vierge* (Paris: Cerf, and Montreal: Fides, 1992).

7. Giovanni Battista Semeria, in *Atti del primo Congresso mariano nazionale* (August 18–21, 1895) (Livorno, 1897), p. 49.

8. Chiara Lubich, *L'avventura dell'Unità* (Milan, 1991).

9. Gertrud Freiin von Le Fort, *The Eternal Woman, the Woman in Time, Timeless Woman* (Milwaukee: Bruce Publishing, 1954).

10. Romana Guarnieri, *Fonti vecchie e nuove per una "storia" dei santuari* (Rome, 1981), p. 502.

11. *La vie du rail,* 1313 (October 24, 1971), p. 44.

12. *Les annales de Lourdes,* 1868.

13. *Journal de la Grotte,* 1867–68.

14. Sofia Boesch Gajano and Lucetta Scaraffia, eds., *Luoghi sacri e spazi della santità* (Turin: Rosenberg e Sellier, 1990).

15. [This is true only of provincial France: the United Kingdom, Germany, Austria, and the north of France not only had well-developed railway systems, but "excursions" had become fairly common by the 1870s. Trans.]

16. Alphone Dupront, *Du Sacré: croisades et pélérinages, images et langages* (Paris: Gallimard, 1987).

17. *Il pellegrinaggio italiano a Lourdes* (Rome, 1899), pp. iv–vii.

18. *Il viaggio a Lourdes—a per tutto la Francia—reso facile agli italiani ovvero schiaramenti e norme sul medesimo ed occorrenti espressioni francesi nella lora pronuncia* (Bergamo, 1900), p. 45.

19. Egle Zoffoli, *Un lungo cammino: diario di un'esperienza* (Bologna, 1978), p. 19.

20. C. Gallini, "Le folle di Lourdes," in Giancarlo Menichelli and Cirillo de Gregorio, eds., *Il terzo Zola, "Emile Zola dopo i Rougon-Macquart"*: Atti del Convegno internazionale, Naples and Salerno, May 27–30, 1987. Studies and Research in French Literature and Linguistics, no. 3, vol. 13 (Naples: Istituto universitario orientale, 1990).

21. L. G. da Fonseca (1959), *Le meraviglie di Fatima* (Milan, 1991).

22. Giovanni Miccoli, *Fra mito della cristianità e secolarizzazione: studi sul rapporto chiesa-società nell'età contemporanea* (Casale Monferrato: Marietti, 1985).

23. Emma Fattorini, *Germania e S. Sede: le nunziature di Pacelli tra la Grande Guerra e la Repubblica di Weimar* (Bologna: Il Mulino, 1992), p. 231. [It is interesting to note, in connection with partisan uses of the Virgin, the transitional "reply" to Lourdes offered by the Marpingen Virgin, who, as though

foreshadowing Fatima, also appeared to three young girls in July 1876, thus creating a specifically "German" Lourdes. See David Blackbourn, *Marpingen: Apparitions of the Virgin Mary in Bismarckian Germany* (Oxford, Clarendon Press, 1993). Trans.]

24. L. Scaraffia, "Devozione di Guerra: identità femminile e simboli religiosi negli anni quaranta," in Anna Bravo, ed., *Donna e uomini nelle guerre mondiali* (Rome: Laterza, 1991).

25. Edouard Dhanis, "Sguardo su Fatima e bilancio di una discussione," in *Civiltà Cattolica*, 2 (1953), pp. 403ff.

26. Giovanni Battista Montini, "Sulla Madonna," in *Discorsi e scritti 1955–1963* (Rome, 1988), p. 9.

27. René Laurentin and G. Maindron, *Les apparitions de Kibeho* (Paris, 1984).

28. W. Christian, "Tapping and Defining New Power. The First Month of Vision at Ezquioga (July 1981)," *American Ethnologist*, 14 (February 1, 1987), pp. 140–166.

29. Paolo Apolito, *Il cielo in terra: costruzioni simboliche di un'apparizione mariana* (Bologna, 1992).

30. M. Carroll, "Visions of the Virgin Mary: The Effect of Family Structures on Marian Apparitions," *Journal for the Scientific Study of Religion*, 22, no. 3 (1983), p. 216. These themes have been taken up systematically by the same author in his *Madonnas That Maim: Popular Catholicism in Italy since the Fifteenth Century* (Baltimore, 1992).

31. *Medjugorje*, no. 26 (Pescara, 1993), pp. 5–6.

32. [Rev. 12:1–6. Trans.]

33. Apolito, *Il cielo in terra*, p. 238.

34. Ibid., p. 235.

35. *Medjugorje*, no. 53 (Turin, 1993), p. 3.

16. Sisters and Saints on the Screen

1. André Bazin, "Santi lo si è solo dopo," in *Che cos'è il cinema?* (Milan: Garzanti, 1973), p. 321.

Index

Abbondanza of Spoleto, 49–50
Academy of the Apatisti, 141
Accademia Clementina, 247
Acts of Paul and Thecla, 9
Adalbert of Canossa, 48
Adam (and Eve), 32, 75
Addolorata, Gabriele dell', 256
Addolorata, Sister, 301
Adelaide, Empress, 48–49, 50
Adelaide of Susa, 225, 227
Adelheid Langmann, 37
Adeodata, Abbess, 24
"Ad virgines" letters (Clement of Rome), 21
Agatha, Saint, 26
Agnella, Abbess, 25
Agnesi, Maria Gaetana, 218, 267
Agnes, Saint, 13, 19, 52, 257
Agolanti, Clare, 189–190
Agreda, Maria de, 188, 214
Alacoque, Margaret-Mary, 6, 178, 188, 214, 255
Alberione, Giacomo, 265
Alberto, Carlo, 228
Albertoni, Ludovica, 185, 236–237
Alcalá, Diego de, 146
Alciati, Andrea, 94
Alessandrini, Goffredo, 297
Alexis, Saint, 65
Alfonso, duke of Ferrara, 39
Alphonsus, Saint, 194
Amadeus IX, duke of Savoy, 219
Ambrose, bishop of Milan, 6, 12–16, 19
Anastasius, 25
Andalò, Diana degli, 57
Angela of Foligno, 37, 63, 65, 114
Angelina of Montegiove, 88
Angel in White, The (film), 301
Angilberga, Empress, 45, 48
Anicius family, 16, 18

Ann (prophetess), 18
Anna (film), 301
Ansa, 27, 45
Anselmi, Tina, 277
Ansperga, Abbess, 27
Antamoro, Giulio C., 297
Anti-Quietist repression, 182–183
Antisatira (Buoninsegni), 142
Antoniano, Cardinal Silvio, 187
Antonini, Sister Theodora, 104
Anzoletti, Luisa, 267, 270
Aratore, Clementina, 230
Arbrissel, Robert d', 58
Arciero, Aniello, 151
Aretino, Pietro, 122
Aribertus II, King, 26
Asella, 22–23
Associations of Christian Mothers, 203
Asterius, bishop of Ansedonia, 22
Athanasius, 18–19, 20, 22
Augustine, bishop of Hippo, 6, 12, 18, 19, 22
Augustinian rule, 28–29
Aurelianus of Arles, 29
Authari, King, 47
Aviso de gente recognida (Pérez de Valdivia), 148, 149
Azione muliebre (magazine), 268–269, 270

Bagno, Giovanna da, 52
Baj, Sister Maria Cecilia, 197, 216
Baldi, Maria, 268
Baldwina, Sister, 223
Barbaro, Francesco, 104
Barberini, Taddeo, 181
Barberini family, 175
Barbero, Alessandro, 65
Barbieri, Clelia, 255
Barelli, Armida (Older Sister), 7, 258, 273, 274, 275

Barnabite order, 115–116
Basilian rule, 28
Batilde, Saint, 222
Battiste de la Salle, Saint Jean, 254–255
Battistoni, Aurelio, 298
Bazzi frescoes (Church of Saint Dominic), 171
"Beata Vergine delle Grazie" (Blessed Virgin of Mercy) cult, 240–241, 242
Beccari, Gualberta, 252
Belgioioso, Cristina di, 252
Bell, Rudolph M., 36, 37, 226
Bellissima (film), 301–302
Benedict of Aniane, 29, 30, 50
Benedict of Nursia, 50
Benedict XI, Pope, 67
Benedict XIII, Pope, 235
Benedict XV, Pope, 211, 273, 275, 288
Benincasa, Caterina, 169–170, 171
Benincasa, Ursula, 151, 211
Berengarius (Berengar II of Ivrea), 48
Berenini, Gianlorenzo, 236
Bergamo, Mino, 206
Bergman, Ingrid, 298
Bernard, Saint, 21
Bernard of Clairvaux, 33
Bernini, Gianlorenzo, 121, 236–237, 238
Bertrán, Luigi, 239, 240
Besozzi, Pietro, 115, 116–117
Bevegnate, Giunta, 64
Bible, the: geographical interpretation of, 127; reinterpretation by John Paul II of, 280; Song of Songs incorporated into, 19, 31–32, 53; studied by female sanctity, 66–67; virgin women of, 18–19
Bindi, Rosy, 277
Biondi, Albano, 153
Birth of Christ (Ruoti), 140, 141
Bizzoche women's groups, 194, 195, 197, 213
Black Death of 1348, 68, 70
Black Virgin of Czestochowa, 288, 290
Blessed Angelina of Montegiove refectory, 82
Bobbio, Giona di, 64
Bobbio Abbey, 50
Boccaccio, Giovanni, 108, 139
Bojani, Benvenuta, 61
Bollandist *Acta sanctorum*, 188
Bolshevik Revolution, 288
Bonaparte, Jerome, 227
Bonaventure, Saint, 208
Bonnard, Mario, 299
Bonnus, Hermannus, 100

Bonomo, Giovanna Maria, 178, 179
Bonucci, Antonio Maria, 184, 190
Book of the History of the Convent of San Cosimato (Formicini), 135
Borgo Pinti convent, 173, 174
Borromeo, Cardinal Federico, 111, 119–120
Borromeo, Carlo, 105, 171, 181, 246
Bosnia-Herzegovina, 291
Bottonio, Timoteo, 116
Brenti, Rosa Teresa, 218
Bridget of Sweden, Saint, 6, 69, 84, 148, 184, 225
Bronzini, Ersilia Majno, 271
Brugnoli, Candido, 154
Bruni, Leonardo, 131
Bugni, Chiara, 85
Buoninsegni, Francesco, 142

Cabrini, Francesca, 257, 258, 263
Cacciaguerra, Bonsignore, 98, 115, 116, 123–124
Caesaria, Abbess, 29
Caesarius of Arles, 8, 29, 30
Cairoli, Maria Adelaide, 252
Cajetan, Saint, 92
Camaldolese congregation, 50, 52
Camerini, Mario, 300, 302
Campori, Pietro Cardinal, 152
Canon 13 (Council of Elvira), 22
Canori Mora, Elisabetta, 199, 200
Canossian Daughters of Charity, 203
"Canticle of the Creatures" (Francis of Assisi), 61
Cantimori, Delio, 85
Canuti, Giovanna, 275
Capitanio, Bartolomea, 255
Cappellani, Alberto, 298
Carena, Cesare, 152
Carlini, Benedetta, 144–145, 147, 150
Carlo Alberto of Piedmont, Prince, 219
Carmelite Church of Santa Maria degli Angeli, 173
Carmelite reform, 111
"Carmen de synodo Ticenensi," 26
Carolingian monarchy, 48–50
Carthusians, 52
Casa, Sister Pautilla della, 139
Casella, Ludovico, 87
Casimira, Maria, 186
Castagno, Andrea del, 79
Castiglione, Sabba da, 95
Cathar movement, 53–54, 55–56, 65
Cathedral of Spilimbergo, 75

Catherine of Alexandria, Saint, 38, 72, 74, 75, 80, 83–84
Catherine of Bologna, Saint, 238, 239, 246–247
Catherine of Bologna with the Infant Jesus (Franceschini), 238–239
Catherine of Genoa, Saint, 92
Catherine of Racconigi, 85
Catherine of Siena, Saint: canonization of, 70; as Counter-Reformation figure, 171; iconography of, 169–172, 236, 238; idealizing image of, 69, 74, 75, 76, 80–81; intellectual understanding of, 66–67; letters of, 113, 114, 121–122, 125; Maria Maddalena identified with, 173, 174; as model for the faithful, 233–236, 252; modern films on, 299; mystical marriage with Christ, 37–38, 40; proclaimed Doctor of the Church, 84, 278; reform discourse of, 5; relics of, 78; stigmata of, 235
Catherine of Siena (film), 299
Catholic Action, 265, 270, 273, 274
Catholic Women's League for the Regeneration of Labor, 268
Cavani, Liliana, 295
Celestinus V, Pope, 68
Celilia, Saint, 7, 297
Cena (del Castagno), 79
Cerchi, Umiliana de', 62, 66, 76
Chantal, Jeanne de, 7
Chapel of Saint Pantaleon (Boccioleto), 77
Charity of Saint Jerome convents, 168
Charles V, Emperor, 96
Charles VIII, King, 92
Charmalières monastery, 30
Chiara d'Assisi (film), 299
Chiara della Passione, 180
Christian Brothers, 255
Christian Democratics, 256, 269–270, 274, 277
Christian feminist movement, 3, 270–272
Christian Ritual, The (Giacomelli), 269
Christina of Sweden, 181
Christus (film), 297
Chronicle of the Convent of the "Vergini" in Venice (anonymous), 135
Chronicle of Corpus Comini (Riccoboni), 135
Chronicle of the Holy Order of Saint Dominic (Frescobaldi), 130, 133–134
Church of the Apostles, 96
Church of Saint Basil, 64, 76, 77
Church of Saint Catherine, 83
Church of Saint Dominic, 74, 78, 171

Church of Saint Gregory of Spoleto, 50
Church, the. *See* Roman Catholic Church
Cielo mistico (Gadda), 218
Cielo sulla palude (film), 299, 300
Cioni, Sister Michelangela, 133
Cistercians, 52
City of God, The (Augustine), 19
Civiltà Cattolica, La, 266, 269
Clare of Assisi, Saint, 7, 36, 57, 60, 63, 74, 79
Clare of Montefalco, 61, 62–63, 64, 65, 66, 80
Clare of Rimini, 80, 189
Clark, Elizabeth Ann, 28
Clement V, Pope, 68
Clement VII, Pope, 67
Clement X, Pope, 185, 223, 237
Clement XI, Pope, 239, 247
Clemente, Maria, 141
Clotilde Adelaide de Bourbon, Maria, 47, 198, 227
Cluniacs, 49, 50
Coari, Adelaide, 268–272
Coccapani, Sigismondo, 168
College of Cardinals, 67
Collegiate Church of San Gimignano, 73
Colomba di Rieti, 88
Colombo, Adele, 268
Colonna, Marcantonio, 136
Colonna, Margaret, 63, 181
Colonna, Vittoria, 131
Colonna family, 181
Colpa di une madre, La (film), 301
Columbus, Christopher, 125, 126, 127
Communism, 291, 293
Companies and Pious Unions of the Daughters of Mary, 203
Company of Saint Ursula, 94–95, 104–105
Comunione e Liberazione, 277
Congregation of the Daughters of Mary, 284
Congregation of the Holy Office, 151, 152
Congregation of the Mother of God, 144
Congregation of Sacred Rites and Ceremonies, 111, 146, 147. *See also* Roman Catholic Church
Conti, Fontana de', 116
Conventual Franciscans, 91, 135
Cordero, Father Emilio, 299
Corner, Patriarch Federico, 157
Coronation of the Virgin (di Pietro), 72
Council of Basel, 69
Council of Elvira, 22
Council of Ephesus, 5

Council of Neo-Cesaream, 22
Council of Nicaea, 98–99
Council's Message to Women, 278
Council of Trent: clarifies policy on
  Eucharist, 166, 169; on criteria of female
  sanctity, 172; efficacy of images affirmed
  by, 233; imposes cloistered life for women
  religious, 39; on principles of marital law,
  225; reforms cult of saints and holy
  images, 99, 100, 101
Counter-Reformation: antimystical
  revolution and, 187–189; artists of, 161;
  expectations of women by, 160; female
  sanctity promoted by, 163–175; on
  Francesca of Rome, 110; monastic model
  of perfect nun by, 177–179; new women's
  communities breaking with, 192–194; true
  holiness defined by, 146–147; unmasking
  of sanctity during, 182–183; virile woman
  model of, 183–185. *See also* Reformation;
  Roman Catholic Church
Cranach, Lucas (the Elder), 83
Crema, Dominican Battista da, 116, 126
Cremonese Inquisition, 152
Crescentia of Kaufbeuren, 188
Cristo, Beneficio di, 98
Crivelli, Giovanni Maria, 215
Croce, Benedetto, 108
Crostarosa, Giulia, 212–214
Crostarosa, Sister Maria Celeste, 205–206,
  210–212
Cult of the Virgin. *See* Marian cult
Cunegund, 65
Cuniperga, 26
Cunipertus, King, 26, 27, 42
Curradi, Francesco, 172–174
Custodiendas virgines (Alciati), 94
Cyprian of Carthage, 10, 22

Damasus, Pope, 14, 16, 19
Danaë paintings, 237
Dante, 21, 56, 139
Da Persico, Elena, 269, 270–721
Darro, Leona, 176
Daughters of Mary the Auxiliary, 262, 278
Daughters of the Queen of the Apostles,
  267
Daughters of the Sacred Heart of Jesus, 203
Daughters of Saint Anne, 264–265
Daughters of Saint Paul of Alba, 265
Death of the Virgin (painting, Caravaggio),
  160
Decameron, 68

De Cesare, Guglielmo, 226, 227
De Juillan, Colomès, 284
De la Cruz, Francisco, 149
Deliberata, Saint, 76
*Della invocazione, della venerazione e delle
  reliquie dei santi e delle sacre immagini*
  (Tridentine decree), 159
Del Rio, Martin, 149–150
De Maio, Romeo, 146
Demetriades, 16, 18, 28
Desert Fathers, 50
Desiderius, King, 27, 45
Diary (Frescodbaldi), 130, 133, 134
Diary (Pioppi), 134
Di Marco, Giulia, 151
Dimesse communities, 109, 149
Diomira del Verbo Incarnato, 247
Direttorio mistico (Scaramelli), 195
Discorso alle zitelle devote (Saint Alphonsus),
  194
Discretio spirituum treatise (Gerson), 84–
  85
Disonorata senza colpa (film), 301
Dominic, Saint, 61
Dominican order, 56–58, 69, 133–134,
  242–243
Dominican sisters of Prato, 196
Dominic of Guzmán, 53
Dominici, Dominican Giovanni, 58, 71
Domnina, 19
Donatists, 19
Donatus, bishop of Besançon, 30
Donizone of Canossa, 52
Donna e i suoi rapporti sociali, La (Mozzoni),
  266
Donna e la Famiglia, La (magazine), 266
Donna nel progresso cristiano, La (Anzoletti),
  267
*Donna vecchia e donna numova: scene di
  domani* (Passivich), 266
Duby, Georges, 52, 56
Duglioli, Elena, 115, 124
Durio, Paolo, 219, 220, 221–222

Ecce Homo (painting, de' Ricci), 246
Edwige of Silesia, 221, 227
Eleanor d'Este, Princess, 97
Elizabeth, Saint, 161, 162
Elizabeth of Hungary, 66, 184
Elizabeth of Portugal, 223
Elizabeth of Thuringia, Saint, 75, 221
Encratites, 11
Enselmini, Elena, 62

Epifania, 27
Epistle 108 (Jerome), 16
Epistle 130 (Ambrose), 21
Epitaphium (Odilo of Cluny), 49
"Epithalamium Christi virginum, Alternatim" (*Speculum virginum*), 35
Ercole d'Este, 39
Eremitic Theatines of the Most Holy Conception, 211
Essai sur la formation du Dogme Catholique (di Belgioioso), 252
Este, Borso d', 87
Eucharist, the, 166, 169
Eugene IV, Pope, 69
Europa '51 (film), 298
Eustochium, Julia, 16, 23, 28, 35
Eve, 32, 75, 280

Famiglia cristiana (weekly), 265
Fanciulla di Corinaldo, La (film), 299
Fatima cult, 283, 287–290
Female Catholic Youth, 258
Feminine Catholicism, 194–204
Ferdinand, duke of Châlon-Arlay, 228, 229, 230
Ferrazzi, Cecilia, 157
Ferrer, Saint Vincenzo, 223, 239
Fiamma viva (magazine), 275
Field of Flowers (Frescobaldi), 130
Filippini, Lucia, 193
Filocolo (Boccaccio), 108, 139
Fina, Saint, 73
Fina of Gimignano, 77
First Women's Congress (1908), 271
Fivoli, Barbera, 127–128
Flagellants, 70
Focolarini (the Hearth movement), 277, 283
Formicini, Orsola, 135–136, 137
Fornari, Chiara Isabella, 215
Fortunatus, 222–223
Fourth Lateran Council (1215), 57
Francesca of Rome, 66, 69, 71, 110, 184
Franceschini, Marc'Antonio, 238
Francia, Renata di, 97
Francis of Assisi, Saint, 7, 34–35, 57, 60, 64, 74, 75
Franciscan Missionary Sisters of the Immaculate Heart of Mary, 263
Franciscan Observants, 88, 91, 135
Franciscan order, 56–58, 188
Franciscan saints, 61
Francis of Sales, 7, 292
Frassinetti, Paola, 262

Frederick Barbarossa, Emperor, 136
Frederick II of Sicily, 56
Frescobaldi, Fiammetta, 129–130, 133–134, 137
Friedan, Betty, 279

Gaiotti de Biase, Paola, 253
Galgani, Gemma, 255, 256, 257
Galluzzi, Maria Domitilla, 40–41
Gandersheim community, 46
Garampi, Count Giuseppe, 189, 190–191
Gattorno, Rosa, 264
Gauthsrude, Abbess, 30
Gemelli, Father, 7, 273, 274
Genealogy of the Gentile Gods (Boccaccio), 139
Genesis, 280
Genina, Augusto, 299
Gentileschi, Artemisia, 167
Geri da Pistoia, Lorenzo, 144
Gernrode community, 46
Gerson, Jean, 84–85
Gertrude of Helfta, 36
Gesù Maria convent, 158
Giacomelli, Antoniette, 269, 271
Gianbattista Piazzetta, 241
Gianbattista Tiepolo, 241
Gill, Katherine, 39
Giordano, Luca, 231, 232, 233
Giovanni of Mantua, 53
Gisulph II, Duke, 43
Giuliana, 15, 16
Giuliani, Veronica, 178, 179, 215
Giuseppa Rossello, Maria, 264
Giussani, Father, 277
Giustiniani Bandini, Cristina, 272–273
Glories of Mary (Liguori), 201
Glory of Catherine in Heaven (painting, Paleotti), 239
Glory of Saint Dominic (chapel ceiling canvas), 241
God: Lutheran "imputed" justice of, 86; male gender image of, 2; marriage between the Church and, 31–35. *See also* Jesus Christ
Golden Legend, The (Vasari), 100, 101, 123, 160, 165, 168
Gonzaga, Gianfrancesco, 118
Gonzaga, Julia, 113, 124
Goretti, Maria, 257, 258, 299, 300
Grattarola, Marc'Aurelio, 149
Great War (1914–1918), 288
Gregory I, Pope (the Great), 24, 25, 30, 47
Gregory VII, Pope, 52

Gregory IX, Pope, 61
Gregory XI, Pope, 67, 68, 110
Gregory XII, Pope, 135
Gregory XVI, Pope, 219
Gregory of Nyssa, 10, 20
Grugni, Father Carlo, 269, 270, 271
Guardia Sanframondo, 241
Guarnieri, Romana, 2
Guastalla College, 95, 109
Guasti, Cesare, 113
Guicciardini, Francesco, 129, 134

"Haili Meidhad," 37
Hatot, Georges, 296, 298
Hermits, 277
Historia Langobardorum (Paul the Deacon), 47
Historia Lausiaca (Palladius), 23
History of Italy (Guicciardini), 129
Holy Family, 161–162
Honorius III, Pope, 56
House of Savoy, 198
Humanae vitae (Paul VI), 279

Ignatian spirituality, 208
Ignatius of Antioch, 9
Ignatius of Loyola, 96, 149, 171
Ignazio Massini, Carlo, 191
Imitation of Christ, 252
Immaculate Conception dogma, 201, 281
Immaculate Mary, 242–243. *See also* Mary (mother of God)
Immensae caritatis, 277
Innocent III, Pope, 57
Innocent VIII, Pope, 90
Inquisition: limited jurisdiction of, 151; revelation of diabolical origin charge by, 149–150; sanctity examined by, 109–110, 183; "soliciting for lewd purposes" charge by, 119–120; witchcraft case procedure by, 152–158. *See also* Roman Catholic Church
Instituzioni analitiche ad uso della gioventù italiana (Gadda), 218
Interior Castle (Maria Maddalena), 111
Io, Caterina (film), 299
Iron Century, 48, 224
Isabel of Castille, 126
Istoria dell'ammirabile Vita della Beata Chiara degli Agolanti (Bonucci), 190
Istoria della vita de Bianca Teresa Massei Buonvisi (Bonucci), 184
Italian Catholic Young Women's Association, 273, 274

Italian Women's Center, 276

Jacob the Patriarch (Ruoti), 140, 141
Jeanne, Mère, 98
Jerome: on ascetic model, 50; on female monastic communities, 22–23, 28, 35; on female religious, 17; on matrimony, 11, 12; saintly women associated with, 185; sister of, 21; Song of Songs translation by, 32; on virginity and chastity, 16, 20
Jesuits, 127, 151, 188
Jesus Christ: as model of chastity, 20; mystical marriage with, 35–38, 40–41; Passion of, 178, 179, 181, 195, 295–297; represented by filmmakers, 295–297; Teresa of Avila's vision of, 40–41. *See also* God
Joachimite movement, 70
Joan of Arc, 69, 85, 255, 297, 298
Joan of Arc at the Stake (film), 298, 299
Joan, Pope (mythical), 91
Joan of Signa, 76, 79
John the Baptist, Saint, 161, 162
John Chrysostom, 22
John of the Cross, Saint, 40, 124, 208
John Paul II, Pope, 280, 290, 293
John XXII, Pope, 68
John XXIII, Pope, 268
Joseph (husband to Mary), 100, 162, 200
Journal de la Grotte, 284
Julia, Abbess, 136
Julia of Certaldo, 73, 78
Juliana Anicia, 18

King of Kings, The (film), 296–297
Kuliscoff, Andreana, 252–253
Kuliscoff, Anna, 252–253
Kurze, Wilhelm, 46, 47

Laity in the Middle Ages, The (Vauchez), 89
Lambertini, Cardinal Prospero, 187, 188
Lancellotti, Vincenzina de Felice, 266
"Last Communion of Saint Mary Magdalene" (iconography, Vanni and Pugliani), 168–169
Last Judgment, The (di Pietro), 72
Last Supper, The (refectory mural), 82
Lazzari, Domenica, 218
Lea, 16, 17, 23
League for the Protection of Women's Interests, 271
Leo III, Pope, 24

Leo XI, Pope, 173
Leo XIII, Pope, 250, 265, 285
Leonviola, Antonio, 298, 299
Lettere spirituali (Negri), 115
Lettres édifiantes et curieuses, 127
Lettres provinciales (Pascal), 116
Liber pontificalis, 24
Libro de la vida (Teresa of Avila), 39, 125
Life, Passion, Death, and Resurrection of Jesus Christ (film), 297
Liguori, Saint Alphonsus, 188, 192, 201, 210, 212, 213
Liguorian Congregation of the Most Holy Redeemer, 205
Lisieux, Thérèse de, 256
Liutprand of Cremona, 44, 48
Lives of the Holy Fathers (Cavalca), 100
Lives of the Most Holy Virgins, The, 100
Lombardi, Father, 256, 257
Lombard monarchy, 42–47
Loredano, Gianfrancesco, 142
Lorenzetti, Pietro, 79, 80
Lothar I, 45, 48
Louise of Savoy, 219–220, 221, 222, 223, 228
Louis XV, King, 198
Louis XVI, King, 198
Lourdes cult, 283, 284–287
Lovere Sisters of Charity, 262
Love of Virtue (del Sera), 139, 141
Lubich, Chiara, 277, 283
Lucia (Fatima child), 289, 290
Lucia Brocadelli of Narni, 39
Lucretia, 19
Lucrezia, Countess (Gambara), 119
Ludovica Albertoni (sculpture, Bernini), 236–237, 238
Luther, Martin, 83, 100

Macinghi Strozzi, Alessandra, 113
Macrina, 10, 17
Madonna, 281–282. *See also* Mary (mother of God)
Madonna alla greca (painting), 154
Madonna dei Bagni cult, 245
Madonna of Fatima. *See* Fatima cult
Maestre Pie Filippini e Venerini congregation, 193, 194, 203
Magdalene in Ecstasy, The (painting, Mehus), 237, 238
Maggiorini, Gilda, 256–257
Magnani, Anna, 301, 302

Malleus maleficarum (Krämer and Sprenger), 90
Mallia Dedalia, 21
Mallio Theodoro, 21
Malnati, Linda, 271
Mamma Rome (film), 302
Mangano, Silvana, 300–301
Manzoni, Vittoria Giorgini, 176, 236
Marcella, 22, 23
Marcellina, 6, 14, 16
Marcellines of Milan, 260–261
Marcellus II, Pope, 96
Margaret of Cortona, 63–64, 74, 77, 79, 198, 299
Margaret of Cortona (film), 299
Margaret of Savoy, 223–224
Margaret of Scotland, 221, 223
Maria Auxilium Christianorum (Pius VII), 202
Maria Cristina of Savoy, 226–230
Maria Crocifissa of the Wounds of Our Lord Jesus Christ, 195
Maria Francesca of the Five Wounds, 195, 197, 198
Maria Maddalena (Caterina de' Pazzi): as Counter-Reformation saint, 171–174, 175; iconography of, 231–232, 238, 246; limited writings of, 114; as model to the faithful, 233–234; sanctity and canonization of, 110–111
Marian congregations, 282–283
Marian congress (1895), 282
Marian cult: "Beata Vergine delle Grazie" (Blessed Virgin of Mercy) form of, 240–241; between 19th and 20th centuries, 283–284; evolution of, 55–56, 73, 100, 102; Fatima and, 283, 287–290; feminization of Catholicism and, 281–282; Lourdes and, 283, 284–287; Medjugorje and, 283–284, 290–293; Reformation challenge to, 102; rejuvenation during 18th century of, 200–204. *See also* Mary (mother of God)
Marriage at Cana, The (refectory mural), 82
Marriage of Hyparchia, Lady Philosopher (Ninci), 143
Martha in Her Kitchen (refectory mural), 82
Martin, Thérèse, 255
Martinengo, Mary Magdalene, 188, 216
Martinengo di Barco, Maria Maddalena, 178
Martin of Tours, 17
Martin V, Pope, 67

Marvelous and Calamitous Things in This World (Frescobaldi), 130
Mary (mother of God): apparitions of, 281–293; as Beata Vergine delle Grazie, 240–241, 242; Council of Ephesus on role of, 5–6; dolls of infant, 244; household images of, 163–164; Immaculate Conception dogma and, 201, 281; as Immaculate Mary, 242–243; as model of virginity, 20–21, 35, 90; as model for women, 2, 54–56, 160–161, 240, 243–244; as protector and mediatrix, 241–242; role in the Passion, 179. *See also* Marian cult
Mary of the Crucifixion Satellico, Sister, 214, 215, 216
Mary Magdalene, 2, 82, 100, 164–169, 237
Mary Magdalene with Mary and the Infant Jesus (painting, Giordano), 231
Mary of Oignies, 62
Mary of Venice, 70
Massei Buonvisi, Bianca Teresa, 184
Matarazzo, Raffaello, 301
Mater Dei (film), 299
Matilda of Canossa ("Great Countess"), 52–53, 72, 252
Maurist school, 188
Maximin, Saint, 165, 168, 169
Maximinian, bishop of Syracuse, 24–25
Maxims of the Saints (de Fénelon), 187, 206
Mazarin, Cardinal, 142
Mazzarello, Maria Domenica, 261
Mazzini feminism, 271
Meal at Martha and Mary (refectory mural), 82
Medici, Anna Maria Louisa de', 243
Medici, Cardinal Alessandro de', 173
Meditationes vitae Christi, 77–78, 160
Medjugorje cult, 283–284, 290–293
Melania the Elder, 16, 17, 23
Melania the Younger, 17, 23, 28
Méliès, Georges, 296, 298
Meliga, Silvana, 301
Mellini, Angela, 213
Memoriale of Monteluce, 135
Memorie ecclesiastiche appartenenti all'istoria e al culto della Beata Chiara di Rimini (Garampi), 189
Mendicant orders, 56–58, 60, 73, 77, 97; saints, 61–67, 68
Merici, Angela, 94, 96, 105
Methodius of Olympus, Bishop, 10–11
Michelangelo, 123, 124

Milanese Women's Federation, 270
Mill, John Stuart, 266
Miriam (sister to Moses), 18
Missionaries of the Sacred Heart, 257
Mistica Ciudad de Dios (de Agreda), 214
Moccheggiani, Dante, 299
Modena, Pellegrino da, 160
Moerl, Maria de, 218
Molinos, Miguel de, 182, 187, 206
Monastic Hell (Tarabotti), 179
Monica, 6
Moniglia, Gian Andrea, 141
Montecassino Abbey, 50
Monteforte group, 53
Monteluce convent, 135
Monteverdi monastery, 46
Morata, Olympia, 97, 113
Mozzoni, Anna Maria, 265–266
Mulieris Dignitatem (John Paul II), 280
Murate convent, 133, 137
Muratori, Ludovico Antonio, 188, 189, 201
Musa Brasovola, Antonio, 97
Muzio, Panacea, 77
Mystica Ciudad de Dios (de Agreda), 188

National Catholic Women's Union, 272, 275
National Feminist Union, 271
Neapolitan Bartolomeo Prignani, 67
Negri, Paola Antonia, 98, 115–117
New Monasticism, 52
New Scholasticism, 208
Nicholas V, Pope, 90
Ninci, Clemenza, 143
Nogarole, Isotta, 113
Nonantola Abbey, 50
Nota sulla inutile straga (Benedict XV), 288
Novelli, Amleto, 297

Oasis of the Sacred Heart, 274
Observant movements, 88, 91, 99
Occitan love poetry, 56
Odilo of Cluny, 49
On Virginity (Methodius of Olympus), 10
Opera dei Congressi, 267–268, 269, 270
Oratory of Divine Love, 92, 96
Order of Preachers, 61
Ordinazioni, 66
Origen of Alexandria, 19, 20, 32
Orsini Borghese, Camilla, 180, 185
Otto II, 49
Otto III, 49, 50
Otto of Saxony, 48, 49, 50
Our Lady of Fatima, 283, 287–290, 291

Our Lady of Sorrows, 289

Pacem in terris (John XXIII), 268
Pachomius, 22, 28
Pagani, Antonio, 105, 149
Palazzo Pubblico (Siena), 75
Paleotti, Alfonso, 107, 111
Paleotti, Gabriele, 239
Paluzzi-Albertoni/Altieri, Cardinal, 237
Pascoli-Angeli, Marianna, 244
Pasolini, Pier Paolo, 295, 302
Pasqualigo, Angela Maria, 155–158
Passion of Christ, 178, 179, 181, 195,
    295–297. *See also* Jesus Christ
Patriarch of Venice, 136–137
Paul IV, Pope, 96, 136
Paul V, Pope, 71, 110, 152
Paul VI, Pope, 75, 278, 279, 290
Paula, 16–17, 23, 185
Paula the Younger, 23, 28
Paul the Deacon, 25, 26, 27, 42, 47
Paulinus of Nola, 16, 17, 20, 23
Paul of Tarsus, 9, 10, 32, 43, 65
Pelagini sect, 182
Pelagius, 16, 18
Penitent Magdalene, The (painting,
    Gentileschi), 167
Pensiero e azione group, 270, 271, 272
Pérez de Valdivia, Diego, 148
Pernoud, Régine, 2
Perpetua, 10
Pesenti, Antonia, 153–155, 157–158
Peter, 15, 25
Petit, Pascale, 300, 301
Petrarch, 56, 139
Philip of Caesarea, 9
Philip II of Spain, 119
Philomena, Saint, 200, 257
Piazza, Abbot Carlo Bartolomeo, 185,
    186–187
Pico della Mirandola, Gianfrancesco, 85
Pietro, Sano di, 72
Pietro of Lucca, 85
Pinzochere communities, 88
Pioppi, Lucia, 134
Pious Association of the Missionaries of the
    Kingship of Christ, 273
Pius VII, Pope, 200, 202
Pius IX, Pope, 177, 200, 201, 249, 252
Pius X, Pope, 261, 265, 269, 270, 272
Pius XI, Pope, 265
Pius XII, Pope, 258, 276, 288, 289, 290
Play of Moses (de' Sernigi), 140

Play of Saint Catherine of Köln (anonymous),
    141
Play of Saint Cecilia Virgin and Martyr
    (Venturelli), 140
Polani, Betta, 142
Policarp of Smyrna, 9
Ponziani, Francesca de', 88
Poor Clare foundations, 57, 75, 104, 105
Postel, Guillaume, 98, 127
Praeceptum ad servos dei (Augustine), 28
Praetextatus, 16
Prattica per procedere neele cause del S. Offizio
    (Scaglia), 152, 153
Prattica spirituale (anonymous nun), 116
"Prophetesses" of Valentano, 196
Prosdoce, 19
Provida mater, 276–277
Puccini, Vincenzo, 172
Pugliani, Domenico, 169

Quedlinburg community, 46
Querini, Cardinal Angelo Maria, 188
Quietism, 149, 178, 182, 187, 194, 196, 208
Quietist crisis, 206, 213
Quinzani, Sister Stefana, 117–118, 119, 120

Raccolte di vite de'santi (Ignazio Massini),
    191
Radegunda, queen of the Franks, 65, 222,
    223
Radio Maria, 292
Ragimbertus, King, 27
Rassegna nazionale, 267
Ratchis, King, 42, 46
Raymond of Capua, 37–38, 69
Razzi, Silvano, 122
Redemptoris Mater (John Paul II), 293
Reformation: Catholic Church official stance
    on, 159; challenge to Marian cult by, 102;
    ecclesiastical authority problem and,
    96–97; Italian women involved in, 97–98.
    See also Counter-Reformation
Refuge of San Giuseppe, 93
Regina Coeli monastery, 181, 182
Registrum epistolarum, 24
Regnun Christi, 257
Regula ad servos dei (Augustine), 29
Regula cuiusdam ad virgines, 30
Regula magistri, 29
Regularis informatio (Augustine), 28–29
Regular Third Orders, 88, 104. *See also* Third
    Orders
Regula tarnantensis (Columbanus), 30

Relations (Teresa of Avila), 40

Renaissance: female sanctity promoted by, 163–175; ideal wife/mother model during, 243–244; naturalism of, 159, 160; positive impact on women by, 108

Rerum Novarum, De (Leo XIII), 250, 268

Ricci, Caterina de', 122, 246, 247

Riccoboni, Dominican Bartolomea, 135

Ricordi (convent of the Murate), 132–133

Risorgimento culture, 252

Rispola, Alfonsina, 151

Rita of Cascia (film), 298, 300

Rita of Cascia, Saint, 254–255, 258, 299

Rodelinda, 26

Roman Catholic Church: feminization of religion and, 194–204; glorification of Mary by, 240–243; *illicterata* model within, 66–67; Marian cult and, 55–56; marriage between God and, 31–35; official stance on Reformation by, 159; place for religious women in, 124–125, 197–198; recognition of Mendicant orders by, 56–57; recognition of women's parity by, 278–280; reconciliation with Eastern Church by, 293; Reformation and women of, 96–98; reforms cult of saints/images, 98–102, 109, 145–147; represented by filmmakers, 294–295; response to flagellants by, 70; sanctity examined by, 84–87, 109–112, 147–153; schism of (1300–1450), 67–69; social Catholicism within, 249–254; Tridentine reform of religious women by, 102–107, 112, 134; virginity overvaluation by, 51–52; witch-hunts sanctioned by, 90–91; women as heretics against, 53–54. *See also* Counter-Reformation; Inquisition

Roman Inquisition, 96

Roman Oddone Colonna, 67

Roncière, Charles de la, 68–69

Rosa of Lima, 238, 239–240, 246

Rose of Viterbo, 75

Rossellini, Roberto, 295, 297, 298, 299

Rossi, Properzia de,' 123

Roussel, Pierre, 218

Rovere, Vittoria della, grand duchess of Tuscany, 142

Rubatto, Anna Maria, 264

Rufinus of Aquila, 17, 32

Ruoti, Maria Clemente, 140, 141

Sabadino degli Arienti, Giovanni, 87

Sacra Famiglia model, 162

Sacred Congregation of Bishops and Regular Clergy, 260, 262, 264

Sacred Congregation of Religious, 261

Sacred Heart of Jesus, 188, 214, 273

Sacrum Commercium Sancti Francisci cum Domina Paupertate, 35

Saint Anne Teaching Mary to Read (Pascoli-Angeli), 244

Saint Dominic chapel (Church of Saints John and Paul), 241

Saint Egidis convent, 181

Saint Juliana of Perugia convent, 79

Saint Mary Magdalene convent, 224

Saint Mary Magdalene in Conversation with the Angels (Pollaiolo), 166

Saint Mary Magdalene in Ecstasy (painting, Coccapani), 168

Saint Paul Without-the-Walls Abbey, 50

Saint Teresa (Bernini), 121

"St. Trudperter Höhe Lied," 35, 37

sancta virginitate, De (Augustine), 20

San Gaggio convent, 138

San Girolamo convent, 133, 141

San Niccolò convent, 139

San Salvatore convent, 27, 44–45

San Sisto convent, 57

Sanson, Yvonne, 301

Santa Caterina convent, 140

Santa Cecilia, regina delle armonie (film), 299

Santa Chiara convent, 139

Santa Giulia community, 46

Santa Maria Church, 55

Santa Maria degli Angeli monastery, 189

Santa Maria del Baraccano (Bologna), 93

Santa Maria della Disciplina convent, 140

Santa Maria della Pusterla monastery, 26, 27

Santa Maria delle Vittorie, 39–40

Santa Maria fuori Porta foundation, 27

Santa Maria Maddalena convent, 93

Santa Maria Maggiore Church, 55

Santa Maria Nova, 59

Santa Maria Theodote monastery, 45

Sant'Anna convent, 142

Savonarola, Girolamo, 87

Scaglia, Desiderio Cardinal, 152–153

Scaramelli, Giovanni Batista, 195, 217

Scholastica, 6

School Missionaries, 265

Scifi, Clare degli, 299

Sebastiani, Lucia, 89–90

Secondo Curione, Celio, 113

Second Vatican Council, 277, 289

Semeria, Father Giovanni Battista, 269, 282
Sera, Beatrice del, 139, 140, 141
Sernigi, Raffaella de', 140
Servants of Charity, 203
Servorum Dei beatificatione et beatorum canonizatione, De (Benedict XV), 187, 211
Sextus Petronius Probus, 18
Sfondrati, Niccolò, 116
Sicambria, Abbess, 136
Simancas, Diego de, 150
Sinelinda, Abbess, 43
Sirani, Elisabetta, 162, 167
Sister Letizia (film), 302
Sixtus V, Pope, 146
Social Realm of the Sacred Heart, 273
Society of Jesus, 196, 198
Solitude of Philagia (de Barry), 112
Song of Songs, 19, 31–33, 53
Soragna, Michelangelo da, 144
Sorelli, Fernanda, 70
Soubirous, Bernadette, 255
Speculum virginum, 35, 37
Sphere of the Universe (Frescobaldi), 129
Spiritual Company, 92
Spiritual Exercises (Ignatius of Loyola), 149
Squilli di resurrezione (newspaper), 274
Stephania, 48
Sticco, Maria, 275
Strict Observance Poor Clare convent (Bologna), 87
Stromboli (film), 298
Student Youth, 277
Subiaco Abbey, 50
Summis desiderantes affectibus (Innocent VII), 90
Syllabus of Errors (Pius IX), 249, 250
Symposium (Methodius of Olympus), 10

Taigi, Anna Maria, 199, 200
Tarabotti, Arcangela, 141–142, 179
Tedeschi, Radini, 266, 268, 269, 270, 271
Teresa of Ahumada, 212
Teresa of Avila: autobiography of, 125; canonization of, 145; as Counter-Reformation figure, 171; fame of, 110; identified with sanctity, 112; letters of, 116; as model to the faithful, 233–234; mystical marriage with Christ and, 39, 40–41; mysticism incarnated in, 211; proclaimed Doctor of the Church, 84, 278; reform discourse of, 5
Teresa of Avila (sculpture, Bernini), 237

Teresa of San Geronimo, Sister, 213
Terracina, Laura, 131
Tertullian, 10
Testimonies (Teresa of Avila), 40
Theatine order, 144, 147, 151
Thecla of Iconium (abbess), 10, 24
Theodelinda, 26, 47
Theodolinda, 43
Theodora, 48
Theodorada, 25
Theodore II Paleologus, 223–224
Theodote, 26–27
Theophanu, 49
Theotokos, 5–6. *See also* Mary
Thiene, Gaetano da, 92, 119, 147
Third Orders, 58, 60, 70, 88–89, 91, 104, 198, 265, 267
Thomas Aquinas, 68, 94
Thomism, 68, 208
Tincani, Luigia, 265
Tomacelli, Lucrezia, 181
Tomasi, Cardinal Giuseppe, 217
Tomasi, Maria Crocifissa, 179, 209, 211, 216, 217, 225
Tommaso of Siena, 76
Torelli, Ludovica, 95, 97
Tormento (film), 301
Tractatus de Officio Sanctissimae Inquisitionis et modo procedendi in causis fidei (Carena), 152
Tragica notte di Assisi, La (film), 299
Traité de l'amour de Dieu, 217
Tre libri dell'educazione christiana de i figliuoli (Antoniano), 187
Tridentine Church, 207–208; decree, 102–107
Tridentine mysticism, 208–209
Troiani, Costanza, 263

Union of the Daughters of Mary, 262
Universal Exhibition of 1834, 230
University of Paris, 68, 83, 84
Urban VI, Pope, 67
Urban VIII, Pope, 147, 153, 157, 174, 176, 181, 182, 187, 227
Ursula, Saint (mythical), 84, 86, 91, 101
Ursuline foundations, 106, 107, 109

Valafredus, 43, 46
Valdés, Juan de, 96, 97, 124
Valier, Agostino, 106, 107
Vallombrosans, 52
Vanni, Andrea, 74

Vasari, Giorgio, 123, 124
Vatican II, 277, 289
Vauchez, André, 62, 66, 68, 69, 89
Venerini, Rosa, 193
Venetian Church, 136
Venturelli, Cherubina, 140
Vera et occulta sanctitate, De (Borromeo), 119
Vera humilitate, De (Demetriades), 18
Vera sposa di Gesù Cristo cioè la monaca santa, La (de' Ligouri), 192
Verdiana of Castelfiorentino, 78–79
Vergini convent, 136, 137
Vernazza, Ettore, 92
Verzieri, Teresa Eustochio, 262
Vespucci, Amerigo, 125, 127
Vettius Praetextatus, 23
Viaggio in Italia (film), 298
Videmari, Marina, 261
Viduis, De (Ambrose), 14
Vigri, Caterina, 87
Vincenzi, Francesco, 153–155
Viotti, Giovanni Maria, 115
Vipereschi, Livia, 180
Virginibus, De (Ambrose), 13, 14, 19, 20
Virginibus velandis, De, 10
Virgin Mary. *See* Mary (mother of God)
Virgin of Medjugorje, 283–284, 290–293

Visconti, Luchino, 301
Vita beata, De (Augustine), 21
Vita (Chiara della Passione), 180, 181
Vita della venerabile serva di Dio Maria Cristina (De Cesare), 226
Vita e miracoli della Beata Madre Cabrini (film), 298–299
Vita nova, 56
Vita Sancti Anselmi (Rangerio of Lucca), 53
Vitry, Cardinal Jacques de, 62
Vittoria Colonna (magazine), 266–267
Vittorio Emanuele II, 198, 227
Voragine, Jacobus da, 101

Waldebert of Luxeuil, 30
Waldensians, 53
Wars of Religion, 101
Way of Perfection (Maria Maddalena), 111
Widow of Sarepta, 18
Wild Rice (film), 301
Woman of the Apocalypse, 243
Women's Fascio, 269, 270
Wycliffe, John, 99

Zeffirelli, Franco, 294, 297
Zeno, bishop of Verona, 13
Zoffoli, Egle, 285–286